17.99

The A-Z of Horror Films

D1585643

The A-Z of Horror Films

Howard Maxford

B.T Batsford Ltd London

For my mate John Dorney… in memory of the time (and money) we spent watching horror videos in the good old days when you could rent practically anything from the video store.

And for Trevor Kersley, carpenter extraordinaire (written quotes upon request), whose collection of sad horror videos helped enormously in the compiling of this book…

First published 1996
© Howard Maxford 1996

Printed in Hong Kong

for the publishers

B.T. Batsford Ltd
4 Fitzhardinge Street
London W1H 0AH

ISBN 0 7134 7973 6

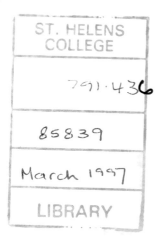
Cover illustrations:

Front: *Hellbound: Hellraiser II*; *Texas Chainsaw Massacre*

Back (clockwise from top): *Scars of Dracula*; *Bride of Frankenstein*;
Food of the Gods; *The Fly*; *Phantom of the Opera*; *Nightmare on Elm Street IV:
The Dream Master*

Contents

Foreword by Ingrid Pitt

I've got a feeling that Horror Films, like TV or the common cold, are here to stay. There's a lot of it about and it's spreading, finding new victims all the time. Like any virus that knows its stuff, just when you think you know all about it, got it nicely catalogued, it mutates. Trouble is that it is not easy to define just what Horror is. Horror is an ordinary woman suddenly and inexplicably taking an axe and chopping her mother to pieces - in Massachusetts or anywhere else. Horror can also be when you bite into a pork pie and find half a mouse. Or is Horror booking in at a motel and finding slashes in the shower curtain? Where does Horror become Fantasy or Fantasy Horror? Does it make any difference? Not really I guess. When the ancient Greeks gathered around in the local bath-house and told each other bowel-stirring stories of neighbours changing shape and howling at the moon, between meals of new-born babies, they were just carrying on a time honoured and respected tradition. The normal work-a-day world is too narrow, too confined, If you've just been out and brought home a brontosaurus to barbie, you can't very well sit by the fire and give a blow by blow description of something that everyone does every day if they want to eat. No - you make up stories about - anything!

It probably all started with The Runt, perhaps played by Elisha Cooke Jnr., trying to grab a bit of attention. So he told about this monster, four woolly mammoths tall and two sabre-toothed tigers wide, that he had cornered by the tar-pit. As he was about to send his specially fire-hardened hickory shafted number 2 spear into its gaping maw, it disappeared with a blood curdling scream into the gathering mist. The story had the value of featuring the Runt as the hero but, as the monster had conveniently vanished, it saved him from having to produce it as proof.

The story got embellished over the millennia. Embellished and added to until there was a whole industry doing nothing else but writing variations on Runt's story. Sounds like the plot of a film I made in Spain in 1966 called *El Sonido Prehistorico* (aka - which means 'also known as' - I only just found that out so I thought I'd share it with you - *The Prehistoric Sound*).

Gothic Horror, the horror of Hammer Films and Universal Studios, has always been the mainstay of the genre. The schlock horror, splatter films are a deviation. They exploit the gore and ghoul at the centre of the tradition and deliver straight to the eyeball without straining it through a shift in perspective. A suitable cypher for today's world, perhaps, but who wants to pay to see on the silver screen what you can see on the TV news 10 times a day - for real!?

For this reason, it seems to me, the move back to the old days of vampires baring fangs - and breasts when I was around - monsters staggering about with their hands stretched out as if someone had pinched their towel and werewolves getting hairy and running sideways when the full-moon comes up over the potting shed, hasn't come a moment too soon.

The late Leslie Halliwell was a friend. The great thing about him was his enthusiasm. He spent most of his life either watching films or writing about them - but he was still ready to discuss productions and answer questions. Like why he was less than enthusiastic about some of the films I've been in. A viewpoint Howard Maxford seems to have taken over, together with the mantle laid aside by Leslie. Still, nobody's perfect. Halliwell was THE MAN in film reference books. Maxford is young and ambitious and, now he's got the taste for it, could become the new Leslie Halliwell.

You may think that already the bookshop shelves groan under the weight of books on the horror genre. And you'd be right. So why *The A-Z of Horror Films*?

The film world suffers from the problem of fecundity. You may hear people moaning about the British film industry being on its last legs or Hollywood pricing itself out of the small picture market and only making mega-buck extravaganzas, but you only

have to stand in the local video shop to be swamped by a cornucopia of goodies, old and new, to appreciate that the canned entertainment industry is breeding like cyborg rabbits with a Spanish fly fix in their hydraulic fluid. What we need is the return of the 'B' picture. Especially Horror, where the miniscule budgets force directors to be inventive to put bums on seats. Not all terrible films do a *Plan 9* half a century on. Horror films should be made on a shoestring, preferably in grainy black and white or colour that is straight out of the primary colour pot, and have a sound-track that adds to the effect by setting your teeth on edge as it mangles the music on the low fidelity sound-track.

Look what happened when they made Branagh's *Frankenstein*, Coppola's *Dracula* and Stephen Woolley's *Interview with a Vampire*? They threw dollars at it like confetti at a Corleone wedding on Valentine's Day. And the result? Magnificent nonsenses that completely missed the point. They worked so hard at suspending belief that in the end you felt it was quite normal to stitch together a Robert de Niro or bump into a Vampire in Piccadilly. Tom Cruise in a blonde wig almost overdid it, but Brad Pitt was so reasonable I began to worry that there was a family connection. The point is I don't want my horror served up like a dog's dinner on a Saturday night out. I want it Ed Wood-ed with

Bela, Vincent and Boris overacting like hell on a set that Jack built in a nightmare - that's horror!

The A-Z of Horror Films lays out the facts in a simple framework that makes it easy to pick out your favourite and unfavourite films. Now you can become a whizz at Trivial Pursuits or bore your friends silly by expounding on the lesser minutae of production from the original *Nosferatu* to the latest Freddie.

Howard Maxford has produced a balanced assessment with an almost cryptic style (unlike mine) as he dissects the films and awards brickbats, bouquets and the occasional raspberry. And I thoroughly recommend this book even if he is less than complimentary about my work!

Introduction

Welcome to *The A-Z of Horror Films*, a film-guide-cum-Who's-Who of films and film-makers featuring the best - and worst - the genre has to offer.

Personally, I've been a horror fan since the age of twelve when, after much begging and pleading, my parents allowed me to stay up late on my own (an event in itself!) to watch *Dracula - Prince of Darkness* on TV. Sitting on the sofa, surrounded by cushions and pillows to protect me from what horrors might emerge from the (black and white) screen, I was immediately hooked, and have remained so ever since. The fact that the BBC soon after ran a series of classic Universal and Hammer horrors also helped to confirm my addiction to the genre, particularly as I'd just bought a copy of Denis Gifford's excellent *Pictorial History of Horror Movies*, and so was able to read and learn about the films at the same time I was watching them. Indeed, those few weeks were a real voyage of cinematic discovery for me.

Though the horror genre is often derided by some of the more serious critics, it has, down the decades, produced many films worthy of comparison with the greatest the cinema has to offer: *Frankenstein*, *King Kong*, *The Bride of Frankenstein*, Hammer's *Dracula* and *The Exorcist* being the *Citizen Kanes* and *Casablancas* of the horror world. Inevitably,

however, amid the highlights there are - as in all genres - clunkers a-plenty. Indeed, for every reasonably good horror film there are at least ten equally bad ones. For every *Halloween* there are at least ten films of the dismal quality of *Aerobicide* and *Night Train to Terror*, movies which no one in their right mind would want to waste time watching, never mind paying money to rent from the video store. But there's always a *Devil Rides Out* or a *Suspiria* or a *Silence of the Lambs* to keep one's hope for better things springing eternal. Therefore, as well as celebrating the best that horror has to offer, this book should also act as a warning against its worst!

Like all film guides, the films included are rated with stars:

no stars poor/avoid
*   average/watchable
**   good/well worth a look
***   excellent/among the genre's best
****   a genre milestone/not to be missed

As well as plot synopses, each entry also contains a paragraph of criticism and the relevant credit and cast lists. The abbreviations for the credit lists are as follows:

w: writer
p: producer
exec p: executive producer
d: director

ph: photographer
m: music
md: music director
ed: editor
pd: production designer
ad: art director
cos: costumes
sp: special effects
sound: sound
2nd unit d: second unit director
story, novel, make-up effects and
stunt co-ordinator are self
explanatory

Each entry also contains the
film's country of origin (GB,
USA, Ger, It, etc.), its year of
release, its running time and the
colour process used
(Technicolor, Metrocolor, De
Luxe, etc., as well as good old
black and white). Given the
proliferation of home movie
systems and stereo televisions
now available, recording systems

used are also noted where
applicable (Dolby, Ultra Stereo,
DTS Stereo, etc.). Meanwhile,
any name recorded within the
body of the cast and credit lists
in capitals denotes a stronger
than usual contribution from the
artist involved (eg: d: TERENCE
FISHER means that the film was
particularly well directed).

With the biographies, I've
attempted to provide as many
key contributors to the genre as
possible - be they actors,
directors, composers, effects
technicians or editors. There
will, I hope, be quite a few
names you haven't come across
before, too. As with most
'people' guides, each entry
contains the subject's birth and
death dates (where available), a
synopsis of his or her career, and
as full a list of their genre work
as possible.

Inevitably, given the enormity
of the task, there are bound to be
some omissions, be they people
or films (unlike the writers of
some film guides, I'd like to
point out that I have actually
watched - for better or worse -
every film reviewed in this
book). Similarly, my views on
certain films may be at variance
with the reader's own personal
taste and even received opinions.
For this I make no apologies, but
hope that the additional
information contained in each
film review (the credit lists are
perhaps the most comprehensive
you'll find in any film guide) will
make amends for any oversights
and slighted feelings.

Happy browsing!

Howard Maxford
May 1996

Top Slots

Inevitably, while working on this book, I have been asked to name my favourite films, directors and stars. In drawing up the lists below, I have tried to distinguish between my purely personal choices, and those films and film-makers who have had an undeniable impact on the genre as a whole.

The Most Important and Influential Horror Films Ever Made

(in order of release)

1. *The Cabinet of Dr Caligari* (1919)
2. *Dracula* (1930)
3. *Frankenstein* (1931)
4. *King Kong* (1933)
5. *The Bride of Frankenstein* (1935)
6. *The Curse of Frankenstein* (1956)
7. *Dracula* (aka *Horror of Dracula* - 1958)
8. *Psycho* (1960)
9. *Night of the Living Dead* (1968)
10. *The Exorcist* (1973)
11. *The Texas Chainsaw Massacre* (1974)
12. *Halloween* (1978)
13. *The Silence of the Lambs* (1990)

The Author's Favourite Horror Films

(in order of release)

1. *Frankenstein* (1931)
2. *King Kong* (1933)
3. *The Bride of Frankenstein* (1935)
4. *Night of the Demon* (aka *Curse of the Demon* - 1957)
5. *Dracula* (aka *Horror of Dracula* - 1958)
5. *Psycho* (1960)
6. *Dracula - Prince of Darkness* (1966)
7. *Carry On Screaming* (1966)
8. *Quatermass and the Pit* (aka *Five Million Years to Earth* - 1967)
9. *The Devil Rides Out* (aka *The Devil's Bride* - 1968)
10. *Vampire Circus* (1971)
11. *Frankenstein and the Monster from Hell* (1973)
12. *The Exorcist* (1973)
13. *Young Frankenstein* (1974)
14. *Deep Red* (aka *Profundo Rosso / The Hachet Murders* - 1975)
15. *Suspiria* (1976)
16. *Halloween* (1978)
17. *Dracula* (1979)
18. *Inferno* (1980)
19. *The Evil Dead* (1980)
20. *The Silence of the Lambs* (1990)

Honourable mentions: *The Abominable Dr Phibes* (1971), *Dr Phibes Rises Again* (1972), *Theatre of Blood* (1973)

Top Horror Stars

(in alphabetical order)

1. John Carradine
2. Lon Chaney
3. Lon Chaney Jr
4. Peter Cushing
5. Boris Karloff
6. Christopher Lee
7. Peter Lorre
8. Bela Lugosi
9. Donald Pleasence
10. Vincent Price
11. Basil Rathbone

Honourable mentions: Evelyn Ankers, Lionel Atwill, Linda Blair, Hazel Court, Jamie Lee Curtis, Robert Englund, Dwight Frye, Paul Naschy, Ingrid Pitt, Robert Quarry, Michael Ripper, Barbara Shelley, Barbara Steele, Fay Wray, George Zucco

Top Horror Directors

(in alphabetical order)

1. Dario Argento
2. Mario Bava
3. Tod Browning
4. John Carpenter
5. Roger Corman
6. Wes Craven
7. David Cronenberg
8. Terence Fisher
9. George Romero
10. Jacques Tourneur
11. James Whale

Honourable mentions: William Castle, Larry Cohen, Brian de Palma, Freddie Francis, Lucio Fulci, Alfred Hitchcock, Tobe Hooper, Roman Polanski

Other Key Contributors to the Genre

(in alphabetical order)

1. Jack Asher (cinematographer)
2. Rick Baker (make-up effects artist)
3. James Bernard (composer)
4. Robert Bloch (author-screen writer)
5. Rob Bottin (make-up effects artist)
6. Michael Carreras (producer)
7. John P. Fulton (special effects technician)
8. Charles D. Hall (art director)
9. Anthony Hinds (producer-writer [writer as John Elder])
10. Stephen King (author-screenwriter)
11. Val Lewton (producer)
12. Richard Matheson (author-writer)
13. Willis O'Brien (stop-motion animator)
14. Jack P. Pierce (make-up effects artist)
15. Bernard Robinson (art director)
16. George Robinson (cinematographer)
17. Jimmy Sangster (writer-producer)
18. Tom Savini (make-up effects artist)
19. Dick Smith (make-up effects artist)
20. Milton Subotsky (screen writer-producer)

AIP

American production and distribution company (the initials stand for American International Productions) formed in 1955 by producers Samuel Z. Arkoff and James H. Nicholson, through which they produced all manner of low-budget horror entries in both America and Britain, several of which have taken on cult status. Arkoff and Nicholson also operated through Alta Vista (through which they made most of the Corman/Poe films for AIP) and Santa Rosa Productions among others. The company disbanded in 1980. Genre filmography:
The She Creature (1956), *The Amazing Colossal Man* (1957), *I Was a Teenage Frankenstein* (1957), *Blood of Dracula* (1957 - aka *Blood Is My Heritage / The Blood Demon*), *War of the Colossal Beast* (1958), *Attack of the Puppet People* (1958), *How to Make a Monster* (1958), *Night of the Blood Beast* (1958), *The Spider* (1958 - aka *Earth vs. the Spider*), *Teenage Caveman* (1958 - aka *Prehistoric World*), *Terror from the Year 5000* (1958), *Attack of the Giant Leeches* (1959 - aka *Demons of the Swamp*), *A Bucket of Blood* (1959), *The Ghost of Dragstrip Hollow* (1959), *The Headless Ghost* (1959), *House of Usher* (1960 - aka *The Fall of the House of Usher*), *The Pit and the Pendulum* (1961), *Tales of Terror* (1962), *The Raven* (1963), *X - The Man with X-Ray Eyes* (1963 - aka *The Man with X-Ray Eyes*), *Dementia 13* (1963 - aka *The Haunted and the Hunted*), *The Comedy of Terrors* (1964), *Die, Monster, Die!* (1965 - aka *Monster of Terror*), *The Ghost in the Invisible Bikini* (1966), *Curse of the Crimson Altar* (1968 - aka *The Crimson Cult / The Crimson Altar*), *De Sade* (1969), *The Haunted House of Horror* (1969 - aka *Horror House*), *Scream and Scream Again* (1969), *The Oblong Box* (1969), *Count Yorga, Vampire* (1970), *The Dunwich Horror* (1970), *The Return of Count Yorga* (1971), *The Abominable Dr Phibes* (1971), *Murders in the Rue Morgue* (1971), *The Thing with Two Heads* (1972), *Frogs* (1972), *Dr Phibes Rises Again* (1972), *Blacula* (1972), *Madhouse* (1974), *Food of the Gods* (1976), *The Island of Dr Moreau* (1977), *Empire of the Ants* (1977), *The People That Time Forgot* (1977), *The Amityville Horror* (1979)

A-Haunting We Will Go
USA 1942 68m bw
Laurel and Hardy are hired to transport a coffin containing a gangster on the run, but get it mixed up with a similar one used in a magic act.
    Haunting doesn't come into this dishevelled comedy-mystery which, even at this length, proves painful to sit through, and though the boys try hard, the material is way below standard. Of note chiefly for the appearance of Dante (real name Harry A. Jansen), a top magician of the day, much of whose act is featured in the film, though many of his illusions now seem somewhat obvious.
p: Sol M. Wurtzel for TCF
w: Lou Beslow
d: Alfred Werker
ph: Glen MacWilliams
m: no credit
ed: Alfred Day
ad: Richard Day, Lewis Creber
Stan Laurel, Oliver Hardy, Dante, Elisha Cook Jr, Sheila Ryan, John Shelton, Willy Best, Don Costello, Addison Richards

Abbott and Costello
see Abbott, Bud

Abbott, Bud (1895-1974)
American vaudeville comic (real name William Abbott) who, with partner Lou Costello (1906-1957 [real name Louis Cristillo]), became one of Universal's top box-office draws in the 1940s with such romps as *One Night in the Tropics*, *Buck Privates* and *In the Navy*, though at no time did their work approach the level of Laurel and Hardy's. When their popularity began to wane, Universal teamed them up with their monsters, whose box-office currency was also in decline, the result being a series of horror comedies that proved extremely popular at the time, though many of them now have to be viewed with a certain degree of sympathy.
Genre credits:
Hold That Ghost (1941), *The Time of Their Lives* (1946), *Abbott and Costello Meet Frankenstein* (1948), *Abbott and Costello Meet the Killer, Boris Karloff* (1949),
Abbott and Costello Meet the Invisible Man (1951), *Abbott and Costello Meet Dr Jekyll and Mr Hyde* (1953), *Abbott and Costello Meet the Mummy* (1955), *The Thirty-Foot Bride of Candy Rock* (1959 - Lou only)

Abbott and Costello Meet Dr Jekyll and Mr Hyde *
USA 1953 79m bw
Two incompetent American policemen visit London to observe British methods and inadvertently help to capture a monster.
    Flat-footed farce with very little to laugh at, though kids and indulgent fans may find it tolerable. A popular enough hit at the time, it was originally filmed in stereophonic sound. Karloff (who replaced first choice Basil Rathbone) plays the Dr Jekyll character, though it is mostly his stuntman Eddie Parker who appears as his alter ego, Mr Hyde. Similarly, when Lou turns into a monster and a giant mouse, it is his stuntman, Vic Parks, who is under the latex. Astonishingly, the film was originally given an X certificate in Britain, disallowing anyone under the age of 16 from seeing it, though it now turns up regularly on children's television!
p: Howard Christie for Universal
w: John Grant, Lee Loeb
story: Sidney Fields, Grant Garrett
d: Charles Lamont
ph: George Robinson
md: Joseph Gershenson
ed: Russell Schoengarth
ad: Bernard Herzbrun, Eric Orbom
cos: Rosemary Odel
sp: David S. Horsley
sound: Leslie I. Carey, Robert Pritchard
ch: Kenny Williams
make-up: Bud Westmore, Jack Kevan
Bud Abbott, Lou Costello, Boris Karloff, Eddie Parker (as Mr Hyde), Craig Stevens, Helen Westcott, Reginald Denny, John Dierkes

Abbott and Costello Meet Frankenstein *
USA 1948 83m bw
Abbott and Costello deliver two crates containing Frankenstein's Monster and

• Poster artwork for *Abbott and Costello Meet Frankenstein*, the first of the duo's encounters with Universal's gallery of fading monsters.

Dracula to a horror museum, and it's not long before the Wolfman turns up on the scene…

Flat, unimaginative comedy thriller, further hampered by the stars' tired routines and mugging. It nevertheless marked their first teaming with Universal's monsters, then on the verge of box-office extinction, and its huge commercial success led to several other 'meetings'. The film, originally to have been called *The Brain of Frankenstein*, was criticized by Lon Chaney Jr who blamed Abbott and Costello for the demise of the classic horror film. The Mummy and Count Alucard (Son of Dracula) were also considered as part of the monster line-up, whilst Ian Keith (the original choice for Universal's 1930 *Dracula*) was offered the role of Dracula before Lugosi. The voice of Vincent Price can be heard at the end of the film in a gag cameo as the Invisible Man, whilst Lon Chaney Jr can be glimpsed briefly playing Frankenstein's Monster, covering for Glenn Strange who'd hurt his ankle on set. Despite the title, Frankenstein himself is nowhere to be seen.
p: Robert Arthur for Universal
w: Robert Lees, Frederic I. Rinaldo, John Grant
d: Charles Barton
ph: Charles Van Enger
m: Frank Skinner
ed: Frank Gross
ad: Bernard Hertzbrun, Hilyard Brown
cos: Grace Houston

sp: David S. Horsley, Jerome Ash
sound: Leslie I. Carey, Robert Pritchard
make-up: Bud Westmore
Bud Abbott, Lou Costello, Lon Chaney Jr (as Larry Talbot, the Wolfman), Bela Lugosi (as Dracula), Glenn Strange (Frankenstein's Monster), Leonore Aubert, Jane Randolph, Vincent Price (as the Invisible Man)

Abbott and Costello Meet the Invisible Man *

USA 1951 82m bw
Abbott and Costello are hired by a boxer to clear him of a murder charge. In the meantime he has made himself invisible with H. G. Wells' serum so as to escape detection.

Laboured excuse for the comedians to meet yet another of Universal's old monsters and gag around, only this time not too brightly. Originally intended as a sequel to *The Invisible Man's Revenge*, the film was provisionally titled *The Invisible Man Strikes Back* before being relegated to Abbott and Costello, who turned it into another hit. Sharp-eyed viewers will spot a picture of Claude Rains, Universal's original Invisible Man, during a laboratory sequence.
p: Howard Christie for Universal
w: Robert Lees, Frederic I. Rinaldo, John Grant
story: Hugh Wedlock Jr, Howard Snyder
d: George Lamont
ph: George Robinson

md: Joseph Gershenson
ed: Virgil Vogel
ad: Bernard Herzbrun, Richard Riedel
sp: David S. Horsley
sound: Leslie I. Carey
Bud Abbott, Lou Costello, Arthur Franz, Nancy Guild, Adele Jergens, Sheldon Leonard, William Frawley, Gavin Muir

Abbott and Costello Meet the Killer, Boris Karloff

USA 1948 84m bw
The boys help solve a series of murders taking place at the lonely Lost Caverns Hotel, with all fingers pointing to Boris Karloff.

Originally intended as a Bob Hope vehicle to have been titled *Easy Does It*, this thin murder romp is perhaps best remembered for its finale in a spooky cavern; otherwise it's a thoroughly routine affair. Boris Karloff doesn't even play the killer but a mad swami (the real killer is Alan Mowbray).
p: Robert Arthur for Universal
w: Hugh Wedlock Jr, Howard Snyder, John Grant
story: Hugh Wedlock, Howard Snyder
d: Charles Barton
ph: Charles Van Enger
m: Milton Schwarzwald
ed: Edward Curtiss
ad: Bernard Herzbraun, Richard H. Riedel
cos: Rosemary Odell
sp: David S. Horsley
sound: Leslie I. Carey, Robert Pritchard
Bud Abbott, Lou Costello, Boris Karloff, Gary Moore, Lenore Aubert, Alan Mowbray

Abbott and Costello Meet the Mummy *

USA 1955 77m bw
Whilst in Egypt, two bumblers hoping to hitch a ride back to America with an archaeologist encounter a revived mummy.

Formularistic Abbott and Costello knockabout with the expected mix of mild thrills and old routines. The Mummy is for some reason here referred to as Klaris (in previous Universal episodes it is called Kharis) and is played by stuntman Eddie Parker, who acted as Lon Chaney's stunt double in *The Mummy's Tomb*, *The Mummy's Ghost* and *The Mummy's Curse*.
p: Howard Christie for Universal
w: John Grant
d: Charles Lamont
ph: George Robinson
md: Joseph Gershenson
ed: Russell Schoengarth
ad: Alexander Goltizen, Bill Newberry
cos: Rosemary Odell

sp: Clifford Stine
sound: Leslie I. Carey, Robert Pritchard
Bud Abbott, Lou Costello, Marie
Windsor, Eddie Parker (as The
Mummy), Michael Ansara. Dan
Seymour, Richard Deacon, Kurt Katch,
Richard Karlan, Peggy King

The Abominable Dr Phibes **
GB 1971 94m Movielab
A disfigured musical genius, thought to
have been killed in a car crash, sets out
to murder the surgeons who failed to
save the life of his beloved wife.

High-camp horror spoof with the
good doctor using the ten curses of
Pharaoh as the themes for each murder.
The low budget is particularly well used
and the cast enters into the fun with
vigour. It was followed by *Dr Phibes Rises
Again* in 1972.
p: Louis M. Heyward, Ron Dunas for
AIP
exec p: Samuel Z. Arkoff, James H.
Nicholson
w: JAMES WHITON, WILLIAM
GOLDSTEIN
d: ROBERT FUEST
ph: NORMAN WARWICK
m: BASIL KIRCHEN, JACK NATHAN
ed: Tristan Cones
pd: BRIAN EATWELL
cos: Elsa Fennell
sp: George Blackwell
sound: Dennis Whitlock, A. W. Lumkin,
Ken Nightingale
make-up: Trevor Crole-Rees
Vincent Price, Joseph Cotten, Peter
Jeffrey, Hugh Griffith, Terry Thomas,
Virginia North, Aubrey Woods, John
Laurie, Susan Travers, Alex Scott,
Edward Burnham, John Cater, Caroline
Munro, Derek Godfrey, Maurice
Kaufman

The Abominable Snowman *
GB 1957 91m bw Hammerscope
Explorers in the Himalayas searching for
the Yeti find their numbers decreasing
one by one.

Eerily effective, intelligently scripted
addition to Hammer's gallery of
monsters, though the Yeti themselves are
only fleetingly glimpsed.
p: Aubrey Baring, Anthony Nelson Keys
for Hammer/Clarion
w: NIGEL KNEALE
d: VAL GUEST
ph: Arthur Grant
m: Humphrey Searle
md: John Hollingsworth
ed: Bill Lenny
pd: Bernard Robinson
cos: Beatrice Dawson
sound: Jock May
make-up: Phil Leakey

PETER CUSHING, Forrest Tucker,
Maureen Connell, Richard Wattis,
ARNOLD MARLE, Robert Brown

The Abominable Snowman of the Himalayas
see The Abominable Snowman

Absolution *
GB 1978 95m Technicolor
A Catholic schoolboy plays a malicious
trick on his schoolmaster priest, but all
is not quite what it seems.

Initially intriguing but finally over
plotted and increasingly far fetched
character thriller, typical of its author.
Fairly watchable despite these faults,
however.
p: Elliott Kastner, Danny O'Donovan
for Bulldog
w: Anthony Shaffer
d: Anthony Page
ph: John Coquillon
m: Stanley Myers
ed: John Victor Smith
pd: Natasha Kroll
cos: Anne Gainsford
sound: Peter Handford, Ken Barker
RICHARD BURTON, Dominic Guard,
Dai Bradley, Billy Connolly, Andrew
Keir, Hilary Mason

Acquanetta (1920-)
Exotic American actress (real name
Burnu Davenport), dubbed the
'Venezuelan Volcano'. A former model,
she found herself featured in several
jungle and horror pictures in the forties,
most notably as Paula Dupree, the ape
woman in *Captive Wild Woman* and its first
sequel, *Jungle Woman*. Her other credits
include *Arabian Nights*, *Flesh and Fantasy*
and *Tarzan* and *The Leopard Woman*.
Genre credits:
Captive Wild Woman (1943), *Jungle Woman*
(1944), *Dead Man's Eyes* (1944), *Lost
Continent* (1951)

Adamson, Al (1919-1995)
American exploitation director whose
films tend to be padded with footage
from others. Featuring actors whose
careers are at a low ebb (Russ Tamblyn,
John Carradine, Lon Chaney Jr, George
Lazenby, etc.), they are archetypal grade
Z fare. Nevertheless, he won an Emmy
for producing the TV movie *Cry Rape*
(1973). Other credits include *Satan's
Sadists*, *Gun Riders*, *Five Bloody Graves*, *The
Female Bunch*, *Girls for Rent*, *The Naughty
Stewardesses* and *Blazing Stewardesses*.
Genre credits:
Two Tickets to Terror (1964), *Blood of
Dracula's Castle* (1969), *Horror of the
Blood Monsters* (1971 - aka *Creatures of the
Prehistoric Planet/Horror Creatures of the*

*Prehistoric Planet/Vampire Men of the Lost
Planet/Space Mission of the Lost Planet),
Blood of Ghastly Horror* (1972), *The Brain
of Blood* (1972), *Doomsday Voyage* (1972),
Dracula vs. Frankenstein (1973), *Death
Dimension* (1978), *Nurse Sherri* (1978 -
aka *Beyond the Living/Hospital of Terror*),
Carnival Magic (1981)

The Addams Family *
USA 1991 99m DeLuxe Dolby
An imposter after the Addams' family
fortune poses as long lost Uncle Fester.

Generally agreeable if somewhat
over-stretched and uncertainly plotted
black comedy via the celebrated *New
Yorker* cartoons and the popular sixties
sit-com.
p: Scott Rudin, Jack Cummins for
Orion
exec p: Graham Place
w: Caroline Thompson, Larry Wilson
cartoons: Charles Addams
d: Barry Sonnenfeld
ph: OWEN ROIZMAN
m: Marc Shaiman
ed: Dede Allen
pd: RICHARD MACDONALD
cos: Ruth Myers
Anjelica Huston, Raul Julia, Christopher
Lloyd, Jimmy Workman, Christina
Ricci, Carel Struycken, Judith Malina,
Dan Hedeya, Elizabeth Wilson,
Christopher Hart (as Thing), Paul
Benedict, John Franklin

Addams Family Values *
USA 1993 94m DeLuxe Dolby
Morticia and Gomez have a new baby,
much to the annoyance of Wednesday
and Pugsley, whilst Uncle Fester falls in
love with their serial killer nanny.

Slimly plotted but generally amusing
collection of macabre gags which should
satisfy fans of the first film.
p: Scott Rudin for Paramount
w: Paul Rudnick
d: Barry Sonnenfeld
ph: Donald Peterman
m: Marc Shaiman
md: Artie Kane
ed: Arthur Schmidt, Jim Miller
pd: Ken Adam
cos: Theoni V. Aldredge
sp: Alan Munro
sound: Peter Kurland, Cecilia Hall
titles: Pablo and Allen Ferro
Anjelica Huston, Raul Julia, Christina
Ricci, Christopher Lloyd, Joan Cusack,
Carol Kane, Jimmy Workman, Carel
Struycken, Christopher Hart, David
Krumholz, Peter MacNicol

Aenigma
It/Yugoslavia 1987 88m Telecolor
Students at an exclusive girls' school are

threatened by the telekinetic powers of a fellow student who has been injured in a prank.

Silly Italian schlocker which plays like a cross between *Carrie* and *Suspiria*. Pretty routine even by this director's standards.
p: Ettore Spagnuolo for AM/Sutjeska
exec p: Walter Bigari
w: Giorgio Mariuzzo, Lucio Fulci
d: Lucio Fulci
ph: Luigi Ciccarese
m: Carlo Maria Cordio
ed: Vanio Amici
ad: Kemo Hrustanovic
cos: Karlo Klemencic
sound: Bruco Monreal
Jared Martin, Lara Naszinski, Ulli Reinthaler, Sophie D'Aulan, Jennifer Naud

Aerobicide

USA 1986 86m colour
The female members of an exercise class are killed off one by one by a maniac.

Cheapjack rubbish, as dismal as it sounds - and then some.
p: Peter Yuval for Winters Group/Maverick
exec p: David Winters, Marc Winters
w/d/ed: David A. Prior
ph: Peter Bouilla
m: Todd Hayen
ad: no credit given
cos: Stacey McFarland
sound: John Hays
2nd unit d: Thomas Baldwin
2nd unit ph: Stephen Blake
ch: Sheila Howard
make-up effects: Robin Beauchesne
Marcia Kerr, David James Campbell, Ted Prior, Teresa Van Der Woude, Fritz Matthews

The Aftermath

USA 1980 89m CFIcolor
Astronauts returning to Earth discover that is has been overrun by mutants, the result of radioactive fallout from World War III.

Little more than a home movie writ large, but with a surprisingly good score.
p: Steve Barkett for Nautilus
w/d/ed: Steve Barkett
ph: Dennis Skotak, Tom Denove
m: John Morgan
pd: Robert Skotak
sp: Robert Skotak, Dennis Skotak, Jim Danforth
make-up effects: Robert Skotak and others
sound: Maurice Allen, Lynne Barkett
Steve Barkett, Lynne Margulies, Sid Haig, Christopher Barkett, Alfie Martin, Forrest J. Ackerman, Jim Danforth

Agar, John (1920-)

American leading man whose first film was John Ford's *Fort Apache* in 1948, which co-starred his then wife Shirley Temple, whom he married in 1945 and divorced in 1949. Majority of film work strictly routine. Other credits include *The Sands of Iwo Jima*, *Waco* and *The St Valentine's Day Massacre*.
Genre credits:
Revenge of the Creature (1955), *Tarantula* (1955), *The Mole People* (1956), *The Brain from Planet Arous* (1956), *Daughter of Dr Jekyll* (1957), *Attack of the Puppet People* (1958 - aka *Six Inches Tall*), *The Invisible Invaders* (1959), *The Hand of Death* (1961), *Journey to the Seventh Planet* (1961), *Women of the Prehistoric Planet* (1965), *Zontar - The Thing from Venus* (1966), *The Curse of the Swamp Creature* (1968), *King Kong* (1976), *Fear* (1989), *Nightbreed* (1990), *The Perfect Bride* (1991), *Body Bags* (1993)

Agutter, Jenny (1952-)

British actress still remembered chiefly for her juvenile roles in both *The Railway Children* and *Walkabout*, though she has since appeared in all manner of international productions, including *The Eagle Has Landed*, *Logan's Run*, *Equus* and *The Riddle of the Sands*.
Genre credits:
Dominique (1978), *An American Werewolf in London* (1981), *Dark Tower* (1987), *Child's Play 2* (1990), *Darkman* (1990)

Aldrich, Robert (1918-1983)

American director and producer who began in films in 1941 as a production clerk at RKO. Gradually worked his way up the ladder, first as a script clerk then as an assistant director, production manager and associate producer. Began directing for television in the early fifties, his first film credit being *The Big Leaguer* in 1953. Formed Associates and Aldrich in 1954, through which he produced many of his own films. He produced and directed *Whatever Happened to Baby Jane?* in 1964, which not only rescued the waning careers of Bette Davis and Joan Crawford, but started a cycle of crazy lady horror flicks (*What's The Matter with Helen? Who Slew Auntie Roo?*). Other credits include *Kiss Me Deadly*, *The Big Knife*, *Flight of The Phoenix*, *The Dirty Dozen* and *The Killing of Sister George*.
Genre credits:
Whatever Happened to Baby Jane? (1962 - p/d), *Hush... Hush, Sweet Charlotte* (1965 - p/d), *Whatever Happened to Aunt Alice?* (1969 - p)

Alias Nick Beal ***

USA 1949 93m bw

A politician finds himself in high office thanks to the help of a mysterious stranger...

Engagingly-conceived fantasy melodrama, a modern day version of *Faust*. All credits A1.
p: Endre Boehm for Paramount
w: JONATHAN LATIMER
story: Mindret Lord
d: JOHN FARROW
ph: LIONEL LINDON
m: FRANZ WAXMAN
ed: Eda Warren
ad: Hans Dreier, Franz Bachelin
cos: Mary Kay Dodson
sound: Phil Wisdom, Gene Garvin
RAY MILLAND, THOMAS MITCHELL, Audrey Trotter, Fred Clark, George Macready

Alien **

GB 1979 117m Eastmancolor Panavision Dolby
After visiting an apparently dead planet, astronauts find that their spaceship has been infiltrated by a vicious alien being whose sole intent appears to be to kill them all.

Technically arresting, genuinely frightening science fiction variation on the Bogey Man theme, with excellent art direction and effects work. A worldwide commercial success, it quickly took on cult classic status and inspired all manner of sequels and rip-offs.
p: Walter Hill, David Giler, Gordon Carroll for TCF/Brandywine
exec p: Ronald Shusett
w: Dan O'Bannon
story: Dan O'Bannon, Ronald Shusett
d: RIDLEY SCOTT
ph: Derek Vanlint
m: JERRY GOLDSMITH
ed: Terry Rawlings, Peter Weatherley
pd: MICHAEL SEYMOUR, LES DILLEY, ROGER CHRISTIAN
cos: John Mollo
sp: CARLO RAMBALDI, H. R. GIGER, BRIAN JOHNSON, RICK ALLDER, DENYS ALING (AA)
sound: Derrick Leather, Bill Rowe
titles: R. Greenberg
stunt co-ordinator: Roy Scammel
Tom Skerritt, Sigourney Weaver, John Hurt, Ian Holm, Veronica Cartwright, Harry Dean Stanton, Yaphet Kotto, Helen Horton (voice only), Bolaji Badejo (as the Alien)

Alien 3 *

USA/GB 1992 115m Rankcolor Panavision Dolby
Ripley unwittingly unleashes an alien on a distant planet, now being used as a prison for murderers and rapists.

Slick looking but imperfectly scripted

addition to the series whose production problems were well publicised at the time. Something of a disappointment compared to the first two entries. Weaver received $5m for her role, which involved the shaving of her head.
p: Gordon Carroll, David Giler, Walter Hill, Sigourney Weaver for TCF/Brandywine
exec p: Ezra Swerdlow
w: David Giler, Walter Hill, Larry Ferguson
story: Vincent Ward (the film's original director)
d: David Fincher
ph: Alex Thomson
m: Elliot Goldenthal
ed: Terry Rawlings
pd: Norman Reynolds
cos: Bob Ringwood, David Perry
sp: George Gibbs, Richard Edlund
sound: Tony Dawe, Harry Snodgrass
alien effects: Alec Gillis, Tom Woodruff Jr
2nd unit d: David Hogan, Martin Brierley
2nd unit ph: Paul Beeson, Nic Morris, Ken Shane, Tony Spratling
titles: John Beach
Sigourney Weaver, Charles Dance, Charles S. Dutton, Paul McGann, Brian Glover, Ralph Brown, Pete Postlethwaite, Danny Webb, Lance Henricksen, Hi Ching

Aliens **
USA/GB 1986 137m Technicolor Panavision Dolby
Officer Ripley and a crew of marines are sent to destroy an army of aliens which have infiltrated a small colony.

Commercially orientated but technically adroit sequel to Alien which, once it gets going, provides a rollercoaster ride of shocks and thrills. A special edition was later released on video, which included 17 minutes of previously unseen footage. Weaver was, somewhat surprisingly, nominated for a best actress Oscar for her performance.
p: Gale Anne Hurd for TCF/Brandywine
exec p: Walter Hill, David Giler, Gordon Carroll
w: James Cameron
story: James Cameron, David Giler, Walter Hill
d: JAMES CAMERON
ph: Adrian Biddle
m: JAMES HORNER
ed: Ray Lovejoy
pd: Peter Lamont
ad: Terence Ackland Snow, Bert Davey, Fred Hole, Ken Court, Michael Lamont
cos: Emma Porteous
sp: Robert Skotak, Stan Winston, John Richardson, Suzanne Benson (aa)
sound: Roy Charman, Graham V.

Hartstone, Nichola Le Messurier, Michael A. Carter
2nd unit d: Stan Winston
stunt co-ordinator: Paul Weston
Sigourney Weaver, Michael Biehn, Paul Reisner, Lance Henricksen, Carrie Henn, Bill Paxton, William Hope, Ricco Ross, Al Matthews

The Aliens Are Coming *
USA 1980 96m Technicolour TVM
Aliens land on earth and begin to possess human bodies, their intention being colonization.

Fair science-fiction hokum in the tried and tested Invasion of the Body Snatchers manner.
p: Quinn Martin for NBC
exec p: Philip Saltzman
w: Robert W. Lenski
d: Harvey Hart
ph: Jacques Marquette
m: William Goldstein
md: John Elizalde
ed: Richard Brockway, Jim Gross
ad: George B. Chan, Norman Newberry
cos/sp: no credits given
sound: Kirk Schuler
Tom Mason, Melinda Lee, Max Gail, Caroline McWilliams, Eric Braeden, Matthew Laborteaux, Fawne Harriman, Ed Harris, Curtis Credel, Laurence Haddon

All That Money Can Buy ***
USA 1941 106m bw
A poor 19th century Massachussetts farmer sells his soul to the devil for good luck and riches.

Clever, highly cinematic Faustian comedy-drama, put together with great style and imagination.
p: William Dieterle for RKO
w: DAN TOTHEROH, STEPHEN VINCENT BENET
story: Stephen Vincent Benet
d: WILLIAM DIETERLE
ph: JOSEPH AUGUST
m: BERNARD HERRMANN (aa)
ed: ROBERT WISE
ad: VAN NEST POLGLASE, AL HERMAN
cos: Edward Stevenson
sp: VERNON L. WALKER
sound: James G. Stewart, Hugh McDowell Jr
WALTER HUSTON, JAMES CRAIG, EDWARD ARNOLD, SIMONE SIMON, Anne Shirley, Jane Darwell, Gene Lockhart, John Qualen, H. B. Warner

Alland, William (1916-)
American producer with a penchant for science fiction (It Came from Outer Space, This Island Earth, The Space Children,

etc.). A former actor and member of Orson Welles' Mercury Theatre troupe, he can be spotted in Citizen Kane as the investigative reporter. Joined the US Air Force during the war, after which he wrote for radio. Turned producer for Universal in 1952 and worked on many of director Jack Arnold's films. Other credits include The Rare Breed and Look in Any Window, which he also directed.
Genre credits:
The Creature from the Black Lagoon (1954), Revenge of the Creature (1955 - & story), Tarantula (1956), The Creature Walks Among Us (1956), The Mole People (1956), The Land Unknown (1957), The Deadly Mantis (1957 - & story), The Colossus of New York (1958)

Allen, Nancy (1950-)
American actress with modelling experience. She began her film career in 1973 in The Last Detail. In 1979 she married director Brian de Palma, many of whose films she has appeared in. They divorced in 1984, since which time she has appeared in all three Robocop films. Other credits include I Wanna Hold Your Hand, Home Movies, 1941, Blow Out and Acting on Impulse.
Genre credits:
Carrie (1975), Dressed to Kill (1980), Strange Invaders (1983), The Philadelphia Experiment (1984), Terror in the Aisles (1984), Poltergeist III (1988)

Allen, Patrick (1919-)
Canadian born actor perhaps best known for his countless television commercial voiceovers, though he has also enjoyed a healthy film career, often in supporting roles. Redubbed Leon Greene in The Devil Rides Out. Other credits include The Long Haul, Puppet On a Chain, The Wild Geese and The Sea Wolves.
Genre credits:
Captain Clegg (1962 - aka Night Creatures), Night of the Big Heat (1967 - aka Island of the Burning Damned), The Devil Rides Out (1968 - aka The Devil's Bride - voice only), The Body Stealers (1969), When Dinosaurs Ruled the Earth (1970), Winter with Dracula (1973 - voice only), Persecution (1974 - aka The Terror of Sheba)

Allied Artists
American studio which, along with its subsidiary Monogram, produced a number of undistinguished second-feature horrors utilizing such talent as William Castle and Roger Corman in his pre-Poe days.
Genre filmography:
The Maze (1953), Daughter of Dr Jekyll

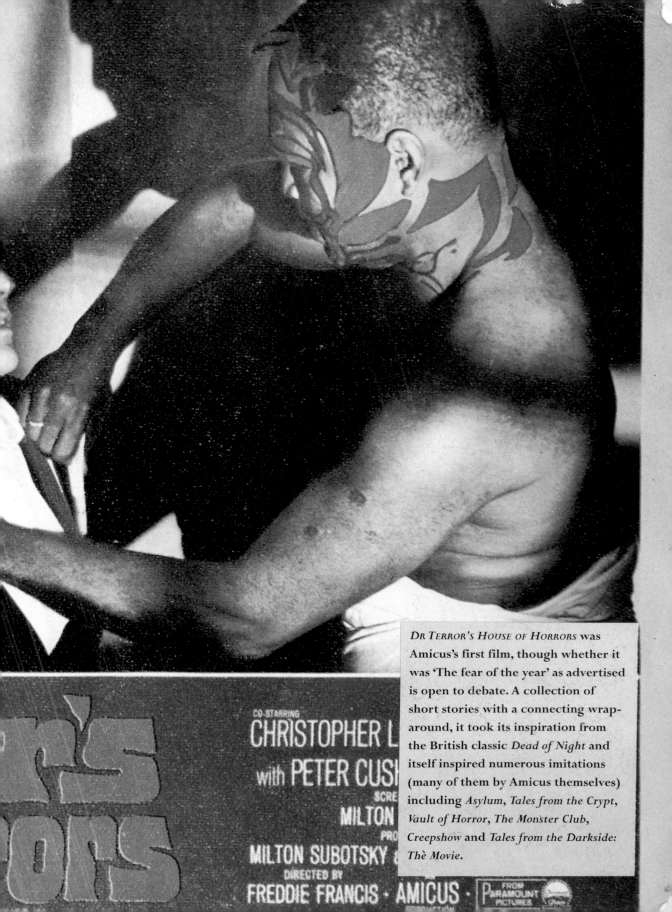

DR TERROR'S HOUSE OF HORRORS was Amicus's first film, though whether it was 'The fear of the year' as advertised is open to debate. A collection of short stories with a connecting wrap-around, it took its inspiration from the British classic *Dead of Night* and itself inspired numerous imitations (many of them by Amicus themselves) including *Asylum*, *Tales from the Crypt*, *Vault of Horror*, *The Monster Club*, *Creepshow* and *Tales from the Darkside: The Movie*.

CO-STARRING
CHRISTOPHER L[EE]
with PETER CUSH[ING]
SCRE[ENPLAY]
MILTON [SUBOTSKY]
PRO[DUCED]
MILTON SUBOTSKY &
DIRECTED BY
FREDDIE FRANCIS · AMICUS ·
FROM PARAMOUNT PICTURES

(1957), *Attack of the Crab Monsters* (1957), *Macabre* (1957), *From Hell It Came* (1957), *The Bride and the Beast* (1957), *Frankenstein 1970* (1958), *Attack of the Fifty Foot Woman* (1958), *The House on Haunted Hill* (1958), *Black Zoo* (1962)

Alligator *

USA 1980 91m DeLuxe
An unwanted pet alligator is flushed down a toilet. In the sewers it grows to an enormous size and years later emerges to terrorize the city.

Quirky low-budget horror comic on similar lines to the same writer's *Piranha*. An unsuccessful sequel, *Alligator II: The Mutation*, appeared in 1991.
p: Brandon Chase for Group 1/Alligator Associates
exec p: Robert S. Bremson
w: John Sayles
d: Lewis Teague
ph: Joseph Mangine
m: Craig Hundley
ed: Larry Bock, Ronald Medico
ad: Michael Erler
cos: Constance Sech
sp: Richard O. Helmer, William F. Short
sound: Arthur Names
2nd unit d: Paul Stader, Miller Drake
2nd unit ph: Hanania Baer, Peter Smokler
underwater ph: Jack Cooperman
stunt co-ordinator: Conrad Palmisano
Robert Forster, Robin Miker, Michael Gazzo, Dean Jagger, Sidney Lassick, John Carter, Perry Lang

Almost Human
see Shock Waves

Alone in the Dark

USA 1982 96m colour
A power failure causes the security system at a mental hospital to break down, and the inmates go on the rampage.

Incredibly inept and tasteless - not to mention boring - horror flick. Inane rubbish with the cast at the end of their tether.
p: Robert Shaye for New Line
w/d: Jack Sholder
ph: Joseph Mangine
m: Renato Serio
ed: Arline Garson
ad: Peter Monroe
make-up effects: Tom Savini, Tom Brumberger, Don Lumpkin
Jack Palance, Donald Pleasence, Martin Landau, Dwight Schultz, Erland Van Lidth, Deborah Hadwell, Lee-Taylor Allen

Altered States **

USA 1980 102m Technicolor
A scientist experiments with an unknown drug whilst in a sensory deprivation tank

and finds himself transmuted back through human evolution.

Super slick amalgam of horror and psychology with a dash of *Dr Jekyll and Mr Hyde*. All very serious but the technical credits are excellent.
p: Howard Gottfried for Warner
exec p: Daniel Melnick
w: Sidney Aaron
novel: Paddy Chayevsky
d: KEN RUSSELL
ph: Jordan Cronenweth
m: John Corigliano
ed: ERIC JENKINS
pd: Richard MacDonald
cos: Ruth Myers
sp: Bran Ferren, Chuck Gaspar
sound: Willie Burton
make-up effects: DICK SMITH, CARL FULLERTON, CRAIG REARDON
William Hurt, Blair Brown, Bob Balaban, Charles Haid, Thaao Penghlis, Dori Brenner, Peter Brandon, Drew Barrymore, Jack Murdoc, George Gaynes

The Amazing Mr Blunden **

GB 1972 99m Eastmancolor
In 1918, two children living in the grounds of a decaying mansion befriend the ghosts of two children murdered there a hundred years previously and travel back in time to save them.

Thoroughly charming ghost story for older children and their parents, done in the style of the same director's *The Railway Children*. Careful period detail and enjoyable performances, particularly from Diana Dors as the wicked housekeeper, always make it worth a look.
p: Barry Levinson for Hemdale/Hemisphere
w/d: LIONEL JEFFRIES
novel: Antonio Barker
ph: Gerry Fisher
m: ELMER BERNSTEIN
ed: Teddy Darvas
pd: Wilfred Shingleton
cos: Elsa Fennell
sp: Pat Moore
sound: Gordon Everett
LAURENCE NAISMITH, James Villiers, Lynn Frederick, DIANA DORS, Dorothy Alison, David Lodge, Rosalyn Lander, Marc Granger, Madeleine Smith, Eric Chitty, Deddie Davies, Paul Eddington, Graham Crowden, Gary Miller, Stuart Lock

American International Productions see A. I. P.

Amicus

Formed in Britain in 1964 by American producers Milton Subotsky and Max J. Rosenberg, Amicus Productions gave

• **Peter Cushing and friend in Amicus's** *From Beyond the Grave*, **one of their better all star portmanteaux produced during sixties and seventies.**

Hammer a run for their money in the sixties and early seventies by churning out a number of horror subjects, often utilizing Hammer talent, including director Freddie Francis and stars Peter Cushing and Christopher Lee. All of the films were either produced or executive produced by Subotsky and Rosenberg, with Subotsky often providing the scripts, too. Their most successful items proved to be compendium films, which were patterned after the 1945 Ealing classic *Dead of Night*, the first of which was *Dr Terror's House of Horrors* in 1964. Subotsky and Rosenberg went their own ways in 1977, the result being that Amicus was wound down as a production company, though their films continue to be late night staples. Non-horror subjects include *Dr Who and the Daleks*, *Daleks Invasion Earth: 2150 A. D.*, *The Terrornauts*, *They Came from Beyond Space* and *The Mind of Mr Soames*.
Genre filmography:
Dr Terror's House of Horrors (1965), *The Skull* (1965), *The Deadly Bees* (1965), *The Psychopath* (1965), *Torture Garden* (1967), *Scream and Scream Again* (1969), *The House That Dripped Blood* (1970), *I, Monster* (1970), *Tales from the Crypt* (1971), *Asylum* (1972), *And Now the Screaming Starts* (1972), *Vault of Horror* (1973), *Madhouse* (1974), *From Beyond the Grave* (1974), *The Beast Must Die* (1974 - aka *Black Werewolf*), *The Land That Time Forgot* (1974), *At the Earth's Core* (1976), *The People That Time Forgot* (1977)

An American Werewolf in London *

USA/GB 1981 97m Technicolor

Whilst exploring the Yorkshire moors, two American tourists are attacked by a werewolf. Subsequently, one of them is turned into a zombie whilst the other becomes a murderous werewolf at every full moon.

Sometimes engaging but not always successful mixture of comedy and horror which nevertheless proved very successful at the box office. Occasionally effective, despite itself, its incredible make-up effects broke new ground at the time.
p: George L. Folsey Jr for Polygram/Lycanthrope
exec p: Jon Peters, Peter Guber
w/d: John Landis
ph: Robert Paynter
m: Elmer Bernstein
ed: Malcolm Campbell
ad: Leslie Dilley
cos: Deborah Nadoolman
make-up effects: RICK BAKER (aa)
sound: Ivan Sharrock, Gerry Humphreys
stunt co-ordinator: Alf Joint
DAVID NAUGHTON, Griffin Dunne, Jenny Agutter, John Woodvine, Brian Glover, Lila Kaye, Frank Oz, Rik Mayall, Paul Kember, Don McKillop, Paddy Ryan, Anne-Marie Davies

Amityville: The Demon see
Amityville 3D

Amityville: The Evil Escapes see
Amityville 4: The Evil Escapes

The Amityville Horror
USA 1979 118m Movielab
An unsuspecting family moves into a house where a series of murders took place and discover a malevolent presence.

Bland haunted house shenanigans, allegedly based on fact. One always expects more than it delivers, though it proved popular enough to provoke several sequels. Worth a glance for Steiger's over-the-top performance as a priest. It was followed by *Amityville II: The Possession* (1982), *Amityville 3D* (1983 - aka *Amityville: The Demon*), *Amityville 4: The Evil Escapes* (1989 -TVM), *The Amityville Curse* (1990), *Amityville 1992: It's About Time* (1992) and *Amityville: A New Generation* (1993 - aka *Amityville 1993: The Image of Evil*).
p: Ronald Saland, Elliot Geisinger for AIP/Cinema 77
exec p: Samuel Z. Arkoff
w: Sandorn Stern
book: Jay Anson
d: Stuart Rosenberg
ph: Fred J. Koenekamp
m: Lalo Schifrin
ed: Robert J. Brown Jr
pd: Kim Swados
sp: William Cruse, Delwyn Rheaume

James Brolin, Margot Kidder, Rod Steiger, Murray Hamilton, Michael Sacks, Natasha Ryan

Amityville II: The Possession
USA 1982 104m DeLuxe
The eldest son of an unsuspecting family turns into a demon after unwittingly moving into the house of horror.

Outlandish 'prequel' which is little more than an artless rip-off of *The Exorcist*.
p: Iran Smith, Stephen R. Greenwald for Orion/Dino de Laurentiis
exec p: Bernard Williams
w: Tommy Lee Wallace
d: Damiano Damiani
ph: Franco Di Giacomo
m: Lalo Schifrin
ed: Sam O'Steen
pd: Pieruigi Basile
cos: William Kellard
sp: Glen Robinson
sound: Kim Ornitz, Dick Vorisek
make-up effects: John Caglione
titles: R. Greenberg
James Olsen, Burt Young, Rutanya Alda, Andrew Prine, Jack Magner, Diane Franklin, Moses Gunn

Amityville 3D
USA 1984 93m Technicolor 3D
A sceptical magazine reporter buys the Amityville house and, after the expected occurrences, discovers it to be a gateway to hell.

Occasionally lively addition to the series thanks to its effective use of 3D. Otherwise just as predictable as the other episodes.
p: Stephen F. Kesten for Universal/Orion/Dino de Laurentiis
w: William Wales
d: Richard Flesicher
ph: Fred Schuler
m: Howard Blake
ed: Frank J. Urioste
pd: Giorgio Postiglione, Justin Scoppa.
make-up effects: John Caglione
Tony Roberts, Tess Harper, Candy Clark, Robert Joy, John Beal, Leora Dana

Amityville 4: The Evil Escapes
USA 1989 96m colour TVM
A weird lamp has a strange effect on the residents of the house of horrors.

Silly tele-sequel to the three theatrical features, neither better nor worse than its predecessors.
p: Bary Bernardi for ACI/Spectator
exec p: Steve White, Sandor Stern
w/d: Sandor Stern
novel: John G. Jones
ph: Tom Richmond
m: Rick Conrad
ed: Skip Schodink
pd: Kandy Berley Stern
cos: Jai Galai
sound: Richard Birnbaum
Patty Duke, Jane Wyatt, Norman Lloyd, Frederic Lehne, Brandy Gold, Aaron Eisenberg, Lou Hancock, Geri Betzler

• **David Naughton watches himself begin to metamorphose into a lycanthrope in John Landis's horror comedy *An American Werewolf in London*. The spectacular make-up effects were provided by Rick Baker, who won an Oscar for his painstaking efforts.**

Amok see Schizo

Amsterdamned
Netherlands 1988 113m colour
The Dutch police search Amsterdam for
a killer who is scuba diving through the
canals as a means of attack and escape.

Intermittently lively thriller with an
interesting premise. Much too long to
sustain itself, however.
p: Laurens Geels, Dick Maas for First
Floor Features/Vestron
w/d/m: Dick Maas
ph: Marc Felperlaan
ed: Hans Van Dongen
pd: Dick Schillmans
cos: Yan Tax
sp: Martin Gutteridge
make-up effects: Sjoerd Didden
2nd unit ph: Erwin Steen
underwater ph: Peter Brugman
Huub Stapel, Monique van de Ven,
Serge-Henri Valcke, Tenneke Hartzuiker,
Wim Zomer, Hidde Maas, Lou Landre.

And Now the Screaming Starts
GB 1973 91m Technicolor
In 1795, events from the past haunt a
bride at her new country home.

Poorish horror movie with just a
couple of shock moments in its favour,
including a convincingly mobile severed
hand.
p: Max J. Rosenberg, Milton Subotsky
for Amicus/Harbour
exec p: Gustav Berne
w: Roger Marshall
novel: David Case
d: Roy Ward Baker
ph: Denys Coop
m: Douglas Gamley
ed: Peter Tanner
ad: Tony Curtis
cos: Betty Adamson.
sound: Norman Bolland
Peter Cushing, Stephanie Beacham,
Herbert Lom, Ian Ogilvy, Patrick
Magee, Geoffrey Whitehead, Guy Rolfe,
Rosalie Crutchley

And Soon the Darkness *
GB 1970 99m Technicolor
Two English girls on a cycling holiday in
France are terrorized by a sex maniac.

Old fashioned murder mystery,
rather typical of its producers' output,
but offering a couple of good thrills
along its overstretched way.
p: Albert Fennell, Brian Clemens for
Associated British
w: Brian Clemens, Terry Nation
d: Robert Fuest
ph: Ian Wilson
m: Laurie Johnson
ed: Anne Chegwidden
pd: Philip Harrison

cos: Roy Ponting
sound: Bill Rowe, Terry Allen
Pamela Franklin, Michele Dotrice,
Sandor Eles, John Nettleton, Clare Kelly

And Then There Were None ***
USA 1945 97m bw
Ten guests on an otherwise deserted
Cornish island are murdered one by one
by a maniac who is among their number.

Stylish murder mystery with a
compelling plot, especially for those
who haven't read the book or seen the
play. The touches of black humour make
it all the more enjoyable. It was remade
in 1947 as Ten Little Niggers (TVM), in
1966 as Ten Little Indians, in 1974 as And
Then There Were None and in 1989 as Ten
Little Indians (aka Death on Safari). The
latter three remakes were all produced
by Harry Alan Towers.
p: Rene Clair for TCF
w: Dudley Nichols
novel/play: Agatha Christie
d: RENE CLAIR
ph: LUCIEN ANDRIOT
m: MARIO CATELNUOVO-TEDESCO
md: Charles Previn
ed: Harvey Manger
ad: Ernest Fetge
BARRY FITZGERALD, WALTER
HUSTON, Louis Hayward, June
Duprez, ROLAND YOUNG, RICHARD
HAYDN, C. Aubrey Smith, JUDITH
ANDERSON, Queenie Leonard, Mischa
Auer, Harry Thurston

Anders, Luana (1940-)
American actress who appeared in a
handful of Corman quickies in the early
sixties. Her other credits include Easy
Rider, Shampoo, The Missouri Breaks, Goin'
South and Personal Best.
Genre credits:
The Pit and the Pendulum (1961), Night
Tide (1963), Dementia 13 (1963)

Angel Heart *
USA 1987 113m Technicolor Dolby
In 1955, a private detective searching
for a missing singer finds himself up to
his neck in black magic, murder and
deception.

Curious supernatural crime thriller
which tries to have its cake and eat it,
but ultimately fails because it never
really explains itself.
p: Alan Marshall, Elliott Kastner for
Tri-Star/Carolco/Winkast-Union
exec p: Mario Kassar, Andrew Vajna
w/d: Alan Parker
novel: William Hjortsberg
ph: Michael Seresin
m: Trevor Jones
ed: Gerry Hambling
pd: Brian Morris

cos: Aude Bronson-Howard
sound: Danny Michael
stunt co-ordinator: Harry Madsen
ch: Louis Falco
Mickey Rourke, Robert de Niro (as
Louis Ciphers), Charlotte Rampling,
Lisa Bonet, Stocker Fontelieu

Ankers, Evelyn (1918-1985)
British actress, a graduate of London's
Royal Academy of Dramatic Art. Made
her film début in 1933 with The Villiers
Diamond which she followed with
appearances in Rembrandt, Over the Moon
and Knight without Armour for producer
Alexander Korda. Went to Hollywood in
1940 and made her first film there,
Burma Convoy, the same year. She
became Universal's leading scream
queen of the early forties. Her other
credits include Bachelor Daddy, The Great
Impersonation, His Butler's Sister and
Sherlock Holmes and the Voice of Terror.
Genre credits:
Hold That Ghost (1941), The Wolf Man
(1941), The Ghost of Frankenstein (1941),
Captive Wild Woman (1943), The Mad
Ghoul (1943), Jungle Woman (1944),
Sherlock Holmes and the Pearl of Death
(1944), The Invisible Man's Revenge
(1944), Weird Woman (1944), The Frozen
Ghost (1945)

Anthropophagus see The
Anthropophagous Beast

The Anthropophagous Beast
It 1980 81m Stacofilm
Tourists on a Greek island find
themselves prey to a killer with a
penchant for eating his victims' viscera.

Straightforward but often extremely
gory shocker including a scene in which
the killer shoves his hand up a pregnant
woman's vagina, pulls out her baby and
eats it! Not for the squeamish. A sequel,
Monster Hunter (aka Anthropophagus
II/Absurd) followed in 1981.
p: RPA/Elettronica Calpini
w: Luigi Montefiore, Aristide
Massaccesi
story: Luigi Montefiore
d: Joe D'Amato
ph: Enrico Birbicchi
m: Marcello Giombini
ed: Ornella Michel
ad: Mario Paladini
cos: Ennio Micchettoni
sound: Goffredo Salvatori
Tisa Farrow, Saverio Vallone, Vanessa
Steiger, George Eastman, Zora Kerova,
Mark Bodin

April Fool's Day
USA 1986 88m Metrocolor Dolby
Friends spending the weekend on a

remote island are killed off one by one - or are they?

Tame attempt to inject some humour into the *Friday 13th* formula. Unfortunately, it doesn't quite go far enough.
p: Frank Mancuso Jr for Paramount/Hometown
w: Danilo Bach
d: Fred Walton
ph: Charles Minskly
m: Charles Bernstein
ed: Bruce Green
ad: Stewart Campbell
cos: Lid Kellas
sp: Martin Becker
sound: Davd Lewis Yewdall
Deborah Foreman, Griffin O'Neal, Thomas F. Wilson, Deborah Goodrich, Ken Olandt, Mike Nomad, Leah King Pinsent, Clayton Rohner, Tom Heaton

Aquarius see Stage Fright

Arachnophobia *
US 1990 109m DeLuxe Dolby
A deadly South American spider causes havoc in a small midwestern township.

Old fashioned scare story which was promoted with the tag line, 'Eight Legs. Two Fangs. And an attitude.' Well enough made, though likely to be more frightening to those with a genuine disaffection for spiders.
p: Kathleen Kennedy, Richard Vane for Hollywood Pictures/Amblin/Tangled Web
exec p: Steven Spielberg, Frank Marshall
w: Don Jakoby, Wesley Strick
story: Don Jakoby, Al Williams
d: Frank Marshall
ph: Mikael Salomon.
m: Trevor Jones
ed: Michael Kahn
pd: James Bissell
sound: Ronald Judkin
creature effects: Chris Walas
stunt co-ordinator: Chuck Waters
Jeff Daniels, John Goodman, Julian Sands, Harley Jane Kozak, Henry Jones, Stuart Pankin, Mark L. Taylor, Brian McNamara

Argento, Asia (1975-)
Italian actress, the daughter of director Dario Argento and actress Daria Nicolodi. Has appeared in several of her father's productions.
Genre credits:
Demons 2 (1986 - aka *Demoni 2*), *The Zoo* (1988), *The Church* (1989), *Trauma* (1993)

Argento, Dario (1940-)
Cult Italian writer-director with a penchant for slick, violent thrillers and

horror films, often with strong colour schemes. The son of producer Salvatore Argento and the brother of writer-producer Claudio Argento, he is a former critic who turned to screenplay writing in the late sixties with such films as *Cemetry Without Crosses*, *Once Upon a Time in the West* (for which he co-wrote the story with Bernardo Bertolucci), *Today Me... Tomorrow You* (aka *Oggi a Me... Domani a Te*), *Sex Revolution*, *Zero Probability* and *Five Man Army* (aka *Un Esercito di 5 Uomini*), etc. His first film as a writer-director was the giallo thriller *The Bird with the Crystal Plumage* in 1969, which successfully launched him on the international scene, where he enhanced his reputation with such films as *The Blow Up*-like *Deep Red*, the gorily garish *Suspiria* (another international hit) and *Inferno*, though his more recent work has failed to live up to these genre classics. Dubbed by many as 'the Italian Hitchcock', his other credits include *One Night at Dinner*, *Cat O'Nine Tails*, *Four Flies on Grey Velvet* (aka *Quattro Mosche di Velluto Grigio*) and *Le Cirque Giornate*. He is now also producing for directors Lamberto Bava and Michele Soavi, two proteges who were both once his assistants.
Genre credits:
Deep Red (1975 - aka *Profondo Rosso*/*The Hatchet Murders* -co-w/d), *Suspiria* (1976 - co-w/d), *Dawn of the Dead* (1979 - aka *Zombies* - oversaw European cut only), *Inferno* (1980 - w/d), *Tenebres* (1982 - aka *Tenebres*/*Unsane*/*Sotto gli Occhi dell'Assassino* - co-w/story/d), *Phenomena* (1985 - aka *Creepers* - co-w/d), *Demons* (1985 - aka *Demoni* - co-w/p), *Opera* (1987 - aka *Terror at the Opera* - co-w/story/d), *Demons 2* (1987 - aka *Demoni 2* - co-w/p), *The Church* (1988 - aka *La Chiesa* - co-w/p), *Two Evil Eyes* (1990 - aka *Due Occhi Diabolici*/*Due Occhi Malocchio* - co-w/co-p/co-d [with George Romero]), *The Sect* (1991 - aka *La Setta*/*The Devil's Daughter* - co-w/co-p), *Trauma* (1993 - co-w/p/d), *The Stendhal Syndrome* (1996 - w/p/d)

Arkoff, Samuel Z. (1918-)
American producer, executive producer and studio executive who co-founded American International Pictures (AIP) with James H. Nicholson in 1955, through which he has presented dozens of low budget horror, sci-fi and exploitation pictures aimed primarily at the teenage/drive-in market. These also include several of Roger Corman's highly successful Poe series (mostly for Alta Vista) as well as early films by such directors as Francis Ford Coppola,

Woody Allen and Martin Scorsese. He later sold AIP to Filmways and set up the Samuel Z. Arkoff Company in 1980 and Arkoff International Productions (AIP!) in 1981. Other credits include *Reform School Girl*, *The Bonnie Parker Story*, *Beach Party*, *Dillinger*, *Futureworld* and *How to Beat the High Cost of Living*.
Genre credits:
The She-Creature (1956 - p), *The Amazing Colossal Man* (1957 -co-exec p), *I Was a Teenage Frankenstein* (1957 - aka *Teenage Frankenstein* - co-exec p), *Blood of Dracula* (1957 - aka *Blood Is My Heritage*/*Blood of the Demon* - co-exec p), *Attack of the Puppet People* (1958 - co-exec p), *How to Make a Monster* (1958 - co-exec p), *Night of the Blood Beast* (1958 - co-exec p), *The Spider* (1958 - aka *Earth vs. the Spider* - co-exec p), *Teenage Caveman* (1958 - aka *Prehistoric World* - co-exec p), *Terror from the Year 5000* (1958 - co-exec p), *War of the Colossal Beast* (1958 - aka *The Terror Strikes* - co-exec p), *Attack of the Giant Leeches* (1959 - aka *Demons of the Swamp* - co-exec p), *A Bucket of Blood* (1959 - co-exec p), *The Ghost of Dragstrip Hollow* (1959 - co-exec p), *The Headless Ghost* (1959 - co-exec p), *House of Usher* (1960 - aka *The Fall of the House of Usher* - p), *The Pit and the Pendulum* (1961 - co-exec p), *Tales of Terror* (1962 - co-exec p), *The Raven* (1963 - co-exec p), *X - The Man with X-Ray Eyes* (1963 - aka *The Man with X-Ray Eyes* - co-exec p), *The Comedy of Terrors* (1964 -co-p), *Die, Monster, Die!* (1965 - aka *Monster of Terror* - co-exec p), *The Ghost in the Invisible Bikini* (1966 - p), *De Sade* (1969 - p), *The Dunwich Horror* (1970 - co-p), *The Abominable Dr Phibes* (1971 - co-exec p), *Murders in the Rue Morgue* (1971 - co-exec p), *Blacula* (1972 - exec p), *Dr Phibes Rises Again* (1972 - co-exec p), *Madhouse* (1974 - exec p), *Food of the Gods* (1975 - exec p), *Empire of the Ants* (1977 - exec p), *The Island of Dr Moreau* (1977 - co-exec p), *The People That Time Forgot* (1977 - exec p), *The Amityville Horror* (1979 - exec p), *Empire of the Ants* (1979 -exec p), *CHOMPS* (1979 - exec p), *Dressed to Kill* (1980 - exec p)

Armstrong, Michael (1944-)
British writer and director who, in the late sixties and early seventies, divided his time between horror films and sexploitation (*The Sex Thief*, *Eskimo Nell*, *Adventures of a Taxi Driver*, *Adventures of a Private Eye*, *Adventures of a Plumber's Mate*, etc.). He began directing in 1969 with a short titled *The Image* (aka *Sex in the Grass*) which starred the then unknown David Bowie.
Genre credits:
The Haunted House of Horror (1969 - aka

The Dark / The Horror House - co-w / d), *Mark of the Devil* (1969 - aka *Austria 1700 / Hexen Geschandet und zu Tode Gequalt* - co-w / d [co-w as Sergio Casstner]), *The Black Panther* (1977 - w), *Dreamhouse* - aka *Scream House / Screamtime* - short - w), *The House of the Long Shadows* (1983 - w)

Armstrong, Robert (1890-1973)

Tough-acting and fast-talking American supporting actor (real name Donald Robert Smith) with many films to his credit, including *G-Men*, *Gangs of the Waterfront*, *Sea of Grass*, *The Paleface*, *Las Vegas Shakedown* and *Those Who Think Young*, though he is perhaps best known for playing producer Carl Denham in *King Kong* and its sequel.

Genre credits:

The Most Dangerous Game (1932 - aka *The Hounds of Zaroff*), *King Kong* (1933), *Son of Kong* (1933), *The Mad Ghoul* (1943), *Mighty Joe Young* (1949)

Army of Darkness *

USA 1992 89m Technicolor

Ash finds himself transported back to medieval times where he is hailed a conquering hero.

Disappointing follow-up to the two *Evil Dead* films which, despite a few good moments and a larger budget, doesn't quite hit its mark. Two different endings were filmed, both of which were used: one for the theatrical release, one for the video.

p: Robert Tapert for Universal / Introvision International
exec p: Dino de Laurentiis
w: Sam Raimi, Ivan Raimi
d: Sam Raimi
ph: Bill Pope
m: Joe LoDuca, Danny Elfman
ed: Bob Morawski, R. O. C. Sandstorm
pd: Tony Tremblay
cos: Ida Gearon
sp: William Mesa, Introvision International
sound: Alan Howarth
make-up effects: Tony Gardner and others
Bruce Campbell, Embeth Davidtz, Marcus Gilbert, Ian Abercrombie, Richard Grove, Michael Earl Reid, Timothy Patrick Quill, Bridget Fonda

Army of Darkness - The Medieval Dead see Army of Darkness

Arness, James (1923-)

Tall American actor (real name James Aurness) perhaps best remembered for Marshal Dillon in TV's long-running *Gunsmoke*, though he was certainly memorable as *The Thing* in the 1952 movie.

Arnold, Jack (1916-1992)

American director with an inclination for science fiction (*It Came from Outer Space*, *The Incredible Shrinking Man*, *The Space Children*, etc.), often in association with producer William Alland. A former actor and stage manager on Broadway and in London's West End, he gained experience as a filmmaker in the Army Signal Corps during World War Two with documentary maker Robert Flaherty. Became a documentary maker himself after the war, turning to films proper in 1953 with *Girls in the Night* (aka *Life After Dark*).

Genre credits:

The Creature from the Black Lagoon (1954), *Revenge of the Creature* (1955), *Tarantula* (1955), *Monster on the Campus* (1958)

Arrighi, Nike (1946-)

Australian-Italian actress with roles in a couple of Hammer horrors to her credit, most notably as Tanith in *The Devil Rides Out*. Other credits include *Women in Love* and *Day for Night*.

Genre credits:

The Devil Rides Out (1968 - aka *The Devil's Bride*), *Countess Dracula* (1970)

Arsenic and Old Lace **

USA 1944 (made in 1942) 118m bw

The nephew of two dear old ladies discovers that, much to his surprise, his aunts are poisoning their gentlemen lodgers.

Frenetic adaptation of the celebrated stage farce which, despite memorable highlights, tends to wear after the first hour.

p: Frank Capra for Warner
exec p: Jack L. Warner
w: Julius J. Epstein, Philip G. Epstein
play: JOSEPH KESSERLING
d: Frank Capra
ph: Sol Polito
m: Max Steiner
md: Leo F. Forbstein
ed: Daniel Mandell
ad: Max Parker
cos: Orry-Kelly
sp: Byron Haskin, Robert Burks
sound: C. H. Riggs
make-up: Perc Westmore
Cary Grant, JOSEPHINE HULL, JEAN ADAIR, Priscilla Lane, Raymond Massey, Peter Lorre, John Alexander, James Gleason, Jack Carson, Edward Everett Horton, Grant Mitchell

Asher, Jack (1916-1994)

Distinguished British cinematographer and colour expert who entered the film industry in 1930 as an assistant cameraman at Gainsborough, where he became their resident camera operator in 1940. His first film as a director of photography was the Technicolor period piece *Jassy* in 1947, which he followed with such films as *Lili Marlene*, *The Young Lovers* and *Reach for the Sky*. In 1956 he photographed *The Curse of Frankenstein* for Hammer, which led to a long association with the studio. The brother of director Robert Asher (1915-), he photographed several of his brother's films in the sixties, including *She'll Have to Go* (which he co-produced), *The Intelligence Men*, *The Early Bird* and *That Riviera Touch*.

Genre credits:

The Curse of Frankenstein (1956), *Dracula* (1958 - aka *The Horror of Dracula*), *The Revenge of Frankenstein* (1958), *The Hound of the Baskervilles* (1959), *The Mummy* (1959), *The Man Who Could Cheat Death* (1959), *The Brides of Dracula* (1960), *The Two Faces of Dr Jekyll* (1960 - aka *House of Fright / Jekyll's Inferno*)

Ashley, John (1934-)

American actor familiar from countless sixties beach films (*Beach Party*, *Beach Blanket Bingo*, *Bikini Beach*, *Muscle Beach Party*, *How to Stuff a Wild Bikini*). He later went to the Philippines where he made a handful of low budget genre pictures for director Eddie Romero, after which he became a producer, most notably with TV's *The A-Team*.

Genre credits:

Frankenstein's Daughter (1958), *The Eye Creatures* (1968), *Brides of Blood* (1968), *The Mad Doctor of Blood Island* (1969), *Beast of Blood* (1970), *Beast of the Yellow Night* (1971), *The Twilight People* (1972), *Beyond Atlantic* (1973), *Savage Sisters* (1974)

Ashton, Roy (1909-1994)

Australian born make-up artist who came to Britain in 1933 to study art and music. Became an apprentice make-up artist at Gaumont shortly after, his first film being *Tudor Rose* in 1936. Following service in World War Two, he became a singer with The English Opera Group, returning to make-up in the late fifties when he became the head of Hammer's make-up department after the departure of former head Phil Leakey. He subsequently worked on all of the studio's key horror films, as well as many non-Hammer horrors for Amicus and Tyburn.

Genre credits:

The Man Who Changed His Mind (1936 - aka *The Man Who Lived Again*), *The Curse of Frankenstein* (1956 - assistant), *The Hound of the Baskervilles* (1959), *The Ugly Duckling* (1959), *The Mummy*

• **David Rintoul displays Roy Ashton's excellent werewolf make-up for Tyburn's** *Legend of the Werewolf.*

(1959), *The Man Who Could Cheat Death* (1959), *The Stranglers of Bombay* (1960), *The Curse of the Werewolf* (1960), *The Brides of Dracula* (1960), *The Two Faces of Dr Jekyll* (1960 - aka *House of Fright / Jekyll's Inferno*), *The Terror of the Tongs* (1961), *The Shadow of the Cat* (1961), *Captain Clegg* (1962 - aka *Night Creatures*), *The Old Dark House* (1962), *The Phantom of the Opera* (1962), *The Damned* (1963 - aka *These Are the Damned*), *Kiss of the Vampire* (1964 - aka *Kiss of Evil*), *Nightmare* (1964), *The Evil of Frankenstein* (1964), *The Curse of the Mummy's Tomb* (1964), *Fanatic* (1965 - aka *Die! Die! My Darling!*), *She* (1965), *Hysteria* (1965), *Dr Terror's House of Horrors* (1965), *Dracula - Prince of Darkness* (1966), *The Plague of the Zombies* (1966), *Rasputin - The Mad Monk* (1966), *The Reptile* (1966), *Tales from the Crypt* (1971), *Asylum* (1972), *Vault of Horror* (1972), *Frankenstein - The True Story* (1973 - TVM), *Persecution* (1974 - aka *The Terror of Sheba*), *Legend of the Werewolf* (1974), *The Ghoul* (1975), *The Monster Club* (1980)

Askwith, Robin (1950-)

British actor who became a star as Timothy Lea in the *Confessions* sex romps of the seventies (*Confessions of a Window Cleaner*, *Confessions of a Pop Performer*, *Confessions of a Driving Instructor*, *Confessions from a Holiday Camp*) and several other similarly themed films (*Stand Up Virgin Soldiers*, *Let's Get Laid*, etc.). He also popped up in a couple of horror films of the period.
Genre credits:
Tower of Evil (1972), *Horror Hospital* (1973)

The Asphyx

GB 1973 99m Eastmancolor Todd-AO
A Victorian gentleman discovers a means of photographing the soul as it leaves the body.
Silly horror hokum, flatly staged and certainly unworthy of the talent involved.
p: John Brittany for Glendale
w: Brian Comfort
story: Christina Beers, Laurence Beers
d: Peter Newbrook
ph: Frederick A. Young
m: Bill McGuffie
ed: Maxine Julius
pd: John Stoll
cos: Evelyn Gibbs
sp: Ted Samuels
sound: Ken Ritchie, Bob Jones
Robert Stephens, Robert Powell, Jane Lapotaire, Alex Scott, Fiona Walker, Ralph Arliss

Astley, Edwin

British composer with many film and television credits to his name, including the themes for TV's *Danger Man* and *The Saint*, many episodes of which he also scored. His other film credits include *Alias John Preston* and *Visa to Canton* (aka *Passport to China*).

Genre credits:
The Devil Girl from Mars (1954), *The Giant Behemoth* (1959 - aka *Behemoth the Sea Monster*), *The Phantom of the Opera* (1962), *Captain Clegg* (1962 - aka *Night Creatures*)

Asylum *

GB 1972 88m Eastmancolor
A doctor applying for a job at an asylum is promised the position if he can identify the former governor from five patients.
Reasonable Amicus horror compendium, typical if not quite the best of its kind.
p: Milton Subotsky, Max J. Rosenberg for Amicus / Harbor
exec p: Gustav Berne
w: Robert Bloch
d: Roy Ward Baker
ph: Denys Coop
m: Douglas Gamley
ed: Peter Tanner
ad: Tony Curtis
cos: Bridget Sellers
sound: Clive Smith, Norman Bolland, Robert Jones
make-up: Roy Ashton
Patrick Magee, Robert Powell, Peter Cushing, Herbert Lom, Richard Todd, Britt Ekland, Geoffrey Bayldon, Barbara Perkins, Sylvia Syms, Barry Morse, James Villiers, Megs Jenkins, Charlotte Rampling

Attack of the Fifty-Foot Woman

USA 1958 69m bw
A mid-western heiress grows to gigantic proportions after an encounter with a radio-active flying saucer.
Lunatic grade Z horror hokum, worth a look for the sheer absurdity of it all. A sort of distaff version of *The Amazing Colossal Man*.
p: Bernard Woolner for Allied Artists
exec p: James Marquette
w: Mark Hanna
d: Nathan Hertz
ph: Jacques Marquette
m: Paul Stein
ed: Edward Mann
ad / cos: no credits given
sound: Philip Mitchell
props: Richard Rubin
Allison Hayes, William Hudson, Roy Gordon, Yvette Vickers, Ken Terrell, George Douglas, Eileen Stevens, Frank Chase, Otto Waldid

Atwill, Lionel (1885-1946)

Intense looking British actor with stage experience from 1904 and film work from 1918. His role in *The Silent Witness* took him to Hollywood for the film

• An intense-looking Lionel Atwill.

version in 1932. He then stayed on to play all manner of mad scientists and burgomasters in horror films of the thirties and forties, his best roles being in *The Mystery of the Wax Museum* and *Son of Frankenstein* as the one-armed police chief. Other credits include *Captain Blood*, *The Road Back*, *The Three Musketeers* and *To Be Or Not To Be*. Also played Moriarty in *Sherlock Holmes and the Secret Weapon*.
Genre credits:
Dr X (1932), *The Mystery of the Wax Museum* (1933), *The Vampire Bat* (1933), *The Secret of the Blue Room* (1933), *Murders in the Zoo* (1933), *The Man Who*

Reclaimed His Head (1934), *Mark of the Vampire* (1935), *Son of Frankenstein* (1939), *The Hound of the Baskervilles* (1939), *The Gorilla* (1939), *Man-Made Monster* (1941), *The Mad Doctor of Market Street* (1941), *The Ghost of Frankenstein* (1942), *Night Monster* (1942), *The Strange Case of Dr RX* (1942), *Frankenstein Meets the Wolf Man* (1943), *House of Frankenstein* (1944), *Fog Island* (1945), *House of Dracula* (1945)

Audrey Rose

USA 1977 113m DeLuxe Panavision
An English professor is led to believe that his dead daughter has been reincarnated into the daughter of a New York couple.
  Vague variation on *The Exorcist*, but with none of that film's style or effect. It long outstays its welcome.
p: Joe Wizan, Frank de Felitta for UA
w: Frank de Felitta from his novel
d: Robert Wise
ph: Victor J. Kemper
m: Michael Small
ed: Karl Kress
pd: Harry Horne
cos: Dorothy Jeakins
sp: Henry Millar
sound: Tom Overton
Marsha Mason, Anthony Hopkins, John Beck, Norman Lloyd, Robert Walden, John Hillerman, Susan Swift

Austin, Ray (1932-)

British exploitation director who combined soft porn and horror in a couple of movies. Other credits include *It's the*

Only Way to Go and *Fun and Games*.
Genre credits:
Virgin Witch (1972), *House of the Living Dead* (1973)

The Awakening

GB 1980 105m Technicolor
An archaeologist lets loose the spirit of an evil Egyptian queen when he discovers her long-lost tomb.
  Dreary horror hokum which fails to achieve the desired effect. Based on Bram Stoker's novella *The Jewell of the Seven Stars*, it was previously filmed by Hammer as *Blood from the Mummy's Tomb*.
p: Robert Solo, Andrew Scheinman, Martin Shafer for EMI/Orion/British Lion/Solofilm
w: Allan Scott, Chris Bryant, Clive Exton
novel: Bram Stoker
d: Mike Newell
ph: Jack Cardiff
m: Claude Bolling
md: Marcus Dods
ed: Terry Rawlings
pd: Michael Stringer
cos: Phyllis Dalton
sp: John Stears
sound: Brian Simmons, Hugh Strain
titles: Maurice Binder
stunt co-ordinator: Alan Stuart
Charlton Heston, Susannah York, Stephanie Zimbalist, Jill Townsend, Patrick Drury, Bruce Myers, Nadim Sawalha, Ian McDiarmid, Ahmed Osman, Miriam Margolyes, Leonard Maguire

B

The Baby
USA 1972 102m colour
Murder follows when a social worker takes on the case of a man-child who is still treated like a baby by his mother and two sisters.

Weird but uninteresting thriller, too flatly handled to disguise the general tastelessness and foolishness.
p: Milton Polsky, Abe Polsky for Quintet
exec p: Elliott Feinman, Ralph Hirsch
w: Abe Polsky
d: Ted Post
ph: Michael Margulies
m: Gerald Fried
ed: Dick Wormeil, Bob Crawford Jr
ad: Michael Devine
cos: Diana Jewett
sound: Robert Harman
Ruth Roman, Anjanette Cromer, Marianna Hill, David Manzy, Suzanne Zenor

Bach, Barbara (1947-)
Glamorous American actress (real name Barbara Goldbach) who began making films in Italy whilst living there (*The Black Belly of the Tarantula*, *Stateline Motel*, etc.) before shooting to stardom as Bond girl Anya Amasova in *The Spy Who Loved Me*, which led to leading roles in such films as *Force Ten from Navarone* and *The Caveman* (in which she co-starred with her future husband Ringo Starr).
Genre credits:
The Humanoid (1979), *Screamers* (1979), *The Great Alligator* (1980), *The Unseen* (1981)

Backwoods see The Geek

Backwoods Massacre see Midnight

Baclanova, Olga (1899-1974)
Russian stage actress who made a few films in America (*Street of Sin*, *Docks of New York*, *Billion Dollar Scandal*), the most memorable of which was Tod Browning's *Freaks* (1932), in which she played a glamorous trapeze artist who marries a midget for his money, only to

be disfigured into a 'chicken' in the shocking climax.

Bad Taste
New Zealand 1987 92m colour
Humans defend themselves against man-eating aliens out to restock their food supplies.

Made over a period of four years, this determinedly gross splatter comedy is often energetically staged and has enough quirky touches to satisfy the late night crowd.
p: Peter Jackson for Wing Nut/New Zealand Film Commission
w: Peter Jackson, Tony Hiles, Ken Hammon
d/ph/sp: Peter Jackson
m: Michelle Scullion
ed: Peter Jackson, Jamie Selkirk
pd: no credit given
sound: Brent Burge
Mike Minett, Peter Jackson, Terry Potter, Pete O'Herne, Craig Smith, Dou Wren

Bakaleinikoff, Constantin (1898-1966)
Prolific Russian musical director, long in America. Headed RKO's musical department for eleven years from 1942, during which period he conducted several of Roy Webb's scores for the Val Lewton horror series.

Baker, Rick (1950-)
American make-up effects artist whose innovative work on *An American Werewolf in London* won him the first official Oscar for make-up, which he later followed with a second for the fantasy comedy *Harry and the Hendersons* (1987 - aka *Bigfoot and the Hendersons*) and a third (with Ve Neill and Yolanda Toussieng) for *Ed Wood*. Following work on a few low-budget pictures, Baker began his career in earnest as an assistant to Dick Smith, working on *The Exorcist*. This led to a solo credit on *It's Alive*, for which he created the demonic baby. Then, in 1974, he and Stan Winston won an Emmy for their old-age make-up on the TV movie *The Autobiography of Miss Jane*

Pittman. In 1977 Baker assisted Stuart Freeborn on the celebrated Cantina sequence in *Star Wars*, after which his career finally took off with *An American Werewolf in London*, for director John Landis. His penchant for ape make-up has also produced sterling work on such films as *Greystoke* and *Gorillas in the Mist*, while in 1976 he both designed the make-up and played the title role in the disastrous remake of *King Kong*. His other credits include *Black Caesar*, *Live and Let Die*, *Flesh Gordon*, *Death Race 2000*, *Tanya's Island*, *Coming to America*, *Moonwalker*, *Baby's Day Out* and *The Nutty Professor*.
Genre credits:
Octaman (1971), *Schlock* (1972), *The Thing with Two Heads* (1972), *Bone* (1972), *The Exorcist* (1973 - assistant), *It's Alive* (1974), *King Kong* (1976 - also actor, as Kong), *Squirm* (1976), *The Incredible Melting Man* (1977), *It's Alive 2* (1978 - aka *It Lives Again*), *Funhouse* (1978), *The Fury* (1978), *The Warning* (1980), *The Howling* (1980 - supervisor), *An American Werewolf in London* (1981), *The Funhouse* (1981), *Ghost Story* (1981 - co-sp), *Videodrome* (1983), *Thriller* (1983 - music video), *Ratboy* (1986), *It's Alive III: Island of the Alive* (1987), *Missing Link* (1989), *Gremlins 2: The New Batch* (1990 - also co-p), *Wolf* (1994), *Ed Wood* (1994)

Baker, Roy Ward (1916-)
British director who began his career at Gainsborough in 1934 as a third assistant, graduating to first assistant in 1938, in which capacity he worked with Hitchcock and Carol Reed. After the war, during which he served with the Army Kinematograph Unit, he returned to film making, his first fully-fledged credit being for the atmospheric thriller *The October Man* in 1947. Experience in Hollywood followed, along with a string of top-class British productions, such as *The One That Got Away* and *A Night to Remember*, the best account yet of the *Titanic* tragedy. During the sixties his career began to decline and he took refuge in television, from which he was saved in 1967 by an offer to direct Hammer's third Quatermass film,

• **Rick Baker not only designed the make-up for producer Dino de Laurentiis's expensive *King Kong* remake, he also played the title character himself.**

Quatermass and the Pit, his best genre effort. After this he became a surprisingly unambitious genre director for both Hammer and Amicus. Returned to television in the eighties with the highly popular *Flame Trees of Thika*.
Genre credits:
Quatermass and the Pit (1967 - aka *Five Million Years to Earth*), *Moon Zero Two* (1969), *The Vampire Lovers* (1970), *Scars of Dracula* (1970), *Dr Jekyll and Sister Hyde* (1971), *Asylum* (1971), *Vault of Horror* (1973), *And Now the Screaming Starts* (1973), *The Legend of the Seven Golden Vampires* (1974 - aka *The Seven Brothers Meet Dracula*), *The Monster Club* (1980)

Baker, Tom (1936-)
British actor, perhaps best known as television's fourth Dr Who. Other credits include *Nicholas and Alexandra* (in which he made a memorable Rasputin), *The Golden Voyage of Sinbad* and TV's *Medics*.

Genre credits:
Vault of Horror (1973), *The Mutations* (1974)

Balderston, John L. (1889-1954)
American screenwriter and playwright, a former journalist, war correspondent and magazine editor. Co-authored several of Universal's key horror films in the 1930s, *Dracula* being based on his stage adaptation of the Bram Stoker novel, co-authored with Hamilton Deane. Other credits include *Lives of a Bengal Lancer*, *The Prisoner of Zenda* and *Gaslight*.
Genre credits:
Dracula (1930 - co-play), *Frankenstein* (1931 - co-w), *The Mummy* (1932 - w), *The Bride of Frankenstein* (1935 - co-w), *Mad Love* (1935 - co-w)

Band, Albert (1924-)
French-born writer, producer and director (real name Alfredo Antonini) working in both Hollywood and Europe. He

began his career at Warner Bros. in the forties as an assistant editor, before moving on to become an assistant to director John Huston, for whom he adapted *The Red Badge of Courage*. The father of producer-director Charles Band and composer Richard H. Band, his other credits include *The Young Guns*, *Face of Fire*, *I Pascali Rossi*, *She Came to the Valley* and *Honey, I Blew Up the Kid* (which he produced).
Genre credits:
I Bury the Living (1958 - p/d), *Dracula's Dog* (1977 - aka *Zoltan, Hound of Dracula* - d), *Troll* (1986 - p), *Terrorvision* (1986 - p), *Ghost Warrior* (1986 - aka *Sword Kill* - p), *Ghoulies II* (1988 - d), *Robot Wars* (1993 - d), *Prehysteria* (1993 - co-d), *Prehysteria 2* (1995 - d)

Band, Charles (1952-)
Prolific American producer, director and executive, almost entirely in the sci-fi, fantasy and horror genres. The son of director Albert Band and the brother of composer Richard H. Band, he founded Meda Home Entertainment, an early video label, in 1978, the success of which led to the formation of both the Empire (1982) and Full Moon Entertainment (1988) production companies, through which he has presented countless low-budget genre items, several of which he has directed himself. He also founded the Moonbeam and Torchlight production companies in 1994 to make films for children and adults respectively, with much of the output going directly to video. His genre credits as a producer, executive producer and/or studio head include *Ghoulies*, *Zone Troopers*, *Re-Animator*, *Troll*, *From Beyond*, *Crawlspace*, *Psychos in Love*, *Prison*, *Puppetmaster*, *Dollman*, *Robot Jox*, *Demonic Toys*, *Beach Babes from Beyond Infinity*, *Test Tube Teens from the Year 2000*, *Puppetmaster 5: The Final Chapter* and *Trancers 5: Sudden Deth*. The following is a list of his directorial credits only.
Genre credits:
Mansion of the Doomed (1975 - aka *The Eyes of Dr Chaney*), *Crash* (1976 - co-d), *Parasite* (1982), *Dungeonmaster* (1983 - co-d), *Metalstorm - The Destruction of Jared Syn* (1983), *Trancers* (1984), *Pulsepounders* (1988), *Crash and Burn* (1990), *Meridian* (1990 - aka *Kiss of the Beast*), *Trancers II: The Return of Jack Deth* (1990), *Doctor Mordrid* (1990 - co-d), *Dollman vs. Demonic Toys* (1993)

Band, Richard H. (1953-)
American composer, son of director Albert Band and brother to producer-director Charles Band, on whose films he primarily works. He

• Doug Bradley as Pinhead in Clive Barker's *Hellraiser*.

co-wrote (with Joel Goldsmith) his first film score in 1977 for *Laserblast*.
Genre credits:
The Day Time Ended (1978), *Dr Heckly and Mr Hype* (1980), *Parasite* (1982), *The House on Sorority Row* (1982 - aka *House of Evil*), *Time Walker* (1983), *Ghoulies* (1985), *The Re-Animator* (1985), *Terrorvision* (1986), *Troll* (1986), *Dolls* (1986 - co-m), *Prison* (1988), *Puppet Master* (1989), *Bride of the Re-Animator* (1990 - aka *Re-Animator 2*), *Puppetmaster 2* (1990), *The Pit and the Pendulum* (1990), *The Resurrected* (1991)

Banks, Don (1923-1980)

Australian-born composer, long resident in Britain. Used the income from his film work to support himself whilst composing classical pieces.
Genre credits:
Captain Clegg (1962 - aka *Night Creatures*), *The Evil of Frankenstein* (1964), *Nightmare* (1964), *Hysteria* (1964), *Die, Monster, Die!* (1965), *Rasputin - The Mad Monk* (1966), *The Reptile* (1966), *The Mummy's Shroud* (1967), *Torture Garden* (1968 - co-m with James Bernard)

Barbeau, Adrienne (1945-)

American leading lady, formerly married to director John Carpenter, in whose films she occasionally appeared (*The Fog*, *Escape from New York*). Has both stage and television experience, primarily in the comedy series *Maude*. Other credits include *The Cannonball

Run, *Back to School* and *Cannibal Women in the Avacado Jungle of Death*.
Genre credits:
Someone's Watching Me (1978 - TVM), *The Fog* (1980), *Swamp Thing* (1982), *Creepshow* (1982), *Open House* (1987), *Two Evil Eyes* (1989 - aka *Due Occhi Diabolici*)

Barker, Clive (1952-)

British horror novelist turned writer-director and producer, whose books have been somewhat variably adapted for the silver screen. Like Stephen King, he has a cult following, thanks to his tendency to revel in the darker, gorier aspects of horror. His best known creation is perhaps the character of Pinhead from the *Hellraiser* series.
Genre credits:
Salome (1973 - short - w/d/actor), *Forbidden* (1978 - short -w/d/actor), *Transmutations* (1986 - aka *Underworld* - w), *Rawhead Rex* (1987 - w), *Hellraiser* (1987 - w/novel/d), *Hellbound: Hellraiser II* (1988 - story/co-exc p), *Nightbreed* (1990 - w/novel/d), *Candyman* (1992 - story/exec p), *Sleepwalkers* (1992 - acting cameo), *Hellraiser III: Hell on Earth* (1993 - exec p), *Candyman 2: Farewell to the Flesh* (1995 - story/exec p)

Barnes, Chris (1938-)

British editor, long associated with Hammer. Began his career as an assistant editor in television in the mid-fifties (*The Buccaneers*, etc.). He joined Hammer in 1958 as an assistant

to their editor in chief James Needs, becoming a fully fledged editor in 1966 with *Dracula - Prince of Darkness*. He stayed with Hammer as either editor or co-editor until the mid-seventies. His other credits include *The Long Haul, Ten Seconds to Hell, I Only Arsked, The Brigand of Kandahar, The Devil-Ship Pirates, A Challenge for Robin Hood* and *The Lost Continent*.
Genre credits include:
The Trollenberg Terror (1958 - co-ed), *Dracula - Prince of Darkness* (1966 - ed), *One Million Years B. C.* (1966 - co-ed), *Plague of the Zombies* (1966 - co-ed), *The Witches* (1966 - aka *The Devil's Own* - co-ed), *The Mummy's Shroud* (1966 - co-ed), *The Lost Continent* (1968), *Crescendo* 1969 - ed), *Taste the Blood of Dracula* (1970 - ed), *Horror of Frankenstein* (1970 - ed), *Creatures the World Forgot* (1971 - ed), *Hands of the Ripper* (1971 - ed), *Demons of the Mind* (1972 - ed), *The Satanic Rites of Dracula* (1973 - ed), *The Legend of the Seven Golden Vampires* (1973 - aka *The Seven Brother Meet Dracula* - ed), *The Last Horror Film* (1981 - co-ed)

Barrymore, Drew (1975-)

American child actress who shot to stardom as Gertie in *E.T.*. Drug and alcohol abuse followed in her early teenage years, though she gradually overcame these problems and emerged as a leading lady/supporting actress in such films as *Wayne's World 2, Bad Girls* and *Batman Forever*. She is the daughter of actor John Barrymore Jr, himself the son of John Barrymore of the famous Barrymore clan (Lionel, Ethel, Diana).
Genre credits:
Firestarter (1984), *Cat's Eye* (1984), *Poison Ivy* (1992)

Bartell, Paul (1938-)

American actor, writer and director with a penchant for offbeat themes. In films from 1969 as an actor (*Hi, Mom, Hollywood Boulevard, Eat My Dust, Heartbeeps, Into the Night, The Pope Must Die*, etc.), he began directing in 1972 with *Private Parts*, though it was *Death Race 2000* that established him as a director to watch. His other directorial credits include *Cannonball* (aka *Carquake*), *Lust in the Dust, Not for Publication, The Longshot* and *Scenes from the Class Struggle in Beverly Hills*.
Genre credits:
Death Race 2000 (1975 - d), *Piranha* (1978 - actor), *Trick or Treats* (1982 - actor), *Eating Raoul* (1982 - co-w/d/ actor), *Chopping Mall* (1986 - aka *Killbots* - actor), *Killer Party* (1986 - actor), *Gremlins 2: The New Batch* (1990 - actor)

Basket Case
USA 1981 90m TV Colour
A young man and his deformed Siamese twin brother, from whom he was separated at birth, go about murdering those responsible for their separation.

Semi-professional horror comic which took on cult status in some circles and provoked two sequels: *Basket Case 2* (1990) and *Basket Case 3: The Progeny* (1992). Amusing moments for those who can take it, but the presentation is often amateur.
p: Edgar Ievins for Ievins-Henenlotter/Basket Case Company
exec p: Arnie Bruck, Tom Kaye
w/d/ed: Frank Henenlotter
ph: Bruce Torbet
m: Gus Russo
ad: Frederick Loren
sound: Peter Thomas
make-up effects: Kevin Haney, John Caglione Jr
Kevin Van Hentenryck, Terri Susan Smith, Beverly Bonner, Robert Vogel, Diana Browne, Lloyd Pace

The Bat Whispers **
USA 1930 82m bw
The inhabitants of a remote country house are menaced by The Bat, a murderous super-criminal in search of hidden loot.

Though much of this talkie remake of the same director's 1926 silent (originally filmed in an experimental widescreen process) now seems stilted and dated, there are moments of arresting camera work as well as such novelties as an epilogue in which the audience is asked not to reveal the identity of The Bat to keep one interested. The comic relief is unfortunate, though the compensations will make it worth a look for connoisseurs. It was also billed as 'A Roland West Attraction' in the end credits.
p: Joseph M. Schenck for UA
w: Roland West
play: Mary Robert Rinehart
d: ROLAND WEST
ph: Robert Planck, Ray June
m: no credit given
ed: James Smith
ad: Paul Roe Crawley
cos: Helen Hallett
sp: Ned Herbert Mann
sound: J. I. Reed, O. E. Lagerstrom, Roger Heman, Charles H. Smith
Chester Morris, Una Merkel, Grayce Hampton, Maude Eburne, Chance Ward, Spencer Charters

Bates, Ralph (1940-1991)
British actor, the great-great nephew of Louis Pasteur! Studied drama at Yale University after which a career in the theatre followed. Came to prominence in the television drama *The Caesars* in 1968, in which he played Caligula. This led to his being cast in Hammer's *Taste the Blood of Dracula*, after which the studio seemed to groom him for stardom. Later returned to television with *Poldark*, *Penmaric* and the sit-com *Dear John*.
Genre credits:
Taste the Blood of Dracula (1970), *Horror of Frankenstein* (1970 - as Frankenstein), *Lust for a Vampire* (1971), *Dr Jekyll and Sister Hyde* (1971), *Fear in the Night* (1972), *Persecution* (1974 - aka *The Terror of Sheba*), *I Don't Want to Be Born* (1975)

Bauer, Michelle
American actress, a former model and, using the name Pia Snow, porno star (*Cafe Flesh*, *Bad Girls*, etc.). She has since appeared in several low-budget horror films, mostly for director Fred Olen Ray. Her other credits include *Assault of the Party Nerds* and *Night of the Living Babes*.
Genre credits:
The Tomb (1986), *The Phantom Empire* (1987), *Beverly Hills Vamp* (1988), *I Was a Teenage Sex Mutant* (1988 - aka *Dr Alien*), *Hollywood Chainsaw Hookers* (1988), *Demon Warp* (1988)

Bava, Lamberto (1944-)
Italian writer and director, the son of director Mario Bava, on whose films he began as an assistant. He often works in collaboration with Dario Argento, who has co-written and produced several of his films. Bava directed the underwater cellar sequence for Argento's *Inferno*, which also contained effects by his father. His other credits include *Blastfighter* and *Monster Shark* (aka *Shark Rosso nell Oceano*).
Genre credits:
Lisa the Devil (1972 - aka *House of Exorcism* - ass d), *Shock!* (1977 - aka *Beyond the Door II* - co-w/ass d), *Inferno* (1980 - ass d), *Macabre* (1980 - aka *Frozen Terror* - d), *Demons* (1985 - aka *Demoni* - co-w/d), *Graveyard Disturbance* (1986 - co-w/d), *Demons 2* (1986 - aka *Demoni 2* - co-w/d), *Demons 3: The Ogre* (1988 - aka *The Ogre* - TVM - co-w/d), *La Mascha del Demonio* (1990 - d)

Bava, Mario (1914-1980)
Italian director, cinematographer and special effects director whose baroque visual style distinguished a number of horror films in the sixties, some of which had a later effect on such directors as Dario Argento, Michele Soavi and his son, Lamberto Bava. He photographed his first film, the short *Il Tacchino Prepotente*, in 1939, after experience as a second assistant director and camera operator. Many other shorts and features as a cinematographer followed, including *Pagliacci*, *Porcellana* and *Antonio di Padova*. His first film as a director was the short *L'Orecchio* in 1946. Other credits as director include *Erik the Conqueror* (aka *Fury of the Vikings*), *Knives of the Avenger*, *The Road to Fort Alamo* and *Danger: Diabolik*. He also directed the special effects sequences for the TV series *Moses*.
Genre credits:
I, Vampiri (1958 - aka *Lust of the Vampire* - ph), *Caltiki - The Immortal Monster* (1958 - *Caltiki, Il Monstro Immortale* - ph), *Black Sunday* (1960 - *Mask of the Demon/Mask of Satan/La Maschera del Demonio* - co-w/ph/d), *Hercules in the Haunted World* (1961 -aka *Hercules at the Centre of the Earth/Ercole al Centro della Terra* - co-w/ph/d), *Black Sabbath* (1963 - aka *I Tre Volti della Paura* - co-w/d), *The Evil Eye* (1963 - aka *La Ragazza che Sapeva Troppo* - co-w/co-story/ph/d), *Night Is the Phantom* (1964 - aka *What!/La Fustra e il Corpo* - co-w/ph/d), *Blood and Black Lace* (1964 - aka *Sei Donne per L'Assassino* - co-w/d), *Planet of the Vampires* (1965 - aka *Planet of Blood/Terrore nello Spazio* - co-w/d), *Curse of the Dead* (1966 - aka *Kill, Baby, Kill/Operzione Paura* - d), *Dr Goldfoot and the Girl Bombs* (1966 - d), *Blood Brides* (1966 - aka *Hatchet for the Honeymoon/Un Macha Para la Luna de Miel* co-w/co-ph/d), *Five Dolls for an August Moon* (1970 - aka *Cinque Bambole per la Luna d'Agosto* - d), *Baron Blood* (1972 - aka *Gli Orrori del Castello de Norimberga* - d), *Bay of Blood* (1972 - aka *Bloodbath: Bay of Blood/Antefatto/Carnage/Twitch of the Death Nerve/Last House on the Left Part 2* - co-w/ph/d), *Lisa and the Devil* (1972 - aka *House of Exorcism* - d [as Mickey Lion]), *Shock* (1977 - aka *Beyond the Door II* - d), *Inferno* (1980 - sp)

Baxter, Les (1922-1996)
American composer who has worked on several of Roger Corman's Poe adaptations. A graduate of the Detroit Conservatory of Music, he began his career as a dance band arranger. Several innovative albums (for Capitol) followed in the fifties, including *Music out of the Moon*, *Perfume Set to Music* and *The Voice of the Xtabay*, which inevitably led to film offers. Other credits include *Goliath and the Barbarians*, *Master of the World*, *Muscle Beach Party* and *Dr Goldfoot and the Bikini Machine*.
Genre credits:
Macabre (1958), *House of Usher* (1960 - aka *The Fall of the House of Usher*), *The Pit and the Pendulum* (1961), *Tales of Terror*

(1962), *The Raven* (1963), *The Comedy of Terrors* (1963), *Black Sabbath* (1964), *The Dunwich Horror* (1970), *Cry of the Banshee* (1970), *Frogs* (1972), *The Beast Within* (1982)

Bay Cove *

USA 1987 96m Technicolor TVM
A successful lady lawyer and her husband buy a house on an exclusive island only to discover that their neighbours are witches.

Silly but good-looking hokum with a cast of familiar TV faces.
p: Stanley M. Brooks, Michael Rhodes for Jerlor
exec p: Jon Peters, Peter Guber, Roger Birnbaum
w: R. Timothy Kring
d: Carl Schenkel
ph: Jack Steyn
m: Shuki Levy
ed: Jimmy B. Frazier
ad: Richard St. John Harrison
cos: Mary Partridge-Raynor
sp: Frank C. Carrere
sound: Tom Hadderley
Tim Matheson, Pamela Sue Martin, Barbara Billingsley, Jeff Conaway, Susan Ruttan, Inga Swenson, Woody Harrelson, James B. Sikking

Bay Coven see Bay Cove

Bay of Blood

It 1970 90m/82m colour
Multiple murders take place in a secluded bay, provoked by the prospect of land development.

Confusingly told giallo thriller, hard to sit through, despite occasional pretensions to style.
p: Giuseppe Zaccariello for Nuovo Linea
w: Mario Bava, Joseph McLee, Filippo Ottoni, Gene Luotto
story: Dardano Sacchetti, Franco Barbieri
d/ph: Mario Bava
m: Stelvio Cipriani
ed: Carlo Reali
ad: Sergio Canvari
Isa Miranda, Claudine Auger, Luigi Pistilli, Laura Betti, Anna M. Rosati, Chris Avram

Bayldon, Geoffrey (1924-)

British character actor with many supporting roles to his credit, though he is still best remembered for the children's TV series *Catweazle*. Other credits include *A Jolly Bad Fellow*, *King Rat*, *Otley* and *The Pink Panther Strikes Again*.
Genre credits:
Dracula (1958), *Scrooge* (1971), *Asylum* (1972)

Beacham, Stephanie (1947-)

Decorative British actress perhaps best known for her television appearances in the likes of *Tenko*, *Connie*, *The Colbys*, *Dynasty* and *Sea Quest DSV*. Also on the stage, her other film credits include *The Games*, *Blue Movie Blackmail*, *Tam Lin* (aka *The Devil's Widow*), *Troop Beverly Hills* and *The Lilac Bus*.
Genre credits:
The Nightcomers (1971), *Dracula A. D. 1972* (1972 - as Jessica Van Helsing), *And Now the Screaming Starts* (1973), *House of Mortal Sin* (1975), *Schizo* (1977), *Inseminoid* (1980), *The Wolves of Willoughby Chase* (1988)

Beal, John (1909-)

American actor, a juvenile lead of the thirties who has since turned to character parts. Much stage experience; during World War Two he directed a number of training films for the USAAF. Other credits include *Madame X*, *Port of Seven Seas*, *The Sound and the Fury* and *Ten Who Dared*.
Genre credits:
The Cat and the Canary (1939), *The Vampire* (1957), *The Funhouse* (1981), *Amityville 3D* (1983)

The Beast from 20,000 Fathoms

USA 1953 80m bw
Atomic experiments at the North Pole thaw out a prehistoric monster, which promptly goes on the rampage.

Archetypal fifties monster flick let down by inferior trick work and cardboard characters. No *King Kong*, that's for sure.
p: Bill Chester, Jack Dietz for Warner
w: Lou Morheim, Fred Friedburger
story: Ray Bradbury
d: Eugene Lourie
ph: Jack Russell
m: David Buttolph
ed/associate p: Bernard W. Burton
ad: Hal Waller
cos: Berman's
sp: Ray Harryhausen, Willis Cook
sound: Max Hutchinson
Paul Christian, Cecil Kellaway, Donald Woods, Lee Van Cleef, Kenneth Tobey, Steve Brodie

The Beast in the Cellar

GB 1970 87m Eastmancolor
Two elderly sisters keep their brother locked up in the cellar for many years, but he escapes and goes on a killing spree.

Embarrassingly bad horror film which degrades its two leading ladies, who perhaps should have known better to begin with.

p: Christopher Neame, Graham Harris for Tigon
exec p: Tony Tenser
w/d: James Kelly
ph: Harry Waxman, Desmond Dickinson
m: Tony Mcauley
ed: Nicholas Napier-Bell
ad: Roger King
cos: Mary Gibson
sound: Tony Dawe, Ted Karnon
Beryl Reid, Flora Robson, Tessa Wyatt, John Hamill, T. P. McKenna, David Dodimead

The Beast Must Die

GB 1974 93m Technicolor
An eccentric millionaire arranges a weekend werewolf hunt.

Silly horror comic with echoes of *The Most Dangerous Game* (aka *The Hounds of Zaroff*) and Agatha Christie's *Ten Little Indians*, as the guests succumb to attack one by one. The film's alternative title, *Black Werewolf*, seems to tie the film in with the blaxploitation horror sub-genre of the seventies (*Blacula*, *Blackenstein*, *Dr Jekyll and Mr Black* etc.) whilst its 'guess who the monster is' break towards the end links it with the gimmick films of William Castle. Despite these points of interest, however, the film itself could have been much better.
p: Max J. Rosenberg, Milton Subotsky, John Dark for British Lion/Amicus
w: Michael Winder
story: James Blish
d: Paul Annett
ph: Jack Hildyard
m: Douglas Gamley
ed: Peter Tanner
ad: John Stoll
cos: John Hilling
sound: Ken Ritchie
Peter Cushing (sporting a thick German accent), Calvin Lockhart, Charles Gray, Anton Diffring, Marlene Clark, Ciaran Madden, Michael Gambon

The Beast of Hollow Mountain

USA 1956 75m DeLuxe Cinemascope/Regiscope
Mexican villagers discover a monster lurking up a nearby mountain.

Cheapjack hokum which seems to consist mostly of padding. The effects are particularly poor. Willis O'Brien, of course, supplied the special effects for the rather better *King Kong*, the story presumably being one of his cast-offs.
p: William Nassour, Edward Nassour, Peliculas Rodriguez for UA/Nassour
w: Robert Hill, Jack DeWitt
story: Willis O'Brien
d: Edward Nassour, Ismael Rodriguez
ph: Jorge Stahl Jr
m: Raul Lavista

ed: Holbrook Todd, Mauty Wright
ad: no credit given
sp: Jack Rabin, Louis DeWitt
sound: James L. Fields, Nick Rosa
Guy Madison, Patricia Medina, Eduardo Noriega, Carlos Rivas, Lupe Carriles, Julio Villareal, Hal Baylor, Garcia Pena

The Beast of Morocco see The Hand of Night

The Beast with Five Fingers *

USA 1946 88m bw
The murderous hand of a dead pianist apparently returns from the grave to wreak havoc.

Much mentioned minor horror comic. Good moments along the way, though the ending is something of a let down.
p: William Jacobs for Warner
w: Curt Siodmak
story: W. F. Harvey
d: Robert Florey
ph: Wesley Anderson
m: Max Steiner
md: Leo F. Forbstein
ed: Frank Magee
ad: Stanley Fleischer
cos: Travilla
sp: William McGann, Henry Koenekamp
sound: Oliver S. Garretson
PETER LORRE, Andrea King, Robert Alda, J. Carrol Naish, Victor Francen, Charles Dingle

Beaudine, William (1892-1970)

American director whose swift (some would say shoddy) working methods earned him the nickname 'One Shot' Beaudine. Began in silents at the age of seventeen as a general assistant at Biograph, but was directing shorts as early as 1916. Made his feature début in 1922 with Watch Your Step, which he followed with well over 300 features and support features. Career highlights include Where There's a Will (starring Will Hay), The Old Fashioned Way (starring W. C. Fields) and Westward Ho the Wagons. Also directed many episodes of TV's Lassie, several of which were produced by his son, William Beaudine Jr. Genre credits:
Condemned Men (1940), Professor Creeps (1942), The Living Ghost (1943), Ghosts on the Loose (1943), The Ape Man (1943), Voodoo Man (1944), Spook Busters (1946), The Face of Marble (1946), Bela Lugosi Meets a Brooklyn Gorilla (1952 - aka The Monster Meets the Gorilla), Billy the Kid vs. Dracula (1966), Jesse James Meets Frankenstein's Daughter (1966)

Bedlam **

USA 1946 80m bw
An eighteenth-century asylum master has a sane girl committed because she knows too much about his nefarious activities.

Less a horror film than a rich melodrama, this nevertheless falls within its producer's celebrated horror cycle and is certainly well enough mounted to retain one's interest. The real Bedlam, situated in Lambeth, South London, is now the British War Museum.
p: Val Lewton for RKO
exec p: Jack J. Gross
w: Mark Robson, Carlos Keith (Val Lewton)
d: MARK ROBSON
ph: Nicholas Musuraca
m: Roy Webb
md: Constantin Bakaleinikoff
ed: Lyle Boyer
ad: Albert S. D'Agostino, Walter E. Keller
cos: Edward Stevenson
sp: Vernon L. Walker
sound: Jean L. Speak, Terry Kellum
Boris Karloff, Anna Lee, Billy House, Richard Fraser, Glenn Vernon

Beetlejuice *

USA 1988 92m Technicolor Dolby
A recently deceased couple hire a bio-exorcist to rid their home of the mortals who have taken it over.

Slick but slackly written spook comedy which, despite amusing sequences, fails to be consistently funny. Sheer novelty value nevertheless brought in large audiences, which led to the Burton-Keaton collaboration on Batman.
p: Michael Bender, Larry Wilson, Richard Hashimoto for Geffen
w: Michael McDowell, Warren Skaaren
story: Michael McDowell, Larry Wilson
d: Tim Burton
ph: Thomas Ackerman
m: DANNY ELFMAN
ed: Jane Curson
pd: Bo Welch
cos: Aggie Guerrard Rodgers
sp: Chuck Gaspar, Alan Munro
make-up effects: Ve Neill, Steve La Porte, Robert Short (aa)
sound: David Ronne
stunt co-ordinator: Fred Lerner
Alec Baldwin, Geena Davis, MICHAEL KEATON, Winona Ryder, Jeffrey Jones, Sylvia Sidney, Catherine O'Hara, Glenn Shadix, Robert Goulet, Dick Cavett, Annie McEnroe

Before I Hang

USA 1940 71m bw
A scientist working to discover a rejuvenation serum turns into a murderer as a consequence.

Archetypal mad doctor hokum with an archetypal star performance. Barely distinguishable from the others of its ilk.
p: Wallace MacDonald for Columbia
w: Robert D. Andrews
d: Nick Grinde
ph: Benjamin Kline
md: W. M. Stloff
ed: Charles Nelson
ad: Lionel Banks
Boris Karloff, Evelyn Keyes, Bruce Bennett, Pedro de Cordoba, Edward Van Sloane, Don Beddoe

The Believers

USA 1987 123m DeLuxe Dolby
A group of Satanists determine on sacrificing the young son of a New York family, but the father fights back.

Over directed mumbo-jumbo which never really begins to make sense, never mind entertain.
p: Beverly Cambe, Michael Childers, John Schlesinger for Orion
exec p: Edward Teets
w: Mark Frost
novel: Nicholas Conde
d: John Schlesinger
ph: Robby Muller
m: J. Peter Robinson
ed: Peter Honess
pd: Simon Holland
cos: Shay Cunliffe
sp: Connie Brink, Ted Ross, Bryan Day
sound: Gerry Humphreys, Todd Maitland
make-up effects: Kevin Hayney
2nd unit d: Michael Childers
2nd unit ph: Peter R. Norman
stunt co-ordinator: Dean Jeffries
Martin Sheen, Helen Shaver, Robert Loggia, Richard Masur, Elizabeth Wilson, Lee Richardson, Harris Yulin, Jimmy Smits, Harley Cross

Ben

USA 1972 92m DeLuxe
A sickly young boy befriends the leader of an enormous pack of rats.

God-awful sequel to Willard, which itself wasn't so hot. The most surprising thing about it is that the title song, which is about a rat, is performed by the young Michael Jackson and was actually nominated for an Oscar.
p: Mort Briskin for Cinerama/Bing Crosby Productions
w: Gilbert A. Ralston
d: Phil Karlson
ph: Russell Metty
m: Walter Scharf
ly: Don Black
ed: Harry Gerstad
ad: Roland M. Brooks
Lee Harcourt Montgomery, Arthur O'Connell, Rosemary Murphy, Meredith Baxter, Kaz Garas, Paul Carr, Kenneth Tobey

Benchley, Peter (1940-)

American novelist, the grandson of actor and humorist Robert Benchley. Remembered solely for authoring *Jaws*, he tried to repeat its success several times.
Genre credits:
Jaws (1975 - co-w/novel), *The Deep* (1977 - co-w/novel), *The Island* (1980 - w/novel)

Bennett, Joan (1910-1990)

American leading lady of the thirties and forties, sister of actresses Barbara and Constance Bennett, daughter of actor Richard Bennett and actress Adrienne Morrison. First appeared on stage in 1928 in *Jarnegan* (with her father) after which Hollywood beckoned with a small part in *Power* in 1928, though she'd previously had bits in such silents as *Valley of Decision* and *The Eternal City*. Stardom followed in 1929 with *Bulldog Drummond* in which she co-starred with Ronald Colman. Subsequent films included *Little Women*, *Private Worlds*, *The Woman in the Window* and *Father of the Bride*. When film roles began to dry up in the sixties she turned to television and the cult horror series *Dark Shadows*, in which she appeared from 1966 to 1971. Several horror films followed.
Genre credits:
The Secret Beyond the Door (1948), *House of Dark Shadows* (1970 - film version of *Dark Shadows*), *Inn of the Damned* (1971), *The Eyes of Charles Sand* (1972 - TVM), *Suspiria* (1976)

Bennett, Richard Rodney (1936-)

Distinguished British composer with many top class film scores to his credit, including *Far from the Madding Crowd*, *Murder on the Orient Express*, *Lady Caroline Lamb* and *Yanks*. Trained at the Royal Academy of Music and entered films at twenty in 1956 with *Face the Night*.
Genre credits:
The Man Who Could Cheat Death (1959), *The Nanny* (1965), *The Witches* (1966 - aka *The Devil's Own*), *Voices* (1973)

Berman, Monty (1913-)

British producer, director and cinematographer, known primarily for his television output, which includes countless episodes of such series as *The Saint*, *The Baron*, *The Champions*, *Department S*, *The Adventurer* and *Randall and Hopkirk Deceased* all of which he produced with partner Robert S. Baker, with whom he co-founded Tempean Films in 1948. They have many low-budget second features to their credit.
Genre credits:
Jack the Ripper (1958 - co-p/ph/co-d), *The Flesh and the Fiends* (1959 - aka *Mania* - co-p/ph), *Blood of the Vampire* (1959 - co-p/ph), *The Hellfire Club* (1960 - co-p/ph/co-d), *What A Carve Up* (1961 - co-p/ph)

Bernard, James (1925-)

British composer, one of Hammer's lynch pins, his scores for their horror classics being among the genre's finest (his three note *Dracula* motif practically became Hammer's signature tune). Began composing during his teenage years and, after wartime service in the RAF, went to study at the Royal College of Music at the suggestion of his friend, Benjamin Britten. Began his professional career scoring for BBC radio, his music for a production of *The Duchess of Malfi* leading to *The Quatermass Experiment*, his first score for Hammer (his *Malfi* score had been conducted by John Hollingsworth, then Hammer's resident musical director). Prior to this, Bernard won an Oscar in 1950 for co-authoring the story (with Paul Dehn) for the thriller *Seven Days to Noon*. His work as a composer has almost been exclusively for Hammer, exceptions being *Windom's Way*, two documentaries for Basil Wright (*The Immortal Land* and *A Place for Gold*), *Torture Garden* (with Don Banks), *Across the Bridge* and *Nor the Moon by Night*.
Genre credits:
The Quatermass Experiment (1955 - aka *The Creeping Unknown*), *X - The Unknown* (1956), *Quatermass 2* (1956 - aka *Enemy from Space*), *The Curse of Frankenstein* (1956), *Dracula* (1958), *The Hound of the Baskervilles* (1959), *The Stranglers of Bombay* (1959), *The Terror of the Tongs* (1961), *Kiss of the Vampire* (1962 - aka *Kiss of Evil*), *The Damned* (1963 - aka *These Are the Damned*), *The Gorgon* (1964), *She* (1965), *Dracula - Prince of Darkness* (1966), *The Plague of the Zombies* (1966), *Frankenstein Created Woman* (1967), *The Devil Rides Out* (1967 - aka *The Devil's Bride*), *Torture Garden* (1967 - co-m with Don Banks), *Dracula Has Risen from the Grave* (1968), *Frankenstein Must Be Destroyed* (1969), *Taste the Blood of Dracula* (1970), *Frankenstein and the Monster from Hell* (1973), *The Legend of the Seven Golden Vampires* (1974 - aka *The Seven Brothers meet Dracula*)

Berryman, Michael (1948-)

Bald American character actor, memorable as Pluto, one of the cannibals in Wes Craven's *The Hills Have Eyes*, which exploited his odd looks, causing some to compare him to Rondo Hatton. His other credits include *One Flew Over the Cuckoo's Nest*, *Another Man*, *Another Chance* and *Armed Response*.
Genre credits:
The Hills Have Eyes (1977), *The Fifth Floor* (1981), *Deadly Blessing* (1981), *The Hills Have Eyes 2* (1984)

Berserker see Berserker: The Nordic Curse

Berserker: The Nordic Curse

USA 1987 85m Alpha Cinecolor
A group of young campers find themselves threatened by a killer bear-cum-werewolf.

Dismal low-budget shocker, a sort of cross between *Grizzly* and *Friday the 13th*.
p: Jules Rivera for Paradise Filmworks/American Video Group
exec p: Robert A. Foti, Robert M. Seibert
w/d: Jef Richard
story: Joseph Kaufman
ph: Henning Shellerup
m: Chuck Francour, Gary Griffin
ed: Marcus Manton
ad: Bill Cornford
cos: Carol Lynn Salonen
sp: Jason Ross Zimmerman
sound: Les Udy
make-up effects: Perri Sorel
Joseph Alan Johnson, Valerie Sheldon, George 'Buck' Flower, Greg Dawson, Rodney Montague, Beth Toussaint

Best, Willie (1916-1962)

Slow talking African-American actor in films from 1930 with *Feet First*. He played the stereotypical frightened servant in a number of thirties and forties comedies. Also known as Sleep 'n' Eat, his work is now no longer deemed politically correct. His other credits include *Annie Oakley*, *Thankyou, Jeeves*, *General Spanky*, *Vivacious Lady*, *Mr Moto Takes a Vacation* and *The Bride Wore Boots*.
Genre credits:
Mummy's Boys (1936), *The Ghost Breakers* (1940), *The Body Disappears* (1941), *The Smiling Ghost* (1941), *The Hidden Hand* (1942), *Whispering Ghosts* (1942), *A-Haunting We Will Go* (1942), *The Monster and the Ape* (1945 - serial)

Beswick, Martine (1941-)

Jamaican-born actress who came to Britain in 1953. She made her film début in 1963 with *Saturday Night Out*, though it was her performance as the gypsy girl in *From Russia with Love* later the same year that brought her to attention. She met James Bond again in *Thunderball*, since when she has appeared in all manner of films in both Britain and America, including *The Penthouse*, *Melvin and Howard* and *Wide Sargasso Sea*,

as well as several Hammer horrors.
Genre credits:
One Million Years B. C. (1966), *Slave Girls* (1968 - aka *Prehistoric Women*), *Dr Jekyll and Sister Hyde* (1971 - aka *Sister Hyde*), *Seizure* (1974), *Devil Dog: The Hound of Hell* (1978 - TVM), *The Offspring* (1987), *Evil Spirits* (1991), *Trancers II: The Return of Jack Deth* (1991), *Evil Spirits* (1991), *Critters 4* (1992 - voice only)

Bey, Turhan (1920-)

Turkish actor in Hollywood films from the early forties, where he tended to play either Arabian princes or mystics, such as Mehemt Bey in *The Mummy's Tomb*. His credits include *Footsteps in the Dark*, *Arabian Nights*, *Ali Baba and the Forty Thieves*, *Sudan*, *Song of India*, *Prisoners of the Casbah* and *Night in Paradise*.
Genre credits:
The Mummy's Tomb (1942), *The Mad Ghoul* (1943), *The Climax* (1944), *The Amazing Mr X* (1948 - aka *The Spiritualist*)

The Beyond

It 1981 85m Technicolor
A Louisiana hotel is discovered to be one of several gateways to hell.
  Outlandish horror brew whose occasional visual flair may commend it to Fulci completists.
p: Fabriziode Angelis for Eagle/Fulvia
w: Lucio Fulci, Giorgio Mariuzzo, Dardano Sacchetti
story: Dardano Sacchetti
d: LUCIO FULCI
ph: Sergio Salvati
m: Fabio Fizzi
ed: Vincenzo Tomassi
pd: Massimo Lentini
pd/cos: Massimo Lentini
sp: Germano Natali
sound: Ugo Celani, Bruno Montreal
make-up effects: Giannetto de Rossi
Katherine McColl, David Warbeck, Sara Keller, Antoine Saint John, Michael Marabella

Beyond the Door 2 see Shock!

The Bird with the Crystal Plumage *

It 1970 98m Technicolor Techniscope
Whilst working in Rome, a American ornithologist witnesses an attempted murder and tries to solve the case himself when his own life is put in jeopardy.
  Argento's first movie as a writer-director is a slickly handled puzzle piece with many of the touches familiar in his later work. A must for connoisseurs.
p: Salvatore Argento for UM
w: Dario Argento

• Bela Lugosi and Boris Karloff relax between takes during the filming of *The Black Cat*.

d: DARIO ARGENTO
ph: Vittorio Storaro
m: Ennio Morricone
ed: Franco Fraticelli
pd/cos: Dario Micheli
Tony Musante, Suzy Kendall, Enrico Maria, Salerno Pino Patti, Guido di Marco, Raf Valenti, Rosa Toros

The Birds **

USA 1963 119m Technicolor
Large flocks of birds unaccountably attack the small coastal township of Bodega Bay in California.
  Despite its vaunted reputation, this relentlessly padded piece of Hitchcockery doesn't quite deserve the adulation that has been heaped upon it over the years, suffering as it does from a particularly childish script and variable special effects. There are, nevertheless, effective and memorable set pieces along the way, even if they are a long time coming. A TV movie sequel, *Birds II: The Land's End*, followed in 1994, the less said about which the better.
p: Alfred Hitchcock for Universal
w: Evan Hunter
story: Daphne Du Maurier
d: ALFRED HITCHCOCK
ph: ROBERT BURKS
m: none
ed: GEORGE TOMASSINI
pd: Robert Boyle
cos: Edith Head
sp: Ub Iwerks, Albert Whitlock, Lawrence A. Hampton

sound: Waldon O. Watson, William Russell
sound consultant: Bernard Herrmann
sound effects: Bernard Herrmann, Reni Gassmann, Oskar Sala
titles: James S. Polak
make-up: Howard Smit
bird trainer: Ray Berwick
Rod Taylor, Tippi Hedren, Jessica Tandy, Suzanne Pleshette, Veronica Cartwright, Ethel Griffies

Birkinshaw, Andrew

British director working in Europe and South Africa, where he has has helmed a handful of Edgar Allan Poe subjects for producer Harry Alan Towers, as well as Towers' third version of *Ten Little Indians* (1989).
Genre credits:
The House of Usher (1989), *The Raven* (1990), *Masque of the Red Death* (1990)

Bissell, Whit (1909-1996)

American bit part actor who has cropped up in countless films (*Holy Matrimony*, *It Should Happen to You*, *The Time Machine*, *Airport*, *Soylent Green*, *Casey's Shadow*, etc.), though he is perhaps best known to genre fans for playing Professor Frankenstein in *I Was a Teenage Frankenstein*, his only leading role.
Genre credits:
The Creature from the Black Lagoon (1954), *Invasion of the Body Snatchers* (1956), *I Was a Teenage Werewolf* (1957), *I Was a*

Teenage Frankenstein (1958 - aka *Teenage Frankenstein*), *Monster on the Campus* (1958), *Psychic Killer* (1975)

Black Carrion
GB 1984 74m Technicolor TVM
A journalist searches for two pop stars who mysteriously disappeared in the sixties.

One of several unwatchable tele-thrillers made under the umbrella title of *Hammer House of Mystery and Suspense*.
p: Roy Skeggs for Hammer/TCF
w/d: John Hough
ph: Brian West
m: Paul Patterson
md: Philip Martell
ed: Bob Dearberg
ad: Carolyn Scott
Season Hubley, Leigh Lawson, Norman Bird, Alan Love, Diana King, Julian Littman, William Hootkins

The Black Cat *
USA 1934 65m bw
A devil worshipper takes in stranded travellers in the hope of using one of them in his ceremonies.

Poorly scripted horror malarkey with occasional flashes of style and some interesting sets.
p: Carl Laemmle Jr for Universal
w: Peter Ruric
story: Edgar G. Ulmer, Peter Ruric, after Edgar Allan Poe
d: Edgar G. Ulmer
ph: John Mescall
md: Heinz Roemheld
ed: Ray Curtiss
ad: CHARLES D. HALL
cos/sp/sound: no credits given
BORIS KARLOFF, BELA LUGOSI, David Manners, Jacquline Wells, Egon Brecher, Lucille Lund, Harry Cording, Henry Armetta, Albert Conti

The Black Cat
USA 1941 70m bw
The family of a cat lover are summoned to her spooky house for the reading of her will and murder follows...

Childish thriller which, especially given the cast, should have been a lot better than it is. The so-called 'comedy relief' kills it stone dead.
p: Burt Kelly for Universal
w: Robert Less, Fred Rinaldo, Eric Taylor, Robert Neville
d: Albert S. Rogel
ph: Stanley Cortez
m: Hans J. Salter
ed: Ted Kent
ad: Jack Otterson
sp: John P. Fulton
Basil Rathbone, Gladys Cooper, Broderick Crawford, Alan Ladd, Bela Lugosi, Hugh Herbert, Gale Sondergaard, Anne Gwynne, Celia Loftus

The Black Cat
GB/It 1981 91m Eastmancolor Technovision
A psychic is influenced by a murderous black cat.

A tedious and poorly handled shocker which needed a lot more style if it was to work at all. Given its director's usual preponderance for gore and viscera, very mild indeed.
p: Guilo Sbarigia for Selinia Cinematografica
w: Biagio Proietti, Lucio Fulci
d: Lucio Fulci
ph: Sergio Salvati
m: Pino Donaggio
ed: Vincenzo Tomassi
pd: Francesco Calabrese
sp: Paolo Ricci
Patrick Magee, Mimsy Farmer, David Warbeck, Al Oliver, Dagmar Lassander, Bruno Corazzari

Black Christmas
Canada 1974 97m Technicolor
Girls in a sorority house are threatened by a mad killer.

Routine killer thriller with the expected quota of shocks and a better cast than it deserves. Its director went on to helm the *Porky's* series.
p: Bob Clark for Film Funding/Vision IV/Famous Players/Canadian Film Development Corp
w: Roy Moore
d: Bob Clark
ph: Reginald Morris
m: Carl Zittrer
ed: Stan Cole
ad: Karen Bromley
Olivia Hussey, Keir Dullea, Margot Kidder, Andre Martin, John Saxon, Art Hindle, Lunne Griffin

Black, Karen (1942-)
American actress (real name Karen Ziegeler) who made a splash in the seventies in such films as *Five Easy Pieces*, *The Great Gatsby*, *Airport '75*, *Nashville*, *Family Plot* and *Capricorn One* before her star began to diminish.
Genre credits:
The Pyx (1973), *Trilogy of Terror* (1975 - TVM), *Burnt Offerings* (1976), *The Strange Possession of Mrs. Oliver* (1977 - TVM), *Invaders from Mars* (1986), *Eternal Evil* (1986), *It's Alive III: Island of the Alive* (1986), *The Invisible Kid* (1987), *Night Angel* (1989), *Overexposed* (1990), *Dead Girls Don't Dance* (1990), *Auntie Lee's Meat Pies* (1991), *The Haunting Fear* (1991), *Evil Spirits* (1991), *Children of the Night* (1992)

The Black Room *
USA 1935 70m bw
The evil twin brother of a nobleman murders him and takes his place.

Lively horror melodrama with some neat directorial touches and a good eye-rolling part for its star.
p: Columbia
w: Henry Myers, Arthur Strawn
story: Arthur Strawn
d: ROY WILLIAM NEILL
ph: Al Siegler

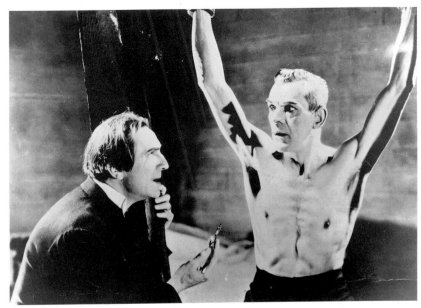

• Bela Lugosi prepares to torture Boris Karloff in *The Black Cat*.

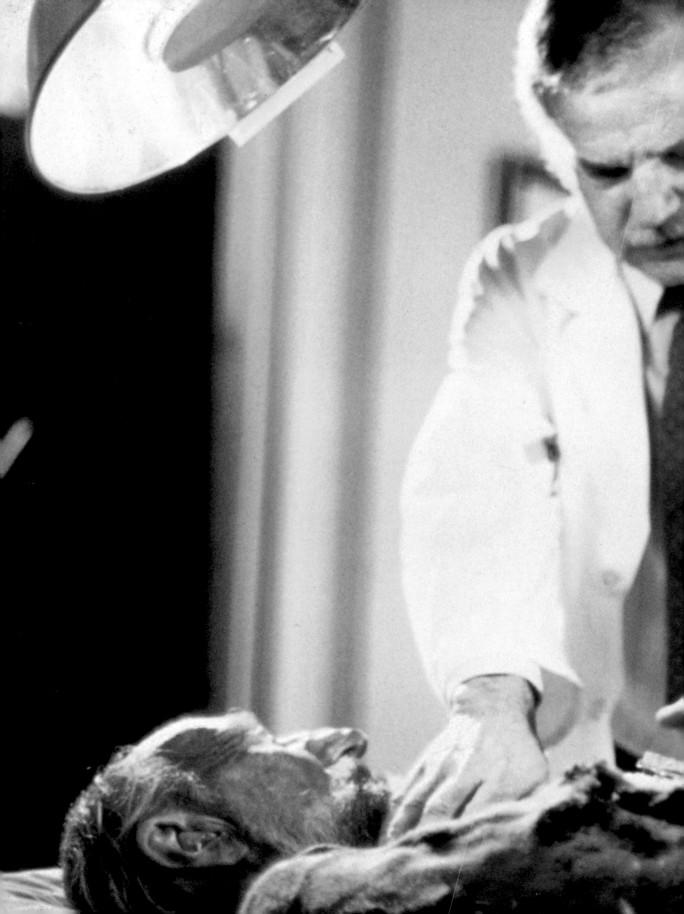

A GRISLY MOMENT from the 1988 remake of *The Blob*. The original had starred the then 28-year-old Steve McQueen and had a title song by Burt ('The Look of Love') Bacharach, but they both seemed to live it down.

md: Louis Silvers
ed: Richard Cahoon
ad: STEPHEN GOOSON
cos: Murray Mayer
sound: no credit given
BORIS KARLOFF, Marian Marsh, Katherine de Mille, Robert Allen, Thurston Hall

The Black Sleep

USA 1956 81m bw
A Victorian scientist uses live victims for his experiments, but they finally turn on him with a murderous vengeance.

Poor low-budget horror with a couple of energetic scenes and a stalwart cast. Tolerable enough for aficionados.
p: Howard W. Koch for UA/Bel-Air
w: John C. Higgins
d: Reginald Le Borg
ph: Gordon Avil
m: Les Baxter
ed: John F. Schreyer
ad: Bob Kinoshita
BASIL RATHBONE, Bela Lugosi, Lon Chaney Jr, John Carradine, Akim Tamiroff, Tor Johnson, Herbert Ridley, Patricia Brake

Black, Stanley (1913-)

Prolific British composer/conductor/ musical director (approaching 200 credits), former bandleader, arranger and record producer who conducted the BBC Dance Orchestra from 1944-1954. Perhaps best known for the three Cliff Richard musicals he worked on, *The Young Ones*, *Summer Holiday* and *Wonderful Life*.
Genre credits:
The Trollenberg Terror (1957 - aka *The Crawling Eye*), *Blood of the Vampire* (1958), *House of Mystery* (1961), *The Full Treatment* (1961 - aka *Stop Me Before I Kill*), *Maniac* (1963)

Black Sunday *

It 1960 83m bw
A seventeenth-century witch rises from the dead two hundred years after being put to death in a spiked mask.

Silly but stylishly handled Italian horror comic which launched its director and leading lady and started a trend.
p: Massimo de Rita for Galatea/Jolly
w: Ennio de Concini, Mario Serandrei
story: Nicolai Gogol
d/ph: MARIO BAVA
m: Robert Nicolai
ed: Mario Serandrei
ad: Giorgio Giovannini
cos: Tina Loriedo Grani
Barbara Steele, John Richardson, Ivo Garrani, Andrea Checchi, Arturo Dominici

The Black Torment *

GB 1964 85m Eastmancolor
After the death of his first wife, an eighteenth-century baronet remarries, but is haunted by what appears to be the ghost of his first wife.

Tolerable shocker for those who haven't been here a dozen times before.
p: Robert Hartford Davies for Compton-Tekli
exec p: Michael Klinger, Tony Tenser
w: Donald Ford, Derek Ford
d: Robert Hartford Davies
ph: Peter Newbrook
m: Robert Richards
ed: Alastair McIntyre
ad: Alan Harris
cos: Elsa Fennell
sound: Bert Ross, John Aldred
fight ch: Peter Brace
Heather Sears, John Turner, Ann Lynn, Peter Arne, Raymond Huntley, Norman Bird, Patrick Troughton, Joseph Tomelty

Black Werewolf see The Beast Must Die

Blackmer, Sidney (1894-1973)

American actor who began his film career in 1914 appearing in *The Perils of Pauline* serial, though he is perhaps best known for playing the devil-worshiping Roman Castevet in *Rosemary's Baby* (1968). His only other genre credit was for *The Lady and the Monster* (1944 - aka *The Lady and the Doctor*).

Blair, Linda (1959-)

American child actress and model who shot to international stardom as the possessed Regan in *The Exorcist*, which earned her an Oscar nomination as Best Supporting Actress, though it has since pigeon-holed her in low-budget horror and exploitation films. Non-genre films include *Sarah T*, *Portrait of a Teenage Alcoholic* (TVM), *Airport '75*, *Victory at Entebbe*, *Roller Boogie* and *Up Your Alley*. She spoofed her *Exorcist* image in the *Airplane*-like *Repossessed*.
Genre credits:
The Exorcist (1974), *Exorcist II: The Heretic* (1977), *Hell Night* (1981), *Grotesque* (1987), *A Woman Possessed* (1989 - aka *Bad Blood*), *Witchery* (1989 - aka *Witchcraft/Ghosthouse II*), *The Chilling* (1989), *Zapped Again!* (1989), *Repossessed* (1990)

Blatty, William Peter (1928-)

American writer, director and novelist, remembered chiefly for penning *The Exorcist*, a long-running number one bestseller which he adapted for the screen to great commercial success, winning a Best Screenplay Oscar for his

efforts. Served with the American Air Force during World War Two, which he followed with work as an editor with the United States Information Agency. Turned to writing in 1959 after experience as a publicity director for USC and Loyola universities. Wrote his first screenplay, *The Man from the Diners' Club*, in 1963, after which he wrote several comedy scripts for director Blake Edwards (*A Shot in the Dark*, *What Did You Do In the War, Daddy? Gunn*, *Darling Lili*).
Genre credits:
The Exorcist (1974 - w/p/novel), *The Ninth Configuration* (1980 - w/novel/ p/d), *Exorcist III* (1990 - w/novel/d)

Blind Terror *

GB 1971 89m Technicolor
A maniac murders a family in a lonely country house and then goes after the only survivor - a defenceless blind girl.

A padded but generally effective and genuinely frightening thriller with a good quota of shocks as well as the expected red herrings.
p: Basil Appleby for Columbia/ Filmways/Genesis
w: Brian Clemens
d: RICHARD FLEISCHER
ph: Gerry Fisher
m: Elmer Bernstein
ed: Thelma Connell
ad: John Hoesli
cos: Evelyn Gibbs
sound: Robert Allen, Ken Scrivener, Colin Miller
MIA FARROW, Robin Bailey, Dorothy Alison, Diane Grayson, Norman Eshley, Brian Rawlinson, Paul Nicholas, Lila Kaye, Michael Elphick

The Blob

USA 1958 83m DeLuxe
A strange jelly-like substance from outer space grows to an enormous size and threatens an American township.

Standard fifties sci-fi/monster hokum; the most surprising thing about which was that it was shot in colour. Handling strictly routine. It was remade, by the same producer, in 1988.
p: Jack H. Harris for Tonylyn
w: Theodore Simonson, Kate Phillips
story: Irvine H. Millgate
d: Irwin S. Yeaworth Jr
ph: Thomas Spalding
m: Ralph Carmichael
title song: Burt Bacharach
ed: Alfred Hillman
ad: William Jersey, Karl Karlson
sp: Bart Sloane
sound: Gottfried Buss, Robert Clement
Steve McQueen, Aneta Corseaut, Olin Howlin, Earl Rowe, Steve Chase

The Blob **
USA 1988 92m Technicolor Ultra Stereo
The small American township of
Arborville is threatened by a blob-like
creature from outer space which absorbs
its victims on contact.
Superior remake of the fifties
schlock classic, with improved effects
and slick production. Ideal video
viewing.
p: Jack H. Harris, Elliott Kastner for
Tri-Star
w: Chuck Russell, Frank Darabont
d: Chuck Russell
ph: Mark Irwin
m: Michael Hoenig
ed: Terry Stokes, Tod Feurman
pd: Craig Stearns
cos: Joseph Porro
sp: Lyle Conway, Hoyt Yeatman, Michael
Fink
sound: Wayne Heitman, Stanley Kastner,
Matthew Iadarola
make-up effects: Terry Gardner
titles: Dan Curry
stunt co-ordinator: Gary Hytnes
Kevin Dillon, Shawnee Smith, Donovan
Leitch, Ricky Paull Goldin, Billy Beck,
Candy Clark, Jeffrey de Munn, Del
Close, Beau Billingslea, Art La Fleur

Bloch, Robert (1917-1994)
Celebrated genre writer with many
short stories to his credit, though he is
perhaps best known for writing the
novel *Psycho*, on which Hitchcock based
his most famous film. His subsequent
work was generally routine, however.
Genre credits:
Psycho (1960 - original author only),
The Cabinet of Dr Caligari (1962 - aka
The Cabinet of Caligari), *Strait Jacket*
(1963), *The Night Walker* (1964), *The
Skull* (1965 - original story only), *The
Psychopath* (1966), *The Deadly Bees*
(1966 - co-w), *Torture Garden* (1967),
The House That Dripped Blood (1970),
Asylum (1972), *The Cat Creature* (1973 -
w/co-story - TVM), *The Dead Don't Die*
(1975 - TVM)

Blood and Black Lace
It 1964 89m Technicolor
Models at a fashion house are threatened
by a masked maniac.
Stylish Italian horror comic let down
by poor scripting and laughable acting,
though the use of colour and lighting is
striking.
p: Emmepi/Gala/Woodner
w: Marcel Fodato, Giuseppe Barilla,
Mario Bava
d: MARIO BAVA
ph: Herman Tarzana
m: Carl Rustic
ad: Harry Brest

Cameron Mitchell, Thomas Reiner,
Mary Arden, Arian Gorin, Dante Di
Paolo

Blood Beach
USA 1980 77m Movielab
A murderous monster lies beneath a
California beach.
'Just when you thought it was safe
to back in the water you can't get to it!'
ran the ads. An artless variation on the
Jaws theme, whose lack of humour
makes its silly story seem all the more
tedious.
p: Steve Nalevansky for Empress
exec p: Gerry Gross, Sir Run Run Shaw,
Sidney Beckerman
w/d: Jeffrey Bloom
ph: Steve Poster
m: Gil Melle
ed: Gary Griffin, Bud S. Isaacs
ad: William Sandell
cos: Lawrence Vallasco
sp: Dellwyn Rheume
sound: Bill Randall
David Huffman, Mariana Hill, John
Saxon, Burt Young, Otis Young

Blood Beast from Outer Space
see The Night Caller

The Blood Beast Terror
GB 1967 88m Eastmancolor/Movielab
A Victorian scientist's daughter has the
ability to turn into a giant Death's Head
moth, and her father tries to create a
mate for her.
Ludicrous horror hokum, lazily
directed on a low budget.
p: Arnold L. Miller for Tigon
exec p: Tony Tenser
w: Peter Bryan
d: Vernon Sewell
ph: Stanley A. Long
m: Paul Ferris
ed: Howard Lanning
ad: Wilfred Woods
cos: Marie Feldwick
sp: Roger Dicken
sound: Alan Hogben
Peter Cushing, Robert Flemyng, Wanda
Ventham, Vanessa Howard, David
Griffin, Kevin Stoney, Glyn Edwards,
Roy Hudd

Blood from the Mummy's Tomb *
GB 1971 94m Technicolor
A young woman is possessed by the
spirit of a mummy discovered by her
father on an expedition.
Competently mounted though less
than wholly satisfactory transcription of
one of Bram Stoker's lesser known
novels, *The Jewell of the Seven Stars*, later
tackled with even less success as *The
Awakening*. Studio head Michael Carreras

stepped in to complete the film when
director Seth Holt died shortly before
the end of production, whilst the
original leading man, Peter Cushing,
was replaced by Andrew Keir after only
one day's filming owing to the sudden
death of his wife.
p: Howard Brandy for Hammer
w: Christopher Wicking
novel: Bram Stoker
d: SETH HOLT (and Michael Carreras)
ph: Arthur Grant
m: Tristam Carey
md: Philip Martell
ed: Peter Weatherley
ad: Scott MacGregor
cos: Rosemary Burrows
sp: Michael Collins
sound: Tony Dawe
Valerie León, Andrew Keir, James
Villiers, Hugh Burdern, George
Coulouris, Rosalie Crutchley, Aubrey
Morris, David Markham

Blood Is My Heritage see Blood of
Dracula

Blood of Dracula
USA 1957 70m bw
The chemistry teacher at a young girls'
preparatory school hypnotizes one of
her pupils into thinking she's a vampire.
Dim low-budgeter, all talk and little
action. Dracula has nothing to do with it.
p: Herman Cohen for AIP
exec p: James H. Nicholson, Samuel Z.
Arkoff
w: Ralph Thornton
d: Herbert L. Strock
ph: Monroe Atkins
m: Paul Dunlap
ed: Robert Moore
ad: Leslie Thomas
cos: Florence Hays
sound: Herman Lewis
Sandra Harrison, Louise Lewis, Gail
Ganley, Jerry Blaine, Heather Ames,
Malcolm Atterbury, Mary Adams

Blood of the Demon see Blood of
Dracula

Blood of the Undead see Schizo

Blood of the Vampire *
GB 1958 85m Eastmancolor
A mad doctor raised from the dead
experiments on the inmates of an insane
asylum.
Fair low-budget horror piece in the
Hammer vein.
p: Robert S. Baker, Monty Berman for
Artistes Alliance
w: Jimmy Sangster
d: Henry Cass
ph: Monty Berman

m: Stanley Black
ed: Douglas Myers
ad: John Elphick
cos: Muriel Dickson
sound: Bill Bulkley
Donald Wolfit, Vincent Ball, Barbara
Shelley, Victor Maddern, Andrew
Faulds, John le Mesurier, Bernard
Bresslaw

Blood on Satan's Claw *

GB 1970 93m Eastmancolor
Inhabitants of a seventeenth-century
English village find their lives influenced
by the unearthing of a devil's claw.

Good looking low-budget horror
piece with a few striking moments, let
down only by its length.
p: Tony Tenser, Malcolm B. Heyworth,
Peter L. Andrews for Tigon/Chilton
w: Robert Wynn-Simmons, Piers
Haggard
d: PIERS HAGGARD
ph: Dick Bush
m: Malcolm Wilkinson
ed: Richard Best
ad: Arnold Chapkis
cos: Dulcie Midwinter
sound: Tony Dawe, Ken Barker
Patrick Wymark, Linda Hayden, Barry
Andrews, Simon Williams, Avice
Landon, Anthony Ainley, Tamara Ustinov,
Michelle Dotrice, Geoffrey Hughes

Blood Sisters see Sisters

Bloodbath, Bay of Blood see Bay
of Blood

Bloodsuckers

GB 1970 87m colour
The wayward son of the British Foreign
Secretary becomes involved with a
vampire cult in Greece.

Tolerable international schlocker
offering a reasonably diverting variation
on the old theme, though with a better
cast than it perhaps deserves.
p: Graham Harris for Lucinda
exec p: Peter Newbrook (uncredited)
w: Julian More
d: Robert Hartford-Davis
ph: Desmond Dickinson
m: Robyn Richards
pd: George Provis
sound: Tony Dawe, Douglas Whitlock
Patrick Macnee, Patrick Mower, Peter
Cushing, Edward Woodward, Alex
Davion, Madeline Hindle, Johnny Sekka,
David Lodge, Imogen Hassal, Valerie Van
Ost

Bloody Bird see Stage Fright

The Blue Boy

GB 1994 65m colour TVM

A young couple - he faithless, she
pregnant - are haunted by the spirit of a
drowned boy whilst holidaying in
Scotland.

Slight, overstretched ghost story,
adequately but unsurprisingly presented.
p: Kate Swan for BBC/WGBH
exec p: Rebecca Eaton, Andrea
Calderwood
w/d: Paul Murton
ph: Stuart Wyld
m: Philip Appleby
ed: Peter Hayes
ad: Graham Rose
cos: David Beeton
sound: Stuart Bruce
Emma Thompson, Adrian Dunbar,
Eleanor Bron, David Horovitch, Joanna
Roth, Phyllida Law, Barry Molloy

Body Count

It 1986 87m Technicolor
Teenagers are murdered by a killer
posing as an Indian spirit.

Lamentable horror trash with the
expected quota of tits and slash.
p: Alessandro Fracassi
w: Alex Capone, David Parker Jr, Sheila
Goldberg, Luca D'Alisera
d: Ruggero Deodato
ph: Emilio Loffredo
m: Claudio Simonetti
ed: Eugenio Alabiso
sp: Roberto Page
Bruce Penhall, Mimsy Farmer, David
Hess, Luisa Maneri, Nicola Farron,
Andrew Lederer, Stefano Madia, Charles
Napier

Body Double

USA 1984 114m Metrocolor Dolby
An out-of-work actor witnesses a
vicious murder, but later meets the
victim's double.

Over-plotted mixture of *Rear
Window*, *Vertigo* and *Dressed to Kill* in
which the director tries too hard to out-
do himself. A few good set pieces along
the way, but the overall silliness ruins
the effect.
p: Brian de Palma for Columbia/Delphi
exec p: Howard Gottfried
w: Brian de Palma, Robert J. Avrech
d/story: Brian de Palma
ph: Stephen H. Burum
m: PINO DONAGGIO
ed: Jerry Greenberg, Bill Pankow
pd: Ida Random
cos: Gloria Gresham
sp: Bill Hansard
sound: James Tanenbaum
stunt co-ordinator: Jerry Brutshe
Craig Wasson, Gregg Henry, Melanie
Griffith, Deborah Shelton, Guy Boyd,
Dennis Franz, David Haskell, Holly
Johnson

The Body Snatcher ***

USA 1945 77m bw
In 1831 Edinburgh, a grave-robber resorts
to murder when bodies run short.

Well mounted melodrama with
strong performances and assured
production. Arguably the best of the
Lewton horrors.
p: Val Lewton for RKO
exec p: Jack J. Gross
w: PHILIP MACDONALD, CARLOS
KEITH (VAL LEWTON)
story: Robert Louis Stevenson
d: ROBERT WISE
ph: ROBERT DE GRASSE
m: Roy Webb
md: Constantin Bakaleinikoff
ed: J. R. Whittredge
ad: Albert S. D'Agostino, Walter E.
Keller
cos: Renie
sound: Bailey Felser, Terry Kellum
BORIS KARLOFF, HENRY DANIELL,
Bela Lugosi, Edith Atwater, Russell
Wade, Mary Gordon

Body Snatchers *

USA 1993 87m Technicolor Dolby
A young girl discovers that the military
base where her father is working has
been taken over by aliens from outer
space.

Third version of the Jack Finney
story and a surprisingly tolerable and
inexplicit one, given its director's usual
taste for extreme violence.
p: Robert H. Solo for Warner
w: Stuart Gordon, Dennis Paoli,
Nicholas St. John
novel: JACK FINNEY
screen story: Raymond Cistheri, Larry
Cohen
d: Abel Ferrara
ph: Bojan Bazelli
m: Joe Delia
ed: Anthony Redman
pd: Peter Jamison
cos: Margaret Mohr
sp: Phil Cory
sound: Michael Barosky
make-up effects: Thomas R. Burman,
Bari Dreiband-Berman
2nd unit d/stunt co-ordinator: Phil
Neilson
2nd unit ph: Henry Link
titles: R. Greenberg
Gabrielle Anwar, Terry Kinney, Meg
Tilly, Reilly Murphy, Billy Wirth,
Christine Élise, R. Lee Ermey, Forest
Whitaker, Kathleen Doyle

Borland, Carol (1914-)

American actress, remembered solely
for playing Luna Mora, the eye-catching
vampire girl in Tod Browning's *Mark of
the Vampire* (1935).

Boswell, Simon

British composer with a penchant for hard rock horror scores.
Genre credits:
Graveyard Disturbance (1986), *Stage Fright* (1987 - aka *Deleria/Bloody Bird/Aquarius*), *Demons 2* (1987 - aka *Demoni 2*), *Demons 3: The Ogre* (1988 - aka *The Ogre*), *Santa Sangre* (1989), *Hardware* (1990), *Dust Devil* (1992 - aka *Demonica*), *Shallow Grave* (1995), *Lord of Illusions* (1995)

Bottin, Rob (1959-)

American make-up effects designer, an Academy Award winner for his work on Paul Verhoeven's *Total Recall* (1990). A former assistant to Rick Baker on such films as *Squirm*, *Star Wars*, *Tanya's Island* and *The Fury*, he began his solo career with Joe Dante's *Piranha*, which led to several other collaborations with the director, including *Explorers* and *Inner Space*. It was his work on Dante's *The Howling* and, more importantly, John Carpenter's superb remake of *The Thing*, that finally confirmed his status as one of the industry's most talented and sought after make-up effects artists. His other credits include *Rock 'n' Roll High School*, *Airplane*, *Legend*, *Robocop* (and sequels), *Bugsy*, *Basic Instinct* and *Toys*.
Genre credits:
Squirm (1976 - assistant), *King Kong* (1976 - assistant), *The Incredible Melting Man* (1978 - assistant), *The Fury* (1978 - assistant), *Piranha* (1978), *The Fog* (1980 - also actor, as Captain Blake), *Humanoids from the Deep* (1980), *The Howling* (1980), *The Thing* (1982), *Twilight Zone - The Movie* (1983), *The Witches of Eastwick* (1987)

Bowie, Les (1913-1979)

Busy British special effects technician who worked on a good many of Hammer's films, his main task usually being to disintegrate Dracula. Worked on a wide variety of projects, including *The Red Shoes*, *The Assassination Bureau*, *Star Wars* and *Superman*, for which he won an Oscar in 1978. Began his career as a scenic artist, which led to his first film, *The School for Secrets* (aka *Secret Fight*) in 1946. His first Hammer film was *The Quatermass Experiment* in 1956, for which he was given a budget of just £30!
Genre credits:
The Quatermass Experiment (1955 - aka *The Quatermass Xperiment/The Creeping Unknown*), *X - The Unknown* (1956 - co-sp), *The Curse of Frankenstein* (1956), *The Trollenberg Terror* (1957 - aka *The Crawling Eye*), *Grip of the Strangler* (1958 - aka *The Haunted Strangler*), *The Day the Earth Caught Fire* (1961), *The Curse of the Werewolf* (1961), *The Shadow of the Cat* (1961), *Captain Clegg* (1962 - aka *Night Creatures*), *The Old Dark House* (1963), *Paranoiac* (1963), *Kiss of the Vampire* (1964 - aka *Kiss of Evil*), *The Evil of Frankenstein* (1964), *She* (1965 - co-sp), *The Face of Fu Manchu* (1965), *Dracula - Prince of Darkness* (1966), *The Plague of the Zombies* (1966), *The Reptile* (1966), *Frankenstein Created Woman* (1966), *One Million Years B. C.* (1966 - co-sp), *The Mummy's Shroud* (1966), *Quatermass and the Pit* (1967), *Vampire Circus* (1971), *Nothing But the Night* (1972), *Dracula A. D. 1972* (1972), *The Satanic Rites of Dracula* (1973), *Legend of the Seven Golden Vampires* (1974 - aka *The Seven Brothers Meet Dracula*), *To the Devil... A Daughter* (1976)

Boyle, Peter (1933-)

American character actor (*Joe*, *The Candidate*, *Outland*, *Hammett*), remembered by genre fans for his hilarious portrayal of Frankenstein's Monster in the Mel Brooks parody *Young Frankenstein* (1974).

Bradley, David (1954-)

British actor whose screen performances as Pinhead in Clive Barker's *Hellraiser* series have earned him a cult following.
Genre credits:
Salome (1973 - short), *Forbidden* (1978 - short), *Hellraiser* (1987), *Hellbound: Hellraiser II* (1988), *Hellraiser III: Hell on Earth* (1992), *Hellraiser IV* (1995)

Brahm, John (1893-1982)

German born director (real name Hans Brahm), a former stage director who moved to Hollywood, via Britain, in the thirties. Brought a certain visual flair to three genre subjects in the forties. Other credits include *Broken Blossoms*, *Escape to Glory*, *The Locket* and *The Brasher Doubloon*.
Genre credits:
The Undying Monster (1942), *The Lodger* (1944), *Hangover Square* (1944), *The Mad Magician* (1954)

The Brain

Canada 1988 90m colour
The residents of a small township find themselves compelled to murderous acts via the hypnotic waves from a giant synthetic brain.
    Foolish nonsense, as hilarious as it is generally inept.
p: Anthony Kramreither for Brightstar/Filmhouse
exec p: Don Haig
w: Barry Pearson
d: Edward Hunt
ph: Gilles Corbeil
m: Paul Zaza
ed: David Nicholson
ad: no credit given
cos: Eva Gord
sound: Jin Hong, Rae Crombie
Tom Breznahan, Cyndy Preston, George Buza, David Gale, Brett Pearson

Brain Damage

USA 1988 90m TVCcolor
A brain-eating parasite attaches itself to a young man who consequently has to do its murderous bidding.
    Comic schlocker, somewhat typical of its writer-director's low-budget output.
p: Edgar Levins for The Brain Damage Company
w/d/exec p: Frank Henenlotter
ph: Bruce Torbet
m: Gus Russo, Clutch Reiser
ed: Frank Henenlotter, James Y. Kwei
ad/cos: Ivy Rosvsky
sound: Joe Warda, Russell Jessum, Aaron Nathanson
make-up effects: Gabe Bartalos, David Kindlon and others
Rick Herbst, Gordon Macdonald, Jennifer Lowry, Theo Barnes, Lucille Saint-Peter, Vicki Darnell

The Brain Eaters

USA 1958 61m bw
The inhabitants of a small American township find themselves prey to leech-like creatures.
    Grade Z hokum, a real Golden Turkey.
p: Edwin Nelson for Corinthian
w: Gordon Urquhart
d: Bruno VeSota
ph: Larry Raimond
m: Tom Jonson
ed: Carlo Lodato
ad: Bert Shonberg
cos: Charles Smith
sound: James Fullerton
titles: Robert Balser
Edwin Nelson, Alan Frost, Jack Hill, Joanna Lee, Jody Fair, David Hughes, Robert Ball, Leonard Nimoy, Greigh Phillips, Orville Sherman

The Brain of Arous

USA 1958 71m bw
A giant floating brain from outer space takes over the mind of a nuclear scientist.
    Ludicrous schlocker in which initial amusement is quickly replaced by tedium.
p: Jacques Marquette for Howco/Marquette
w: Ray Buffam
d: Nathan Hertz
ph: Jacques Marquette
m: Walter Greene

ed: Irving Schoenberg
ad: no credit given
sound: Philip Mitchell
John Agar, Joyce Meadows, Robert
Fuller, Tom Browne Henry, Henry
Travis, Tim Graham

Braindead

New Zealand 1992 104m Technicolor
A monkey bite turns a middle aged
housewife into a man-eating zombie,
and her wimpish son attempts to destroy
the others she has infected.

Determinedly sick and outrageous
comedy schlocker in the *Evil Dead* manner, wholly typical of its director's horror output. Perhaps best remembered
for the gore-filled finale, in which the
zombies are destroyed by a flymower.
p: Jim Booth for Wingnut
w: Stephen Sinclair, Frances Walsh,
Peter Jackson
story: Stephen Sinclair
d: Peter Jackson
ph: Murray Milne
m: Peter Dasnet
ed: Jamie Selkirk
pd: Kenneth Leonard-Jones
cos: Chris Elliott
sp: Richard Taylor
sound: Mike Hedges, Sam Negri
make-up effects: Bob McCarron,
Marjory Hamlin
Timothy Balme, Diana Penalver,
Elizabeth Moody, Ian Watkin, Brenda
Kendall, Stuart Devenie, Jed Brophy

Brainwave

USA 1985 80m colour
The brain of a young woman
electrocuted to death by her boyfriend is
transferred into the body of a woman
seriously injured in a road accident.

Low-budget horror hokum which
needed tighter handling if its central
premise was to be at all effective. Not
entirely unwatchable, though.
p: Ulli Lommel
w/d: Ulli Lommel
ph: Jon Kranhouse
m: Robert O. Ragland
ed: Richard Brummer
ad: Stephen E. Graff
cos: Irma Cleef
sound: Ed Christiane, John Huck
Keir Dullea, Tony Curtis, Vera Miles,
Suzanna Love, Percy Rodrigues, Paul
Willson, Corrine Alphen, Ryan Seitz

Bram Stoker's Dracula *

USA 1992 128m Technicolor Dolby
Count Dracula travels to England in
search of new blood, and falls in love
with the reincarnation of his wife, who
committed suicide four hundred years
earlier.

Opulent, reasonably faithful but
over-directed version of the oft told
story which manages to turn up every
visual cliche in the book - and then
some. All of which becomes tiresome
well before the end.
p: Francis Ford Coppola, Fred Fuchs,
Charles Mulvehill for
Columbia/American Zoetrope/Osiris
exec p: Michael Apted, Peter O'Connor
w: James V. Hart
novel: BRAM STOKER
d: Francis Ford Coppola
ph: Michael Balhaus
m: Wojciech Kilar
ed: Nicholas C. Smith, Glen
Scantlebury, Anne Goursard
pd: Thomas Sanders
cos: Eiko Ishioka (aa)
sp/2nd unit d: Roman Coppola
sound: Leslie Shatz, Robert Janiger
sound effects ed: Tom C. McCarthy,
David E. Stone (aa)
make-up effects: Greg Cannom, Michele
Burke, Matthew W. Mungle (aa)
titles: Gary Gutierrez
2nd unit ph: Steve Yaconelli
stunt co-ordinator: Billy Burton
Gary Oldman, Winona Ryder, Anthony
Hopkins (as Van Helsing), Keanu
Reeves, Richard E. Grant, Cary Elwes,
Bill Campbell, Sadie Frost, Tom Waits,
Jay Robinson

Brand, Neville (1921-1992)

American character actor, perhaps best
remembered for playing Al Capone in
the TV series *The Untouchables*. Began
studying drama in New York after being
discharged from the army in 1946 as
the fourth most decorated GI in World
War Two. Other credits include *Riot in
Cell Block Eleven*, *The Scarface Mob* (as Al
Capone again), *Cry Terror* and *The
Birdman of Alcatraz*.
Genre credits:
Killdozer (1974 - TVM), *Psychic Killer*
(1975), *Death Trap* (1976 - aka *Eaten
Alive*), *The Ninth Configuration* (1980),
Alligator (1980)

Brandt, Carolyn

American actress who, since marrying
director Ray Dennis Steckler, has
appeared mostly in his zero-budget
exploitation films, including *Rat Pfink a
Boo Boo* and *Wild Guitar*.
Genre credits:
Eegah! (1963), *The Incredibly Strange
Creatures Who Stopped Living and Became
Mixed-Up Zombies* (1963), *The Thrill
Killers* (1964), *The Lemon Grove Kids Meet
the Monsters* (1966), *Body Fever* (1969),
Blood Shack (1971 - aka *The Chopper*), *The
Hollywood Strangler Meets the Skid Row
Slasher* (1972)

• Christopher Lee's career might have
taken a different turn indeed had
Carry On star Bernard Bresslaw been
cast as the Creature in *The Curse of
Frankenstein* as was originally
planned.

Breakfast at the Manchester Morgue

see The Living Dead at the
Manchester Morgue

Bresslaw, Bernard (1933-1993)

Tall, gormless-looking British comedy
actor, a mainstay of the *Carry On* series.
Was considered for the role of the
Creature in Hammer's *The Curse of
Frankenstein* in 1956, but the part went
to Christopher Lee instead.
Genre credits:
Blood of the Vampire (1958), *The Ugly
Duckling* (1959), *Carry On Screaming*
(1966), *Vampira* (1974 - aka *Old
Dracula*), *Jabberwocky* (1977), *Hawk the
Slayer* (1980)

Bresslee, Bobbie

American actress, a former model, who
has appeared in a handful of low-budget
genre entries.
Genre credits:
Mausoleum (1982), *Evil Spawn* (1987),
Surf Nazi Must Die (1987)

Briant, Shane (1946-)

British actor whom Hammer seemed to
be grooming for stardom in the early
seventies.
Genre credits:
Demons of the Mind (1972), *Straight on Till
Morning* (1972), *Captain Kronos - Vampire
Hunter* (1973 - aka *Kronos*), *Frankenstein
and the Monster from Hell* (1973)

The Bride

GB/USA 1985 118m Technicolor Dolby

Baron Frankenstein creates a mate for his Monster, but falls in love with her himself.

Good looking but otherwise inadequate reworking of *The Bride of Frankenstein*, with ill-starred leads.
p: Victor Drai for Columbia
exec p: Keith Addis
w: Lloyd Fonvielle
d: Franc Roddam
ph: Stephen H. Burum
m: Maurice Jarre
ed: Michael Ellis
pd: Michael Seymour
cos: Shirley Russell
sp: Peter Hutchinson
sound: David John, Hugh Strain
make-up: Sarah Monzani
stunt co-ordinator: Gerry Crampton
Sting, Jennifer Beals, Clancy Brown, David Rappaport, Quentin Crisp, Geraldine Page, Anthony Higgins, Phil Daniels, Cary Elwes, Timothy Spall, Janine Duvitsky

The Bride of Frankenstein ★★★★
USA 1935 85m bw
With the assistance of the mysterious Dr Pretorious, Baron Frankenstein creates a mate for his Monster.

One of the silver screen's most fondly regarded horror movies, this splendid sequel to *Frankenstein* offers an excellent blend of black humour and thrills, and shows all concerned in top form. Lighting, photography, sets and direction could hardly be better.
p: Carl Laemmle Jr for Universal
w: JOHN L. BALDERSTON, WILLIAM HURLBUTT
novel: MARY WOLLSTONECRAFT SHELLEY
d: JAMES WHALE
ph: JOHN MESCALL
m: FRANZ WAXMAN
md: Constantin Bakaleinikoff
ed: MAURICE PIVAR, TED KENT
ad: CHARLES D. HALL
cos: no credit given
sp: JOHN P. FULTON
sound: no credit given
make-up: JACK P. PIERCE
BORIS KARLOFF, COLIN CLIVE, Valerie Hobson, ELSA LANCHESTER, ERNEST THESIGER, Dwight Frye, O. P. Heggie, E. E. Clive, UNA O'CONNOR, Ann Darling, Neil Fitzgerald, Reginald Barlow, Glinnis Davis, Temple Piggott, John Carradine, Mary Gordon, Gavin Gordon

The Brides of Dracula ★★
GB 1960 85m Technicolor
A lady traveller staying at a lonely castle unwittingly frees a vampire.

Well mounted vampire saga in the best Hammer tradition, with plenty of

• **Boris Karloff enjoys a sandwich between takes during the filming of** *The Bride of Frankenstein*

pace and atmosphere. Because Christopher Lee was unwilling to reprise the role of Dracula at this stage in his career, one of his disciples, Baron Meinster (David Peel) is the centre of attention instead.
p: Anthony Hinds for Hammer/Universal/Hotspur
w: Jimmy Sangster, Peter Bryan, Edward Percy
d: TÉRENCE FISHER
ph: JACK ASHER
m: Malcolm Williamson
md: John Hollingsworth
ed: James Needs, Alfred Cox
cos: Molly Arbuthnot
sp: Sydney Pearson
sound: Jock May
make-up: Roy Ashton
PETER CUSHING, DAVID PEEL, MARTITA HUNT, Yvonne Molnaur, Andree Melly, Mona Washborne, FREDA JACKSON, Henry Oscar, Miles Malleson

The Brides of Fu Manchu ★
GB 1966 94m Technicolor

Fu Manchu kidnaps the daughters of several scientists and politicians in order to influence their fathers.

Fair sequel to *The Face of Fu Manchu*, with plenty of serial-like thrills.
p: Harry Alan Towers for Anglo-EMI/Hallam
w: Peter Welbeck (Harry Alan Towers)
d: DON SHARP
ph: Ernest Steward
m: Bruce Montgomery
ed: Alan Morrison
ad: FRANK WHITE
Christopher Lee, Douglas Wilmner, Marie Versini, Burt Kwouk, Howard Marion Crawford, Tsai Chin, Kenneth Fortescue, Eric Young, Rupert Davies, Roger Hanin

Brimstone and Treacle ★
GB 1976 75m colour TVM
The devil takes the form of a charming young man and insinuates himself into the home of a businessman whose brain damaged daughter he later rapes.

Extremely black religious comedy which was deemed worthy of banning for eleven years. Contemporary audiences may well wonder why, especially as the play is not one of its author's best and the production is pretty slack.
p: Kenith Trodd for BBC
w: Dennis Potter
d: Barry Davis
ph: Peter Bartlett
m: various
ed: Tony Woolard
ad: Colin Shaw
cos: John Bloomfield
sound: Tony Millier
Denholm Elliott, Michael Kitchen, Patricia Lawrence, Malcolm Newell, Paul Williamson, Patricia Quayle, James Greene

Brimstone and Treacle

GB 1982 87m Technicolor Dolby
A mysterious young man insinuates himself into the home of a writer of epitaphs and doggerel and rapes his comatose daughter.

Anaemic rehash of the play previously filmed and then banned by the BBC. A stronger sense of style and the supernatural was needed if it were to work any better on the big screen.
p: Kenith Trodd for Namara
exec p: Alan E. Salke
w: Dennis Potter, from his play
d: Richard Loncraine
ph: Peter Hannan
m: Sting, Michael Nyman
ed: Paul Green
pd: Milly Burns
cos: Shauna Harwood
sound: Tony Jackson, Hugh Strain
Sting, Denholm Elliott, Joan Plowright, Suzanna Hamilton, Benjamin Whitrow, Dudley Sutton

The Brood

Canada 1979m 91m Technicolor
The rage of a woman under the psychiatric observation of a mad doctor manifests itself as murderous dwarfs.

Fairish exploitation horror which could have done with more zip. Now something of a cult item, it helped to establish its director's reputation for visceral horror.
p: Claude Heroux for Mutual/Elgin/Montreal
w/d: David Cronenberg
ph: Mark Irwin
m: Howard Shore
ed: Alan Collins
ad: Carol Spier
Oliver Reed, Samantha Eggar, Art Hindle, Cindy Hinds, Nuala Fitzgerald, Henry Beckman

Brooks, Jean (1915-1963)

American actress (real name Ruby M. Kelly), in films from 1935 as Jeanne Kelly (*Obeah*, *Frankie and Johnnie*, *Tango Bar*, *The Crime of Dr Crespi*, etc.), though best known for a handful of films in the forties, most notably Val Lewton's *The Seventh Victim*, in which she played the Cleopatra-wigged Jacqueline Gibson. A former nightclub singer, she also acted in American made Spanish films under the name Robina Duarte. Her other English speaking film credits include *A Miracle on Main Street*, *Son of Roaring Dan*, *Fighting Bill Fargo*, *The Falcon Strikes Back* (unbilled), *The Falcon in Danger*, *The Falcon and the Co-Eds*, *The Falcon's Alibi* and *The Bamboo Blonde*, after which she disappeared into obscurity.
Genre credits:
Obeah (1935), *The Leopard Man* (1943), *The Seventh Victim* (1943)

Brooks, Mel (1926-)

American actor, comedian, writer, producer and director (real name Melvin Kaminsky) responsible for a series of hit and miss movie parodies, the best of which is the horror spoof *Young Frankenstein*. Founded Brooksfilms in the early eighties through which he has also produced a number of non-comedy subjects. Other credits include *The Producers*, *Blazing Saddles*, *Silent Movie*, *High Anxiety* and *Robin Hood: Men in Tights*.
Genre credits:
Young Frankenstein (1974 - co-w/d), *The Elephant Man* (1980 - exec p), *The Doctor and the Devils* (1985 - exec p), *The Fly* (1986 - exec p), *Dracula: Dead and Loving It* (1995 - d)

Browning, Ricou (1930-)

American stuntman and second unit director, a former Olympic swimmer who specializes in underwater sequences. He played the Creature in *The Creature from the Black Lagoon* and its sequels and has directed the underwater sequences for such films as *Flipper* and *Around the World Under the Sea*.
Genre credits:
The Creature from the Black Lagoon (1954), *Revenge of the Creature* (1955), *The Creature Walks Among Us* (1956)

Browning, Tod (1880-1962)

American writer, producer and director, perhaps best known for directing *Dracula* in 1930. A former actor, circus performer and vaudevillian, he began working in films in 1912 as an actor. Began writing scenarios in 1916, working on D. W. Griffith's *Intolerance*, by which time he'd also started directing shorts. Made his feature début in 1919 with *Jim Bludso*. In the twenties he directed horror star Lon Chaney in several popular vehicles, with whom he intended to work on *Dracula* before the actor's untimely death, whilst his 1932 feature, *Freaks*, was banned for almost 30 years and disowned by its producing studio, MGM. Despite the importance of several of his films in the development of the genre, many of them now seem rather stagey and slow moving. He retired from movies in 1939 and went into real estate.
Genre credits:
The Unholy Three (1925 - p/d), *The Mystic* (1925 - story/d), *The Black Bird* (1926 - story/d), *The Show* (1927 - p/d), *The Unknown* (1927 - story/d), *London After Midnight* (1927 - aka *The Hypnotist* - story/p/d), *The Thirteenth Chair* (1929 p/d), *Dracula* (1930 - d), *Freaks* (1932 - d), *Mark of the Vampire* (1935 - a remake of *London After Midnight* - d), *The Devil-Doll* (1936 - adaptation/d)

Bryan, Peter

British writer, producer, director and camera operator, the brother of Oscar winning production designer John Bryan (1911-1969). Joined Hammer in 1949 as a camera operator and worked on several of their early B thrillers, such as *Meet Simon Cherry* and *Room to Let*. Later directed a number of travelogues and shorts for them. Genre work mostly as a writer.
Genre credits:
The Hound of the Baskervilles (1959 - w), *The Brides of Dracula* (1960 - co-w), *Plague of the Zombies* (1966 - w), *The Blood Beast Terror* (1967 - w)

Buchanan, Larry (1923-)

American director who, in the mid-sixties, made a number of zero-budget horror pictures, most of which are practically unwatchable. He began his directorial career in 1952 with the western *Apache Gold*. His other credits include *A Taste of Venom*, *Free White and 21*, *Naughty Dallas*, *The Other Side of Bonnie and Clyde*, *Bullet for a Pretty Boy*, *Rebel Jesus* and *Mistress of the Apes*.
Genre credits:
The Naked Witch (1961), *Mars Needs Women* (1964), *The Eye Creatures* (1965), *Curse of the Swamp Creature* (1966), *Zontar, the Thing from Venus* (1966), *Creature of Destruction* (1967), *In the Year 2889* (1967), *It's Alive!* (1968), *The Loch Ness Horror* (1978)

Buechler, John Carl

American make-up effects artist working

chiefly for producer Charles Band. He has directed several low-budget genre entries, also for Band.
Genre credits:
Mausoleum (1982 - sp), *Dungeonmaster* (1983 - co-d), *Ghoulies* (1984 - sp), *Zone Troopers* (1984 - sp), *Troll* (1986 - d), *Crawlspace* (1986 - sp), *From Beyond* (1986 - co-sp), *Dolls* (1986 - co-sp), *Demonwarp* (1987 - co-w/sp), *Slave Girls from Beyond Infinity* (1987 - co-sp), *Ghoulies 2* (1987 - sp), *Prison* (1988 - sp), *Halloween 4: The Return of Michael Myers* (1988 - sp), *Friday the Thirteenth Part VII - The New Blood* (1988 - d), *Demonic Toys* (1990 - sp), *Ghoulies III: Ghoulies Go to College* (1991 - aka *Ghoulies Go to College* - d)

Buffy the Vampire Slayer
USA 1992 94m DeLuxe
A school cheerleader is trained to become a vampire slayer.

Poor horror spoof, neither funny enough nor scary enough and with a better supporting cast than it deserves. Not even worthy of comparison to *Fright Night*.
p: Kaz Kuzui, Howard Rosenman for TCF/Sandollar/Kuzui Enterprises
exec p: Sandy Gallin, Carol Baum, Fran Rubel Kuzui
w: Joss Whedon
d: Fran Rubel Kuzui
ph: James Hayman
m: Carter Burwell
ed: Camilla Toniolo, Jill Savitt
pd: Lawrence Miller
cos: Marie France
sp: Joseph Mercurio
sound: Steve Aaron
2nd unit d/stunt co-ordinator: Terry J. Leonard
Kristy Swanson, Donald Sutherland, Paul Reubens, Rutger Hauer, Luke Perry, Michele Abrams, Hilary Swank, Paris Vaughan, David Arquette, Candy Clark

Buono, Victor (1938-1982)
Obese American character actor whose first film, as the pianist in *Whatever Happened to Baby Jane?* earned him an Oscar nomination for Best Supporting Actor. Consequent roles a mixture of the comic and the villainous.

Genre credits:
Whatever Happened to Baby Jane? (1962), *The Strangler* (1964), *Hush... Hush, Sweet Charlotte* (1965), *The Mad Butcher* (1972 - aka *The Strangler of Vienna/Il Stranglatore de Vienna/Meat is Meat*), *Arnold* (1975), *The Evil* (1978)

Burn, Witch, Burn! see Night of the Eagle

The Burning (1980) see Don't Go Into the House

The Burning
USA 1981 87m Palcolor
Kids at a summer camp play a trick on the evil caretaker, but it backfires and he later returns to extract a murderous revenge.

Another sick variation on *Friday the 13th*. Just an excuse for killing people in dark places - and very bloodily.
p: Harvey Weinstein for Miramax
w: Pater Lawrence, Bob Weinstein
d: Tony Maylam
ph: Harvey Harrison
m: Rick Wakeman
ed: Jack Sholder
ad: Peter Politanoff
make-up effects: Tom Savini
Brian Matthews, Leah Ayres, Brian Backer, Larry Joshua, Lou David

Burns, Marilyn
American actress, remembered chiefly for playing Sally Hardesty, the unfortunate victim in Tobe Hooper's notorious *Texas Chainsaw Massacre*.
Genre credits:
The Texas Chainsaw Massacre (1974), *Eaten Alive* (1976 - aka *Death Trap/Starlight Slaughter/Horror Hotel Massacre/Legend of the Bayou*), *Future Kill* (1985)

Burnt Offerings
USA 1976 115m DeLuxe Panavision
A family rent a decaying house for their vacation only to find themselves caught in a web of evil.

A fair but overstretched horror story which would have been twice as effective at half the length. A few goodish moments.
p: Robert Singer for UA/PEA
exec p: Dan Curtis

w: William Nolan, Dan Curtis
novel: Robert Marasco
d: Dan Curtis
ph: Jacques Marquette, Stevan Larner
m: Robert Cobert
ed: Dennis Virkler
ad: Eugene Lourie
sp: Cliff Wenger
Karen Black, Oliver Reed, Bette Davis, Burgess Meredith, Eileen Heckart, Lee Montgomery, Dub Taylor, Anthony James

Burstyn, Ellen (1932-)
Respected American actress who earned herself an Oscar nomination for Best Actress as the mother in *The Exorcist* (1974). Other films include *Alice Doesn't Live Here Anymore* (which won her an Oscar), *Same Time Next Year*, *Resurrection* and *Twice in a Lifetime*.

Burton, Tim (1960-)
American director with a strong visual sense but little narrative grip. A former Disney animator, he is perhaps best known for his two Batman films, *Batman* and *Batman Returns*. He produced the third Batman film, *Batman Forever*, leaving the directorial chores to Joel Schumacher.
Genre credits:
Vincent (1982 - short - d), *Frankenweenie* (1984 - short - d), *Beetlejuice* (1988 - d), *Edward Scissorhands* (1990 - story/d), *The Nightmare Before Christmas* (1993 - aka *Tim Burton's The Nightmare Before Christmas* - co-p/story), *Ed Wood* (1994 - co-p/d)

Bush, Dick (1931-)
British cinematographer with several Ken Russell credits to his name, including *Savage Messiah*, *Tommy* and *Crimes of Passion*. Has also worked on several Blake Edwards comedies, including *Trail of the Pink Panther*, *Victor/Victoria*, *Curse of the Pink Panther* and *Switch*.
Genre credits:
Whistle and I'll Come to You (1968 - TVM) *When Dinosaurs Ruled the Earth* (1970), *Blood on Satan's Claw* (1970 - aka *Satan's Skin*), *Twins of Evil* (1971), *Dracula A. D. 1972* (1972), *Phase IV* (1973), *The Hound of the Baskervilles* (1977 - co-ph), *The Legacy* (1978 - co-ph), *The Fan* (1981), *Lair of the White Worm* (1988), *Little Monsters* (1989)

C

The Cabinet of Dr Caligari ***
Ger 1919 69m bw silent
The proprietor of a fairground sideshow uses a somnambulist to carry out a series of murders.

Seminal expressionist melodrama regarded by many as the first true horror film. Though time and imitation have faded its impact, its influences are still being felt today. Of particular note for its stylized art direction and its twist ending, in which the story turns out to be the ravings of a madman.
p: Erich Pommer for Decla/Bioscop
w: Carl Mayer, Hans Janowitz
story: Hans Janowitz
d: ROBERT WIENE
ph: WILLY HAMEISTER
ad: HERMANN WARM, WALTER REIMAN, WALTER ROHRIG
cos: WALTER REIMANN
WERNER KRAUSS, CONRAD VEIDT (as Cesare), Lil Dagover, Friedrich Feher, Hans H. Von Twardowski, Rudolf Lettinger, Rudolf Klein-Rogge

Cacavas, John (1930-)
Workaday American composer with many routine film and television credits to his name, including *Airport 1975*, *Airport 1977* and countless episodes of TV's *Kojak*.
Genre credits:
Horror Express (1972), *The Satanic Rites of Dracula* (1973), *Mortuary* (1981)

Cage of Doom see Terror from the Year 5,000

Cahn, Edward L. (1899-1963)
American producer and director who began his career as a cutter at Universal, working his way up to editor-in-chief in 1926. Turned to direction in 1931 with *Homicide Squad*, though by the fifties he'd been reduced to directing second feature science fiction and horror subjects. Other credits include *Invasion of the Saucer Men* (aka *Invasion of the Hell Creatures*), *It! The Terror from Beyond Space* and *Invisible Invaders*.
Genre credits:
The Creature with the Atom Brain (1955 -

d), *The She-Creature* (1956 - d), *Voodoo Woman* (1957 - d), *The Zombies of Mora Tau* (1957 - aka *The Dead That Walk* - d), *The Curse of the Faceless Man* (1958 - d), *The Four Skulls of Jonathan Drake* (1959 - d), *Beauty and the Beast* (1963 - d)

Cahn, Phil
American editor with many credits for Universal and PRC.
The Mummy's Hand (1940), *The Brute Man* (1946), *House of Horrors* (1946 - aka *Joan Medford is Missing*), *Bela Lugosi Meets a Brooklyn Gorilla* (1952 - aka *The Monster Meets the Gorilla*)

Cameron, James (1954-)
American writer, producer and director of high-octane action thrillers such as *The Abyss*, *True Lies* and the *Terminator* films, though he began rather more humbly as an art director for Roger Corman.
Genre credits:
Piranha II: The Spawning (1983 - aka *Piranha II: The Flying Killers* - d), *The Terminator* (1984 - co-w/d), *Aliens* (1986 - co-w/d), *Terminator 2: Judgement Day* (1991 - co-w/d)

Campbell, Bruce
American actor who first came to attention as the hero of Sam Raimi's cult classic *The Evil Dead*. He has since appeared in many of Raimi's subsequent films, as well as a number of other genre titles. He has also recently turned to direction.
Genre credits:
The Evil Dead (1980), *Crimewave* (1985), *Evil Dead 2: Dead by Dawn* (1987), *Maniac Cop* (1988), *Moontrap* (1988), *Maniac Cop 2* (1990), *Darkman* (1990 - gag cameo), *Sundown - The Vampire in Retreat* (1990), *Waxwork 2: Lost in Time* (1992), *Lunatics* (1992), *Army of Darkness* (1993 - aka *Army of Darkness: The Medieval Dead/The Medieval Dead/Evil Dead III*), *The Man with the Screaming Brain* (1994 - actor/d), *Congo* (1995)

Candyman *
USA 1992 99m Technicolor
A college student investigating a mythical

murderer finds him to be all too real.

Standard horror story with standard jolts, though the fact that it is set amid the urban decay of an American city seems to hint that it's also trying to 'say something'. *Candyman 2: Farewell to the Flesh* followed in 1995.
p: Steve Golin, Sigurjon Sighvatsson, Alan Poul for Polygram/Propaganda
exec p: Clive Barker
w/d: Bernard Rose
story: Clive Barker
ph: Anthony B. Richmond
m: Philip Glass
ed: Daniel Rae
pd: Jane Stewart
cos: Leonard Pollock
sp: Marty Bresin
sound: Reinhard Sterger
make-up effects: Bob Keen
stunt co-ordinator: Walter Scott
Virginia Madsen, Tony Todd, Xander Berkeley, Kasi Lemmons, Dejuan Guy, Vanessa Williams, Marianna Elliott, Ted Raimi, Gilbert Lewis

Cannom, Greg
American make-up effects artist, an Oscar winner (with Michele Burke and Matthew W. Mungle) for his work on *Bram Stoker's Dracula* (1992) and (with Ve Neill and Yolanda Toussieng) *Mrs Doubtfire* (1993). His other credits include *Hook*.
Genre credits:
Curtains (1983), *Vamp* (1986), *The Lost Boys* (1987), *A Nightmare on Elm Street Part 3: The Dream Warriors* (1987), *Meridian* (1990 - aka *Kiss of the Beast*), *The Pit and the Pendulum* (1990), *Bram Stoker's Dracula* (1992), *The Puppet Masters* (1994), *The Mask* (1994)

The Canterville Ghost *
USA 1943 95m bw
A young heiress discovers her castle ghost not to be so fierce after all.

Mild fantasy comedy, remembered chiefly for its stars rather than any sparkle in the script or handling. Remade for TV in 1996.
p: Arthur Field for MGM
w: Edwin Blum

novel: Oscar Wilde
d: Jules Dassin
ph: Robert Planck
m: George Bassman
ed: Chester W. Schaeffer
ad: Cedric Gibbons, Edward Carfagno
cos: Irene Sharaff, Valles
sp: no credit given
sound: Douglas Shearer
CHARLES LAUGHTON, MARGARET O'BRIEN, Robert Young, William Gargan, Rags Ragland, Peter Lawford, Una O'Connor, Mike Mazurki

Cape Fear *
USA 1962 106m bw
An ex-convict terrorizes the family of the lawyer who testified against him.

Good looking but over stretched thriller with suspenseful sequences.
p: Sy Bartlett for Universal/Melville/Talbot
w: James R. Webb
novel: John D. MacDonald
d: J. Lee-Thompson
ph: SAM LEAVITT
m: BERNARD HERRMANN
ed: George Tomasini
ad: Alexander Golitzen, Robert Boyle
cos: Mary Willis
sound: Waldon O. Watson, Corson Jowett
Gregory Peck, ROBERT MITCHUM, Polly Bergen, Martin Balsam, Telly Savalas, Lori Martin, Jack Kruschen

Cape Fear **
USA 1991 128m Technicolor Panavision Dolby
A vicious psychopath returns after fourteen years in prison to avenge himself on the attorney who failed to get him acquitted.

Slick, determinedly shocking remake, worth a look for some of its more melodramatic directorial touches. It was originally to have been directed by Steven Spielberg.
p: Barbara de Fina for Universal/Amblin/Cappa/Tribeca
exec p: Frank Marshall, Kathleen Kennedy
w: Wesley Strick
novel: John D. MacDonald
d: MARTIN SCORSESE
ph: Freddie Francis
m: Elmer Bernstein, after Bernard Herrmann
ed: Thelma Schoonmaker
pd: Henry Bumstead
cos: Rita Ryack
sp: J. B. Jones and others
sound: Tod Maitland
titles: ELAINE AND SAUL BASS
underwater ph: Pete Romano
ROBERT DE NIRO, Nick Nolte, Jessica

Lange, Juliette Lewis, Joe Don Baker, Robert Mitchum, Gregory Peck, Martin Balsam, Illena Douglas, Fred Dalton Thomas, Zully Montero, Domenica Scorsese, Catherine Scorsese, Charles Scorsese

Captain Clegg *
GB 1962 82m Technicolor
A pirate disguises himself as a mild mannered parish vicar whilst carrying on with his smuggling activities.

Lively adventure thriller of the kind Hammer did well in their earlier days. Perhaps best remembered for its sequences involving the night creatures, horse riding smugglers dressed as luminous skeletons. Disney tackled the same subject the following year as *Dr Syn*, which stars Patrick McGoohan.
p: John Temple Smith for Hammer/Universal
w: John Elder (Anthony Hinds), Barbara S. Harper
d: PETER GRAHAM SCOTT
ph: Arthur Grant
m: Don Banks
ed: James Needs, Eric Boyd-Perkins
pd: Bernard Robinson
ad: Don Mingaye
sp: Les Bowie
Peter Cushing, Patrick Allen, Oliver Reed, Michael Ripper, Derek Francis, Milton Reid, Martin Benson, David Lodge

Captain Kronos - Vampire Hunter *
GB 1972 96m Technicolor
A professional vampire hunter and his hunchback sidekick rid a European township of vampires.

Low-budget latter day Hammer horror, quite inventively handled in its writer-director's *Avengers* manner. Late night hokum for addicts, its failure at the box office unfortunately meant that the proposed sequels never appeared.
p: Albert Fennell, Brian Clemens for Hammer
w: Brian Clemens
d: BRIAN CLEMENS
ph: Ian Wilson
m: Laurie Johnson
md: Philip Martell
ed: James Needs
pd: Robert Jones
cos: Dulcie Midwinter
sound: A. W. Lumkin, Jim Willis
Horst Janson, John Cater, Caroline Munro, Ian Hendry, John Carson, Shane Briant, Wanda Ventham, Lois Diane, William Hobbs

The Car
USA 1977 98m Technicolor Panavision

A car with a will of its own threatens a small town, killing those who try to stop it.

Inept shocker which never begins to work. The theme was also explored in *Killdozer* and *Christine*.
p: Peter Saphier for Universal
w: Dennis Shryack, Michael Butler, Lane Slate
d: Elliott Silverstein
ph: Gerald Hirschfeld
m: Leonard Rosenman
ed: Michael McCrosky
ad: Lloyd S. Papez
sp: Albert Whitlock
James Brolin, Kathleen Lloyd, John Marley, R. G. Armstrong, John Rubenstein

Cardiff, Jack (1914-)
Celebrated British cinematographer whose credits include *A Matter of Life and Death*, *Black Narcissus* (which won him an Oscar), *The Red Shoes*, *War and Peace*, *Summertime*, *The Vikings* and *Death on the Nile*. Turned to direction in the late fifties, but with the exception of *Sons and Lovers*, the results were much less distinguished.
Genre credits:
The Mutations (1974), *The Awakening* (1980 - ph), *Ghost Story* (1981 - ph)

Carlson, Richard (1912-1977)
American actor who progressed from juvenile roles. Much theatre experience, including *Broadway*. He also directed three films: *Riders to the Stars* (one of the first films to seriously attempt to depict space travel), *Four Guns to the Border* and *Appointment with a Shadow* (aka *The Big Story*). Other credits include *The Young in Heart*, *The Little Foxes*, *King Solomon's Mines* and *It Came from Outer Space*.
Genre credits:
The Ghost Breakers (1941), *The Magnetic Monster* (1953), *The Maze* (1954), *The Creature from the Black Lagoon* (1954), *The Power* (1968), *The Valley of Gwangi* (1969)

Carlson, Veronica (1944-)
Glamorous British actress (real name Veronica Mary Glazier) and model who came to notice in a number of Hammer horrors after fleeting appearances in a few sixties comedies (*The Best House in London*, *Smashing Time*, etc.). Her other credits include *Crossplot* and *Pussycat, Pussycat, I Love You*.
Genre credits:
Dracula Has Risen From the Grave (1968), *Frankenstein Must Be Destroyed* (1969), *The Horror of Frankenstein* (1970), *Vampira* (1974 - aka *Old Dracula*), *The Ghoul* (1975), *Freakshow* (1993)

• Director John Carpenter on the set of *The Fog* with his then wife Adrienne Barbeau, Jamie Lee Curtis and her mother, Janet Leigh.

Carmilla

First published in 1872, J. Sheridan LeFanu's novella *Carmilla* has been filmed in several guises, most of which tend to accentuate the story's implied lesbianism in the name of better box office. The story's most notable interpretations are Roger Vadim's *Blood and Roses* (1960), in which she was portrayed by Annette Vadim, and Hammer's *The Vampire Lovers* (1970), in which she was played by Ingrid Pitt. Carmilla Karnstein herself has also popped up in several other films as a minor character. Back in 1946, producer Val Lewton and director Robert Wise planned a colour version of *Carmilla* to add to Lewton's gallery of horrors for RKO. Unfortunately the film, which would have transposed the story to colonial America (just as *Jane Eyre* had been transposed to the West Indies for *I Walked with a Zombie*), was never made. Key filmography:
Blood and Roses (1960 - aka *Et Mourir de Plaisir*), *Carmilla* (1964 - aka *Crypt of Horror/Terror in the Crypt/The Vampire's Crypt/The Crypt of the Vampire/The Crypt and the Nightmare/The Curse of the Karnsteins/Karnstein/El Cripta e L'Incubo/La Maledizione dei Karnstein/La Maldicion de los Karnstein*), *The Vampire Lovers* (1970), *Lust for a Vampire* (1971), *Twins of Evil* (1971 - aka *The Gemini Twins/Virgin Vampires/Twins of Dracula*), *The Blood Spattered Bride* (1972 - aka *La Novia Ensangrentada/Bloody Fiancée/A Frenzy of Blood/Till Death Do Us Part*), *Carmilla* (1989 - TVM), *Carmilla* (1994)

Carnage see Bay of Blood

Carnival of Souls
USA 1962 85m bw
A young woman apparently survives a car crash only to discover later that she is in fact dead.

Low-budget, semi-professional horror story, over-praised in some quarters, but not without its eerily effective moments.
p: Herk Harvey for Herts-Lion
w: John Clifford
d: Herk Harvey

• John Carradine played Dracula more times than Bela Lugosi officially did. Unfortunately, *Billy the Kid vs Dracula* was not one of his true moments of glory.

ph: Maurice Prather
m: Gene Moore
ed: Dan Palmquist, Bill de Jarnette
sound: Ed Dawn, Don Jessup
titles: Dan Fitzgerald
Candice Hilligoss, Frances Feist, Sidney Berger, Art Ellison, Stab Levitt, Tom McGinnis, Herk Harvey

Carpenter, John (1948-)
American writer, producer, composer and director who, in the late seventies, helped to establish the stalk and slash genre with the hugely successful (and genuinely frightening) *Halloween*. A graduate of California's film school, where he made the Oscar winning short *The Resurrection of Broncho Billy* in 1970. This led to the making of his first feature *Dark Star*. The siege drama *Assault on Precinct 13* followed and established him as a talent to watch, though the success of *Halloween* saw him subsequently mostly tied to the horror genre. Other credits include *Elvis* (TVM), *Escape from New York*, *Starman*, *Big Trouble in Little China*, *Memoirs of an Invisible Man* and *Escape from L.A.*. His remake of *The Thing*, critically reviled on its release, is now considered a genre classic.
Genre credits:
Halloween (1978 - co-w/m/d), *The Eyes of Laura Mars* (1978 - co-w), *Someone's Watching Me* (1978 - TVM - w/d), *The Fog* (1979 - co-w/m/d), *Halloween II* (1980 - co-w/co-m/co-p), *The Thing* (1982 - d), *Halloween III: Season of the Witch* (1983 - co-p/co-m), *Christine* (1983 - co-m/d), *Prince of Darkness* (1987 - w/co-m/d [w as Martin Quatermass]), *They Live* (1988 - co-m/d), *Body Bags* (1993 - TVM - co-d/co-m/actor), *In the Mouth of Madness* (1995 - d/co-m), *Village of the Damned* (1995 - d/co-m/actor)

Carradine, John (1906-1988)
Prolific American actor (real name Richmond Reed Carradine, also used the name John Peter Richmond in the early thirties), the father of actors David, Keith and Robert Carradine. After training in New York at the Graphic Arts School, he first turned to painting and sculpture before making his stage début in 1926 in a production of *Camille* in New Orleans. Went to Hollywood in 1927, first working as a set designer for Cecil B. De Mille. Further stage work followed in Los Angeles, after which he made his film début in 1930 (as John Peter Richmond) in the remake of *Tol'able David*. Many character parts followed, though he increasingly found himself cast in horror movies, particularly in

old age, which he countered with tours of Shakespeare readings. Other notable credits include *Stagecoach*, *The Grapes of Wrath*, *The Last Hurrah* and *The Man Who Shot Liberty Valance*. One of the busiest horror stars, he lent many a low-budget film a much needed touch of dignity.
Genre credits:
The Invisible Man (1933 - as John Peter Richmond), *The Black Cat* (1934 - aka *House of Doom* - as John Peter Richmond), *The Bride of Frankenstein* (1935), *The Hound of the Baskervilles* (1939), *Whispering Ghosts* (1942), *Captive Wild Woman* (1943), *Revenge of the Zombies* (1943 - aka *The Corpse Vanished*), *Jungle Woman* (1944), *Voodoo Man* (1944), *The Invisible Man's Revenge* (1944), *Return of the Ape Man* (1944 - aka *Lock Your Doors*), *The Mummy's Ghost* (1944), *Bluebeard* (1944 - title role), *House of Frankenstein* (1944 - as Dracula), *House of Dracula* (1945 - as Dracula), *Face of Marble* (1946), *Half Human* (1955 - aka *Jujin Yukiotoko*), *The Black Sleep* (1956), *The Unearthly* (1957), *The Cosmic Man* (1958), *The Incredible Petrified World* (1959), *Terror in the Midnight Sun* (1960 - aka *Invasion of the Animal People*), *The Curse of the Stone Hand* (1965), *House of Black Death* (1965), *The Wizard of Mars* (1965), *Munster Go Home!* (1966 - TVM), *Billy the Kid vs. Dracula* (1966 - as Dracula), *Night of the Beast* (1966), *Hillbillys in a Haunted House* (1967), *Blood of Dracula's Castle* (1967 - aka *Dracula's Castle*), *The Fiend with the Electronic Brain* (1967), *Dr Terror's Gallery of Horrors* (1967 - aka *The Blood Suckers / Gallery of Horrors / Return from the Past*), *Autopsy on a Ghost* (1967 - aka *Autopsia de un Fantasma*), *The Astro-Zombies* (1968), *La Senora Muerte* (1968 - aka *Mrs. Death / The Death Woman*), *The Vampire Girls* (1968 - aka *Las Vampiras / The Vampires*), *Diabolical Pact* (1968 - *Pacto Diabolico / Pact with the Devil*), *Blood of the Iron Maiden* (1969), *Bigfoot* (1969), *Daughter of the Mind* (1969 - TVM), *Crowhaven Farm* (1970 - TVM), *Horror of the Blood Monsters* (1970 - aka *Horror Creatures of the Prehistoric Planet / Creatures of the Prehistoric Planet / Vampire Men of the Lost Planet*), *Shock Waves* (1970 - aka *Death Corps / Almost Human*), *Blood of Ghastly Horror* (1970), *Dracula vs. Frankenstein* (1970 - aka *Blood of Frankenstein*), *Threshold* (1971), *The Night Strangler* (1972 - TVM), *Moonchild* (1972), *House of the Seven Corpses* (1972), *Richard* (1972), *Legacy of Blood* (1972), *Silent Night, Bloody Night* (1973 - aka *Night of the Full Dark Moon / Death House*), *Hex* (1973), *The Cat Creature* (1973 -TVM), *House of Dracula's Daughter* (1973),

Terror in the Wax Museum (1973), *One Million AD* (1973), *Mary, Mary, Bloody Mary* (1975), *The Killer Inside Me* (1976), *Death at Love House* (1976 - TVM), *The Sentinel* (1976) *Crash* (1977), *Journey into the Beyond* (1977 - narrator), *Satan's Cheerleader* (1977), *Missile X* (1978), *The Bees* (1978), *Vampire Hookers* (1978), *Nocturna* (1979), *Monster* (1979), *The Howling* (1980), *The Monster Club* (1980), *The Nesting* (1980), *Monstroid* (1980), *Phobia* (1980), *The Boogey Man* (1980 - aka *The Bogey Man*), *Scarecrow* (1981), *Frankenstein Island* (1981), *House of the Long Shadows* (1983), *Boogey Man II* (1983), *Evils of the Night* (1983), *The Tomb* (1985), *Reel Horror* (1985), *Monster in the Closet* (1986), *Evil Spawn* (1987), *Buried Alive* (1988)

Carras, Anthony
American editor whose genre credits have been solely in association with the films of Roger Corman.
Genre credits:
A Bucket of Blood (1959), *House of Usher* (1960 - aka *The Fall of the House of Usher*), *The Pit and the Pendulum* (1961), *Tales of Terror* (1962), *X - The Man With X-Ray Eyes* (1963 - aka *The Man With X-Ray Eyes*), *The Comedy of Terrors* (1963)

Carreras, Enrique (1880-1950)
Spanish born entrepreneur who came to England in the early 1900s. After several business ventures, which met with variable success, he formed Exclusive Films in the late 20s, which eventually became a subsidiary of Hammer Films. Sadly, he died five years before the studio's fortunes saw an upturn with *The Quatermass Experiment* and *The Curse of Frankenstein*. Father of James Carreras and grandfather of Michael Carreras.

Carreras, Sir James (1909-1990)
British production executive, very much the driving force behind Hammer Films and its subsidiary, Exclusive. A skilful negotiator and promoter, his links with American producer Robert Lippert assured Exclusive their first substantial American distribution deal in the fifties. Educated at Stonehurst, he served with the HAC during World War Two, was awarded an MBE in 1944 and was demobbed a Lieutenant-Colonel, hence his nickname, The Colonel. Steered Hammer through their most successful period, greenlighting such box office hits as *The Curse of Frankenstein*, *Dracula*, *The Mummy*, *Taste of Fear* and *One Million Years BC*. Was knighted in 1970 and retired from Hammer in 1972, after which he concentrated on charity work. Though he was never actively involved

in the making of films on the studio floor, his influence was present in all of Hammer's product.

Carreras, Michael (1927-1994)
British producer, executive producer, writer, director and, for Hammer Films, studio head. After National Service in the Grenadier Guards (1946-1948), worked his way up through the ranks at Exclusive, from the publicity department to assistant producer. Became a board director of Hammer Films after the death of his grandfather, Enrique Carreras, in 1950. First producer credit was for the B thriller *The Dark Light* in 1951, after which he seemed to have a finger in most Exclusive/Hammer productions, either as a producer or executive producer. Wrote his first script, *The Stranger Came Home*, in 1951, whilst in 1955 he produced and directed a number of widescreen musical featurettes for the company. Disgruntled with the studio's diet of horror, he left Hammer in 1961 to form Capricorn Films, for whom he made a western, *The Savage Guns*, and a musical, *What a Crazy World*, though he still regularly contributed to Hammer's output, either as a writer (using the pen names Henry Younger and Michael Nash), producer or director. However, his output was routine at best. Returned to Hammer full time in the early seventies as managing director, purchasing the company after his father's retirement and a hostile takeover bid. Unfortunately, this coincided with the collapse of the British film industry and the general decline of Hammer. During the seventies they seemed to concentrate mostly on sit-com spin offs, one of which, *On the Buses*, ironically proved to be one of their biggest moneymakers. His last credit was as an executive producer on the ill-fated remake of *The Lady Vanishes*. Following his departure from the then bankrupt Hammer, he involved himself in several ventures, including a travel company and The Palladium Cellars, a Tussaud like horror exhibition which started off well but soon ran into financial difficulties.
Genre credits:
The Curse of Frankenstein (1956 - exec p), *Quatermass 2* (1957 - aka *Enemy from Space* - exec p), *The Abominable Snowman* (1957 - aka *The Abominable Snowman of the Himalayas* - exec p), *Dracula* (1958 - aka *The Horror of Dracula* - exec p), *The Revenge of Frankenstein* (1958 - exec p), *The Hound of the Baskervilles* (1959 - exec p), *The Mummy* (1959 - exec p), *The Ugly Duckling* (1959 - p), *The Man*

Who Could Cheat Death (1959 - exec p), *The Stranglers of Bombay* (1960 - exec p), *The Brides of Dracula* (1960 - exec p), *The Two Faces of Dr Jekyll* (1960 - aka *House of Fright/Jekyll's Inferno* - p), *Taste of Fear* (1961 - aka *Scream of Fear* - exec p), *The Terror of the Tongs* (1961 - exec p), *Maniac* (1963 - d), *The Damned* (1963 - aka *These Are the Damned* - exec p), *The Curse of the Mummy's Tomb* (1964 - d/p/w [w as Henry Younger]), *Fanatic* (1965 - aka *Die! Die! My Darling!* - exec p), *She* (1965 - p), *One Million Years BC* (1966 - w/p), *Slave Girls* (1968 - aka *Prehistoric Women* - d/w [w as Henry Younger]), *The Lost Continent* (1968 - p/d/w [w as Michael Nash]), *Crescendo* (1970 - p), *Creatures the World Forgot* (1970 - w/p), *Blood from the Mummy's Tomb* (1971 - co-d), *Fear in the Night* (1972 - exec p), *Straight on Till Morning* (1972 - exec p), *That's Your Funeral* (1973 - p), *Legend of the Seven Golden Vampires* (1974 - aka *The Seven Brothers Meet Dracula* - exec p), *To the Devil... A Daughter* (1976 - exec p)

Carrie *

USA 1976 98m DeLuxe
A schoolgirl with telekinetic powers is persecuted by her fellow pupils and her fanatically religious mother - but she has the last laugh.

Flashy if rather ugly horror hokum, further marred by a stream of unnecessary bad language. There are some stylish moments, though and at least one good jolt. The cast and credits also have their interest.
p: Paul Monash for UA/Red Bank
w: Laurence D. Cohen
novel: Stephen King
d: BRIAN DE PALMA
ph: Mario Tosi
m: Pino Donaggio
ed: Paul Hirsch
pd: William Kenney, Jack Fisk
cos: Rosanna Norton
sp: Gregory M. Auer
sound: Bertil Hallberg
stunt co-ordinator: Richard Zieker
SISSY SPACEK, PIPER LAURIE, Amy Irving, William Katt, John Travolta, Nancy Allen, P. J. Soles, Betty Buckley

Carruth, Milton

American editor, long with Universal. Worked on several of their key horror films of the thirties.
Genre credits:
Dracula (1930), *The Mummy* (1932), *Murders in the Rue Morgue* (1932), *Werewolf of London* (1935), *Dracula's Daughter* (1936), *The Mad Ghoul* (1943), *The Mummy's Tomb* (1942), *Cult of the Cobra* (1955)

• 'Frying tonight!': Kenneth Williams as Dr Watt, Fenella Fielding as Valeria and Tom Clegg as Oddbod in the British horror spoof *Carry On Screaming*, one of the best entries in the much-loved *Carry On* series. Note the arc lamp left.

Carry On Screaming **

GB 1966 97m Technicolor
When several girls disappear near a sinister house, Detective Sergeant Bung and his assistant investigate.

Enjoyable haunted house spoof in which the cast clearly seem to be having fun. One of the best - if not *the* best - entry in the *Carry On* series, this was number twelve in a series of thirty (thirty-one if the compilation film *That's Carry On* is included).
p: Peter Roger for Anglo Amalgamated
w: TALBOT ROTHWELL
d: Gerald Thomas
ph: ALAN HUME
m: ERIC ROGERS
ed: Rod Keys
ad: Bert Davey
cos: Emma Selby-Walker
sound: C. C. Stevens, Ken Barker
HARRY H. CORBETT, KENNETH WILLIAMS, FENELLA FIELDING, JOAN SIMS, PETER BUTTERWORTH, JIM DALE, Bernard Bresslaw, CHARLES HAWTREY, Angela Douglas, Jon Pertwee, Frank Thornton, Michael Ward, Tom Clegg (as Oddbod), Billy Cornelius (as Oddbod Junior), Anthony Sagar, Sally Douglas, Marianne Stone, Dennis Blake

The Cars That Ate Paris

Australia 1974 88m Eastmancolor
Panavision
Inhabitants of a backroads township make a living by murdering passers through.

Overlong anecdote which wears its single idea pretty thin. Notable chiefly as one of its director's earlier endeavours.
p: Jim McElroy, Howard McElroy for Saltpan/AFDC
exec p: Royce Smeal
w/d: Peter Weir
ph: John McClean
m: Bruce Smeaton
ed: Wayne Le Clos
Terry Camilleri, John Meillon, Melissa Jaffa, Kevin Miles

Cartwright, Veronica (1949-)

British child actress in Hollywood films, sister of Angela Cartwright. She later matured into offbeat adult roles. Her other credits include *Inserts*, *Goin' South*, *The Right Stuff* and *Flight of the Navigator*.
Genre credits:
The Birds (1963), *Invasion of the Body Snatchers* (1978), *Alien* (1979), *Nightmares* (1983 - TVM), *The Witches of Eastwick* (1987)

Cary, Tristam (1925-)

British composer who trained at Oxford's Trinity College of Music. Began in films by scoring documentaries before moving into features. Became the Dean of Music at Adelaide University, Australia, in the 1980s. He is the son of actress and writer Joyce Carey. Credits include *The Ladykillers*, *The Prince and the Pauper* and *Sammy Going South*.
Genre credits:
Quatermass and the Pit (1967 - aka *Five*

Million Years to Earth), *Blood from the Mummy's Tomb* (1971)

Cassevetes, John (1929-989)
Distinguished American actor, writer and director whose experimental films made him a darling of the critics, though this didn't prevent him from occasionally stooping to horror, most notably as Guy Woodhouse in Roman Polanski's *Rosemary's Baby* and the evil Childress in Brian de Palma's *The Fury*. His work as a director includes *Shadows*, *Too Late the Blues*, *Faces*, *Husbands*, *A Woman Under the Influence*, *Gloria* and *Love Streams*.
Genre credits:
Rosemary's Baby (1968), *The Fury* (1978), *The Incubus* (1982)

Castle of Doom see Vampyre

Castle, William (1914-1977)
American writer, producer and director (real name William Schloss) with a penchant for low-budget horror films which were dependent on such gimmicks as insurance policies for death by fright, wiring up seats to provide mild electric shocks, fright breaks and Emergo, which involved skeletons being trundled over the heads of unsuspecting audiences. He did produce one classic, however, the box office smash *Rosemary's Baby*, which was directed by Roman Polanski. A former stage actor (he can be spotted making cameos in several of his films), Castle turned to stage direction in the mid-thirties before moving into radio, working for a time with Orson Welles. Moved to Hollywood in the early forties where he became a dialogue director and an assistant director. Made his directorial début in 1943 with *The Chance of a Lifetime*. One of the last old time showmen, his image was successfullly spoofed by John Goodman in the 1993 movie *Matinee*.
Genre credits:
Macabre (1957 - p/d), *The House on Haunted Hill* (1958 - p/d), *The Tingler* (1959 - p/d), *Thirteen Ghosts* (1960 - p/d), *Homicidal* (1960 - p/d/narrator), *Mr Sardonicus* (1960 - p/d/narrator), *The Old Dark House* (1962 - co-p/d), *Strait-Jacket* (1963 - p/d), *The Night Walker* (1964 - p/d), *I Saw What You Did* (1965 - p/d), *Let's Kill Uncle* (1966 - p/d), *Project X* (1967 - p/d), *Rosemary's Baby* (1968 - p), *Shanks* (1974 - p/d), *Bug* (1975 - co-w/p)

The Cat and the Canary ***
USA 1939 72m bw
Relatives of a rich recluse assemble in his swampland home to hear the reading of his will.

Fairly delightful haunted house comedy thriller, a highly satisfactory piece of entertainment, with fine production and a first rate cast. Remade in 1977.
p: Arthur Hornblow Jr for Paramount
w: WALTER DE LEON, LYNN STARLING
play: JOHN WILLARD
d: ELLIOTT NUGENT
ph: CHARLES LANG
m: ERNST TOCH
ed: Archie Marshek
ad: HANS DREIER, ROBERT USHER
cos: Edith Head
sound: Philip Wisdom, Richard Olson
BOB HOPE, PAULETTE GODDARD, GALE SONDERGAARD, John Beal, Douglas Montgomery, NYDIA WESTERN, ELIZABETH PATTERSON, GEORGE ZUCCO, John Wray

The Cat and the Canary
GB 1977 95m Technicolor
A murderer threatens relatives assembled in an old dark house for the reading of a will.

Mild, rather creaky remake which misses several good opportunities. Mainly of interest for its cast.
p: Richard Gordon for Grenadier/Gala
w/d: Randy Metzger
ph: Alex Thomson
m: Steven Cagan
ed: Roger Harrison
pd: Anthony Pratt
cos: Monica Howe, Lorna Hillyard
sound: Clive Winter, David Sutton
Honor Blackman, Michael Callan, Edward Fox, Wendy Hiller, Olivia Hussey, Beatrix Lehmann, Carol Lynley, Daniel Massey, Peter McEnery, Wilfred Hyde White

The Cat Creature *
USA 1973 74m colour TVM
The theft of an Egyptian amulet revives a murderous cat god.

Tolerable horror malarkey with a better cast than it deserves.
p: Douglas S. Cramer for Columbia
w: Robert Bloch
story: Douglas S. Cramer, Wilford Lloyd Baumes, Robert Bloch
d: Curtis Harrington
ph: Charles Rosher
m: Leonard Rosenman
ed: Stan Ford
ad: Ross Bellah, Carey Odell
sp: Roy Maples
titles: Phil Norman
sound: no credit given
Meredith Baxter, Stuart Whitman, David Hedison, Gale Sondergaard, Keye Luke, John Carradine, Kent Smith, Peter Lorre Jr, John Abbott

Cat People **
USA 1944 73m bw
A mysterious Balkan girl living in New York believes that she has the power to turn into a murderous panther.

Economically produced horror thriller which uses shadow and suggestion to the maximum effect. The first of the Lewton horror packages for RKO, its refraining from showing its monster proved revolutionary at the time and, despite a few sloshy spots, it still has the ability to thrill. It was remade in 1982.
p: VAL LEWTON for RKO
w: DE WITT BODEEN
d: JACQUES TOURNEUR
ph: Nicholas Musuraca
m: Roy Webb
md: Constantin Bakaleinikoff
ed: Mark Robson
ad: Albert S. D'Agostino, Walter E. Keller
cos: Renie
sound: John L. Cass
SIMONE SIMON, Kent Smith, Tom Conway, Jane Randolph, Jack Holt

Cat People
USA 1982 118m Technicolor
A beautiful young woman turns into a savage panther whenever she makes love and cannot change back again until she has killed.

Tediously trendy remake of the 1942 classic, full of fashionable and repellent gore and fornication. Pretty awful.
p: Charles Fries for Universal/RKO
w: Alan Ormsby
d: Paul Schrader
ph: John Bailey
m: Giorgio Moroder
ed: Jacqueline Cambas
pd: Ferdinando Scarfiotti
sp: Albert Whitlock
make-up effects: Tom Burman
Natassja Kinski, Malcolm McDowell, John Heard, Annette O'Toole, Ruby Dee, Ed Begley Jr

Catacombs *
USA 1988 84m DeLuxe Ultra Stereo
A demon, holed up in a monastery since 1506, causes havoc when he escapes in the present.

Good-looking hokum with good scenes along the way, including an effective prologue. It plays like a cross between *The Name of the Rose* and *The Exorcist* and was later rereleased as *Curse IV: The Ultimate Sacrifice*, even though it has nothing to do with the previous episodes.
p: Hope Perello for Empire/Eden
exec p: Charles Band
w: Giovanni Di Marco, R. Baker Price

d: David Schmoeller
ph: Sergio Salvati
m: Pino Donaggio
md: Natale Massara
ed: Tom Meshelski
pd: Giovanni Natalucci
cos: Robin Lewis
sp: Renato Agostini
sound: Primiano Muratori, Luciano Muratori
make-up effects: Tom Floutz
Laura Shaeffer, Timothy Van Patten, Jeremy West, Mapi Galan, Ian Abercrombie, Feodor Chaliapin

Cat's Eye *
USA 1985 98m Technicolor Dolby
Three tales of horror, linked by a wandering feline.

Reasonably amusing horror compendium, adequately enough packaged and presented. Keep an eye out for Cujo and Christine in the opening credit sequence.
p: Milton Subotsky, Martha Schumacher for MGM/UA/Famous Films/FC
exec p: Dino de Laurentiis
w: Stephen King
d: Lewis Teague
ph: Jack Cardiff
m: Alan Silvestri
ed: Scott Conrad
pd: Giorgio Postiglione
cos: Clifford Capone
sp: Carlo Rambaldi, Barry Nolan
sound: Donald Summer
2nd unit ph: Paul Ryan
James Woods, Drew Barrymore, Alan King, Kenneth McMillan, Robert Hayes, Candy Clark, James Naughton

The Cellar
USA 1989 92m Technicolor
An ancient Indian demon manifests itself in the cellar of a remote house.

Fair, low-budget horror piece.
p: Patrick Wells for Indian Neck Entertainment
w: John Woodward
story: John Woodward, Brian Wimberley, David Henry Keller
d: Kevin S. Tenney
ph: Thomas Jewett
m: Will Sumner
ed: Sally Allen
make-up effects: Kevin Brennan, Elaine Alexander
Patrick Kilpatrick, Suzanne Savoy, Chris Miller, Ford Rainey

Cellar Dweller
USA/It 1987 92m Technicolor Ultra Stereo
A lady cartoon artist discovers that her creations have a life of their own.

Mildy amusing horror comic from

the Empire conveyor belt.
p: Bob Wynn for Empire/Dove
w: Kit du Bois
d: John Buechler
ph: Sergio Salvati
m: Carl Dante
ed: Barry Zetlin
ad: Angelo Santucci
cos: Claire Joseph
sp: John Buechler
sound: Primlano Muratori, Jan Brodin
Debrah Mullowney, Brian Robbins, Pamela Bellwood, Jeffrey Combs, Yvonne de Carlo, Vince Edwards, Cheryl-Ann Wilson

C'est Arrive Pres de Chez Vous
see Man Bites Dog

Chaffey, Don (1917-1990)
British director on the international scene who began his career as an assistant in Gainsborough's art department in 1944, becoming an art director in his own right in 1946. He began directing in 1950 with the children's feature *The Mysterious Poacher*. Many more children's films followed (*Greyfriars Bobby*, *The Prince and the Pauper*, *Peter's Dragon*, *The Magic of Lassie*), a good many of them for Disney's British arm. He also directed several key fantasy films (*Jason and the Argonauts*, *One Million Years BC*, etc.).
Genre credits:
One Million Years BC (1966), *Creatures the World Forgot* (1971), *Persecution* (1973 - aka *The Terror of Sheba*)

Chamber of Horrors
USA 1966 99m Warnercolor
Two amateur criminologists track down a murderous necrophile who has escaped the electric chair.

Mild horror comic which just about passes muster, though the script is pretty awful and the added gimmicks of a 'fear flasher' and 'horror horn' don't help much.
p: Hy Averback for Warner
w: Stephen Kandell
story: Ray Russell, Stephen Kandel
d: Hy Averback
ph: Richard Kline
m: William Lava
ed: David Wages
ad: Art Loel
sound: I. A. Merrick
Caesare Danova, Wilfred Hyde White, Patrick O'Neal, Laura Devon, Patrice Wymore, Suzy Parker, Jeanette Nolan, Tony Curtis (in a one-line cameo)

Chaney, Lon (1883-1930)
Celebrated silent horror star (real name Alonzo Chaney) whose experiments

• Lon Chaney and Edna Tichenor in the sadly lost *London After Midnight*, one of several films Chaney made with director Tod Browning.

with make-up produced some of the screen's most famous early monsters, hence his nickname: The Man of a Thousand Faces. Began working as a prop boy for a local theatre in his early teens after which he gained experience as an actor in a variety of touring and repertory companies. Moved to California in 1912, where he made his film début, in *Poor Jake's Promise*, in 1913. Signed a contract with Universal in 1915, for whom he also directed a number of films starring J. Warren Kerrigan. Began making genre films in 1919, which reached a peak with *The Hunchback of Notre Dame* and *The Phantom of the Opera* in the mid-twenties. He made his first and only talkie in 1930, a remake of his 1925 film *The Unholy Three*. In the same year he also added a few snatches of dialogue to the sound re-release of *The Phantom of the Opera*. Was preparing to make the screen version of *Dracula* with director Tod Browning (who'd helmed several of his silents) when he died of throat cancer. The father of actor Lon Chaney Jr, he is protrayed by James Cagney in the 1957 biopic *Man of a Thousand Faces*. Other credits include *The Miracle Man*, *Oliver Twist* (as Fagin), *The Black Bird* and *Mr Wu*.
Genre credits:
While Paris Sleeps (1919), *The Penalty* (1920), *A Blind Bargain* 1922), *The Hunchback of Notre Dame* (1923), *The Monster* (1925), *The Phantom of the Opera* (1925), *The Unholy Three* (1925), *The Unknown* (1927), *London After Midnight* (1927), *The Unholy Three* (1930)

• Lon Chaney Jr as Lawrence Talbot, better known as the Wolf Man. Chaney loved playing the character so much he referred to him as 'my baby'. The superb make-up was supplied by Universal veteran Jack P. Pierce.

Chaney Jr, Lon (1906-1973)
American actor (real name Creighton Chaney), the son of silent horror star Lon Chaney. Began making films in 1932 with *Girl Crazy* using his real name, changing his name to Lon Chaney Jr in 1935. Minor roles in a slew of nondescript films followed, all of which gradually led up to his performance as Lennie in the 1939 classic *Of Mice and Men*. Began to follow his father's footsteps in the early forties with a number of top genre films for Universal, his most famous role being the lycanthrope Lawrence Talbot in *The Wolf Man*, which he reprised several times. He also played the Mummy, Frankenstein's Monster and Count Alucard, Son of Dracula. However, his career began to wind down in the fifties and he found himself cast in increasingly smaller parts in increasingly inferior horror films. Other credits include *Northwest Mounted Police*, *My Favorite Brunette*, *The Defiant Ones* and the TV series *The Last of the Mohicans* (in which he played Chingachook). In the Lon Chaney biopic *Man of a Thousand Faces* he is portrayed by Roger Smith.
Genre credits:
Undersea Kingdom (1936 - serial), *One Million BC* (1940 - aka *Man and His Mate / The Cave Dwellers*), *The Wolf Man* (1941 - title role), *Man Made Monster* (1941 - aka *The Electric Man*), *Ghost of Frankenstein* (1942 - as the Monster), *The Mummy's Tomb* (1942 - as the Mummy), *Frankenstein Meets the Wolf Man* (1943 - as the Wolf Man), *Son of Dracula* (1943 - as Count Alucard), *The Ghost Catchers* (1944), *Weird Woman* (1944), *The Mummy's Ghost* (1944 - as the Mummy), *Dead Man's Eyes* (1944), *The Mummy's Curse* (1944 - as the Mummy), *House of Frankenstein* (1944 - as the Wolf Man), *House of Dracula* (1945 - as the Wolf Man), *Pillow of Death* (1945), *Abbott and Costello Meet Frankenstein* (1948 - as the Wolf Man), *Bride of the Gorilla* (1951), *The Black Castle* (1952), *The Black Sleep* (1956), *The Indestructable Man* (1956), *The Cyclops* (1957 - title role), *Face of the Screaming Werewolf* (1959 - aka *La Casa del Terror*), *The Alligator People* (1959), *The Phantom* (1961), *The Devil's Messenger* (1962), *The Haunted Palace* (1963), *Witchcraft* (1964), *Night of the Beast* (1966), *Hillbillys in a Haunted House* (1967), *The Vulture* (1967), *Dr Terror's Gallery of Horrors* (1967 - aka *The BloodSuckers / Gallery of Horrors / Return from the Past*), *Spider Baby* (1969 - aka *The Maddest Story Ever Told / Cannibal Orgy / The Liver Eaters*), *Jungle of Terror* (1970 - aka *Fireball Jungle*), *Dracula vs. Frankenstein* (1970 - aka *Blood of Frankenstein*), *Satan's Sadists* (1970)

Chattaway, Jay
American composer with many synth scores to his credit, a good deal of them for the horror genre.
Genre credits:
Maniac (1981), *Maniac Cop* (1987), *Maniac Cop 2* (1990)

La Chiesa see The Church

Children of the Corn
USA 19874 92m CFIcolor
Murderous children take over a small mid-western community.
Good looking but over stretched thriller with a fashionable emphasis on blood letting. *Children of the Corn II: The Final Sacrifice* followed in 1992 and *Children of the Corn III: Urban Harvest* in 1995.
p: Donald P. Borchers, Terence Kirby for New World / Cinema Group / Hal Roach / Gatlin
w: George Goldsmith
novel: Stephen King
d: Fritz Kiersch
ph: Raoul Lomas
m: Jonathan Elias
ed: Harry Keranudas
ad: Craig Stearns
sp: Max W. Anderson
Peter Horton, Linda Hamilton, R. G. Armstrong, John Franklin

Children of the Damned *
GB 1964 91m bw
Scientific research reveals that the world's most intelligent children hail from another planet.
Acceptable follow-up to *Village of the Damned*, though the results aren't quite so effective the second time round.
p: Ben Arbeid for MGM
w: John Briley
d: Anton M. Leader
ph: Davis Boulton
m: Ron Goodwin
ed: Ernest Walter
ad: Elliot Scott
sp: Tom Howard
sound: A. W. Watkins, Dave Browne, J. B. Smith
Ian Hendry, Alan Badel, Barbara Ferris, Sheila Allen, Alfred Burke, Harold Goldblatt, Martin Miller, Ralph Michael, Bessie Love

Children of the Night
USA 1991 91m colour Ultra Stereo
A small township in America's bible belt is infested by vampires.
Tame shocker that fails to add much new to an overworked subject.
p: Christopher Webster for Fangoria
exec p: Norman Jacobs, Steven Jacobs
w: William Hopkins, Nicolas Falacci
story: Christopher Webster, Nicolas Falacci, Tony Randel
d: Tony Randel
ph: Richard Michalak
m: Daniel Licht
ed: Rick Roberts
pd: Kim Hix
cos: Pamela Goldman
sound: Hans Roland
make-up effects: KNB
Karen Black, Peter De Luise, Evan MacKenzie, Ami Dolenz, Garrett Morris, Maya McLaughlin, Josette De Carlo

Child's Play *
US 1972 100m Movielab
An unpopular schoolteacher is taunted by his pupils at a Catholic school for boys, and it transpires that they are being manipulated by another, more liked tutor.
Quietly gripping melodrama with interesting plot developments, including hints of diabolism. Quite enjoyable.
p: David Merrick for Paramount
w: Leon Pochnik
novel: Robert Marasco
d: Sidney Lumet
ph: Gerald Hirschfeld
m: Michale Small
ed: Joanne Burke, Edward Warschilka
pd: Philip Rosenberg
JAMES MASON, ROBERT PRESTON, Beau Bridges, Ronald Weyand, Charles White, David Rounfs, Kate Harrinton

Child's Play
GB 1984 74m Technicolor TVM
A family wake up to discover that their house is surrounded by an impenetrable wall.

A mildly intriguing idea is drawn out to undue length in yet another almost unwatchable entry in the disappointing *Hammer House of Mystery and Suspense* series of tele-thrillers.
p: Roy Skeggs for Hammer/TCF
w: Graham Wassell
d: Val Guest
ph: Frank Watts
m: David Bedford
md: Philip Martell
ed: Peter Weatherley
ad: Heather Armitage
Mary Crosby, Nicholas Clay, Debbie Chasan, Suzanne Church, Joanna Joseph

Child's Play
USA 1988 87m Technicolor Dolby
A dying murderer imparts his soul into a doll which subsequently goes on the rampage.

Initially amusing but increasingly foolish horror hokum. Chucky the doll reappeared in two sequels: *Child's Play 2* (1990) and *Child's Play 3* (1991).
p: David Kirschner for MGM/UA
exec p: Barrie M. Osborne
w: Don Mancini, John Lafia, Tom Holland
story: Don Mancini
d: Tom Holland
ph: Bill Butler
m: Joe Renzetti
ed: Edward Warschilka, Roy E. Peterson
pd: Daniel A. Lomino
cos: April Ferry
sp: Peter Donen
sound: James E. Webb, Donald O. Mitchell
doll design: Kevin Yagher
titles: Wayne Fitzgerald
2nd unit ph: James Blandford
2nd unit d/stunt co-ordinator: Bud Davis
Catherine Hicks, Chris Sarandon, Alex Vincent, Brad Dourif, Dinah Manhoff, Tommy Swerdlow, Jack Colvin, Neil Giuntoli

Chiller
USA 1985 96m Technicolor TVM
A cryogenically preserved man is brought back to life, but it isn't long before things start to go wrong.

Slick but silly thriller which doesn't quite live up to its premise.
p: J. D. Feigelson for CBS/Polar
w: J. D. Feiglson
d: Wes Craven
ph: Frank Thackery
m: Dana Kaproff

ed: Duane Hartzell
ad: Charles Hughes
cos: Darryl Athons, Deborah Hopper
sp: Ken Pepiot
sound: Tom Causey, Don MacDougall, John Mack
make-up effects: Stan Winston
stunt co-ordinator: Tony Cecere
Michael Beck, Beatrice Straight, Paul Sorvino, Jill Schoeler, Dick O'Neill, Laura Johnson

Chopping Mall *
USA 1986 76m DeLuxe
An electrical storm causes three new security robots to go on a killing spree in a shopping mall where a group of teenagers are holding a midnight party.

Surprisingly tolerable (and commendably brief) horror comic, quite slickly done. Ideal late-night video viewing.
p: Julie Corman for Trinity/Concorde
w: Jim Wynorski, Steve Mitchell
d: Jim Wynorski
ph: Tom Richmond
m: Chuck Cirino
ed: Leslie Rosenthal
ad: no credit given
cos: Katie Sparks
sp: Roger George
sound: Walt Martin, George Mahlberg
make-up effects: Anthony Shaw
killbots: Robert Short
2nd unit d: Steve Mitchell
2nd unit ph: Steve Carpenter
Tony O'Dell, John Terlesky, Kelli Maroney, Russell Todd, Barbara Crampton, Gerrit Graham, Mel Welles, Paul Bartel, Dick Miller (as Walter Paisley)

The Chosen see Holocaust 2000

Christensen, Benjamin (1879-1959)
Danish writer and director, remembered chiefly for the long banned *Witchcraft Through the Ages*, a visually arresting 'documentary' on the practices of witchcraft. After studying to become a doctor he turned to the stage before writing screenplays. He directed his first film, *The Mysterious X*, in 1913, which was followed by such films as *Night of Revenge*, *His Mysterious Adventure* and *The Woman Who Did*. It was the notoriety of *Witchcraft* that saw Christensen invited to Hollywood in the late twenties, where he directed a variety of films, including *The Devil's Circus* (which starred Norma Shearer), *Mockery* (a Lon Chaney melodrama) and *The Hawk's Nest*, as well as a handful of horror comedies. He later returned to Denmark, where he worked mostly in the theatre, though he did

occasionally return to the cinema with the likes of *The Child*, *Come Home with Me* and *The Lady with the Coloured Gloves*.
Genre credits:
The Mysterious X (1913 - w/d/actor), *Witchcraft Through the Ages* (1922 - aka *Haxan* - w/d/actor), *The Haunted House* (1928 - d), *Seven Footprints to Satan* (1929 - d), *The House of Horror* (1929 - d)

Christine *
USA 1983 110m Metrocolor Panavision Dolby
A put upon teenager buys a clapped out Chevy and restores it to its former glory, but it takes on a murderous life of its own.

Slick but silly retread of *The Car* and *Killdozer*, marred by an over abundance of bad language.
p: Richard Korbitz for Columbia/Delphi
w: Bill Phillips
novel: Stephen King
d: John Carpenter
ph: Donald M. Morgan
m: John Carpenter, Alan Howarth
ed: Marion Rothman
pd: Daniel Lomino
cos: Darry Levine, Dawn Jackson
sp: Roy Arbogast
sound: Thomas Causey
stunt co-ordinator: Terry Leonard
Keith Gordon, John Stockwell, Alexandra Paul, Harry Dean Stanton, Robert Prosky. Christine Belford

The Church
It 1989 98m Technicolor
Demonic forces make themselves felt in a crumbling medieval church.

Ludicrous fantasy horror in the Italian tradition. Good to look at, but the plot makes very little sense and the director's hand seems to have been controlled by the producer's.
p: Dario Argento for ADC/Cecchi Gori/Tiger/Reteitalia
w: Dario Argento, Franco Ferrini, Michele Soavi
d: Michele Soavi
ph: Renato Tafuri
m: Keith Emerson, Goblin
ed: Franco Fraticelli
ad: Anotello Geleng
Hugh Quarshie, Tomas Arana, Feodor Chaliapin, Asia Argento, Giovanni Lombardo Radice, Barbara Cupisti

Circus of Horrors
GB 1960 91m Eastmancolor
A plastic surgeon with a criminal record takes over a rundown circus and peoples it with his victims.

Crude horror melodrama with moments of vigour.

p: Norman Priggen for Anglo Amalgamated/Lynx/Independent Artists
w: George Baxt
d: Sidney Hayers
ph: Douglas Slocombe
m: Franz Reizenstein
md: Muir Mathieson
ed: Reginald Mills
ad: Jack Shamp
cos: Vi Murray
make-up: Trevor Crole-Rees
Anton Diffring, Erika Remberg, Yvonne Molnaur, Donald Pleasence, Jane Hylton, Jack Gwyllim, Kenneth Griffith, Conrad Phillips, William Mervyn

Citta dei Morti Viventi see City of the Living Dead

City of the Dead *
GB 1960 78m bw
A student discovers that the inhabitants of an isolated Massachusetts town are witches, one of whom was burned at the stake 250 years previously.
  An atmospheric and sometimes chillingly effective horror story with a few goose-pimply moments. Made on a small budget, it shows that good movies can be made cheaply if the talent is there. In this case it is.
p: Donald Taylor for Vulvan/Britannia/British Lion
exec p: Seymour S. Dorner, Milton Subotsky
w: George Baxt
story: Milton Subotsky
d: JOHN MOXEY
ph: DESMOND DICKINSON
m: Douglas Gamley, Ken Jones
ed: John Pomeroy
ad: John Blezzard
cos: Freda Gibson
sp: Cliff Richardson
sound: Richard Bird
ass d: Tom Pevsner
PATRICIA JESSEL, Christopher Lee, Betta St. John, Dennis Lotis, VALENTINE DYALL, Venetia Stevenson, Norman McCowan, Fred Johnson

City of the Living Dead
It 1983 94m Technicolor
The people of Dunwich find themselves in mortal danger from the resurrected dead.
  Ridiculously plotted schlock horror with revolting detail. For gorehounds only.
p: Giovani Masini for Dania/Medusa/National Cinematografica
w: Lucio Fulci, Dardano Sacchetti
d: Lucio Fulci
ph: Sergio Salvati

m: Fabio Frizzi
ed: Vincenzo Tomassi
pd/cos: Massimo Anotello Geleng
make-up: Franco Rufini
Christopher George, Katherine McColl, Carlo de Mejo, Anotello Interlenghi, Giocvani Lombardo Radic

The Clairvoyant *
GB 1934 80m bw
A music hall mind reader discovers that he really does possess supernatural powers of prediction.
  Good little suspense thriller, interestingly dated and with several effective sequences.
p: Michael Balcon for Gainsborough
w: Charles Bennett, Bryan Edgar Wallace, Robert Edmunds
novel: Ethel Lother
d: MAURICE ELVEY
ph: Glen MacWilliams
m: Arthur Benjamin
md: Louis Levy
ed: Paul Capon
ad: Alfred Junge
cos: J. Strassner, Marianne
sound: H. Hand
CLAUDE RAINS, Fay Wray, Jane Baxter, Mary Clare, Athole Stewart, Ben Field, Felix Aylmer, Donald Calthrop

Clark, Bob (1941-)
American writer, producer and director, perhaps best known for the raucous Porky's comedies, though he started by directing horror films in Canada. Other credits include Tribute, A Christmas Story, Rhinestone and Turk 182.
Genre credits:
Children Shouldn't Play with Dead Things (1970 - co-w/co-p/d), Dead of Night (1972 - aka Deathdream/Deranged - w/co-p/d), Black Christmas (1974 - aka Silent Night, Evil Night - p/d), Murder by Decree (1978 - co-p/story/d)

Claws
USA 1977 94m colour
A giant bear goes on the rampage in an Alaskan reserve.
  Dismal low-budget shocker on very similar lines to Grizzly, though the plot is again little more than a reworking of Jaws (hence the title).
p: Chuck D. Keen for Alaska Pictures
w: Chuck D. Keen, Brian Russell
d: Richard Bansbach, Robert E. Pierson
ph: Chuck D. Keen
Jason Evers, Leon Ames, Anthony Caruso, Carla Layton, Glenn Sipes, Buck Young

Clemens, Brian (1931-)
Prolific British writer, producer and director with many television credits,

most notably for The Avengers, The Professionals and The New Avengers, almost always in association with his partner, producer Albert Fennell.
Genre credits:
The Tell-Tale Heart (1960 - co-w), And Soon the Darkness (1970 - co-w/co-p), See No Evil (1971 - w), Dr Jekyll and Sister Hyde (1971 - w/co-p), Captain Kronos - Vampire Hunter (1972 - aka Kronos - w/co-p/d), The Golden Voyage of Sinbad (1973 - co-w), The Watcher in the Woods (1980 - co-w), Mark of the Devil (1984 - TVM - w), The Sweet Smell of Death (1984 - TVM - w)

Clive, Colin (1898-1937)
British leading man of the old school. Went to Hollywood in 1930 to film Journey's End for director James Whale and stayed on to play Frankenstein in two films. Other credits include Christopher Strong, Jane Eyre and The Man Who Broke the Bank at Monte Carlo.
Genre credits:
Frankenstein (1931), The Bride of Frankenstein (1935), Mad Love (1935)

Clive, E. E. (1879-1940)
British character actor who, in Hollywood, found employment playing all manner of minor supporting roles, including butlers, cabbies and burgomeisters.
Genre credits:
The Invisible Man (1933), The Bride of Frankenstein (1935), Dracula's Daughter (1936), The Hound of the Baskervilles (1939)

Clouzot, Henri-Georges (1907-1977)
French writer and director, dubbed 'the French Hitchcock'. A former editor, he directed his first film, the short La Terreur des Batignolles, in 1931. Work as an assistant director followed, along with (controversially) screenplays for the pro-Vichy Continental Film Company during the Nazi occupation of France, for whom he also directed his first feature, L'Assassin Habite au 21 in 1942. Le Corbeau and The Wages of Fear (aka La Salaire de la Peur) secured his reputation as a maker of thrillers, though it is for Les Diaboliques (1956 - aka Diabolique/The Fiends) that he is chiefly remembered. A highly influential murder thriller with a much copied twist in its tail, it even said to have influenced Hitchcock's work on Psycho. His other credits include The Picasso Mystery, The Truth and La Prisonnière.

Clownhouse
USA 1988 84m DeLuxe
Three escaped lunatics disguise

HAMMER HORROR WAS NEVER LIKE THIS! An arresting moment from *The Church*. Many regard its director, Michele Soavi, as the new Dario Argento.

themselves as clowns and terrorize three young brothers.

Tame horror hokum, indifferently presented. A real missed opportunity.
p: Michael Danty, Robin Mortarotti, Victor Salva for Commercial Pictures
w/d: Victor Salva
ph: Robin Mortarotti
m: Michael Becker, Thomas Richardson
ed: Roy Anthony Cox, Sabrina Plisco-Morris
pd: Roy Anthony Cox
cos/make-up: Brenda Cox Ciguerre
sound: Sabrina Plisco-Morris, Richard Beggs
stunt co-ordinator: Nick Sanza
Nathan Forrest Winters, Brian McHugh, Sam Rockwell, Tree, Byron Weible, David C. Reinecker, Viletta Skillman, Timothy Enos

Code Name: Trixie see The Crazies

Cohen, Herman (1928-1985)
American writer and producer of low-budget exploitation horror fare which usually revel in ludicrous titles. A former cinema usher, film salesman and exhibitor, he formed his own production company in 1953.
Genre credits:
Bela Lugosi Meets a Brooklyn Gorilla (1952 - aka *The Monster Meets the Gorilla* - associate p), *Target Earth* (1954 - p), *I Was a Teenage Werewolf* (1957 - p), *I Was a Teenage Frankenstein* (1957 - aka *Teenage Frankenstein* - p), *Blood of Dracula* (1957 - aka *Blood is My Heritage* - p), *How to Make a Monster* (1958 - co-w/p), *The Headless Ghost* (1958 - co-w/p), *Horrors of the Black Museum* (1959 - co-w/p), *Konga* (1960 - co-w/p), *Black Zoo* (1963 - co-w/p), *A Study in Terror* (1965 - exec p), *Berserk!* (1967 - co-w/p), *Trog* (1970 - p), *Craze* (1974 - co-w/p)

Cohen, Larry (1938-)
American writer, producer and director, a former actor who broke into the industry via television, first as a pager at NBC, then as a writer (episodes of *The Defenders, Branded, Invaders, Cool Millions*, etc.). Began writing for films in the sixties (*I, the Jury, Return of the Seven, El Condor*, etc.) before moving on to writing and directing horror films in the seventies, the most successful of which was *It's Alive*, which spawned two sequels. Perhaps his most interesting film, however, is the non-horror subject, *The Private Files of J. Edgar Hoover*. His other credits include *Black Caesar, Hell Up in Harlem* and *Perfect Strangers* (aka *Blind Alley*).
Genre credits:
Daddy's Gone a-Hunting (1969 - w), *Bone*

(1972 - aka *Beverly Hills Nightmare / Dial Rat for Terror / Housewife* - w/p/d), *It's Alive* (1974 - w/p/d), *Demon* (1976 - aka *God Told Me To* - w/p/d), *It's Alive 2* (1978 - aka *It Lives Again* - w/p/d), *Full Moon High* (1981 - w/p/d), *Q - The Winged Serpent* (1981 - aka *The Winged Serpent* - w/p/d), *Special Effects* (1985 - w/d), *The Stuff* (1985 - w/d/exec p), *It's Alive III: Island of the Alive* (1987 - w/d/exec p), *Return to Salem's Lot* (1987 - w/d), *Maniac Cop* (1988 - w/p), *Wicked Stepmother* (1988 - w/d/exec p), *Maniac Cop 2* (1990 - w/p), *The Ambulance* (1990 - w/d), *Maniac Cop 3: Badge of Silence* (1992 - w/p)

Collins, Joan (1933-)
Glamorous British actress, in Hollywood since the mid-fifties, though best known for her role as Alexis Carrington in the long running TV soap *Dynasty*, which made her a worldwide star in the eighties. In the seventies, when her career seemed to take a dip, she appeared in a number of genre pictures, at least two of which marked the nadir of her career. She is the sister of novelist Jackie Collins.
Genre credits:
Fear in the Night (1972), *Dark Places* (1973), *Tales That Witness Madness* (1973), *I Don't Want To Be Born* (1975 - aka *The Devil Within Her*), *Empire of the Ants* (1977)

The Colossus of New York
USA 1958 69m bw
The father of a famous scientist killed in an automobile accident transplants his son's brain into a robot.

Stupefyingly boring low-budget science fiction dross.
p: William Alland for Paramount
w: Thelma Schnee
story: Willis Goldbeck
d: Eugene Lourie
ph: John F. Warren
m: Van Cleave
ed: Floyd Knudtson
ad: Hal Pereira, John Goodman
sp: John P. Fulton, Farciot Edouart
sound: John Wilkinson, Winston Leverett
Otto Kruger, Robert Hutton, Ross Martin, John Baragrey, Mala Powers

Columbia (Columbia-Tri Star)
Formed in 1924 by Harry Cohn, one of Hollywood's most feared studio heads, Columbia's fortunes were a little shaky at first, though in the forties they began to grow in stature, thanks to the success of such films as *The Jolson Story*. By the late fifties/early sixties the studio was producing such epic blockbusters such as *The Bridge on the River Kwai, Lawrence*

of Arabia and *Oliver!*, since when it has become one of Hollywood's major players. The studio's genre output has been a mixed bag, however (though like many other US studios, Columbia invested in and distributed a number of Hammer films in the sixties).
Genre filmography:
The Black Room (1935), *The Man They Could Not Hang* (1939), *The Man with Nine Lives* (1940 - aka *Behind the Door*), *The Devil Commands* (1941), *The Boogie Man Will Get You* (1944), *It Came from Beneath the Sea* (1955), *The Man Who Turned to Stone* (1957), *Night of the Demon* (1957 - aka *Curse of the Demon*), *The Zombies of Mora Tau* (1957 - aka *The Dead That Walk*), *The Tingler* (1959), *Thirteen Ghosts* (1960), *Bunny Lake Is Missing* (1965), *The Mad Room* (1969), *Blind Terror* (1971 - aka *See No Evil*), *Ghostbusters* (1984), *The Blob* (1988), *Ghostbusters II* (1989), *Flatliners* (1990)

Coma *
USA 1978 1134m Metroclor
A lady doctor discovers that patients are deliberately being put into coma so that their organs can later be sold on the black market by a sinister organization.

Watchable variation on the old lady in peril theme which, after a slowish build up, provides its share of thrills.
p: Martin Erlichman for MGM
w/d: Michael Crichton
novel: Robin Cooks (Michael Crichton)
ph: Victor J. Kemper, Gerald Hirschfeld
m: Jerry Goldsmith
ed: David Bretherton
pd: Albert Brenner
cos: Eddie Marks, Yvonne Kubis
sp: Joe Day
sound: Bill Griffith, William McCaughey, Michael J. Kohut, Aaron Rachin
Genevieve Bujold, Michael Douglas, Richard Widmark, Rip Torn, Elizabeth Ashley, Lois Chiles, Harry Rhodes, Tom Selleck, Ed Harris

Combes, Jeffrey
American actor with much genre work to his credit, though he is perhaps best known for playing Herbert West in the two *Re-Animator* movies.
Genre credits:
Re-Animator (1984), *From Beyond* (1986), *Pulsepounders* (1988), *The Phantom Empire* (1988), *Re-Animator 2* (1989 - aka *Bride of the Re-Animator*), *Dr Mordrid* (1990), *Trancers II: The Return of Jack Deth* (1990), *The Pit and the Pendulum* (1991), *Lurking Fear* (1994)

The Comeback
GB 1977 93m Technicolor

A singing star making a comeback finds himself in mortal danger from a homicidal maniac.

Old hat horror thriller with nothing to distinguish it from all the countless others of its kind.
p: Pete Walker for Heritage
w: Murray Smith, Michael Sloan
d: Pete Walker
ph: Peter Jessop
m: Stanley Myers
ed: Alan Brett
ad: Mike Pickwoad
Jack Jones, Pamela Stephenson, David Doyle, Bill Owen, Sheila Keith, Holly Palance, Richard Johnson, Peter Turner, Patrick Brook

The Comedy of Terrors
USA 1963 88m Pathecolor Panavision
Faced with bankruptcy, a funeral director decides to create a few extra customers of his own.

Desperate would be black comedy which forces a reliable cast to overplay more than usual. An opportunity sadly missed.
p: James H. Nicholson, Samuel Z. Arkoff, Anthony Carras, Richard Matheson for Alta Vista/AIP
w: Richard Matheson
d: Jacques Tourneur
ph: Floyd Crosby
m: Les Baxter
ed: Anthony Carras
pd/ad: Daniel Haller
sp: Pat Dinga, Butler-Glouner
sound: Dan Rush
Vincent Price, Peter Lorre, Boris Karloff, Basil Rathbone, Joe E. Browne, Joyce Jameson, Beverly Hills, Buddy Mason, Linda Rogers

The Coming
USA 1980 86m CFIcolor
In Salem in 1692, the spirit of the father of a young girl accused of being a witch travels through time to the present to enlist the aid of another young girl, the reincarnation of her accuser, in saving her.

Involved mumbojumbo, often so poorly lit as to be practically invisible.
p: Bert I. Gordon for Alan Landsburg Productions
w/d: Bert I. Gordon
ph: Daniel Yarussi
m: Arthur Kempel
ed: Ron Sawade
ad: Charles Adair
cos: E. Huntington Parker
sp: Fred Yawhick
sound: Jim Tanenbaum
make-up effects: Charles Schram
Susan Swift, Tisha Sterling, Beverly Ross, David Rounds, John Peters, Guy Stockwell, Albert Salmi, Jennie Babo

Connor, Kevin (1937-)
British director, a former editor, who with producer John Dark made a number of variable fantasy films in the seventies before turning to straight drama subjects. Credits include *At the Earth's Core*, *Warlords of Atlantis* and *Arabian Adventure*.
Genre credits:
The Land That Time Forgot (1975), *From Beyond the Grave* (1975), *The People That Time Forgot* (1977), *Motel Hell* (1980), *The House Where Evil Dwells* (1982)

Connors, Chuck (1921-1992)
American actor, familiar from such TV shows as *Rifleman*, *Branded* and *Cowboy in Africa*, as well as roles in the likes of *Geronimo*, *Ride Beyond Vengeance*, *Captain Nemo and the Underwater City* and *Pancho Villa*. Equally adept at good guy as well as bad guy roles, he popped up in several low-budget horror films later in his career.
Genre credits:
Horror at 37,000 Feet (1972 - TVM), *Tourist Trap* (1979), *Virus* (1980), *Summer Camp Nightmare* (1985 - aka *The Butterfly Nightmare*), *Kill and Enjoy* (1988), *Taxi Killer* (1988)

The Conqueror Worm see
Witchfinder General

Conway, Gary (1936-)
American actor (real name Gareth Carmody), popular on TV in the sixties in such series as *Burke's Law* and *Land of the Giants*, though remembered by genre fans for his film début, *I Was a Teenage Frankenstein*, in which he played the monster, a role he also repeated in the sequel, *How to Make a Monster*. His other film credits include *Young Guns of Texas*, *Black Gunn* and *Once Is Not Enough*. He now also produces and writes.
Genre credits:
I Was a Teenage Frankenstein (1957 - aka *Teenage Frankenstein*), *The Saga of the Viking Women and Their Voyage to the Waters of the Giant Sea Serpent* (1957), *How to Make a Monster* (1958)

Conway, Tom (1904-1967)
Suave British actor (real name Thomas Sanders) in Hollywood from the early forties. The brother of actor George Sanders, his voice, looks and manner greatly resembled those of his brother, so much so that he took over Sanders' role as The Falcon in the popular forties crime series after three episodes, playing his screen brother. Other credits include *Repeat Performance*, *One Touch of Venus* and *Confidence Girl* as well as three of the Val Lewton horrors.

Genre credits:
Cat People (1942), *I Walked With a Zombie* (1943), *The Seventh Victim* (1943), *The She-Creature* (1956)

Coodley, Ted
American make-up artist with three Corman horrors to his credit along with several low-budgeters.
Genre credits:
Pharaoh's Curse (1956), *The Pit and the Pendulum* (1961), *X - The Man With X-Ray Eyes* (1963 - aka *The Man With X-Ray Eyes*), *The Haunted Palace* (1963), *Billy the Kid vs. Dracula* (1965), *Jesse James Meets Frankenstein's Daughter* (1965)

Cook Jr, Elisha (1903/6-1995)
Mournful-looking American actor from the stage, with countless supporting roles to his credit. Perhaps most memorable as Wilmer the neurotic gunsel in *The Maltese Falcon*, his success in this part led to many other 'heavy' roles in such films as *The Phantom Lady* and the Laurel and Hardy comedy *A-Haunting We Will Go* (in which he is asked how much he charges to haunt a house).
Genre credits:
Wake Up Screaming (1941), *A-Haunting We Will Go* (1942), *Voodoo Island* (1957), *The House on Haunted Hill* (1959), *Black Zoo* (1963), *The Haunted Palace* (1963), *Rosemary's Baby* (1968), *The Night Stalker* (1971 - TVM), *Blacula* (1972), *Messiah of Evil* (1973), *The Phantom of Hollywood* (1974 - TVM), *Dead of Night* (1978 - TVM), *Salem's Lot* (1979 - TVM)

Coop, Denys (1920-1981)
British cinematographer with several key sixties films to his credit, including *A Kind of Loving*, *Billy Liar* and *This Sporting Life*. Won an Oscar in 1978 for the photographic special effects for *Superman*.
Genre credits:
Bunny Lake is Missing (1965), *10, Rillington Place* (1970), *Asylum* (1972), *And Now the Screaming Starts* (1973), *Vault of Horror* (1973)

Cooper, Merian C. (1893-1973)
American producer, director and executive with credits of all varieties, including documentaries (*Chang*, *Grass*), westerns (including several with director John Ford, with whom he formed Argosy Pictures in 1947) and adventure epics (*The Four Feathers*). He is, however, perhaps best remembered for producing and co-directing *King Kong*.
Genre credits:
The Most Dangerous Game (1932 - aka *The Hounds of Zaroff* - p), *King Kong* (1933 - p/co-d/actor), *Son of Kong*

(1933 - p), *She* (1935 - p), *Mighty Joe Young* (1949 - p)

Coquillon, John

British cinematographer who has lent a certain visual flair to a number of horror films. Other credits include *Triple Echo, Cross of Iron* and *Clockwise*.
Genre credits:
Witchfinder General (1968 - aka *The Conqueror Worm*), *The Oblong Box* (1969), *Scream and Scream Again* (1969), *Absolution* (1978), *The Changeling* (1979)

Corday, Mara (1932-)

American actress (real name Marilyn Watts), a former model. She was a familiar face in fifties westerns and potboilers including *Drums Across the River, Man Without a Star, The Man from Bitter Ridge* and *Girls on the Loose*.
Genre credits:
The Black Castle (1952), *Tarantula* (1955), *The Black Scorpion* (1957), *The Giant Claw* (1957)

Corman, Roger (1926-)

Legendary writer, producer, director and executive of horror and exploitation subjects, renowned for their low budgets and short shooting schedules. Started as a messenger boy at TCF, working his way up to story analyst. After a stint in England studying at Oxford University, he became a literary agent before turning to screenwriting (with *Highway Dragnet* in 1953) and producing. Tied himself to the newly formed AIP (American International Pictures) in 1954, making his directorial début the following year with *Oklahoma Woman*. Many low-budget titles followed, aimed primarily at the teenage and drive-in markets. These included such titles as *Rock All Night, She Gods of Shark Reef, Teenage Doll, Sorority Girl* and *Machine Gun Kelly*. However, in 1960, he looked to Edgar Allan Poe for inspiration and turned out a number of highly acclaimed films based on the author's writings, most of which starred Vincent Price. From the sixties he also helped to nurture up and coming talent both in front of and behind the cameras, including the likes of Francis Ford Coppola, Peter Bogdanovich, Martin Scorsese, Joe Dante, Jonathan Demme, Jack Nicholson and Robert de Niro. From 1971 onwards, following the box office disappointment of his long cherished World War One aerial drama *Von Richthofen and Brown*, he concentrated on producing through his company New World (formed in 1970), through whom he also distributed foreign art house titles (*Cries and Whispers, Amarcord, Breaker Morant*, etc.) as well as exploitation and horror (*Scream of the Demon, Night of the Cobra Woman, Rabid, Deathsport*, etc.). He sold New World in 1983 (for $17m) and set up Millenium, New Horizons and Corncorde. It wasn't until 1990 that he returned to directing with *Frankenstein Unbound*. He also acts occasionally in other directors' movies, such as Jonathan Demme's *The Silence of the Lambs* and John Carpenter's *Body Bags*. Non horror credits include *Five Guns West, I, Mobster, The St. Valentine's Day Massacre, Bloody Mama, Boxcar Bertha* and *Hollywood Boulevard*.
Genre credits:
The Monster from the Ocean Floor (1954 - p), *The Day the World Ended* (1955 - p/d), *It Conquered the World* (1956 - p/d), *Attack of the Crab Monsters* (1956 - p/d), *Not of This Earth* (1956 -p/d), *The Undead* (1956 - p/d), *The Viking Women and the Sea Serpent* (1958 - p/d), *War of the Satellites* (1958 - p/d), *Teenage Caveman* (1958 - aka *Prehistoric World* - p/d), *A Bucket of Blood* (1959 - p/d), *The Wasp Woman* (1959 - p/d), *The Little Shop of Horrors* (1960 - p/d), *The Last Woman on Earth* (1960 - p/d), *The Creature from the Haunted Sea* (1960 - p/d), *House of Usher* (1960 - aka *The Fall of the House of Usher* - p/d), *The Pit and the Pendulum* (1961 - p/d), *The Premature Burial* (1962 - p/d), *Tales of Terror* (1962 - p/d), *Dimentia 13* (1962 - aka *The Haunted and the Hunted* - p), *The Tower of London* (1962 - d), *The Raven* (1963 - p/d), *The Terror* (1963 -p/d), *X - The Man with X-Ray Eyes* (1963 - aka *The Man with X-Ray Eyes* - p/d), *The Haunted Palace* (1963 - p/d), *The Masque of the Red Death* (1964 - p/d), *The Tomb of Ligeia* (1964 - co-p/d), *Queen of Blood* (1965 - p), *The Dunwich Horror* (1969 - exec p), *Gas-s-s-s!* (1970 - aka *It Became Necessary to Destroy the World in Order to Save It* - p/d), *Piranha* (1978 - exec p), *Humanoids from the Deep* (1980 - aka *Monster* - exec p), *Galaxy of Terror* (1981 - exec p), *Forbidden World* (1982 - exec p), *Not of This Earth* (1988 - exec p), *Watchers* (1988 - exec p), *The Masque of the Red Death* (1989 - p), *The Terror Within* (1989 - exec p), *The Haunting of Morella* (1990 - exec p), *Frankenstein Unbound* (1990 - co-w/ co-p/d), *Transylavia Twist* (1990 - exec p), *Watchers II* (1990 - exec p), *Dead Space* (1991 - exec p), *The Terror Within* (1991 - exec p), *Dracula Rising* (1991 - exec p), *Carnosaur* (1993 - exec p)

Corri, Adrienne (1930-)

Glamorous British (Scottish) actress (real name Adrienne Riccobini) whose presence has livened up a variety of films, including *The Kidnappers, Three Men in a Boat, The Viking Queen, Moon Zero Two* and *A Clockwork Orange*.
Genre credits:
Devil Girl from Mars (1954), *Corridors of Blood* (1958 - aka *The Doctor from Seven Dials*), *The Hell-Fire Club* (1961), *The Tell-Tale Heart* (1961), *A Study in Terror* (1965), *Bunny Lake Is Missing* (1965), *Vampire Circus* (1972), *Madhouse* (1974)

Corridors of Blood ✶

GB 1958 86m bw
In 1840, a London surgeon experiments with anaesthesia.
    Stark horror melodrama with well done scenes, though it didn't see the light of day until 1964.
p: John Croydon for Producers' Associates
w: Jean Scott Rogers
d: ROBERT DAY
ph: GEOFFREY FAITHFUL
m: Buxtor Orr
ed: Peter Mayhew
ad: ANTHONY MASTERS
cos: Emma Selby Walker, Doris Turner
sound: Cyril Swern, Maurice Askew
BORIS KARLOFF, Finlay Currie, Christopher Lee, FRANK PETTINGELL, Betta St. John, Francis Matthews, Adrienne Corri, Marian Spencer

Cortez, Stanley (1908-)

Celebrated American cinematographer (real name Stanley Kranz) who has made important contributions to such films as *The Magnificent Ambersons, Night of the Hunter* and *The Bridge at Remagen*, though later in his career he involved himself in a number of low-budget horror films clearly unworthy of his talents. He began as a portrait photographer's assistant before becoming a camera assistant in 1926. Became a cinematographer proper in 1937 with *Four Day Wonder*.
Genre credits:
The Black Cat (1940), *Flesh and Fantasy* (1943 - co-ph), *The Secret Beyond the Door* (1948), *Night of the Hunter* (1955), *Dinosaurus!* (1960), *They Saved Hitler's Brain* (1963 - aka *Madmen of Mandoras*), *Shock Corridor* (1963), *The Navy vs. the Night Monsters* (1965), *The Ghost in the Invisible Bikini* (1966), *Damien: Omen II* (1978 - effects ph only)

The Corvini Inheritance

GB 1984 74m Technicolor TVM
A video security expert helps a neighbour to trap a man in a ski mask who has been terrorizing her.
    Adequate but overstretched tele-thriller, part of the disappointing *Hammer House of Mystery and Suspense* series.
p: Roy Skeggs for Hammer/TCF
w: David Fisher
d: Gabrielle Beaumont

ph: Frank Watts
m: David Bedford
md: Philip Martell
ed: Peter Weatherley
ad: Carolyn Scott
David McCallum, Jan Francis, Terence Alexander, Stephen Yardley, Paul Bacon, Timothy Morand, Johnny Wade

Coscarelli, Don (1954-)
American writer, producer, director, editor, etc., who had a low-budget hit with *Phantasm* but has subsequently failed to repeat its success. His other credits include *Jim - The World's Greatest*, *The Beastmaster* and *The Survival Game*.
Genre credits:
Phantasm (1979 - w/p/d/ph/ed), *Phantasm II* (1988 - w/d), *Phantasm III* (1995 - aka *Phantasm: Lords of the Dead* - w/d)

Costello, Lou see Abbott, Bud

Cotten, Joseph (1905-1994)
American leading man who began his film career in Welles' *Citizen Kane* in which he played the reporter. A former drama critic for the *Miami Herald*, he began acting in the late twenties, first as an understudy and stage assistant, then later on Broadway. He joined Orson Welles' Mercury Theatre company in 1937 and worked with the actor-director on such acclaimed films as *The Magnificent Ambersons*, *Journey into Fear* (which he co-wrote with Welles) and *The Third Man*. Other films include Hitchcock's *Shadow of a Doubt* (in which he played The Merry Widow Murderer), *Duel in the Sun* and *Niagra*.
Genre credits:
Portrait of Jennie (1948), *Hush... Hush, Sweet Charlotte* (1964), *The Abominable Dr Phibes* (1971), *Lady Frankenstein* (1971), *Baron Blood* (1971 - aka *Gli Orrori del Castello di Norimnerga/Chamber of Tortures/The Thirst of Baron Blood/The Torture Chamber of Baron Blood*), *The Devil's Daughter* (1972 - TVM), *Island of Mutations* (1979 - aka *Screamers/Island of the Fishermen/L'Isola degli Uomini Pesci*), *The Hearse* (1980), *Delusion* (1981 - aka *The House Where Death Lives*)

Coulouris, George (1903-1989)
British character actor who was long in Hollywood before returning to Britain. Films include *Citizen Kane*, *Watch on the Rhine* and *Outcast of the Islands*.
Genre credits:
The Man Without a Body (1957), *Womaneater* (1957 - aka *The Woman Eater*), *The Skull* (1965), *Blood from the Mummy's Tomb* (1971), *The Antichrist* (1975 - aka *L'Anticristo/The Tempter*)

Count Dracula *
GB 1977 145m (or varying formats) colour TVM
Count Dracula leaves his castle in Transylvania and travels to England in search of new life to feed upon.
   Surprisingly tolerable and faithful tele-version of the oft filmed story. A prestige production of its day, it stands up better than many of the big screen adaptations, and is let down only by the the look of its interior sequences, which were shot on videotape.
p: Morris Barry for BBC/WNET
w: Gerald Savoury
novel: BRAM STOKER
d: Philip Saville
ph: Peter Hall
m: Kenyon Emrys-Roberts
ed: Richard Bedford, Rod Waldron
ad: Michael Young
cos: Ken Morey
sp: Tony Harding
sound: John Pritchard, Derek Miller-Timmins
titles: Dick Bailey
Louis Jourdan, Frank Finlay, Susan Penhaligon, Jack Shepherd, Mark Burns, Judi Bowker

Count Yorga, Vampire *
USA 1970 90m Movielab
A Bulgarian count terrorizes a group of friends in modern day Los Angeles.
   Low-budget vampire saga with a few minor virtues and an engaging star performance. *The Return of Count Yorga* appeared in 1971.
p: Michael Macready for Erica
w/d: Bob Kelljian
ph: Arch Archembault
m: William Marx
ed: Tony de Zarraga
ad: Bob Wilder
cos: Nancy Stone
sp: James Tanenbaum
sound: Robert Dietz, Lowell Brown
narrator: George Macready
ROBERT QUARRY, Michael Murphy, Roger Perry, Michael Macready, Donna Anders, Judith Lang

Countess Dracula
GB 1971 93m Eastmancolor
An ageing countess discovers that bathing in the blood of virgins restores her youth.
   Based on the Elizabeth Bathory legend, this is an initially promising but ultimately disappointing variation on a well worn theme. A little more style would have worked wonders, though the star gives it a note of distinction, despite being dubbed.
p: Alexander Paal for Hammer/Rank
w: Jeremy Paul
story: Alexander Paal, Peter Sasdy,

Gabriel Ronay
d: Peter Sasdy
ph: Ken Talbot
m: Harry Robinson
md: Philip Martell
ed: Henry Richardson
ad: Philip Harrison
cos: Raymond Hughes
sp: Bert Luxford
sound: Kevin Sutton, Ken Barker
make-up: Tom Smith
ch: Mia Nardi
INGRID PITT, Nigel Green, Sandor Eles, Maurice Denham, Lesley-Anne Downe, Patience Collier, Peter Jeffrey, Jessie Evans

Court, Hazel (1926-)
British actress, a former model who made her screen début in the Tommy Trinder musical *Champagne Charlie* in 1944. Her English rose qualities made her the perfect heroine/victim in a wide variety of gothic horrors, including work for both Hammer and Roger Corman.
Genre credits:
Ghost Ship (1952), *Devil Girl from Mars* (1954), *The Curse of Frankenstein* (1956), *The Man Who Could Cheat Death* (1959), *Dr Blood's Coffin* (1961), *The Raven* (1963), *The Premature Burial* (1963), *The Masque of the Red Death* (1964), *The Final Conflict* (1981)

Crampton, Barbara
American actress who came to note in Stuart Gordon's *Re-Animator*.
Genre credits:
Re-Animator (1985), *From Beyond* (1986)

Crash!
USA 1977 98m DeLuxe Panavision
A strange amulet turns a lady driver into a monster.
   Ludicrous, even by low-budget standards.
p: Charles Band for Group One/Charles Band Ltd
w: Marc Marais
d: Charles Band
ph: Andrew Davis, Bill Williams
m: Andrew Belling
ed: Harry Keramidas
ad: Patrick McFadden
cos: Sterling Von Franck
sp: Harry Wollman
sound: John Hayes
2nd unit ph: John Huneck, Don Clark
stunt co-ordinator: Von Deming
Sue Lyon, Jose Ferrer, John Carradine, John Erickson, Leslie Parrish, Richard Band

The Crater Lake Monster
USA 1977 82m colour
A crashing meteor resurrects a prehistoric monster, which subsequently goes on the rampage.

Grade Z monster hokum of the kind familiar in the less critical fifties. Laughable when it isn't embarrassing.
p: William R. Stromberg for Crown International
w: William R. Stromberg, Richard Cardella
d: William R. Stromberg
ph: Paul Gentry
m: James West
ed: Nancy Grossman, Steve Neilson
pd: Roger Heisman
sp: Dave Allen, Tom Scherman
Richard Cardella, Glenn Roberts, Mark Siegel, Kacey Cobb, Richard Garrison, Michael Hoover, Suzanne Lewis, Bob Hyman

Craven, Wes (1949-)

American writer and director at home in the horror genre, where he is best known for creating the character of child killer Freddy Krueger for the successful *Nightmare on Elm Street* series, though his other films haven't quite reached the same commercial heights. A former production assistant, he broke into directing via editing low-budget films such as *You've Got To Walk It Like You Talk It Or You'll Lose That Beat*. His son Jonathan is now also directing, his début being *Mind Ripper* (1994), of which his father was executive producer.
Genre credits:
Last House on the Left (1972 - w/d/ed), *The Hills Have Eyes* (1977 - w/d/ed), *Summer of Fear* (1978 - aka *Stranger in Our House* - TVM - d), *Deadly Blessing* (1981 - co-w/d), *Swamp Thing* (1981 - w/d), *A Nightmare on Elm Street* (1984 - w/d), *Invitation to Hell* (1984 - TVM - d), *The Hills Have Eyes II* (1985 - w/d), *Chiller* (1985 - TVM - d), *Deadly Friend* (1986 - d), *A Nightmare on Elm Street Part Three: The Dream Warriors* (1987 - co-w/story/ co-exec p), *The Serpent and the Rainbow* (1987 - d), *Shocker* (1989 - w/d/exec p), *Night Visions* (1990 - TVM - d), *The People Under the Stairs* (1991 - w/d/co-exec p), *Body Bags* (1994 - actor only), *Wes Craven's New Nightmare* (1994 - w/d/ co-exec p/actor), *Mind Ripper* (1994 - exec p), *A Vampire in Brooklyn* (1996 - d)

Crawford, Joan (1904-1977)

American star actress who began in silent flapper comedies before maturing into one of Hollywood's most durable leading ladies, at best in soapy melodramas where she suffered in mink. She won a Best Actress Oscar in 1945 for her performance in *Mildred Pierce*. However, in the 1960s, when her career began to wind down, she happily turned to horror movies in an attempt to sustain it, the best of these being

Whatever Happened to Baby Jane?
Genre credits:
Whatever Happened to Baby Jane? (1962), *Strait Jacket* (1964), *I Saw What You Did* (1965), *Berserk* (1967), *Night Gallery* (1969 - TVM), *Trog* (1970)

Crawlspace

USA/It 1986 80m colour
A mad behavioural scientist uses the female residents of his rooming house as guinea pigs, and resorts to murder to keep his experiments secret.
Mildly diverting though mostly predictable mad-scientist saga with a few slick touches.
p: Roberto Bessi for Altar
exec p: Charles Band
w/d: David Schmoeller
ph: Sergio Salvati
m: Pino Donaggio
md: Natel Massara
ed: Bert Glatstein
pd: Giovanni Natalucci
cos: C. J. Strawn
sp: Phil Foreman
sound: Dino Raini
make-up effects: John Buechler
Klaus Kinski, Talia Balsam, Carol Francis, Barbara Whinnery, Jack Heller

Craze

GB 1973 95m Technicolor
A middle-aged antiques dealer sacrifices victims to an African idol in return for monetary gain.
Undernourished horror hokum, undignified even by its cast.
p: Herman Cohen for EMI/Harbor
exec p: Gustav Berne
w: Aben Kandel, Herman Cohen
novel: Henry Seymour
d: Freddie Francis
ph: John Wilcox
m: John Scott
ed: Henry Richardson
ad: George Provis
cos: Rita Wakely
sound: Ken Ritchie
Jack Palance, Diana Dors, Edith Evans, Trevor Howard, Suzy Kendall, Hugh Griffith, Julie Ege, Michael Jayston, Percy Herbert, Kathleen Byron, Martin Potter

The Crazies

USA 1973 103m colour
A contaminated water supply turns the inhabitants of a small township into murderous maniacs.
Overlong and rather tedious horror flick, not quite among its director's best work, but owing much to *Night of the Living Dead*.
p: Alvin C. Croft for Pittsburg/Latent Image/Cambist

exec p: Lee Hessell
w: George A. Romero, Paul McCollough
d/ed: George A. Romero
ph: S. William Hinzman
m: Bruce Roberts, Doris Dodds
Lane Carroll, W. G. McMillan, Harold Wayne Jones, Lloyd Hollar, Richard Liberty

The Creature from the Black Lagoon

US 1954 79m bw 3D
An amphibious monster threatens members of an exploration team.
Archetypal fifties monster pic, a little on the tame side, but with effective underwater sequences. It was followed by *Revenge of the Creature* (1955) and *The Creature Walks Among Us* (1956).
p: William Alland for Universal
w: Harry Essex, Arthur Ross
d: Jack Arnold
ph: William E. Snyder, James C. Havens
md: Joseph Gershenson
ed: Ted J. Kent
ad: Bernard Herzbrun, Hilyard Brown
make-up: Bud Westmore, Jack Kevan
Richard Carlson, Julie Adams, Richard Denning, Antonio Moreno, Nestor Pavia, Ricou Browning (as the Creature)

The Creature Walks Among Us

US 1956 78m bw
A group of scientists capture the Gill Man but he escapes and goes on the rampage.
Third and final of Universal's creature features. Good underwater scenes, but otherwise the mixture is as before.
p: William Alland for Universal
w: Arthur Ross
d: John Sherwood
ph: Maury Gertsman
md: Joseph Gershenson
ed: Edward Curtiss
ad: Alexander Golitzen, Robert E. Smith
cos: Jay A. Morley Jr
sp: Clifford Stine
sound: Leslie I. Carey, Robert Pritchard
make-up: Bud Westmore
Jeff Morrow, Rex Reason, Leigh Snowden, Gregg Palmer, Maurice Manson, Ricou Browning (as the Creature)

Creatures the World Forgot

GB 1970 95m Technicolor
The lives and battles of a prehistoric tribe.
Dull and rather silly follow up to Hammer's other prehistoric adventures, lacking both imagination and monsters.
p: Michael Carreras for Hammer/ Columbia
w: Michael Carreras

d: Don Chaffey
ph: Vincent Cox
m: Mario Nascimbene
md: Philip Martell
ed: Chris Barnes
pd: John Stoll
cos: Rosemary Burrows
sp: Sydney Pearson
sound: John Streeler
2nd unit ph: Ray Sturgess
Julie Ege, Brian O'Shaughnessy, Robert John, Marcia Fox, Rosalie Crutchley

Creepers see Phenomena

The Creeping Flesh *
GB 1972 91m Eastmancolor
A scientist returns from an archaeological expedition with the remains of a Neanderthal man, which returns to life when touched by water.

Quietly effective horror film with a couple of nice touches along the way, including a twist in the tail that can be traced back to The Cabinet of Dr Caligari.
p: Michael Redbourne for Tigon/World Film Services/Columbia/LMG
exec p: Norman Priggen, Tony Tenser
w: Peter Spencerley, Jonathan Rumbold
d: Freddie Francis
ph: Norman Warwick
m: Paul Ferris
ed: Oswald Haffenrichter
ad: George Provis
cos: Bridget Sellers
sound: Norman Bolland, Nolan Roberts
make-up: Roy Ashton
Christopher Lee, Peter Cushing, Lorna Heilbron, George Brenson, Kenneth J. Warren, Harry Locke, Duncan Lamont, Michael Ripper, Jenny Runacre

The Creeping Unknown see The Quatermass Experiment

Creepshow *
USA 1982 120m Technicolor
Five tales of terror and the supernatural emanate from a schoolboy's comic book.

Generally lively blend of horror and humour, though in the end perhaps one story too many. Creepshow 2 followed in 1987.
p: Richard P. Rubinstein for UFD/Laurel
w: Stephen King
d: GEORGE ROMERO
ph: Michael Gornick
m: John Harrison
ed: George Romero, Paul Hirsch, Pasquale Buba, Michael Spolan
pd: Cletus Anderson
cos: Barbara Anderson
sound: Peter Huddal
make-up effects: Tom Savini
Hal Holbrook, Adrienne Barbeau, Viveca

Lindfors, Ed Harris, E. G. Marshall, Stephen King, Leslie Nielsen, Ted Danson, Carrie Nye, Fritz Weaver, Tom Atkins

The Creeping Terror
USA 1964 100m bw
America is threatened by what appear to be man-eating carpets from outer space.

Another Golden Turkey. Good for a few laughs, but only a few.
p: Art J. Nelson for Metropolitan International
w: Robert Silliphant
d/ed: Art J. Nelson
ph: Frederick Janczak
m: Frederick Kopp
ad: Bud Raab
monster design: Jon Lackey
Vic Savage (Art J. Nelson), Shannon O'Neill, William Thourlby, John Caresio, Norman Boone, Byra Holland

Creepzoids
USA 1987 72m colour
In the future, five army deserters find themselves stalked by an alien creature in an abandoned installation.

Dim, low-budget Alien rip-off with a mutant baby thrown into the brew for good measure.
p: David De Coteau, John Schouweiler for Titan
w: Burford Hauser, David De Coteau
d: David De Coteau
ph: Thomas Calloway
m: Guy Moon
md: Jonathan Scott Bogner
ed: Miriam L. Preissel
pd: Royce Matthew
cos: Wilma Rubble (!)
sp: Tom Calloway, John Criswell
sound: Marty Kasparian
make-up effects: Thom Floutz, Peter Carsillo
Linnea Quigley, Richard Hawkins, Joi Wilson, Michael Aranda, Kim McKamy, Ken Abraham

Cregar, Laird (1916-1944)
American character actor in the Orson Welles mould. Though he died at the age of just twenty-eight, he was best known for playing middle-aged parts in such films as Charley's Aunt, The Black Swan and Heaven Can Wait.
Genre credits:
I Wake Up Screaming (1941), The Lodger (1944), Hangover Square (1944)

Crescendo *
GB 1969 95m Technicolor
A girl researching the life of a great composer goes to stay with his widow only to find herself involved in a macabre plot.

Highly derivative thriller in typical Hammer style. Fair enough for those who haven't been here a hundred times before.
p: Michael Carreras for Hammer/Warner
w: Jimmy Sangster, Alfred Shaughnessy
story: Alfred Shaughnessy
d: ALAN GIBSON
ph: Paul Beeson
m: Malcolm Williamson
md: Philip Martell
ed: Chris Barnes
ad: Scott MacGregor
cos: Jackie Breed
sound: Claude Hitchcock
Stefanie Powers, James Olson, Margaretta Scott, Jane Lapotaire, Joss Ackland

Cries and Shadows see Naked Exorcism

Crimes at the Dark House
GB 1939 69m bw
An imposter posing as Sir Percival Glyde has to murder in order to conceal his true identity.

Dated, cloakswirling melodrama with the star at his most dastardly. Loosely based on Wilkie Collins' The Woman in White.
p: George King for Pennant
w: Edward Dryhurst, Frederick Hayward, H. F. Maltby
novel: Wilkie Collins
d: George King
ph: Hone Glendinning
ed: Jack Beaver
ad: Jack Harris
TOD SLAUGHTER, Hilary Evans, Sylvia Marriott, Hay Petrie, David Horne

The Crimes of Stephen Hawk
GB 1936 69m bw
A moneylender is revealed as a notorious murderer.

Swaggering star vehicle with the expected amount of barnstorming.
p: George King
w: A. F. Maltby, Paul White, Jack Celestin
d: George King
ph: Ronald Neame
m: no credit given
ed: John Seabounre
ad: Philip Mewcombe
Tod Slaughter, Eric Portman, Marjorie Taylor, Gerald Barry

Criswell (1907-1982)
American mystic (real name Charles Criswell King), popular on television in the fifties. Allied himself to the low-budget films of Edward D. Wood Jr and

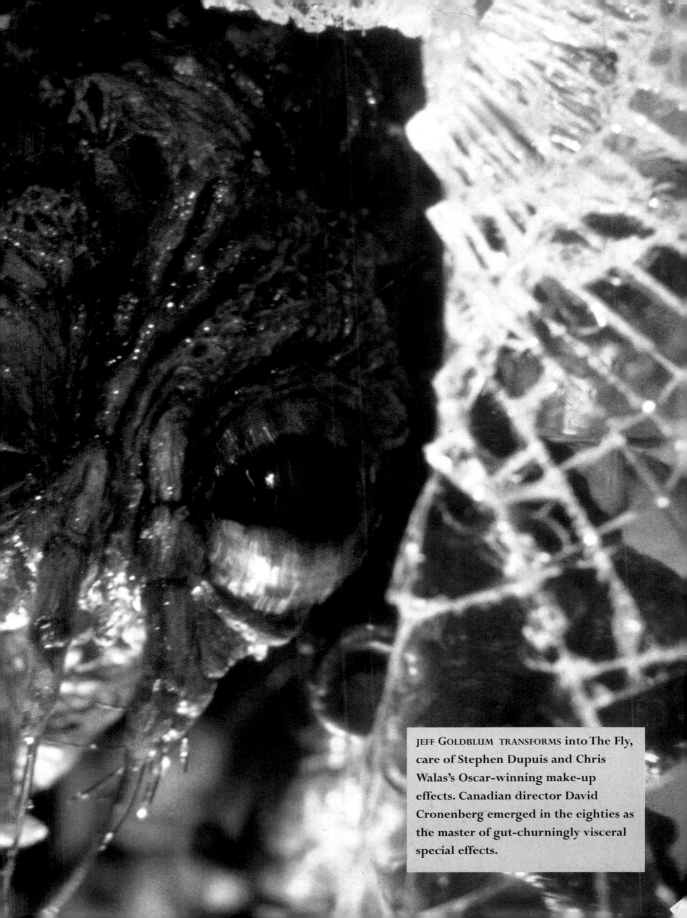

JEFF GOLDBLUM TRANSFORMS into The Fly, care of Stephen Dupuis and Chris Walas's Oscar-winning make-up effects. Canadian director David Cronenberg emerged in the eighties as the master of gut-churningly visceral special effects.

was portrayed by Jeffrey Jones in the 1994 biopic *Ed Wood*.
Genre credits:
Plan 9 from Outer Space (1958 - aka *Grave Robbers from Outer Space*), *Night of the Ghouls* (1959), *Orgy of the Dead* (1965)

Critters

USA 1988 86m DeLuxe
A Kansas farming community finds itself prey to an invasion of man-eating critters from outer space.

Juvenile horror comic which is neither funny enough nor scary enough. It did, however, provoke a number of sequels: *Critters 2* (1988 - aka *Critters 2: The Main Course*), *Critters 3* (1992) and *Critters 4* (1992).
p: Rupert Harvey for New Line/SHO/Smart Egg
exec p: Robert Shaye
w: Stephen Herek, Dominic Muir
story: Dominic Muir
d: Stephen Herek
ph: Chris Tufty, Tim Suhrstedt
m: David Newman
ed: Larry Bock
pd: Gregg Fonseca
sp: Chiodo Brothers Production
sound: Dale Johnston
stunt co-ordinator: Mike Cassidy
titles: Ernest D. Farino
Dee Wallace Stone, M. Emmett Walsh, Scott Grimes, Billy Green Bush, Billy Zane

Crole-Rees, Trevor

British make-up artist, responsible for the look of the disfigured Dr Phibes.
Genre credits:
Circus of Horrors (1960), *The Abominable Dr Phibes* (1971), *Dr Phibes Rises Again* (1972)

Cronenberg, David (1943-)

Canadian writer and director who began by directing visceral horror films before taking the slightly more psychological approach which earned him the respect of the critics. One of the genre's most distinguished talents, though he is still perhaps best remembered for the exploding head in *Scanners*.
Genre credits:
Stereo (1969 - w/p/d/ph/ed), *Crimes of the Future* (1970 - w/p/d/ph/ed), *Shivers* (1974 - aka *They Came from Within/The Parasite Murders* - w/d), *Rabid* (1976 - w/d), *The Brood* (1979 - w/d), *Scanners* (1980 - w/d), *Videodrome* (1982 - w/d), *The Dead Zone* (1983 - d), *The Fly* (1986 - co-w/d/actor), *Dead Ringers* (1988 - co-w/co-p/d), *Nightbreed* (1990 - actor), *Naked Lunch* (1991 - w/d)

Cronos *

Mexico 1992 Foto-Kem Dolby
An antiques dealer discovers a mysterious mechanical device, the work of a fifteenth century alchemist, which has the ability to make one immortal, though one of the side effects proves to be a lust for human blood.

Stylish horror story with a few unsettling moments which may upset the squeamish.
p: Arthur H. Gorson, Bertha Navarro for October/Iguana/Ventana
w/d: Guillermo Del Toro
ph: Guillermo Navarro
m: Javier Alvarez
ed: Raul Davalos
ad: Tolita Figueroa
cos: Genoveva Petitpierre
sp: Laurencio Cordeo
sound: Fernando Camara, Thom Ehle
Federico Luppi, Ron Perlman, Claudio Brooks, Margarita Isabel, Mario Ivan Martinez

Crosby, Floyd (1889-1985)

American cinematographer, a former stockbroker, who began photographing documentaries for the likes of Robert Flaherty and Joris Ivens in the twenties. Won an Oscar in 1931 for photographing *Tabu* after which he worked on such films as *The River*, *My Father's House* and *High Noon* before turning to low-budget horror and exploitation films, which later included Roger Corman's Poe cycle.
Genre credits:
The Monster from the Ocean Floor (1954), *The Snow Creature* (1954), *Attack of the Crab Monsters* (1954), *Teenage Caveman* (1958), *The Screaming Skull* (1958), *House of Usher* (1960 - aka *The Fall of the House of Usher*), *Hand of Death* (1961), *The Premature Burial* (1962), *Tales of Terror* (1962), *The Raven* (1963), *Black Zoo* (1963), *The Haunted Palace* (1963), *X - The Man with X-Ray Eyes* (1963 - aka *The Man with X-Ray Eyes*), *The Comedy of Terrors* (1963)

Crowhaven Farm *

USA 1970 74m Tecnicolor TVM
Having inherited a remote farm, a New York housewife finds herself terrified by local diabolists.

Fair horror hokum which passes the time well enough.
p: Walter Grauman for Aaron Spelling
w: John McGeevey
d: Walter Grauman
ph: Fleet Southcott
m: Robert Drasnin
md: George Duning
ed: Art Seid, Aaron Stell
ad: Tracy Bousman
cos: Robert Harris Sr, Shannon Litton

sound: Barry Thomas
Hope Lange, Paul Burke, John Carradine, Lloyd Bochner, Virginia Gregg

Crucible of Terror

GB 1971 89m colour
A corrupt artist uses real people as the bases for his sculptures.

Yes, that old chestnut again, and very poorly done in this case.
p: Tom Parkinson for Peter Newbrook
w: Ted Hooker, Tom Parkinson
d: Ted Hooker
ph: Peter Newbrook
m: Paris Rutherford
ed: Maxine Julius
ad: Arnold Chapkis
cos: Mary Gibson
sound: Ken Ritchie
Mike Raven, James Bolam, Mary Maude, Ronald Lacey, Marissa Stribling

Cruise into Terror

USA 1978 96m Technicolor TVM
Spirits from an Egyptian sarcophagus threaten passengers on a cruise to Mexico.

Routine, thoroughly uninventive shipboard thriller.
p: Jeff Hayes for Aaron Spelling, Douglas Cramer
w: Michael Braverman
d: Bruce Kessler
ph: Arch Dalzel
Hugh O'Brian, Ray Milland, John Forsythe, Dirk Benedict, Stella Stevens, Christopher George, Linda Day George, Frank Converse, Lee Meriweather, Marshall Thompson

A Cry in the Dark see Naked Exorcism

Crypt of the Living Dead

It/Turkey 1972 83m Metrocolor
A beautiful thirteenth-century vampire returns to life when her tomb is discovered in a cave.

Drawn out but occasionally atmospheric canter through familiar territory and situations.
p: Lou Shaw for Atlas/Coast Industries
exec p: Wolf Schmidt
w: Lou Shaw
story: Lois Gibson
d: Ray Danton
ph: Juan Gelpi
m: Phillip Lambro
ed: David Rawlins
ad: Juan Alberto
sp: A. Molina
sound: Marv Kerner
Mark Damon, Andrew Prine, Patty Sheppard, Teresa Gimpera, Mariano Rey

Cujo
USA 1983 91m CFIcolor
A rabid dog threatens a young mother and her son.

A slick but rather empty-headed horror story centring on too thin a premise.
p: Daniel H. Blatt, Robert Singer for Sunn Classic/Taft
w: Don Carlos Dunaway, Lauren Currier
novel: Stephen King
d: Lewis Teague
ph: Jan de Bont
m: Charles Bernstein
ed: Neil Travis
pd: Guy Comtois
cos: Jack Beuhler
sp: Rick Josephson
sound: Mark Ulano
make-up effects: Peter Knowlton
Dee Wallace, Christopher Stone, Ed Lauter, Daniel-Hugh Kelly, Danny Pintauro

Cundey, Dean
American cinematographer who hitched a ride to the top with director John Carpenter before moving on to bigger things with Robert Zemeckis and Steven Spielberg. Other credits include *Escape from New York*, *Romancing the Stone*, *Back to the Future* (and its sequels), *Who Framed Roger Rabbit* and *The Flintstones*.
Genre credits:
Halloween (1978), *The Fog* (1979), *Halloween II* (1981), *The Thing* (1982), *Halloween III: Season of the Witch* (1983), *Psycho II* (1983), *Welcome to Hell* (1984 - TVM), *Death Becomes Her* (1992), *Jurassic Park* (1993), *Casper* (1995)

Cunningham, Sean S. (1941-)
American producer and director with stage experience as both an actor and producer. He began making industrial films and commercials in the early seventies, following which he began making features in 1971 with the soft-core horror film *The Case of the Full Moon Murders*. His biggest success to date has been the first *Friday the 13th* movie, which spawned a long running series.
Genre credits:
The Case of the Full Moon Murders (1971 - aka *The Case of the Smiling Stiffs/Sex on the Groove Tube* - d), *The Last House on the Left* (1972 - p), *Friday the 13th* (1980 - p/d), *A Stranger Is Watching* (1982 - p/d), *Deepstar Six* (1989 - co-p/d), *The Horror Show* (1989 - aka *House III* - p), *House IV* (1992 - p), *Jason Goes to Hell* (1993 - aka *Friday the 13th Part 9: Jason Goes to Hell* - p)

Curry, Tim (1946-)
British actor with a penchant for offbeat roles, the best known of which is Frank N. Furter in *The Rocky Horror Picture Show*. Other films include *The Shout*, *The Ploughman's Lunch*, *Baby*, *The Hunt for Red October* and *Home Alone 2: Lost in New York*.
Genre credits:
The Rocky Horror Picture Show (1974), *Legend* (1985), *It* (1991 - aka *Stephen King's It* - TVM), *Congo* (1995)

Curse IV: The Ultimate Sacrifice see Catacombs

The Curse of Frankenstein **
GB 1957 83m Eastmancolor
Baron Frankenstein experiments with reanimating the dead, the result being a mutant which goes on the rampage.

Generally spirited and efficient retelling of the Frankenstein story, notable for establishing Hammer as Britain's leading purveyors of horror and for launching Cushing and Lee as stars of the genre.
p: Anthony Hinds, Anthony Nelson Keys for Hammer/Warner
exec p: Michael Carreras
w: JIMMY SANGSTER
novel: MARY SHELLEY
d: TERENCE FISHER
ph: JACK ASHER
m: JAMES BERNARD
md: John Hollingsworth
ed: James Needs
pd: Bernard Robinson
ad: Ted Marshall
cos: no credit given
sound: no credit given
make-up: Phil Leakey
PETER CUSHING, CHRISTOPHER LEE, Hazel Court, Robert Urquhart, Melvyn Hayes, Valerie Gaunt, Noel Hood

The Curse of King Tutankhamun's Tomb
GB/USA 1980 96m Technicolor TVM
When the tomb of King Tutankhamun is discovered, death follows those who despoil it.

Ridiculous account of the 1922 expedition, more laughable than thrilling, and with some hilariously miscast actors.
p: Peter Graham Scott for HTV/Columbia
w: Herb Meadow
novel: Barry Wynne
d: Philip Leacock
ph: Bob Edwards
ed: Adrian Bernard
narrator: Paul Schofield
Raymond Burr, Robin Ellis, Harry Andrews, Angharad Rees, Wendy Hiller, Eva Marie Saint, Faith Brooks, Tom Baker, Rupert Frazer

Curse of the Black Widow
USA 1978 96m Technicolor TVM
The killer responsible for several deaths turns out to be a giant spider.

Ho-hum horror nonsense, not too brightly done.
p: Steven North for ABC/Circle
w: Robert Blees, Earl Wallace
d: Dan Curtis
ph: Paul Lohmann, Steven Larner
m: Robert Cobert
Tony Franciosa, Donna Mills, Patty Duke-Astin, June Allyson, Sid Caesar

The Curse of the Cat People **
USA 1944 70m bw
A lonely child, shunned by her schoolfriends, is befriended by the spirit of her father's first wife.

A mild but rather engaging sequel to Lewton's *Cat People*, with sequences of style and an atmosphere of gentle fantasy rather than horror.
p: VAL LEWTON for RKO
w: DE WITT BODEEN
d: Gunther Fritsch, Robert Wise
ph: NICHOLAS MUSURACA
m: Roy Webb
md: Constantin Bakaleinikoff
ed: J. R. Wittredge
ad: Albert D'Agostino, Walter E. Keller
cos: Edward Stevenson
sound: Francis M. Sarver, James G. Stewart
Simone Simon, Kent Smith, Jane Randolph, Julia Anne Carter, Elizabeth Russell

Curse of the Crimson Altar
GB 1968 89m Eastmancolor
A young antiques dealer searching for his missing brother discovers a witches' coven in a quiet English village.

Tolerable but dated and somewhat slow moving horror hokum with a better cast than it deserves, though Miss Steele looks suitably striking in her green make-up and elaborate headgear.
p: Tony Tenser for Tigon/AIP
exec p: Louis M. Heyward
w: Mervyn Haisman, Henry Lincoln
story: Jerry Stohl
d: Vernon Sewell
ph: John Coquillon
m: Peter Knight
ed: Howard Lanning
ad: Derek Barrington
cos: Michael Southgate
sound: Kevin Sutton
Boris Karloff, Christopher Lee, Mark Eden, Barbara Steele, Michael Gough, Rupert Davies

Curse of the Demon see Night of the Demon

Curse of the Faceless Man *

USA 1958 66m bw
A 2,000-year-old gladiator comes back to life after being excavated by archaeologists working in Pompeii.

Eerie little horror filler which, despite some obvious padding, raises a few thrills along the way.
p: Robert E. Kent for Vogue
w: Jerome Bixby
d: EDWARD L. CAHN
ph: Kenneth Peacock
m: Gerald Fried
ed: Grant Whytock
ad: William Glasgow
cos: Elmar Boyrman, Von Lee Vlokaris
sp: Ira Anderson
sound: Frank Webster Sr
make-up: Charles Gemorra
Richard Anderson, Elaine Edwards, Adele Mara, Luis van Roote, Gar Moore, Felix Locher, Bob Ryan

Curse of the Fly

GB 1965 83m bw Cinemascope
The Delambre family continue their teletransportation experiments, this time across the Atlantic.

Low-budget attempt to continue the series at a British studio.
p: Robert L. Lippert, Jack Parsons for TCF
w: Harry Spalding
d: Don Sharp
ph: Basil Emmott
m: Bert Shefter
ed: Robert Winter
ad: Harry White
sound: Jock May
make-up effects: Harold Fletcher
Brian Donlevy, George Baker, Carole Gray, Michael Graham, Rachel Kempson, Yvette Rees, Burt Kwouk, Jeremy Wilkin, Mary Manson

The Curse of the Mummy's Tomb

GB 1964 80m Technicolor Techniscope
At the turn of the century members of an archaeological expedition are murdered one by one by a vengeful mummy which has been put on display by an unscrupulous American showman.

Childishly scripted and slackly directed hokum which takes forever to get nowhere in particular. The mummy's first appearance is a long time coming and the widescreen is poorly used. A sequence on a street stairway and a climax in the sewers stay in the mind, however.
p: Michael Carreras for Hammer/Columbia/Swallow
w: Henry Younger (Michael Carreras)
d: Michael Carreras
ph: Otto Heller
m: Carlo Martelli
md: Philip Martell
ed: James Needs, Eric Boyd Perkins
pd: Bernard Robinson
cos: Betty Adamson, John Briggs
sound: Claude Hitchcock
make-up: Roy Ashton
Ronald Howard, Terence Morgan, Fred Clark, Jeanne Roland, George Pastell, Jack Gwillim, John Paul, Dickie Owen (as the Mummy), Michael Ripper, Harold Goodwin

Curse of the Werewolf *

GB 1961 92m Technicolor
Having been raped by a raving beggar, a mute servant girl gives birth to a boy who grows up to become a werewolf.

Slow moving addition to the Hammer horror cycle which, despite goodish production values, is mostly ineffective, though Roy Ashton's werewolf make-up is superb. Filmed on sets originally intended for a film about the Spanish Inquisition to be called *The Rape of Sabena*, it was Hammer's only foray into lycanthropy.
p: Anthony Hinds for Hammer/Universal
exec p: Michael Carreras
w: John Elder (Anthony Hinds)
novel: Guy Endore
d: Terence Fisher
ph: Arthur Grant
m: Benjamin Frankel
md: John Hollingsworth
ed: James Needs, Alfred Cox
ad: Bernard Robinson
cos: Molly Arbuthnot
sp: Les Bowie
sound: Jock May
make-up: Roy Ashton
Oliver Reed, Clifford Evans, Catherine Feller, Yvonne Romain, Anthony Dawson, Richard Wordsworth, Warren Mitchell, Michael Ripper, Desmond Llewellyn, Peter Sallis

The Curse of the Wraydons

GB 1946 94m bw
In 1805 Epping, the locals live in fear of a vengeful killer known as Springheeled Jack.

Dated, highly theatrical barnstormer in the best/worst Slaughter tradition.
p: Gilbert Church, J. L. Jones for Bushey
w: Owen George
d: Victor M. Grover
ph: S. D. Onions
m: De Woolfe
ed: Victor M. Grover, John E. House
ad: Victor Hembrow
sound: K. Wiles
Tod Slaughter, Gabriel Toyne, Bruce Seton

Curtains

Canada 1983 88m colour
A star about to make a new film has a nervous breakdown, but the actresses lined up to replace her are murdered one by one.

A slasher pic from a slightly different angle. Unfortunately, it is rather artlessly put across.
p: Peter R. Simpson for Simcom/Curtains Productions
exec p: Richard Simpson
w: Robert Guza Jr
d: Jonathan Stryker (Richard Ciupka)
ph: Robert Paynter, Fred Guthe
m: Paul Zaza
ed: Michael McLaverty
pd: Ray Forge Smith
cos: Mary Jane McCarty
sp: Colin Chilvers
sound: Doug Ganton, Thomas Hidderley
make-up effects: Greg Cannom
Samantha Eggar, John Vernon, Linda Thorson, Lesley Donaldson, Lynne Griffin, Anne Ditchburn

Curtis, Dan (1928-)

American producer and director, perhaps best known for creating the daytime horror soap *Dark Shadows* (1966-1970), which led to a variety of genre productions for both television and the big screen, though he has since turned to large scale international productions, including *The Winds of War* and its sequel, *War and Remembrance*. He also created the horror series *Kolchak: The Night Stalker*. Other credits include *Melvin Purvis, G-Man*, and *The Raid on Coffeyville*.
Genre credits:
The Strange Case of Dr Jekyll and Mr Hyde (1968 - TVM - p), *House of Dark Shadows* (1970 - p/d), *Night of the Dark Shadows* (1971 - co-story/p/d), The Night Stalker (1972 - TVM - p), The Norliss Tapes (1973 - TVM - p), Frankenstein (1973 - TVM - p), *The Picture of Dorian Gray* (1973 - TVM - p), *The Turn of the Screw* (1974 - TVM - p/d), *Shadow of Fear* (1974 - TVM - p), *The Invasion of Carol Enders* (1974 - TVM - p), *Scream of the Wolf* (1974 - TVM - p/d), *Dracula* (1974 - TVM - p/d), *Trilogy of Terror* (1975 - TVM - p/d), *Burnt Offerings* (1976 - co-w/ p/d), *Curse of the Black Widow* (1977 - TVM - exec p/d), *Intruders* (1992 - p)

Curtis, Jamie Lee (1958-)

American actress, the daughter of actor Tony Curtis and actress Janet Leigh. Began working on television in the series *Operation Petticoat* before coming to prominence as a scream queen in a string of low-budget horror films, though she wisely decided to break away into mainstream films. Other credits include *Trading Places*, *A Fish Called Wanda*, *Forever Young* and *True Lies*.

key directors, his films are notable for their Germanic style and crisp photography.
Genre credits:
The Mad Genius (1931), *Dr X* (1932), *The Mystery of the Wax Museum* (1933), *The Walking Dead* (1936)

Cushing, Peter (1913-1994)

British actor who, along with Christopher Lee, came to personify Hammer Films, though he appeared in horror films for a variety of other companies. He began his professional life as a surveyor, but a keen interest in amateur dramatics led to his joining the Worthing Repertory Company. After four years' experience, he travelled to Hollywood on a one way ticket in 1939, gaining work on the Laurel and Hardy comedy *A Chump at Oxford* and as Louis Hayward's double in *The Man in the Iron Mask*. Returned to Britain in 1942 and joined ENSA for the duration, after which he was cast by Laurence Olivier as Osric in both his film and touring productions of *Hamlet*. In the fifties he fortuitously tied his career to television, in which he quickly became recognized for a series of memorable performances in such productions as *The Creature* and *1984* (as Winston Smith); the latter won him the British Television Actor of the Year award and led to his being cast as Baron Frankenstein in Hammer's 1956 film *The Curse of Frankenstein*. Following the success of this, Cushing became almost synonymously tied with the horror genre, particularly with the roles of Baron Frankenstein and vampire hunter Van Helsing. Many of the films he subsequently appeared in weren't worthy of his presence, but he always gave his best, his own mild persona earning him the nickname 'the gentleman of horror'. Meanwhile, in 1977, he found a whole new generation of fans when he played Grand Moff Tarkin in George Lucas's phenomenally successful *Star Wars*. His non-horror credits include *Fury at Smugglers' Bay*, *Dr Who and the Daleks* (as Dr Who), *Daleks Invasion Earth: 2150 A.D.*, *Shatter*, *Trial by Combat*, *Top Secret* and *Biggles*.
Genre credits:
The Curse of Frankenstein (1956), *The Abominable Snowman* (1957 - aka *The Abominable Snowman of the Himalayas*), *Dracula* (1958 - aka *The Horror of Dracula*), *The Hound of the Baskervilles* (1959 - as Sherlock Holmes), *The Mummy* (1959), *The Flesh and the Fiends* (1959 - aka *The Fiendish Ghouls / Mania / Psycho Killers*), *The Brides of Dracula* (1960), *The Hellfire Club*

(1962), *Captain Clegg* (1962 - aka *Night Creatures*), *The Evil of Frankenstein* (1964), *The Gorgon* (1964), *Dr Terror's House of Horrors* (1964), *She* (1965), *Dracula - Prince of Darkness* (1966 - prologue recap only), *The Skull* (1965), *Island of Terror* (1966), *Frankenstein Created Woman* (1967), *Night of the Big Heat* (1967 - aka *Island of the Burning Damned*), *The Torture Garden* (1967), *The Blood Beast Terror* (1967 - aka *The Vampire Beast Craves Blood*), *The Mummy's Shroud* (1967 - narrator), *Corruption* (1968), *One More Time* (1969 - gag cameo as Baron Frankenstein), *Frankenstein Must Be Destroyed* (1969), *Scream and Scream Again* (1970), *The Vampire Lovers* (1970), *I, Monster* (1970), *Bloodsuckers* (1970 - aka *Incense of the Damned*), *The House That Dripped Blood* (1970), *Twins of Evil* (1971), *Fear in the Night* (1972), *Asylum* (1972), *Dr Phibes Rises Again* (1972), *Nothing But the Night* (1972), *Dracula AD 1972* (1972), *Tales from the Crypt* (1972), *The Creeping Flesh* (1972), *Horror Express* (1972 - aka *Panico en el Transiberio*), *The Satanic Rites of Dracula* (1973), *Frankenstein and the Monster from Hell* (1973), *And Now the Screaming Starts* (1973), *From Beyond the Grave* (1973), *The Beast Must Die* (1974 - aka *Black Werewolf*), *The Legend of the Seven Golden Vampires* (1974 - aka *The Seven Brothers Meet Dracula*), *Tender Dracula* (1974 - aka *La Grand Trouille*), *Madhouse* (1974), *Legend of the Werewolf* (1975), *The Ghoul* (1975), *Death Corps* (1976 - aka *Almost Human / Shock Waves*), *The Devil's Men* (1976 - aka *Land of the Minotaur*), *At the Earth's Core* (1976), *The Uncanny* (1977), *The Mystery of Monster Island* (1980), *House of the Long Shadows* (1982)

Czech Mate

GB 1984 74m Technicolor TVM
A woman's husband disappears whilst they are in Prague and she finds herself in mortal danger.
   Watchable what's-going-on thriller, one of the better examples from the *Hammer House of Mystery and Suspense* series.
p: Roy Skeggs for Hammer/TCF
w: Jeremy Burnham
d: John Hough
ph: Brian West
m: John McCabe
md: Philip Martell
ed: Peter Weatherley
ad: Carolyn Scott
Susan George, Patrick Mower, Richard Heffer, Peter Vaughan, Stefan Gryff, Sandor Eles, Catherine Nielson

• **Scream queen Jamie Lee Curtis in a posed still on the set of *Halloween*, the John Carpenter classic that made her a star.**

Genre credits:
Halloween (1978), *The Fog* (1979), *Prom Night* (1980), *Terror Train* (1980), *Halloween II* (1981), *Road Games* (1981), *Mother's Boys* (1994)

Curtis, Tony

British art director with many Amicus credits to his name.
Genre credits:
The Sorcerers (1967), *I, Monster* (1970), *The House That Dripped Blood* (1970), *Asylum* (1972), *Vault of Horror* (1973), *And Now the Screaming Starts* (1973), *Madhouse* (1974), *The Monster Club* (1980)

Curtiz, Michael (1888-1962)

Hungarian director (real name Mihakly Kertesz) who began his career in 1912 with *The Last Bohemian*. He directed over fifty films in Hungary before moving to Hollywood, via Germany and France, where he also directed several features. Went to work for Warner Bros. in 1927, where his first film was *The Third Degree*, after which he gradually worked his way up to the top of his profession with such classics as *Captain Blood*, *The Charge of the Light Brigade*, *The Adventures of Robin Hood*, *Angels with Dirty Faces*, *The Sea Hawk*, *The Sea Wolf*, *Yankee Doodle Dandy*, *Casablanca* (which won him an Oscar) and *Mildred Pierce*. One of the cinema's

Dagover, Lil (1897-1980)

German leading lady who was memorable as the abducted Jane in *The Cabinet of Dr Caligari* in 1919. She made her film début earlier the same year in Fritz Lang's *Harakiri*. Her other credits include *Destiny*, *Orient Express* and *End of the Game* (aka *Der Richter und sein Henker*)
Genre credits:
The Cabinet of Dr Caligari (1919), *Doctor Mabuse, The Gambler* (1922 - aka *Doctor Mabuse, Der Spieler*), *Phantom* (1922)

Dallesandro, Joe (1948-)

American actor, noted for his appearances in the films of Andy Warhol (*Flesh*, *Trash*, *Heat*, *Lonesome Cowboys*, etc.) as well as such other films as *The Cotton Club*, *Sunset*, *Cry-Baby* and *Sugar Hill*.
Genre credits:
Andy Warhol's Frankenstein (1974 - aka *Flesh for Frankenstein*), *Andy Warhol's Dracula* (1974 - aka *Blood for Dracula*), *Killer Nun* (1978 - aka *Suor Omicidi*)

D'Amato, Joe (1936-)

Italian exploitation director (real name Aristide Massaccesi) who works under such pseudonyms as Kevin Mancuso, Steve Benson, David Hills and Michael Wotruba. Was responsible for much of the *Black Emanuelle* series of the seventies and the *Ator* series of the eighties.
Genre credits:
Emanuelle and the Last Cannibals (1977 - aka *Trap Them and Kill Them/Emanuelle e Gli Ultimi Cannibali*), *Beyond the Darkness* (1979 - aka *Buio Omega*), *The Anthropophagus Beast* (1980 - aka *Grim Reaper/Anthropophagus*), *Buried Alive* (1984), *Return from Death* (1991)

Damiani, Damiano (1922-)

Italian director with plenty of action films to his credit.
Genre credits:
Amityville II: The Possession (1982)

Damien: Omen II *

USA 1978 109m DeLuxe Panavision
Now a teenager, Antichrist Damien Thorn continues on his path of death and destruction.

Lively sequel to *The Omen*, inventively enough staged, though little more than a rehash of the first movie. Also see *The Final Conflict* (1981) and *Omen IV: The Awakening* (1991).
p: Harvey Bernhard for TCF
exec p: Mace Neufeld
w: Stanley Mann, Michael Hodges (the film's original director)
story: Harveu Bernhard
d: DON TAYLOR
ph: Bill Butler, Gilbert Taylor
m: JERRY GOLDSMITH
md: Lionel Newman
ed: Robert Brown, Jr
pd: Philip M. Jeffries, Fred Harpman
cos: Burton Miller
sp: Ira Anderson Jr, Chuck Taylor
sound: Al Overton
stunt co-ordinator: Max Kleven
effects ph: Stanley Cortez
William Holden, Lee Grant, Jonathan Scott Taylor (as Damien), Robert Foxworth, Lucas Donat, Lew Ayres, Sylvia Sidney, Elizabeth Shepherd, Nicholas Pryor

Damon, Mark (1935-)

American actor remembered for playing Philip Winthrop in Roger Corman's *The Fall of the House of Usher*. He appeared in several other horror films and as a support in the likes of *The Longest Day*, *This Rebel Breed*, *The Young Racers* and *Anzio* before becoming a successful producer with such films as *The Choirboys*, *The Never Ending Story*, *Short Circuit*, *The Lost Boys*, *High Spirits*, *9 1/2 Weeks*, *Mac and Me*, *Wild Orchid* and *Wild Orchid II: Two Shades of Blue*.
Genre credits:
The Fall of the House of Usher (1960 - aka *House of Usher*), *Beauty and the Beast* (1963), *Black Sabbath* (1963), *The Devil's Wedding Night* (1973 - aka *Il Pleniluno delle Vergini*), *Crypt of the Living Dead* (1973 - aka *Queen of the Vampires*)

Dance of the Vampires see The Fearless Vampire Killers

Danning, Sybil (1950-)

Curvaceous Austrian born actress with many low-budget and exploitation films

to her credit including *Jungle Warriors*, *The Seven Magnificent Gladiators* and *Amazon Women on the Moon*. Other credits include *The Three Musketeers*, *The Four Musketeers*, *The Prince and the Pauper*, *Meteor* and *Battle Beyond the Stars*.
Genre credits:
Bluebeard (1972), *Howling II: Your Sister is a Werewolf* (1986), *The Tomb* (1986)

Dano, Royal (1922-1994)

American character actor, most memorable as the tattered soldier in John Huston's *Red Badge of Courage*. Other credits include *Johnny Guitar*, *Moby Dick*, *Huckleberry Finn* and *Hammett*.
Genre credits:
The Seven Faces of Dr Lao (1964), *Moon of the Wolf* (1972 - TVM), *Messiah of Evil* (1976), *Something Wicked This Way Comes* (1983), *Ghoulies II* (1988), *The Dark Half* (1993)

Dante, Joe (1947-)

American director with a penchant for big-budget fantasy films crammed with cameos from old time actors (Dick Miller, Kenneth Tobey, etc.). Following experience as a journalist he went to work for Roger Corman, for whom he edited together trailers. He made his directorial début in 1977 for Corman, co-directing (with Allan Arkush) *Hollywood Boulevard*, which he also co-edited. He had a hit with the *Jaws* rip off *Piranha*, which in turn led to the equally successful *Howling*, to which it was but a short step to *Gremlins*. His other credits include *Explorers*, *Innerspace*, *Amazon Women on the Moon*, *The Burbs* and *Matinee*.
Genre credits:
Piranha (1978 - co-ed/d), *The Howling* (1981 - co-ed/d), *Twilight Zone: The Movie* (1983 - co-d), *Gremlins* (1984 - d), *Gremlins 2: The New Batch* (1990 - d), *Sleepwalkers* (1992 - actor)

Dante's Inferno **

USA 1935 89m bw
An out of work stoker hits it rich when he joins a carnival sideshow.

Visually striking melodrama, most notable for its vision of hell sequence

and a climax on board a blazing ship.
p: Sol M. Wurtzel for TCF
w: Philip Klein, Robert M. Yost
d: HARRY LACHMAN
ph: RUDOLPH MATE
md: Samuel Kaylin
ed: Al de Gaetano
ad: DUNCAN CRAMER, DAVID S. HALL
cos: Royer
sp: Fred M. Sersen, Ralph Hammeras, Louis J. White
sound: George Leverett
ch: Sammy Lee
SPENCER TRACY, Claire Trevor, Henry B. Walthall, Alan Dinehart, Scott Beckett, Rita Cansino (Rita Hayworth)

Darabont, Frank
American writer and director who received much praise for writing and directing *The Shawshank Redemption*. Genre credits:
A Nightmare on Elm Street Part Three: The Dream Warriors (1987 - co-w), *The Blob* (1988 - co-w), *The Fly II* (1989 - co-w), *Buried Alive* (1990 - TVM - d), *Mary Shelley's Frankenstein* (1994 - co-w)

The Dark (1969) see The Haunted House of Horror

The Dark
USA 1979 92m Technicolor Panavision
A chameleon like alien roams Los Angeles in search of victims.
　Indifferently directed hokum with all elements strictly routine.
p: Edward L. Montoro, Dick Clark for Film Ventures International
exec p: Derek Power
w: Standford Whitmore
d: John Cardos
ph: John Morrill
m: Roger Kellaway
ed: Martin Dreffke
ad: no credit given
cos: Valrae, Eva Paulette Frye
sp: Robby Knott, Harry Moreau, Peter Kuran
sound: Robert Dietz
2nd unit d: Ray Clevenger
2nd unit ph: Les Frost
stunt co-ordinator: Bobby Clark
titles: Dave Tate.
make-up effects: Steve Neil
William Devane, Cathy Lee Crosby, Richard Jaekel, Keenen Wynn, Vivian Blaine

Dark Eyes of London *
GB 1939 75m bw
A blind mute is used to drown wealthy policy holders so that his master can collect on the insurance.
　Enjoyably dated horror hokum.

p: John Argyle for Pather / Argyle
w: John Argyle, Walter Summers, Patrick Kirwan
novel: Edgar Wallace
d: WALTER SUMMERS
ph: Bryan Langley
m: Guy Jones
ed: E. G. Richards
ad: Duncan Sutherland
sound: H. Benson, A. E. Rudolph
Bela Lugosi, Hugh Williams, Greta Gynt, Wilfred Walter, Edmond Ryan

The Dark Half
USA 1991 121m DeLuxe Dolby
A writer finds himself threatened by his murderous alter ego.
　Over stretched horror story which plays like a cross between *Misery* and *The Birds*. Tolerable of its kind.
p: Declan Baldwin for Orion
exec p: George A. Romero
w/d: George A. Romero
novel: Stephen King
ph: Tony Pierce-Roberts
m: Christopher Young
ed: Pasquale Buba
pd: Cletus Anderson
cos: Barbara Anderson
sound: Gregory H. Watkins, Carlos de Larios, Bill W. Benton
make-up effects: John Vulick, Everett Burrell
Timothy Hutton, Amy Madigan, Michael Rooker, Julie Harris, Patrick Brannan

Dark Waters
It / USSR 1993 99m colour
An English heiress travels to a remote abbey to visit her friend and finds herself amid murder and demon worship.
　Good looking but risibly plotted shocker which tries too hard to emulate the Argento style.
p: Victor Zuev for Tea and Co. / Mosfilm / Belarius / A. Dovzhenko / Gidropribor Plant / Teleserial / Kinotechnika / Pontida / Odessafilm / Aquapolis / Institute of Cinematography
exec p: Svetlana Polyarush, Igor Trimasov
w: Mariano Baino, Andrew M. Bank
d: Mariano Baino
ph: Alex Howe
m: Igor Clark
ed: Mariano Baino, Rick Littler
ad: Ivan Pulenko
cos: Antonina Petrova
sound: Josef Goldman
make-up effects: Richard Field, David Mundin
Louise Salter, Maria Kapnist, Venera Simmons, Valeriy Bassel, Sergey Rugens

Darkman *
USA 1990 91m DeLuxe Dolby
A scientist working to perfect a form of

synthetic skin is hideously deformed when his laboratory is blown up by gangsters, but he later uses his invention to gain revenge.
　Quirky horror comic, basically an excuse for its director to show off his technical flair, which he does somewhat relentlessly. Amusing touches along the way, though. It was later followed by *Darkman 2: The Return of Darkman* and *Die, Darkman, Die!*
p: Robert Tapert for Universal / Renaissance
w: Chuck Pfarrar, Sam Raimi, Ivan Raimi, Daniel Goldin, Joshua Goldin
d/story: Sam Raimi
ph: Bill Pope
m: Danny Elfman
ed: Bud Smith, Scott Smith
pd: Randy Ser
cos: Grania Preston
sp: Spectacular Effects Unlimited
sound: Don Summer
2nd unit ph: Peter Deming
stunt co-ordinator: Chris Doyle
Liam Neeson, Frances McDormand, Colin Friels, Larry Drake, Nelson Mashita, Theodore Raimi, Danny Hicks, Rafael H. Robledo, Bruce Campbell

Daughter of Darkness
USA 1989 96m Technicolor TVM
A young woman travels to Romania to search for her long lost father and finds herself up to her neck with vampires.
　Predictable horror fare which never quite takes off. Also, too little is made of the locations.
p: Andra Hamori for Accent / King Phoenix Entertainment
w: Andrew Laskos
d: Stuart Gordon
ph: Ivan Mark
m: Colin Towns
ed: Andy Horvitch
cos: Eva Lord
Mia Sara, Anthony Perkins, Robert Reynolds, Jack Coleman, Erika Bodnar, Dezso Garas

Daughter of the Mind *
USA 1969 74m Technicolor TVM
A scientist believes he has seen the ghost of his recently deceased daughter, but an investigation reveals foul play.
　Acceptable mystery thriller, quite well done of its kind.
p: Walter Grauman for TCF
w: Luther Davis
novel: Paul Gallico
d: Walter Grauman
ph: Jack Woolf
m: Robert Drasnin
ad: Jack Martin Smith, Philip Barber
Ray Milland, Gene Tierney, Don Murray, George Macready, John Carradine

Daughters of Darkness
Belgium/Fr/Ger 1970 98m
Eastmancolor
Newlyweds waylaid at an Ostend hotel
fall victim to the Countess Bathory and
her companion.

Unremarkable erotic horror which
seems to have gained cult status in some
circles. The story is perhaps better
known as the not much better *Countess
Dracula*.
p: Henry Lange, Paul Collet for
Showking/Maya/Roxy/Cine Vog
exec p: Alain-Claude Guilleaume
w: Pierre Drouot, Jean Ferry, Harry
Kumel, Jo Amiel
d: Harry Kumel
ph: Edward Van Der Roubaix
m: Francois de Roubaix
ed: Gust Verscheuren, Denis Bonan
ad: Francoise Hardy
cos: Bertrand Perris
sp: Eudene Hendricks, Thierry Hallard
sound: Jack Eippers
Delphine Seyrig, Daniele Quimet, John
Karlen, Andree Rau, Paul Esser, Georges
Jamin

Davis, Bette (1908-1989)
Celebrated American star actress,
twice an Oscar winner (for *Dangerous*
and *Jezebel*), and top box office
attraction of the thirties and forties.
When her career began to slide in the
sixties, she turned to the horror genre
with *Whatever Happened to Baby Jane?*
the success of which recharged her
career. Further genre outings
subsequently followed.
Genre credits:
Whatever Happened to Baby Jane?
(1962), *Hush... Hush, Sweet Charlotte*
(1964), *The Nanny* (1965), *Scream,
Pretty Peggy* (1974 - TVM), *Burnt
Offerings* (1976), *The Dark Secret of
Harvest Home* (1978 - TVM), *Return
from Witch Mountain* (1978), *The
Watcher in the Woods* (1980), *Wicked
Stepmother* (1989)

Davis, Geena (1957-)
Respected American leading lady,
notable in *The Accidental Tourist* (which
won her a Best Supporting Actress
Oscar), *Thelma and Louise* and *A League of
Their Own*.
Genre credits:
Transylvania 6-5,000 (1984), *The Fly*
(1986), *Beetlejuice* (1988)

Davis, Warwick
Diminutive British actor who came to
attention as the title character in George
Lucas's *Willow* in 1988, following work
on Lucas's *Return of the Jedi*.
Leprechaun (1992), *Leprechaun II: Bride of*

the *Leprechaun* (1993 - aka *One Wedding
and Lots of Funerals*), *Leprechaun 3* (1994)

Dawn of the Dead
USA 1979 127m Technicolor
Survivors of a zombie onslaught take
refuge in a large shopping mall.

Overstretched and rather artless
follow up to Romero's groundbreaking
Night of the Living Dead that is
nevertheless held in high esteem in
some quarters. A few good moments
among the longueurs for gore-hounds. It
was followed in 1985 by *Day of the Dead*.
A European cut of the film was overseen
by Dario Argento.
p: Richard P. Rubinstein for Laurel/
Target/Dawn Associates
w/d/ed: George A. Romero
ph: Michael Gornick
m: Goblin, Dario Argento
ad: Barbara Lifsher, Jodie Caruso
cos: Josie Caruso
sound: Tony Buba
make-up effects: Tom Savini
script consultant: Dario Argento
David Emge, Ken Force, Scott H.
Reininger, Gaylen Ross, George A.
Romero, Tom Savini

Dawn of the Mummy
USA 1981 88m Technicolor
A group of models, in Egypt for a fashion shoot, find themselves prey to a
murderous mummy whose tomb has
been desecrated.

Laughably inept nonsense with over-
the-top performances - on which count
it is quite enjoyable.
p: Frank Agrama for Harmony Gold
exec p: Lew Horwitz
w: Frank Agrama, David Price, Ronald
Dobrin
story: David Price, Ronald Dobrin
d: Frank Agrama
ph: Sergio Rubini
m: Shuki Y. Levy
ed: Jonathan Braum
ad: Maher Abdel Nour
cos: Sousou
sp: Luigi Batistelli, Farid Abdoul Hai,
Tony Di Dio Jr
sound: Allan Emara, Andrew Kramer,
Dan McIntire
2nd unit d: Ahmed Sabawi
Barry Sattels, Brenda King, George
Peck, Ellene Faison, John Salvo, Joan
Levy

Dawson, Anthony M. see Antonio
Margheriti

The Day It Came to Earth
USA 1979 84m colour
Two college students help destroy a zom-
bie reactivated by a crashed meteorite.

Dismal low-budget schlocker.
Enough said.
p: John Braden for Rainbow/Atlas
exec p: Harry Thomason
w: Paul J. Fisk
d: Harry Thomason
ph: Mike Varner
m: Joe Southerland
ed: LeRoy Slaughter
ad: Mike Frey
Wink Roberts, Roger Manning, Bob
Ginnaven, Delight de Bruine, Rita
Wilson, George Gobel

Day of the Animals
USA 1976 DeLuxe Todd AO
A party of climbers is mysteriously
attacked by a variety of animals whilst
walking through the High Sierras.

Artless exploitation piece, somewhat
typical of its director. At no point does it
ever approach Hitchcock's *The Birds*,
after which it was all too obviously
patterned.
p: Edward L. Montero for Film Ventures
International
w: Edwin Norton, Eleanor Norton
story: Edwin Norton
d: William Girdler
ph: Robert Sorrentino
ed: Bub Asman, James Mitchell
ad: no credit given
cos: Michael Faeth
sp: Sam Burney
sound: Sally Rodin
2nd unit ph: Tom McHugh
Christopher George, Leslie Nielsen,
Lynda Day George, Richard Jaeckel,
Ruth Roman, Michael Ansara, Andrew
Stevens

Day of the Dead
USA 1986 120m Technicolor
A handful of survivors lock themselves
away in an underground bunker when
the world is taken over by carniverous
zombies.

The third entry in Romero's zombie
cycle is unfortunately as tedious as it is
gruesome. Also see *Night of the Living
Dead* and *Dawn of the Dead*.
p: Richard P. Rubinstein, Daniel Ball for
Laurel
w/d: George A. Romero
ph: Michael Gornick
m: John Harrison
ed: Pasquale Buba
pd: Cletius Anderson
cos: Barbara Anderson
make-up effects: Tom Savini
Lori Cardille, Terry Alexander, Joe
Pilato, Jarlath Conroy, Antoine DiLeo,
Richard Liberty, Howard Sherman

The Day the Screaming
Stopped see The Comeback

The Day the World Ended
USA 1955 82m bw Scope
Survivors of a nuclear war find
themselves threatened by mutants.

Grade Z nonsense, for Corman
completists only.
p: Roger Corman for Golden State
exec p: James H. Nicholson, Samuel Z.
Arkoff
w: Lou Rusoff
d: Roger Corman
ph: Jock Feindel
m: Ronald Stein
ed: Ronald Sinclair
ad: no credit given
cos: Gertrude Reai
sp: Paul Blaisdell
sound: Jean Speak
Richard Denning, Lori Nelson, Adele
Jergens, Touch (Mike) Connors, Paul
Birch, Raymond Hatton, Paul Dubov,
Paul Blaisdell, Jonathan Haze

De Carlo, Yvonne (1922-)
Canadian actress (real name Peggy
Middleton), best known for playing Lily
in TV's The Munsters. A glamorous
leading lady in the forties and fifties, she
appeared in a mixture of 'easterns'
(Salome Where She Danced, The Song of
Scheherezade, Casbah) and westerns (Black
Bart [aka Black Bart, Highwayman],
Calamity Jane and Sombrero). Her other
credits include Criss Cross, The Ten
Commandments, McLintock, The Man with
Bogart's Face and Oscar.
Genre credits:
Munster, Go Home! (1966 - TVM), The
Power (1967), Satan's Cheerleaders (1977),
Nocturna (1979 - aka Nocturna, Dracula's
Granddaughter), Silent Scream (1980), The
Munsters' Revenge (1981 - TVM), Play
Dead (1983), American Gothic (1987),
Cellar Dweller (1988), Mirror, Mirror
(1991)

De Coteau, David (1964-)
American producer and director who
began his career as a production assistant
to Roger Corman. He made his
directorial début in the hard core adult
market before crossing over into the
horror genre with Dreamaniac in 1986
for Full Moon producer Charles Band,
for whom he has since made several
more genre titles (including a handful of
soft core entries for Band's subsidiary
label Torchlight). His other credits
include Linnea Quigley's Horror Work Out,
Crash and Burn, Shock Cinema Volume One,
Shock Cinema Volume Two, Steel and Lace,
Virgin Hunters, Beach Babes from Beyond,
Huntress and Blonde Heaven.
Genre credits:
Dreamaniac (1986 - d), Creepozoids (1987
- d), Sorority Babes in the Slime

Bowl-a-Rama (1987 - d), Nightmare Sisters
(1987 - d), Assault of the Killer Bimbos
(1987 - d), Deadly Embrace (1987 - d),
Murder Weapon (1988 - d [as Ellen
Cabot!]), Dr Alien (1988 - aka I Was a
Teenage Sex Mutant - d), Ghostwriter
(1989 - p), Skinned Alive (1990 - d),
Puppetmaster II (1991 - p), Ghoul School
(1991 - p), Beasties (1992 - d), Trancers
II: The Two Faces of Jack Deth (1992 - p),
Puppetmaster III: Toulon's Revenge (1992 -
p/d)

De Laurentiis, Dino (1919-)
Italian producer and executive with
many big-budget international
spectaculars to his credit including
Barabbas, The Bible, Waterloo, The Bounty
and Dune.
Genre credits:
King Kong (1976), Orca - Killer Whale
(1977), The Dead Zone (1983), Cat's Eye
(1985), Manhunter (1986), Evil Dead 2:
Dead by Dawn (1986), Army of Darkness
(1992 - aka The Medieval Dead/Evil Dead
III: The Medieval Dead)

De Ossorio, Armando (1926-)
Spanish writer and director, responsible
for the Blind Dead series about the
Knights Templar. He began directing in
1956 with the short La Bandera Negra.
He turned to features in 1963 with La
Tumba del Pistolero, though it would be
nearly a decade before he made his first
Blind Dead epic in 1971. His other
credits include Noche de Embrujo (short),
Rebeldes en Canada (documentary), Pasto
de Fieras, La Nina de Patio and Pasion
Prohibida.
Genre credits:
Fangs of the Living Dead (1968 - aka
Malenka/Malenka, Niece of the Vampire/La
Sobrina del Vampiro - w/d), Tombs of the
Blind Dead (1971 - aka The Blind
Dead/Tombs of the Blind Zombies/Night of
the Blind Dead/Those Cruel and Bloody
Vampires/Crypt of the Blind Dead/La
Noche del Terror Ciego - w/d), When the
Screaming Stops (1973 - aka The Lorelei's
Grasp/Las Garras de Lorelei -w/d), Return
of the Evil Dead (1973 - aka Return of the
Blind Dead/Revenge of the Evil
Dead/Attack of the Eyeless Dead/El Ataque
de los Muertos Sin Ojos - w/d), Night of
the Sorcerers (1973 - aka La Noche de los
Brujos - d), Ghost Ship of the Blind Dead
(1974 - aka Ship of Zombies/Horror of the
Zombies/Ghost Galleon/El Buque Maldito -
d), The Possessed (1974 - aka Demon Witch
Child/La Endemoniada - d), Night of the
Seagulls (1975 - aka Bloodfeast of the Blind
Dead/Night of the Death Cult/Terror
Beach/La Noche de las Gaviotas - w/d),
The Sea Serpent (1985 - aka Hydra, the Sea
Serpent/Serpiente de Mar - d)

De Palma, Brian (1940-)
American writer, director and producer
who, in the seventies, directed a number
of effective Hitchcockian thrillers and
horror films before moving on to more
serious projects such as Scarface, The
Untouchables, Casualties of War, Bonfire of
the Vanities and Carlito's Way.
Genre credits:
Sisters (1973 - aka Blood Sisters -
co-w/d), The Phantom of the Paradise
(1974 - w/d), Carrie (1976 - d), The
Fury (1978 - d), Dressed to Kill (1980 -
w/d)

De Wit, Louis
American special effects technician with
several low-budget credits to his name.
Genre credits:
The Black Sleep (1956 - co-sp), Pharaoh's
Curse (1956 - co-sp), Macabre (1957 -
co-sp), The Monster from Green Hell (1957
- co-sp), Behemoth the Sea Monster (1958 -
aka The Giant Behemoth - co-sp),

Dead and Buried
USA 1981 98m Technicolor Panavision
In a small seaside town, the inhabitants
kill all visitors whom the local mortician
then turns into living corpses.

Tasteless horror story, poorly done
and with the graphic detail expected
from this period.
p: Ronald Shusett, Robert Fentress for
Richard R. St. Johns, Ronald Shusett
Productions
w: Ronald Shusett, Dan O'Bannon
d: Gary A. Sherman
ph: Steve Poster
m: Joe Renzetti
ed: Alan Balsam
ad: Bill Sandell, Joe Aubel
make-up effects: Stan Winston
James Farrentino, Jack Albertson,
Melody Anderson, Dennis Redfield,
Nancy Locke Hauser

The Dead Don't Die *
USA 1975 74m Technicolor TVM
In 1934, a man wrongly executed for
murder returns from the grave to reveal
the real culprit.

Mild attempt to resurrect the old
Karloff-Lugosi type of chiller from the
thirties and forties. Some scares, but
more overall style was needed.
p: Henry Colman for Douglas S.
Cramer Productions
exec p: W. L. Baums
w: Robert Bloch
d: Curtis Harrington
ph: James Crabe
George Hamilton, Ray Milland, Ralph
Meeker, Joan Blondell, Linda Cristal,
James McEachin

Dead of Night ★★★★

GB 1945 104m bw

An architect visits a country house about which he has been having a recurring dream, is told five supernatural stories by the people he meets there, and then wakes up, only to find the whole thing starting over again.

Superior horror compendium with just the right mixture of chills, thrills and laughter. Excellent stories (the most famous one involving a ventriloquist's dummy), polished production and a cleverly engineered sting in the tail make this a model of its kind. Its premise was much copied in the sixties and seventies with such films as *Dr Terror's House of Horrors*, *Torture Garden*, *Asylum* and *Vault of Horror*.

p: MICHAEL BALCON for Ealing
w: JOHN BAINES, ANGUS MACPAHIL, T. E. B. CLARK
stories: H. G. Wells, E. F. Benson, John Baines, Angus Macpahil
d: CHARLES CRICHTON, BASIL DEARDEN, ALBERTO CAVALCANTI, ROBERT HAMER
ph: STAN PAVEY, DOUGLAS SLOCOMBE
m: GEORGES AURIC
ed: Charles Hasse
ad: MICHAEL RELPH
cos: Bianca Mosca, Marion Horn
sp: Cliff Richardson, L. Banes
sound: Eric Williams, Len Page, A. E. Rudolph
MERVYN JOHNS, ROLAND CULVER, MARY MERRALL, GOOGIE WITHERS, SALLY ANNE HOWES, Judy Kelly, Anthony Baird, MICHAEL RÉDGRAVE, FRÉDERICK VALK, BASIL RADFORD, NAUNTON WAYNE, Ralph Michael, Esme Percy, Miles Malleson, Elizabeth Welch, Hartley Power, Peter Jones

The Dead Pit

USA 1989 98m colour

A mad doctor with a penchant for performing lobotomies without anaesthetic returns from the dead to wreak even more havoc.

Low-budget schlock horror, bereft of both wit and style.

p: Imperial Entertainmet
d: Brett Leonard
Cheryl Lawson, Jeremy Slate, Danny Gochnauer, Steffen Gregory Foster, Joan Bechtel, Geha Getz

The Dead Zone ★★

USA 1983 103m Technicolor Dolby

After a near fatal road accident, a teacher discovers that he has psychic powers.

Slick psychic thriller which does quite well by its theme and certainly comes off a lot better than most of the King adaptations of this period. Strong performances also an asset.

p: Debra Hill for Lorimar
exec p: Dino de Laurentis
w: Jeffrey Boam
novel: Stephen King
d: DAVID CRONENBERG
ph: MARK IRWIN
m: MICHAEL KAMEN
ed: Ronald Sanders
pd: Carol Spier
cos: Olga Dimitrov
sp: Jon Belyeu, Calvin Acord
sound: Bryan Day
sound ed: David Yewdall
titles: Robert Greenberg
stunt co-ordinator: Dick Warlock, Carey Loftin
CHRISTOPHER WALKEN, Brooke Adams, HERBERT LOM, MARTIN SHEEN, Tom Skerritt, Anthony Zerbe, Colleen Dewhurst, Nicholas Campbell, Sean Sullivan, Jackie Burroughas, Geza Kovacs, Simon Craig

Deadly Blessing

USA 1981 103m Metroclor

Members of a Hittite sect are murdered by an incubus.

Good looking but mostly ineffective horror story with a few mild shocks for addicts.

p: William Gilmore for UA/Polygram/Inter Planetary
exec p: Jack Marty
w: Glenn M. Benest, Matthew Barr, Wes Craven
story: Glenn M. Benest, Matthew Starrt
d: Wes Craven
ph: Robert Jessup
m: James Horner
ed: Richard Bracken
pd: Jack Marty
cos: Patricia McKiernan
sp: Jack Bennett
sound: Bob Wald
Maren Jensen, Ernest Borgnine, Susan Buckner, Jeff East, Lois Nettleton, Lisa Hartman

Deadly Eyes

Canada 1982 87m colour

A horde of giant rats, the product of toxic waste, infest Toronto.

Just about tolerable version of James Herbert's book *The Rats*, with dachshunds playing the rats! Generally padded, but with a few tense sequences along the way, including a subway-set finale.

p: Jeffrey Schechtman, Paul Kahmert for Northshore/J. G. Arnold Associates Ltd/ACFC
exec p: J. Gordon Arnold
w: Charles Eglee, London Smith
novel: James Herbert
d: Robert Clouse
ph: René Verzier
m: Anthony Guefen
ed: Ron Wisman
ad: Ninkey Dalton
cos: Sharon Purdy
sound: Stuart French
make-up effects: Allan A. Apone and others
Sam Groom, Sara Botsford, Lisa Langlois, Cec Linder, Scatman Crothers, Lesley Donaldson

Deadly Friend

USA 1986 99m Technicolor

A teenager revives his dead girlfriend and turns her into a robot so that she can avenge herself.

More silly than frightening, this off-beat shocker is something of a disappointment given that it was directed by *A Nightmare on Elm Street*'s Wes Craven.

p: Robert M. Sherman for Warner/Pan Arts
w: Bruce Joel Rubin
novel: Diana Hensetll
d: Wes Craven
ph: Philip Lathrop
m: Charles Bernstein
ed: Michael Eliot
pd: Daniel Lomino
cos: Barton Kent James, Carole Brown-James
sound: Richard Church
titles: Dan Perri
stunt co-ordinator: Terry Leonard, Tony Cecere
Kristy Swanson, Matthew Laborteaux, Anne Twomey, Michael Sharrett, Richard Marcus, Anne Ramsey

Death Becomes Her ★★

USA 1992 103m DeLuxe Dolby

The film star wife of an eminent plastic surgeon resorts to black magic to retain her looks, but with drastic consequences.

Lively, technically adroit black comedy with superior effects work and game performances.

p: Robert Zemeckis, Steve Starkey for Universal
w: Martin Donovan, David Koepp
d: Robert Zemeckis
ph: Dean Cundey
m: Alan Silvestri
ed: Arthur Schmidt
pd: Rick Carter
cos: Joanna Johnston
sp: Ken Ralston, Doug Chiang, Doug Smythe, Tom Woodruff (aa)
sound: William B. Kaplan
make-up effects: Dick Smith, Kevin Haney, Tom Woodruff Jr, Alec Gillis
2nd unit d: Max Kleven, Ken Ralston
Meryl Streep, Bruce Willis, Goldie

Hawn, Isabella Rossellini, Ian Ogilvy, Adam Storke, Nancy Fish, Alaina Reed Hall, Mary Ellen Trainor, Jonathan Silverman, Sidney Pollack

Death Corps see Shock Waves

Death House see Silent Night, Bloody Night

Death Line
GB 1972 87m Technicolor
Police investigating a series of disappearances on London's underground system discover the culprits to be a group of subterranean cannibals.

Tacky horror flick with no redeeming features, though some consider it a cult item.
p: Paul Maslansky for K-L
w: Ceri Jones
d/story: Gary Sherman
ph: Alex Thomson
m: Jeremy Rose, Wil Malone
ed: Geoffrey Foot
ad: Danis Gordon-Orr
sp: John Horton
sound: Cyril Collick
make-up: Harry Frampton
Donald Pleasence, Christopher Lee, Norman Rossington, David Ladd, Sharon Gurney, Hugh Armstrong, James Cossins, June Turner, Clive Swift, Heather Stoney

Death Ship
Canada 1980 91m Technicolor
Shipwreck survivors take refuge on an empty ship, which then sets about killing them one by one.

Unspeakably dreadful variation on a theme already explored in *The Car* and *Killdozer*.
p: Derek Gibson, Harold Greenberg for Astral Bellevue
Pathe/Bloodstar/Lamitas
w: John Robins
d: Alvin Rakoff
ph: Rene Verzier
m: Ivor Slaney
ed: Mike Campbell
pd: Chris Burke
sp: Mike Albrechtsen, Peter Hughes
sound: Bill Trent
George Kennedy, Richard Crenna, Sally Ann Howes, Nick Mancuso, Kate Reid, Jennifer McKinney

Death Trap
USA 1974 89m Technicolor
At a lonely motel, the proprietor viciously murders his guests and feeds them to an enormous crocodile.

Sadistic cheapjack horror of the most boring and tasteless kind.
p: Alvin L. Fast, Mardi Rustam

w: Alvin L. Fast, Mardi Rustam, Kim Henkel
d: Tobe Hooper
ph: Robert Caramaco
m: Tobe Hooper, Wayne Bell
ed: Michael Brown
Neville Brand, Mel Ferrer, Carolyn Jones, Stuart Whitman

Death Valley
USA 1981 88m Technicolor
A killer threatens a family holidaying in Death Valley.

Routine shocker with only the child's performance worth noting.
p: Elliott Kastner, Richard Rothstein, Stanley Beck for Universal
w: Richard Rothstein
d: Dick Richards
ph: Stephen H. Burum
m: Dana Kaproff
ed: Joel Cox
pd: Allen H. Jones
cos: Patrick Cummings
sound: James E. Webb Jr, Donald O. Mitchell
titles: Wayne Fitzgerald
stunt co-ordinator: Whitey Hughes
Paul Le Mat, Catherine Hicks, Stephen McHattie, PETER BILLINGSLEY, Edward Herrmann, A. Wilford Brimley

Deep Red **
It 1976 98m/105m/120m
Eastmancolor Panavision
A passerby witnesses a violent murder and decides to investigate it himself but the clues he discovers become more puzzling as he progresses.

Despite poor dubbing in the English version, this is a compellingly plotted thriller with an abundance of macabre events and plenty of dexterous camerawork. Required viewing for Argento buffs.
p: Claudio Argento for Rizzilio/Techni
exec p: Salvatore Argento
w: Dario Argento, Bernardino Zapponi
d: DARIO ARGENTO
ph: Luigio Kuveiller
m: Giorgio Gaslini, Goblin
ed: Franco Fraticelli
pd: Giuseppe Bassan
sp: Carlo Rambaldi, Germano Natali
sound: Mario Faraoni
David Hemmings, Daria Nicolodi, Gabrielle Lavia, Macha Meril, Eros Pagni

Deezen, Eddie
American actor who specializes in geeks, most memorably in *I Wanna Hold Your Hand* and *1941*. Now turning to horror films, his other credits include *War Games*, *Desperate Moves* and *The Rosebud Beach Hotel*.

Genre credits:
A Polish Vampire in Burbank (1985), *Beverly Hills Vamp* (1988)

Dekker, Albert (1905-1968)
American character actor, remembered for playing the title role in *Dr Cyclops* (1940). His other credits include *The Great Garrick*, *Among the Living*, *The Killers*, *The Silver Chalice*, *Suddenly Last Summer* and *The Wild Bunch*.

Dekker, Fred (1959-)
American writer and director who began his career with a couple of quirky low-budget horror comics. His other credits include *Robocop 3*.
Genre credits:
Night of the Creeps (1986 - w/d), *The Monster Squad* (1987 - co-w/d)

Deleria see Stage Fright

Demented
USA 1980 89m colour
A doctor's wife goes on a killing spree after being gang raped.

Sleazy shocker with little to recommend it.
p: Sandy Cobe, Arthur Jeffries, Mike Smith for IWDC/Four Features Partners Ltd
exec p: Alex Rebar, Rick Whitfield
w: Alex Rebar
d: Arthur Jeffreys
ph: Jim Tynes
m: Richard Tufo
ed: William J. Waters
ad: no credit given
cos: Bryan Ryman
sound: Bob Fisher
Sallee Elyse, Bruce Gilchrist, Deborah Altar, Bryan Charles, Chip Matthews, Kathryn Clayton

The Demon
South Africa 1981 93m colour
A psychic tracks down a maniac with a penchant for abducting girls and suffocating his victims with plastic.

Overstretched low-budget killer thriller, murkily photographed into the bargain (the credits are barely readable, hence the short list).
p: Percival Rubens
w/d: Percival Rubens
ph: Vincent Cox
m: Nick Cabuschagne
sound: Bernard Buys, Sid Knowles
Cameron Mitchell, Jennifer Holmes, Zoli Markey, Craig Gardner

The Demon Murder Case
USA 1983 96m Technicolor TVM
Various professionals are brought in to exorcize a young man who appears to

be demonically possessed.

Passable but somewhat belated, not to mention tame, variation on *The Exorcist* which saw theatrical release in some countries.
p: Len Steckler for Dick Clark Cinema Productions
exec p: Dick Clark, Preston Fischer
w: William Kelley
d: Billy Hale
ph: John Lindley
m: George Aliceson Tipton
ed: Scott Eyler
pd: Marc Donnenfeld
cos: Irene Baldassano
sp: Peter Kunz, Mark Mann
sound: Chat Gunter
Cloris Leachman, Eddie Albert, Andy Griffith, Richard Masur, Kevin Bacon, Joyce Van Patten, Charlie Fields, Lione Landland

Demon of Paradise

USA 1987 87m colour
Fishermen using explosives disturb a demon which subsequently goes on the rampage in a Hawaiian resort.

Dismal zero-budget rubbish. Avoid.
p: Leonard Hermes for Santa Fe
w: Frederick Bailey, C. J. Santiago
d: Ciro H. Santiago
ph: Ricardo Remias
md: Edward Achacoso
ed: Gervacio Santos
pd/2nd unit d: Joe Mari Avellana
cos: Elvie Santos
sound: Rollie Ruta
Kathryn Witt, William Steis, Lesley Huntly, Laura Banks, Frederick Bailey, Nick Nicholson, Joe Mari Avellana, Henry Strazalkowski

Demoni see Demons

Demoni 2 see Demons 2

Demons

It/Ger 1985 89m Technicolor
A movie audience find themselves being attacked by murderous demons.

Italian schlock horror. Not much sense, but plenty of blood and guts for gorehounds.
p: Dario Argento for Dacfilm
w: Dario Argento, Lamberto Bava
d: Lamberto Bava
m: Claudio Simonetti and others
ed: Franco Fraticelli
Urbano Barberini, Nathsha Hovey, Fiore Argento, Karl Zinny, Paolo Cozzo, Fabiola Toldeo

Demons 2 *

It 1987 98m Technicolor Dolby
Murderous demons take over an apartment building.

Slicked-up sequel with improved effects and action sequences.
p: Dario Argento for Dacfilm
w: Dario Argento, Lamberto Bava, Franco Ferrini, Dardano Sacchetti
d: Lamberto Bava
ph: Gianlorenzo Battaglia
m: Simon Boswell and others
ed: Franco Fraticelli, Pietro Bozza
ad: Davide Bassan
cos: Nicola Trussardi
sp: Sergio Stivaletti
sound: Rataele De Lucca
make-up effects: Rosario Presotpino
David Knight, Nancy Brilli, Carolina Catildi Tassoni, Asia Argento, Bobby Rhodes, Virginia Bryant

Demons 3: The Ogre

It 1988 90m Eastmancolor TVM
A family staying at a remote castle fear that someone - or something - is watching them.

Tame TV follow-up to the two previous films, of note only for an underwater sequence blatantly ripped off from Dario Argento's *Inferno*.
p: Massimo Manasse, Marlo Grillo Spina
w: Dardano Sacchetti, Lamberto Bava
story: Dardano Sacchetti
d: Lamberto Bava
ph: Gianfranco Transanto
m: Simon Boswell
ed: Mauro Bonanni
ad: Antonello Di Palma
sp: Angelo Mattei, Ditta Ricci
sound: Giullano Piermarioli
make-up effects: Fabrizio Sforza
ass d: Fabrizio Bava
Virginia Bryant, David Flosey, Sabrina Ferilli, Stefanio Montorsi, Patrizio Vinci, Alice di Giuseppe, Davide Flosi

Demons of the Mind *

GB 1972 85m Technicolor
In 1830, a Bavarian count locks up his children, believing them to be mad.

Good looking though confusingly plotted psychological thriller in typical Hammer style.
p: Frank Godwin for Hammer
w: Christopher Wicking
story: Frank Godwin
d: Peter Sykes
ph: Arthur Grant
m: Harry Robinson
md: Philip Martell
ed: Chris Barnes
ad: Michael Stringer
cos: Rosemary Burrowas
sound: John Purchese
Paul Jones, Patrick Magee, Yvonne Mitchell, Robert Hardy, Michael Hordern, Kenneth J. Warren, Shaned Briant, Virginia Wetherell, Deidre Costello, Barry Stanton, Sidonie Bond

Demonwarp

USA 1987 colour
A series of Big Foot attacks in a dense backwood area turns out to be a diversion for zombie-making aliens (!).

Increasingly foolish low-budgeter that takes some swallowing.
p: Richard L. Albert for Design Projects Incorporated/Vidmark
exec p: Mark Amin
w: John Buechler, Jim Bertges, Bruce Akiyama
d: Emmett Alston
ph: R. Michael Stringer
m: Dan Slider
ed: W. Peter Miller
sp: John Buechler
George Kennedy, David Michael O'Neill, Michelle Bauer, Bill Jacoby, Colleen McDermott, Pamela Gilbert

Denberg, Susan (1944-?)

Polish born model (*Playboy*'s Miss August, 1966) and actress (real name Dietlinde Ortrun Zechner), in London from 1963, where she became an au pair and a Bluebell Girl. She made her film début in America in *See You In Hell, Darling* (aka *An American Dream*) in 1966, though she is remembered chiefly for her role as Christina in Hammer's *Frankenstein Created Woman* (1967). She succumbed to drug addiction after this, then mysteriously disappeared from the film scene, the persistent rumour being that she died soon after.

Destroy All Monsters

Japan 1969 89m Technicolor
Aliens release Godzilla and his fellow monsters from captivity on a Pacific island.

Monster packed hokum, just as ludicrous as its many predecessors.
p: Tomoyuki Tanaka for Toho
w: Kaoru Mabuchi
d: Ishori Honda
m: Akira Ifukube
ed: Ryohei Fujii
sp: Sanemas Arikawa, Eiji Tsuburaya
sound: Hisashi Shimonaga
Akira Kubo, Yukiko Kobayashi, Kyoko Ai, Jan Tazaki, Yoshio Tzuchiya

The Devil and Daniel Webster

see All That Money Can Buy

The Devil Commands *

USA 1941 65m bw
A scientist tries to communicate with his dead wife via a series of experiments which include the use of corpses.

One of the better low-budget mad doctor flicks of the forties.
p: Wallace MacDonald for Columbia
w: Robert D. Andrews, Milton Gunzberg

story: William Sloan
d: Edward Dmytryk
ph: Allan G. Siegler
md: M. W. Stoloff
ed: Al Clark
ad: Lionel Banks
sound: no credit given
Boris Karloff, Richard Fiske, Anne Revere, Amanda Duff, Ralph Penney

The Devil-Doll *

USA 1936 79m bw
An escaped convict disguises himself as an old woman and uses life-like dolls to murder those who sent him to prison.

Foolish but engaging fantasy-horror which never even attempts to be convincing. Also of interest for its credits.
p: E. J. Mannix for MGM
w: Tod Browning, Garrett Fort, Erich Von Stroheim, Guy Ednore
novel: A. A. Merritt
d: TOD BROWNING
ph: Leonard Smith
m: Franz Waxman
ed: Frederick Y. Smith
ad: Cedric Gibbons, Stan Rogers, Edwin B. Willis
cos: Dolly Tree
sound: Douglas Shearer
LIONEL BARRYMORE, Maureen O'Sullivan, Frank Lawton, Henry B. Walthall, Rafaela Ottiano, Grace Ford, Arthur Hohl

Devil Doll *

GB 1963 80m bw
A newspaper reporter investigates *The Great Vorelli*, a magician-cum-ventriloquist whose dummy seems to have a life of its own.

Better than average low-budget thriller, not without its moments of style, though some claim it was mostly the work of director Sidney J. Furie, who oversaw the project whilst preparing to film *The Ipcress File*.
p: Lindsay Shonteff for Galaworld/Gordon
w: George Barclay, Lance Z. Hargreaves
d: Lindsay Shonteff
ph: Gerald Gibbs
m: no credit given
ed: Ernest Bullingham
ad: Stan Shields
cos: Mary Gibson
sound: Derek McColm
Bryant Halliday, William Sylvester, Yvonne Romain, Karel Stepanek, Francis de Wolff

The Devil Rides Out **

GB 1968 95m Technicolor
The Duke de Richleau discovers that one of his friends is a member of a Satanic ring and sets out to save him, only to cross paths with the Devil himself.

Enjoyable, full blooded, persuasively handled Hammer horror, with plenty going on to keep one watching. One of the studio's key films.
p: Anthony Nelson Keys for Hammer/Associated British
w: Richard Matheson
novel: Dennis Wheatley
d: TERENCE FISHER
ph: ARTHUR GRANT
m: JAMES BERNARD
md: Philip Martell
ed: James Needs, Spencer Reeve
ad: BERNARD ROBINSON
cos: Rosemary Burrows
sp: Michael Stalmer-Hutchins
sound: Ken Rawkins, A. W. Lumkin
CHRISTOPHER LEE, CHARLES GRAY, Leon Greene (dubbed by Patrick Allen), Patrick Mower, Gwen Ffrangcon, Paul Eddington

The Devils ***

GB 1970 111m Technicolor Panavision
In 17th century Loudun, a publicity seeking exorcist colludes with the authorities to accuse a convent of nuns of being possessed by the Devil, and their priest, Father Grandier, is burned at the stake as a consequence.

Much has been written about this censorship milestone, which leaves nothing to the imagination. Yet, despite the hysteria both on the screen and in the press, this is a compelling and intelligently handled adaptation of the play and book which has important things to say about the hypocrisies of religion amid the (justifiable) sensationalism.
p: Robert H. Solo, Ken Russell for Warner/Russo
w/d: KEN RUSSELL
book: Aldous Huxley
play: JOHN WHITING
ph: DAVID WATKIN
m: Peter Maxwell Davies
ed: Michael Bradsell
ad/sets: ROBERT CARTWRIGHT, DEREK JARMAN
cos: Shirley Russell
ch: Terry Gilbert
OLIVER REED, Vanessa Redgrave, Murray Melvin, Dudley Sutton, Gemma Jones, Graham Armitage, Michael Gothard, Max Adrian, Georgina Hale, Brian Murphy, Christopher Logue, John Woodvine, Andrew Faulds, Kenneth Colley, Catherine Wilmer

The Devil's Daughter *

USA 1972 74m Technicolor TVM
When she turns twenty-one, a young woman learns that she has been promised to the Devil.

Fairly enjoyable diabolical thriller in typical TV style.
p: Edward J. Mikis for Paramount
w: Colin Higgins
d: JEANNOT SZWARC
ph: J.J. Jones
m: Laurence Rosenthal
ed: Rita Roland
ad: William Cambell
cos: Gerald Alpert, Jennifer Parsons
sp: Howard A. Anderson
sound: William Andrews
titles: Phil Norman
SHELLEY WINTERS, Belinda Montgomery, Robert Foxworth, Joseph Cotten, Jonathan Frid, Martha Scott, Diane Ladd, Lucille Benson, Thelma Carpenter, Abe Vigoda

Devils of Darkness

GB 1964 91m Eastmancolor
400 years after being staked, Count Sinistre terrorizes modern day Brittany.

Undernourished vampire yarn hampered chiefly by its obviously low budget.
p: Tom Blakeley for Planet
w: Lynn Fairhurst
d: Lance Comfort
ph: Reg Wyer
m: Bernie Fenton
ed: John Trumper
ad: John St. John Earl
cos: Muriel Dickson
sound: Robert T. MacPhee, Gordon K. McCallum
ch: Leo Kharibian
William Sylvester, Hubert Noel, Tracy Reed, Carol Gray, Rona Anderson, Peter Illing, Avril Angers, Eddie Byrne

The Devil's Own see The Witches

The Devil's Rain

USA 1975 76m Technicolor Todd AO
A coven of witches is discovered in a small mid-west town, but they melt away when routed out by the forces of goodness.

And how they melt! Unfortunately a few pretensions to style can't quite save this harkback to the B movies of the forties, even with all these stars at hand.
p: James V. Cullen, Michael S. Glick for Sandy Howard Productions
w: Gabe Essoe, James Ashton
d: Robert Fuest
ph: Alex Phillips, Jr
m: Al De Lory
ed: Michael Kahn
pd: Nikita Katz
make-up effects: Tom Burman
Ernest Borgnine, Eddie Albert, Ida Lupino, William Shatner, Keenan Wynn, Tom Skerritt, John Prather, John Travolta

The Devil's Skin see The Blood on
Satan's Claw

Diary of a Madman
USA 1962 96m Technicolor
A diary reveals that a murderer was, in
fact, possessed by an evil spirit.

Thin horror melodrama with more
energy than style.
p: Robert E. Kent for UA / Admiral
w: Robert E. Kent
story: Guy de Maupassant
d: Reginald Le Borg
ph: Ellis W. Carter
m: Richard La Salle
ed: Grant Whytock
ad: Daniel Haller
cos: Marjorie Corso
sp: Norman Breedlove
sound: Ralph Butler
Vincent Price, Nancy Kovack, Chris
Warfield. Lewis Martin, Elaine Dervy,
Stephen Roberts

Diabolique see Les Diaboliques

Les Diaboliques **
Fr 1954 114m bw
The wife and mistress of a much
despised headmaster plot to murder
him but after the deed is done his body
mysteriously disappears ...

Much copied since its original
release, this influential thriller has
consequently lost much of its surprise,
but for those not familiar with its
twists and turns it should remain fairly
engrossing, despite a rather slow start.
It was remade as a TV movie, Reflections
of Murder, in 1976, and as Diabolique in
1996.
p: Henri-Georges Clouzot for
Filmsonor
w: Henri-Georges Clouzot, G.
Geronimi, Rene Masson, Frederic
Grendel
d: HENRI-GEORGES CLOUZOT
ph: Armand Thirard
m: Georges Van Parys
ed: Madeleine Gug
ad: Leon Barsacq
sound: William-Robert Sivel
SIMONE SIGNORET, VERA
CLOUZOT, Charles Vanel, Paul
Meurisse

Dicken, Roger
British special effects technician.
Genre credits:
The Blood Beast Terror (1967 - aka The
Vampire Beast Craves Blood), Witchfinder
General (1967 - aka - The Conqueror
Worm), Scars of Dracula (1970),

Dickinson, Desmond (1904-)
Prolific British cinematographer with

• When not playing Nazi officers,
which wasn't very often, Anton
Diffring popped up in the occasional
horror film, such as Circus of Horrors,
one of his few leading roles.

credits on all manner of productions,
including Hamlet, The History of Mr Polly
and The Importance of Being Earnest.
Genre credits:
Horrors of the Black Museum (1959), Konga
(1960), The Hands of Orlac (1960), City
of the Dead (1960 - aka Horror Hotel),
Berserk (1967), The Beast in the Cellar
(1970 - co-ph), Bloodsuckers (1970 - aka
Incense for the Damned / Doctors Wear
Scarlet), The Fiend (1971)

Diffring, Anton (1918-1989)
German actor in international films,
more often than not as a Nazi in such
films as The Colditz Story, Where Eagles
Dare and Zeppelin.
Genre credits:
The Man Who Could Cheat Death (1959),
Circus of Horrors (1960), The Iguana with
the Tongue of Fire (1970), Seven Deaths in
the Cat's Eye (1973 - aka La Morte Negli
Occhi del Gatto), Kiss Me and Die (1974),
The Beast Must Die (1974 - aka Black
Werewolf), Mark of the Devil Part 2
(1975), Le Mutant (1977), Les Predateurs
de la Nuit (1988 - aka Faceless)

Dinga, Pat
American special effects technician with
several credits for Roger Corman.
Genre credits:
Bride of the Monster (1955), House of Usher
(1960 - aka The Fall of the House of Usher
- co-sp), The Pit and the Pendulum
(1961), Tales of Terror (1962), The Raven
(1963), The Comedy of Terrors (1963),
Black Zoo (1965)

Dinosaurus!
USA 1960 85m DeLuxe Cinemascope
A caveman and two dinosaurs are
revived on a remote tropical island.

Amateur low-budgeter with dismal
effects.
p: Jack H. Harris for Universal
w: Jean Yeaworth, Dan E. Weisburd
story: Jack H. Harris
d: Irwin S. Yeaworth, Jr
ph: Stanley Cortez
m: Ronald Stein
ed: John H. Bishelman
ad: Jack Senter
cos: Bill Edwards
sp: Tim Baar, Wan Chang, Gene Warren
sound: Vic Appel
underwater d: Paul Stader
Ward Ramsey, Paul Lukather, Alan
Roberts, Kristina Hanson

A Distant Scream
GB 1984 74m Technicolor TVM
A dying man dreams the truth about a
murder he did not commit but for
which he was sent to prison.

Another time filler from the Hammer
House of Mystery and Suspense stable, most
of which are indistinguishable from each
other.
p: Roy Skeggs for Hammer / TCF
w: Martin Worth
d: John Hough
ph: Brian West
m: Paul Patterson
md: Philip Martell
ed: Peter Weatherley
ad: Carolyn Scott
David Carradine, Stephanie Beacham,
Stephen Greif, Stephen Chase, Fanny
Carby, Lesley Dunlop

The Doctor and the Devils
USA 1985 93m Technicolor Panavision
A nineteenth-century Edinburgh surgeon
condones grave robbing and murder in
order to procure the bodies needed for
his research.

Straight faced account of events
which might have worked better if
treated as out and out horror.
p: Jonthan Sanger for Brooksfilm
exec p: Mel Brooks
w: Ronald Harwood
original script: Dylan Thomas
d: Freddie Francis
ph: Norman Warwick, Gerry Turpin
m: John Morris
ed: Laurence Mery-Clark
pd: Robert Laing
cos: Imogen Richardson
Timothy Dalton, Twiggy, Jonathan Pryce,
Julian Sands, Lewis Fiander, Stephen
Rea, Phyllis Logan, Beryl Reid, T. P.
McKenna, Sian Phillips, Patrick Stewart

Doctor Blood's Coffin

GB 1960 92m Eastmancolor

In Cornwall, a doctor experiments with heart transplants and brings back to life a corpse which inevitably goes on the rampage.

Undernourished horror lacking the wit and style needed to bring it off, never mind make it interesting.

p: George Fowler for UA/Carlan
w: Jerry Juran, James Kelly, Peter Miller
d: Sidney J. Furie
ph: Stephen Dade
m: Buxton Orr
md: Philip Martell
ed: Anthony Gibbs
ad: Scott MacGregor
Kieron Moore, Hazel Court, Ian Hunter, Gerald C. Lawson, Lenneth J. Warren

Dr Cyclops

USA 1940 76m Technicolor

In the jungles of Brazil, a research scientist miniaturizes five of his colleagues for experimentation.

Routine mad doctor hokum ineptly scripted and acted but with good use of colour. Effects work variable.

p: Dale Van Every for Paramount
w: Tom Kilpatrick
d: Ernest B. Shoedsack
ph: HENRY SHARP, WINTON C. HOCH
m: Ernst Toch, Gerard Carbonara, Albert Hay Malotte
ed: Ellsworth Hoagland
ad: Hans Dreier, Earl Hedrick
sp: Farciot Edouart, Wallace Kelley
sound: Harry Lindgren, Richard Olson
Albert Dekker, Janice Logan, Victor Kilian, Thomas Coley, Charles Halton, Paul Fix

The Doctor from Seven Dials

see Corridors of Blood

Dr Giggles

USA 1992 95m Technicolor Dolby

A lunatic with a penchant for performing operations without anaesthetic escapes an asylum and goes on the rampage in his home town.

Over stretched horror hokum with a little more style and black humour than most - but not enough to save it.

p: Stuart M. Besser for Largo/JVC/Dark Horse
w: Manny Coto, Graeme Whifler
d: Manny Coto
ph: Robert Draper
m: Brian May
ed: Debra Neil
pd: Bill Malley
cos: Sandra Culotta
sp: Phil Cory

• John Barrymore as Mr Hyde in the 1921 version Robert Louis Stevenson's oft filmed novella *The Strange Case of Dr Jekyll.*

make-up effects: Kurtzman, Nicotero and Berger EFX Group
sound: Jim Stuebe
stunt co-ordinator: John Moio
Larry Drake, Holly Marie Combs, Cliff DeYoung, Keith Diamond, Richard Bradford, Michelle Johnson, Glenn Quinn

Dr Jekyll and Mr Hyde

First published in 1886, Robert Louis Stevenson's novella *The Strange Case of Dr Jekyll* has been one of the horror genre's staples, with film versions dating back to as early as 1908. The silent period was a particularly prolific time for the story, there being five versions between 1910 and 1915 alone, though the first classic interpretation didn't appear until 1921 when John Barrymore played the dual roles. In 1932, Fredric March won a Best Actor Oscar for playing Jekyll and Hyde in the celebrated Rouben Mamoulian version, the only actor to win a Best Actor award for a horror film until Anthony Hopkins' win for *The Silence of the Lambs* in 1990. Other key versions include MGM's lavish 1941 adaptation with Spencer Tracy, Universal's *Abbott and Costello Meet Dr Jekyll and Mr Hyde*, Hammer's *The Two Faces of Dr Jekyll* and Amicus's *I, Monster* which had Christopher Lee playing Dr Charles Marlowe and his alter ego Edward Blake, who were Jekyll and Hyde in all but name. As to be expected, there have been a number of spoofs (*The Ugly Duckling*, *The Nutty Professor*, *Dr Heckly and Mr Hype*, etc.) as well as a couple of sex change versions (*Dr Jekyll*

and Sister Hyde, Dr Jekyll and Ms Hyde).
Key filmography:
Dr Jekyll and Mr Hyde (1908, 1909, 1912, 1913 x 2, 1914), *Horrible Hyde* (1915), *Der Januskopf* (1920), *Dr Jekyll and Mr Hyde* (1920 x 2, 1921), *Dr Pickle and Mr Pride* (1925 - Stan Laurel comedy short), *Dr Jekyll and Mr Hyde* (1932, 1941), *El Hombre Y la Bestia* (1951), *Il Dottor Jekyll* (1951), *Son of Dr Jekyll* (1951), *Abbott and Costello Meet Dr Jekyll and Mr Hyde* (1953), *Daughter of Dr Jekyll* (1957), *The Doctor's Horrible Experiment* (1959 - aka *Experiment in Evil/Le Testament du Dr Cordelier*), *The Ugly Duckling* (1959), *Il Mio Amico Jekyll* (1960), *The Two Faces of Dr Jekyll* (1960 - aka *House of Fright/Jekyll's Inferno*), *The Nutty Professor* (1962), *Dr Jekyll's Mistress* (1964 - aka *El Secreto del Dr Orloff/Dr Orloff's Monster*), *Dottor Jekyll* (1964), *The Mad Monster Party?* (1967 - puppetoon), *The Strange Case of Dr Jekyll and Mr Hyde* (1968 - TVM), *Pacto Diabolico* (1968), *The Adult Version of Jekyll and Hide* (1971), *I, Monster* (1971), *The Man with Two Heads* (1971 - aka *Dr Jekyll and Mr Blood*), *Dr Sexual and Mr Hyde* (1971), *Dr Jekyll and Sister Hyde* (1971), *Doctor Jekill Y el Hombre Lobo* (1971 - aka *Dr Jekyll and the Werewolf*), *The Adult Version of Jekyll and Hyde* (1972), *Dr Black, Mr Hyde* (1976), *Dr Heckyl and Mr Hype* (1980), *Dr Jekyll and Mr Hyde* (1980 - TVM), *Dottor Jekyll e Gentile Signora* (1980 - aka *Jekyll Jr./Dr Jekyll Jr./Il Dottore Jekyll Jr./Dr and Mrs. Jekyll*), *Dr Jekyll et les Femmes* (1982 - aka *The Strange Case of Dr Jekyll and Lady Osbourne/Dr Jekyll and His Wives/Dr Jekyll and Miss Osbourne/Blood of Dr Jekyll*), *Jekyll and Hyde... Together Again* (1982), *Dr Jekyll's Dungeon of Death* (1982), *Edge of Sanity* (1988 - aka *Dr Jekyll and Mr Hyde*), *Jekyll and Hyde* (1990 - TVM), *Dr Jekyll and Ms. Hyde* (1995), *The Nutty Professor* (1996), *Mary Reilly* (1996)

Dr Jekyll and Mr Hyde *

USA 1921 63m bw silent
A London doctor separates the good and evil in him by drinking a potion he has concocted.

Relatively early version of the oft filmed story, though certainly not the most imaginative. It did prove to be a popular vehicle for Barrymore at the time.
p: Adolph Zukor for Paramount
w: Clara S. Beranger
novel: ROBERT LOUIS STEVENSON
d: John S. Robertson
ph: Roy Overtaugh
ad: Robert Haas, Charles O. Seesel
JOHN BARRYMORE, Brandon Hurst, Martha Mansfield, Charles Lane, Nita Naldi, Cecil Clavelly, Louis Wolheim

Dr Jekyll and Mr Hyde **

USA 1931 98m bw
A Victorian scientist works on a chemical to separate the good from the evil in his soul only to discover the evil predominating.

Though generally regarded as the definitive version of the Stevenson story, this adaptation of one of the cinema's most oft told tales now comes across as rather dated and, despite occasional inventiveness, proves to be tiresome to sit through. March tied with Wallace Beery for *The Champ* for the Best Actor Oscar. It would be almost sixty years before another actor (Anthony Hopkins for 1990's *The Silence of the Lambs*) would win the award again for a horror role.
p: Rouben Mamoulian for Paramount
w: Samuel Hoffenstein, Percy Heath
novel: ROBERT LOUIS STEVENSON
d: ROUBEN MAMOULIAN
ph: Karl Struss
m: no credit given
ed: William Shea
ad: HANS DREIER
make-up: Wally Westmore
sound: no credit given
FREDRIC MARCH (aa), MIRIAM HOPKINS, Rose Hobart, Holmes Herbert, Halliwell Hobbes, Edgard Norton

Dr Jekyll and Mr Hyde *

USA 1941 122m bw
Expensive remake, obviously intended as

a prestige production, but fatally compromised by too leaden a pace and a misguided sense of its own worth. Only of occasional interest despite the talent involved.
p: Victor Saville, Victor Fleming for MGM
w: John Lee Mahin
novel: ROBERT LOUIS STEVENSON
d: Victor Fleming
ph: Joseph Ruttenberg
m: Franz Waxman
ed: Harold F. Kress
ad: CEDRIC GIBBONS, DANIEL B. CATHCART
cos: Adrian, Gile Steele
sp: Warren Newcombe
sound: Douglas Shearer
montage: Peter Ballbusch
ch: Ernst Matray
make-up: Jack Dawn
Spencer Tracy, Ingrid Bergman, Lana Turner, Ian Hunter, C. Aubrey Smith, Sara Allgood, Donald Crisp

Dr Jekyll and Sister Hyde *

GB 1971 Technicolor
Dr Jekyll experiments with female hormones in the search for a life extending serum, only to discover himself periodically turning into a woman.

It had to come, one supposes, and, despite a predictable plot and some restricted sets, the results aren't too bad though the promises of sex changes before our very eyes never materialize.

• **Vincent Price as Dr Phibes and Valli Kemp as Vulnavia in the high camp horror comedy *Dr Phibes Rises Again*, one of Price's most entertaining films.**

p: Brian Clemens, Albert Fennell for Hammer/EMI
w: Brian Clemens
d: Roy Ward Baker
ph: Norman Warwick
m: David Whitaker
md: Philip Martell
ed: James Needs
ad: Robert Jones
cos: Rosemary Burrows
sound: Bill Rowe
make-up: Trevor Crole-Rees
Ralph Bates, Martine Beswick, Gerald Sim, Lewis Fiander, Susan Broderick, Dorothy Alison, Ivor Dean, Tony Calvin, Paul Whitsun-Jones, Philip Madoc

Doctor Mabuse the Gambler **
Ger 1922 101m bw silent
A ruthless criminal mastermind uses hypnotism and elaborate disguises to achieve his ends but he is finally revealed to be insane.

Fairly fascinating silent melodrama with moments of great style in the German manner. It was followed by *The Testament of Dr Mabuse* (1933) and *The Thousand Eyes of Dr Mabuse* (1960), both of them directed by Lang.
p: UFA
w: Thea Von Harbou, Fritz Lang
novel: Norbert Jacques
d: FRITZ LANG
ph: CARL HOFFMANN
ad: OTTO HUNTE, STAHL URACH
cos: Vally Reinecke
RUDOLPH KLEIN-ROGGE, Alfred Abel, Lil Dagover, Paul Richter, Gertrude Welcker

Dr Phibes Rises Again **
GB 1972 89m DeLuxe
The immortal Dr Phibes rises from the grave to search for the elixir of life, the secret of which lies in an Egyptian tomb. But he is not the only interested party...

Good looking, high camp sequel to *The Abominable Dr Phibes*, with plenty of black humour and some nifty art direction. Horror hokum at its very best.
p: Richard Dalton for AIP
exec p: James H. Nicholson, Samuel Z. Arkoff
w: ROBERT FUEST, ROBERT BLEES
d: ROBERT FUEST
ph: ALEX THOMSON
m: JOHN GALE
ed: Tristan Cones
ad: BRIAN EATWELL
cos: Ivy Baker Jones, Brian Cox
sound: Les Hammond, Dennis Whitlock, A. W. Watkins
make-up: Trevor Crole-Rees
VINCENT PRICE, ROBERT QUARRY, Valli Kemp, Fiona Lewis, Peter Cushing, Terry Thomas, Beryl Reid, Hugh

Griffith, PETER JEFFREY, JOHN CATER, Gerald Sim, John Thaw, Lewis Fiander, John Comer

Dr Terror's House of Horrors
GB 1966 98m Technicolor Techniscope
The futures of passengers on a train are foretold by a mysterious stranger.

Poorly handled horror compendium with just a few lively touches - but not enough.
p: Max J. Rosenberg, Milton Subotsky for Amicus
w: Milton Subotsky
d: Freddie Francis
ph: Alan Hume
m: Elisabeth Lutyens
ed: Thelma Connell
ad: Bill Constable
cos: Bridget Sellers
sp: Ted Samuels
sound: Buster Ambler, John Cox
make-up: Roy Ashton
Peter Cushing, Christopher Lee, Roy Castle, Ursula Howells, Alan Freeman, Max Adrian, Bernard Lee, Kenny Lynch, Donald Sutherland, Michael Gough, Jeremy Kemp, Judy Cornwell, Neil McCallum, Peter Madden, Edward Underdown, Katy Wild, Isla Blair, Laurie Leigh

Dr X **
USA 1932 82 Technicolor
A reporter sets out to discover which of a group of doctors is responsible for a series of grizzly 'moon' murders.

Foolishly plotted but stylishly executed Germanic horror comic with many points of interest for connoisseurs. Though shot in three strip Technicolor, it is now almost always shown in black and white. In many ways a dress rehearsal for the same team's *The Mystery of the Wax Museum*, which appeared the following year.
p: Hal B. Wallis for Warner
w: Earl Baldwin, Robert Tasker
play: Howard W. Comstock, Allen C. Miller
d: MICHAEL CURTIZ
ph: RICHARD TOWERS, RAY RENNAHAN
md: Leo F. Forbstein
ed: George Amy
ad: ANTON GROT
cos/sound: no credits given
make-up: The Max Factor Co
Lee Tracy, Lionel Atwill, Fay Wray, Preston Foster, George Rosener, Mae Busch, Arthur Edmund Carewe, John Wray, Harry Beresford

Dolls *
USA/It 1986 89m Technicolor Ultra Stereo

Travellers waylaid by a storm take refuge at a remote country mansion only to be murdered one at a time by the owner's collection of killer dolls.

Mildly amusing horror comic in the Empire tradition, distinguished chiefly by lively effects work.
p: Brian Yuzna for Empire/Taryn
exec p: Charles Band
w: Ed Naha
d: Stuart Gordon
ph: Mac Ahlberg
m: Richard Band, Fuzzbee Morse, Victor Spiegel
ed: Lee Percy
pd: Giovanni Natalucci
cos: Angee Beckett
sp: John Brunner, Vivian Brunner, Giancarlo Del Brocco, David Allen
sound: Mario Bramonti
make-up effects: John Carl Beuchler
titles: Robert Dawson
Ian Patrick Williams, Carolyn Purdy-Gordon, Hilary Mason, Carrie Lorraine, Guy Rolfe, Bunty Bailey, Cassie Stuart, Stephen Lee

Dominique
GB 1978 99m Technicolor
A wealthy woman believes that her husband is trying to drive her mad.

Old hat thriller whose derivative plot needed much more style than is on show here to bring it off. A television half hour might have been more suitable.
p: Milton Subotsky, Andrew Donally for Grand Prize/Sword and Sorcery
exec p: Melvin Simon
w: Edward Abraham, Valerie Abraham
story: Harold Lawlor
d: Michael Anderson
ph: Ted Moore
m: David Whitaker
ed: Richard Best
pd: David Minty
cos: Will Hemmink, Douglas Hayward
sound: David Bowen, Bob Jones
Cliff Robertson, Jean Simmons, Jenny Agutter, Simon Ward, Ron Moody, Judy Geeson, Jack Warner, Michael Jayston, Flora Robson, David Tomlinson

Donaggio, Pino (1941-)
Italian composer (real name Giuseppe Donaggio) with a penchant for fantasy and thriller scores. He has worked on several of Brian de Palma's films including *Blow Out*, *Body Double* and *Raising Cain*. Other credits include *Hercules*, *Appointment with Death* and *Night Game*.
Genre credits:
Don't Look Now (1973), *Haunts* (1976 - aka *The Veil*), *Carrie* (1976), *Piranha* (1978), *Tourist Trap* (1979), *Beyond Evil* (1980), *The Black Cat* (1980 - aka *Il Gatto*

Nero), *Dressed to Kill* (1980), *The Howling* (1981), *The Fan* (1981), *Crawlspace* (1986), *Catacombs* (1988 - aka *Curse IV: The Ultimate Sacrifice*), *Phantom of Death* (1989), *Two Evil Eyes* (1989 - aka *Due Occhi Diabolici*), *Meridian* (1990 aka - *Kiss of the Beast*), *The Sect* (1991 - aka *La Setta*), *Trauma* (1993)

Donlevy, Brian (1899-1972)
Burly Irish-American character actor with much Hollywood experience (*Beau Geste, Brigham Young, The Great McGinty, The Glass Key*, etc.). Came to England to portray Professor Quatermass in two films for Hammer: *The Quatermass Experiment* (1955 - aka *The Creeping Unknown*) and *Quatermass 2* (1957 - aka *Enemy from Space*). Also appeared in *The Curse of the Fly* (1965).

Don't Be Afraid of the Dark
USA 1973 74m Technicolor TVM
Supernatural creatures threaten a couple in their new home.

Old fashioned haunted house thriller, watchable enough on the comic book level.
p: Allen Epstein for Lorimar
exec p: Lee Rich
w: Nigel McKeand
d: John Newland
ph: Andrew Jackson
m: Billy Goldenberg
ed: Gene Fowler Jr, Michael McCrosky
ad: Ed Graves
sp/titles: Howard A. Anderson
cos: Patricia Norris
sound: Charles Knight
Jim Hutton, Kim Darby, Barbara Anderson, William Demarest, William Sylvester, Pedro Armendariz Jr

Don't Go Into the House
USA 1979 83m DeLuxe
A disturbed young man takes to torching young women after years of abuse at the hands of his recently deceased mother.

Depressing, misogynistic low-grade stuff for the tail end of the exploitation market.
p: Ellen Hammill for Turbinew: Joseph R. Mansfield, Joseph Ellison, Ellen Hammill
story: Joseph R. Mansfield
d: Joseph Ellison
ph: Oliver Wood
m: Richard Einhorn
ed: Jane Kurson
ad: no credit given
cos: Sharon Lynch
sp: Matt Vogel
sound: Jimmy Kwol
make-up effects: Tom Brumberger
Dan Grimaldi, Robert Osth, Johanna Bushay, Ruth Dardick, Gail Turner

Don't Look Now ***
GB 1973 110m Technicolor
After the death of their young daughter, an architect and his wife go to Venice where they meet two elderly sisters who claim to have contact with the dead girl.

Puzzling, brilliantly detailed and thoroughly absorbing thriller which makes excellent use of its locations and has many thought provoking passages. A modern day classic.
p: Peter Katz for British Lion/Casey/Elodorado
w: ALLAN SCOTT, CHRIS BRYANT
novel: Daphne Du Maurier
d: NICOLAS ROEG
ph: ANTHONY RICHMOND
m: PINO DONAGGIO
ed: GRAEME CLIFFORD
pd: Giovanni Soccoli
cos: Annamaria Fed, Marit Lieberson, Andrea Galler
sound: Peter Davies, Bob Jones
sound ed: Rodney Holland
stunt co-ordinator: Richard Grayden
DONALD SUTHERLAND, JULIE CHRISTIE, Clelia Matania, HILARY MASON, Massimo Serrato, Renato Scarpa, Adelina Poerio

Don't Open the Window see The Living Dead at the Manchester Morgue

Don't Open Till Christmas
GB 1983 86m colour
A maniac with a penchant for killing Father Christmases is on the loose in London.

Cheap-looking slasher pic for the bin end of the market.
p: Dick Randall, Steve Minasian for Spectacular International Films (!)
w: Derek Ford, Al McGoohan
d: Edmund Purdom
ph: Alan Pudney
m: Des Dolan
ed: Ray Selfe
ad: no credit given
sp: Peter Litton
sound: no credit given
Edmund Purdom, Alan Lake, Belinda Mayne, Caroline Munro, Gerry Sundquist, Mark Jones

Don't Panic
Mexico 1987 89m colour
After messing about with a ouija board at a birthday party, one of two teenage boys becomes possessed by a demon.

Stupid horror nonsense, of no abiding interest.
p: Raul Galindo, Bruce Glenn for Dynamic Films
w/d: Ruben Galindo Jr
ph: Miguel Arana, Daniel Lopez
m: Pedro Plascenci

ad: no credit given
cos: Antonia Cortez
sp: Screaming Mad George, Miguel Vasquez
sound: Jesus Carrasco
make-up effects: Richard Davison
Jon Michael Bischoff, Gabriela Hassel, Helen Rojo, George Luke, Juan Ignacio Aranda

Donovan's Brain
USA 1953 81m bw
A scientist keeps alive the brain of a dead business tycoon only to find himself increasingly dominated by it.

Silly but not entirely unengaging sci-fi/horror which at least has the courage of its own convictions. Co star Nancy Davis later married Ronald Reagan and became America's First Lady.
p: Tom Gries for UA/Dowling
w: Felix Feist, Hugh Brook
novel: Curt Siodmak
d: Felix Feist
ph: Joseph Biroc
m: Eddie Dunsteder
ed: Herbert L. Strock
pd: Boris Leven
cos: Chuck Keehne
sp: Harry Redmond Jr
sound: Earl Snyder
Lew Ayres, Nancy Davis, Gene Evans, Steve Brodie, Lisa K. Howard, Tom Powers, Victor Sutherland, Michael Colgan

Don't Take it to Heart *
GB 1944 90m bw
A castle ghost helps a researcher clear a bankrupt lord with the help of some ancient manuscripts.

Dotty British farce with a roster of favourite British character actors giving it their best.
p: Sydney Box for GFD/Two Cities/Central
w: JEFFREY DELL
d: Jeffrey Dell
ph: Eric Cross
m: MISCHA SPOLIANSKY
ed: Frederick Wilson
ad: Alex Vetchinsky
cos: Navratil
sp: Henry Harris, George Blackwell
sound: George Burgess, Stan Jolly
Richard Greene, Patricia Medina, EDWARD RIGBY, Alfred Drayton, RICHARD BIRD, Wylie Watson, Moore Marriott, BREFNI O'ROURKE, Amy Veness, Claude Dampier, Joan Hickson, Joyce Barbour, Ronald Squire, ERNEST THESIGER, Esma Cannon, Harry Fowler, Edie Martin

Doomed to Die see Eaten Alive
(1980)

Doomwatch

GB 1972 92m Technicolor

Pollution in a Cornish village causes some of the locals to mutate.

An overstretched and rather too slowly paced shocker, based on a popular TV series. No great shakes.

p: Tony Tenser for Tigon
w: Clive Exton
d: Peter Sasdy
ph: Kenneth Talbot
m: John Scott
ed: Keith Palmer
ad: Colin Grimes
Ian Bannen, Judy Geeson, John Paul, Simon Oates, George Sanders, Percy Herbert, Geoffrey Keen, Joseph O'Connor, Norman Bird

Dors, Diana (1931-1984)

Glamorous actress (real name Diana Fluck), Britain's answer to the Hollywood bombshells. Proved that she could act in such films as *Yield to the Night* and *The Amazing Mr Blunden*, though her talents, particularly her comic ones, were often under used. Guested in a few horror films towards the end of her career as well as several mild sex romps (*Adventures of a Taxi Driver*, *Swedish Wildcats*, *Adventures of a Private Eye*, etc.).

Genre credits:

Nothing But the Night (1972), *The Amazing Mr Blunden* (1972), *Theatre of Blood* (1973), *Craze* (1973), *From Beyond the Grave* (1973)

Dourif, Brad (1950-)

American character actor with a liking for offbeat roles who came to films via the stage and television. Other credits include *One Flew Over the Cuckoo's Nest*, *Wise Blood*, *Ragtime*, *Dune* and *Blue Velvet*.

Genre credits:

The Eyes of Laura Mars (1978), *I Desire* (1982), *Sonny Boy* (1987), *Child's Play* (1988), *Child's Play 2* (1990 - voice only), *Exorcist III* (1990), *Spontaneous Combustion* (1990), *Graveyard Shift* (1990), *Grim Prairie Tales* (1990), *Body Parts* (1991), *Child's Play 3* (1991 - voice only), *Critters 4* (1993), *Trauma* (1993), *Death Machine* (1994)

Doyle, Patrick

British (Scottish) composer and actor who studied at The Royal Scottish Academy of Music and Drama. Came to films via his association with actor-director Kenneth Branagh, for whose Renaissance Theatre Company he scored several stage productions. Other credits include *Henry V*, *Much Ado About Nothing* (in which he also appeared as Balthazar), *Indochine*, *Carlito's Way*, *Sense and Sensibility* and *The Little Princess*.

Genre credits:

Dead Again (1991), *Needful Things* (1993), *Mary Shelley's Frankenstein* (1994)

• **Frank Langella makes a suave Dracula in director John Badham's underrated remake.**

Dracula

First published in 1897, Bram Stoker's *Dracula* remains one of the horror genre's most often filmed subjects, though like Mary Shelley's *Frankenstein*, few versions could be described as faithful. Taking its inspiration from the historical character Vlad the Impaler, Stoker's book was first filmed in disguised form as *Nosferatu* in Germany in 1922, with Max Schreck playing Graf Orlok, much to the annoyance of Stoker's widow, who sued for copyright infringement. Universal's 1930 version, which stars Bela Lugosi as the vampire count, was for many years seen as the definitive adaptation and, though Dracula himself popped up in all manner of spin offs (*Dracula's Daughter*, *Son of Dracula*), it wasn't until the Hammer version of 1958, starring Christopher Lee as Dracula and Peter Cushing as Van Helsing, that the character became identified with another actor. Lugosi himself only played the part officially twice, the second time in *Abbott and Costello Meet Frankenstein*. The Hammer series (1958-1973) ran to seven episodes plus assorted offshoots (*The Brides of Dracula*, *Kiss of the Vampire*, *The Legend of the Seven Golden Vampires*, etc.), whilst the seventies produced all manner of variations, including blaxploitation entries (*Blacula* and *Scream, Blacula, Scream*), the inevitable adult versions (*Dracula Sucks*, *Spermula*) and even a hearing impaired version (*Deafula*). Other so-called faithful versions of the novel popped up in 1970 (*El Conde Dracula* with Christopher Lee), 1979 (*Dracula* with Frank Langella), 1979 (*Nosferatu* with Klaus Kinski) and 1993 (*Bram Stoker's Dracula* with Gary Oldman). As with Shelley's *Frankenstein*, there have also been all manner of spoofs and hard core versions. Also see *Vampires* and *Carmilla*.

Key filmography:

Nosferatu (1922 - aka *Nosferatu - Eine Symphonie des Graunes*), *Dracula* (1930), *Dracula's Daughter* (1936), *Son of Dracula* (1943), *House of Frankenstein* (1944), *House of Dracula* (1945), *Abbott and Costello Meet Frankenstein* (1948), *Blood of Dracula* (1957 - aka *Blood Is My Heritage*), *The Return of Dracula* (1957 - aka *The Curse of Dracula / The Fantastic Disappearing Man*), *Dracula* (1958 - aka *Horror of Dracula*), *The Brides of Dracula* (1960), *Kiss of the Vampire* (1964 - aka *Kiss of Evil*), *Billy the Kid vs. Dracula* (1965), *Dracula - Prince of Darkness* (1966), *Mad Monster Party?* (1966 - puppetoon), *El Imperio de Dracula* (1966), *Batman Fights Dracula* (1967), *Dracula's Wedding Day* (1967), *Dracula Has Risen from the Grave* (1968), *Dracula Meets the Outer Space Chicks* (1968), *Santo Y el Tesoro de Dracula* (1968), *Taste the Blood of Dracula* (1969), *Dracula - The Dirty Old*

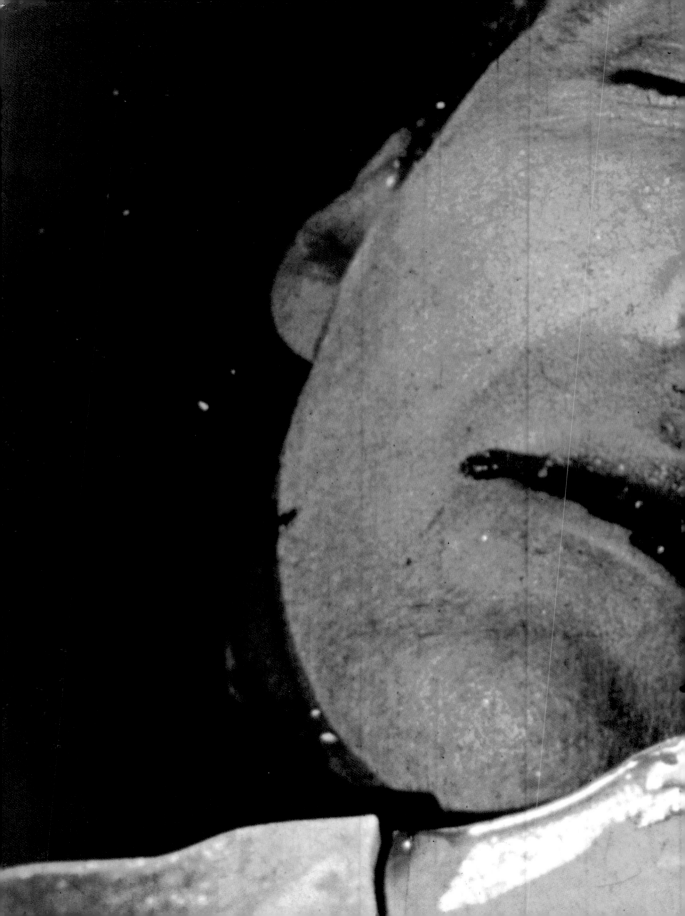

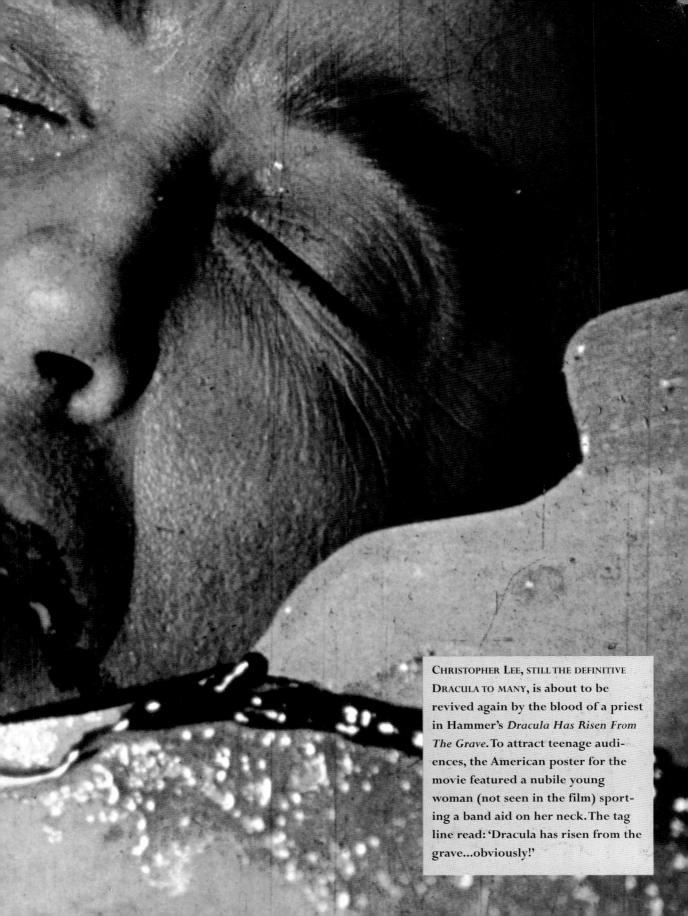

CHRISTOPHER LEE, STILL THE DEFINITIVE DRACULA TO MANY, is about to be revived again by the blood of a priest in Hammer's *Dracula Has Risen From The Grave*. To attract teenage audiences, the American poster for the movie featured a nubile young woman (not seen in the film) sporting a band aid on her neck. The tag line read: 'Dracula has risen from the grave...obviously!'

SHOWMAN'S MANUAL

HORROR OF DRACULA

ADVERTISING · PUBLICITY · EXPLOITATION

• The showman's manual for the American release of Hammer's *Dracula*. Inside, promotional suggestions for cinemas include a nurse in attendance in the lobby, an ambulance out front and a hearse with banners driven round town.

Man (1969), *Dracula vs. Frankenstein* (1969 - aka *El Hombre que Vino del Ummo/Los Monstuos del Terror*), *Guess What Happened to Count Dracula?* (1970 - aka *The Master of the Dungeon*), *Dracula vs. Frankenstein* (1970 - aka *Blood of Frankenstein/They're Coming to get You/The Revenge of Dracula*), *Countess Dracula* (1970), *Vampyros Lesbos die Erbin des Dracula* (1972 - aka *Las Vampiras*), *El Conde Dracula* (1970 - aka *Bram Stoker's Count Dracula/Count Dracula*), *Lake of Dracula* (1971 - aka *Chi O Suu Me*), *In Search of Dracula* (1971 - aka *In Search of the Real Dracula* - documentary), *Blacula* (1972), *La Fille de Dracula* (1972 - aka *La Hija de Dracula*), *Dracula, Prisoner of Frankenstein* (1972 - aka *Dracula Contra Frankenstein*), *The Dracula Saga* (1972 - aka *Saga of the Draculas/Dracula - The Bloodline/La Saga de Los Dracula*), *Santo Y Blue Demon Contra Dracula Y el Hombre Lobo* (1972), *Dracula AD 1972* (1972), *The Mystery in Dracula's Castle* (1972 - TVM), *Dracula's Great Love* (1972 - aka *El Gran Amor del Conde Dracula/Dracula's Virgin Lovers/Cemetary Girls/Vampire Playgirls*), *Andy Warhol's Dracula* (1973 - aka *Blood for Dracula*), *The Satanic Rites of Dracula* (1973), *Scream, Blacula, Scream* (1973), *Son of Dracula* (1973 -aka *Count Downe*), *Dracula* (1973 - TVM), *Tender Dracula* (1974 -aka *La Grande Trouille/Tendre Dracula*), *The Legend of the Seven Golden Vampires* (1974 - aka *The Seven Brothers Meet Dracula*), *Il Cavaliere Costante Nicosia Demoniaco Ovvero Dracula in Brianza* (1975), *Spermula* (1975),

Deafula (1975), *Dracula and Son* (1976 - aka *Dracula, Pere et Fils*), *Dracula's Dog* (1977 - aka *Zoltan, Hound of Dracula*), *Lady Dracula* (1977), *Dracula* (1977 - TVM), *Doctor Dracula* (1977), *La Dinastia Dracula* (1978), *Dracula* (1979), *Dracula Blows His Cool* (1979), *Love at First Bite* (1979), *Mama Dracula* (1979), *Dracula Sucks* (1979 - aka *Lust at First Bite/Dracula's Bride*), *Nocturna* (1979 - aka *Nocturna, Granddaughter of Dracula*), *Nosferatu* (1979 - aka *Nosferatu the Vampyre/Nosferatu: Phantom der Nacht*), *Dracula's Last Rites* (1980 - aka *Last Rites*), *Dracula* (1980 - cartoon), *Dracula Exotica* (1981 - aka *Love at First Gulp*), *Hysterical* (1982), *Dracula Rises from the Coffin* (1982), *Dracula - The Great Undead* (1982 - aka *Vincent Price's Dracula* - documentary), *Dracula Tan Exarchia* (1983), *Gayracula* (1983), *The Monster Squad* (1987), *Vampires in Venice* (1988 - aka *Nosferatu a Venezia*), *Dracula's Widow* (1988), *Rockula* (1990), *Bram Stoker's Dracula* (1992), *Dracula Rising* (1992), *Dracula's Hair* (1992), *Children of Dracula* (1994) *Dracula - Dead and Loving It* (1995)

Dracula **

USA 1930 84m bw

A vampire Count begins a new reign of terror when he moves from his home in Transylvania to seek fresh victims in England.

Important for being one of the first major horror movies to come out of America, this adaptation of the famous Stoker novel (or rather the stage adaptation) made both its star and studio synonymous with such productions throughout the thirties and forties though, ironically, Lugosi would only officially play Dracula once more in the movies - in *Abbott and Costello Meet Frankenstein* (1948). As a piece of cinema, the film now seems unbearably slow and the acting somewhat stilted, though the early scenes in Transylvania still retain their effect. A simultaneously shot Spanish language version of the film, directed by George Melford and starring Carlos Villarias as Dracula, is generally regarded to be superior.

p: Carl Laemmle Jr for Universal
w: Garrett Fort
novel: BRAM STOKER
play: Hamilton Deane, John L. Balderston
d: TOD BROWNING
ph: KARL STRUSS
m: Tchaikowsky
ed: Milton Carruth, Maurice Pivar
ad: CHARLES D. HALL
make-up: Jack P. Pierce
BELA LUGOSI, Helen Chandler, David Manners, DWIGHT FRYE, Edward Van Sloane, Herbert Bunston, Frances Drake

Dracula ****

GB 1958 82m Technicolor

Dracula is pursued to his castle in Transylvania by his nemesis Professor Van Helsing.

Arguably the best of the Hammer horrors, this pacy, richly coloured and splendidly detailed remake of the 1930 movie has everyone working hard to preserve the spirit if not the letter of the book. Also notable for giving Cushing and Lee the roles which would quickly become synonymous with them and for its imaginative use of limited sets.

p: Anthony Hinds for Hammer
exec p: Michael Carreras
w: JIMMY SANGSTER
novel: BRAM STOKER
d: TERENCE FISHER
ph: JACK ASHER
m: JAMES BERNARD
md: John Hollingsworth
ed: James Needs, Bill Lenny
pd: BERNARD ROBINSON
cos: Molly Arbuthnot
sp: Sydney Pearson
sound: Jock May
make-up: Phil Leakey
associate p: Anthony Nelson Keys
PETER CUSHING, CHRISTOPHER LEE, Melissa Stribling, Michael Gough, Carol Marsh, Miles Malleson, Geoffrey Bayldon, John Van Eyssen, Valerie Gaunt

Dracula **

USA/GB 1979 112m Technicolor

Panavision Dolby
Rich, stylish remake, taking up the story with the Count's arrival in Yorkshire. Though no more faithful than all the other versions, it is consistently good to look at and its technical credits are more than satisfactory.
p: Marvin Mirisch, Tom Pevsner for Universal/Mirisch
w: W. D. Richter
novel: BRAM STOKER
play: Hamilton Deane, John L. Balderston
d: JOHN BADHAM
ph: GILBERT TAYLOR
m: JOHN WILLIAMS
ed: John Bloom
pd: PETER MULLINS
cos: Julie Harris
sp: Albert Whitlock, Roy Arbogast
sound: Robin Gregory, Gerry Humphreys
visual consultant: Maurice Binder
2nd unit d: Gerry Gavigan
add ph: Leslie Dear, Harry Oakes
stunt co-ordinator: Eddie Powell
make-up: Peter Robb-King
ch: Jan Francis
FRANK LANGELLA, Laurence Olivier, DONALD PLEASENCE, Kate Nelligan, Jan Francis, Trevor Eve, Sylvester McCoy, Janine Duvitsky, Tony Haygarth, Teddy Turner, Joe Belcher, Kristine Howarth

Dracula (1992) see Bram Stoker's Dracula

Dracula *
USA/GB 1972 96m colour TVM
Miscast but otherwise quite acceptable tele-version of the story, helped by good location work.
p: Dan Curtis for Latglen
w: Richard Matheson
novel: BRAM STOKER
d: Dan Curtis
ph: Oswald Morris
m: Robert Cobert
ed: Richard A. Harris, Tony Palk
ad: Trevor Williams
cos: Ruth Myers
sp: Kit West
sound: Roy Charman, Gerry Humphreys
Jack Palance, Simon Ward, Nigel Davenport, Pamela Brown, Fiona Lewis, Penelope Horner, Sarah Douglas

Dracula AD 1972
GB 1972 95m Eastmancolor
A Satanist revives Dracula in a desanctified church in modern day Chelsea.
    Abysmal fang and cross flick without even the saving grace of humour. The worst of the Hammer *Draculas*, its

would be hip dialogue has to be heard to be believed. Quickly becoming a cult item.
p: Josephine Douglas for Hammer/Warner
w: Don Houghton
d: Alan Gibson
ph: Dick Bush
m: Mike Vickers
md: Philip Martell
ed: James Needs
ad: Don Mingaye
cos: Rosemary Burrows
sp: Les Bowie
sound: A. W. Lumkin, Claude Hitchcock, Bill Rowe
Christopher Lee, Peter Cushing, Christopher Neame (as Johnny Alucard), Stephanie Beecham, Michael Coles, William Ellis, Caroline Munro, Lally Bowers, Michael Kitchen, Marsha Hunt, Janet Key, Philip Muller, David Andrews

Dracula Has Risen from the Grave
GB 1968 92m Technicolor
Resuscitated by the blood of a priest, Dracula again terrorizes the countryside near his castle.
    Lame but commercially successful addition to Hammer's *Dracula* series, lacking both excitement and invention. Script and acting are alike of the lowest order, whilst the use of colour filters during several key sequences is an unwarranted distraction.
p: Aida Young for Hammer/Warner
w: John Elder (Anthony Hinds)
d: Freddie Francis
ph: Arthur Grant
m: James Bernard
md: Philip Martell
ed: James Needs, Spencer Reeve
ad: Bernard Robinson
cos: Jill Thompson
sp: Frank George, Peter Melrose
sound: Ken Rawkins
Christopher Lee, Rupert Davies, Veronica Carlson, Barbara Ewing, Ewan Hooper, Barry Andrews, Michael Ripper

Dracula - Prince of Darkness **
GB 1965 90m Technicolor Techniscope
Four stranded travellers unwittingly spend the night at Castle Dracula.
    The first and best of the direct sequels to Hammer's own *Dracula*, the script itself being little more than a clever reworking of its predecessor. Filmed back-to-back with *Rasputin - The Mad Monk* with much the same team.
p: Anthony Nelson Keys for Hammer/Warner
w: John Sanson
story: John Elder (Anthony Hinds)

d: Terence Fisher
ph: Michael Reed
m: JAMES BERNARD
md: Philip Martell
ed: James Needs, Chris Barnes
ad: Bernard Robinson
cos: Rosemary Burrows
sp: Les Bowie
sound: Ken Rawkins
Christopher Lee, Francis Matthews, BARBARA SHELLEY, Charles Tingwell, Suzan Farmer, PHILIP LATHAM, Andrew Keir, Thorley Walters

Dracula, Prisoner of Frankenstein
Sp 1972 82m Telecolor
Frankenstein revives the remains of Count Dracula and, with the help of his Monster, makes him do his bidding.
    Cheapjack horror, somewhat typical of its director's amateurish output, with every shot seeming to consist of a zoom.
p: Interfilm/Fenix/Prodif Ets
w: Jess Franco, Paul D'Ales
d: Jeff Franco
ph: Jose Climent
m: Bruno Nicolai
ed: R. Aventer
make-up: Elisa Villenevue
Dennis Price, Howard Vernon, Mary Francis, Genevieve Deloir, Jossiane Gilbert, Fernando Bilbao

Dracula's Daughter *
USA 1936 70m bw
The dead Count's daughter comes to London to cremate her father's body and stays on to taste the city's society life.
    By turns intriguing and tedious, this is a sometimes half hearted sequel to Universal's earlier smash hit, though its lesbian overtones are interesting for the period and Miss Holden is mesmerising.
p: E. M. Asher for Universal
w: Garrett Fort
d: LAMBERT HILLYER
ph: George Robinson
m: Heinz Roemheld
ed: Maurice Pivar, Milton Carruth
ad: Albert S. D'Agostino
sp: John P. Fulton
GLORIA HOLDEN, Otto Kruger, Margueritte Churchill, Edward Van Sloane (as Van Helsing), IRVING PICHEL, Nan Grey, Hedda Hopper, Gilbert Emery, Claud Allister, E. E. Clive, Halliwell Hobbes, Billy Bevan

Dracula's Dog see Zoltan - Hound of Dracula

Dream Demon
GB 1988 89m colour
A young woman, about to be married, finds herself haunted by horrific dreams.

Tame horror hokum lacking both spirit and originality - especially originality.
p: Paul Webster for Filmscreen/British Screen/Palace/Spectrafilm
w: Christopher Wicking, Harley Cokliss
d: Harley Cokliss
ph: Ian Wilson
m: Bill Nelson
ed: Ian Crafford, David Martin
pd: Hugo Luczyc-Whyowski
Jemma Redgrave, Kathleen Wilhoite, Timothy Spall, Jimmy Nail, Nickolas Grace, Susan Fleetwood, Annabelle Lanyon

Dressed to Kill **
USA 1980 105m Technicolor
When a woman is slashed to death after a visit to her psychiatrist, a witness teams up with her son and goes after the killer but all is not what it seems.
Slick and clever variation on themes from *Psycho*, sometimes brilliantly done. Arguably its director's best film and certainly the best of his Hitchcock homages.
p: George Litto for Filmways/Cinema 77
exec p: Samuel Z. Arkoff
w/d: BRIAN DE PALMA
ph: Ralf D. Bode
m: PINO DONAGGIO
md: Natale Massara
ed: JERRY GREENBERG
pd: Gary Weist
cos: Ann Roth
sound: John Bolz, Dick Vorisek
MICHAEL CAINE, ANGIE DICKINSON, Nancy Allen, Keith Gordon, Dennis Franz

The Driller Killer
USA 1979 89m colour

A mad artist goes about murdering tramps with a cordless drill.
Tawdry, depressing, absolutely worthless killer thriller that gloats over the death agonies of its victims. It later gained a certain notoriety for being banned on video in Britain. Its director-star nevertheless went on to direct such films as *King of New York*, *Bad Lieutenant* and, most notably, *Body Snatchers*.
exec p: Rochelle Weisbberg
w: N. G. St John
d: Abel Ferrara
ph: Ken Kelsch
m: Joseph Delia
ed: Orlando Gallini and others
ad: no credit given
sp: David Smith
sound: J. MacIntyre, Richard Wiggte
Jimmy Laine (Abel Ferrara), Carolyn Marz, Harry Schultz, Baybi Day, Rhodney Montreal, Richard Howorth

Dullea, Keir (1936-)
American actor, best known for playing astronaut Dave Bowman in Stanley Kubrick's *2001: A Space Odyssey*. In films from 1961 with *Hoodlum Priest*, he began his career on stage in stock, reaching Broadway in 1959. His other film credits include *David and Lisa*, *Pope Joan*, *Leopard in the Snow* and *2010: Odyssey Two*.
Genre credits:
Bunny Lake is Missing (1965), *De Sade* (1969), *Black Christmas* (1975 - aka *Silent Night, Evil Night*), *Full Circle* (1976 - aka *The Haunting of Julia*), *Brainwaves* (1982)

Dust Devil
GB/South Africa 1993 105m Technicolor Dolby

A murderous hitchhiker uses the blood of his victims to paint horrific murals.
Good looking but uninvolving scare story.
p: Joanne Sellar for Palace/Film Four/British Screen/Miramax
exec p: Bob Weinstein, Harvey Weinstein, Nik Powell, Stephen Woolley, Paul Trybits
w/d: Richard Stanley
ph: Steven Chivers
m: Simon Boswell
ed: Derek Trigg
pd: Joseh Bwennett
cos: Michele Clapton, Ruy Filipe
sp: The Dream Machine
sound: Richard Rhys-Davies, Robin Harris
Robert Burke, Chelsea Field, Zake Mokae, John Matshikiza, Rufus Swart, William Hootkins, Marianne Sagebrecht

Dyall, Valentine (1908-1985)
Velvet voiced British actor with much stage and radio experience, in films from 1943 with Powell and Pressburger's *The Life and Death of Colonel Blimp*. His gaunt appearance lent itself well to horror films, though he made only a few. His other credits include *Caesar and Cleopatra*, *Brief Encounter*, *The Man in Black*, *The Slipper and the Rose* and *Britannia Hospital*.
Genre credits:
The Ghost of Rashmon Hall (1949), *City of the Dead* (1960 - aka *Horror Hotel*), *The Haunting* (1963), *The Horror of It All* (1964), *The Naked World of Harrison Marks* (1967 - voice only), *Lust for a Vampire* (1970 - voice only, dubbing Mike Raven)

E

Earles, Harry (1902-1985)

Diminutive, baby-faced German-born actor (real name Kurt Schnieder), remembered for playing Hans the midget in Tod Browning's *Freaks* and the 'baby' in both versions of *The Unholy Three*. His other credits include *Baby Mine* and *The Wizard of Oz* (as a Munchkin). He sometimes went by the name Harry Doll.
Genre credits:
The Unholy Three (1925), *The Unholy Three* (1930 - sound remake), *Freaks* (1932)

Earth vs the Spider

USA 1958 70m bw
A giant spider threatens a small isolated township.
   Grade Z fifties hokum with poor effects work.
p: Bert I. Gordon for AIP
exec P: James H. Nicholson, Samuel Z. Arkoff
w: Lazslo Gorog, George Worthington Yates
d/sp/story: Bert I. Gordon
ph: Jack Marta
m: Albert Glasser
ed: Ronald Sinclair
ad: Walter Keller
sound: Al Overton
Ed Kemmer, June Kenney, Gene Persson, Gene Roth, Hal Torey, Mickey Finn, Sally Fraser, Troy Patterson

Eaten Alive (1976) see Death Trap

Eaten Alive

It 1979 87m colour
A woman searching for her missing sisters on a tropical island is confronted by cannibals.
   Zero-budget schlock horror which isn't even good exploitation.
d: Umberto Lenzi
Robert Kerman, Janet Agren, Mel Ferrer, Ivan Rassimov, Meg Fleming, Me Me Lai, Paola Senatore

Ebirah - Horror of the Deep

Japan 1966 86m Tohoscope
Eastmancolor

Godzilla teams up with Mothra to destroy a giant lobster.
   Pretty juvenile, even for a Godzilla movie, which is saying something.
p: Tomoyuki Tanaka for Toho
w: Shinichi Seyizawa
d: Jun Fukuda
ph: Kazuo Yamada
m: Masaru Sato
ad: Takeo Kita
sp: Eiji Tsuburaya
sound: Schici Yoshizawa
Akira Takarada, Toru Watanabe, Hideo Sunazuka, Kumi Mizuno, Jun Tazaki

Eburne, Maude (1875-1960)

Canadian character actress, on Broadway from 1914 and in films from 1918 in *A Pair of Sixes*, in which she recreated her stage role of Coddles. She didn't make another film until *The Bat Whispers* in 1930 after which she was much in demand. Her other credits include appearances in *Lonely Wives*, *Blonde Crazy*, *Polly of the Circus*, *Fog*, *Ruggles of Red Gap*, *The Secret Life of Walter Mitty* and *Mother Wore Tights*.
Genre credits:
The Bat Whispers (1930), *The Vampire Bat* (1932), *The Return of the Terror* (1934), *Among the Living* (1941), *The Boogie Man Will Get You* (1944)

Echoes

USA 1981 93m Technicolor
A young man has weird recurring nightmares and cannot tell if it is reality or a past life.
   Thoroughly boring psycho-horror drama with nothing of interest whatever.
p: George R. Nice, Valerie Y. Belsky for Herberval/Siedelman/Shiffman
exec p: Barry Rosenthal
w: Richard J. Anthony
d: Arthur Allan Siedelman
ph: Hanania Baers
m: Stephen Swartz, Gerard Bernard Cohen
ed: Dan Perry
Richard Alfieri, Nathalie Nell, Ruth Roman, Mercedes McCambridge, Mike Kelin, Gale Sondergaard, John Spencer

Ecoglia del Delitto see Bay of Blood

Ed Wood **

USA 1994 139m bw Dolby
The life and grade Z movies of angora-loving Edward D. Wood Jr, Hollywood's worst director.
   Highly engaging biopic with many points of interest along the way for buffs, not least of which is Martin Landau's excellent performance as the drug addicted Bela Lugosi.
p: Denise Di Novi, Tim Burton for Touchstone
exec p: Michael Lehmann
w: Scott Alexander, Larry Karaszewski
d: TIM BURTON
ph: STEFAN CZAPSKY
m: HOWARD SHORE
ed: Chris Lebenzon
pd: TOM DUFFIELD
make-up: Rob Bottin, V. E. Neill, Yolanda Toms (aa)
JOHNNY DEPP, MARTIN LANDAU (AA), Sarah Jessica Parker, Patricia Arquette, Jeffrey Jones, Bill Murray

Edeson, Arthur (1891-1970)

Distinguished American cinematographer who worked on many important silent productions, including several with Douglas Fairbanks (*The Three Musketeers*, *Robin Hood*, *The Thief of Baghdad*), before photographing three of Universal's key thirties horror films for director James Whale. A former portrait photographer, he entered the film industry in 1911, first working as a camera operator for Elcair before graduating to full blown cinematographer with *Cheating Cheaters* in 1919. Other credits include *All Quiet on the Western Front*, *Mutiny on the Bounty*, *The Maltese Falcon*, *Casablanca* and *The Mask of Dimitrios*.
Genre credits:
The Lost World (1925), *The Bat* (1926), *The Gorilla* (1927), *Frankenstein* (1931), *The Old Dark House* (1932), *The Invisible Man* (1933)

Edge of Sanity

GB 1988 92m Eastmancolor Dolby

Dr Jekyll's experiments turn him into Jack the Ripper.

Failed attempt to add something more to the classic story. Tedium sets in well before the end.
p: Edward Simons, Harry Alan Towers for Allied Vision
w: J. P. Felix, Ron Raley
story: Robert Louis Stevenson
d: Gerard Kikoine
ph: Tony Spratling
m: Fredric Talgorn
ed: Malcolm Cooke
pd: Jean Charles Dedieu
cos: Valerie Lanee
sound: Paul Sharkey
Anthony Perkins, Glynis Barber, Sarah Maur-Thorp, Ben Cole, Ray Jewers, David Lodge, Jill Melford

Edge of Terror
GB 1986 91m Technicolor Dolby
A lady writer holidaying in Greece finds herself stalked by a madman.

Wholly unremarkable variation on an over-used theme with a much better cast than it deserves.
p: Nico Mastorakis for Omega Entertainment
exec p: Isabel Mastorakis
w: Nico Mastorakis, Fred C. Perry
d/story: Nico Mastorakis
ph: Andrew Bellis
m: Stanley Myers, Hans Zimmer
ed: Nico Mastorakis, Bruce Cannon
ad: no credit given
cos: Richard Abramson
sound: Blake Wilcox
Meg Foster, Wings Hauser, David McCallum, Robert Morley, Steve Railsback, Michael Yannatos

Ege, Julie (1943-)
Curvaceous Norwegian actress in Britain from 1969. A former model, she was signed to star in Hammer's *Creatures the World Forgot* following minor roles in *On Her Majesty's Secret Service*, *Every Home Should Have One* and *Up Pompeii*. Her other film credits include *The Magnificent Seven Deadly Sins*, *Rentadick* and *Not Now, Darling*.
Genre credits:
Creatures the World Forgot (1971), *Craze* (1973), *The Mutations* (1974), *The Legend of the Seven Golden Vampires* (1974 - aka *The Seven Brothers Meet Dracula*)

Ekerot, Bengt
Swedish actor with much stage experience, remembered for his appearance as Death in Ingmar Bergman's *The Seventh Seal* (1956), a role that has since been spoofed in such films as *Bill and Ted's Bogus Journey* and *Last Action Hero*.

Ekland, Britt (1942-)
Swedish born actress (real name Britt-Marie Eklund) in international films from the mid-sixties. Formerly married to Peter Sellers, her credits include *After the Fox*, *Baxter* and *The Man with the Golden Gun*, in which she played Bond girl Mary Goodnight, though she is perhaps best remembered by genre fans for her naked dance in *The Wicker Man*.
Genre credits:
The Night Hair Child (1971), *Asylum* (1972), *The Wicker Man* (1973), *Satan's Mistress* (1982)

Elder, John see Hinds, Anthony

The Electric Man see Man Made Monster

Eles, Sandor (1936-)
Hungarian actor who came to Britain in 1956 following the uprising. In films from the early sixties, his credits include *Guns of Darkness*, *The Naked Edge*, *The Rebel*, *French Dressing* and *The Magnificent Two* as well as much stage and television work.
Genre credits:
The Evil of Frankenstein (1964), *Countess Dracula* (1970), *And Soon the Darkness* (1970)

Elfman, Danny (1954-)
American composer with a penchant for dark fantasy themes. A singer, songwriter and performer with rock group Oingo Boingo, he began scoring films in the early eighties and linked himself to the career of director Tim Burton, scoring *Pee-Wee's Big Adventure*, *Beetlejuice*, *Batman*, *Edward Scissorhands*, *Batman Returns* and *The Nightmare Before Christmas*, singing the role of Jack Skellington (voiced by Chris Sarandon) in the latter. Other credits include *Dick Tracy*, *Sommersby* and *Black Beauty* and TV themes for *Sledgehammer*, *The Simpsons* and *Tales from the Crypt*. Brother of director Richard Elfman.
Genre credits:
Beetlejuice (1988), *Scrooged* (1988), *Darkman* (1990), *Nightbreed* (1990), *Edward Scissorhands* (1990), *The Nightmare Before Christmas* (1993 - aka *Tim Burton's The Nightmare Before Christmas* - also voice), *Shrunken Heads* (1995 - theme)

Embryo
USA 1976 104m Technicolor
A scientist experiments with a human foetus and produces a super intelligent woman.

Frankenstein-like goings on without the wit, style or taste to make it even remotely interesting.
p: Arnold H. Orgolini, Anita Doohan for Cine Artists/Sandy Howard Productions
w: Anita Doohan, Jack W. Thomas
d: Ralph Nelson
ph: Fred J. Koenekamp
m: Gil Melle
ed: John Martinelli
pd: Joe Alves
Rock Hudson, Barbara Carrera, Diane Ladd, Roddy McDowall, Ann Schedeen

Emerson, Keith (1944-)
British composer with several synth scores to his credit, most notably Dario Argento's *Inferno*. A former member of the rock group Emerson, Lake and Palmer, his other credits include *Nighthawks* and *Best Revenge*.
Gebre credits:
Inferno (1980), *Murderock* (1984 - aka *Murderock: Uccide a Passo di Danza*), *Two Evil Eyes* (1990 - aka *Due Occhi Diabolici*)

Empire of the Ants
USA 1977 89m Movielab
Tourists are threatened by giant radioactived ants on a quiet stretch of the Florida coast.

Dismal low-budget shocker which isn't even unintentionally funny. Regarded even by its star as the nadir of her career (which is saying something).
p: Bert I. Gordon for AIP/Cinema 77
exec p: Samuel Z. Arkoff
w: Jack Turley
story: H. G. Wells
d/sp: Bert I. Gordon
ph: Reginald Morris
m: Dana Kaproff
ed: Michael Luciano
ad: Charles Rosen
Joan Collins, Robert Lansing, John David Carson, Albert Salmi, Jacqueline Scott, Pamela Shoop, Brook Palance, Robert Pine

Endangered Species
USA 1982 97m Metrocolor
A cop visiting Wyoming on his vacation uncovers the truth about a series of cattle mutilations with the help of a local policewoman.

Reasonable amalgam of mystery, melodrama and horror which keeps one watching simply to find out what's going on.
p: Carolyn Pfeiffer for MGM/Alive
w: Alan Rudolph. John Binder
story: Judson Klinger, Richard Woods
d: Alan Rudolph
ph: Paul Lohmann
m: Gary Wright
ed: Tom Walls
pd: Trevor Williams
cos: Betsy Cox

sp: Jonnie Burke, Steve Garlich
sound: Jim Tananbaum
add ph: Jan Keisser
Robert Urich, JoBeth Williams, Paul
Dooley, Peter Coyote, Hoyt Axton

Endore, Guy (1900-1970)
American novelist and screenwriter
whose novel, *Werewolf of Paris*, has been
filmed twice, as *The Curse of the Werewolf*
and *Legend of the Werewolf*.
Genre credits:
Mark of the Vampire (1935 - co-w), *Mad
Love* (1935 - aka *The Hands of Orlac* -
co-w), *The Devil Doll* (1936 - co-w),
Curse of the Werewolf (1961 - novel),
Legend of the Werewolf (1974 - novel)

Enemy from Space see
Quatermass 2

English, Marla (1930-)
Decorative American actress who made
a handful of low-budget pictures in the
fifties, among them *Desert Sands*, *Flesh
and the Spur* and *A Strange Adventure*, as
well as two horror films for director
Edward L. Cahn.
Genre credits:
The She-Creature (1956), *Voodoo Woman*
(1957)

Englund, Robert (1948-)
American actor who, after playing bit
parts for nearly ten years in films and
on television, shot to stardom as Freddy
Krueger in the *Nightmare on Elm Street*
series and the TV show *Freddy's
Nightmares*. His other credits include
Buster and Billie, *A Star is Born* and *St.
Ives*, though more recent attempts to
break away from the Freddy image have
been met with a certain indifference.
He has also directed one genre film,
976-Evil.
Genre credits:
Death Trap (1976 - aka *Eaten Alive*),
Dead and Buried (1981), *Galaxy of Terror*
(1981), *A Nightmare on Elm Street*
(1984), *A Nightmare on Elm Street Part II:
Freddy's Revenge* (1985), *A Nightmare on
Elm Street Part Three - The Dream Warriors*
(1987), *A Nightmare on Elmstreet Part 4 -
The Dream Master* (1988), *976-Evil* (1988
- aka *Horrorscope* - d only), *A Nightmare
on Elm Street Part 5 - The Dream Child*
(1989), *The Phantom of the Opera* (1989),
Freddy's Dead: The Final Nightmare
(1991), *Dance Macabre* (1992), *Night
Terrors* (1993 - aka *Tobe Hooper's Night
Terrors/Tobe Hooper's Nightmare*), *Wes
Craven's New Nightmare* (1994), *The
Mangler* (1995)

The Entity
USA 1981 125m Technicolor Panavision

• **Robert Englund as Freddy Krueger
in Wes Craven's *A Nightmare on Elm
Street*, the success of which spawned
six sequels (to date) and a television
series, *Freddy's Nightmares*.**

Dolby
A woman is sexually attacked by an
entity and seeks help from psychiatrists
and supernaturalists to dispel it.
  Allegedly based on fact (it says here),
this film was made before *Poltergeist* but
not released until after its box office
success. In itself tolerable enough, with
many sequences in its director's most
typical (ie: flashy) style.
p: Harold Schneider for TCF/PI/
American Cinema
w: Frank DeFelitta from his novel
d: Sidney J. Furie
ph: Stephen H. Burum
m: Charles Bernstein
ed: Frank J. Urioste
pd: Charles Rosen
sp: William Cruse, Joe Lombardi
make-up effects: Stan Winston, James
Kagel
Barbara Hershey, Ron Silver, David
Labiosa, George Coe, Jacqueline Brookes

Eraserhead
USA 1976 90m bw
A young man depressed over life and his
surroundings becomes even more so
when his girfriend presents him with a
mutated baby.
  Open to interpretation, this occa-
ionally clever but ultimately depressing
and boring piece of surrealism has been
acclaimed as a masterpiece by some and
garbage by others. For the most part an

• **Robert Englund sans Freddy
make-up, here seen in a publicity
portrait for the TV series *V*.**

alienating and tasteless experience,
whatever one's consideration.
p: David Lynch for American Institute
w/d/ed/pd/sp: David Lynch
ph: David Elmes, Herbert Cardwell
Jack Nance, Charlotte Stewart, Allen
Joseph, Jeanne Bates, Juduth Anna
Roberts, Jennifer Lynch, Peggy Lynch,
Laurel Near

The Escape of Mechagodzilla
see Terror of Mechagodzilla

Eternal Evil
Canada 1985 86m colour
A commercials director with the ability
to leave his body may or may not be
responsible for a series of killings.
  Tired variation on a theme already
explored in *Psychic Killer*.
p: Peter Kroonenberg for Filmline/
Telefilm Canada/Global Television
exec p: Nicolas Clermont, David J.
Patterson
w: Robert Geoffrion
d: George Milhalka
ph: Paul Van Der Linden
m: Marvin Dolgay
ed: Yves Langlois, Nick Rotundo
ad: John Meighen
cos: Paul-André Guerin
sound: Gabor Vadnay
Winston Reckert, Karen Black, Lois
Maxwell, Patty Talbot, John Novak,
Andrew Bednarsky

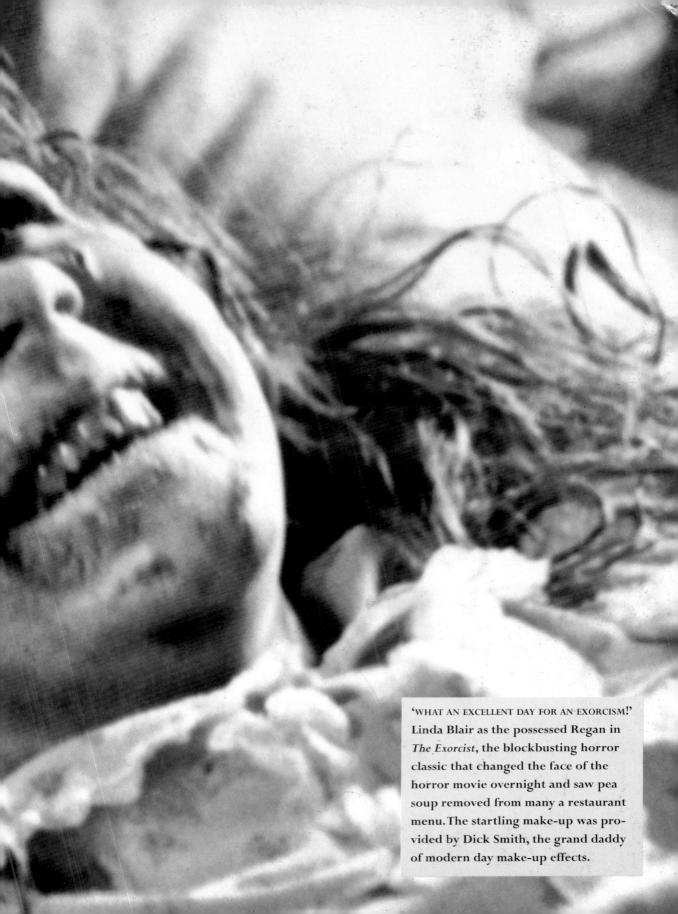

'WHAT AN EXCELLENT DAY FOR AN EXORCISM!'
Linda Blair as the possessed Regan in
The Exorcist, the blockbusting horror
classic that changed the face of the
horror movie overnight and saw pea
soup removed from many a restaurant
menu. The startling make-up was provided by Dick Smith, the grand daddy
of modern day make-up effects.

Evans, Clifford (1912-1985)

Welsh character actor memorable as the vampire hunter in Hammer's *Kiss of the Vampire*. Other films include *Love on the Dole*, *The Foreman Went to France*, *Twist of Sand* and TV's *Stryker of the Yard*.
Genre credits:
Curse of the Werewolf (1961), *Kiss of the Vampire* (1962 - aka *Kiss of Evil*)

Evans, Jimmy

British make-up artist with a smattering of low-budget horrors to his credit.
Genre credits:
Blood of the Vampire (1958), *Monster of Terror* (1965 - aka *Die, Monster, Die!*), *Crucible of Terror* (1971), *Captain Kronos - Vampire Hunter* (1972 - aka *Kronos*), *Legend of the Werewolf* (1974 - co-make-up)

The Evil

USA 1978 89m Movielab
When an allegedly haunted house is reopened it begins to murder its new inhabitants. Later events reveal the place to be a gateway to hell.

Middling horror film in the *Amityville* manner. Effective touches along the way but no overall style.
p: Ed Carlin for New World/Rangoon
exec p: Paul A. Joseph, Malcolm Levinthal
w: Donald G. Thompson
d: Gus Trikonis
ph: Mario Di Leo
m: Johnny Harris
ed: Jack Kerscher
ad: Peter Jamison
cos: Barbara Andrews
sound: Bill Kaplan Jr
Richard Crenna, Joanna Pettet, Andrew Prine, Cassie Yates, Victor Buono, Lynne Maddy

The Evil Dead *

USA 1982 85m DuArt
A group of teenagers find themselves threatened by dormant demons whilst staying at an isolated woodland cabin.

Superior exploitation horror which won't be to everyone's taste (it was banned outright as a so-called 'video nasty' in Britain for several years). However, it is certainly imaginatively made with an inventive use of camera and plenty of shocks and gore to keep aficionados glued. It was followed by *Evil Dead 2: Dead by Dawn* (1986) and *Army of Darkness* (1992).
p: Robert Tappert for Renaissance
exec p: Robert Tappert, Bruce Campbell, Sam Raimi
w: Sam Raimi
d: SAM RAIMI
ph: Tim Philo

m: Joe Loduca
ed: Edna Ruth Paul, Joel Coen
ad: no credit given
sp: Bart Pierce
sound: John Mason, Jerry Frederick, Mel Zelniker, Josh Becker
make-up effects: Tom Sullivan
Bruce Campbell, Hal Delrich, Betsy Barker, Sarah York, Ellen Sandweiss

Evil Dead 2: Dead by Dawn *

USA 1986 86m Technicolor
The sole survivor of *The Evil Dead* finds himself stranded in the demon infested cabin for a second night.

Basically a remake of the first movie, with a bigger budget and improved special effects. Nevertheless, a good rollercoaster ride of shocks and laughs for the late night crowd.
p: Robert Tapert, Bruce Campbell for Renaissance/De Laurentiis Entertainment Group/Rosebud
exec p: Irvin Shapiro, Alec de Benedetti
w: Sam Raimi, Scott Spiegel
d: Sam Raimi
ph: Peter Deming, Eugene Schluglett
m: Joe Loduca
ed: Kaye Davis
ad: Philip Duffin, Randy Bennet
cos: Vicki Graef
sp: Doug Beswick
sound: Tom Morrison
make-up effects: Mark Shostrom
2nd unit ph: Tim Philo
stunt co-ordinator: Gary Jensen
Bruce Campbell, Sarah Berry, Kassie Wesley, Dan Hicks, Theodore Raimi, Denise Dixler, Richard Domeier, John Peaks, Lou Hancock, William Preston Robertson (voice only)

Evil Dead III see Army of Darkness

Evil Dead III: The Medieval Dead see Army of Darkness

The Evil Eye see Possessed

The Evil of Frankenstein *

GB 1964 94m Technicolor
Frankenstein revives one of his previous creations found preserved in a glacier.

Variably handled third entry in Hammer's ongoing Frankenstein series in which the Monster's make-up verges on the ludicrous.
p: Anthony Hinds for Hammer/Universal
w: John Elder (Anthony Hinds)
d: Freddie Francis
ph: John Wilcox
m: DON BANKS
md: Philip Martell
ed: James Needs
d: Don Mingaye

cos: Rosemary Burrows
sp: Les Bowie
sound: Ken Rawkins
make-up: Roy Ashton
Peter Cushing, Sandor Eles, Peter Woodthorpe, Duncan Lamont, David Hutcheson, Katy Wild, Kiwi Kingston (as the Monster)

Evilspeak

USA 1982 89m colour
A army cadet, tormented by his classmates, contacts the Devil via his computer and extracts a bloody revenge.

Taps meets *Carrie* in this fitfully diverting shocker with a few good moments along the way for gore-hounds (including a sequence involving a pack of man-eating pigs).
p: Eric Weston
exec p: Sylvio Tabet, Eric Weston
w: Joseph Garofalo, Eric Weston
d: Eric Weston
ph: Irv Goodnoff
m: Roger Kellaway
ed: Charles Tefoni
Clint Howard, R. G. Armstrong, Joseph Cortese, Haywood Nelson, Charles Tyner, Lynn Hancock, Hamilton Camp, Claude Earl Jones

Ewing, Barbara

New Zealand-born actress on stage in Britain from the mid-sixties and in films from 1967 with *Torture Garden*. Much theatre work as well as television appearances in such programmes as *Country Matters*, *Hard Times* and *Brass*.
Genre credits:
Torture Garden (1967), *Dracula Has Risen from the Grave* (1968)

The Exorcist ****

USA 1973 122m Metroclor
When a twelve-year-old girl apparently becomes possessed by the Devil a priest who is beginning to question his faith helps to exorcize her.

A brilliantly conceived and intelligently executed horror movie which has a lot more to it than might at first meet the eye. The religious parallels make the story all the more compelling (the Devil is out to get the priest, not the girl) and the technical effects are most believable. A seminal film indeed, it spawned several imitators and was a smash hit at the box office with sensation hungry audiences. A modern classic, not to be missed, it was followed by *Exorcist II: The Heretic* (1977) and *Exorcist III* (1990).
p: William Peter Blatty for Warner/Hoya
exec p: Noel Marshall
w/novel: WILLIAM PETER BLATTY (AA)
d: WILLIAM FRIEDKIN

ph: OWEN ROIZMAN, BILLY WILLIAMS
m: George Crumb, Jack Nitzsche, Mike Oldfield and others
ed: Bud Smith, Jordan Leondopoulos, Evan Lottman, Norman Gay
pd: Bill Malley
cos: Florence Foy, Bill Beattie
sound: ROBERT KNUDSON, CHRIS NEWMAN (AA)
sp: MARCEL VERCOUTERE
make-up effects: DICK SMITH
ELLEN BURSTYN, Max Von Sydow (as the exorcist), JASON MILLER, LINDA BLAIR (as Regan), LEE J. COBB, Kitty Winn, JACK McGOWRAN, MERCEDES McCAMBRIDGE (as the voice of the Devil)

Exorcist 1990 see Exorcist III

Exorcist II: The Heretic
USA 1977 117m Technicolor
It transpires that the demon inside Regan wasn't properly exorcized after all…

Pointless sequel which tries and fails to exploit the success of its illustrious predecessor, but with nothing new to offer of its own, save some po-faced psychological mumbo jumbo and an exciting finale involving a plague of locusts. But it's a long time in coming.
p: Richard Lederer, John Boorman for Warner
w: William Goodhart
d: John Boorman
ph: William A. Fraker
m: Ennio Morricone
ed: Tom Priestley
pd: Richard MacDonald
cos: Robert DeMora
sp: Albert Whitlock, Frank Van Der Veer, Chuck Gaspar
sound: Walter Goss
sound effects ed: Jim Atkinson
make-up effects: Dick Smith
titles: Dan Perri
creative associate/2nd unit d: Rospo Pallenberg
locust ph: Sean Morris, David Thompson
Richard Burton, Linda Blair, Louise Fletcher, Kitty Winn, Max Von Sydow (as the exorcist, in flashback after his death in the first film), Paul Henreid, James Earl Jones, Ned Beatty

Exorcist III: Cries and Shadows (1975) see Naked Exorcism

Exorcist III *
USA 1990 110m DeLuxe Dolby
Lieutenant Kinderman traces a series of grizzly murders back to the spirit which possessed Regan in The Exorcist.

Complexly plotted sequel to The Exorcist via Blatty's own sequel, Legion. Intelligently handled hokum for those who can pick up the threads, let down only by a formularistic denouement.
p: Carter de Haven for TCF/Morgan Creek
exec p: James G. Robinson, Joe Roth
w/novel/d: WILLIAM PETER BLATTY
ph: Gerry Fisher
m: Barry de Vorzon
ed: Todd Ramsay, Peter Lee
pd: Leslie Dilley
cos: Dana Lyman
sp: Bill Purcell, Norman Reynolds
sound: Richard Van Dyke
make-up effects: Greg Cannom
stunt co-ordinator/2nd unit d: Paul Baxley
George C. Scott, Jason Miller, Brad Dourif, Ed Flanders, Nicol Williamson, Scott Wilson, Nancy Fish, George di Cenzo, Viveca Lindfors

Eye of the Cat *
USA 1969 102m Technicolor
A young man with a fear of cats goes to live with his rich, cat loving aunt in the hope that he will inherit.

Good-looking but rather elementary horror story which takes a while to get going and suffers from the usual holdback of movies of this kind: cats just aren't frightening.
p: Bernard Schwarz, Philip Hazelton for Universal
exec p: Joseph M. Schenck
w: Joseph Stefano
d: David Lowell Rich
ph: RUSSELL METTY, ELLSWORTH FREDERICKS
m: Lalo Schifrin
md: Stanley Wilson
ed: J. Terry Williams
ad: Alexander Golitzen, William O. De Cincey
cos: Edith Head
sound: Waldon O. Watson, Frank Wilkinson
titles: Wayne Fitzgerald
animal trainer: Ray Berwick
Michael Sarrazin, Gayle Hunnicutt, Eleanor Parker, Tim Henry, Laurence Naismith

Eye of the Demon see Bay Cove

Eye of the Evil Dead see Possessed

The Eyes of Charles Sand *
USA 1972 74m Technicolor TVM
A man who has inherited the family curse of second sight helps a girl who claims her brother has been murdered.

Fair horror story containing a series of well staged shock effects, though finally it's a shade too hysterical.
p: Hugh Benson for Warner
w: Henry Farrell, Stanford Whitmore
story: Henry farrell
d: Reza S. Badiyi
ph: Ben Colman
m: Henry Mancini (an uncredited use of his score from Wait Until Dark)
ed: Carroll Sax
ad: Walter M. Simmons
sound: Everett Hughes
titles: Reza S. Badiyi
Peter Haskell, Joan Bennett, Barbara Rush, Sharon Farrell, Bradford Dillman, Adam West, Ivor Francis, Gary Clarke

The Eyes of Laura Mars
USA 1978 104m Metrocolor
A female fashion photographer has pre-monitions about murders not yet committed.

Glossy killer-thriller which seems to be concerned more about its fashion element than about providing shocks. Considering the talent involved it should have been a lot better than it is.
p: Jack H. Harris for Columbia
exec p: Jon Peters
w: John Carpenter, David Zelag Goodman
d: Irvin Kershner
ph: Victor J. Kemper
m: Artie Kane
md: Charles A. Koppelman
title song sung by: Barbra Streisand
ed: Michael Kahn
pd: Gene Callahn
cos: Bernardene Mann, James Hagerman, Marilyn Bishop
sp: Edward Drohan, James Liles
sound: Les Lazarowitz
Faye Dunaway, Tommy Lee Jones, Brad Dourif, Rene Auberjonois, Frank Adonis, Raul Julia, Lisa Taylor, Meg Mundy

F

The Face **
Sweden 1958 103m bw
The arrival of a mesmerist and his troupe in a small Swedish village has a curious effect on the townsfolk.

Beautifully lit gothic melodrama in its director's best style. Great to look at though perhaps a fraction overlong.
p: Allan Ekelund for Svensk Filmindustri
w/d: INGMAR BERGMAN
ph: GUNNAR FISCHER
m: Erik Nordgren
ed: E. Eckert-Lundin
ad: P. A. Lundgren
cos: Manne Lindholm, Greta Johansson
sound: Aaby Wedin, Ake Hansson
Max Von Sydow, Ingrid Thulin, Gunnar Bjornstrand, Naima Wifstrand, Ake Fridell, Lars Ekborg, Bengt Ekerot

The Face at the Window
GB 1939 65m bw
In Paris, a murderer uses his half-brother, a dim-witted moron, to distract his victims.

Hoary melodrama with a succulently hammy performance from its barnstorming star.
p: George King for Ambassador/Pennant
w: A. Rawlinson, Ronald Faye
play: Brooke Warren
d: George King
ph: Home Glendining
m: Jack Beaver
ed: Jack Harris
ad: Philip Bawcombe
sound: Harold King
Tod Slaughter, Marjorie Taylor, John Warwick, Leonard Henry, Aubrey Mallalieu, Harry Terry (as The Face)

The Face Behind the Mask *
USA 69m bw
A Hungarian immigrant turns to a life of crime after his face has been disfigured in a fire.

Silly but mildly diverting second feature with horror overtones.
p: Wallace MacDonald for Columbia
w: Allen Vincent, Paul Jarrico
play: Thomas O'Connell
ph: Franz Planer

md: M. W. Stoloff
ed: Charles Nelson
ad: Lionel Banks
PETER LORRE, DON BEDDOE, Evelyn Keyes, George E. Stone

The Face of Fu Manchu *
GB 1965 96m Technicolor Techniscope
Thought to have been executed, the Yellow Peril is discovered to be at the head of a new crime wave, so Nayland Smith of Scotland Yard investigates.

Competent thriller on similar lines to the old Saturday morning serials and all the better for it, with the period detail particularly well judged. It was followed by *The Brides of Fu Manchu* (1966), *The Vengeance of Fu Manchu* (1967), *The Castle of Fu Manchu* (1968) and *The Blood of Fu Manchu* (1968), all of them starring Lee.
p: Harry Alan Towers for Anglo-EMI/Hallam
w: Peter Welbeck (Harry Alan Towers)
d: DON SHARP
ph: ERNEST STEWARD
m: Christopher Whelan
ed: John Trumper
ad: FRANK WHITE
sound: Dorothy Edwards
CHRISTOPHER LEE, NIGEL GREEN, Tsai Chin, Howard Marion Crawford, Joachim Fuschburger, James Robertson Justice, Walter Rilla

Fade to Black
USA 1980 100m Metrocolor
A maladjusted teenager with a movie fixation goes on a murder spree in the guise of his favourite movie characters.

Over long, notably under produced horror parody which wastes a basically interesting premise.
p: George S. Braunstein, Ron Hamady for Leisure Investment/American Cinema/Movie Ventures/Fade to Black venture
exec p: Irwin Yablans, Sylvio Tabet
w/d: Vernon Zimmerman
ph: Alex Phillips, Jr
m: Craig Safan
ed: James Mitchell, Howard Kunin
Dennis Christopher, Tim Thomerson, Gwynne Giford, Norman Burton,

Mickey Rourke, Linda Kerridge, Morgan Paul

The Fall of the House of Usher
see House of Usher (1960)

The Fan
USA 1981 95m Technicolor
A star is pestered by a fan who turns out to be homicidal.

Unremarkable killer thriller, distinguished only by its cast, who should have known better.
p: Robert Stigwood for Paramount/Filmways
exec p: Kevin McCormick
w: Priscilla Chapman, John Hartnell
novel: Bob Randall
d: Edward Bianchi
ph: Dick Bush
m: Pino Donaggio
songs: Marvin Hamlisch, Tim Rice, Louis St. Louis.
ed: Alan Heim
pd: Santo Loquasto
cos: Jeffrey Kurlan, Tom McKinley
sound: Chris Newman, Arthur Bloom, Dick Vorisek
ch: Arlene Phillips
Lauren Bacall, Michael Biehn, James Garner, Maureen Stapleton, Hector Elizondo, Anna Marie Horsford, Kurt Johnson, Griffin Dunne

Fanatic (1980) see The Last Horror Film

The Fantastic Disappearing Man see The Return of Dracula

Farrow, Mia (1945-)
American actress, the daughter of director John Farrow and actress Maureen O'Sullivan, best known for her roles in the films of her one-time partner Woody Allen. Came to prominence on television in the soap opera *Peyton Place* before achieving international stardom with the film version of *Rosemary's Baby*. Other credits include *The Great Gatsby*, *Death on the Nile*, *Supergirl* and *Widows' Peak*.
Genre credits:
Rosemary's Baby (1968), *Blind Terror*

(1971 - aka *See No Evil*), *Full Circle* (1977
- aka *The Haunting of Julia*)

Farrow, Tisa
American actress, the younger sister of
Mia Farrow, who has appeared in a few
gory European horrors.
Genre credits:
Zombie Flesheaters (1980 - aka *Zombies*),
The Anthropophagus Beast (aka
Anthropophagus/The Grim Reaper - 1980)

The Fear see City of the Living Dead

Fear in the Night *
GB 1972 85m Technicolor
Following a nervous breakdown a young
woman and her schoolteacher husband
move to the country where he has a
teaching job. However, when a prowler
starts to threaten her she begins to
suspect foul play.
    Routine variation on Hammer's
various other psychodramas which
began with *A Taste of Fear* back in 1961.
Just about watchable for those who
haven't seen all the others.
p: Jimmy Sangster for Hammer
w: Jimmy Sangster, Michael Syson
d: Jimmy Sangster
ph: Arthur Grant
m: John McCabe
md: Philip Martell
ed: Peter Weatherley
ad: John Picton
Peter Cushing, Ralph Bates, Joan
Collins, Judy Geeson, Gillian Lind,
James Cossins

The Fearless Vampire Killers **
GB/USA 1967 124m Metrocolor
Panavision
An eccentric professor and his dim-witted
assistant go to Transylvania in search of
vampires.
    Frequently laboured and somewhat
claustrophobically photographed horror
spoof whose heavy handed sense of style
nevertheless produces an effectively off
beat atmosphere, though strain frequently
shows in both script and performances.
p: Gene Gutowski for MGM/Cadre/
Filmways
w: Gerard Brach, Roman Polanski
d: Roman Polanski
ph: DOUGLAS SLOCOMBE
m: CHRISTOPHER KOMEDA
ed: Alastair MacIntyre
pd; WILFRED SHINGLETON
cos: SOPHIE DEVINE
sound: George Stephenson
titles: Andre Francois
ch: Tutte Lemkow
cam op: Chic Waterson
fangs: Dr Ludwig Von Krankheit
Jack McGowran, Roman Polanski, Sharon

• **Actor-director Roman Polanski in a moment from his vampire spoof** *The
Fearless Vampire Killers.*

Tate, ALFIE BASS, FERDY MAYNE, Iain
Quarrier, Terry Downes, Jessie Robbins,
Fiona Lewis, Ronald Lacey, Tutte Lemkow

Feitshans Jr, Fred
American editor with credits for
Universal and, later, AIP.
Genre credits:
Jungle Captive (1944), *The Mummy's Curse*
(1944), *The Neanderthal Man* (1953), *The
Dunwich Horror* (1969 - co-ed), *Frogs*
(1972)

Feldman, Corey (1971-)
American child actor who graduated to
more adult roles via a variety of films,
including *The Goonies*, *Stand By Me*,
Meatballs IV and *National Lampoon's Last
Restort*.
Genre credits:
Time After Time (1979), *Friday the
Thirteenth - The Final Chapter* (1984),
Gremlins (1984), *Friday the Thirteenth Part
V - A New Beginning* (1985), *The Lost Boys*
(1987), *The 'burbs* (1989)

Feldman, Marty (1933-1983)
Bug-eyed British comedy actor, director
and scriptwriter, perhaps best known to
genre fans for his performance as Igor
the hunchback in Mel Brook's horror
parody *Young Frankenstein* (1974).

The Fiend Without a Face
GB 1957 75m bw
A scientist's experiments produce a force
which sucks the brains from its victims.

Low-budget horror entry of little
abiding interest, save the effects in the
final reel.
p: John Croydon for Producers'
Associates
w: H. J. Leder
story: Amelia Reynolds Long
d: Arthur Crabtree
ph: Lionel Banes
m: Buxton Orr
md: Frederic Lewis
ed: R. Q. McNaughton
ad: John Elphick
cos: Anna Duse
sp: Peter Nielson, Ruppel and Nordhoff
sound: Peter Davies
ass d: Douglas Hickox
2nd unit ph: Martin Curtis
Marshall Thompson, Terence Kilburn,
Kim Parker, Stanley Maxted, Kynaston
Reeves, Michael Balfour, Robert
Mackenzie

The Fiends see Les Diaboliques

Fin de Sermana Para los
Muertos see The Living Dead at the
Manchester Morgue

Fine, Harry
Irish-born producer who, with his partner Michael Styles, produced Hammer's
Carmilla trilogy. A former actor, stage
manager and television casting director,
he became an associate producer on TV's
Sir Francis Drake, progressing to fully
fledged producer on *Man of the World*

and *Sentimental Agent*. First film as a producer *The Pleasure Girls* in 1965, which he followed with *The Penthouse*, *Up the Junction* and *The Rise and Rise of Michael Rimmer*. Later formed Fantale Films with Michael Styles.
Genre credits:
The Vampire Lovers (1970 - co-p), *Lust for a Vampire* (1971 - co-p), *Twins of Evil* (1971 - co-p), *Fright* (1971 - co-p)

Fisher, Gerry (1926-)
British cinematographer who has worked on several of director Joseph Losey's films, including *Accident*, *Secret Ceremony*, *The Romantic Englishwoman*, *A Doll's House*, *The Go-Between*, *Mr Klein* and *Don Giovanni*. Began his career as a camera operator before graduating to cinematographer on such large scale films as *Juggernaut*, *Fedora*, *Highlander* and several for director John Frankenheimer (*The Holcraft Covenant*, *Dead Bang* and *The Fourth War*).
Genre credits:
Blind Terror (1971 - aka *See No Evil*), *The Amazing Mr Blunden* (1972), *The Island of Dr Moreau* (1977), *The Ninth Configuration* (1980), *Wolfen* (1981), *Exorcist III* (1990)

Fisher, Terence (1904-1980)
British director, most associated with Hammer Horror. Began his film career as a clapper boy in 1928 after experience in the navy and as a window dresser. Worked his way up to become an apprentice editor, his first solo credit being *Brown on Resolution* in 1935. After editing for several years, became a trainee director with Rank, his first credit being for *Colonel Bogey* in 1947, which he followed with *Portrait from Life*, *Marry Me*, *The Astonished Heart* and *So Long at the Fair*. His first film for Hammer/Exclusive was the 1952 B thriller *The Last Page* (aka *Man Bait*) which he followed with several more undistinguished programme fillers, including *Wings of Danger*, *Face the Music* (aka *The Black Glove*) and *The Stranger Came Home* (aka *The Unholy Four*). Was given *The Curse of Frankenstein* to direct as he was owed a picture by Hammer on his contract. The film's huge international success led Fisher to direct new versions of *Dracula* and *The Mummy* for Hammer, after which he went on to direct many of the studio's key films. Criticized by many for being little more than a journeyman director, many of his films are now nevertheless considered classics of the genre, though he often fell below the high standards of his best films. His television work includes many episodes for *Douglas Fairbanks Presents* (1954-1956).

• Director Terence Fisher, one of Hammer's most important talents.

Genre credits:
Stolen Face (1952), *Four-Sided Triangle* (1953), *Spaceways* (1953), *The Curse of Frankenstein* (1956), *Dracula* (1958 - aka *The Horror of Dracula*), *The Revenge of Frankenstein* (1958), *The Hound of the Baskervilles* (1959), *The Mummy* (1959), *The Man Who Could Cheat Death* (1959), *The Stranglers of Bombay* (1960), *The Brides of Dracula* (1960), *The Two faces of Dr Jekyll* (1961 - aka *House of Fright/Jekyll's Inferno*), *The Phantom of the Opera* (1962), *Sherlock Holmes and the Deadly Necklace* (1962 - aka *Sherlock Holmes und der Halsband des Todes*), *The Horror of It All* (1964), *The Earth Dies Screaming* (1964), *The Gorgon* (1964), *Dracula -Prince of Darkness* (1966), *Frankenstein Created Woman* (1966), *Island of Terror* (1966), *Night of the Big Heat* (1966 - aka *Night of the Burning Damned*), *The Devil Rides Out* (1968 - aka *The Devil's Bride*), *Frankenstein Must Be Destroyed* (1969), *Frankenstein and the Monster from Hell* (1973)

Five Million Years to Earth see
Quatermass and the Pit

Flagg, Cash see Steckler, Ray Dennis

Flatliners
USA 1990 114m DeLuxe Panavision Dolby
A group of medical students experiment on themselves to see if there really is life after death.
    Visually arresting but thoroughly foolish and tedious slice of science fiction-horror in which the director seems more concerned with baroque imagery than the narrative. Charmless garbage which nevertheless did pretty well at the box office thanks to the presence of Miss Roberts in the cast.
p: Michael Douglas, Rick Bieber for Columbia/Tri-Star
exec p: Scott Rudin, Michael Rachmil, Peter Filardi
w: Peter Filardi
d: Joe Schumacher
ph: Jan de Bont
m: James Newton Howard
ed: Robert Brown
pd: Eugenio Zanetti
cos: Susan Becker
sp: Philip Cory, Hans Metz, Peter Donen
sound: David MacMillan
Kiefer Sutherland, Julia Roberts, Kevin Bacon, William Baldwin, Oliver Platt, Kimberly Scott, Joshua Rudoy, Benjamin Mouton

Flavia - La Monaca Musulamane see Flavia - The Heretic

Flavia - La Nonne Musulmane see Flavia - The Heretic

Flavia - Priestess of Violence see Flavia - The Heretic

Flavia - The Heretic
Fr/It 1974 95m Technicolor
In the 15th century, a young woman is banished to a convent and endures all manner of horrors, culminating in martyrdom by flaying, when the Muslims invade Italy.
    Part historical drama part shock horror, this film inevitably falls between two stools by trying to have it both ways, whilst its less savoury aspects will repel most viewers.
p: Gianfranco Mingozzi for PAC/ROC
w: Fabrizio Onofri, Gianfranco Mingozzi, Bruno Di Geronimo, Sergio Tau
story: Ramaro Di Giovanbattista, Sergio Tau, Francesco Vietri
d: Gianfranco Mingiozzi
ph: Alfio Contini
m: Nicole Piovani
ed: Ruggero Maastroianni
ad/cos: Guido Josia
Florinda Bolkan, Maria Casares, Claudio Cassinelli, Anthony Corlan, Spiros Focas

Flesh and Fantasy *
USA 1943 94m bw
Three tales of mystery, murder and the supernatural.
    A nicely judged portmanteau of stories, stylishly handled and with a choice cast.
p: Charles Boyer, Julien Duvivier for Universal

w: Ernest Pascal, Samuel Hoffenstein, Ellis St. Joseph
stories: Ellis St. Joseph, Laslo Vadnay, Oscar Wilde
d: JULIEN DUVIVIER
ph: STANLEY CORTEZ, PAUL IVANO
m: Alexander Tansman
md: Charles Previn
ed: Arthur Hilton
ad: John Goodman, Arthur Riedel, Robert Boyle
make-up: Jack P. Pierce
Robert Benchley, EDWARD G. ROBIN-SON, Barbara Stanwyck, Charles Boyer, Betty Field, Robert Cummings, Thomas Mitchell, C. Aubrey Smith, DAME MAY WHITTY, Edgar Barrier, David Hoffman

Flesh-Eating Mothers

USA 1988 90m colour
Suburban housewives become cannibals following the outbreak of a mysterious virus.

Failed would-be comedy horror lacking the required madcap sense of humour to bring it off.
p: Miljan Peter Ilich for Indigo
exec p: Fred Martin, Peter Lewnes
w: James Martin, Zev Shlasinger
d: James Aviles Martin
ph: Harry Eisenstein
m: Minerva
ed: Harry Eisenstein, James Martin
ad: Michael Veasey
sp: Carl Sorensen
sound: Chris Lombardozzi
Donatella Hecht, Robert Lee Oliver, Valerie Hubbard, Neal Rosen, Terry Hayes

Florey, Robert (1900-1979)

French writer and director, long in Hollywood. Began working in films in Switzerland as an actor, making his directorial début in 1919 with *Heureuse Intervention*. In the early twenties he worked as a film critic in France before moving to America as a correspondent where he also became a publicity director and gag writer. He made his US directorial début in 1923 with *Fifty-Fifty*. For a while he was attached to Universal's *Frankenstein*, both as an uncredited writer (it was apparently he who came up with the idea of giving the Monster a damaged brain) and director before being ousted by James Whale. His other genre subjects are somewhat variable, making one wonder what he would have made of *Frankenstein* had he in fact directed it. His other credits include the Marx Brothers comedy *The Cocoanuts*, *The Woman in Red* and *God Is My Co-Pilot*.
Genre credits:
Frankenstein (1931 - co-w [uncredited]),

Murders in the Rue Morgue (1932 - d), *The Face Behind the Mask* (1941 - d), *The Beast with Five Fingers* (1946 - d)

The Fly *

USA 1958 93m Eastmancolor Cinemascope
A scientist working on the transmission of matter finds himself turning into a giant fly when the experiment goes wrong.

Routinely presented science fiction horror in the fifties manner, surprisingly shot in colour and wide screen. Regarded with affection in certain quarters, it was followed by *The Return of the Fly* (1959), and *Curse of the Fly* (1965). It was remade in 1986, which itself was followed by a sequel, *The Fly II* (1989).
p: Kurt Neumann for TCF
w: James Clavell
story: George Langelaan
d: Kurt Neumann
ph: Karl Struss
m: Paul Sawtell
ed: Merrill G. White
ad: Lyle Wheeler, Theobald, Holsopple
cos: Charles Le Maire, Adele Balkan
sp: L. B. Abbott
sound: Eugene Grossman, Harry M. Leonard
make-up effects: Ben Nye
Vincent Price, David Hedison, Herbert Marshall, Patricia Owens, Kathleen Freeman, Betty Lou Gerson, Charles Herbert, Eugene Borden, Torben Meyer

The Fly *

USA/Canada 1986 96m DeLuxe Dolby
A scientist experimenting with teleportation fails to notice a fly in the compartment when he tries the gadget out himself and as a result he begins to mutate into a giant insect.

Slick remake with improved script and production values, as well as a pretty high gross-out factor.
p: Stuart Cornfield, Marc-Ami Boyman, Kip Ohman for TCF/Brooksfilms
w: Charles Edward Pogue, David Cronenberg
story: George Langelaan
d: DAVID CRONENBERG
ph: Mark Irwin
m: Howard Shore
ed: Ronald Sanders
pd: Carl Spier
sound: Bryan Day, Michael Lacrois, Gerry Humphreys, Robin O'Donoghue
make-up effects: CHRIS WALAS, STEPHEN DUPUIS (AA)
stunt co-ordinator: Wayne McLean
titles: Wayne Fitzgerald
Jeff Goldblum, Geena Davis, John Getz, Joy Boushel, Les Carlson, George Chuvalo, Michael Coepman, Carol

Lazare, David Cronenberg (in a cameo, delivering a pupae!)

The Fly II

USA 1989 105m DeLuxe Dolby
Martin Brundle begins to show signs that he might be about to follow in his father's footsteps.

Slick but rather leisurely paced sequel to a remake which fails to add anything new to the formula. An adequate time filler for horror addicts.
p: Steven-Charles Jaffe for TCF/Brooksfilm
exec p: Stuart Cornfield
w: Mick Garris, Jim Wheat, Ken Wheat, Frank Darabont
story: Mick Garris
d: Chris Walas
ph: Robin Vidgeon
m: Christopher Young
ed: Sean Barton
pd: Michael S. Bolton
sp: Chris Walas, Jon Berg, Stephen Dupuis
sound: Leslie Shatz, John Wardlow
titles: Sam Alexander
Eric Stoltz, Daphne Zuniga, Lee Richardson, Ann Marie Lee, Gary Chalk, Harley Cross, Frank C. Turner, John Getz

The Fog **

USA 1979 91m Metrocolor Panavision
A township celebrating its centenary is threatened by murderous spectres.

Amiable, old fashioned scare story, very competently handled with several well timed shocks typical of its director.
p: Debra Hill for Avco
w: John Carpenter, Debra Hill
d: JOHN CARPENTER
ph: Dean Cundey
m: John Carpenter
ed: Tommy Lee Wallace, Charles Bornstein
pd: Tommy Lee Wallace
cos: Richard Bloore
sp: James F. Liles
sound: Craig Felburg, William Stevenson
make-up effects: Rob Bottin
Jamie Lee Curtis, Janet Leigh, Adrienne Barbeau, Tom Atkins, John Houseman, Hal Holbrook, Nancy Loomis, Charles Cyphers, John Carpenter, Rob Bottin

Foreman, Deborah

American actress who played teenage roles in a number of eighties comedies and horrors, including *Valley Girl*, *My Chauffeur* and *3:15 - The Moment of Truth*.
Genre credits:
April Fool's Day (1986), *Destroyer* (1986), *Waxwork* (1988)

Foster, Jody (1963-)

American actress, a former child star, who matured from innocuous musicals and Disney comedies (*Tom Sawyer, Bugsy Malone, Candleshoe, Freaky Friday*) into a leading actress of distinction, winning Best Actress Oscars for both *The Accused* (1988) and *The Silence of the Lambs* (1991), in which she played FBI trainee Clarice Starling. Her other key films include *Alice Doesn't Live Here Anymore, Taxi Driver, Carny, Sommersby, Maverick* and *Nell*. She has also turned to direction with equal success with *Little Man Tate*.
Genre credits:
The Little Girl Who Lives Down the Lane (1976), *Svengali* (1982 - TVM), *The Silence of the Lambs* (1991)

Fraidy Cat **

USA 1942 6m Technicolor
After hearing a ghost story on the radio, Jerry tries to scare Tom by pretending to be a ghost.
Excellent early Tom and Jerry cartoon.
p: Fred Quimby for MGM
d: William Hanna, Joseph Barbera

Fraker, William A. (1923-)

Important American cinematographer, a former stills photographer who turned to cinematography after experience as a camera operator. His credits include such films as *Bullitt, Paint Your Wagon, Heaven Can Wait* and *1941*. He has also directed three films: *Monte Walsh, A Reflection of Fear* and *Legend of the Lone Ranger*.
Genre credits:
Rosemary's Baby (1968 - ph), *Exorcist II: The Heretic* (1977 - ph), *Reflection of Fear* (1971 - d), *Memoirs of An Invisible Man* (1992 - ph)

Francis, Freddie (1917-).

Celebrated British cinematographer, an Oscar winner for both *Sons and Lovers* (1960) and *Glory* (1989). Began as a stills photographer then joined Gainsborough as a clapperboy in 1936, where his first film was *Joy Ride*. Work as a camera assistant at Pinewood followed, whilst during the war he joined the Army Kinematograph Services. After the war he became a camera operator on such films as *The Macomber Affair* and *Mine Own Executioner*, and second unit photographer on John Huston's *Moby Dick*. First film as a fully-fledged cinematographer came in 1957 with *A Hill in Korea*, which was followed by such films as *Room at the Top* and *The Innocents*. Turned to direction in 1962 with *Two and Two Make Six* and *Vengeance*, then slipped into the horror genre. His talents as a top cinematogra-

pher are undeniable, though as a director his work is much less assured. Francis returned to cinematography in 1981 with *The French Lieutenant's Woman*, which was followed by sterling work on *The Elephant Man, Dune, Glory, Cape Fear* and *The Princess Caraboo*. He is the father of producer Kevin Francis, for whom he directed *Legend of the Werewolf* and *The Ghoul*.
Genre credits:
The Innocents (1961 - ph), *Paranoiac* (1963 - d), *Nightmare* (1964 - d), *The Evil of Frankenstein* (1964 - d), *Hysteria* (1964 - d), *The Psychopath* (1965 - d), *The Skull* (1965 - d), *The Deadly Bees* (1966 - d), *They Came from Beyond Space* (1966 - d), *Torture Garden* (1967 - d), *Dracula Has Risen from the Grave* (1968 -d), *Mumsy, Nanny, Sonny and Girly* (1969 - aka *Girly* - d), *Trog* (1970 - d), *Tales from the Crypt* (1971 - d), *The Vampire Happening* (1971 - aka *Gebissen wird nur Nachts / Happening der Vampire* - d), *Asylum* (1972 - d), *The Creeping Flesh* (1973 - d), *Craze* (1973 - d), *Tales That Witness Madness* (1973 - d), *Son of Dracula* (1974 - aka *Count Downe* - d), *Legend of the Werewolf* (1974 - d), *The Ghoul* (1975 - d), *The Elephant Man* (1981 - ph), *The Doctor and the Devils* (1986 - d), *Dark Tower* (1987 - d [as Ken Barnett]), *Cape Fear* (1991 - ph)

Francis in the Haunted House

USA 1956 79m bw
Francis the talking mule and his friend solve a murder in an apparently haunted castle.
Seventh and last in a series of increasingly tatty and threadbare farces. Its success led to the later television series, *Mr Ed*.
p: Robert Arthur for Universal
w: Herbert Margolis, William Raynor
d: Charles Lamont
ph: George Robinson
md: Joseph Gershenson
ed: Milton Carruth
ad: Alexander Golitzen, Richard H. Riedel
cos: Jay A. Morley Jr
sp: Clifford Stine
sound: Leslie I. Carey, Robert Pritchard
Mickey Rooney, Virginia Welles, Paul Cavanaugh, David Janssen, Mary Ellen Kay, James Flavin, Richard Deacon

Francis, Kevin (1944-)

British producer, the son of director / cinematographer Freddie Francis. A former production manager (from 1967) he began producing in 1971 with *Trouble with Canada*. In 1972 he founded Tyburn Productions, two of whose films were directed by his father (*Legend of the Werewolf* and *The Ghoul*). Other credits include *The Masks of Death*

(a Sherlock Holmes TV movie which he executive produced) and the documentary *Peter Cushing: The Gentleman of Horror*, which was photographed by his father.
Genre credits:
Persecution (1974 - aka *The Terror of Sheba*), *The Legend of the Werewolf* (1974), *The Ghoul* (1975).

Franco, Jesus (1930-)

Spanish actor, writer and director (real name Jesus Franco Manera) who has churned out a seemingly endless stream of low-budget genre films in various European languages, most of which rely heavily on sex and sadism for their effect. A former detective novelist (under the name David Khunne) and film critic, he worked his way up the industry ladder via work as a dubbing supervisor, assistant director (*Comicos, La Justicia del Coyote, Felices Pascuas*, etc.), production manager and second unit director (*Solomon and Sheba*) before directing his first feature, *Tenemos 18 Anos* (aka *We Are 18 Years Old*) in 1959, which followed directorial duties on a handful of documentary shorts (*El Arbol de Espana, El Destierro del Cid, Estampas Guipuzcoanas*, etc.). His first horror film, *The Awful Dr Orloff*, appeared in 1961. A filmmaker of minimal technique (most of which seems to involve zooming), his movies vary from the marginally interesting to the downright amateur. His various screen pseudonyms include Jess Frank, Clifford Brown, Frank Hollman and, most often, Jess Franco. He also directed the second unit for Orson Welles' *Chimes at Midnight* (aka *Falstaff*). His other (countless) credits include *La Muerte Silba un Blues, El Llanero, The Girl from Rio, Los Amantes de la Isla del Diablo, Les Nonnes en Folie, Midnight Party* and, in the eighties, many hard core titles.
Genre credits:
The Awful Dr Orloff (1961 - aka *The Demon Doctor / L'Horrible Dr Orloff / Gritos en la Noche* - w/d/actor/novel [novel as David Khunne / d as Jess Franco]), *La Mano de un Hombre Muerto* (1962 - d/novel [d as Jess Frank/novel as David Khunne]), *El Secreto del Doctor Orloff* (1964 - aka *Dr Orloff's Monster* - w/d/novel/actor [w and d as Jess Frank/novel as David Khunne]), *Miss Muerte* (1965 - aka *The Diabolical Dr Z / Dr Z & Miss Death* - co-w/novel/d/ actor [co-w and novel as David Khunne/actor as Jess Frank]), *Cartas Boca Arriba* (1966 - aka *Cartes sur Table / Attack of the Robots* - w/d/actor), *Necronomicon* (1967 - aka *Succubus* - co-w/d [as Jess Franco]), *Blood of Fu Manchu* (1967 - aka *Fu Manchu and the*

Kiss of Death / Kiss and Kill / Against All Odds / Fu Manchu y el Beso de la Muerte - co-w/d [as Jess Franco]), *The Castle of Fu Manchu* (1968 - aka *Assignment Istambul / The Torture Chamber of Dr Fu Manchu / El Castillo de Fu Manchu* -d/actor [d as Jess Frank]), *Venus in Furs* (1968 - aka *Paroxismus* - co-w/d/actor [co-w/d as Jess Franco]), *Justine* (1968 - aka *Justine et Juliet / Marquis de Sade: Justine* - co-w/d/actor [co-w/d as Jess Franco]), *Night of the Blood Monster* (1969 - aka *The Bloody Judge / El Proceso de las Brujas* - w/d [as Jess Franco]), *Count Dracula* (1969 - aka *Bram Stoker's Count Dracula / Les Nuits de Dracula / El Conde Dracula* - co-w/d/actor [co-w/d as Jess Franco]), *Sex Charade* (1970 -w/d), *Les Cauchemars Naissent la Nuit* (1970 - w/d [as Jess Franco]), *Virgin Among the Living Dead* (1970 - aka *Christina, Princesse de L'Erotisme* - w/d [w as J. Franco Manera]), *Vampyros Lesbos* (1970 - aka *Las Vampiras / Sexualite Speciale* - w/d/actor [w/d as J. Franco Manera]), *Sie Totete in Ekstase* (1970 -aka *Ms Hyde* - w/d/actor [w/d as Frank Hollman]), *El Diablo que Vino de Akasava* (1970 - aka *The Devil Came from Akasava* - d/actor [d as Jess Frank]), *La Vengaza del Doctor Mabuse* (1970 - co-w/d [d as Frank Manero/w as Jess Franco]), *Dracula Contra Frankenstein* (1971 - aka *Dracula, Prisoner of Frankenstein* - co-w/d), *La Fille de Dracula* (1972 - w/d/actor [w/d as Jess Franco]), *La Maldición de Frankenstein* (1972 - aka *The Erotic Rites of Frankenstein / Les Experiences Erotiques de Frankenstein* - w/d/actor [w/d as Jess Franco]), *Les Demons* (1972 - aka *The Demons / The She-Demons* - w/d/novel [w as Jess Franco/d as Clifford Brown/novel as David Khunne]), *Los Ojos Siniestros del Doctor Orloff* (1973 - w/d/actor), *Plaisir a Trois* (1973 - aka *How to Seduce a Virgin / Ultra Tumba* - w/d/co-ph [w as J. Franco Manera/d as Clifford Brown/ph as Jess Franco]), *La Comtesse Perverse* (1973 - w/d [w as J. Franco Manera/d as Clifford Brown]), *La Noche de los Asesinos* (1973 - w/d), *La Comtesse Noire* (1973 - aka *Les Avaleuses / The Bare-Breasted Countess / Erotikill / The Loves of Irina* - w/d/actor [d as James P. Johnson]), *Exorcisme* (1974 - aka *Sexorcismes* - co-w/d/actor [co-w as David Khunne/d as James P. Johnson/actor as Jess Frank]), *Lorna, L'Exorciste* (1974 - aka *Lorna / Les Possedees du Diable / Sexy Diabolic Story* - co-w/d/actor [co-w as J. Franco Manera/d as Clifford Brown]), *Jack the Ripper* (1976 - aka *Jack L'Eventreur* - co-w/d [as Jess Franco]), *Das Bildnis der Doriana Gray* (1976 - aka *Dirty Dracula / Ejaculations* - w/d/ph [d as Jess Franco/w/ph as

David Khunne]), *Poseida* (1978 - aka *L'Osceno Desiderio* - m only), *La Sadique de Notre-Dame* (1979 - aka *Demoniac / Chains and Black Leather* - w/d/actor [w as Jeff Maner/d as Jess Franco]), *Mondo Cannibale* (1980 - aka *Les Cannibales / White Cannibal Queen / The Cannibalss* - w/d/actor [w as Jeff Manner/d as Jess Franco]), *Die Sage des Todes* (1980 - aka *Bloody Moon / Colegialas Violadas* - d), *El Sexo Esta Loco* (1980 w/d [as Jess Franco]), *Sexo Canibal* (1980 - aka *The Man Hunter / The Devil Hunter / Mandingo Hunter* - co-w/d [co-w as Jess Franco/d as Clifford Brown]), *La Tumba de los Muertos Vivientes* (1981 - aka *L'Abime des Morts-Vivants* -co-w/d [as Jess Franco]), *Macuma Sexual* (1981 - w/d/actor [w/d as Jess Franco]), *El Siniestro Dr Orloff* (1982 - w/d/actor [w/d as Jess Franco]), *Mil Sexos Tiene la Noche* (1982 w/d [as Jess Franco]), *La Mansion de los Muertos Vivientes* (1982 - w/d [as Jess Franco]), *Sola Ante el Terror* (1983 - w/d [w as Jess Franco/d as Clifford Brown]), *El Hundimiento de la Casa Usher* (1983 - aka *Revenge in the House of Usher / Nevrose / Neurosis* - w/d), *Voces de Muerte* (1984 - w/d [as Jess Franco]), *Les Predateurs de la Nuit* (1988 - aka *Faceless* - w/d [as Jess Franco])

Frankel, Benjamin (1921-1983)
British composer and musical director with many important credits to his name, including *The Seventh Seal*, *Mine Own Executioner* and *Night of the Iguana*.
Genre credits:
The Curse of the Werewolf (1960), *The Old Dark House* (1962)

Frankenhooker
USA 1990 91m TVCcolor Dolby
After the death of his girlfriend in a lawnmowing accident (!), a scientist attempts to rebuild her with the body parts of prostitutes he's murdered with explosive crack cocaine.
Fitfully amusing spoof with plenty of over-the-top-comic gore. A must for Henenlotter devotees.
p: Edgar Ievens for Shapiro Glickenhaus Entertainment
exec p: James Glickenhaus
w: Robert Martin, Frank Henenlotter
d: Frank Henenlotter
ph: Robert M. Baldwin
ed: Kevin Tent
pd: Charles Bennett
cos: Artemis Pizarro
sp: Al Magliochetti
sound: Dominick Tavella, Paul Bang
make-up effects: Gabe Bartalos
James Lorintz, Patty Mullen, Charlotte Heimkamp, Louise Lasser, Shirley Stoler, Joseph Gonzales

Frankenstein
Mary Wollstonecraft Shelley's 1818 novel *Frankenstein* (aka *A Modern Prometheus*) remains, along with Bram Stoker's *Dracula* and Robert Louis Stevenson's *The Strange Case of Dr Jekyll*, not only one of the horror genre's most oft filmed novels but also one of the cinema's. First filmed in America in 1910 with Augustus Phillips as Frankenstein and Charles Ogle playing the Monster, several more silent versions followed (including such early variations as *Alraune*, *The Eleventh Dimension*, *Homonculus* and *Legally Dead*). It wasn't until Universal's 1931 version, which starred Colin Clive as Frankenstein and Boris Karloff as the Monster, that the novel took off as a movie subject despite its much altered storyline. It was much influenced by the German *Golem* films. The success of this version produced several sequels from Universal (*The Bride of Frankenstein*, *Son of Frankenstein*, *Frankenstein Meets the Wolf Man*, etc.) as well as countless mad doctor variations (*The Man They Could Not Hang*, *The Man with Nine Lives*, *Black Friday*, *Man Made Monster*, etc.). The link between the Universal films was the Monster, which itself became synonymous with the name Frankenstein. It wasn't until the Hammer series (1956-1973) that this mistake was rectified, when Peter Cushing's Baron Frankenstein became the mainstay of the series as opposed to his Creation, a new one of which was now provided for each instalment. Since the demise of the Hammer series there have been all manner of *Frankenstein* rip-offs and variations (including several hard core versions), most of them a million miles from the source material. Nevertheless, the name of Frankenstein remains a key element of the horror genre, be it in such far out films as *Jesse James Meets Frankenstein's Daughter* or Kenneth Branagh's $60m 'straight' version.
Key filmography:
Frankenstein (1910 - short), *Life without Soul* (1915), *Il Mostro di Frankenstein* (1920), *Frankenstein* (1931), *The Bride of Frankenstein* (1935), *Son of Frankenstein* (1939), *The Ghost of Frankenstein* (1942), *Frankenstein Meets the Wolf Man* (1943), *House of Frankenstein* (1944), *House of Dracula* (1945), *Abbott and Costello Meet Frankenstein* (1948), *The Curse of Frankenstein* (1956), *I Was a Teenage Frankenstein* (1957), *Frankenstein 1970* (1958), *Frankenstein's Daughter* (1958), *How to Make a Monster* (1958), *The Revenge of Frankenstein* (1958), *Orlak, El Infierno de Frankenstein* (1960),

• **Charles Ogle as the Monster in Thomas Edison's** *Frankenstein*, **the screen's first ever version of the oft filmed Mary Shelley novel.**

Frankenstein, El Vampiro Y Cia (1961), *The Evil of Frankenstein* (1964), *Frankenstein Conquers the World* (1964 - aka *Furankenshut ain tai Baragon*), *Jesse James Meets Frankenstein's Daughter* (1965), *Frankenstein Meets the Space Monster* (1965 - aka *Duel of the Space Monsters / Marte Invade a Puerto Rico*), *Frankenstein Created Woman* (1966), *Munster, Go Home!* (1966 - TVM), *Carry On Screaming* (1966), *Mad Monster Party?* (1966 - puppetoon), *Frankenstein's Bloody Terror* (1967), *Dracula vs. Frankenstein* (1969 - aka *El Hombre que Vino del Ummo*), *Frankenstein Must Be Destroyed* (1969), *The Horror of Frankenstein* (1970), *Dr Frankenstein on Campus* (1970 - aka *Frankenstein on Campus*), *Dracula vs Frankenstein* (1970 -

aka *Blood of Frankenstein / They're Coming to Get You / The Revenge of Dracula*), *Santo Contra la Hija de Frankenstein* (1971 - aka *La Hija de Frankenstein*), *Lady Frankenstein* (1971), *Pastel de Sangre* (1971 - segment), *Blackenstein* (1972 - aka *Black Frankenstein*), *Dracula, Prisoner of Frankenstein* (1972 - aka *Dracula Contra Frankenstein*), *The Erotic Rites of Frankenstein* (1972 - aka *La Maldición de Frankenstein / Les Experiences Erotiques de Frankenstein*), *Frankenstein '80* (1972), *Andy Warhol's Frankenstein* (1973 - aka *Flesh for Frankenstein*), *Frankenstein* (1973 - TVM), *Frankenstein's Castle of Freaks* (1973), *Frankenstein: The True Story* (1973 - TVM), *Frankenstein and the Monster from Hell* (1973), *Young Frankenstein* (1974),

Sevilmi Frankestayn (1975), *Frankenstein Italian Style* (1975 - aka *Frankenstein All'Italiana*), *The Rocky Horror Picture Show* (1975), *Victor Frankenstein* (1976 - aka *Terror of Frankenstein*), *Dr Franken* (1980 - TVM), *Frankenstein Island* (1981), *The Munsters' Revenge* (1981 - TVM), *Frankenstein - Legend of Terror* (1981 - aka *Kaiki Furankenshutain* - cartoon), *Britannia Hospital* (1982), *Frankenstein's Great Aunt Tillie* (1983), *Prototype* (1983 - TVM), *Frankenstein '88* (1984 - aka *The Vindicator*), *Frankenweenie* (1984 - short), *Frankenstein* (1984 - TVM), *Frankenstein '90* (1984), *Transylvania 6-5000* (1985), *Re-Animator* (1985), *The Bride* (1985), *Dr Hackenstein* (1987), *The Monster Squad* (1987), *Frankenstein General Hospital* (1988), *Bride of the Re-Animator* (1989 - aka *Re-Animator 2*), *Edward Scissorhands* (1990), *Frankenhooker* (1990), *Frankenstein's Baby* (1990 - TVM), *Frankenstein Unbound* (1990), *Frankenstein* (1990 - documentary), *Frankenstein: The College Years* (1991 - TVM), *Last Frankenstein* (1991), *Frankenstein* (1992), *Frankenstein: The Real Story* (1993 - TVM), *Mary Shelley's Frankenstein* (1994)

Frankenstein ****
USA 1931 71m bw
A scientist obssesed by the mysteries of life and death creates from the remains of various corpses what he believes to be the perfect man, but he unwittingly gives it the brain of a lunatic...
  One of the most influential horror movies ever made, this stylish and still effective adaptation of the celebrated Mary Shelley novel made an instant star out of Karloff and, along with *Dracula* (1930), made its studio synonymous with such genre offerings for the next two decades. Despite its age and hurried running time it remains vastly enjoyable and has many points of interest along the way.
p: Carl Laemmle Jr for Universal
w: GARRETT FORT, FRANCIS EDWARD FARAGOH, JOHN L. BALERSTON, Robert Florey
novel: MARY WOLLSTONECRAFT SHELLEY
d: JAMES WHALE
ph: ARTHUR EDESON
m: David Broekman
ed: Maurice Pivar, Clarence Kolster
ad: CHARLES D. HALL
sp: John P. Fulton
sound: C. Roy Hunter
make-up: JACK P. PIERCE
COLIN CLIVE (as Frankenstein),

BORIS KARLOFF (as the Monster), MAE CLARK, John Boles, EDWARD VAN SLOANE, FREDERICK KERR, DWIGHT FRYE, Lionel Belmore, Michael Mark

Frankenstein

USA 1973 96m colour TVM

Victor Frankenstein fashions a creature from bodies stolen from the graveyard.

Poor, studio bound tele-version of the oft told story, taped on video and looking it.
p: Dan Curtis for DCP
w: Sam Hall, Dan Curtis
novel: MARY WOLLSTONECRAFT SHELLEY
d: Dan Curtis
ph: Dean Hall
m: Robert Cobert
ad: Trevor Williams
cos: John Perry, Thalia Phillips
sound: Chips Brooks
make-up: Mike Westmore
Robert Foxworth, Susan Strasberg, Bo Svenson, Heidi Vaughan, Philip Bourneuf, Robert Gentry, John Iormer, William Hansen, John Karlen

Frankenstein and the Monster from Hell *

GB 1973 99m Technicolor

Baron Frankenstein continues his experiments from within the confines of a lunatic asylum.

Silly but quite lively final entry in Hammer's Frankenstein series, with slightly more style than had been seen in some of the previous episodes.
p: Roy Skeggs for Hammer
w: John Elder (Anthony Hinds)
d: TERENCE FISHER
ph: Brian Probyn
m: JAMES BERNARD
md: Philip Martell
ed: James Needs
ad: SCOTT MACGREGOR
cos: Dulcie Midwinter
sound: Les Hammond
make-up: Eddie Knight
PETER CUSHING, Shane Briant, Madeleine Smith, Dave Prowse (as the Monster), Bernard Lee, John Stratton, Patrick Troughton, Clifton Mollison, Charles Lloyd Pack

Frankenstein Created Woman *

GB 1966 86m Technicolor

The Baron restores the soul of a wrongly executed man into the body of his dead fiancée.

Comparatively mild addition to Hammer's Frankenstein cycle, perhaps because there is no actual marauding monster. The cutting of the central laboratory scene doesn't help matters either

especially as it wrecks the narrative. But there are spirited moments.
p: Anthony Nelson Keys for Hammer/Seven Arts
w: John Elder (Anthony Hinds)
d: Terence Fisher
ph: Arthur Grant
m: James Bernard
md: Philip Martell
ed: James Needs, Spencer Reeve
ad: James Bernard
sp: Les Bowie
Peter Cushing, Susan Denberg, THOR-LEY WALTERS, Robert Morris, Duncan Lamont, Peter Blythe, Barry Warren

Frankenstein General Hospital

USA 1988 92m colour

Dr Bob Frankenstein, a descendent of Baron Frankenstein, builds his own monster in the basement of LA General Hospital.

Dismal would-be spoof. No Young Frankenstein, that's for sure.
p: Dimitri Villard for New Star Entertainment
exec p: Robby Wald
w: Michael Kelly, Robert Deal
d: Deborah Roberts
ph: Tom Fraser
m: John Ross
ed: Ed Cotter
pd: Don Day
cos: Virginia Kramer
sound: Izak Ben-Meir, John Ross
make-up effects: Dave White
Mark Blankfield, Leslie Jordan, Jonathan Farwell, Irwin Keyes (as the Monster), Kathy Shower, Lou Cutell

Frankenstein Meets the Wolf Man *

USA 1943 73m bw

Wolf Man Lawrence Talbot comes across the Frankenstein Monster whilst travelling through Europe to find a cure for his lycanthropy.

Serial-like teaming of the famous monsters, originally made to revive interest in a flagging series. Occasionally atmospheric despite a rather silly script.
p: George Waggner for Universal
w: Curt Siodmak
d: ROY WILLIAM NEILL
ph: GEORGE ROBINSON
m: Hans J. Salter
ed: Edward Curtiss
ad: JOHN B. GOODMAN, MARTIN OBZINA
sp: John P. Fulton
make-up: Jack P. Pierce
LON CHANEY Jr, Ilona Massey, Bela Lugosi (as the Monster), Patric Knowles, Lionel Atwill, MARIA OUS-ENESKAYA, Dwight Frye

• **Bela Lugosi's Frankenstein Monster grapples with Lon Chaney Jr's Wolf Man in this posed publicity still from** *Frankenstein Meets the Wolf Man.*

Frankenstein Must Be Destroyed *

GB 1969 96m Technicolor

Frankenstein transplants the brain of an old associate into a new body so as to save the secrets it holds.

Full blooded Hammer horror, perhaps the liveliest of their various Frankenstein sequels.
p: Anthony Nelson Keys for Hammer/Columbia
w: Bert Batt
story: Bert Batt, Anthony Nelson Keys
d: TERENCE FISHER
ph: Arthur Grant
m: James Bernard
md: Philip Martell
ed: Gordon Hales
ad: Bernard Robinson
cos: Rosemary Burrows
sp: Studio Locations Ltd
sound: Tony Lumkin, Ken Rawkins
make-up: Eddie Knight
ass d: Bert Batt
PETER CUSHING, Simon Ward, Veronica Carlson, Freddie Jones, Thorley Walters, Geoffrey Bayldon, Frank Middlemass, Maxine Audley, Harold Goodwin, Peter Copley, Colette O'Neil, Windsor Davies

Frankenstein: The College Years

US 1991 91m colour

Two college students revive Frankenstein's Monster on which their recently deceased science teacher had been working.

Dismal teenage comedy.

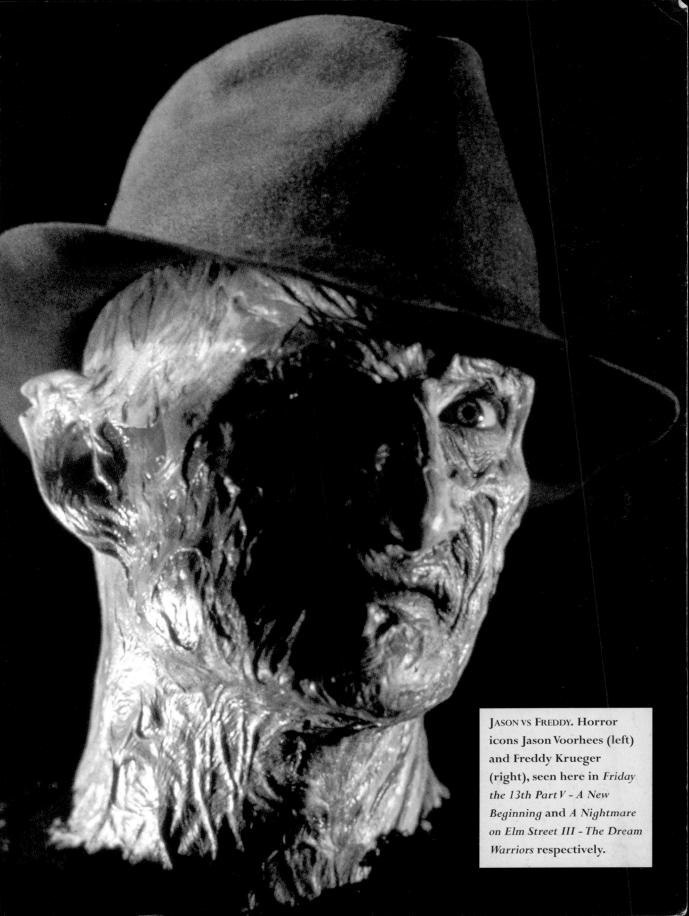

JASON VS FREDDY. Horror icons Jason Voorhees (left) and Freddy Krueger (right), seen here in *Friday the 13th Part V - A New Beginning* and *A Nightmare on Elm Street III - The Dream Warriors* respectively.

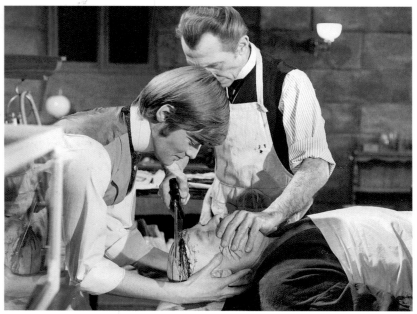

• Peter Cushing and Simon Ward get down to business in *Frankenstein Must be Destroyed.*

p: Bob Engelamn for FNM/Spirit
exec p: Richard E. Johnson, Scott D. Goldstein
w: Bryant Christ, John Trevor Wolff
d: Tom Shadyac
ph: Steve Confer
m: Joel McNeely
ed: David Garfield
pd: Mick Strawn
cos: Diah Wymont
sp: Tom Bellissimo, Charlie Belardinelli
sound: Russell Fager, John Ross
William Ragsdale, Christopher Daniel Barnes, Vincent Hammond, Larry Miller, Andrea Elson

Frankenstein - The Real Story
GB 1992 110m Technicolor TVM
In 1820, Frankenstein pursues his creature to the Arctic in an attempt to destroy it.

Reasonably faithful but otherwise unremarkable retelling of a story already told several times too often.
p: David Wickes for Turner/David Wickes
w/d: David Wickes
novel: MARY WOLLSTONECRAFT SHELLEY
ph: Jack Conroy
m: John Cameron
ed: John Grover
pd: William Alexander
cos: Raymond Hughes
sp: Graham Longhurst
sound: Peter Glossop, John Hayward
make-up: Mark Coulier
2nd unit d/stunt co-ordinator: Peter Brayham

2nd unit ph: Geoff Glover
Patrick Bergin, Randy Quaid (as the Monster), John Mills, Lambert Wilson, Fiona Gillies, Jacinta Mulcahy

Frankenstein - The True Story *
GB/USA 1973 176m (or varying formats) colour TVM
The title leads one to believe this to be a faithful rendition of the story, but it proves to be no more so than all the other versions. A long, flatly directed but mostly worthwhile production nevertheless, with passages of interest.
p: Hunt Stromberg Jr for Universal
w: Christopher Isherwood, Don Bachardy
novel: MARY SHELLEY
d: Jack Smight
ph: Arthur Ibbetson
m: Gil Melle
md: Philip Martell
ed: Richard Marden
pd: Wilfred Shingleton
cos: Elsa Fennell
sp: Roy Whybrow
sound: Don Sharpe, Gordon Everett, Ken Barker
make-up: Roy Ashton
ch: Sally Gilpin
Leonard Whiting, JAMES MASON, David McCallum, Jane Seymour, MICHAEL SARRAZIN (as the Monster), Nicola Pagett, John Gielgud, Ralph Richardson, Michael Wilding, Tom Baker, Agnes Moorehead, Clarissa Kaye, Margaret Leighton, Yootha Joyce, Peter Sallis

Frankenstein Unbound *
USA 1990 87m DeLuxe
A scientist from the twenty-first century finds himself transported back to nineteenth century Switzerland where he encounters Dr Frankenstein, the Monster and the young Mary Shelley.

Agreeable mixture of genres, silly certainly, but most of it comes off quite well. It was Corman's first film as a director for nineteen years, his last effort being *Von Richthofen and Brown* in 1971.
p: Roger Corman, Thom Mount, Kobi Jaeger for Warner/Mount
w: Roger Corman, F. X. Feeney, Ed Neumeier
novel: Brian W. Aldiss
d: ROGER CORMAN
ph: Armando Nannuzzi, Michael Scott
m: Carl Davis
ed: Jay Cassidy
pd: Enrico Tovaglieri
cos: Franca Zucchelli
sp: Renato Agostini
sound: Gary Alper
2nd unit d: Thierry Notz
make-up effects: Nick Dudman
John Hurt, Raul Julia, Bridget Fonda, Jason Patric, Michael Hutchence, Nick Brimble, Catherine Rabett, Bruce McGuire, Grady Clarkson

Franklin, Pamela (1949-)
British child actress who graduated to mature roles via such films as *Our Mother's House*, *The Prime of Miss Jean Brodie* and *David Copperfield*. Trained as a ballet dancer, she made her film début in Jack Clayton's *The Innocents*.
Genre credits:
The Innocents (1961), *The Nanny* (1965), *And Soon the Darkness* (1970), *Necromancy* (1972), *Satan's School for Girls* (1973 - TVM), *The Legend of Hell House* (1973), *Screamer* (1974), *Terror from Within* (1976), *Food for the Gods* (1976)

Franklin, Richard (1948-)
Australian producer and director with a penchant for horror themes, often in imitation of Alfred Hitchcock, whom he knew in the late sixties. Came to the cinema via documentaries and television, his most prominent film being *Psycho 2*. Other credits include *The True Story of Eskimo Nell* (aka *Dick Down Under*), *Cloak and Dagger* and *F/X 2: The Deadly Art of Illusion*.
Genre credits:
Patrick (1978 - co-p/d), *Road Games* (1981 - co-p/co-story/d), *Psycho 2* (1983 - d), *Link* (1986 - co-p/d)

Freaks *
USA 1932 64m bw

A glamorous trapeze artist marries a midget for his money and then tries to poison him, but she reckons without the intervention of the other circus freaks who turn her into a human chicken!

More famous for being disowned by its studio and banned for thirty years than anything else, this horror story uses real freaks to get its point across and thus seems all the more tasteless. As it is there is much tedium before the long delayed climax.

p: Tod Browning for MGM
w: Willis Goldbeck, Leon Gordon, Edgar Allan Woolf
d/story: Tod Browning
ph: Merrit G. Gerstad
m: no credit given
ed: Basil Wrangell
ad: Cedric Gibbons
sound; Douglas Shearer
Wallace Ford, Olga Baclanova, Leila Hyams, Roscoe Ates, Henry Victor, Harry Earles, Rose Dione, Daisy and Violet Hilton, Josephine Joseph, Randion

Freeman, Kathleen (1919-)

American comedy character actress with a strong line in battleaxes, most memorably opposite Jerry Lewis (*The Ladies' Man*, *The Errand Boy*, *The Nutty Professor*, *The Disorderly Orderly*, *Hook, Line and Sinker*, *Three On a Couch*, *Which Way to the Front?* etc.). Her other credits include *The Naked City*, *The Bad and the Beautiful*, *Houseboat*, *Point Blank*, *Dragnet*, *Innerspace* and *Reckless Kelly*, as well as countless bit parts and cameo appearances.
Genre credits:
The Magnetic Monster (1953), *The Fly* (1958), *Psycho Sisters* (1969 - aka *So Evil, My Sister/La Sorelle*), *Teen Wolf, Too* (1987 -TVM), *Gremlins 2: The New Batch* (1990)

Freund, Karl (1890-1969)

Important Czechoslovakian cinematographer and director who photographed many German silents (including *The Last Laugh* and *Metropolis*) before moving first to Britain and then to America. A projectionist in 1906, he photographed his first film, *Der Hauptmann Von Kopenick*, in 1907 and became a Pathe newsreel cameraman in 1908. Started his own film processing lab in 1919, which eventually led to the formation of Movie Colour Ltd in Britain in 1928. Signed a contract with Universal in 1930 and as a result became involved in several of the studio's key horror films, to which he brought many Germanic influences. Later in his career he moved into television, most notably for Desilu, for whom

he developed the three camera technique of photographing sit-coms. His other credits include *Camille*, *The Good Earth* (which won him an Oscar for best cinematography), *Pride and Prejudice* and *Key Largo*.
Genre credits:
Satanas (1919 - ph), *Der Januskopf* (1920 - ph), *The Golem* (1920 - ph), *Dracula* (1931 - ph [English and Spanish versions]), *Murders in the Rue Morgue* (1931 - ph), *The Mummy* (1932 - d), *Mad Love* (1935 - aka *The Hands of Orlac* - d)

Friday the Thirteenth

USA 1980 95m Technicolor
A series of grizzly murders take place at an isolated summer camp.

The surprising success of this gory shocker helped to establish the stalk and slash genre of the eighties. Quite frightening in places but, like its sequels and its countless imitators, its gore revolts rather than frightens. Now seems quite tame.

p: Sean S. Cunningham for Paramount/Georgetown
exec p: Alvin Geiler
w: Victor Miller
d: Sean S. Cunningham
ph: Barry Abrams
m: Harry Manfredini
ed: Bill Freda
ad: Virginia Field
cos: Caron Coplan
sound: Richard Murphy, Lee Dicter
make-up effects: Tom Savini
Betsy Palmer, Adrienne King, Jeannie Taylor, Robbi Morgan, Kevin Bacon, Ari Lehman (as Jason)

Friday the Thirteenth Part Two

USA 1981 87m DeLuxe
More murders take place at Camp Crystal Lake, the culprit being the son of the previous murderer.

You can't keep a good killer down, especially if he's good box office. Just another excuse for gore and mayhem, though Jason Voorhees became the Norman Bates of the eighties. Otherwise, full of the expected sex-starved teenagers willing to go into dark places for no apparent reason other than to get murdered.

p: Steve Miner for Paramount/Georgetown
exec p: Tom Gruenberg, Lisa Bargamian
associate p: Frank Mancuso Jr
w: Ron Kurz
d: Steve Miner
ph: Peter Stein
m: Harry Manfredini
ed: Susan E. Cunningham
ad: Virginia Field
make-up effects: Carl Fullerton

cos: Ellen Lutter
sound: Richard Murphy
Amy Steel, Adrienne King, Kristen Baker, John Furey, Stu Charno, Warrington Gillette

Friday the Thirteenth Part III in 3D

USA 1982 95m Movielab 3D
The kids still keep coming back to Camp Crystal Lake, where murder is still the order of the day.

The worst of the series (which is saying something). The 3D gimmick drew the crowds in, most of whom left disappointed. The dialogue simply fills in the gaps between the murders, which are full of the expected gore and graphic detail.

p: Frank Mancuso Jr for Paramount/Georgetown
exec p: Lisa Barsmian
w: Martin Kitrosser, Carol Watson
d: Steve Miner
ph: Gerald Feil
m: Harry Manfredini (title theme: Harry Manfredini, Michael Zager)
ed: George Hively
ad: Robb Wilson King
cos: Sandi Love
make-up effects: Douglas J. White, Allan Apone, Frank Carrisosa
sound: Bill Nelson, William J. McCaughey, Kent F. Cleary
Dana Kimmell, Richard Brooker, Catherine Parks, Paul Kratka

Friday the Thirteenth - The Final Chapter

USA 1984 91m Movielab
More sex and slashing up at Camp Crystal Lake, with the demented Jason presiding over all.

Just as mindlessly sick as its predecessors yet box office takings made sure it was far from the final chapter in the series.

p: Frank Mancuso Jr for Paramount/Georgetown
exec p: Lisa Barsamian
w: Barney Cohen
story: Bruce Hidemi Sakow
d: Joseph Zito
ph: Joao Fernades
m: Harry Manfredini
ed: Joel Goodman
ad: Shelton H. Bishop III
pd: Shelton Bishop III
cos: Steagall
sound: Gary Rich, John 'Doc' Wilkinson
make-up effects: Tom Savini
Kimberly Beck, Peter Barton, Crispin Glover, Barbara Howard, Alan Hayes, Judie Aronson, E. Erich Anderson

Friday the Thirteenth Part V - A New Beginning

USA 1985 95m Metrocolor
Jason's killer is let out of the state mental institute and the murders begin again.

Just as sick and sadistic as all the others.
p: Timothy Silver for Paramount
exec p: Frank Mancuso Jr
w: Martin Kitrosser, David Cohen, Danny Steinmann, Tina Landau
story: Martin Kitrosser, David Cohen
d: Danny Steinmann
ph: Stephen L. Posey
m: Harry Manfredini
ed: Bruce Green
pd: Robert Howland
cos: Image Makers
sound: Mark Vlano, Ray West
make-up effects: Martin Becker
John Shepherd, Melanie Kinnaman, Shavar Ross, Richard Young, Narco St John, Corey Feldman

Friday the Thirteenth Part VI - Jason Lives

USA 1986 93m Metrocolor Ultra Stereo
A bolt of lightning brings Jason back to life.

The most professional entry in the series, though the basic recipe remains the same.
p: Don Behrns for Paramount/Terror Inc.
w/d: Tom McLaughlin
ph: John Kranhouse
m: Harry Manfredini
ed: Bruce Green
pd: Joseph T. Garrity
cos: Maria Mancuso
sp: Martin Becker
sound: James Thornton
make-up effects: Chris Swift, Brian Wade
titles: Dan Curry
add ph: J. Patrick Daily
underwater ph: Barry Herror
Thom Matthews, Jennifer Cooke, Kerry Noona, Renee Jones, Tom Fridley, C. J. Graham, Alan Blumenthal, Matthew Fraison, Ann Riverson, Tony Goldwyn

Friday the Thirteenth Part VII - The New Blood

US 1988 90m Technicolor Ultra Stereo
Jason meets his match with a girl who possesses lethal telekinetic powers.

Slick but comparatively mild entry. Otherwise, the mixture as before.
p: Iain Paterson for Paramount/Friday Four Inc.
w: Daryl Haney, Manuel Fidelloo
d: John Carl Buechler
ph: Paul Elliott
m: Harry Manfredini, Fred Molin
ed: Barry Zetlin, Maureen O'Connell, Martin Jay Sadoff
pd: Richard Lawrence
cos: Jacqueline Johnson
sp: Lou Carlucci
sound: Jan Brodin
stunt co-ordinator: Kane Hodder
Jennifer Banko, John Otrin, Susan Blu, Lar Park Lincoln, Terry Kiser, Kevin Blair, Jennifer Sullivan, Heidi Kozak, Kane Hodder, William Clarke Butler

Friday the Thirteenth Part VIII - Jason Takes Manhattan

USA 1989 100m Technicolor Ultra Stereo
Jason leaves Camp Crystal Lake for Manhattan.

More motiveless mayhem, with most of the action taking place on board a ship, not in New York.
p: Randolph Cheseldave for Paramount/Horror Inc.
w/d: Bob Hedden
ph: Bryan England
m: Fred Molin
ed: Steve Mirkovich
pd: David Fischer
cos: Carla Hetland
sound: Lars Ekstrom
make-up effects: Jamie Brown
stunt co-ordinator: Key Kirzinger
Jensen Daggett, Peter Mark Richman, Scott Reeves, Barnara Bingham, V. C. Dupree, Sharlene Martin, Kane Hodder

Friday the Thirteenth Part IX - Jason Goes to Hell see Jason Goes to Hell

Friedkin, William (1939-)

American director, producer and writer, from television, whose career hit a high in the early seventies with two blockbusters: *The French Connection* (1971), which won him a Best Director Oscar, and *The Exorcist*, which changed the nature of the horror film overnight. His career has since been somewhat variable, including such films as *Sorcerer*, *Cruising*, *To Live and Die in LA* and *Jade*.
Genre credits:
The Exorcist (1973), *The Guardian* (1990)

Friedman, David F.

American producer of gory low-budget exploitation pictures. A former carnival press agent he began his career in 1960 in tandem with director Herschell Gordon Lewis, with whom he made a handful of soft core sex films (*The Prime Time, The Adventures of Lucky Pierre, Nature's Playmates, etc.*) before success-

fully turning to horror with *Blood Feast*. He later split with Lewis and went on to produce and occasionally write a string of horror and sexploitation items, including *The Notorious Daughter of Fanny Hill, Space Thing, The Ribald Tales of Robin Hood, The Erotic Adventures of Zorro, Trader Hornee, Ilsa - She Wolf of the SS, The Budding of Brie* and *Sex and Buttered Popcorn*.
Genre credits:
Blood Feast (1963), *2000 Maniacs* ((1964), *Color Me Blood Red* (1965), *She Freak* (1967), *The Adult Version of Jekyll and Hyde* (1972), *The Flesh and Blood Show* (1973)

Fright

GB 1971 87m Eastmancolor
A teenage girl babysitting at a remote country house is menaced by a homicidal maniac.

Childishly scripted screamer, strictly for the uncritical.
p: Harry Fine, Michael Styles for Fantale/British Lion
w: Tudor Gates
d: Peter Collinson
ph: Ian Wilson
m: Harry Robinson
ed: Raymond Poulton
ad: Disley Jones
cos: Jean Fairlie
sound: Spencer Reeve
Susan George, Honor Blackman, George Cole, Ian Bannen, John Gregson, Maurice Kaufman

Fright Night *

USA 1985 105m Metroclor Panavision Dolby
A teenager discovers that his new next door neighbour is a vampire and enlists the aid of a has-been horror film star to help dispose of him.

Agreeable modern day variation on a well worn theme, helped by good effects and a willing cast. *Fright Night Part 2* appeared in 1988.
p: Herb Jaffe for Columbia/Delphi IV/Vistar
w/d: Tom Holland
ph: Jan Keisser
m: Brad Fiedel
ed: Kent Beyda
pd: John De Cuir Jr
cos: Robert Fletcher
sp: Richard Edlund and others
sound: John T. Reitz, David E. Campbell, David K. Kimball
stunt co-ordinator: Bill Couch Jr
Chris Sarandon, William Ragsdale, Roddy McDowell, Amanda Bearse, Stephen Geoffreys, Jonathan Stark, Dorothy Fielding, Art J. Evans

Fright Night Part 2 *

USA 1988 99m DeLuxe Panavision
Ultra Stereo
The young hero of *Fright Night* finds
himself threatened by the sister of the
vampire he disposed of at the end of the
first episode.

Generally slick and lively
sequel/rehash which picks up after a
slowish start.
p: Herb Jaffe, Mort Engelberg for Vista
w: Tim Metcalfe, Miguel Tejada-Flores,
Tommy Lee Wallace
d: Tommy Lee Wallace
ph: Mark Irwin
m: Brad Fiedel
ed: Jay Lash Cassidy
pd: Dean Tschetter
cos: Joseph Porro
sp: Gene Warren, Jr
sound: Bobby Anderson, Jr
make-up effects: Bart J. Mixon, Greg
Cannom
stunt co-ordinator: Edward James
Ulrich
titles: David Aaron
Roddy McDowall, William Ragsdale,
Traci Lin, Julie Carmen, Russell Clark,
Brian Thompson, Merritt Butrick, Ernie
Sabella

Le Frisson des Vampires

Fr 1970 90m colour
A honeymooning couple find themselves
at the mercy of modern day vampires.

Occasionally striking though mostly
incomprehensible vampire yarn with
dollops of the nudity expected from this
director.
p: Sam Selsky for Cinetheque/Les Films
Modernes/ABC
w/d: Jean Rollin
ph: Jean-Jacques Renon
m: Acan Thus
ed: Olivier Gregoire
ad: Michel Delesalles
sound: Jean-Paul Loublier
Sandra Julien, Nicole Nacel, Michel
Delahaye, Jacques Robiolles,
Marie-Pierre Tricot, Kuelan, Jean-Marie
Durand

Frogs *

USA 1972 91m Movielab
On an island in the Everglades the
inhabitants are killed off by the swamp
life, which appears to be rebelling
against the pollution.

Those with a dislike of creepy
crawlies will certainly be looking under
their chairs with this one. Otherwise,
just another ecological shocker on the
lines of *The Birds*.
p: George Edwards, Peter Thomas for
AIP
w: Robert Hutchinson, Robert Blees
d: George McCowan
ph: Mario Tosi
m: Les Baxter
ed: Fred R. Feitshans
Ray Milland, Sam Elliott, Joan Van Ark,
Adam Roarke, Judy Pace, Lynn Borden,
Mae Mercer, David Gilliam

From Beyond

USA/It 1986 88m DeLuxe Ultra Stereo
A scientist's experiments with sensory
equipment result in murder and madness.

Gory fantasy horror whose plot loses
its way about halfway through.
p: Brian Yuzna, Roberto Bessi for
Empire/Tarvin
exec p: Charles Band
w: Brian Yuzna, Dennis Paoli, Stuart
Gordon
novel: H. G. Lovecraft
d: Stuart Gordon
ph: Mac Ahlberg
m: Richard Band
ed: Lee Percy
ad: Giovanni Natalucci
cos: Angee Beckeett
sp: John Beuchler, Mark Shostrom, John
Naulin, Anthony Doublin
titles: Robert Dawson
Jeffrey Combs, Barbara Crampton, Ted
Sorel, Ken Foree, Carolyn
Purdey-Gordon, Bunny Summers

From Beyond the Grave *

GB 1973 98m Technicolor
Customers visiting a dusty antiques shop
get more than they bargained for when
they try to cheat its elderly owner.

Effectively handled horror compendium, above average of its kind, with one
of the stories (concerning a haunted
mirror) borrowed from *Dead of Night*.
p: Milton Subotsky, Max J. Rosenberg
for Warner/Amicus
w: Robin Clark, Raymond
Christodoulou
stories: R. Chetwyn-Hayes
d: KEVIN CONNOR
ph: Alan Hume
m: Douglas Gamley
ed: John Ireland
pd: Maurice Carter
ad: Bert Davey
cos: John Hilling
sound: Peter Handford, Nolan Roberts
Peter Cushing, Ian Bannen, Ian
Carmichael, Diana Dors, MARGARET
LEIGHTON, Donald Pleasence, Nyree
Dawn Porter, David Warner, Ian Ogilvy,
Lesley-Anne Down, Jack Watson, Angela
Pleasence

From Dusk to Dawn *

USA 1996 108m Technicolor Dolby
A preacher and his family on an RV
vacation are taken hostage by two brothers on the run to Mexico following a
bank robbery. Unfortunately, the bar
chosen for the brothers to rendezvous
with their boss happens to be a haunt
for local vampires.

A curious mixture of genres, not
quite as successful as it could have been
in terms of style and content, but with
energetic moments for those who don't
mind an excess of gore and bad language.
p: Gianni Nunnar, Meir Teper for
Miramax/A Band Apart/Los Hooligans
exec p: P. Lawrence Bender, Quentin
Tarantino, Robert Rodriguez
w: Quentin Tarantino
story: Robert Kurtzman
d/ed/steadicam op: Robert Rodriguez
ph: Guillermo Navarro
m: Graeme Revell
pd: Cecilia Montiel
cos: Graciela Mazon
sound: Mark Ulano
make-up effects: Kurtzman, Nicotero,
Berger EFX Group Inc.
Harvey Keitel, George Clooney,
Quentin Tarantino, Juliette Lewis,
Ernest Liu, Tom Savini, Cheech Marin
(in three roles)

From Hell It Came

USA 1957 71m bw
Natives of Kali are threatened by a
murderous tree stump.

Inept low-budgeter, as ludicrous as
its sounds.
p: Jack Milner for Allied Artists/Milner
Brothers
w: Richard Bernstein
story: Richard Bernstein, Jack Milner
d: Dan Milner
ph: Brydon Baker
m: Darrell Calker
ed: Jack Milner
ad: Rudi Field
cos: Frank Delmar
sound: Frank Webster Sr
Tod Andrews, Tina Carver, Linda
Watkins, John McNamara, Gregg
Palmer, Robert Swan

Frye, Dwight (1899-1943)

American character actor with much
stage experience, in films from 1927
with *The Night Bird*. After his appearance as Renfield in *Dracula*, however,
he found himself typecast in horror
roles, more often than not as a lunatic.
He also played Fritz the hunchback
assistant in *Frankenstein* and turned up
in several of the sequels in different
roles. A top Broadway star in the
1920s, he ended his career playing
uncredited bit parts in films unworthy
of his talents. Other credits include *The
Maltese Falcon* (1931 version, as Wilmer
the gunsel), *Sea Devils*, *The Great*

Impersonation, The Man in the Iron Mask, The People vs Dr Kildare and Renfrew of the Royal Mounted.
Genre credits:
Dracula (1930), Frankenstein (1931), The Invisible Man (1933), The Vampire Bat (1933), The Crime of Dr Crespi (1935), The Bride of Frankenstein (1935), The Cat and the Canary (1939), Son of Frankenstein (1939), The Drums of Fu Manchu (1940 - serial), The Ghost of Frankenstein (1942), Frankenstein Meets the Wolf Man (1943), Dead Men Walk (1943)

Fuest, Robert (1927-)

British director who, after experience as a graphic designer, entered television in the late fifties as an art director. Turned to direction with programmes and commercials before directing his first film, Just Like a Woman, in 1966. Helmed several interesting films in the early seventies, including the two classic Dr Phibes films. His other credits include Wuthering Heights, The Final Programme (aka The Last Days of Man on Earth) and Aphrodite.
Genre credits:
And Soon the Darkness (1970), The Abominable Dr Phibes (1971), Dr Phibes Rises Again (1972), The Devil's Rain (1972), The Revenge of the Stepford Wives (1980 - TVM)

Fukuda, Jun

Japanese director associated with the Japanese monster cycle which featured men romping about in rubber suits.
Genre credits:
Godzilla vs. the Sea Monster (1966 - aka Nankai No Dai Ketto), Son of Godzilla (1968 - aka Gojira No Musuko), Godzilla on Monster Island (1971 - aka Gojira Tai Gaigan / Godzilla vs. Gigan), Godzilla vs. Megalon (1973 - aka Gojira Tai Megaro), Godzilla vs. the Bionic Monster (1974 - aka Gojia Tai Meka-Gojira / Godzilla vs. Mecha Godzilla / Godzilla vs. the Cosmic Monster / The Terror of Mecha Godzilla)

Fulci, Lucio (1927-1996)

Italian director with a penchant for gut churning, viscera filled exploitation and horror movies, most of which are usually cut for video release in the UK. Perhaps best known for Zombie Flesh Eaters (aka Zombi 2).

Genre credits:
Don't Torture the Duckling (1972), Schizoid (1973), The Psychic (1978), Zombi Flesh Eaters (1979 - aka Zombi 2), City of the Living Dead (1980 - aka Paura Nella Citta dei Morti Viventi), The Black Cat (1980 - aka Il Gatto Nero di Park Lane), The Beyond (1981 - aka The Gates of Hell), Seven Doors of Death (1981), The House By the Cemetery (1981), The New York Ripper (1982), Eye of the Evil Dead (1983), Aenigma (1987), Zombie 3 (1988), House of Doom (1989 - TVM - co-d), Nightmare Concert (1990), Voices from the Deep (1990 - aka Voices from Beyond), Cat in the Brain (1990)

Fulton, John P. (1902-1965)

Pioneering American special effects technician at Universal from 1930 where he worked on many of their key horror films, most notably The Invisible Man and several other James Whale-directed productions. He later moved to Samuel Goldwyn and Paramount, winning Oscars for his effects work on the Danny Kaye comedy Wonder Man (1945), The Bridges at Toko-Ri (1954), and The Ten Commandments (1956). A former surveyor and electrical engineer, he began his movie career as a camera assistant in the late twenties, graduating to cinematographer in 1929 on such films as Hell's Harbour, Eyes of the World and The Great Impersonation before sidelining into special effects. His other credits include Waterloo Bridge, Show Boat, Elephant Walk, Rear Window and The Disorderly Orderly.
Genre credits:
Frankenstein (1931), The Murders in the Rue Morgue (1932), The Mummy (1932), The Old Dark House (1932), The Invisible Man (1933), The Werewolf of London (1935), The Bride of Frankenstein (1935), Dracula's Daughter (1936), The Invisible Ray (1936), Dracula's Daughter (1936), The Invisible Man Returns (1939), Son of Frankenstein (1939), The Invisible Woman (1940), The Black Cat (1941), Man-Made Monster (1941 - aka The Electric Monster), The Invisible Agent (1942), Calling Dr Death (1943), Son of Dracula (1943), Frankenstein Meets the Wolf Man (1943), Dead Man's Eyes (1944), Cobra Woman (1944), House of Frankenstein (1944), The Ghost Catchers (1944), The Invisible Man's

Revenge (1944), Weird Woman (1944), The Scarlet Claw (1944), House of Dracula (1945), Pillow of Death (1945), Abbott and Costello Meet the Invisible Man (1951), The Colossus of New York (1958), I Married A Monster from Outer Space (1958), The Space Children (1958)

The Funhouse

USA 1981 97m Technicolor Panavision Dolby
A group of college kids decide to spend the night in the ghost train of a touring funfair and wish they hadn't.
  Very average horror fare, typical of both its period and its director.
p: Mace Neufeld, Derek Power for Universal
w: Larry Block
d: Tobe Hooper
ph: Andrew Laszlo
m: John Beal
ed: Jack Hofstra
pd: Morton Rabinowitz
make-up effects: RICK BAKER
titles: Murray Naidich
Elizabeth Berridge, Shawn Carson, Largo Woodruff, Miles Chapin, Vera Miles, Kevin Conway, Wayne Doba, Cooper Huckabee, William Finley

The Fury **

USA 1978 117m DeLuxe
The father of a boy with lethal telekinetic powers gives chase when his son is kidnapped by terrorists, and is helped by a girl with similar abilities.
  Complex but technically accomplished horror movie with various points of interest for connoisseurs of its director.
p: Frank Yablans for TCF
exec p: Ron Preissman
w: John Farris from his novel
d: BRIAN DE PALMA
ph: Richard H. Kline
m: JOHN WILLIAMS
ed: Paul Hirsch
pd: Bill Malley
cos: Theoni V. Aldredge
sp: A. D. Flowers
sound: Hal Etherington, Dick Vorisek
make-up effects: Rick Baker
stunt co-ordinator: Mickey Gilbert
Kirk Douglas, John Cassavetes, Carrie Snodgress, Amy Irving, Andrew Stevens, Charles Durning, Fiona Lewis, Daryl Hannah

G

Galeen, Henrik (1882-1949)
Dutch writer and director who became a key figure of the German silent cinema. A former stage actor and director, he began acting in films in 1910, turning to direction in 1913 as a co-director with Paul Wegener, with whom he worked on several other films. He lived in America for the last sixteen years of his life but never directed a film there.
Genre credits:
The Student of Prague (1913 - co-w/co-d), *The Golem* (1914 - aka *Der Golem* - co-w/co-d), *The Golem* (1920 - aka *Der Golem* - co-w), *Nosferatu* (1922 - aka *Eine Symphonie des Grauens* - w), *Waxworks* (1924 - aka *Das Wachsfigurenkabinett* - w), *The Student of Prague* (1926 - aka *The Man Who Cheated Life* - co-w/d), *Alraune* (1927 - w/d)

Galligan, Zach (1963-)
American actor who came to notice as the teenage lead of *Gremlins* though subsequent roles have failed to build on this success.
Genre credits:
Gremlins (1984), *Waxwork* (1988), *Gremlins 2: The New Batch* (1990), *Psychic* (1991), *Waxwork II: Lost in Time* (1992), *Warlock II: The Armageddon* (1993)

Gamley, Douglas (1924-)
Australian born composer long in Britain. Scores include *The Admirable Crichton*, *Watch It, Sailor!* and *Spring and Port Wine*. Genre credits mostly for Amicus.
Genre credits:
The Ugly Duckling (1959), *The Horror of it All* (1964), *Tales from the Crypt* (1972), *Asylum* (1972), *Vault of Horror* (1973), *And Now the Screaming Starts* (1973), *From Beyond the Grave* (1973), *Madhouse* (1974), *The Beast Must Die* (1974), *The Land That Time Forgot* (1975), *The Monster Club* (1980)

Gargoyles
USA 1972 74m Technicolor TVM
In Mexico to research a book, a demonologist and his daughter discover a secret race of gargoyles.

Silly fantasy thriller which could have been better handled, though it passes the time. The gargoyle make-up won its creators an Emmy.
p: Bob Christiansen, Rick Rosenberg for Tomorrow Entertainment
exec p: Norman Gimbel
w: Elinor Karpf, Stephen Karpf
d: B. W. L. Norton
ph: Earl Rath
m: Robert Prince
ed: Frank P. Keller
sp: Milt Rice, George Peekham
gargoyle make-up: Tom Burman, Stan Winston, Ross Wheat
Cornel Wilde, Jennifer Salt, Grayson Hall, Scott Glenn

Garland, Beverly (1926-)
American actress (real name Beverly Fessenden) in films from 1950 with *DOA*. Many fifties B movies followed, a good deal of them for Roger Corman (*The Gunslinger*, *Swamp Women*, *Thunder Over Hawaii*, etc.). Her early genre work aside, however, she is perhaps best known for her roles in such TV series as *Decoy*, *My Three Sons* and *The Scarecrow and Mrs King*. Her other film credits include *The Glass Web*, *The Joker is Wild*, *Pretty Poison*, *Airport '75*, *Roller Boogie* and *It's My Turn*.
Genre credits:
The Neanderthal Man (1953), *The Rocket Man* (1954), *It Conquered the World* (1956), *Not of This Earth* (1956), *Curucu, Beast of the Amazon* (1956), *The Alligator People* (1959), *Twice Told Tales* (1963), *The Mad Room* (1969)

Garris, Mick
American writer (the story editor for TV's *Amazing Stories*) and director whose genre projects have grown in size.
Genre credits:
Critters 2 (1988 - aka *Critters 2: The Main Course* - co-w/d), *Psycho IV* (1990 - TVM - d), *Sleepwalkers* (1992 - d), *The Stand* (1994 - TVM - d)

The Gate *
Canada 1986 84m Technicolor Dolby
Two young boys accidentally release a

horde of demons from a hellhole in their garden.
Bright little horror comic, a little slow to start, but with sufficient special effects in its latter half to redeem itself. *The Gate II* followed in 1992.
p: John Kemeny for New Century Entertainment/Vista/Alliance/The Gate Film Productions
w: Michael Nankin
d: Tibor Tacaks
ph: Thomas Vamos
m: Michael Hoenig, J. Peter Robinson
ed: Rit Wallis
pd: William Beeton
cos: Trysha Bakker
sp: Randall William Cook
sound: Doug Granton, Joe Grimaldi, Dino Pigat
make-up effects: Craig Reardon
2nd unit ph: Peter Benison
Stephen Dorff, Louis Tripp, Christa Denton, Kelly Rowan, Jennifer Irwin, Sean Fagan, Deborah Grover

Gates of Hell see City of the Living Dead

Gates, Tudor
British screenwriter and novelist, a former stage manager. Credits include *Troubled Waters*, *Barbarella*, *Dateline Diamonds* and episodes for TV's *The Avengers*, though he is perhaps best known for penning Hammer's 'Carmilla' trilogy. He also wrote and directed two soft-core sex films: *Sex Thief* and *Love Box*.
Genre credits:
Cry Nightmare (1966), *The Vampire Lovers* (1970), *Lust for a Vampire* (1971), *Twins of Evil* (1971), *Fright* (1971)

Il Gatto Nero see The Black Cat (1981)

Il Gatto di Park Lane see The Black Cat (1981)

Gay, Ramon (1917-1960)
Mexican actor who appeared in a handful of absurd home grown horror films, some of which were dubbed and

released in English.
Genre credits:
Cry of the Bewitched (1960), *The Aztec Mummy* (1957), *The Robot vs the Aztec Mummy* (1959), *The Curse of the Aztec Mummy* (1959), *The Curse of the Doll People* (1960)

The Geek

USA 1986 87m Astrocolor
Two campers fall prey to the maniac son of a backwoods family.

Tired shocker, as predictable as it is boring.
p: Maureen Sweeney for Overlook
w: Charles Joseph
d: Dean Crow
ph: Jon Gerard
m: Skeet Bushor
ed: Chris Hodapp
pd: Bob Smith
cos: Jacque Workman
sound: Chuck Rapp
make-up effects: Phil Yeary
Christina Noonan, Jack O'Hara, Brad Armacost, Dick Kreusser, Lesley Denise

Geeson, Judy (1948-)

British actress on stage from the age of nine. She has appeared in a variety of films, often as a sexy young thing. She is the sister of actress Sally Geeson (1950-), who herself has appeared in such genre films as *The Oblong Box* (1969) and *Cry of the Banshee* (1970). Her other credits include *Here We Go Round the Mulberry Bush*, *Three Into Two Won't Go*, *Carry On England* and *The Eagle Has Landed*.
Genre credits:
Berserk (1967), *10, Rillington Place* (1970), *Doomwatch* (1972), *Fear in the Night* (1972), *Dominique* (1978), *Inseminoid* (1980 - aka *Horror Planet*)

George, Screaming Mad

Japanese make-up effects technician working in America, where he has provided gut-churning effects for a variety of genre films, perhaps most notoriously for *Society*.
Genre credits:
Don't Panic (1987 - co-sp), *A Nightmare on Elm Street Part Four: The Dream Master* (1988), *Society* (1989), *Bride of the Re-Animator* (1991 - aka *Re-Animator 2*), *Necronomicon* (1993), *Freaked* (1994)

George, Susan (1950-)

British actress who began her career as a child in such films as *Come Fly with Me* and *Cup Fever* before graduating to 'sexpot' roles in such films as *Twinky*, *All Neat in Black Stockings* and *Mandingo*. She now also produces films with her her husband, actor Simon MacCorkindale

(*Stealing Heaven*, *That Summer of White Roses*, etc.). Her other credits include *Spring and Port Wine*, *Eyewitness*, *Dirty Mary*, *Crazy Larry*, *Out of Season* and *The Jigsaw Man*.
Genre credits:
The Sorcerers (1967), *Die Screaming, Marianne* (1970), *Fright* (1971), *Straw Dogs* (1971), *Dr Jekyll and Mr Hyde* (1973 - TVM), *Venom* (1981), *The House Where Evil Dwells* (1982), *Czech Mate* (1984 - TVM), *Jack the Ripper* (1988 - TVM)

Gershenson, Joseph (1904-)

Russian born music director in films from 1920 as a musician. From 1941 he headed Universal's music department, conducting many of the studio's genre pictures, often uncredited.
Genre credits:
Abbott and Costello Meet the Invisible Man (1950), *The Creature from the Black Lagoon* (1953), *Abbott and Costello Meet Dr Jekyll and Mr Hyde* (1953), *Cult of the Cobra* (1955), *Abbott and Costello Meet the Mummy* (1955), *Revenge of the Creature* (1955), *The Creature Walks Among Us* (1956), *The Deadly Mantis* (1957), *Monster on the Campus* (1958), *The Thing That Couldn't Die* (1958)

Gertsman, Maury (1910-)

Prolific American cinematographer whose credits include *Terror by Night*, *Meet Danny Wilson* and *Gunfight in Abilene*.
Genre credits:
The Brute Man (1946), *The Creature Walks Among Us* (1956)

Ghost *

USA 1990 126m Technicolor Dolby
The ghost of a murdered stockbroker returns from the dead and, with the assistance of a fake medium and his girlfriend, helps to bring his killer to justice.

Curious but generally entertaining mish-mash of fantasy, comedy, drama, thrills, romance and detection. *Topper* did it better but it found huge favour with audiences.
p: Lisa Weinstein for Paramount
w: Bruce Joel Rubin (aa)
d: Jerry Zucker
ph: Adam Greenberg
m: Maurice Jarre
ed: Walter Murch
pd: Jane Musky
cos: Ruth Morley
sp: Richard Edlund
sound: Jeff Wexler
Patrick Swayze, Demi Moore, Whoopi Goldberg (aa), Tony Goldwyn, Stanley Lawrence, Christopher J. Keene, Susan Breslau, Martina Degnan

The Ghost and Mr Chicken *

USA 1965 Technicolor Techniscope
A nervous reporter investigates a spooky mansion where a series of murders were committed.

Thin hayseed comedy. Children are probably its best audience; they'll certainly enjoy the mild scares.
p: Edward J. Montague for Universal
w: James Fritzell, Everett Greenbaum
d: Alan Rafkin
ph: William Margulies
m: Vic Mizzy
DON KNOTTS, Skip Homeier, Joan Stanley, Reta Shaw, Dick Sargent, Liam Redmond

The Ghost and Mrs Muir **

USA 1947 104m bw
After the death of her husband a widow moves into a seaside house where she meets the ghost of the former occupier, with whom she writes a book.

A warm hearted and engaging piece of whimsy with charming performances and excellent photography. Most likeable.
p: Fred Kohlmar for TCF
w: PHILIP DUNNE
novel: R. A. Dick
d: Joseph L. Mankiewicz
ph: CHARLES LANG JR
m: BERNARD HERRMANN
ed: Dorothy Spencer
ad: Richard Day, George Davis
cos: Charles Le Maire, Eleanor Bohm, Oleg Cassini
sp: Fred Sersen
sound: Bernard Freericks, Roger Heman
GENE TIERNEY, REX HARRISON, George Sanders, Edna Best, Natalie Wood, Vanessa Brown, Anna Lee, Robert Coote, Isobel Elsom

The Ghost Breakers ***

USA 1940 85m bw
A radio announcer on the run from gangsters helps an heiress who has inherited a haunted castle in Cuba.

Sprightly comedy thriller, an agreeable blend of wisecracks and thrills on very similar lines to the same team's earlier success *The Cat and the Canary*. Production excellent.
p: Arthur Hornblow Jr for Paramount
w: Paul Dickey, Walter de Leon
play: Paul Dickey, Charles W. Goddard
d: GEORGE MARSHALL
ph: CHARLES LANG
m: ERNST TOCH
md: Andreo Setaro
ed: Ellsworth Hoagland
ad: HANS DREIER, ROBERT USHER
cos: Edith Head
sp: Farciot Edouart
sound: Harold Lewis, Richard Olsen

BOB HOPE, PAULETTE GODDARD, Paul Lukas, WILLIE BEST, Richard Carlson, Lloyd Corrigan, Anthony Quinn (as twins), Pedro de Cordova, Noble Johnson (as the zombie)

Ghost Dad
USA 1990 84m DeLuxe
An uninsured father, killed in a car crash, returns as a ghost and has just three days to sort out his children's futures before being sent on to the afterlife.

Thin, sentimental, overplayed and rather self-satisfied supernatural comedy which failed to make a movie star out of a TV sitcom star.
p: Terry Nelson for Universal
exec p: Stan Robertson
w: Chris Reese, Brent Maddock, S. S. Wilson
story: Brent Maddock, S. S. Wilson
d: Sidney Poitier
ph: Andrew Laszlo
m: Henry Mancini
ed: Pembroke Herring
pd: Henry Humstead
Bill Cosby, Denise Nicholas, Kimberley Russell, Ian Bannen, Christine Ebersole, Barry Corbin

The Ghost Goes West **
GB 1935 85m bw
When an ancient Scottish castle is transported stone by stone to America by a millionaire, he doesn't reckon with the castle ghost going too.

Fondly remembered but now largely disappointing fantasy comedy with which the director appears to have been a little out of his depth. Amusing touches but not enough of them.
p: Alexander Korda for London Films
w: Robert E. Sherwood, Geoffrey Kerr
story: Eric Keown
d: Rene Clair
ph: Harold Rosson
m: Mischa Spoliansky
md: Muir Mathieson
ed: William Hornbeck, Harold Earle-Fischbacher
ad: Vincent Korda
cos: Rene Hubert, John Armstrong
sp: Ned Mann
sound: A. W. Watkins
ROBERT DONAT, Jean Parker, EUGENE PALLETTE, Elsa Lanchester, Ralph Bunker, Patricia Hilliard, Morton Selten

The Ghost of Frankenstein *
US 1942 67m bw
A second son of Frankenstein implants the brain of an evil shepherd into the Monster.

Preposterous, often unintentionally funny, addition to Universal's Frankenstein series, a follow on to *Son of Frankenstein*. A few energetic moments help to liven things up.
p: George Waggner for Universal
w: W. Scott Darling
d: Erle C. Kenton
ph: Milton Krasner, Woody Bredell
m: Hans J. Salter
ed: Ted Kent
ad: Jack Otterson, Harold H. MacArthur
cos: Vera West
make-up: Jack P. Pierce
Cedric Hardwicke, Lon Chaney Jr, BELA LUGOSI, Ralph Bellamy, Lionel Atwill, Evelyn Ankers

The Ghost of Rashmon Hall
GB 1949 62m bw
A young couple rent a large house only to discover that it's haunted.

Dim programmer, amateurishly filmed.
p: Harold Baum for British Animated Federate
w: no credit given
d: Dennis Kavanagh
ph/sp: Ray Densham
m: no credit given
ed: Dorothy Elliott
ad: George Ward
sound: B. Brightwell, R. Littlejohn, G. Webster
Valentine Dyall, Anne Howard, Alec Faversham, Howard Douglas, Beatrice Marsden, Frank Dunlop

The Ghost of St Michael's *
GB 1941 82m bw
Evacuated to a remote Scottish castle, a class of schoolboys and their seedy master discover that an enemy agent is using an old ghost legend to scare off the locals.

Fitfully amusing Will Hay comedy. Not quite one of his best but with a few good situations along the way. Perhaps he just needed Graham Moffatt and Moore Marriott.
p: Michael Balcon, Basil Dearden for Ealing
w: Angus Macphail, John Dighton
d: Marcel Varnel
ph: Derick Williams
md: Ernest Irving
ed: E. B. Jarvis
ad: Wilfred Shingleton
sound: Eric Williams
WILL HAY, CLAUDE HULBERT, Charles Hawtrey, Felix Aylmer, Raymond Huntley, Eliot Makeham, John Laurie, Roddy Hughes, Hay Petrie, Manning Whiley

The Ghost Ship *
USA 1943 69m bw
A sadistic sea captain systematically murders his crew and the third officer attempts to expose him.

Something of a disappointment when compared to this producer's supernatural thrillers, this slow moving, misleadingly titled psychological drama, long unavailable, is, however, not without its moments of interest.
p: Val Lewton for RKO
w: Donald Henderson
story: Leo Mitler
d: Mark Robson
ph: Nicholas Musuraca
m: Roy Webb
md: Constantin Bakaleinikoff
ed: John Lockert
ad: Albert S. D'Agostino, Walter E. Keller
cos: Edward Stevenson
sp: Vernon L. Walker
sound: Francis M. Sarver
Richard Dix, Russell Wade, Edmund Glover, Ben Bard, Skelton Knaggs, Edith Barrett

Ghost Story *
GB/India 1974 89m Fujicolor
Three former college acquaintances spend the weekend together at a country house which turns out to have one or two nasty secrets.

Atmospheric but amateurish little ghost story, not without its minor virtues but, even at this length, much too long.

• A gooey moment from *Ghost Story*, with make-up effects care of Dick Smith, whose work has influenced such luminaries as Rick Baker and Rob Bottin.

p: Stephen Weeks for Stephen Weeks Company
w: Rosemary Sutcliffe, Stephen Weeks, Philip Norman
d: Stephen Weeks
ph: Peter Hurst
m: Ron Geesin
ed: Jon Costelloe
pd: Peter Young
cos: Joelle Weeks
sound: Doug Turner
Murray Melvin, Anthony Bate, Larry Dann, Vivian Mackerell, Marianne Faithfull, Leigh Lawson, Barbara Shelley, Penelope Keith

Ghost Story *
USA 1981 110m Technicolor
Four elderly gentlemen are haunted by a dark secret from their past.

Involved, over plotted adaptation of a complex novel. Quite frightening in places for all that and with sufficient style and atmosphere to keep one watching.
p: Ronald G. Smith, Douglas Green for Universal
w: Lawrence D. Cohen
novel: Peter Straub
d: John Irvin
ph: JACK CARDIFF
m: PHILIPPE SARDE
ed: Tom Rolf
ad: Norman Newberry
cos: May Routh
sp: Albert Whitlock
sound: Jim Alexander
make-up effects: Dick Smith
titles: Phil Norman
visual consutant: Michael Seymour
Fred Astaire, John Housemann, Melvyn Douglas, Douglas Fairbanks Jr, Craig Wasson, Patricia Neal, Alice Krige, Jacqueline Brooks, Miguel Fernandez, Lance Holcomb, Mark Chamberlain, Tim Choate, Kurt Johnson, Ken Olin, Robin Curtis

The Ghost Train **
GB 1941 85m bw
Passengers stranded at a Cornish halt during a thunder storm find themselves menaced by gun runners posing as ghosts.

Lively comedy thriller, previously filmed in 1927 and 1931, but here adapted as a vehicle for Arthur Askey. Creaky fun in the music hall manner.
p: Edward Black for Gainsborough
w: Mariot Edgar, J. O. C. Orton, Val Guest
play: ARNOLD RIDLEY
d: WALTER FORDE
ph: Jack Cox
md: Louis Levy
ed: R. E. Dearing
ad: Alex Vetchinsky

sound: M. Hobbs
ARTHUR ASKEY, RICHARD MURDOCH, KATHLEEN HARRISON, Morland Graham, Linden Travers, Peter Murray Hill, HERBERT LOMAS, Raymond Huntley

Ghostbusters **
USA 1984 105m Technicolor Panavision Dolby
When a series of weird hauntings take New York by surprise, three unemployed parapsychologists open a ghost disposal business and find themselves faced with saving the world.

Lively supernatural farce which, despite a couple of lapses in pace, provides a fair amount of harmless entertainment. It also made a pot of money at the box office. Who you gonna call?
p: Ivan Reitman for Columbia-Delphi/Black Rhino
exec p: Bernie Brillstein
w: Dan Aykroyd, Harold Ramis
d: Ivan Reitman
ph: LASZLO KOVACS
m: Elmer Bernstein
song m/ly: RAY PARKER JR
ed: Sheldon Kahn, David Blewitt
pd: John de Cuir
cos: Theoni V. Aldrege
sp: RICHARD EDLUND
sound: Richard Beggs, Tom McCarthy Jr, Gene Cantamessa
stunt co-ordinator: Bill Couch
titles: R. Greenberg
BILL MURRAY, Dan Aykroyd, Harold Ramis, Sigourney Weaver, Ernie Hudson, Rick Moranis, Annie Potts, William Atherton, David Margulies

Ghostbusters II
USA 1989 103m DeLuxe Panavision Dolby
When New York is again menaced by monsters from the spirit world the Ghostbusters come to the rescue.

Expensive but unimaginative and much delayed sequel which does little other than to regurgitate the plot of the first film - and to much less effect. A prime example of eighties take-the-money-and-run filmmaking.
p: Ivan Reitman for Columbia
w: Harold Ramis, Dan Aykroyd
d: Ivan Reitman
ph: Michael Chapman
m: Randy Edelman
ed: Sheldon Kahn, Donn Cambern
pd: Bo Welch
cos: Gloria Gresham
sp: Dennis Muren
sound: Gene Cantamessa
2nd unit d: Michael Moore
Bill Murray, Sigourney Weaver, Harold Ramis, Ernie Hudson, Annie Potts, Rick

Moranis, Peter MacNicol, Kurt Fuller, David Margulies

Ghosthouse
USA/It 1987 94m Telecolor Dolby
A radio ham tracks down a series of weird messages to a remote house where many strange events - including murder - take place.

Fairish Poltergeist clone with a few effective moments for the uncritical. Witchery, which was also released as Ghosthouse II, followed in 1989.
p: Filmirage
w: Cinthia McGavin, Sheila Goldberg
d/story: Humphrey Humbert (Umberto Lenzi)
ph: Franco Delli Colli
m: Piero Montanari
ed: Kathleen Stratton
ad: Alexander Colby
cos: Kuo Ami
sp: Dan Maklansky, Robert Gould, Rolanda Park
sound: Hubrecht Nijhuis, David Lee
Lara Wendel, Donald O'Brian, Mary Sellars, Greg Scott, Kate Silver, Ron Houck

Ghosthouse II see Witchery

Ghosts in the Night see Spooks Run Wild

The Ghosts of Berkeley Square *
GB 1947 89m bw
At a spooks' reunion two ghosts recall their various adventures, which involve haunting a house in Berkeley Square until royalty visits.

Slight supernatural comedy, little more than a collection of linked sketches, though not without its moments of amusement.
p: Louis H. Jackson for British National
w: James Seymour
novel: S. J. Simon, Caryl Brahms
d: Vernon Sewell
ph: Ernest Palmer
m: Hans May
ed: Dan Birt, George Adams
ad: Wilfred Arnold
sound: Harold V. King
cam op: Moray Grant
Robert Morley, Felix Aylmer, Claude Hulbert, Marie Lohr, Yvonne Arnaud, Abraham Sofaer, A. E. Matthews, Ernest Thesiger, Mary Jerrold, Wally Patch, Martin Miller, Esme Percy, Martita Hunt, John Londgen, Ronald Fankau, Wilfred Hyde White

The Ghoul *
GB 1933 79m bw
A dying Egyptologist vows to return from the tomb.

• **Boris Karloff in** *The Ghoul,* **his first British horror film following his successes in** *Frankenstein, The Mummy* **and** *The Old Dark House.*

Interestingly cast and dated horror thriller, very much of its period but notably underlit.
p: Michael Balcon for Gaumont
w: Frank King, Leonard Hines, L. DuGarde Peach, Roland Pertwee, John Hastings
d: T. Hayes Hunter
ph: Gunther Krampf
m: Louis Levy
md: Rupert Downing
ed: Ian Dalrymple, Ralph Kemplen
ad: Alfred Junge
sound: A. Birch
Boris Karloff, Cedric Hardwicke, Kathleen Harrison, Ralph Richardson, Ernest Thesiger, Dorothy Hyson, Anthony Bushell, D. A. Clarke-Smith

The Ghoul
GB 1975 87m Eastmancolor
In the twenties, a former clergyman lures travellers to his home to satisfy the murderous lusts of his depraved son.
Over stretched shocker which wastes too much time on preliminaries.
p: Kevin Francis for Tyburn
w: John Elder (Anthony Hinds)
d: Freddie Francis
ph: John Wilcox
m: Harry Robinson
md: Philip Martell
ed: Henry Richardson
ad: Jack Shapman, Peter Williams
cos: Anthony Mendleson
sp: Charles Staffell
sound: John Brommage, Ken Barker
make-up: Roy Ashton
Peter Cushing, Veronica Carlson,

Alexandra Bastedo, John Hurt, Gwen Watford, Don Henderson (as the Ghoul)

The Giant Spider Invasion
USA 1975 76m Eastmancolor
Strange crystals from outer space hatch spiders which grow to a giant size and threaten a small township.
Abysmal low-budget farrago with absolutely nothing going for it.
p: Bill Rebane, Richard L. Ruff for Transcentury/Cinema Group 75
w: Richard L. Huff, Robert Easton
d: Bill Rebane
ph: Jack Willoughby
ed: Barbara Pokras
ad: Ito Rebane
Barbara Hale, Steve Brodie, Leslie Parrish, Alan Hale, Robert Easton, Bill Williams

Gibson, Alan (1938-1987)
Canadian-born director who came to Britain in 1967. An ex-actor, he became a trainee director with the BBC. Much television work, including several episodes of Hammer's *Journey to the Unknown,* before moving into films.
Genre credits:
Crescendo (1969), *Goodbye, Gemini* (1970), *Dracula AD 1972* (1972), *The Satanic Rites of Dracula* (1973), *Crash!* (1977 - uncredited co-d)

Giger, H. R.
Swiss designer whose often disturbing work has been used in only a handful of movies, most notably *Alien,* which won him a Best Visual Effects Oscar (with Carlo Rambaldi, Brian Johnson, Nick Allder and Denys Aylin).

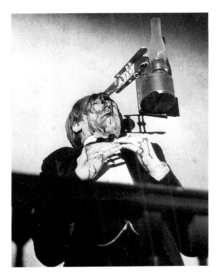

• **Ian McCulloch in a gory moment from Tyburn's 1975 remake of** *The Ghoul.*

Genre credits:
Alien (1979), *Poltergeist II* (1986), *Species* (1995)

Gilling, John (1912-1985)
British writer-producer-director, a former clerk, extra and stunt man. Began his film career as an assistant director for BIP in 1933. Served in the Royal Naval Volunteer Reserve during the war after which he turned his talents to writing. His first screenplay, *Black Memory,* was filmed in 1947. He turned to direction in 1948 with *Escape from Broadmoor.* All manner of low-budget crime thrillers and programmes followed, though his best work was for Hammer in the sixties for whom he also made a number of swashbucklers, *The Pirates of Blood River* and *The Scarlet Blade* among them.
Genre credits:
The Greed of William Hart (1948 - w), *Mother Riley Meets the Vampire* (1952 - aka *My Son the Vampire/Vampire Over London/King Robot* - p/d), *The Flesh and the Fiends* (1959 - aka *The Fiendish Ghouls/Mania/Psycho Killers* - co-w/d/story), *The Shadow of the Cat* (1961 - d), *The Gorgon* (1964 - w), *The Night Caller* (1965 - aka *Blood Beast from Outer Space* - d), *The Plague of the Zombies* (1966 - d), *The Reptile* (1966 -d), *The Mummy's Shroud* (1967 -w/d), *Trog* (1970 - co-story)

Girdler, William
American producer and director, often exploiting established box office trends, *Grizzly* being a dry land variation on *Jaws* and *The Manitou* a variation on *The Exorcist,* etc.
Genre credits:
Grizzly (1976 - d), *Day of the Animals* (1976 - d), *The Manitou* (1977 - co-w/p/d)

Glen or Glenda
USA 1953 61m bw
A young man reveals to his girlfriend that he is a transvestite with a passion for angora.
Hilariously then tediously inept, semi-autobiographical schlocker, one of several cult items written and directed by the notorious Edward D. Wood Jr.
p: Edward D. Wood Jr for Screen Classics
w/d: Edward D. Wood Jr
ph: William C. Thompson
md: Sandford Dickinson
ed/ad/cos: no credits given
sound: Ben Winkler
Daniel Davis (Edward D. Wood Jr), Bela Lugosi, Dolores Fuller, Tim Farrell, Lyle Talbot, Tommy Haynes, Charles Crafts

THE GILL MAN LOOKS LIKE HE'S APPLIED A
LITTLE TOO MUCH LIPSTICK in this rare
colour still from the 1954 black and
white shocker which was also filmed
in 3D. The unfortunate person underneath all the rubber is stunt man
Ricou Browning, whose swimming
skills were put to much use in the
movie.

Glickenhaus, James (1950-)

American writer, producer, director and executive, the founder in 1987 (with Lenny Shapiro) of Shapiro-Glickenhaus Entertainment, which produces low-budget genre films of varying quality. Genre credits include:
The Suicide Club (1977 - aka *The Astrologer* - d), *The Exterminator* (1980 - w/d), *Frankenhooker* (1990 - co-exec p)

Godzilla

This prehistoric monster with radioactive breath has appeared in countless Japanese monster marathons, the first of which was 1954's *Godzilla* (original title *Gojira*). As with the sequels, Godzilla was played by a man in a monster suit to save on the expense of stop motion animation. The film climaxed with the destruction of Tokyo, also a feature of many of the sequels. A dubbed American version of this film, with extra scenes involving Raymond Burr as a reporter, was released the following year. In the sixties sequels came thick and fast with Godzilla, originally the aggressor, often the hero of the piece. Teamed at various stages with King Kong, Megalon and Mothra, the films became increasingly childish as the series progressed. Close cousins include *Gigantis the Fire Monster* (Godzilla under another name in the US because of copyright laws), Britain's *Gorgo* and *Ebirah - Horror of the Deep*. Key filmography:
Godzilla (1954/5 - aka *Godzilla, King of the Monsters/Gojira*), *Gigantis the Fire Monster* (1955 - aka *The Return of Godzilla/Gojira No Gyakushyu*) *King Kong vs. Godzilla* (1962 - aka *Kingu Kongu Tai Gojira*), *Godzilla vs the Thing* (1964 - aka *Gojira Tai Mosura*), *Godzilla vs the Sea Monster* (1966 - aka *Nankai No Dai Ketto*), *Godzilla's Revenge* (1967 - aka *Ord Kaiju Daishingeki*), *Son of Godzilla* (1968 - aka *Gojira No Musuko*), *Destroy All Monsters* (1968 - aka *Kaiju Soshingeki*), *Godzilla vs the Smog Monster* (1971 - aka *Gojira Tai Hedora*), *Godzilla on Monster Island* (1971 - aka *Godzilla vs Gigan/Gojira Tai Gaigan*), *Godzilla vs Megalon* (1973 - aka *Gojira Tai Megaro*), *Godzilla vs the Cosmic Monster* (1974 - aka *Godzilla vs Mecha-Godzilla/Godzilla vs the Bionic Monster/Gojira Tai Meka-Gojira*), *Godzilla 1985* (1984 - aka *Gojira*), *Godzilla vs Biollante* (1989 - aka *Gojira Tai Biollante*), *Godzilla vs King Ghidorah* (1991 - aka *Gojira Tai Kingu Gidora*), *Godzilla vs Queen Mothra* (1992 - aka *Gojira Tai Mosura*), *Godzilla vs. Mechagodzilla* (1993), *Godzilla vs.Space Godzilla* (1995), *Godzilla vs. the Destroyer* (1995)

Godzilla on Monster Island

Japan 1971 91m Eastmancolor
Godzilla teams up with Angurus to save the world from Ghidra and Gigan and a bunch of cockroach aliens (no kidding!).

Hilarious rubber-suited nonsense, good for a laugh but not for too long. Also known as *Godzilla vs Gigan* and *Gojira Tai Gaigan*.
p: Tomoyuki Tanaka for Toho
w: Shinichi Sekizawa
d: Jun Fukuda
m: Akira Ifukube
ed: Yoshio Tamura
pd: Yoshifumi Honda
sp: Akiyoshi Nakano
Hiroshi Ishikawa, Tomoko Umeda, Zan Fujita, Yuriko Hishimi, Minora Takashima

Godzilla vs. Gigan see Godzilla on Monster Island

Godzilla vs. Megalon

Japan 1973 86m Eastmancolor
Godzilla joins forces with Jet Jaguar to destroy the Setopians and the monsters they have under their control.

Ludicrous monster epic, indistinguishable from all the others. Also known as *Gojira Tai Megaro*.
p: Tomoyaki Tanaka for Toho
w: Jun Fukuda, Shinichi Sekizawa
story: Shinichi Sekizawa
d: Jun Fukuda
ph: Yuzuru Aizawa
m: Riichiro Manabe
ed: Michiko Ikeda
ad: Yoshibum Honda
sp: Akiyoshi Nakano
sound: Teishiro Hayashi
Katsushiko Sasaki, Hiroyuki Kawase, Ytaka Hayshi, Kotaro Tomita

Godzilla vs. Monster Zero see Invasion of the Astro Monsters

Goldblum, Jeff (1952-)

Offbeat American actor who, after brief appearances in such films as *California Split*, *Death Wish* and *Nashville* gradually grew to leading man status via appearances in the likes of *The Big Chill*, *Silverado* and *Into the Night*. His other credits include *Beyond Therapy*, *Earth Girls Are Easy*, *The Tall Guy*, *Deep Cover* and *Independence Day*, though horror fans remember him for playing Seth Brundle in David Cronenberg's remake of *The Fly*. Genre credits:
The Sentinel (1976), *Invasion of the Body Snatchers* (1978), *Transylvania 6-5000* (1986), *The Fly* (1987), *Mr Frost* (1990), *Jurrassic Park* (1993)

Godzilla vs. the Sea Monster

see Ebirah - Horror of the Deep

Goldsmith, Jerry (1929-)

Prolific American composer (real name Jerrald Goldsmith), comfortable in most genres, but with a predeliction for action and sci-fi themes. Studied music at USC where he was tutored by Miklos Rozsa. Began his career by composing for radio and then television, breaking into films in 1957 with *Black Patch*. In 1976 he won an Oscar for scoring *The Omen*, whose Latin chanting added immeasurably to the atmosphere of the film. Of his many other scores, highlights include *The Blue Max*, *Planet of the Apes*, *Capricorn One*, *The First Great Train Robbery*, *Star Trek - The Motion Picture*, *First Blood* and *Basic Instinct*.
Genre credits:
The Mephisto Waltz (1971), *The Reincarnation of Peter Proud* (1975), *The Omen* (1976), *Damien: Omen II* (1978), *The Boys from Brazil* (1978), *Coma* (1978), *Magic* (1978), *Alien* (1979), *The Final Conflict* (1981 - aka *Omen III*), *Poltergeist* (1982), *Psycho 2* (1983), *Gremlins* (1984), *Poltergeist II* (1985), *Warlock* (1989), *Gremlins 2: The New Batch* (1990 - also actor)

The Golem

A clear influence on such Universal classics as *Frankenstein*, the silent Golem films, particularly the 1920 German version directed by Paul Wegener and Carl Boese and photographed by Karl Freund (who would later photograph *Dracula* and direct *The Mummy*), were based on the Czech legend about a sixteenth-century rabbi who builds and gives life to a giant man of clay so as to protect his people from a pogrom. The first version of the story appeared in 1914, though there have also been several sound remakes/variations, all of them European in origin.
Genre filmography:
Der Golem (1914 - aka *The Monster of Fate*), *Der Golum und Die Tanzerin* (1917), *Der Golem: Wie Er in Die Welt Kam* (1920 - aka *The Golem*), *Le Golem* (1936 - aka *The Legend of Prague*), *Cisaruv Pekar a Pekaruv Cisar* (1951 - aka *The Emperor's Baker*), *Le Golem* (1966), *It* (1967)

Golitzen, Alexander (1904-)

Prolific Russian born art director long with Universal where he worked on several of their genre pictures in the fifties. He won Oscars for his design work on *The Phantom of the Opera* (1943 [with John Goodman]), *Spartacus* (1961 [with Eric Obrom]) and *To Kill a Mocking Bird* (1962 [with Henry Bumstead]). Other key credits include *Letter from an Unknown Woman*, *The Glenn Miller Story*,

Sweet Charity, Play Misty for Me and Earthquake.
Genre credits:
The Phantom of the Opera (1943 - co-ad), *Cult of the Cobra* (1955 - co-ad), *Abbott and Costello Meet the Mummy* (1955 - co-ad), *Tarantula* (1955 - co-ad), *The Creature Walks Among Us* (1956 - co-ad), *The Deadly Mantis* (1957 - co-ad), *Monster on the Campus* (1958 - ad), *The Thing That Couldn't Die* (1958 - co-ad), *Curse of the Undead* (1959 - co-ad),

Goodman, John B.
American art director long with Universal where he worked on several of their key horror films of the forties. Won an Oscar for his work on *The Phantom of the Opera* (1943 [with Alexander Golitzen]).
Genre credits:
Captive Wild Woman (1942 - co-ad), *Son of Dracula* (1943 - ad), *The Mad Ghoul* (1943 - co-ad), *The Phantom of the Opera* (1943 - co-ad), *Frankenstein Meets the Wolf Man* (1943 - ad), *The Mummy's Ghost* (1943 - co-ad), *Jungle Woman* (1944 - co-ad), *The Mummy's Curse* (1944 - ad), *Jungle Captive* (1944 - co-ad), *House of Frankenstein* (1944 - co-ad), *House of Dracula* (1945 - co-ad), *The Brute Man* (1946 - co-ad), *House of Horrors* (1946 - aka *Joan Medford is Missing* - co-ad)

Goodwin, Harold (1917-)
Chirpy British character actor often in gormless or dim-witted roles. Films include *The Happiest Days of Your Life*, *The Man in the White Suit* and *All Creatures Great and Small*. Often popped up in Hammer films as a coachdriver, etc.
Genre credits:
The Mummy (1959), *The Ugly Duckling* (1959), *The Terror of the Tongs* (1961), *The Phantom of the Opera* (1962), *The Curse of the Mummy's Tomb* (1964), *Die, Monster, Die!* (1967 - aka *Monster of Terror*), *Frankenstein Must Be Destroyed* (1969), *Jabberwocky* (1977)

Gordon, Bert I. (1922-)
American writer, producer, director and effects technician with numerous low-budget horrors to his credit, though few of them are of outstanding merit. Came to films in 1957 via television and commercials. He also writes for the horror magazine *Fangoria*.
Genre credits:
King Dinosaur (1957 - co-story/co-p/ d), *The Amazing Colossal Man* (1957 - co-w/p/sp/d), *The Beginning of the End* (1957 - co-w/p/sp/co-d), *The Cyclops* (1957 - w/p/sp/d), *Attack of the Puppet People* (1958 - aka *Six Inches Tall* - story/sp/p/d), *The Earth vs the Spider*

(1958 - aka *The Spider* - story/co-sp/ p/d), *War of the Colossal Beast* (1958 - aka *The Terror Strikes* -story/co-sp/ p/d), *Tormented* (1960 - story/co-sp/ co-p/d), *St George and the Seven Curses* (1962 - aka *The Magic Sword* - story/ co-sp/p/d), *Village of the Giants* (1965 - co-sp/p/d), *Picture Mommy Dead* (1966 - p/d), *Necromancy* (1971 - w/p/d), *Food of the Gods* (1976 - w/sp/p/d), *Empire of the Ants* (1977 -story/sp/p/d), *The Coming* (1983 - d), *Satan's Princess* (1989 - aka *Malediction/Princess of Darkness* - d)

Gordon, Ruth (1896-1985)
American actress, playwright and screenplay writer who, with her husband, director Garson Kanin, penned such movie classics as *A Double Life*, *Adam's Rib* and *Pat and Mike*. A busy stage actress, she made her first film appearance in 1915 in *Camille*. Other film appearances include *Abe Lincoln in Illinois*, *Two-Faced Woman* and *Edge of Darkness*, though it wasn't until old age that she became a character actress of note in such films as *Inside Daisy Clover*, *Harold and Maude*, *Every Which Way But Loose* and, of course, *Rosemary's Baby* which won her a Best Supporting Actress Oscar for playing the devil-worshipping Minnie Castevet.
Genre credits:
Rosemary's Baby (1968), *Whatever Happened to Aunt Alice?* (1969), *Isn't It Shocking?* (1973 - TVM), *Look What Happened to Rosemary's Baby* (1977 - TVM)

Gordon, Stuart (1947-)
American writer, producer and director who, since the success of *Re-Animator* in 1985, has concentrated his career almost entirely on horror films, though not always to the same effect. He often works in association with producer Brian Yuzna.
Genre credits:
Re-Animator (1985 - co-w/d), *From Beyond* (1986 - aka *H. P. Lovecraft's From Beyond* - co-story/d), *Dolls* (1987 - d), *Daughter of Darkness* (1989 - TVM - d), *Robojox* (1989 - aka *Robot Jox* - d), *The Pit and the Pendulum* (1990 - d), *Body Snatchers* (1993 -co-w), *Castle Freak* (1994 - d)

Gorgo
GB 1960 78m Technicolor
A prehistoric monster is captured and brought to London, but its mother follows and wreaks a path of destruction.

Silly but good looking monster hokum let down by unconvincing effects work, most of which involve a man sweating it out in a rubber Godzilla suit.
p: Wilfred Eades for King Brothers
exec p: Frank King, Maurice King
w: John Loring, Daniel Hyatt
story: Eugene Lourie, Daniel Hyatt
d: Eugene Lourie
ph: Frederick A. Young
m: Angelo Lavagnino
md: Muir Mathieson
ed: Eric Boyd-Perkins
ad: Elliott Scott
cos: Harry Haynes

• **Gorgo's mother goes on the rampage in a not too convincing model set in the Godzilla-like *Gorgo*.**

sp: Tom Howard
sound: John Bramall, A. W. Watkins
Bill Travers, William Sylvester, Vincent
Winter, Christopher Rhodes, Joseph
O'Connor, Bruce Seton, Martin Benson,
Nigel Green

The Gorgon *
GB 1964 83m Technicolor
A small European village is terrorized by
Magera, a Gorgon who can turn those
who dare look into her eyes to stone.
   Slow moving and rather talkative
minor Hammer horror with the studio
obviously looking for another monster
to exploit. A few moments of suspense
but otherwise nothing at all new.
p: Anthony Nelson Keys for Hammer
w: John Gilling
d: Terence Fisher
ph: Michael Reed
m: James Bernard
md: Marcus Dods
ed: James Needs, Eric Boyd-Perkins
pd: Bernard Robinson
cos: Rosemary Burrows
sp: Syd Pearson
sound: Ken Rawkins
Peter Cushing, Christopher Lee, Barbara
Shelley, Richard Pasco, Patrick
Troughton

The Gorilla *
USA 1939 66m bw
In a spooky house several people are
threatened by a murderous gorilla.
   Good looking but otherwise tame
mixture of comedy and mild thrills,
somewhat over played by its resistable
comic leads.
p: Harry Joe Brown for TCF
w: Rian James, Sid Silvers
play: Ralph Spence
d: ALLAN DWAN
ph: EDWARD CRONJAGER
md: David Buttolph
ed: Allen McNeill
ad: Richard Day, Lewis Creber
cos: Gwen Wakeling
sound: George Leverett, Roger Heman
The Ritz Brothers, Bela Lugosi,
LIONEL ATWILL, Patsy Kelly, Joseph
Calleia, Anita Louise, Edward Norris,
Wally Vernon

Gothic
GB 1986 87m Technicolor
An account of the famous weekend in
1816 at Lake Geneva which inspired
Mary Shelley to write Frankenstein.
   A relently hysterical barrage of images
in its director's most deplorable manner.
Laughable when it isn't sickening.
p: Al Clark, Robert Devereaux for
Virgin Vision
w: Stephen Volk

• Distinguished character actor
Michael Gough, whose career
encompasses several not so
distinguished horror movies.

d: Ken Russell
ph: Robert Southon
m: Thomas Dolby
ed: Michael Bradsell
pd: Christopher Hobbs
cos: Victoria Russell
sound: Bruce White
Gabriel Byrne, Natasha Richardson,
Julian Sands, Myriam Cyr, Timothy
Spall, Alec Mango, Andreas Wisniewski,
Dexter Fletcher, Pascal King, Tom
Hickey

Gough, Michael (1917-)
Distinguished looking British character
actor on stage since 1936 and in films
from 1947 with Blanche Fury. His first
horror film was Hammer's Dracula in
which he played Arthur Holmwood. All
manner of low-budget genre items
followed, including several for producer
Herman Cohen, though he is now
perhaps best known for playing Alfred
the butler in Batman, Batman Returns and
Batman Forever.
Genre credits:
Dracula (1958 - aka Horror of Dracula),
Horrors of the Black Museum (1959),
Konga (1961), What A Carve Up (1961),
The Phantom of the Opera (1962), The
Black Zoo (1963), Dr Terror's House of
Horrors (1964), The Skull (1965), They
Came from Beyond Space (1967), Berserk!
(1967), The Curse of the Crimson Altar
(1968 - aka The Crimson Cult), Trog

(1970), Crucible of Horror (1970 - aka
The Corpse / Velvet House), Horror Hospital
(1973), The Legend of Hell House (1973),
Satan's Slaves (1976), The Boys from
Brazil (1978), The Serpent and the
Rainbow (1987), Nostradamus (1994)

Graham, Gerrit (1949-)
American actor in films from 1968 with
Brian de Palma's Greetings, which he has
followed with a wide variety of subjects,
including Cannonball, Pretty Baby, Used
Cars, Home Movies, Soup for One and The
Last Resort.
Genre credits:
The Phantom of the Paradise (1974),
Tunnelvision (1976), Demon Seed (1977),
Rat Boy (1986), It's Alive III: Island of the
Alive (1987), Child's Play 2 (1990)

Grand Guignol
Established in Paris in 1899 by one Max
Maurey, Theatre du Grand Guignol was
very much a precursor of the modern-
day splatter film in that it presented
plays and illusions with a high gore
content. To this day, horror films are still
often described as being Grand Guignol
in style. The Theatre des Vampires
sequence in director Neil Jordan's film
version of Anne Rice's novel Interview
with the Vampire was influenced by the
Theatre du Grand Guignol and its
presentations, though here the gory
deeds were played out for real.

Grant, Arthur (1915-1972)
Prolific British cinematographer who,
along with Jack Asher, helped give
Hammer films their rich look. Began
his film career in 1929 at the studios of
Cecil Hepworth. Became a camera
operator in 1947 with When You Came,
graduating to cinematography in 1950
with The Dragon of Pendragon Castle.
Non-genre films include Hell is a City,
Jigsaw and 80,000 Suspects.
Genre credits:
The Dragon of Pendragon Castle (1950),
The Abominable Snowman (1957 - aka The
Abominable Snowman of the Himalayas),
The Stranglers of Bombay (1960), Curse of
the Werewolf (1960), Terror of the Tongs
(1961), The Shadow of the Cat (1961),
Captain Clegg (1962 - aka Night
Creatures), Phantom of the Opera (1962),
The Old Dark House (1962), The Damned
(1963 - aka These Are the Damned),
Paranoiac (1963), The Tomb of Ligeia
(1964), The Plague of the Zombies
(1966), The Reptile (1966), The Witches
(1966 - aka The Devil's Own),
Frankenstein Created Woman (1967),
Quatermass and the Pit (1967 - aka Five
Million Years to Earth), The Devil Rides
Out (1968 - aka The Devil's Bride),

Dracula Has Risen from the Grave (1968), *Frankenstein Must Be Destroyed* (1969), *Taste the Blood of Dracula* (1970), *Blood from the Mummy's Tomb* (1971), *Fear in the Night* (1972), *Demons of the Mind* (1972)

Grant, Moray (1917-1977)
British (Scottish) cinematographer (no relation to Arthur Grant) with many Hammer films to his credit. Began as a clapper boy at Denham in 1935. Became a camera operator in 1937 at British National. Subsequent films many and various, though work mostly routine.
Genre credits:
Kiss of the Vampire (1962 - aka *Kiss of Evil* - cam-op), *The Mummy's Shroud* (1966 - cam-op), *The Devil Rides Out* (1968 - aka *The Devil's Bride* - cam-op), *The Horror of Frankenstein* (1970 -ph), *Scars of Dracula* (1970 - ph), *I, Monster* (1970 - ph), *The Vampire Lovers* (1970 - ph), *Vampire Circus* (1972 - ph)

Grave Secrets
USA 1989 89m Technicolor Dolby
A professor of the paranormal is invited to investigate a haunted hotel and discovers the ghost to be that of the owner's brutal father.
Lethargic, cliche ridden spooker with nothing at all new of its own to add to the genre.
p: Michael Alan Shores for New Sky/ Planet/Shapiro Glickenhaus
w: Jeffrey Polman, Lenore Wright
story: David Polman
d: Donald P. Borchers
ph: Jamie Thompson
m: Jonathan Elias
ed: James Gavin Bedford
pd: Janna Sheehan
Paul LeMat, Renee Soutendijk, David Warner, Lee Ving, Olivia Barash

Graveyard Disturbance
It 1986 105m Kodacolor
Teenage tearaways spend the night in a haunted crypt for a bet.
Standard Italian horror junk, strictly for the initiated.
p: Massimo Manasse, Marco Grillo Spina for Devon/Dania/Rere Italia
w: Dardano Sacchetti, Lamberto Bava
story: Dardano Sacchetti
d: Lamberto Bava
ph: Gianlorenzo Battaglia
m: Simon Boswell
ed: Mauro Bonanni
ad: Anonello Geleng
cos: Valentina DiPalma
sp: Angelo Mattei
sound: Guiliano Pier Mariolo
make-up effects: Fabrizio Storza

titles: Aldo Matera
Gregory Lech, Thaddeus Martino, Beatrice Ring, Gianmarco Tognazzi, Karl Zinny, Lino Salemmer, Gianpaolo Saccarola

Graveyard Shift
USA 1986 89m colour
A vampire working for the Black Cat Taxi Co. preys on his women passengers.
Passable video fodder that has a minor cult following. It was followed by *The Understudy: Graveyard Shift II* in 1988.
p: Lester Berman, Michael Bockner for Cinema Ventures/Lightshow/Bockner/ Ciccoriti/Bergman
exec p: Arnold H. Bruck, Stephen R. Flaks
w/d: Gerard Ciccoretti
ph: Robert Bergman
m: Nicholas Pike
ed: Robert Bergman, Norman Smith
ad: no credit given
cos: Janet Shacter
sp: Tim Mogg
sound: Jeremy Gauthier
Silvio Oliviero, Helen Papas, Dan Rose, Cliff Stoker, Kim Cayer, Dorin Ferber, Frank Procopio (as a character named Mario Bava)

Graveyard Shift
USA 1990 86m DeLuxe Dolby
Night workers at a run-down mill find themselves in mortal danger from a giant rodent.
Lamentable rubbish which should never have seen the light of day. One of the worst King adaptations - which is saying something.
p: William J. Dunn, Ralph S. Singleton for Graveyard Inc.
w: John Esposito
novel: Stephen King
d: Ralph S. Singleton
ph: Peter Stein
m: Anthony Matinelli, Brian Banks
ed: Jim Gross, Randy Jon Morgan
pd: Gary Wissner
cos: Sarah Lemire
sp: Syd Dutton, Bill Taylor, Albert Whitlock
sound: Bernie Blynder
David Andrews, Kelly Wolf, Stephen Macht, Brad Dourif, Andrew Divoff, Vic Polizos, Robert Alan Beuth

Gray, Charles (1928-)
Distinguished sounding British actor (real name Donald M. Gray), perhaps best known to horror fans for his chilling performance as Mocata in Hammer's *The Devil Rides Out* - and for teaching us how to do The Time Warp in *The Rocky Horror Picture Show*! Much

stage and TV work, he has also appeared in two Bond films (*You Only Live Twice* and *Diamonds Are Forever*), playing Blofeld in the second of them. His vocal similarities to actor Jack Hawkins saw him dub many of that star's later films (*Waterloo*, *Kidnapped*, *Nicholas and Alexandra*, *Theatre of Blood*, *Tales That Witness Madness*, etc.), a result of Hawkins losing his own voice after an operation in 1966. Gray's other screen credits include *The Entertainer*, *Cromwell*, *The Mirror Crack'd* and *An Englishman Abroad* (TVM). He has also played Mycroft Holmes several times, first in the film *The Seven Per Cent Solution*, and in the Granada TV series starring Jeremy Brett as Holmes.
Genre credits:
The Devil Rides Out (1968 - aka *The Devil's Bride*), *The Beast Must Die* (1974 - aka *Black Werewolf*), *The Rocky Horror Picture Show* (1975), *The Legacy* (1978)

The Greed of William Hart
GB 1948 78m bw
In seventeenth-century Edinburgh resurrectionists resort to murder to keep an anatomist supplied with corpses.
Tame variation on an old story which has also seen life as *The Body Snatcher*, *The Flesh and the Fiends*, *Burke and Hare* and *The Doctor and the Devils*. Here it is reduced to a star vehicle for the barnstorming Tod Slaughter
p: Gilbert Church for Bushey
w: John Gilling
d: Oswald Mitchell
ph: S. D. Onions
m: no credit given
ed: John F. House
ad: no credit given
sound: Ken Wiles
Tod Slaughter, Henry Oscar, Aubrey Woods, Arnold Bell, Jenny Lynn, Mary Love

Green, Hilton A.
American producer who began his career as an assistant director for Alfred Hitchcock on his television series *Alfred Hitchcock Presents*. He served in the same capacity on *Psycho* and later produced all three *Psycho* sequels.
Psycho (1960 - ass d), *Psycho II* (1983 - p), *Psycho III* (1986 -p), *Psycho IV* (1990 - TVM - co-p)

Gremlins **
USA 1984 106m Technicolor Dolby
A quiet American town is threatened by hordes of destructive creatures who multiply when they come in contact with water.
An enjoyable hark back to the monster movies of the 1950s, this black

fantasy has a good smattering of humour, thrills, in-jokes and gag cameos.
p: Michael Finnell for Warner/Amblin
exec p: Steven Spielberg, Kathleen Kennedy, Frank Marshall
w: Chris Columbus
d: JOE DANTE
ph: John Hora
m: Jerry Goldsmith
ed: Tina Hirsch
pd: James H. Spencer
cos: Norman Burza, Linda Matthews
gremlin design/sp: CHRIS WALAS
sound: Ken King, Bill Varney, Steve Maslow, Kevin O'Connell
stunt co-ordinator: Terry Leonard
Zach Galligan, Hoyt Axton, Frances Lee McCain, Phoebe Cates, Polly Holliday, Scott Brady, Dick Miller, Keye Luke, Chuck Jones, Edward Andrews, Kenneth Tobey, Judge Reinhold, Steven Spielberg and the voices of Howie Mandell, Frank Walker and Fred Newman

Gremlins 2: The New Batch *

USA 1990 105m Technicolor Dolby
The gremlins take over a Donald Trump-style skyscraper in Manhattan.

Zany, *Hellzapoppin'*-like sequel in which anything goes. It tends to outstay its welcome, but buffs will have a field day spotting all the in-jokes and gag cameos.
p: Michael Finnell, Rick Baker for Warner/Amblin
exec p: Steven Spielberg, Frank Marshall, Kathleen Kennedy
w: Charles Haas
d: Joe Dante
ph: John Hora
m: Jerry Goldsmith
ed: Kent Beyda
pd: James Spencer
cos: Rosanna Norton
sp: Doug Beswick, Dennis Michelson
sound: Ken King, Douglas Vaughan
sound effects: Mark Mangini, David Stone
gremlin effects: Rick Baker
2nd unit d: James Spencer
stunt co-ordinator: Mike McGaughy
Zach Galligan, Phoebe Cates, John Glover, Robert J. Prosky, Christopher Lee, Robert Picardo, Kathleen Freeman, John Astin, Kenneth Tobey, Dick Miller, Joe Dante, Jerry Goldsmith, Paul Bartell, Hulk Hogan, Henry Gibson, Leonard Maltin, Haviland Morris, Jackie Joseph, Keye Luke, Don Stanton, Dan Stanton, Charlie Haas, Dick Butkus, Bubba Smith and the voices of Howie Mandell, Tony Randall, Frank Walker and Jeff Bergman

Grim Prairie Tales

USA 1990 94m Technicolor
Two travellers making their way through the old west spin stories round the campfire.

Mild portmanteau, watchable enough, but no better than four stories from *The Twilight Zone* strung together.
p: Richard Hahn for East West
w/d: Wayne Coe
ph: Janusz Kaminski
m: Steve Dancz
ed: Earl Ghaffari
pd: Anthony Zierhut
sound: Anthony Zierhut
Brad Dourif, James Earl Jones, Will Hare, Lisa Eichhorn, William Astherton, Marc McClure, Wendy Cooke, Michelle Joyner

The Grim Reaper see The Anthropophagus Beast

Grip of the Strangler *

GB 1958 78m bw
A social reformer investigating an old murder case discovers that he was the culprit himself.

Tame low-budget horror, all rather predictable. Also known as *The Haunted Strangler*.
p: John Croydon for Producers' Associates
w: Jan Read
d: Robert Day
ph: Lionel Banes
m: Buxtor Orr
ed: Peter Mayhew
ad: John Elphick
sp: Les Bowie
make-up: Jim Hydes
Boris Karloff, Elizabeth Allen, Jean Kent, Anthony Dawson, Vera Day

Grizzly

USA 1976 91m Movielab Todd-AO 35
An enormous grizzly bear threatens tourists in a national park.

An horrendous attempt to do for grizzlies what *Jaws* did for sharks. Absolutely abysmal.
p: David Sheldon, Harvey Flazman for Film Ventures
w: Harvey Flazman, David Sheldon
d: William Girdler
ph: William Asman
m: Robert O. Ragland
ed: Bud Asman
sp: Phil Corey
Christopher George, Andrew Prine, Richard Jaechel, Joan McCall

Grot, Anton (1884-1974)

Influential Polish born art director in Hollywood. Emigrated to America when he was sixteen and began designing in 1913. Worked for a variety of companies until 1927 after which he remained with Warner Bros. for the remainder of his career. His angular sets added visual interest to a number of thirties horror films. His other credits include *The Thief of Baghdad* (silent version), *Little Caesar*, *Footlight Parade*, *A Midsummer Night's Dream*, *Anthony Adverse*, *The Sea Hawk* and *Mildred Pierce*.
Genre credits:
Outward Bound (1930), *Svengali* (1931), *The Mad Genius* (1931), *Dr X* (1932), *The Mystery of the Wax Museum* (1933)

The Guardian

USA 1990 93m Technicolor Dolby
A nanny turns out to be the murderous handmaiden of an evil tree god.

Slick but over stretched horror hokum which might have worked better as a television half hour.
p: Joe Wizan for Universal
w: Stephen Volk, Dan Greenburg
novel: Dan Greenburg
d: William Friedkin
ph: John A. Alonzo
m: Jack Hues
ed: Seth Flaum
pd: Gregg Fonsecca
cos: Denise Cronenberg
sp: Phil Cory
sound: Mark Berger
make-up effects: Matthew W. Mungle
Jenny Seagrove, Dwier Brown, Carey Lowell, Brad Hull, Miguel Ferrer

Guardian of Hell see The Other Hell

Guest, Val (1911-)

Prolific British actor, writer, producer, director and lyricist, a former trade journalist who began his film career as a writer on a number of classic British comedies, including *Good Morning, Boys*, *Oh, Mr Porter*, *Alf's Button Afloat* and *The Frozen Limits*, which starred the likes of Will Hay and The Crazy Gang. He made his directorial debut on the Arthur Askey comedy *Miss London Ltd* in 1943, which he followed with all manner of comedies and lightweight musicals (*Mr Drake's Duck*, *The Runaway Bus*, *Penny Princess*, etc.). His first film for Hammer was the domestic comedy *Life with the Lyons*, though it was *The Quatermass Experiment* which changed both his career and the path of the studio for which he made it. Subsequent non-genre films include *The Camp on Blood Island*, *Up the Creek*, *Expresso Bongo*, *Jigsaw*, *Casino Royale*, *Confessions of a Window Cleaner* and TV's *Shillingbury Tales*.
Genre credits:

Oh, Mr Porter (1937 - co-w), *Ask a Policeman* (1938 - co-w), *The Ghost Train* (1941 - co-w), *The Quatermass Experiment* (1955 - aka *The Creeping Unknown* - co-w/d), *Quatermass 2* (1957 - aka *Enemy from Space* - co-w/d), *The Abominable Snowman* (1957 - aka *The Abominable Snowman of the Himalayas* - d), *The Day the Earth Caught Fire* (1962 - co-w/p/d), *When Dinosaurs Ruled the Earth* (1970 - w/d) *In Possession* (1984 - TVM - d), *The Scent of Fear* (1984 - TVM - d), *Child's Play* (1984 - TVM - d), *Mark of the Devil* (1984 - TVM - d)

Gwynne, Anne (1918-)

American actress (real name Marguerite Gwynne Trice) who appeared in a handful of horror films for Universal in the forties, most memorably as Rita the hunchbacked nurse in *House of Frankenstein*. Her other credits include *Flash Gordon Conquers the Universe* (serial), *Sandy Is a Lady*, *South of Dixie* and *Adam at 6am*.
Genre credits:
The Black Cat (1941), *Man Made Monster* (1941 - aka *The Electric Monster*), *The Strange Case of Dr RX* (1942), *Weird Woman* (1944), *House of Frankenstein* (1944), *The Ghost Goes Wild* (1947), *Teenage Monster* (1957 - aka *Meteor Monster*).

H

H. P. Lovecraft's From Beyond
see From Beyond

H. P. Lovecraft's The Unnameable
see The Unnameable

H. P. Lovecraft's The Unnameable Returns
see The Unnameable Returns

Hafenrichter, Oswald
German-born editor working in Britain where he has cut a variety of subjects, including several horror films for Amicus.
Genre credits:
The Hands of Orlac (1962), *The Skull* (1965), *The Psychopath* (1965), *The Creeping Flesh* (1972), *Vault of Horror* (1973)

Hall, Charles D. (1899-1968)
British art director who, after stage experience at home, went to Hollywood via Canada where he started as an assistant designer in 1912. He became a fully fledged art director in 1921 with *Smiling All the Way*, which was followed by such films as Chaplin's *The Gold Rush* and *The Hunchback of Notre Dame*. He worked on several of Universal's key horror films of the twenties and thirties including some for director James Whale. Other credits include *The Circus*, *Broadway*, *All Quiet on the Western Front*, *City Lights*, *Showboat* and *Modern Times*.
Genre credits:
The Hunchback of Notre Dame (1923 - co-ad), *The Phantom of the Opera* (1926 - co-ad), *The Cat and the Canary* (1927 - ad), *The Man Who Laughs* (1928 - co-ad), *Dracula* (1930 - ad), *Frankenstein* (1931 - ad), *The Old Dark House* (1932 - ad), *The Invisible Man* (1933 - ad), *The Black Cat* (1934 - ad), *The Bride of Frankenstein* (1935 - ad), *One Million BC* (1940 - co-ad), *The Devil with Hitler* (1942 - ad), *The Unearthly* (1957 - ad)

Haller, Daniel (1929-)
American art director and director who has worked on many of Roger Corman's films. A former stage designer, he also worked on commercials before moving to Hollywood in 1955. He turned to direction in 1965 but is perhaps best remembered for his atmospheric sets for Corman's Poe cycle. His other films as a director include *Devil's Angels*, *The Wild Racers* and *Buck Rogers in the 25th Century* (TVM).
Genre credits:
Teenage Caveman (1958 - ad), *The Devil's Partner* (1958 - ad), *Night of the Blood Beast* (1958 - ad), *War of the Satellites* (1958 - ad), *The Ghost of Dragstrip Hollow* (1959 - ad), *A Bucket of Blood* (1959 - ad), *The Wasp Woman* (1959 - ad), *The Giant Leeches* (1959 - ad), *House of Usher* (1960 - aka *The Fall of the House of Usher* - ad), *The Little Shop of Horrors* (1960 - ad), *Master of the World* (1961 - ad), *The Pit and the Pendulum* (1961 - ad), *The Premature Burial* (1961 - ad), *Tales of Terror* (1961 - ad), *Diary of a Madman* (1962 - ad), *Tower of London* (1962 - ad), *The Comedy of Terrors* (1963 - ad), *X - The Man with X-Ray Eyes* (1963 - aka *The Man with X-Ray Eyes* - ad), *The Raven* (1963 - ad), *The Terror* (1963 - ad), *Die, Monster, Die* (1965 - aka *Monster of Terror* - d), *The Ghost in the Invisible Bikini* (1966 - ad), *The Dunwich Horror* (1968 - d)

Halloween **
USA 1978 91m Metrocolor Panavision
A young boy murders his sister and is put into a mental institution. Fifteen years later he escapes and returns to terrorize his home town.

Genuinely frightening and inventively handled killer-thriller whose success helped to launch its director and a much overworked genre. Unlike the many sequels and rip-offs, this film is literally blood free. It was followed by *Halloween II* (1981), *Halloween III: Season of the Witch* (1983), *Halloween IV: The Return of Michael Myers* (1988), *Halloween V: The Revenge of Michael Myers* (1989), *Halloween VI: The Curse of Michael Myers* (1995).
p: Debra Hill for Falcon International/ Compass
exec p: Moustapha Akaad, Frank Yablans
w: JOHN CARPENTER, DEBRA HILL
d/m: JOHN CARPENTER
ph: Dean Cundey
ed: Tommy Wallace, Charles Bornstein
pd: Tommy Wallace
cos: Bess Rodgers
sound: Tommy Causey
DONALD PLEASENCE, JAMIE LEE CURTIS, Nancy Loonis, P. J. Soles, Charles Cyphers, Kyle Richards, Tony Moran, Brian Andrews, Nick Castle (as Michael Myers)

Halloween II
USA 1981 95m Metrocolor Panavision Dolby
Michael Myers continues his murder spree, this time centring on the hospital where Laurie is recovering from her first ordeal.

Repetitive and unnecessary sequel, well enough made and not without its frightening moments, though containing enough repellent detail to make most audiences head for the exit.
p: John Carpenter, Debra Hill for Universal
exec p: Dino de Laurentiis, Moustapha Akaad, Irwin Yablans, Joseph Wolf
w: John Carpenter, Debra Hill
d: Rick Rosenthal
ph: Dean Cundey
m: John Carpenter, Alan Howarth
Donald Pleasence, Jamie Lee Curtis, Charles Cyphers, Jeffrey Kramer

Halloween III: Season of the Witch *
USA 1983 99m Technicolor Panavision
A mysterious industrialist plans a nasty surprise for the children of America on Hallowe'en.

Fairly inventive change of direction for the series let down by scenes of

fashionable but unattractive and unnecessary gore, on which count the original author had his name removed from the credits. Michael Myers can be spotted briefly in a walk-on gag cameo.
p: John Carpenter, Debra Hill for Moustapha Akaad
exec p: Irwin Yablans, Joseph Wolf
w/d: Tommy Lee Wallace
original w: NIGEL KNEALE
ph: Dean Cundey
m: John Carpenter, Alan Howarth
ed: Millie Moore
pd: Peter Jamison
cos: Jane Riehm, Francis Aubrey
sp: John G. Belyeu
sound: Bill Varney, Steve Maslow, James S. Cavarette Jr
make-up effects: Tom Burman
titles: John Walsh
masks: John Post
Tom Atkins, Stacey Nelkin, DAN O'HERLIHY, Michael Currie, Ralph Strait, Judeen Barber, Gary Stephens, Dick Warlock

Halloween IV - The Return of Michael Myers *
USA 85m Technicolor Panavision Ultra Stereo
Michael Myers returns to Haddonfield to terrorize the family living in his childhood home.

Quite reasonable return to the original formula which picks up the story ten years after Halloween II.
p: Paul Freeman for Trancas/Hallowe'en IV Partnership
exec p: Mustapha Akaad
w: Alan B. McElroy
story: Dhani Lipuis, Larry Rattner, Benjamin Ruffner, Alan B. McElroy
d: Dwight H. Little
ph: Peter Lyons Collister
m: Alan Howarth
ed: Curtiss Clayton
ad: Roger S. Crandall
sp: Larry Fioritto
sound: Mark McNabb
make-up effects: John Beuchler
titles: Howard A. Anderson
Donald Pleasence, Ellie Cornell, Danielle Harris, Michael Pataki, Beau Starr, Kathleen Kenmont, Sasha Jenson, George P. Wilbur

Halperin, Victor (1895-?)
American writer, director and producer who, after experience on the stage as both an actor and director, entered films in 1924 directing When a Girl Loves, which he also wrote and co-produced. He is best known for directing the Bela Lugosi vehicle White Zombie, after which little was heard from him. He is the brother of producer Edward Halperin.

Other credits include I Conquer the Sea, Nation Aflame and Girls' Town.
Genre credits:
White Zombie (1932 - d), Supernatural (1933 - co-p/d), Revolt of the Zombies (1936 - co-w/d)

Hamilton, Linda (1956-)
American actress who, after experience on television (in the soap opera Secrets of Midland Heights), broke into movies and shot to fame in the two Terminator films. She also appeared in the cult TV series Beauty and the Beast.
Genre credits:
The Terminator (1984), Children of the Corn (1984), King Kong Lives (1986), Terminator 2: Judgement Day (1991)

Hammer Films
British production company, synonymous with the making of horror films. Formed in 1935 by William Hinds (aka Will Hammer) and his partner Enrique Carreras, the original Hammer films produced a handful of light comedies and dramas in the mid-thirties, including The Public Life of Henry the Ninth, Song of Freedom and Sporting Love. Their nearest brush with horror at this stage was a verion of The Mystery of the Marie Celeste (aka The Phantom Ship) starring Bela Lugosi. The advent of World War Two forced the fledgling Hammer into bankruptcy, though Carreras's distributing company, Exclusive, continued to operate throughout the war years. Hammer reformed as an adjunct to Exclusive in 1947 and entered the quota quickie market, churning out countless thrillers and no-budgeters, many of them based on popular radio series, among them three Dick Barton adventures, Dr Morelle - The Case of the Missing Heiress, Meet Simon Cherry, The Man in Black and two PC 49 romps. By this time Hammer/Exclusive had turned into something of a family business, with executive and production posts taken by by Enrique Carreras's son James and his son Michael, who would see the company through to the seventies. William Hinds' son Anthony also became a producer. During the fifties, Hammer's quota policy became more adventurous with downward sliding American stars brought in to make the films more appealing to American audiences and distributors, the result being such films as The Last Page (with George Brent), Wings of Danger (Zachary Scott), Stolen Face (Paul Henreid), Cloudburst (Robert Preston) and The Saint Returns (Louis Hayward). Then, in 1955, Hammer almost accidentally stumbled on The Quatermass

Experiment, a top-rated television serial by Nigel Kneale of which they decided to make a film version. The success of this astonished the industry and provoked Hammer into remaking the Frankenstein legend as The Curse of Frankenstein, which again broke box office records. A successful version of Dracula followed and, though they continued to make comedies and war films, Hammer had by this time become the world market leader in horror films, a position they continued to hold until the late sixties/early seventies, winning the Queen's Award to Industry along the way. They were the first film company ever to do so. The collapse of the British film industry in the seventies combined with some unwise choices and an apparent inability to move with the times eventually saw the demise of Hammer in 1979, though their product remains a television and video favourite and several fan magazines devoted to the studio's history (Little Shoppe of Horrors, Dark Terrors, Hammer Horror) have since sprung up. Reformed by Roy Skeggs (who produced a number of Hammer television projects in the eighties, including Hammer House of Horror and Hammer House of Mystery and Suspense [aka Fox Mystery Theatre]), the company now stands on the brink of a new era, with several big-budget remakes of their classic films supposedly in the pipeline.
Genre filmography:
The Mystery of the Marie Celeste (1936 - aka The Phantom Ship), Stolen Face (1952), Four-Sided Triangle (1953), The Quatermass Experiment (1955 - aka The Quatermass Xperiment/The Creeping Unknown), X - The Unknown (1956), The Curse of Frankenstein (1956), Quatermass 2 (1957 - aka Enemy from Space), The Abominable Snowman (1957 - aka The Abominable Snowman of the Himalayas), Dracula (1958 - aka Horror of Dracula), The Revenge of Frankenstein (1958), The Hound of the Baskervilles (1959), The Mummy (1959), The Man Who Could Cheat Death (1959), The Stranglers of Bombay (1960), The Brides of Dracula (1960), The Two Faces of Dr Jekyll (1960 - aka House of Fright/Jekyll's Inferno), Curse of the Werewolf (1961), Taste of Fear (1961 - aka Scream of Fear), The Terror of the Tongs (1962), The Phantom of the Opera (1962), The Old Dark House (1962), Captain Clegg (1962 - aka Night Creatures), Maniac (1963), The Damned (1963 -aka These Are the Damned), Paranoiac (1963), Kiss of the Vampire (1964 - aka Kiss of Evil), Nightmare (1964), The Gorgon (1964), The Curse of the Mummy's Tomb (1964), Fanatic (1965

- aka *Die! Die! My Darling!*), *She* (1965), *Hysteria* (1965), *The Nanny* (1965), *Dracula - Prince of Darkness* (1966), *Rasputin - The Mad Monk* (1966), *The Plague of the Zombies* (1966), *The Reptile* (1966), *The Witches* (1966 - aka *The Devil's Own*), *One Million Years BC* (1966), *Frankenstein Created Woman* (1966), *The Mummy's Shroud* (1967), *Quatermass and the Pit* (1967 - aka *Five Million Years to Earth*), *The Vengeance of She* (1968), *The Devil Rides Out* (1968 - aka *The Devil's Bride*), *Slave Girls* (1968 - aka *Prehistoric Women*), *Dracula Has Risen from the Grave* (1968), *The Lost Continent* (1968), *Frankenstein Must Be Destroyed* (1969), *Crescendo* (1969), *Taste the Blood of Dracula* (1969), *Horror of Frankenstein* (1970), *Scars of Dracula* (1970), *The Vampire Lovers* (1970), *When Dinosaurs Ruled the Earth* (1970), *Lust for a Vampire* (1971), *Countess Dracula* (1971), *Creatures the World Forgot* (1971), *Hands of the Ripper* (1971), *Dr Jekyll and Sister Hyde* (1971), *Blood from the Mummy's Tomb* (1971), *Vampire Circus* (1972), *Fear in the Night* (1972), *Straight on Till Morning* (1972), *Demons of the Mind* (1972), *Dracula AD 1972* (1972), *The Satanic Rites of Dracula* (1973), *Frankenstein and the Monster from Hell* (1973), *Captain Kronos: Vampire Hunter* (1973 - aka *Kronos*), *The Legend of the Seven Golden Vampires* (1974 - aka *The Seven Brothers Meet Dracula*), *To the Devil... A Daughter* (1976), *And the Wall Came Tumbling Down* (1984 - TVM), *Black Carrion* (1984 - TVM), *Child's Play* (1984 - TVM), *The Corvini Inheritance* (1984 - TVM), *Czech Mate* (1984 - TVM), *A Distant Scream* (1984 - TVM), *In Possession* (1984 - TVM), *Last Video and Testament* (1984 - TVM), *The Late Nancy Irving* (1984 - TVM), *Mark of the Devil* (1984 - TVM), *Paint Me a Murder* (1984 - TVM), *The Sweet Smell of Death* (1984 - TVM), *Tennis Court* (1984 - TVM)

Hammer, Will see Hinds, William

The Hammond Mystery see The Undying Monster

The Hand
USA 1981 104m Technicolor Dolby
A comic strip artist loses his hand in a freak accident, but it apparently returns with a life of its own.

A silly premise is handled adequately enough but at far too great a length to be of lasting interest. Is this really the same Oliver Stone who went on to direct *Salvador*, *Platoon*, *Born on the Fourth of July* and *JFK?*

p: Edward R. Pressman for Warner/ Orion
w/d: Oliver Stone
novel: Mark Hobel
ph: King Baggot
m: James Horner
ed: Richard Marks
pd: John Michael Riva
cos: Ernest Misko
sp: Carlo Rambaldi
sound: Darin Knight
Michael Caine, Andrea Marcovicci, Rosemary Murphy, Viveca Lindfors, Bruce McGill, Mara Hobel

The Hand of Night
GB 1966 73m Eastmancolor
An archaeologist visiting Morocco falls into the hands of a group of vampires.

Well enough made low-budget shocker which unfortunately lacks surprise.
p: Harry Field for Associated British
w: Bruce Stewart
d: Frederic Goods
ph: William Jordan
m: Joan Shakespeare
md: John Shakespeare
ed: John Blair, Frederick Ives
ad: Peter Moll
sound: John Bromage, Trevor Pyke
titles: Biographie Films
William Sylvester, Diane Clare, Alizia Cur, Edward Underdown, Terence de Marney, William Dexter

Hands of the Ripper *
GB 1971 85m Technicolor
Jack the Ripper's daughter shows signs of following in her father's footsteps after a nasty childhood experience.

Nicely detailed latter day Hammer horror with a climax taking place in the Whispering Gallery of St Paul's Cathedral.
p: Aida Young for Hammer
w: L. W. Davidson
d: PETER SASDY
ph: Kenneth Talbot
m: CHRISTOPHER GUNNING
md: Philip Martell
ed: Chris Barnes
ad: ROY STANNARD
cos: Rosemary Burrows
sp: Cliff Culley
sound: Kevin Sutton
Eric Porter, Angharad Rees, Dora Bryan, Jane Merrow, Derek Godfrey, Keith Bell, Marjorie Rhodes, Norman Bird, Linda Baron

Hangover Square **
USA 1945 77m bw
In turn of the century London a composer is revealed to be a psychopath.

Silly but stylish period thriller in the Hitchcock manner. A must for

connoisseurs, its credits are impeccable.
p: Robert Bassler for TCF
w: Barre Lyndon
novel: Patrick Hamilton
d: JOHN BRAHM
ph: JOSEPH LA SHELLE
m: BERNARD HERRMANN
ed: Harry Reynolds
ad: LYLE WHEELER, MAURICE RANSFORD
cos: Rene Hubert, Kay Nelson
so: Fred Sersen
sound: Bernard Freericks, Harry M. Leonard
LAIRD CREGAR, Linda Darnell, George Sanders, Glenn Langan, Faye Marlowe, Frederick Worlock, Alan Napier

Hannah: Queen of the Vampires
see Crypt of the Living Dead

Hansen, Gunnar
American actor remembered for playing Leatherface in Tobe Hooper's notorious *Texas Chainsaw Massacre*, though he failed to reprise the role for the sequels.
Genre credits:
The Texas Chainsaw Massacre (1974), *The Demon Lover* (1976), *Hollywood Chainsaw Hookers* (1988)

Hardware
GB 1990 92m Technicolor
Post-apocalypse mercenaries attempt to destroy an android whose job it is to modulate the population.

Flashy pot-pourri of *Mad Max*, *Bladerunner*, *Alien* and *The Terminator*, with a noisy soundtrack and plenty of gratuitous violence and gore. It has its admirers, though the film ran into legal problems for allegedly ripping off the story from a *2000 AD* comic strip without permission.
p: Joanne Sellar, Paul Trybits for Wicked Films
w/d: Richard Stanley
ph: Steven Chivers
m: Simon Boswell
ed: Derek Trigg
pd: Joseph Bennett
cos: Michael Baldwin
sp: Image Imagination, Barney Jeffrey
sound: Jonathan Miller, Kate Hopkins
Dylan McDermott, Stacey Travis, John Lynch, William Hootkins, Iggy Pop (voice only), Mark Northover, Oscar James, Paul McKenzie, Carl McCoy

Hardwicke, Sir Cedric (1893-1964)
Distinguished British actor on stage from 1912. Made his film début in 1913 in the silent short *Riches and Rogues*. He was knighted in 1934, by

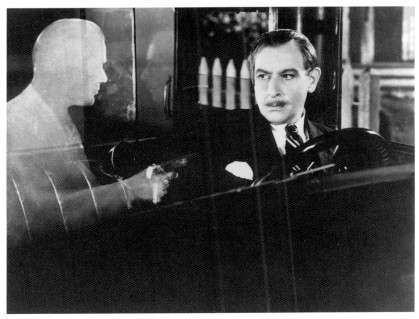

• Cedric Hardwicke meets the Invisible Man care of John P. Fulton's special effects in *The Invisible Man Returns.*

which time he'd made several films in England. Hollywood inevitably called where he lent his name to countless productions, including *Becky Sharp*, *King Solomon's Mines* (in which he played Allan Quatermain), *Stanley and Livingstone* and *I Remember Mamma*. He is the father of actor Edward Hardwicke, best known for playing Dr Watson opposite Jeremy Brett's Sherlock Holmes in the Granada TV series.
Genre credits:
The Ghoul (1933), *The Hunchback of Notre Dame* (1939), *The Invisible Man Returns* (1940), *Invisible Agent* (1942), *The Ghost of Frankenstein* (1942)

Harlequin

Australia 1980 94m Technicolor Panavision
A mystic makes himself indispensable to the family of an Australian politician but his motives seem to be sinister.
   Curious but unsuccessful fantasy drama which ends up being neither one nor the other. It could have been promising in other hands.
p: James Scott, Anthony Ginnane for FG
exec p: William Fayman
w: Everett de Roche, Jon George, Neill Hicks
d: Simon Wincer
ph: Gary Hansen
m: Brian May
ed: Adrian Carr
pd: Bernard Hides
sp: Conrad C. Rothman

sound: Gary Wilkins
Robert Powell, David Hemmings, Broderick Crawford, Carmen Duncan

Harper, Jessica (1949-)

American actress who has appeared in a wide variety of films, including *Inserts*, *My Favorite Year*, *Pennies from Heaven*, *Stardust Memories* and *The Blue Iguana*, as well as a handful of horror pictures, most notably Dario Argento's *Suspiria*.
Genre credits:
Phantom of the Paradise (1974), *Suspiria* (1976), *Shock Treatment* (1981), *Big Man on Campus* (1989 - aka *The Hunchback of UCLA*)

Harrington, Curtis (1928-)

American writer and director, a former executive assistant at TCF from 1955. He turned to direction in 1963 though by this time he'd already directed several amateur films, including a version of *The Fall of the House of Usher*.
Genre credits:
Night Tide (1961 - w/d), *Queen of Blood* (1966 - w/d), *Games* (1967 - co-story/d), *Voyage to a Prehistoric Planet* (1965 - w/d [as Jonathan Sebastian]), *How Awful About Alan* (1970 - TVM - d), *What's the Matter with Helen?* (1971 - d), *Who Slew Auntie Roo?* (1972 - d), *The Cat Creature* (1973 - TVM - d), *The Killing Kind* (1973 - d), *Killer Bees* (1974 - TVM - d), *The Dead Don't Die* (1975 - TVM - d), *Ruby* (1977 - d), *Devil Dog: The Hound of Hell* (1978 - TVM - d)

Harris, Len (1916-1995)

Prolific British camera operator, long with Hammer (1952-1962) where he worked on many of their classic horror films. Began his career in the camera-loading department at Gaumont British, working his way up to second assistant at Gainsborough's Islington Studios. After wartime experience with the army's Film and Photographic Unit he returned to Gainsborough before moving over to Hammer/Exclusive. He worked at Shepperton after leaving Hammer but occasionally returned to do 2nd unit work.
Genre credits:
The Quatermass Experiment (1955 - aka *The Creeping Unknown*), *The Curse of Frankenstein* (1956), *Quatermass 2* (1956 - aka *Enemy from Space*), *The Abominable Snowman* (1957 - aka *The Abominable Snowman of the Himalayas*), *Dracula* (1958 - aka *Horror of Dracula*), *The Revenge of Frankenstein* (1958), *The Hound of the Baskervilles* (1959), *The Man Who Could Cheat Death* (1959), *The Mummy* (1959), *The Two Faces of Dr Jekyll* (1960 - aka *House of Fright/Jekyll's Inferno*), *The Brides of Dracula* (1960), *The Terror of the Tongs* (1961), *The Curse of the Werewolf* (1961), *Captain Clegg* (1962), *The Phantom of the Opera* (1962), *The Reptile* (1966), *Quatermass and the Pit* (1967 - aka *Five Million Years to Earth*)

Harryhausen, Ray (1920-)

American special effects wiz, known for his stop motion effects which have graced a number of spectacular fantasy adventures, including *The Seventh Voyage of Sinbad*, *The Three Worlds of Gulliver*, *Mysterious Island*, *Jason and the Argonauts*, *The Golden Voyage of Sinbad* and *Clash of the Titans*. Began experimenting with stop frame animation after seeing *King Kong* in 1933, which eventually led to work with George Pal on his *Puppetoon* series in the early forties. Worked with his hero Willis O'Brien on *Mighty Joe Young* in 1949. Teamed up with producer Charles H. Schneer in the fifties with whom he has worked almost exclusively since. He is also the inventor of the effects process Superdynamation.
Genre credits:
Mighty Joe Young (1949 - co-sp), *The Beast from 20,000 Fathoms* (1953 - sp), *It Came from Beneath the Sea* (1955 - co-sp), *Twenty-Million Miles to Earth* (1957 -sp), *One Million Years BC* (1966 - sp), *The Valley of Gwangi* (1968 - sp)

Hartford-Davis, Robert (1923-1977)

British producer and director with a number of oddities to his credit,

including *The Yellow Teddy Bears*, *Gonks Go Beat* and *The Sandwich Man*.
Genre credits:
The Black Torment (1964 - p/d), *Corruption* (1968 - d), *Bloodsuckers* (1970 - aka *Incense for the Damned/Doctors Wear Scarlet* - d [as Michael Burrowes]), *The Fiend* (1971 - p/d), *Nobody Ordered Love* (1971 - d)

Harvey, Forrester (1890-1945)

Irish character actor, on stage in Britain and Ireland from World War One and in films (in Britain) from 1920, with brief appearances in *London Pride* and *The Glad Eye*. Travelled to America with a stage production of *Havoc* in 1924 and returned in 1931 to take up a film career beginning with MGM's *A Tailor-Made Man*. A reliable comic support, he subsequently appeared in such films as *Possession*, *Guilty Hands*, *Tarzan the Ape Man*, *Red Dust*, *Shanghai Express*, *Captain Blood* and *Lloyds of London* - as well as a handful of genre titles, most memorably as Herbert Hall, the landlord of The Lion's Head Inn in *The Invisible Man*.
Genre credits:
The Invisible Man (1933), *The Invisible Man Returns* (1940), *Dr Jekyll and Mr Hyde* (1941), *The Wolf Man* (1941), *The Lodger* (1944), *The Man in Half Moon Street* (1944)

The Hatchet Murders see Deep Red

Hatton, Rondo (1894-1946)

Billed as the monster who needed no make-up, this once handsome American actor suffered from acromegaly, a bone deforming disease which distorted his face. Consequently, the only roles he could get were in low-budget horror films where he played the heavy. Perhaps best known for his role as the back-breaking Hoxton Creeper in the Sherlock Holmes adventure *Pearl of Death*. His image was later spoofed in the Disney action adventure *The Rocketeer* (1991). Early credits include *Hell Harbour*, *In Old Chicago* and *Alexander's Ragtime Band*.
Genre credits:
The Hunchback of Notre Dame (1939), *Pearl of Death* (1944), *Jungle Captive* (1945), *The Spider Woman Strikes Back* (1946), *Joan Medford is Missing* (1946 - aka *House of Horrors*) *The Brute Man* (1946)

Haunted Honeymoon

USA/GB 1986 82m DeLuxe
In the thirties, a radio star and his fiancee encounter all kinds of monsters at his family's spooky mansion.

Hamfisted rehash of *The Cat and the Canary*. Silly rather than funny.
p: Susan Ruskin for Orion
w: Gene Wilder, Terence Marsh
d: Gene Wilder
ph: Fred Schuler
m: John Morris
ed: Christopher Greenbury
pd: Terence Marsh
cos: Ruth Myers
sp: John Stears
sound: Simon Kaye, Tommy Staples, Bill Rowe
titles: Robert Dawson
Gene Wilder, Gilda Radner, Dom DeLuise, Jonathan Pryce, Peter Vaughan, Bryan Pringle, Ann Way

The Haunted House *

USA 1921 20m bw silent
A small town bank clerk exposes a gang of counterfeiters who have been using a supposedly haunted house as their hideaway.

Reasonably inventive star comedy.
p: Joseph M. Schenck for Metro
w/d: Buster Keaton, Eddie Cline
ph: Elgin Lessley
Buster Keaton, Virginia Fox, Joe Roberts, Eddie Cline

The Haunted House of Horror

GB 1969 89m Eastmancolor
A group of teenagers spend the night in an apparently haunted house and find themselves being menaced by an axe murderer.

Cheap is hardly the word for this low grade British effort.
p: Tony Tenser for Tigon
w: Michael Armstrong, Peter Marcus
d: Michael Armstrong
ph: Jack Atchelor
m: Reg Tilsley
ed: Peter Pitt
ad: Haydon Pearce
cos: Kathleen Moore, Hilda Geerdts
sound: Alan Kane
Frankie Avalon, Jill Haworth, Marc Wynter, Dennis Price. George Sewell, Gina Warwick, Richard O'Sullivan, Jan Holden

The Haunted Palace

USA 1963 85m Pathecolor Panavision
A nineteenth-century New Englander finds himself possessed by the spirit of an evil ancestor who was burned at the stake.

Pedestrian Corman horror which never quite shifts into first gear. For Corman completists only.
p: Roger Corman for AIP/Alta Vista
w: Charles Beaumont
d: Roger Corman
ph: Floyd Crosby

m: Ronald Stein
ed: Ronald Sinclair
ad: Daniel Haller
cos: Marjorioe Corso
sound: John Bury
titles: Armand Acosta
Vincent Price, Debra Paget, Lon Chaney Jr, Elisha Cook Jr, Leo Gordon, Barboura Morris, Frank Maxwell, John Dierkes

The Haunting *

GB 1963 112m bw Panavision
Four people investigate an apparently haunted house just outside Boston and several presences make themselves felt.

Over long ghost story with a surplus of dull chat. A few effective moments - the 'breathing' door is memorable - but the remake, *The Legend of Hell House*, proved to be more satisfactory - and frightening.
p: Robert Wise for MGM/Argyle
w: Nelson Gidding
novel: Shirley Jackson
d: Robert Wise
ph: DAVIS BOULTON
m: Humphrey Searle
ed: Ernest Walter
pd: Elliot Scot
cos: Maude Churchill, Mary Quant
sp: Tom Howard
sound: A. W. Watkins, Gerry Turner, J. B. Smith
Richard Johnson, Julie Harris, Claire Bloom, Russ Conway, Lois Maxwell, Valentine Dyall, Fay Compton, Janet Mansell, Amy Dalby, Rosalie Crutchley

Haunts of the Very Rich *

USA 1972 74m Technicolor TVM
Guests at an exclusive island resort find that they cannot escape and may, in fact, be in hell.

Promising fantasy thriller which seemed much more effective at the time.
p: Lillian Gallo for Worldvision/ABC
w: William Wood
story: T. K. Brown
d: Paul Wendkos
ph: Ben Colman
m: Dominic Frontiere
ed: Fredric Steinkamp
ad: Eugene Lourie
cos: John Perry
sound: Harold Lewis
Lloyd Bridges, Cloris Leachman, Ed Asner, Moses Gunn, Robert Reed, Donna Mills, Tony Bill

Hayden, Linda (1951-)

British actress (real name Linda Higginson) who came to attention in the *Lolita*-like *Baby Love* in 1968, after which she decorated a few horror films of the late sixties and early seventies. Her other credits include *Something to Hide*, *Confessions of a Window Cleaner* and *Let's Get Laid*.

Genre credits:

Taste the Blood of Dracula (1969), *Blood on Satan's Claw* (1970 - aka *Satan's Skin*), *Night Watch* (1973), *Madhouse* (1974), *Vampira* (1974 - aka *Old Dracula*), *The House on Straw Hill* (1975), *The Boys from Brazil* (1978), *Black Carrion* (1984 - TVM)

Hayes, Alison (1930-1977)

American actress (real name Mary Jane Hayes) remembered for playing Nancy Archer, the title role in *Attack of the Fifty Foot Woman*. Her other credits include *Francis Joins the WACs*, *The Blackboard Jungle*, *The Purple Mask* and *Tickle Me*, though all her genre appearances were in low-budget Bs at best.

Genre credits:

The Undead (1957), *Zombie of Mora Tau* (1957), *The Unearthly* (1957), *The Disembodied* (1957), *Attack of the Fifty Foot Woman* (1958), *The Hypnotic Eye* (1960), *The Crawling Hand* (1963)

Haze, Jonathan (1929-)

American actor who appeared in countless Corman quickies of the fifties and sixties (*Five Guns West*, *Gunslinger*, *The Oklahoma Woman*, *Carnival Rock*, *The Viking Women and The Sea Serpent*, etc.), most memorably as Seymour Krelboin in *Little Shop of Horrors*. His other credits include *East of Eden*, *Poor White Trash*, *Stakeout on Dope Street* and *Vice Squad*.

Genre credits:

The Monster from the Ocean Floor (1954), *The Day the World Ended* (1956), *It Conquered the World* (1956), *Not of This Earth* (1957), *Teenage Caveman* (1958), *Little Shop of Horrors* (1960), *The Terror* (1963), *X - The Man with X-Ray Eyes* (1963 - aka *The Man with X-Ray Eyes*)

He Knows You're Alone

USA 1980 92m Metrocolor
A maniac goes after brides-to-be on their wedding days.

Cheaply made killer-thriller with all the expected cliches on hand.
p: George Manasse for MGM/ Lansbury-Beruh
w: Scott Parker
d: Armand Mastroiani
m: Alexander Perskanov, Mark Perskanov
Lewis Arlt, Caitlin O'Heaney, Patsy Pease, Elizabeth Kemp, James Carroll, Don Scardino, Tom Hanks

Headhunter

South Africa 1988 92m colour stereo
A head-hunting killer at bay in Miami

turns out to be a Nigerian demon.

Unremarkable stalk-and-kill stuff with the twist barely worth waiting for, though a slightly higher quota of gore than usual.
p: Jay Davidson for Gibraltar
exec p: Joel Levine
w: Len Spinelli
d: Francis Schaeffer
ph: Hans Kuhle
m: Julian Laxton
ed: no credit given
ad: no credit given
cos: Elaine Downing
sound: Colin Macfarlane, Darryl Martin
make-up effects: Elaine Alexander, Kevin Brennan
Kay Lenz, Wayne Crawford, Sam Williams, June Chadwick, Steve Canaly, John Fatooh

The Hearse

USA 1980 85m Metrocolor
In order to recover from a series of personal traumas, a woman goes to stay in her aunt's isolated country home, only to find herself threatened by an apparently driverless hearse.

Mild thriller with familiar situations.
p: Charles Russell for Crown International/Marimark
exec p: Newton P. Jacobs
w: Bill Blech
story: Mark Tenser
d: George Bowers
ph: Mori Kawa
m: Webster Lewis

ed: George Berndt
ad: Keith Michl (sic)
cos: Kristine Chadwick
sound: John Brodin
Trish Van Devere, Joseph Cotten, David Gautreaux, Donald Hotton, Med Flory

Hell Night

USA 1981 100m Metrocolor
A group of college kids spend the night in a supposedly haunted house for a dare, only there is a real killer on the loose.

Yet another 'let's kill the kids' flick. Of very little interest indeed.
p: Irwin Yablans, Bruce Colmcurtis for Compass International
w: Randolph Feldman
d: Tom de Simone
ph: Mac Ahlberg
m: Dan Wyman
ed: Tony di Marco
ad: Steven G. Legler
Linda Blair, Vincent Van Patten, Peter Barton, Kevin Brophy, Jenny Neuman, Hal Ralston

Hellbound: Hellraiser II

GB 1988 93m Technixolor Dolby
Direct sequel to *Hellraiser* in which the main protagonists now find themselves in hell itself.

Relentlessly gory even in its cut down version, this tasteless enterprise is made to seem even more so because of its technical flair. Strong stomachs a requirement.

• **Oliver Smith and Clare Higgins in Clive Barker's** *Hellraiser*, **one of the British cinema's few horror successes in the past decade.**

p: Christopher Figg for New World
exec p: Clive Barker, Christopher Webster
w: Peter Atkins
story: Clive Barker
d: Tony Randel
ph: Robin Vidgeon
m: Christopher Young
ed: Richard Marden
pd: Mike Buchanan
cos: Jane Wildgoose, Daryl Bristow
sp: Graham Longhurst
sound: John Midgley, Otto Snell, Kevin Taylor, Mike Carter
make-up effects: Image Animation, Geoff Portass
2nd unit d: Christopher Figg
2nd unit ph: Wally Byatt
Clare Higgins, Kenneth Cranham, Ashley Laurence, Imogen Boorman, Sean Chapman, William Hope, Doug Bradley, Barbie Wilde, Simon Bamford, Nicholas Vince, Oliver Smith, Angus McInnes

Hellraiser *
GB 1987 93m Technicolor
A man resurrected from the other side of hell coaxes his ex-lover into murdering for him.

Determinedly stylish if somewhat gory horror movie which went down well with schlock fans, the Pinhead character becoming something of a cult hero. It was followed by *Hellbound: Hellraiser II* (1988), *Hellraiser III: Hell on Earth* (1992) and *Hellraiser IV: Bloodlines* (1995).
p: Christopher Figg for New World/Cinemarque/Film Futures
w/d: Clive Barker from his novel
ph: Robin Vidgeon
m: Christopher Young
ed: Richard Marden
pd: Mike Buchanan
cos: Daryl Bristow
sound: John Midgley
make-up effects: Bob Keen
Andrew Robinson, Clare Higgins, Ashley Lawrence, Sean Chapman, Oliver Smith

Hellraiser III: Hell on Earth
USA/GB 1992 93m Technicolor
Pinhead manifests himself from a statue and wreaks havoc in a New York nightclub, but Nemesis is at hand in the form of a lady television reporter.

More gore filled nonsense, though an improvement on the indulgences of its direct predecessor.
p: Lawrence Mortoff for Arrow
exec p: Clive Barker
w: Peter Atkins
d: Anthony Hickox
ph: Gerry Lively
m: Randy Miller

ed: Chris Cibelli
pd: Steve Hardie
make-up effects: Bob Keen
stunt co-ordinator: Bob Stephens
Terry Farrell, Doug Bradley, Paula Marshall, Kevin Bernhardt, Ken Carpenter, Larry Mortoff, Aimee Leigh, Brent Bolthouse, Chris Frederick, Anthony Hickox

Henenlotter, Frank
American writer, producer and director with an inclination for low-budget horror films, usually infused with a streak of black humour. A former graphic designer, he began by making amateur films on 8mm (*Son of Psycho*, *Slash of the Knife*, *Queen Gorilla*, *Lurid Women*, etc.) before turning 'professional' with *Basket Case* in 1982.
Genre credits:
Basket Case (1982 - w/d/ed), *Brain Damage* (1988 - w/d/exec p/co-ed), *Frankenhooker* (1990 - co-w/d), *Basket Case 2* (1990 - w/d/exec p), *Basket Case 3: The Progeny* (1992 - co-w/d)

Henriksen, Lance
American character actor, often in villainous roles, though he is perhaps best known for playing Bishop the android in *Aliens*. His other credits include *Dog Day Afternoon*, *The Right Stuff*, *Super Mario Bros.*, *Jennifer 8*, *Boulevard* and *Color of Night*.
Genre credits:
Mansion of the Doomed (1975 - aka *The Eyes of Dr Chaney*), *Damien: Omen 2* (1978), *The Visitor* (1978), *Piranha 2: The Spawning* (1983 - aka *Piranha 2: The Flying Killers*), *Nightmares* (1983 - TVM), *The Terminator* (1984), *Aliens* (1986), *Near Dark* (1987), *Pumpkinhead* (1988), *The Horror Show* (1989 - aka *House III: The Horror Show*), *The Pit and the Pendulum* (1991), *Alien 3* (1992), *No Escape* (1994), *Mind Ripper* (1995)

Henry: Portrait of a Serial Killer *
USA 1986 83m Technicolor
The daily activities of a serial killer, from the mundane to the murderous.

Low-budget case study which doesn't quite live up to its critical reputation but is well enough made and acted given its subject matter, which certainly won't be to everyone's taste. Though made in 1986 it didn't receive a proper release until 1990 following the box office success of *The Silence of the Lambs*.
p: John McNaughton, Lisa Dedmond, Steven A. Jones for Maljack
w: Richard Fire, John McNaughton
d: John McNaughton
ph: Charlie Lieberman

m: John McNaughton, Ken Hale, Steven A. Jones
ad: Rick Paul
cos: Patricia Hart
sound: Thomas T. Yore, Rick Coken
Michael Rooker, Tom Towles, Tracy Arnold, Ray Atherton, Eric Young, David Katz, Kurt Naebig, Lisa Temple

Here Is a Man see All That Money Can Buy

Hero and the Terror
USA 1988 96m Technicolor
A police detective tracks down an escaped killer with a penchant for necrophilia.

Curious mixture of action heroics and shocks in the *Friday the 13th* vein. Not a goer by any stretch of the imagination.
p: Raymond Wagner for Cannon/Golan-Globus
w: Dennus Shryack
novel: Michael Blodgett
d: William Tannen
ph: Eric Van Haren Norman
m: David M. Frank
ed: Christian A. Wagner
Chuck Norris, Brynn Thayer, Steve James, Jack O'Halloran, Michael Blodgett

Herrmann, Bernard (1911-1975)
Celebrated American composer and conductor, remembered for his productive association with director Alfred Hitchcock (*Vertigo*, *North By Northwest*, *Psycho*, etc.). Trained at Juilliard, after which he began composing for CBS radio, where he became a member of Orson Welles' Mercury Theatre group, working on a variety of programmes, including *War of the Worlds*. When Welles went to Hollywood in 1941 to direct *Citizen Kane*, Herrmann followed. He won an Oscar the following year for scoring *All That Money Can Buy*, worked with Welles again on *The Magnificent Ambersons*, then contributed a string of standout scores to a variety of productions (several of the later ones often unworthy of his talents). He is also noted for his associations with producer Charles H. Schneer and effects wiz Ray Harryhausen (*The Seventh Voyage of Sinbad*, *The Three Worlds of Gulliver*, *Mysterious Island*, *Jason and the Argonauts*) and Brian de Palma (*Sisters*, *Obsession*). Other credits include *Jane Eyre*, *The Day the Earth Stood Still*, *Journey to the Centre of the Earth*, *Fahrenheit 451* and *Taxi Driver*. He'd just finished scoring Scorsese's *Taxi Driver* and was about to start on de Palma's *Carrie* when he died.

Genre credits:
All That Money Can Buy (1941 - aka *The Devil and Daniel Webster* - AA), *The Ghost and Mrs Muir* (1947), *Psycho* (1960), *Cape Fear* (1961), *Twisted Nerve* (1969), *The Night Diggers* (1971), *Sisters* (1973), *It's Alive* (1974), *It Lives Again* (1978 - aka *It's Alive 2* - themes only), *Cape Fear* (1991 - themes only)

Hessler, Gordon (1925-)

German producer and director working in both Britain and Hollywood. He helmed a number of stylish horror pictures in the late sixties and early seventies before moving on to more routine productions. Began his career in 1950 as a documentary maker before moving into television in the early sixties where he worked primarily on *Alfred Hitchcock Presents*, first as a story editor then later as a producer and director. Turned to films in 1964 with the thriller *Catacombs*. Other credits include *Embassy*, *The Golden Voyage of Sinbad* and *A Cry in the Wilderness* (TVM). Genre credits:
The Oblong Box (1969 - p/d), *Scream and Scream Again* (1970 - d), *Cry of the Banshee* (1971 - p/d), *Murders in the Rue Morgue* (1971 - d), *Scream, Pretty Peggy* (1973 - TVM - d), *The Strange Possession of Mrs Oliver* (1977 - TVM - d)

Heyward, Louis M. (1920-)

American producer and executive producer (also known as Deke Heyward) with many AIP credits to his name, all of them filmed in Britain. *Curse of the Crimson Altar* (1968 - aka *The Crimson Cult* - p), *Witchfinder General* (1968 - aka *The Conqueror Worm* - co-p), *The Oblong Box* (1969 - exec p), *Scream and Scream Again* (1969 - exec p), *Murders in the Rue Morgue* (1971 - p), *The Abominable Dr Phibes* (1971 - co-p), *Dr Phibes Rises Again* (1972 - p)

Hi, Honey, I'm Dead

USA 96m colour TVM
A self-centred architect killed in a lift accident is returned to earth in the body of a no-hoper.
  Dismal rehash of *Heaven Can Wait*, itself a remake of *Here Comes Mr Jordan*. Steer well clear.
p: Paul A. Rudnick for FMN
w: Carl Kleinschmitt
d: Alan Myerson
ph: James Hayman
m: Roger Bellon
ed: Gary Karr
pd: Michael Clausen
cos: Nancy Fox
sound: Ed Novick, John Ross
Curtis Armstrong, Catherine Hicks, Kevin Conroy, Robert Briscoe Evans, Joseph Gordon-Levitt, Harvey Jason, Paul Rodriguez

Hickox, Anthony

British writer and director with a penchant for quirky genre pictures which he makes in America. He is the son of director Douglas Hickox (1929-1988) whose own genre credits include *The Giant Behemoth* (1959 - aka *Behemoth the Sea Monster* - co-d), the excellent *Theatre of Blood* (1973 - d) and *The Hound of the Baskervilles* (1983 - TVM - d). Genre credits:
Waxwork (1988 - w/d), *Sundown* (1990 - aka *Sundown: The Vampire in Retreat* -d), *Waxwork II: Lost in Time* (1992 - w/d), *Hellraiser III: Hell on Earth* (1992 - d/actor), *Warlock II: The Armageddon* (1993 - d), *Full Eclipse* (1994 - TVM - d)

The Hidden Hand

USA 1942 67m bw
A madman escapes from a lunatic asylum and makes his way to his sister's house.
  Half-baked spooky house thriller with one or two laughs. More wit and style might have produced a little gem.
p: Warner
w: Anthony Coldeway, Raymond Schrock
play: Rufus King
d: Ben Stoloff
ph: Henry Sharp
m: no credit given
ed: Harold McLernon
ad: Stanley Fleischer
Craig Stevens, Elizabeth Fraser, Julie Bishop, Willie Best, Milton Parsons

The Hideous Sun Demon

USA 1959 74m bw
As a result of a laboratory experiment, a scientist finds himself turning into a giant lizard whenever exposed to the sun.
  Poorly made schlock horror, too bad to be amusing.
p: Robert Clarke, Robin Kirkman for Pacific International
w: E. S. Seelet Jr, Doane Hoag
story: Robert Clarke, Phil Hiner
d: Robert Clarke, Thomas Cassarino
ph: John Morrill, Vilis Lapenieks, Stan Follis
m: John Seely
ed: Tom Boutross
ad: Gianbattista Cassarino
sound: Doug Menville
Robert Clarke, Patricia Manning, Nan Peterson, Patrick Whyte, Fred La Porta

High Spirits

GB 1988 96m Technicolor
The owner of a crumbling Irish castle fakes haunting so as to attract tourists, only to find himself with some real ghosts on his hands.
  Raucous supernatural comedy which very quickly wears out its welcome.
p: Stephen Woolley, David Saunders for Palace/Vision PDG
w/d: Neil Jordan
ph: Alex Thomson
m: George Fenton
ed: Michael Bradsell
pd: Anton Furst
sp: Derek Meddings
Peter O'Toole, Steve Guttenberg, Beverly D'Angelo, Donald McCann, Liz Smith, Mary Koughlan, Peter Gallagher, Daryl Hannah, Liam Neeson, Ray McAnally, Jennifer Tilly

Hill, Debra

American writer and producer who, after gaining experience on documentaries as an assistant, worked her way up the ladder to writer-producer status. In the late seventies she teamed up with director John Carpenter and made a big splash with *Halloween*. For a while she seemed stuck in the horror genre but has since produced such non-genre films as *Escape from New York*, *Clue*, *Big Top Pee-Wee* and *The Fisher King*. Genre credits:
Halloween (1978 - co-w/p), *The Fog* (1979 - co-w/p), *Halloween II* (1981 - co-w/co-p), *Halloween III: Season of the Witch* (1983 - co-p), *The Dead Zone* (1983 - p)

Hilligoss, Candace

American actress remembered for playing Mary Henry, the leading role in the semi-professional cult favourite *Carnival of Souls* (1963). Her only other credit is *Curse of the Living Corpse* (1964).

Hinds, Anthony (1922-)

British producer and writer (always using the pseudonym John Elder), son of William Hinds (aka Will Hammer, who founded Exclusive Films with Enrique Carreras). Joined Exclusive for a brief period in 1939 as a bookings clerk before war service in the RAF. Rejoined Exclusive in 1946, gaining experience overseeing the quota quickies made on their behalf for distribution. Became a fully-fledged producer when Exclusive/Hammer turned to production themselves, producing 37 of the studio's first 50 features/programmers. Went on to produce many of Hammer's classic horror films. Left Hammer in 1969 after producing their TV series *Journey to the Unknown*, though he carried on writing for them and for Tyburn.

Genre credits:
Stolen Face (1952 - p), *The Quatermass Experiment* (1955 - aka *The Creeping Unknown* - p), *The Curse of Frankenstein* (1956 - p), *X - The Unknown* (1957 -p), *Quatermass 2* (1957 - aka *Enemy from Space* - p), *Dracula* (1958 - aka *Horror of Dracula* - p), *The Hound of the Baskervilles* (1959 - p), *The Revenge of Frankenstein* (1958 - p), *The Man Who Could Cheat Death* (1959 - p), *The Stranglers of Bombay* (1960 - p), *The Brides of Dracula* (1960 - p), *Curse of the Werewolf* (1961 - w/p [w as John Elder]), *The Phantom of the Opera* (1962 - w/p [w as John Elder]), *Captain Clegg* (1962 - aka *Night Creatures* [as John Elder]), *The Old Dark House* (1962 - co-p), *The Damned* (1963 - aka *These Are the Damned* - p), *Paranoiac* (1963 - p), *Kiss of the Vampire* (1964 - aka *Kiss of Evil* - w/p [w as John Elder]), *The Evil of Frankenstein* (1964 - w/p [w as John Elder]), *Fanatic* (1965 - aka *Die! Die! My Darling!* - p), *Dracula - Prince of Darkness* (1966 - story [as John Elder]), *The Reptile* (1966 - w [as John Elder]), *Frankenstein Created Woman* (1967 - w [as John Elder]), *The Mummy's Shroud* (1967 - story [as John Elder]), *Dracula Has Risen from the Grave* (1968 - w [as John Elder]), *Scars of Dracula* (1970 - w [as John Elder]), *Frankenstein and the Monster from Hell* (1973 - w [as John Elder]), *The Legend of the Werewolf* (1974 - w [as John Elder]), *The Ghoul* (1975 - w [as John Elder])

Hinds, William (1887-?)
British producer who, with partner Enrique Carreras, founded Hammer Films in the thirties, which churned out a number of mostly forgettable quota quickies. The company disappeared during World War Two, but emerged in the late forties as an adjunct to Exclusive Films, though it wouldn't be until the mid-fifties that it became synonymous with the horror genre.

Hinwood, Peter
British actor, a former model and photographer, whose only film appearance has been as the creature in *The Rocky Horror Picture Show* (1975).

Hirsch, Paul
American editor who won an Oscar for co-editing *Star Wars* in 1977. Perhaps best known for his association with Brian de Palma, his credits include *The Empire Strikes Back*, *Ferris Bueller's Day Off*, *Trains, Planes and Automobiles*, *Raising Cain* and *Mission: Impossible*.
Genre credits:
Sisters (1973), *Phantom of the Paradise* (1974), *Creepshow* (1982)

Hitchcock, Alfred (1889-1980)
British director and producer, known the world over as The Master of Suspense. Famous primarily as a maker of thrillers, many of which are rightly considered classics (*The Lodger*, *The Thirty-Nine Steps*, *Rebecca*, *Vertigo*, *North By Northwest*). He only occasionally broached the horror genre, most notably with *Psycho* (1960) and *The Birds* (1963).

The Hitcher *
USA 1986 98m Metroclor Panavision Dolby
A young man driving to California finds himself menaced by a murderous hitch-hiker.
Slick thriller which, despite its fairly familiar premise, at least keeps moving and has several well-staged sequences.
p: David Bombyk, Kip Ohman, Paul Lewis for HBO/Silver Screen Partners
exec p: Edward S. Feldman, Charles R. Meeker
w: Eric Red
d: Robert Harmon
ph: John Seale
m: Mark Isham
ed: Frank J. Urioste
pd: Dennis Gassner
cos: Simon Tuke, Parker Poole
sound: Art Names
stunt co-ordinator: Eddie Donno
Rutger Hauer, C. THOMAS HOWELL, Jennifer Jason Leigh, Jeffrey de Munn, Billy Green Bush, John Jackson, Henry Darrow

Hobbes, Halliwell (1877-1962)
British character actor with many supporting roles in Hollywood to his name, usually as a plummy butler (most memorably in *Sherlock Holmes Faces Death*). On stage since 1898, and in America from 1923, he made his film début in 1929 in *Jealousy*. His many other credits include *You Can't Take It With You*, *Lady Hamilton*, *The Sea Hawk* and *Gaslight*.
Genre credits:
Dr Jekyll and Mr Hyde (1932), *Dracula's Daughter* (1936), *The Undying Monster* (1942 - aka *The Hammond Mystery*), *Sherlock Holmes Faces Death* (1943), *The Invisible Man's Revenge* (1944)

Hold That Ghost *
USA 1941 86m bw
Two incompetents inherit an apparently haunted house.
Laboured comedy thriller, very typical of its period and its stars. One or two bright moments.
p: Burt Kelly, Glenn Tyron for Universal
w: Robert Lees, Fred Rinaldo, John Grant
story: Robert Lees, Fred Rinaldo

d: Arthur Lubin
ph: Elwood Bredell, Joe Valentine
md: Hans J. Salter
ed: Philip Cahn
ad: Jack Otterson, Harold H. MacArthur
cos: Vera West
sound: Bernard B. Brown, William Fox
ch: Nick Castle
Bud Abbott, Lou Costello, JOAN DAVIS, Evelyn Ankers, Marc Lawrence, Mischa Auer, Ted Lewis and his Orchestra, The Andrews Sisters

Holden, Gloria (1908-1991)
British actress in Hollywood movies (*Test Pilot*, *The Corsican Brothers*, *The Eddy Duchin Story*), though recalled primarily for playing the title role in *Dracula's Daughter* (1936).

Holland, Tom (1943-)
American screenwriter who turned to direction. Comfortable with horror themes, he is perhaps best known for scripting *Psycho 2*. Other credits include *Cloak and Dagger*, *Fatal Beauty* and *The Temp*.
Genre credits:
The Beast Within (1982 - w), *Psycho 2* (1983 - w), *Scream for Help* (1984 - w), *Fright Night* (1985 - w/d), *Child's Play* (1988 - co-w/d)

Hollingsworth, John (1916-1963)
British conductor who, in 1954, became Exclusive/Hammer's first in-house musical supervisor, a post he retained until his death in 1963, when he was succeeded by Philip Martell. Trained at London's Guildhall School of Music. Joined the RAF during the war, following which he conducted several orchestras, including those of the Royal Opera House and BBC Radio, which is where he discovered James Bernard, offering him his first film scoring assignment, *The Quatermass Experiment*, in 1955.

Holocaust 2000
GB/It 1977 102m Technicolor Technovision
An executive discovers that his son is the Anti-Christ and that he is attempting to destroy the world with the thermo-nuclear plant he is in charge of.
Silly, over plotted all star horror thriller, a long way behind *The Exorcist* and *The Omen*.
p: Edmondo Amati for Rank/Aston/Embassy
w: Sergio Donati, Alberto de Martino, Michael Robson
story: Sergio Donati, Alberto de Martino
d: Alberto de Martino

ph: Erico Menczer
m: Ennio Morricone
ed: Vincenzo Tomassi
ad: Umberto Bertacca
cos: Enrico Sabbatini
sound: Peter Handford
Kirk Douglas, Simon Ward, Agostina Belli, Anthony Quayle, Virginia McKenna, Spiros Focas, Alexander Knox, Adolfo Celi, Denis Lawson, Peter Cellier, Geoffrey Keen

Holt, Seth (1923-1971)

Palestinian born director. Began his career as an editor at Ealing working on such classics as *Mandy*, *The Lavender Hill Mob* and *The Titfield Thunderbolt*. His first film as a director was *Nowhere to Go* in 1958. His three Hammer films aside, he directed only two more films: *Danger Route* and *Station Six Sahara*. Died during the filming of *Blood from the Mummy's Tomb*, which was completed by Michael Carreras. His best work (*Taste of Fear* and *The Nanny*) is easily comparable with that of Hitchcock.
Genre credits:
Taste of Fear (1961 - aka *Scream of Fear*), *The Nanny* (1965), *Blood from the Mummy's Tomb* (1971)

Homicidal *

USA 1961 87m bw
A murderous young blonde isn't quite what she seems.
    Low-budget shocker, rather obviously inspired by *Psycho*. Introduced by the director himself, his gimmick this time involves a 'fright break' near the end to allow the nervy to leave the theatre before the final bloodbath.
p: William Castle for Columbia
w: Robb White
d: William Castle
ph: Burnett Guffey
m: Hugo Friedhoffer
ed: Edwin Bryant
ad: Cary Odell
sound: Lambert Day, Charles J. Rice
Jean Arliss, Glenn Corbett, Patricia Breslin, Eugenie Leontovitch, Alan Bunce, Richard Rust

Honda, Inoshiro (1911-1993)

Japanese director who tied himself to the Godzilla series and its various off-shoots, all of which featured men romping about in rubber monster suits.
Genre credits:
Godzilla, King of the Monsters (1954 - aka *Gojira* - co-w/d), *Half Human* (1955 -aka *Jujin Yukiotako*), *Rodan* (1957), *The H-Man* (1958 - aka *Uomini H/Bijyo to Ekitainingen*), *Mothra* (1962 - aka *Mosura*), *King Kong vs Godzilla* (1962 - aka *Kingu Kongu Tai Gojira*), *Godzilla vs*

Mothra (1964), *Attack of the Mushroom People* (1964 - aka - *Curse of the Mushroom People/Matango, the Fungus of Terror* - co-d), *Dagora the Space Monster* (1964 - aka *Uchu Daikaiju Dogora*), *Godzilla vs The Thing* (1964 - aka *Gojira Tai Mosura)*, *Frankenstein Conquers the World* (1964 - aka *Fuharankenshutain Tai Baragon*), *Ghidrah the Three-Headed Monster* (1965 - aka *Sandai Kaiji Chikyu Saidai No Kessen*), *Invasion of the Asto-Monsters* (1967 - aka *Godzilla vs Monster Zero/Invasion of Planet X/Monster Zero*), *King Kong Escapes* (1968), *Godzilla's Revenge* (1969 - aka *Ord Kaiju Daishingeki* - co-w/d), *Destroy All Monsters* (1969 - aka *Kaiju Soshingeki*), *The War of the Gargantuas* (1970 - aka *Sanda Tai Gailah* - co-w/d), *Yog, Monster from Space* (1971), *Monsters from an Unknown Planet* (1975)

The Honeymoon Killers *

USA 1969 108m bw
A gigolo and a nurse murder lonely women for their money.
    Based on actual events, this is a fairly compulsive low-budget thriller, helped immeasurably by Stoler's chilling performance as the weighty killer.
p: Warren Steibel for Roxanne
w/d: Leonard Kastle
ph: Oliver Wood
m: Mahler
ed: Stan Warnow, Richard Brophy
ad: no credit given
cos: Martha Fogg
sound: Fred Kanniel, Tom Dillinger
Tony Lo Bianco, SHIRLEY STOLER, Mary Jane Highby, Kip McArdie, Doris Roberts

Hooper, Tobe (1943-)

American writer, producer, director and composer. Gained experience as a director of documentaries, commercials and industrial films before becoming notorious in the mid-seventies for his feature début *The Texas Chainsaw Massacre*, a viscera-filled splatter flick which, though it was much banned, proved to be a trendsetter. His most commercial film to date has been *Poltergeist*, in which his directorial hand was allegedly controlled by his producer, Steven Spielberg. His films since have often been a disappointment. His other credits include *Lifeforce* and *Invaders from Mars*. He can also be spotted in *Sleepwalkers*.
Genre credits:
The Texas Chainsaw Massacre (1974 - co-w/co-m/p/d), *Death Trap* (1976 - aka *Eaten Alive/Horror Hotel* - co-m/d), *Salem's Lot* (1979 - TVM - d), *The Funhouse* (1981 - d), *Poltergeist* (1982 - d), *Texas Chainsaw Massacre 2* (1986 -co-m/co-p/d), *Spontaneous Combustion*

(1989 - co-w/d), *I'm Dangerous Tonight* (1990 - TVM), *Sleepwalkers* (1992 - actor only), *Body Bags* (1993 - TVM - co-d), *Night Terrors* (1993 - aka *Tobe Hooper's Night Terrors/Tobe Hooper's Nightmare* - d), *The Mangler* (1995 - co-w/d)

Hopkins, Sir Anthony (1937-)

British (Welsh) actor in the Richard Burton tradition. His career has seen as many highs as lows, though he became known the world over for his portrayal of Hannibal the Cannibal Lecter in the 1991 film *The Silence of the Lambs,* which deservedly won him a Best Actor Oscar, only the second awarded for a horror performance (the other went to Fredric March for his performance in *Dr Jekyll and Mr Hyde* in 1932). Other credits include *The Lion in Winter*, *When Eight Bells Toll*, *Howards End*, *The Remains of the Day* and *Shadowlands*.
Genre credits:
Audrey Rose (1977), *Magic* (1978), *The Elephant Man* (1980), *The Hunchback of Notre Dame* (1982 - TVM - as Quasimodo), *The Silence of the Lambs* (1991), *Bram Stoker's Dracula* (1992 - as Van Helsing)

Horror at 37,000 Feet *

USA 1972 74m Technicolor
A transatlantic jet is threatened by a mysterious force that appears to be emanating from the stones of an English abbey being transported to the States.
    Watchable horror hokum, quite smoothly done.
p: Anthony Wilson for CBS
d: David Lowell Rich
Buddy Ebsen, William Shatner, Chuck Connors, Tammy Grimes, Frances Nuyen, Lyn Loring, Roy Thinnes, Paul Winfield

Horror Express *

Sp 1974 97m Technicolor
Passengers on a train travelling through Siberia are threatened by the remains of a fossilized being that has returned to life.
    Curious horror piece with a few interesting touches along the way.
p: Bernard Gordon for Granada/Benmar/Scottia Inc.
w: Arnaud D'Usseau, Julian Halevy
d/story: Gene Martin
ph: Alejandro Ulloa
m: John Cacavas
ed: Robert Dearberg
ad: Ramiro Gomez Guardiana
cos: Charles Simminger
sp: Brian Stevens, Pablo Perez
sound: Antonio Man, Enrique Molinaro
make-up: Julian Ruiz
Peter Cushing, Christopher Lee, Telly Savalas, Silvia Tortosa, Jorge Rigaud

Horror Hospital

GB 1973 91m Rank colour

A young man discovers that the health farm he has gone to visit for a holiday is in fact a front for a mad doctor who is carrying out experiments on the 'guests'.

Inept horror comic with a silly script, bad acting and poor continuity, though a car with a beheading device is memorable.

p: Richard Gordon for Noteworthy
w: Antony Balch, Alan Watson
d: Antony Balch
ph: David McDonald
m: De Wolfe
ed: Robert Dearberg
as: David Bill
sound; Paul Le Mare, Tony Ascombe
stunt co-ordinator: Martin Grace
Michael Gough, Robin Askwith, Dennis Price, Skip Martin, Vanessa Shaw, Ellen Pollack, Kurt Christian

Horror Hotel (1960) see City of the Dead

Horror Hotel (1976) see Death Trap

The Horror House see The Haunted House of Horror

Horror of Dracula see Dracula (1958)

Horror of Frankenstein

GB 1970 95m Technicolor

Victor Frankenstein's experiments with life produce a muscle-bound mutant with a taste for murder.

Wholly unsuccessful rehash of Hammer's own Curse of Frankenstein with Peter Cushing sadly missed in the title role. Wooden acting and a few unwise attempts at humour only make matters worse. The film marked Sangster's directorial début.

p: Jimmy Sangster for Hammer
w: Jimmy Sangster, Jeremy Burnham
d: Jimmy Sangster
ph: Moray Grant
m: Malcolm Williamson
md: Philip Martell
ed: Chris Barnes
ad: Scott Macregor
cos: Laura Nightingale
sound: Claude Hitchcock, Terry Lumkin
make-up: Tom Smith
Ralph Bates, Kate O'Mara, Graham Jones, Veronica Carlson, James Hayter, Joan Rice, Dennis Price, Bernard Archand, Dave Prowse (as the Monster), James Cossins, Jon Finch, Terry Duggan

Horror Planet see Inseminoid

The Horror Show

USA 1989 96m DeLuxe

A cop tracks down a killer who has lived through the electric chair to emerge as an apparently indestructable monster.

Despite the title, this is the third episode in the House series, a gory low-budget schlocker with Friday the 13th-style shocks. Wes Craven's Shocker, made the same year, uses a similar premise.

p: Sean S. Cunningham for UA
w: Allyn Warner (billed Alan Smithee), Leslie Bohem
d: James Isaac
ph: Mac Ahlberg
m: Harry Manfredini
ed: Edward Anton
pd: Stewart Campbell
Lance Henriksen, Brion James, Rita Taggart, Dedee Pfeiffer, Lawrence Tierney, Matt Clark

Hough, John (1941-)

British director from television (The Avengers, The Saint) whose strong visual sense is well suited to horror films and thrillers. Other credits include Eyewitness, Dirty Mary, Crazy Larry, Escape to Witch Mountain, Brass Target and Triumphs of a Man Called Horse. Returned to television in the late 1980s to direct Barbara Cartland romances for Lew Grade (A Hazard of Hearts, Dangerous Love, The Lady and the Highwayman, etc.). His best film is the supernatural thriller The Legend of Hell House.

Genre credits:
Twins of Evil (1971), The Watcher in the Woods (1980), The Incubus (1982), A Distant Scream (1984 - TVM), Black Carrion (1984 - TVM - w/d), Czech Mate (1984 - TVM), American Gothic (1987), Howling IV: The Original Nightmare (1988)

Houghton, Don (1933-1991)

Paris born British screenwriter and story editor (for TV's Hammer House of Mystery and Suspense), the son of novelist George W. Houghton. Began writing for television (Emergency Ward 10, Dr Who, The Flaxton Boys) before moving on to Hammer horrors. Also scripted the dialogue for two Hammer records: Dracula and The Legend of the Seven Golden Vampires.

Genre credits:
Dracula AD 1972 (1972), The Satanic Rites of Dracula (1973), The Legend of the Seven Golden Vampires (1974 - aka The Seven Brothers Meet Dracula)

The Hound of the Baskervilles **

USA 1939 80m bw

When an apparently supernatural hound terrorizes a landed Dartmoor family, Sherlock Holmes is requested to investigate.

The first of the Rathbone-Holmes mysteries is a rather dated and stately affair, hampered chiefly by its lack of a full music score, though connoisseurs will find things to enjoy along the way.

p: Gene Markey for TCF
exec p: Darryl F. Zanuck
w: Ernest Pascall
novel: Arthur Conan Doyle
d: Sidney Lanfield
ph: Peverell Marley
md: Cyril Mockridge
ed: Robert Simpson
ad: Richard Day, Hans Peters.
cos: Gwen Wakeling
sound: W. D. Flick, Roger Heman
BASIL RATHBONE, NIGEL BRUCE, Richard Greene, Wendy Barrie, Lionel Atwill, John Carradine, Morton Lowry, Barlowe Borland, E. E. Clive, Mary Gordon, Eily Malyon, Ralph Forbes, Beryl Mercer

The Hound of the Baskervilles **

GB 1959 86m Technicolor

Sherlock Holmes discovers the truth about a legendary hound from hell.

Well-mounted Hammer remake with plenty of atmosphere, let down only by the familiarity of the story itself.

p: Anthony Hinds for Hammer
exec p: Michael Carreras
w: Peter Bryan
novel: Arthur Conan Doyle
d: TERENCE FISHER
ph: JACK ASHER
m: JAMES BERNARD
md: John Hollingsworth
ed: James Needs, Alfred Cox
pd: BERNARD ROBINSON
cos: Molly Arbuthnot
sp: Sydney Pearson
sound: Jock May
PETER CUSHING, ANDRE MORELL, CHRISTOPHER LEE, Francis de Wolff, Maria Landi, Ewen Solon, Miles Malleson, Sam Kydd, John Le Mesurier

The Hound of the Baskervilles

GB 1977 85m Technicolor Panavision

Carry On meets Hammer in this camped up spoof of the familiar story which quickly resolves itself into a series of end of term sketches (including an Exorcist send-up) which tend to be silly rather than funny, though star fans may derive a few giggles from the awful puns. The urinating chihuahuas are also memorable.

p: John Goldstone for Hemdale
exec p: Michael White, Andrew Braunsberg
w: Peter Cook, Dudley Moore, Paul Morrisey

novel: Arthur Conan Doyle
d: Paul Morrissey
ph: Dick Bush, John Wilcox
m: Dudley Moore
ed: Richard Marden, Glenn Hyde
pd: Roy Smith
cos: Charles Knode
sp: Ian Wingrove
sound: Brian Simmons, George Stephenson, Gerry Humphreys
Peter Cook, Dudley Moore, Terry-Thomas, Denholm Elliott, Joan Greenwood, Max Wall, Irene Handl, Kenneth Williams, Hugh Griffiths, Spike Milligan, Roy Kinnear, Penelope Keith, Jessie Matthews, Prunella Scales, Dana Gillespie, Lucy Griffiths

The Hound of the Baskervilles
GB/USA 1983 96m Technicolor TVM
Poorly scripted and handled tele-version of a story already filmed once too often.
p: Otto Plaschkes for Sy Weintraub
w: Charles Edward Pogue
novel: Arthur Conan Doyle
d: Douglas Hickox
ph: Ronnie Taylor
m: Michael J. Lewis
ed: Malcolm Cooke
pd: Michael Stringer
cos: Julie Harris
sp: Alan Whibley
sound: Tony Dawe, Ken Barker
Ian Richardson, Donald Churchill, Denholm Elliott, Nicholas Clay, Martin Shaw, Glynis Barker, Edward Judd, Eleanor Bron, Brian Blessed, Ronald Lacey, Connie Booth, David Langton

The Hounds of Zaroff see The Most Dangerous Game

House
USA 1985 85m Technicolor
An author writing about his experiences in Vietnam moves into an aunt's old house which proves to be haunted.
   Mild horror comic with predictable scares. Fair enough for its intended market, it inspired three sequels: House II: The Second Story (1988), The Horror Show (1989 - aka House III) and House IV (1992).
p: Sean S. Cunningham for New World
w: Ethan Wiley
story: Fred Dekker
d: Steve Miner
ph: Mac Ahlberg
m: Harry Manfredini
ed: Michael J. Knue
pd: Gregg Fonseca
make-up efects: Kirk Thatcher, James Cummins
William Katt, George Wendt, Richard Moll, Mary Stavin, Michael Ensign, Erik Silver, Mark Silver, Susan French

House II: The Second Story
USA 1987 88m Technicolor
A young couple discover that their house is haunted by the ghost of a gunslinger in search of a crystal skull.
   Ramshackle comedy thriller for undemanding late night audiences. The connection to the first film is non-existent.
p: Sean S. Cunningham for New World
w/d: Ethan Wiley
ph: Mac Ahlberg
m: Harry Manfredini
ed: Marty Nicholsaon
pd: Gregg Fonsecca
make-up effects: Chris Walas
Arye Gross, Jonathan Stark, Royal Dano, Bill Maher, John Ratzenberger, Amy Yasbeck

House III see The Horror Show

House by the Cemetery
It 1981 78m colour
A writer and his family move into a strange house where murders took place - and still do.
   Yet more of the usual sick nonsense expected from this director. For completists only.
p: Fabrizzio de Angelis for Fulvia Films
w: Dardano Sacchetti, Giorgio Mariuzzo, Lucio Fulci
d: Lucio Fulci
ph: Sergo Salvati
m: Walter Rizzati
Katherine McColl, Paolo Malco, Ania Pierono, Giovanni Frezza, Silvia Collatina, Dagmar Lessander

The House in Nightmare Park *
GB 1973 95m Technicolor
An Edwardian actor is hired to read at a remote country house only to find his life in peril.
   Camp comedy thriller which plays like a cross between a Carry On and The Cat and the Canary. Amusing moments for star fans.
p: Clive Exton, Terry Nation for EMI/Associated London/Extonation
w: Clive Exton, Terry Nation
d: Peter Sykes
ph: Ian Wilson
m: Harry Robinson
ed: Bill Blunden
ad: Maurice Carter
cos: Judy Moorcroft
sound: Rene Borisewitz, Ken Barker
FRANKIE HOWERD, Ray Milland, Hugh Burden, Kenneth Griffith, Rosalie Crutchley, Ruth Dunning, John Bennett

House of Doom see The Black Cat (1934)

House of Dracula *
USA 1945 67m bw
Count Dracula visits an eminent surgeon in order to to be cured of his blood lust only to discover the Wolf Man and Frankenstein's Monster at hand too.
   Unbelievably plotted horror farrago, a last attempt by Universal to wring a few more bucks out of their horror series. Stuff and nonsense for lovers of the absurd.
p: Paul Malvern for Universal
exec p: Joseph Gershenson
w: Edward T. Lowe
d: EARLE C. KENTON
ph: GEORGE ROBINSON
md: Edgar Fairchild
ed: Russell Schoengarth
ad: John B. Goodman, Martin Obzina
cos: Vera West
sp: John P. Fulton
make-up: Jack P. Pierce
sound: Bernard B. Brown, Jess Moulin
Lon Chaney Jr, John Carradine, Martha O'Driscoll, Lionel Atwill, Jane Adam, Onslow Stevens, Glenn Strange, Skelton Knaggs (is that a great name or what?)

House of Evil (1982) see The House on Sorority Row

House of Exorcism see Lisa and the Devil

House of Fear **
USA 1945 68m bw
When the members of an exclusive club begin to be murdered one by one Sherlock Holmes investigates, his only clue being an envelope containing several orange pips.
   Rather good Holmes mystery with plenty of inventive touches and a plot not that dissimilar to And Then There Were None.
p: Roy William Neill for Universal
w: ROY CHANSLOR
story: Arthur Conan Doyle
d: ROY WILLIAM NEILL
ph: Virgil Miller
md: Paul Sawtell
ed: Saul Goodkind
ad: John B. Goodman, Eugene Lourie
cos: Vera West
sound: Bernard B. Brown
BASIL RATHBONE, NIGEL BRUCE, Dennis Hoey, AUBREY MATHER, Paul Cavanaugh, Holmes Herbert, Gavin Muir, Sally Shepherd

House of Frankenstein *
USA 1944 71m bw
Using a travelling horror show as cover, a mad doctor has confrontations with Dracula, Frankenstein's Monster and Larry Talbot, the Wolf Man.

Beguilingly silly horror nonsense, energetically handled and with a cast of old faithfuls.
p: Paul Malvern for Universal
w: Edward T. Lowe
story: Curt Siodmak
d: ERLE C. KENTON
ph: GEORGE ROBINSON
m: Hans J. Salter
ed: Philip Cahn
ad: John B. Goodman, Martin Obzina
sp: John P. Fulton
make-up: Jack P. Pierce
BORIS KARLOFF, John Carradine, Lon Chaney Jr, George Zucco, J. Carrol Naish, Glenn Strange, Elena Verdugo, Lionel Atwill, Sig Rumann

House of Mystery
GB 1961 56m bw
A young couple looking to buy a country cottage are told that it is haunted.

Mildly diverting programmer with a well-telegraphed twist in the tail.
p: Julian Wintle, Leslie Parkyn for Anglo Amalgamated/Independent Artists
w/d: Vernon Sewell
ph: Ernest Steward
m: Stanley Black
ed: John Trumper
ad: Jack Shapman
cos: Vi Murray
sound: John W. Mitchell, Ken Cameron
Jane Hylton, Peter Dyneley, Nanette Newman, Maurice Kaufman, John Merivale

House of the Long Shadows
GB 1982 102m Technicolor
A young author takes up a bet that he can't write a gothic novel during one night in a haunted house.

Disappointing horror comic that wastes its cast of old favourites.
p: Meneham Golan, Yoram Globus for Cannon
w: Michael Armstrong
d: Peter walker
ph: Norman Langley
m: Richard Harvey
ed: Robert Dearberg
ad: Mike Pickwode
sound: Pete O'Connor
Vincent Price, Christopher Lee, Peter Cushing, John Carradine, Desi Arnaz Jr, Sheila Keith, Julie Peasgood, Richard Todd, Louise English, Richard Hunter, Norman Rossington

House of Usher *
USA 1960 85m Eastmancolor
Cinemascope
A young man discovers that his fiancee is cataleptic and has been buried alive by her brother in their crumbling mansion.

Slow and rather hesitant horror film whose success established the popular Corman Poe cycle of the sixties. It was remade in 1990 with much less success.
p: Roger Corman for AIP/Alta Vista
exec p: Samuel Z. Arkoff, James H. Nicholson
w: Richard Matheson
story: Edgar Allan Poe
d: Roger Corman
ph: Floyd Crosby
m: Les Baxter
ed: Anthony Carras
pd: Daniel Haller
cos: Marjorie Corso
sp: Larry Butler, Pat Dinga, Ray Mercer
sound: Al Bird, Phil Mitchell
Vincent Price, Mark Damon, Myrna Fahey, Harry Ellerbe

House of Wax *
USA 1953 88m Warnercolor 3D
Disfigured in a fire, a wax sculptor avenges himself by using real people as the bases for the models in his new exhibition.

Gimmicky horror fare which came at the height of the 3D cycle in the fifties. Quite lively in places, its success helped make Price synonymous with the horror genre.
p: Bryan Foy for Warner
w: Crane Wilbur
story: Charles Belden
d: Andre de Toth
ph: Bert Glennon, Peverell Marley
m: David Buttolph
ed: Rudi Fehr
ad: Stanley Fleischer
cos: Howard Shoup
sound: Charles Lang
make-up: Gordon Bau
VINCENT PRICE, Frank Lovejoy, Phyllis Kirk, Carolyn Jones, Paul Picerni, Roy Roberts, Paul Cavanaugh, Charles Buchinsky (later Charles Bronson), Reggie Rymal, Angela Clarke, Dobbs Greer

House of Whipcord
GB 1974 101m Eastmancolor
A lunatic magistrate imprisons young women whom he considers immoral in his mansion.

Cheap and interminable exploitation piece which has gained cult status in some quarters.
p: Pete Walker for Heritage
w: David McGillivray
d/story: Pete Walker
ph: Peter Jessop
m: Stanley Myers
ed: Matt McCarthy
ad: Mike Pickwode
Barbara Markham, Patrick Barr, Sheila Keith, Ray Brooks, Ann Michelle, Celia Imrie, Penny Irving

The House on Haunted Hill
USA 1958 75m bw Emergo
A millionaire holds a party in a haunted house, offering $10,000 to those who will stay the night.

There's more energy than sense in this camp exploitation piece, typical of its producer's gimmicky output, but it's enjoyable enough.
p: William Castle for Allied Artists

• **Vincent Price amid the flames in** *House of Wax*.

• Promotional artwork for producer-director William Castle's *The House on Haunted Hill*.

w: Robb White
d: William Castle
ph: Carl Guthrie
m: Von Dexter
ed: Roy Livingston
ad: David Milton
cos: Rosemary Weinberg, Ward Sharipter
sound: Charles Schelling, Ralph Butler
Vincent Price, Richard Long, Carol Ohmart, Alan Marshall, Elisha Cook Jr, Carolyn Craig

The House on Sorority Row

USA 1982 91m Technicolor
Sorority girls are stalked and killed by a slasher, out to avenge the death of his mother.

Mild shocker, slightly better made than most, though sticking to the expected clichés.

p: Mark Rosman, John G, Clark for VAE
exec p: John Ponchock, W. Thomas McMahon
w/d: Mark Rosman
ph: Timothy Suhrstedt
m: Richard Band
ed: Jean-Marc Vasseur
ad: Vincent Peranio
cos: Susan Perez Prichard
sp: Rob E. Holland
sound: Steve Rogers
Kathryn McNeil, Lois Kelso Hunt, Robin Meloy, Christopher Lawrence, Jodi Draigie, Ellen Davidson, Janis Zido

The House That Dripped Blood *

GB 1970 102m Eastmancolor
Four tales of terror centred on the same old house.

Tepid horror compendium lacking the necessary style and atmosphere, not to mention horror.
p: Max J. Rosenberg, Milton Subotsky for Amicus
w: Robert Blochy
d: Peter Duffell
ph: Robert Parslow
m: Michael Dress
ed: Peter Tanner
ad: Tony Curtis
coa: Laurel Staffel
sound: Ken Ritchie
Peter Cushing, Christopher Lee, Jon Pertwee, Ingrid Pitt, Denholm Elliott, Nyree Dawn Porter, Joanna Dunham, John Bennett, Geoffrey Bayldon

The House That Would Not Die

USA 1970 74m Technicolor
A remote house takes over the soul of one of its new occupants.

Standard creepy house chiller, too flatly handled to be as effective as it might have been.
p: Steve Kibler for Aaron Spelling
w: Henry Farrell
d: John Llewellyn Moxey
ph: Fleet Southcott
m: Laurence Rosenthal
md: George Duning
ed: Art Seid
ad: Tracy Bousman
cos: Robert Harris, Sr, Jerrie Woods, Nolan Miller
sound: Barry Thomas
Barbara Stanwyck, Richard Egan, Michael Anderson Jr, Mabel Albertson

The House Where Evil Dwells

USA 1982 88m Technicolor
An American couple living in Japan find themselves affected by the deaths of their house's one-time occupants, involved in a love triangle, back in 1840.

Tediously overstretched (even at this length) ghost story, a poor attempt at a mainstream genre picture.
p: Martin B. Cohen for MGM/UA
w: Robert Suhosky
novel: James Hardiman
d: Kevin Connor
ph: Jacques Haitkin
m: Ken Thorne
ed: Barry Peters
ad: Yoshikazu Sano
cos: Shannon
sound: Teruhiko Arakawa
Susan George, Doug McClure, Edward Albert, Amy Barrett, Mako Hattori, Toshiyuki Sasaki, Henry Mitowa

How Awful About Alan *

USA 1970 74m Technicolor TVM
After a fire in which his father was killed, a young man goes blind and is later taunted by strange voices.

Predictable twist in the tail thriller which nevertheless keeps one watching.
p: George Edwards for Aaron Spelling
w: Henry Farrel from his novel
d: Curtis Harrington
ph: Fleet Southcott
m: Laurence Rosenthal
md: George Duning
ed: Richard Farrell, Art Seid
ad: Tracy Bousman
cos: Robert Harris, Sr, Jerrier Woods
sp: Joe Lombardi
sound: Gene Eliot, Bill Ford
Anthony Perkins, Julie Harris, Joan Hackett, Kent Smith, Gene Lawrence, Jeanette Howe, Robert H. Harris, Bill Bowles, Trent Dolan

How to Make a Monster

USA 1958 73m bw/Technicolor
A disgruntled make-up man, fired after twenty-five years, hypnotizes actors made up as monsters to murder his bosses.

Foolish low-budget romp, a sequel of sorts to *I Was a Teenage Werewolf* and *I Was a Teenage Frankenstein*, the make-ups from which it uses. Of passing interest for its studio backgrounds and for its last few moments which are in colour. The script and acting, however, are atrocious.
p: Herman Cohen for AIP
exec p: Samuel Z. Arkoff, James H. Nicholson
w: Kenneth Laughty, James H. Nicholson
d: Herbert L. Strock
ph: Maury Gertzman
m: Paul Dunlap
ed: Jerry Young
ad: Leslie Thomas
cos: Oscar Rodriguez
sound: Herman Lewis
make-up: Phil Scheer
Robert H. Harris, Paul Brinegar, Gary Conway, Gary Clarke, Dennis Cross

Howard, Tom

British special effects technician with countless credits to his name of varying quality, including *Blithe Spirit*, *Tom Thumb*, *Children of the Damned*, *The Gamma People*, *Battle Beneath the Earth* and *2001: A Space Odyssey*.
Genre credits:
Gorgo (1960), *The Haunting* (1963), *The Man Who Haunted Himself* (1970), *The Legend of Hell House* (1973)

Howarth, Alan

American composer and synth player who has co-written many film scores in association with director-composer John Carpenter, with whom he also performs them. His credits include *Dark Star* and *Escape from New York* (both with Carpenter).
Genre credits:
Halloween II (1981 - co-m), *Christine* (1983 - co-m), *Halloween III: Season of the Witch* (1983 - co-m), *Prince of Darkness* (1987 - co-m), *Halloween 4: The Return of Michael Myers* (1988 - m), *They Live* (1988 - co-m), *Retribution* (1988 - m), *Halloween 5: The Revenge of Michael Myers* (1989 - m), *Halloween 6: The Curse of Michael Myers* (1995 - m)

The Howling *

USA 1981 90m CFIcolor
A lady reporter goes to stay at a secluded health resort to recover from a nasty experience only to find herself surrounded by werewolves.

Quirky, well-mounted horror comic with excellent make-up effects during the transformation sequences. It was followed by *Howling II: Your Sister Is a Werewolf* (1985 - aka *Howling II: Stirba, Werewolf Bitch*), *Howling III: The Marsupials* (1987), *Howling IV: The Original Nightmare* (1988), *Howling V: The Rebirth* (1989), *Howling VI: The Freaks* (1991) and *Howling VII* (1994).
p: Michael Finnel, Jack Conrad for Avco Embassy/Wescom
w: John Sayles, Terence J. Winkles
novel: Gary Brander
d: JOE DANTE
ph: John Hora
m: PINO DONAGGIO
ed: Mark Goldblatt, Joe Dante
pd: Robert A. Burns, Steve Legler
cos: Jack Buehler
sp: Doug Beswick, Dave Allen
sound: Ken King
make-up effects: ROB BOTTIN, RICK BAKER
titles: Peter Kuran, Jack Rabin
Dee Wallace, Patrick Macnee, Dennis Dugan, Christopher Stone, John Carradine, Belinda Belaski, Dick Miller, Kevin McCarthy, Kenneth Tobey, Elizabeth Brooks, Slim Pickens

Howling II: Stirba, Werewolf Bitch see Howling II: Your Sister Is a Werewolf

Howling II: Your Sister Is a Werewolf

USA 1985 91m Technicolor
An occult expert and the brother of a werewolf victim travel to Transylvania to destroy the ringleaders.

Dismal sequel (the first, unfortunately, of many), lacking the humour and panache of its predecessor.
p: Steven Lane for EMI/Hemdale/Granite
w: Robert Sarno, Gary Brandner
d: Philippe Mora
ph: G. Stephenson
sp: Jack Bricker, Scott Wheeler, Steve Johnson
Christopher Lee, Reb Brown, Annie McEnroe, Ferdy Mayne, Sybil Danning, Marsha A. Hunt, Jimmy Naill

Howling III: The Marsupials

Australia 1987 94m Technicolor
A scientist discovers a pack of lycanthropic marsupials in the Australian outback.

Poorly judged blend of horror and humour, lacking the required touch to bring it off.
p: Charles Waterstreet, Philippe Mora for Baccanial
w/d: Philippe Mora
novel: Gary Brandner
ph: Louis Irving
m: Allan Zavod
ed: Lee Smith
pd: Ross Major
sp: Bob McCarron
Imogen Annesley, Barry Otto, Dasha Blahova, Barry Humphries, Frank Thring, Michael Pate, Ralph Cotterill

Howling IV: The Original Nightmare

GB 1988 92m Technicolor
A successful authoress is haunted by visions of a wolf-like creature whilst vacationing at her cottage retreat.

Howlingly inept fourth episode in a series that should have quit with number one. This is the pits.
p: Harry Alan Towers for Allied Entertainment
w: Clive Turner, Freddie Rowe
story: Clive Turner
d: John Hough
ph: Godfrey Godar
m: David George, Barrie Guard
ed: Claudia Finkle, Malcolm Burns-Errington
pd: Robbie Jenkinson
cos: Elaine Downing

sp: Noel Henry
sound: Colin McFarline
make-up effects: Steve Johnson, Lennie MacDonald
stunt co-ordinator: Red Ruiters
2nd unit d: Cedric Sundstorm
Romy Windsor, Michael T. Weiss, Antony Hamilton, Suzanne Sevreid, Lamya Derval, Norman Anstey, Kate Edwards, Clive Turner

Howling V: The Rebirth

USA 1989 96m Eastmancolor Dolby
Tourists visting an ancient castle are murdered one by one by a werewolf.

Tedious variation on a by now tired theme, whose plot seems to have been borrowed from *And Then There Were None*.
p: Clive Turner for Allied Vision
exec p: Edward Simons, Gary Barber, Stephen Lane, Robert Pringle
w: Clive Turner, Freddie Rowe
story: Clive Turner
d: Neal Sundstrom
ph: Arledge Armenaki
m: The Factory
ed: Claudia Finkle, Bill Swenson
pd: Nigel Triffitt
sound: Paul Sharkey, Clive Pendry, Hugh Strain
make-up effects: Max Effects
Ben Cole, Mark Siversen, William Shockley, Philip Davis, Elizabeth She, Clive Turner

Howling VI - The Freaks

US 1991 102m Foto-Kem Ultra Stereo
A werewolf drifter has a run in with a circus of monsters.

Marginally better entry in this seemingly endless series, but that isn't really saying much. Incredibly, it was followed by *Howling VII* (1994).
p: Robert Pringle for Allied Lane Pringle
exec p: Steve Lane, Edward Simons, Ronna B. Wallace
w: Kevin Rock
d: Hope Perello
ph: Edward Pei
m: Patrick Gleeson
ed: Adam Wolfe
pd: Richard Reams
cos: Lynn Marie Murdock
sp: John P. Cazin
sound: Charles Kelly
make-up effects: Todd Masters, Steve Johnson
Brendan Hughes, Michele Matheson, Sean Gregory, Carol Lynley, Antonio Fargas, Jered Barclay.

Hugo, Victor

French novelist whose 1831 novel *Notre Dame de Paris* (*The Hunchback of Notre*

Dame) has been filmed several times, most notably in 1923, 1939, 1956, 1978, 1982 and 1996 (Disney cartoon). His other filmed genre work includes *The Man Who Laughs* (1928), along with countless versions of *Les Miserables*. Also see *The Hunchback of Notre Dame*.

Hull, Henry (1890-1977)

American character actor with a variety of film roles to his credit, including appearances in *The Great Waltz*, *High Sierra* and *Objective Burma*, though he is perhaps best known to genre fans for playing the title role in Universal's *Werewolf of London*, which set the tone for their later *Wolf Man* series.
Genre credits:
Werewolf of London (1935), *Portrait of Jennie* (1948)

The Human Monster see Dark Eyes of London

Hume, Alan (1924-)

Prolific British cinematographer who began his career as a camera operator, especially on the *Carry Ons* and TV's *The Avengers*. Photographed many of the later *Carry Ons* before moving on to big international productions, including *Eye of the Needle*, *For Your Eyes Only*, *Return of the Jedi*, *Supergirl*, *Runaway Train*, *A View to a Kill* and *A Fish Called Wanda*.
Genre credits:
Svengali (1954 - cam op), *Kiss of the Vampire* (1964 - aka *Kiss of Evil*), *Dr Terror's House of Horrors* (1965), *From Beyond the Grave* (1973), *The Legend of Hell House* (1973), *The Land That Time Forgot* (1974), *Trial by Combat* (1976), *The Legacy* (1978 - co-ph), *The Hunchback of Notre Dame* (1982 - TVM), *Lifeforce* (1985), *Jack the Ripper* (1988 - TVM), *Eve of Destruction* (1991)

Humongous

USA 1981 93m Technicolor
Teenagers stranded on an island are murdered by a deformed maniac.
Standard horror fare with absolutely nothing new to offer.
p: Anthony Kramreithen for Manesco/Humongous
w: William Gray
d: Paul Lynch
ph: Brian R. R. Hebb
m: John Mills Cockell
ed: Nick Rotundo
ad: Carol Spier, Barbara Dunphy
Janet Julian, David Wallace, John Wildnman, Janit Baldwin, Joy Boushel

The Hunchback of Notre Dame

Victor Hugo's 1831 novel *Notre Dame de Paris* has been filmed several times down the decades. The most notable incarnations of Quasimodo have been by Lon Chaney (1923), Charles Laughton (1939), Anthony Quinn (1956), Warren Clarke (1978 - TVM) and Anthony Hopkins (1982 - TVM). 1989 brought a comedy, *Big Man on Campus* (aka *The Hunchback of UCLA*), whilst 1996 brought a musical cartoon version of the story from the Disney studio.

The Hunchback of Notre Dame *

USA 1923 119m bw silent
The deformed bellringer of Notre Dame cathedral falls in love with a gypsy dancer whom he later rescues from the hands of a tyrant.
The enormous sets and Chaney's performance are one thing, but the unimaginative handling and the length, especially to modern audiences, are another. Not quite the classic some would have it be, but with interesting moments for those who can stay the course.
p: Carl Laemmle for Universal
w: Percy Poore Sheehan, Edward T. Lowe Jr
novel: Victor Hugo
d: Wallace Worsley (and William Wyler)
ph: Robert S. Newhard, Tony Kornman
ed: Sidney Singerman, Edward Curtis, Maurice Pivar
ad: E. E. Sheeley, Sidney Ullman, Stephen Goosson
LON CHANEY, Patsy Ruth Miller, Norman Kerry, Kate Lester, Ernest Torrence, Gladys Brockwell

The Hunchback of Notre Dame ★★★★

USA 1939 117m bw
Quasimodo, the deformed bellringer of Notre Dame, rescues a beautiful gypsy girl from the gallows in return for a kindness she once showed him.
A splendid depiction of medieval life, with vast sets, milling crowds, lustrous photography, strong direction and a memorable star performance, all drawn together by a compelling narrative. One of the silver screen's greatest triumphs.
p: PANDRO S. BERMAN for RKO
w: SONYA LEVIEN, BRUNO FRANK
novel: Victor Hugo
d: WILLIAM DIETERLE
ph: JOSEPH H. AUGUST
m: ALFRED NEWMAN
ed: WILLIAM HAMILTON, ROBERT WISE
ad: VAN NEST POLGLASE, AL HERMAN
cos: WALTER PLUNKETT
sp: VERNON L. WALKER
sound: John E. Tribby
ch: Ernst Matray
make-up: Perc Westmore
CHARLES LAUGHTON, CEDRIC HARDWICKE, MAUREEN O'HARA, Edmond O'Brien, THOMAS MITCHELL, HARRY DAVENPORT, Walter Hampden, Alan Marshall, George Zucco, Katherine Alexander, Etienne Girardot, Rod La Rocque, Helene Whitney, Fritz Lieber

• Lon Chaney, the original Quasimodo, in the 1923 version of the much filmed Victor Hugo classic *The Hunchback of Notre Dame*.

• **Anthony Quinn as Quasimodo in the French remake of** *The Hunchback of Notre Dame.*

The Hunchback of Notre Dame

Fr/It 1956 106m Eastmancolor
Cinemascope
Hunchbacked bellringer Quasimodo falls in love with a gypsy girl called Esmerelda.

Poor and rather pointless international remake with a surprising star. Of very little abiding interest.
p: Robert Hakim, Raymond Hakim for Panitalia/Paris
w: Jacques Prevert, Jean Aurenche
novel: Victor Hugo
d: Jean Delannoy
ph: Michel Kelber
m: Georges Auric
Anthony Quinn, Gina Lollobrigida, Jean Danet, Alain Cuny, Robert Hirsch

The Hunchback of Notre Dame

GB 1982 96m Technicolor TVM
Inevitable television version of the oft told story. Sincere, but in no way comparable to the Laughton version.
p: Norman Rosemont for Columbia
w: John Gay
novel: Victor Hugo
d: Michael Tuchner
ph: Alan Hume
m: Ken Thorne
make-up: Christopher Tucker

Anthony Hopkins, John Gielgud, Derek Jacobi, Lesley Anne Down

The Hunger *

USA 1983 100m Metroclor Panavision
A beautiful vampire loses her lover and searches for a new one, but is killed in the process.

Visually arresting if rather silly modern day vampire yarn which plays like a hundred minute commercial.
p: Richard Shepherd for MGM/UA
w: Ivan Davis, Michael Thomas
novel: Whitney Strieber
d: TONY SCOTT
ph: STEPHEN GOLDBLATT
m: Michael Rubini, Denny Jaeger, David Lawson
md: Howard Blake
ed: Pamela Power
pd: BRIAN MORRIS
cos: Milena Canonero
sp: Graham Longhurst
sound: Clive Winter, Bill Rowe, Ray Merrin
make-up effects: DICK SMITH, CARL FULLERTON, Antony Clavet
titles: John O'Driscoll
add ph: Hugh Johnson, Tom Mangravite
Catherine Deneuve, David Bowie, Susan Sarandon, Cliff de Young, Beth Enlers, Dan Hedoya, Rufus Collins, Shane Rimmer, Bessie Love, Willem Dafoe

Hunter's Blood

USA 1987 101m colour
A group of city folk on an adventure weekend in the Oklahoma backwoods find themselves prey to a family of psychos.

Little more than a tedious low-budget reworking of *Deliverance* with added gore.
p: Myrl A. Schreibman
exec p: Judith F. Schuman
w: Emmett Aston
novel: Jere Cunningham
d: Robert C. Hughes
ph: Tom De Nove
m: John D'Andrea
songs: Dan Hamilton
ed: Barry Zetlin
ad: Douglas Forsmith
cos: Jacqueline Johnson
sp: Scott Haas
sound: Larry Hooberg

make-up effects: Douglas J. White, John R. Fifel, Allan A. Apone
stunt co-ordinator: Rawn Hutchinson
Sam Bottoms, Joey Travoltra, Kim Delaney, Clu Gulagher, Ken Swofford, Mayf Nutter

Huntley, Raymond (1904-1990)

British character actor usually in supercilious authority roles in countless films, including *Night Train to Munich* (aka *Night Train*), *Passport to Pimlico* and *Hobson's Choice.* Played Dracula on stage in the original London production, for which he had to supply his own evening dress!
Genre credits:
The Ghost of St Michael's (1941), *The Ghost Train* (1941), *The Mummy* (1959), *The Black Torment* (1964), *Symptoms* (1974)

Hush... Hush, Sweet Charlotte *

USA 1964 133m bw
A middle-aged Southern belle who believes she butchered her lover to death many years before begins to doubt her sanity when she is haunted by his headless corpse.

Grand Guignol à la *Whatever Happened to Baby Jane?* Not quite as effective as its predecessor, despite almost identical credits, though the stalwart cast give it their all. Joan Crawford turned down the role played by Olivia de Havilland following her fall-out with Davis on *Baby Jane.*
p: Robert Aldrich for TCF/Associates and Aldrich
w: Henry Farrell, Lukas Heller
story: Henry Farrell
d: Robert Aldrich
ph: JOSEPH BIROC
m: Frank de Vol
ly: Mack David
ed: Michael Luciano
ad: William Glasgow
cos: Norma Koch
sound: Herman Lewis, Bernard Freericks
BETTE DAVIS, OLIVIA DE HAVILLAND, Joseph Cotten, AGNES MOOREHEAD, CECIL KELLAWAY, Victor Buono, Bruce Dern, Mary Astor, William Marshall, George Kennedy

I

I Changed My Sex see Glen or Glenda

I Drink Your Blood
USA 1971 83m DeLuxe
A young boy avenges himself on the blood-drinking cultists who poisoned his grandfather by selling them rabies-injected pies in his mother's bakery.

This once notorious low-budget shocker is no longer as stomach-churning as it must once have been simply because it has been succeeded by far gorier films.
p: Jerry Gross for Jerry Gross Productions
w/d: David Durstob
ph: Jacques Demarceaux
m: Clay Pitts
ed: Lyman Hallowell
ad: Charles Baxter
sound: Stan Goldstein
make-up effects: Irvin Carlton
Bhaskar, Jadine Wong, Lynn Lowry, Richard Bowler, Elizabeth Manner-Brooks, Ronda Fultz

I Led Two Lives see Glen or Glenda

I Married a Monster from Outer Space *
USA 1958 78m bw
A young housewife discovers that her husband's body has been taken over by an alien whose people are intent on colonizing Earth.

Despite a silly title and some bad lapses in continuity, this is an otherwise acceptable addition to the cycle of paranoid fifties sci-fi shockers.
p: Gene Fowler for Paramount
w: Louis Vittes
d: Gene Fowler
ph: Haskell Boggs
m: no credit given
ed: George Tomasini
ad: Hal Pereira, Henry Bumstead
sp: John P. Fulton
sound: Charles Granzbach, Phil Wilsdon
Tom Tyron, Gloria Talbot, Peter Baldwin, Robert Ivers, Chuck Wassil, Valerie Allen, Ty Hungerford, Ken Lynch, Alan Dexter, John Eldredge, James Anderson, Jean Carson, Maxie Rosenbloom

I Married a Witch **
USA 1942 82m bw
A Salem witch returns to haunt the descendant of the Puritan who sent her to the stake but she accidentally drinks a love potion and falls in love with him.

An expert mixture of comedy, romance, fantasy and zaniness, smartly assembled and enjoyably performed by a cast of reliables.
p: René Clair for UA/Cinema Guild
w: ROBERT PIROSH, MARC CONNELLY
story: Thorne Smith, Norman Matson
d: RENE CLAIR
ph: Ted Tatzlaff
m: Roy Webb
ed: Eda Warren
ad: Hans Dreier, Ernest Fetge
cos: Edith Head
sp: Gordon Jennings
sound: Harry Mills, Richard Olson
FREDRIC MARCH, VERONICA LAKE, CECIL KELLAWAY, ROBERT BENCHLEY, SUSAN HAYWARD, Elizabeth Patterson, Robert Warwick

I, Monster *
GB 1970 75m Eastmancolor
A Victorian doctor experiments on himself with a new drug that gradually transforms him into a raging monster.

Carefully mounted and commendably brief variation on Dr Jekyll and Mr Hyde, originally shot, but not released, in 3D (which explains why so many things lurch towards the camera). Despite its qualities, one does not remember it with fondness.
p: Milton Subotsky, Max J. Rosenberg for Amicus
w: Milton Subotsky
d: Stephen Weeks
ph: Moray Grant
m: Carl Davis
ed: Peter Tanner
ad: Tony Curtis
cos: Bridget Sellers
sound: Buster Ambler, Nolan Roberts
make-up: Harry Frampton, Peter Frampton
Christopher Lee, Peter Cushing, Mike Raven, Michael Hurndall, George

Merritt, Kenneth J. Warren, Susan Jameson

I Wake Up Screaming *
USA 1941 79m bw
A girl joins forces with an innocent murder suspect in order to clear him of the murder of her glamorous sister.

Good-looking mystery thriller, somehow very typical of its period.
p: Milton Sperling for TCF
w: Dwight Taylor
novel: Steve Fisher
d: H. BRUCE HUMBERSTONE
ph: EDWARD CRONJAGER
md: Cyril Mockridge
ad: Richard Day, Nathan Juran
cos: Gwen Wakeling
sound: Bernard Freericks, Roger Heman
Betty Grable, VICTOR MATURE, Carole Landis, LAIRD CREGAR, William Gargan, Alan Mowbray, Allyn Joslyn, Elisha Cook Jr

I Walked with a Zombie *
USA 1943 68m bw
A nurse goes to the Caribbean to look after the wife of a plantation owner only to discover that voodoo may have had a hand in her illness.

Thin but atmospheric entry in the Lewton gallery of horrors with echoes of Jane Eyre and the later Wide Sargasso Sea.
p: VAL LEWTON for RKO
w: Curt Siodmak, Ardel Wray
story: Inez Wallace
d: JACQUES TOURNEUR
ph: J. Roy Hunt
m: Roy Webb
md: Constantin Bakaleinikoff
ed: Mark Robson
ad: Albert S. D'Agostino, Walter E. Keller
sound: John C. Grubb
Frances Dee, Tom Conway, James Ellison, James Bell, Christine Gordon, Edith Barrett, Sir Lancelot

I Was a Teenage Frankenstein
US 1957 72m bw/colour
Professor Frankenstein assembles a human being from the bodies of teenage car crash victims.

ZOMBIE

ONE OF PRODUCER VAL LEWTON'S CLASSIC RKO HORRORS, *I Walked with a Zombie* was actually a variation on Charlotte Bronte's *Jane Eyre*.

SCREEN PLAY BY CURT SIODMAK AND ARDEL WRAY

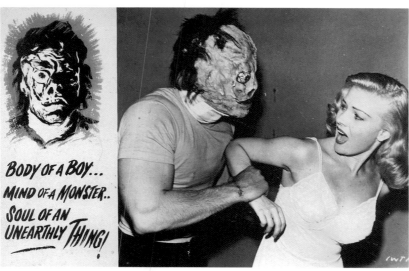

**BODY OF A BOY...
MIND OF A MONSTER..
SOUL OF AN
UNEARTHLY THING!**

• Promotional lobby card featuring Gary Conway as the monster in *I Was a Teenage Frankenstein*.

Disappointingly talkative low-budget horror hokum in the fifties manner, the last few minutes of which are in colour.
p: Herman Cohen for American International/Santa Rosa
exec p: James H. Nicholson, Samuel Z. Arkoff
w: Kenneth Langtry
d: Herbert J. Strock
ph: Lothrop Worth
m: Paul Dunlap
ed: Jerry Young
ad: Leslie Thomas
cos: Einar Bourman
sound: Al Overton
make-up: Philip Scheer
Whit Bissell, Gary Conway, Phyllis Coates, Robert Burton, George Lynn, John Cliff, Marshall Bradford

I Was a Teenage Werewolf
USA 1957 76m bw
A college student periodically turns into a werewolf.

Artless low grade hokum, though not the worst example of its kind. A cult item in some circles, it inspired two sequels: *I Was a Teenage Frankenstein* (1957) and *How to Make a Monster* (1958). It was more or less remade in 1985 as the comedy *Teen Wolf*.
p: Herman Cohen for AIP/Sunset
w: Ralph Thornton
d: Gene Fowler Jr
ph: Joseph La Shelle
m: Paul Dunlap, Jerry Blain
ed: George Gittens
ad: Leslie Thomas
cos: Oscar Rodruiguez
sound: James S. Thomson
make-up: Philip Scheer

Michael Landon, Yvonne Lime, Whit Bissell, Tony Marshall, Dawn Richard, Barney Phillips, Ken Miller

If a Body Meets a Body
USA 1945 20m bw
In order for Curly to claim an inheritance, The Three Stooges have to spend the night in a spooky house.

Better than average Three Stooges romp.
p: Jules White for Columbia
w: Jack White
story: Gil Pratt
d: Jules White
ph: Benjamin Kline
ed: Charles Hochberg
ad: Charles Clague
Curly Howard, Larry Fine, Moe Howard, Theodore Lorch, Fred Kelsey

Ifukube, Akira (1914-)
Japanese composer who has scored many of Japan's monster epics involving Godzilla and Rodan, etc.
Genre credits:
Godzilla, King of the Monsters (1954 - aka *Gojira*), *Rodan* (1957), *King Kong vs Godzilla* (1963 - aka *Kingu Kongu Tai Gojira*), *Destroy All Monsters* (1969 - *Kaiju Soshingeki*), *Yog, Monster from Space* (1971), *The Revenge of Mecha Godzilla* (1977)

Images
GB 1972 101m Technicolor Panavision
A woman has trouble separating her real life from her daydreams.

An interesting though finally defeating psycho drama in which the audience will probably find themselves as baffled as the leading lady.
p: Tommy Thompson for Lion's Gate/Hemdale
w/d: Robert Altman
ph: Vilmos Zsigmond
m: John Williams

• Can that really be Michael Landon underneath all the yak hair? Though *I Was a Teenage Werewolf* may not be a classic, it does have its followers, and its success provoked two sequels: *I Was a Teenage Frankenstein* and *How to Make a Monster*.

ed: Graeme Clifford
pd: Leon Erickson
SUSANNAH YORK, Rene Auberjonois, Marcel Bozzuffi, Hugh Millais, Cathryn Harrison

In Possession
GB 1984 74m Technicolor TVM
A married couple find themselves experiencing a series of strange visions.

Perhaps the most tolerable of the *Hammer House of Mystery and Suspense* tele-thrillers.
p: Roy Skeggs for Hammer/TCF
w: Michael J. Bird
d: Val Guest
ph: Brian West
m: Paul Patterson
md: Philip Martell
ed: Peter Weatherley
ad: Carolyn Scott
Carol Lynley, Christopher Cazenove, Bernard Kay, Vivienne Burgess, Judy Loe, David Healey

In the Mouth of Madness *
USA 1994 94m Deluxe Dolby
An insurance investigator is hired to search for a missing horror writer, Sutter Kane, only to find himself caught up in a fictional world of the author's devising.

Slick horror anecdote which doesn't quite live up to its original promise, though it passes the time well enough.
p: Sandy King for New Line
w/exec p: Michael De Luca
d: John Carpenter
ph: Gary K. Kibbe
m: John Carpenter, Jim Lang
ed: Edward Warschilka
pd: Jeff Steven Ginn
sp: Bruce Nicholson, ILM
sound: Oliver A. Langevin
make-up effects: Robert Kurtzman, Howard Berger, Gregory Nicolette
stunt co-ordinator: Jeff Imada
Sam Neill, Charlton Heston, Julie Carmen, David Warner, Jurgen Prochnow (as Sutter Kane), John Glover, Bernie Casey, Peter Jason

Incense for the Damned see
Bloodsuckers

The Incredible Melting Man
USA 1977 84mm Movielab
An astronaut begins to melt upon his return to earth following a trip to Saturn.

The Quatermass Experiment twenty years on, with added gore in the make-up effects. Still very much a B item, though.
p: Max J. Rosenberg for AIP/Quartet
w/d: William Sachs
ph: Willy Curtis

m: Arlon Ober
make-up effects: Rick Baker
Alex Rebar, Myron Healey, Michael Alldredge, Burr De Benning, Rainbeaux Smith, Jonathan Demme

Incubus
Canada 1981 93m Technicolor
A homicidal maniac turns out to be a devil trying to propagate a race on earth.

Reasonably well crafted but overstretched shocker with a twist ending that's hardly worth waiting for.
p: Mark Boyman, John M. Eckert for Mark Films/John M. Eckert Productions
exec p: Stephen Friedman
w: George Frankling
d: John Hough
ph: Albert J. Dunk
m: Stanley Myers
ed: George Appleby
pd: Ted Watkins
John Cassavetes, Kerrie Keane, Helen Hughes, Eric Flannery, Duncan McIntosh, John Ireland

Inferno *
It 1980 104m Technicolor Technovision Dolby
A young woman is murdered when she discovers that her apartment building is one of three gateways to hell.

Confusingly plotted but slickly directed occult horror with excellent set pieces and some dazzling camera work. One of Argento's key films.
p: Claudio Argento for Roduzzioni Intersound
exec p: Salvatore Argento
w: Dario Argento

d: DARIO ARGENTO
ph: Romano Abani
m: KEITH EMERSON
ed: Franco Fraticelli
pd: GIUSEPPE BASSAN
cos: Massimo Lentini
sp: Germano Natali
sound: Francesco Groppioni, Romano Pampaloni
ass d: Lamberto Bava
underwater sequence: Lorenzo Battaglia
Leigh McLoskey, Eleanor Giorgi, Gabrielle Lavia, Veronica Lazar, Leopoldo Mastelloni, Irene Miracle, Daria Nicolodi, Alida Valli

Inseminoid *
GB 1980 97m Technicolor
A female astronaut is impregnated by an alien and goes on the rampage when others on the crew try to help her.

Reasonable exploitation piece, not too badly done, though it won't be to everyone's taste.
p: Richard Gordon, David Speechley for Jupiter
exec p: Sir Run Run Shaw
w: Nick Maley, Gloria Maley
d: Norman J. Warren
ph: John Metcalfe
m: John Scott
ed: Peter Boyle
pd: Hayden Pearce
make-up effects: Nick Malley
Judy Geeson, Stephanie Beecham, Robin Clarke, Jennifer Ashley, Stephen Grives, Barry Houghton, Victoria Tennant

Interview with the Vampire *
USA 1994 122m Technicolor Dolby

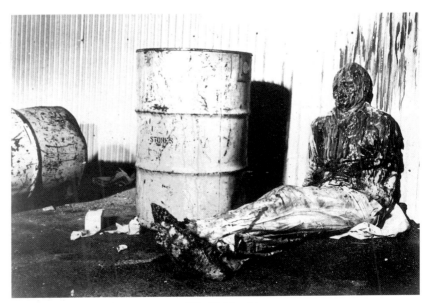

• **A gooey moment from** *The Incredible Melting Man.*

The Intruder Within

A vampire recalls his centuries-long existence to a young reporter.

Expensive but slow moving and overly talkative version of the Anne Rice novel, good to look at but ultimately a bit of a yawn. The casting of Tom Cruise as the vampire Lestat caused some controversy, with Anne Rice being particularly vocal in her condemnation, though she later publicly recanted.
p: David Geffen, Stephen Woolley for Geffen
w: Anne Rice from her novel
d: Neil Jordan
ph: Philippe Rousselot
m: Elliot Goldenthal
pd: Dante Ferrati
make-up effects: Stan Winston
Tom Cruise, Brad Pitt, Antonio Banderas, Stephen Rea, Christian Slater, Kirsten Dunst, Roger Lloyd Pack

The Intruder Within
USA 1981 96m Technicolor TVM
Workers on an oil-rig are menaced by a humanoid sea monster.

In other words, *Alien* on an oilrig. Pretty awful.
p: Neil T. Maffeo for ABC
exec p: John Furia Jr, Barry Orringer
w: Ed Waters
d: Peter Carter
ph: James Pergola
m: Gil Melle
Chad Everett, Joseph Bottoms, Jennifer Warren, Rockne Tarkington, Paul Larsen, James Hayden

Invasion of Planet X see Invasion of the Astro Monsters

Invasion of the Astro Monsters
Japan 1965 94m Fujicolor
Earth helps Planet X overcome a three-headed monster by sending Godzilla and Rodin to sort things out.

Hilarious Japanese monster epic of the men-in-rubber-suits variety.
p: Tomoyuki Tanaka for Benedict/Henry G. Saperstein Enterprises
exec p Reuben Bercovitch
w: Shinichi Sekizawa
d: Ishiro Honda, Eiji Tsuburaya
ph: Hajime Konzami
md: Akira Ifuchine
ed: Rhyohei Fuji
ad: Takeo Kita
sp: Sadamas Arikawa and others
sound: Hiroshi Mulayma, Wataski Kinimara
Nick Adams, Akira Takadara, Kumi Nizumo, Akira Kubo, Keiko Sawai, Jun Tazaki, Goro Naya

Invasion of the Body Snatchers **

USA 1956 80m bw SuperScope
The small American township of Santa Mira is invaded by pods from outer space which have the ability to duplicate humans.

Much revered science-fiction thriller which, after a careful start, builds to scenes of genuine alarm.
p: Walter Wanger for Allied Artists
w: Daniel Mainwairing, Sam Peckinpah (uncredited)
novel: JACK FINNEY
d: DON SIEGEL
ph: Ellsworth Fredericks
m: Carmen Dragon
ed: Robert S. Eisen
ad: Ted Haworth
sp: Milt Rice
sound: Ralph Butler
KEVIN MCCARTHY, Dana Wynter, Larry Gates, King Donovan, Carolyn Jones, Virginia Christie, Sam Peckinpah, Pat O'Malley

Invasion of the Body Snatchers ***
USA 1978 115m Technicolor Panavision Dolby
Strange pods from outer space threaten the survival of mankind.

Clever, unsettling, technically adroit retelling of the 1956 classic, here relocated to the city of San Francisco. A must for science-fiction buffs.
p: Robert H. Solo for UA/Solofilm
w: W. D. RICHETER
novel: JACK FINNEY
d: PHILIP KAUFMAN
ph: MICHAEL CHAPMAN
m: Danny Zeitlin
ed: DOUGLAS STEWART
pd: Charles Rosen
cos: Agnes Anne Rogers
sp: Ron Dexter, Howard Preston
make-up effects: Tom Burman, Edouardo Henriques
sound: Art Rochester
stunt co-ordinator: David Ellis
Donald Sutherland, Brooke Adams, Leonard Nimoy, Jeff Goldblum, Veronica Cartwright, Art Hindle, Kevin McCarthy (cameo, reprising his role in the 1956 version), Don Siegel (cameo), Leila Goldoni, Robert Duvall (uncredited cameo)

Invasion of the Body Snatchers (1993) see Body Snatchers

Invasion of the Saucermen
USA 1957 88m bw
Aliens with the ability to kill by injecting their victims with pure alcohol land in a small American township.

Would-be comic low-budget sci-fi horror with a notable lack of genuine wit though quite a few unintentional laughs.
p: James H. Nicholson, Robert J. Gurney Jr, for AIP/Malibu
exec p: Samuel Z. Arkoff
w: Al Martin, Robert J. Gurney Jr
story: Paul Fairman
d: Edward L. Cahn
ph: Fred West
m: Ronald Stein
ed: Ronald Sinclair, Charles Gross Jr
ad: Don Ament
cos: Marjory Corso
sp: Paul Blaisdell, Alex Weldon
sound: Phil Mitchell
Steve Terrell, Frank Gorshin, Gloria Castillo, Ed Nelson, Raymond Hatton

Invisibility
Invisibility has provided plenty of opportunities for horrific fun in the movies down the decades, most notably via adaptations and variations on H. G. Wells' 1897 novel *The Invisible Man*, though the cinema's first encounter with invisiblity came a year before Wells' book was published. This was in the form of Georges Melies' 1896 trick film *The Vanishing Lady*, which he followed in 1904 with *Siva the Invisible*. Only a few other silent films used the theme of invisibility as a subject, and it wasn't until 1933 that the definitive adaptation of Wells' book appeared care of Universal and director James Whale, the part of Jack Griffin, the 'Invisible One', turning Claude Rains into a star over night. As with *Dracula*, *Frankenstein*, *The Mummy* and *The Wolf Man*, Universal followed this film up with a number of sequels, all of which inevitably led to an encounter with Abbott and Costello in the fifties, since when invisibility has had a fairly chequered movie career. The most notable of recent efforts is the $40m adaptation of H. F. Saint's comic novel, *Memoirs of an Invisible Man*. Surprisingly, Hammer never tackled the subject.
Genre filmography:
The Vanishing Lady (1896), *Siva the Invisible* (1904), *The Invisible Fluid* (1908), *The Invisible Thief* (1909), *The Invisible Cyclist* (1912), *The Invisible Man* (1933), *The Vanishing Shadow* (1934 - serial), *The Invisible Ray* (1935), *The Invisible Man Returns* (1940), *The Invisible Woman* (1941), *The Invisible Agent* (1942), *The Invisible Man's Revenge* (1944), *Abbott and Costello Meet Frankenstein* (1948 - gag cameo at the end of the film), *Abbott and Costello Meet the Invisible Man* (1951), *The Invisible Avenger* (1958), *El Hombre que Logro ser Invisible* (1958), *Invisible Invaders* (1959), *Los Invisibles* (1961), *Der Unsichtbare*

(1963), *Now You See Him, Now You Don't* (1972), *The Invisible Man* (1975 - TVM), *Mr Superinvisible* (1976), *The Gemini Man* (1976 -TVM), *The Invisible Strangler* (1976), *The Invisible Woman* (1983 - TVM), *The Invisible Kid* (1987), *The Invisible Maniac* (1990), *Memoirs of an Invisible Man* (1992), *Invisible - The Chronicles of Benjamin Knight* (1993)

Invisible Agent
USA 1942 84m bw
An American uses an invisibility potion to help him become a spy in Nazi Germany.

Light hearted wartime fantasy that is played more for laughs than thrills. It passes the time.
p: George Waggner for Universal
w: Curt Siodmak
d: Edwin L. Marin
ph: Lester White
m: Hans J. Salter
ed: Edward Curtiss
ad: Jack Otterson
sp: JOHN P. FULTON
Jon Hall, Ilona Massey, Peter Lorre, Cedric Hardwicke, Edward Bromberg, John Litel, Albert Basserman, Holmes Herbert

The Invisible Man **
USA 1933 71m bw
A scientist goes mad after taking a potion that makes him invisible, and he is finally tracked down in the snow.

Dated but generally sprightly horror comic, one of several that established Universal as the major purveyors of such entertainments during the thirties and forties. Gaffe spotters should note that though the Invisible Man is obviously naked during his pursuit through the snow, he leaves behind shoeprints instead of footprints!
p: Carl Laemmle Jr for Univeral
w: R. C. SHERIFF, PHILIP WYLIE
novel: H. G. WELLS
d: JAMES WHALE
ph: Arthur Edeson, John Mescall
m: W. Frank Harling (uncredited)
ed: Maurice Pivar, Ted Kent
ad: Charles D. Hall
sp: JOHN P. FULTON
sound: no credit given
CLAUDE RAINS (as Jack Griffin, the 'Invisible One'), Gloria Stuart, William Harrigan, Dudley Digges, Una O'Connor, Henry Travers, Donald Stuart, E. E. Clive, Merle Tottenham, Holmes Herbert, Walter Brennan, John Carradine, Dwight Frye

The Invisible Man
USA 1975 74m Technicolor TVM
A scientist working on a teleportation experiment discovers that the side effects include invisibility.

Mild update of the Wells novel with the expected modern day military angle.
p: Steve Bochco for Universal/NBC/Silverston
exec p: Harve Bennett
w: Steven Bochco
novel: H. G. WELLS
d: Robert Michael Lewis
ph: Enzo A. Martinelli
m: Richard Clements
ed: Richard Belding, Robert F. Shugrue
ad: Frank T. Smith
sp: Universal Title
sound: Terry Kellum
David McCallum, Melinda Fee, Jackie Cooper, Henry Darrow, Arch Johnson

The Invisible Man Returns *
USA 1940 81m bw
A man wrongly accused of murder uses an invisibility potion to help him track down the real culprit.

Acceptable low-budget sequel with improved special effects. Price played the invisible man once more in a vocal gag cameo at the end of *Abbott and Costello Meet Frankenstein*.
p: Ken Goldsmith for Universal
w: Curt Siodmak, Lester Cole
story: Joe May, Curt Siodmak
d: Joe May
ph: Milton Krasner
m: Hans J. Salter, Frank Skinner
ed: Frank Gross
ad: Jack Otterson, Martin Obzina
cos: Vera West
sp: JOHN P. FULTON
sound: Bernard B. Brown, William Hedgcock
Vincent Price, Cedric Hardwicke, John Sutton, Nan Gray, Cecil Kellaway, Alan Napier, Forrester Harvey

The Invisible Man's Revenge
USA 1944 77m bw
A psychopath escapes a mental home, returns to England and hides out with an old friend who has perfected an invisibility potion.

Adequate second feature thriller that marked the tailing off of Universal's *Invisible Man* series until Abbott and Costello met him in 1951.
p: Ford Beebe for Universal
w: Bertram Millhauser
d: Forde Beebe
ph: Milton Krasner
m: Hans J. Salter
ed: Saul Goodkind
ad: John B. Goodman, Harold H. MacArthur
cos: Vera West
sp: JOHN P. FULTON
sound: Bernard B. Brown, William Hedgcock
Jon Hall, Leon Errol, Evelyn Ankers, John Carradine, Alan Curtis, Gale Sondergaard, Halliwell Hobbes, Doris Lloyd, Ian Wolfe

•The authorities finally track down the Invisible One (Claude Rains) in director James Whale's horror comic *The Invisible Man*. But if he's naked, why are the footprints of shoes instead of feet?

The Invisible Woman *

USA 1941 72m bw
A scientist advertises for a guinea pig to
try out his new invisibility potion.

Wacky comedy variation on the old
theme with everyone trying hard. On
the whole, quite likeable.
p: Burt Kelly for Universal
w: Robert Lees, Fred Rinaldo, Gertrude
Purcell
story: Curt Siodmak, Joe May
d: A. Edward Sutherland
ph: Elwood Bredell
md: Charles Previn
ed: Frank Gross
ad: Jack Otterson, Richard H. Riedel
cos: Vera West
sp: John P. Fulton
sound: Bernard B. Brown, Joseph Lapis
Virginia Bruce, JOHN BARRYMORE,
John Howard, CHARLIE RUGGLES,
MARGARET HAMILTON, Anne Nagel,
Maria Montes, Oscar Homolka, Charles
Lane, Mary Gordon

Invitation to Hell

USA 1984 96m Technicolor TVM
Having moved to a new city and a new
job a computer expert and his family
find themselves in mortal danger.

Bland tele-thriller somewhere in the
wake of *Poltergeist*.
p: Robert N. Sertner for
ABC/Moonlight
exec p: Frank Von Zerneck
w: Richard Rothstein
d: Wes Craven
ph: Dean Cundey
m: Sylvester Levay
ed: Gregory Prange, Ann Mills
ad: Hub Braden
Robert Urich, Joanna Cassidy, Susan
Lucci, Joe Regalbuto, Kevin McCarthy,
Barrett Oliver, Bill Erwin

The Island

USA 1980 115m Technicolor Panavision
A newspaper reporter and his son find
themselves at the mercy of savage
modern day pirates after their plane
crash-lands on a tropical island.

Misconceived blood and thunder,
as senseless as it is brutal. An
embarrassment for all concerned, who
were no doubt hoping for another *Jaws*-
sized hit.
p: Richard Zanuck, David Brown for
Universal
w: Peter Benchley from his novel
d: Michael Ritchie
ph: Henri Decae
m: Ennio Morricone
ed: Richard A. Harris
pd: Dale Hennesy
cos: Ann Roth
sp: Albert Whitlock

sound: Bernard Bats, Swede Sorensen,
David Parker
stunt co-ordinator: Ted Grossman
Michael Caine, David Warner, Angela
Punch-McGregor, Frank Middlemass,
Dudley Sutton, Colin Jeavons, Don
Henderson, Zakes Mokae, Brad Sullivan,
Jeffrey Frank

The Island of Dr Moreau *

USA 1977 98m Movielab
On a remote Pacific island, a mad
doctor turns animals into humans but
they revolt and kill him.

Flat and rather lifeless version of a
story previously filmed as *Island of Lost
Souls* in 1932. Lacklustre performances
don't help matters much, either.
p: Skip Steloff, John Temple-Smith for
AIP/Cinema 77
exec p: Samuel Z. Arkoff, Sandy
Howard
w: John Herman Shaner, Al Ramrus
novel: H. G. Wells
d: Don Taylor
ph: Gerry Fisher
m: Laurence Rosenthal
ed: Marion Rosenthal
pd: Philip Jeffries
cos: Richard La Motte
sp: Cliff Wenger
sound: David Hildyard
make-up: John Chambers, Tom Burman,
Dan Striepeke
2nd unit ph: Ronnie Taylor
stunt co-ordinator: Erik Cord
Burt Lancaster, Michael York, Barbara
Carrera, Nigel Davenport, Richard
Basehart, Nick Cravat, Bob Ozman,
Gary Baxley, John Gillespie, David Cass

Island of Terror

GB 1966 89m Eastmancolor
A remote Irish island is threatened by
monsters that get their nourishment
from bone.

Minor low-budget horror with
unconvincing monsters. Also see *Night of
the Big Heat*, a similarly plotted film
which appeared the following year with
much the same talent.
p: Tom Blakeley for Planet
w: Edward Andrew Mann, Alan Ramsen
d: Terence Fisher
ph: Reg Wyer
m: Malcolm Lockyer, Barry Gray
ed: Thelma Connell
ad: John St John Earl
cos: Rosemary Burrows
sp: John St John Earl, Billy Partleton,
Michael Albrechtson
sound: Bob McPhee
Peter Cushing, Edward Judd, Carole
Gray, Eddie Byrne, Sam Kydd, Niall
MacGinnis

Island of the Burning Damned
see Night of the Big Heat

Island of the Living Dead see
Zombie Flesh-Eaters

Isle of the Dead *

USA 1945 72m bw
In 1912, a group of people stranded on
a Balkan island fear that one of their
number may be a vorvolaka, a form of
vampire.

Atmospheric but otherwise tediously
drawn out chiller with just a couple of
mild frissons towards the end.
p: Val Lewton for RKO
w: Ardel Wray, Josef Mischel
d: Mark Robson
ph: Jack Mackenzie
m: Leigh Harline
md: Constantin Bakaleinikoff
ed: Lyle Boyer
ad: Albert S. D'Agostino, Walter E.
Keller
cos: Edward Stevenson
sound: Jean L. Speak, Jack J. Gross
Boris Karloff, Ellen Drew, Helene
Thimig, Marc Cramer, Katherine
Emery, Alan Napier, Jason Robards

Isn't It Shocking? **

USA 1973 74m Technicolor TVM
When a series of fatal heart attacks
plague the senior citizens of a small
New England township the local sheriff
gradually realizes that there is a
murderer on the loose.

Engagingly etched and performed
black comedy-thriller, something of a
rarity from American television.
w: LANE SLATE
d: JOHN BADHAM
ph: Jack Woolf
m: David Shire
ed: Henry Berman
ad: Joseph M. Alves Jr
cos: John S. Perry, Betsy Cox
sound: Donald F. Johnson, Don Bassman
ALAN ALDA, Lloyd Nolan, Louise
Lasser, Ruth Gordon, Edmond O'Brien,
Will Geer, Dorothy Tristan, Pat Quinn,
Liam Dunn, Michael Powell, Jacqueline
Allan McClure

It *

USA 1990 2x96m Technicolor TVM
Seven children find their lives
threatened by a demonic clown that also
returns to haunt them thirty years later.

Better than average King adaptation
that, despite a couple of longeurs in its
second segment, generally holds one's
interest.
p: Matthew O'Connor for Lorimar/
Konigsberg-Sanitsky
w: Lawrence D. Cohen, Tommy Lee Wallace

novel: Stephen King
d: Tommy Lee Wallace
ph: Richard Leitman
m: Richard Bellis
ed: Robert F. Shugrue, David Blangsted
pd: Douglas Higgins
cos: Monique Stranan
sp: Gene Warren Jr, Fantasy II
sound: Rick Patton
make-up effects: Bart J. Mixon
Richard Thomas, John Ritter, Anette
O'Toole, Tim Curry, Dennis
Christopher, Olivia Hussey, Michael
Cole, Sheila Moore, Harry Anderson,
Richard Masur, Tim Reid

It Came from Beneath the Sea

USA 1955 79m bw
An atomic powered submarine disturbs
a giant octopus which subsequently
goes on the rampage and half destroys
San Francisco.

Hackneyed low-budget monster flick
in the fifties tradition. Close inspection
reveals the creature to have only six tentacles, owing to the restricted budget.
p: Charles H. Schneer for Columbia
exec p: Sam, Katzman
w: George Worthington Yates, Hal
Smith
story: George Worthington Yates
d: Robert Gordon
ph: Henry Freulich
md: Mischa Bakaleinikoff
ed: Jerome Thoms
ad: Paul Palmentola
sp: Ray Harryhausen
sound: Josh Westmoreland
Kenneth Tobey, Faith Domergue, Ian
Keith, Donald Curtis, Harry Lauter,
Chuck Griffiths

It Came from Hollywood

USA 1982 80m bw/colour
A selection of clips from some of the
worst science fiction and horror movies
ever made.

Initially amusing pot-pourri of awful-
ness that eventually outstays its welcome.
p: Susan Strausberg, Jeff Stein for
Paramount
w: Diana Olsen
d: Malcolm Leo, Andrew Solt
Introduced by: Dan Aykroyd, John

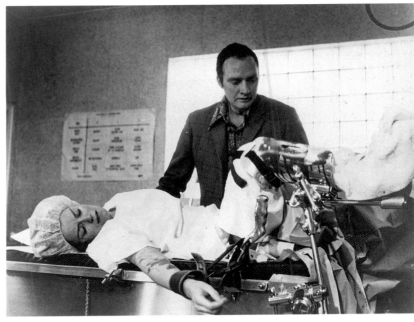

• A scene of post natal trauma in writer-director Larry Cohen's *It's Alive*.

Candy, Cheech and Chong, Gilda
Radner

It! The Terror from Beyond Space

USA 1958 69m bw
In 1973 (!), astronauts returning from
Mars are picked off one by one by an
alien which thrives on blood.

Hilariously dated yet fairly endearing
science fiction nonsense whose premise
resurfaced twenty years later in *Alien*.
p: Robert E. Kent for Vogue
w: Jerome Bixby
d: Edward L. Cahn
ph: Kenneth Peach
m: Paul Sawtell, Bert Shefter
ed: Grant Whytock
ad: William Glasgow
cos: Jack Masters
sp: Robert Carlisle
sound: Al Overton
Marshall Thompson, Shawn Smith, Paul
Langton, Ann Doran, Kim Spalding,
Dabbs Greer, Richard Hervey, Tom

Carney, Ray 'Crash' Corrigan (as It)

It's Alive

USA 1974 91m Technicolor
A woman gives birth to a mutant baby
which goes on a murderous rampage.

Over padded horror comic whose
effective moments are rather too few
and far between. A box-office success, it
was followed by *It Lives Again* (aka *It's
Alive 2* - 1978) and *It's Alive III: Island of
the Alive* (1988).
p: Larry Cohen for Warner/Larco
w/d: Larry Cohen
ph: Fenton Hamilton
m: Bernard Herrmann
ed: Peter Honess
ad: no credit given
sound: Robert Biggart, Patrick Somerset
titles: Gary Leonard
make-up effects: Rick Baker
John Ryan, Sharon Farrell, Andrew
Duggan, James Dixon, Guy Stockwell,
Michael Ansara, Robert Emhardt,
William Wellman, Shamus Locke

JUST AS *PSYCHO* PUT A WHOLE GENERATION OFF TAKING SHOWERS, *Jaws* did the same for bathing in the sea. It also brought new meaning to the word blockbuster and put the name of its then little-known director on the map. Whatever became of Steven Spielberg?

Jabberwocky *
GB/USA 1977 101m Technicolor
In the Middle Ages, a cooper's apprentice manages to slay a monster.

Medieval romp which can now be seen to be very typical of its director's pictorially cluttered style, with the usual emphasis on schoolboy scatology.
p: Sandy Lieberson for Umbrella Entertainment Productions
exec p: John Goldstone
w: Charles Alverson, Terry Gilliam
d: TERRY GILLIAM
ph: Terry Bedford
m: De Wolfe
ed: Michael Bradsell
pd: ROY SMITH
cos: Hazel Pethig, Charles Knode
sp: John Brown
sound: Garth Marshall
Michael Palin, Max Wall, Warren Mitchell, Harry H. Corbett, Deborah Fallender, John Le Mesurier, Bernard Bresslaw, Rodney Bewes, Annette Badland, Brenda Cowling, Dave Prowse, Peter Cellier, Derek Francis, Bryan Pringle, Simon Williams, Frank Williams, Terry Gilliam, Brian Glover, Graham Crowden, Gordon Kaye, Neil Innes, Janine Duvitsky

Jack Be Nimble
New Zealand 93m Eastmancolor Dolby
A brother and sister, separated after being deserted by their parents, later join forces to avenge themselves on those who have done them wrong.

Uninvolving horror drama with supernatural elements.
p: Jonathan Dowling, Kelly Rogers for Essential/New Zealand Film Commission
exec p: Murray Newey, John Barnett
w: Garth Maxwell, Rex Pilgrim
d: Garth Maxwell
ph: Don Duncan
m: Chris Neal
ed: John Gilbert
ad: Grant Major
cos: Ngila Dickson
sound:, Dick Reade, Gethin Creagh
Alexis Arquette, Sarah Smuts Kennedy, Bruno Lawrence, Tony Barry, Elizabeth Hawthorne, Brenda Simmons

Jack the Ripper *
GB 1988 4x55m or various formats TVM
A Scotland Yard detective tracks down Jack the Ripper.

An over padded, variably scripted and acted version of the famous case, whose ghoulish goings on nevertheless manage to keep one watching. According to its makers the final denouement is actually what happened.
p: David Wickes for Thames/Euston
exec p: Lloyd Shirley
w: Derek Marlowe, David Wickes
d: David Wickes
ph: Alan Hume
m: John Cameron
ed: Keith Palmer
pd: John Blezard
cos: Raymond Hughes
Michael Caine, Lewis Collins, Armand Assante, Jane Seymour, Susan George, Harry Andrews, Lysette Anthony, Hugh Fraser, Michael Gothard, T. P. McKenna, Gerald Sim, Ray McAnally, David Swift, Denys Hawthorne, Jon Laurimore, Richard Morant, Jon Croft, George Sweeney, Michael Hughes, Marc Culwick

Jackson, Freda (1909-1990)
Diminutive British character actress remembered for her role as Greta the evil housekeeper in Hammer's *The Brides of Dracula*. She began her busy stage career in 1934 turning to films in 1938 with an appearance in *Mountains O' Mourne*. Other film credits include *A Canterbury Tale*, *Henry V*, *Great Expectations*, *No Room at the Inn* (reviving her stage role), *Tom Jones*, *The Third Secret* and *The Clash of the Titans*.
Genre credits:
The Brides of Dracula (1960), *The Shadow of the Cat* (1961), *Die, Monster, Die!* (1965 - aka *Monster of Terror*), *The Valley of Gwangi* (1969)

Jackson, Peter (1961-)
New Zealand writer and director with a penchant for gore-filled low-budget horror packed with the blackest of humour, though he has since gone 'straight' with *Heavenly Creatures*.

Genre credits:
Bad Taste (1987 - co-w/p/d/ph/co-ed/sp/act), *Meet the Feebles* (1989 - co-w/co-p/d), *Braindead* (1992 - co-w/d), *The Frighteners* (1996 - d/co-exec p)

Jason Goes to Hell
USA 1993 84m DeLuxe Dolby
Jason's spirit takes over several unsuspecting victims before finally being destroyed by his long lost sister.

Surprisingly tolerable finale to the series with a little more style and humour than the rest. The film ends with an in-joke; Jason is pulled to hell by Freddy Krueger's glove!
p: Sean S. Cunningham for New Line
w: Dean Lorey, Jay Huguely
story: Jay Huguely, Adam Marcus
d: Adam Marcus
ph: William Dill
m: Harry Manfredini
ed: David Handman
pd: W. Brooke Wheeler
cos: Julie Ray Engelsman
sp: Al Magliochetti
make-up effects: Kurtzman, Nicotero and Berger EFX Group
sound: Oliver L. Moss, Philip Seretti
stunt co-ordinator: Kane Hodder
John D. LeMay, Kari Keegan, Kane Hodder (as Jason), Steven Williams, Erin Gray, Steven Culp, Billy Green Bush

Jaws ****
USA 1975 125m Technicolor Panavision
An enormous man-eating shark threatens the summer resort of Amity and three men go after it in an undersized boat.

The biggest box office grosser of its day, this well crafted and often frightening thriller, made under the most arduous of conditions, did for sharks what *Psycho* did for showers fifteen years earlier. Notable for its effective use of music and for making a household name of its director, it lingers in the mind well after viewing.
p: Richard Zanuck, David Brown for Universal
exec p: William S. Gilmore Jr
w: Peter Benchley, Carl Gottlieb

novel: Peter Benchley
d: STEVEN SPIELBERG
ph: Bill Butler
m: JOHN WILLIAMS (AA)
ed: VERNA FIELDS (AA)
pd: Joe Alves
sp: Robert A. Mattey
sound: Robert Hoyt, Roger Heman, Earl Madery, John Carter (aa)
underwater ph: Rexford Metz
live shark ph: Ron and Valerie Taylor
ROBERT SHAW, ROY SCHEIDER, RICHARD DREYFUSS, LORRAINE GARY, MURRAY HAMILTON, Carl Gottlieb, Jeffrey C. Kramer, Ted Grossman, Peter Benchley, Susan Backlinie (as the first victim)

Jaws 2 *
USA 1978 117m Technicolor Panavision
A second man-eating shark threatens the island of Amity.

Made with an exploitative eye on the box office, this inevitably repetitive sequel does, nevertheless, manage to work up a certain degree of tension, though the unused storylines - an account of the sinking of the SS *Indianapolis* and a comedy titled *Jaws 2, People 0* - might have been more fun!
p: Richard Zanuck, David Brown for Universal
w: Carl Gottlieb, Howard Sackler
d: Jeannot Szwarc
ph: Michael Butler
m: JOHN WILLIAMS
ed: Neil Travis
pd/2nd unit d/associate p: Joe Alves
cos: Bill Jobe
sp: Robert Mattey, Roy Arbogast
sound: Jim Alexander
2nd unit ph: David Butler, Michael McGowan
live shark ph: Ron and Valerie Taylor
stunt co-ordinator: Ted Grossman
Roy Scheider, Lorraine Gary, Murray Hamilton, Joseph Mascolo, Collin Wilcox, Keith Gordon, Anne Dusenberry, Jeffrey Kramer, Susan French, Barry Coe, Mark Gruner, Cynthia Grover

Jaws 3D
USA 1983 99m Technicolor Arrivision 3D
Yet another man-eating shark menaces tourists, this time at an ocean theme park.

Lame attempt to continue the series with the central gimmick variable at best.
p: Alan Landsburg, Howard Lipstone, Rupert Hipsig for Universal
w: Richard Matheson
story: Gordon Trueblood
d: Joe Alves
ph: James Contner
m: Alan Parker

ed: Randy Roberts
pd: Woods Macintosh
sp: Chuck Comisky, Larry Benson, Ken Jones
Bess Armstrong, Dennis Quaid, Louis Gossett Jr, Simon McCorkindale, John Putch, Lea Thompson, P. H. Moriarty

Jaws - The Revenge
USA 1987 100m DeLuxe Panavision Dolby
The Brody family is threatened by another great white shark, this time in the Bahamas.

Lame excuse to milk a few more bucks out of a series that had already more than outstayed its welcome. The script is lamentable.
p: Joseph Sargent for Universal
w: Michael de Gusman
d: Joseph Sargent
ph: John McPherson
m: Michael Small
ed: Michael Brown
pd: John J. Lloyd
cos: Maria Denis Schlom, Hugo Pend
sp: Henry Miller
sound: Willie Burton, John J. Stephens
underwater d: Jordan Klein
aerial d: James W. Gavin
aerial ph: Frank Holgate
Lorraine Gary, Michael Caine, Lance Guest, Mario Van Peebles, Karen Young, Judith Barsi, Lynn Whitfield, Melvin Van Peebles

Jayston, Michael (1935-)
Distinguished British actor (real name Michael James) whose velvety voice has been much sought after for commercial voice overs. Much stage experience, his credits include prominent roles in *Cromwell*, *Nicholas and Alexander* (as Tsar Nicholas II), *Follow Me*, *The Internecine Project* and *Zulu Dawn*.
Genre credits:
Tales That Witness Madness (1973), *Craze* (1973), *Dominique* (1978)

Jeffries, Lionel (1926-)
British comedy character actor who later turned to direction with equal success (*The Railway Children*, *The Amazing Mr Blunden*, *Baxter*, etc.).
Genre credits:
The Quatermass Experiment (1955 - aka *The Creeping Unknown*), *The Revenge of Frankenstein* (1958), *The First Men in the Moon* (1963), *Who Slew Aunty Roo?* (1971), *The Amazing Mr Blunden* (1972 - d), *Jekyll and Hyde* (1990 - TVM)

Jekyll and Hyde
GB 1990 96m colour TVM
In 1889 London, the respected Dr Jekyll experiments with a potion that turns him

into the monstrous Mr Hyde.

Melodramatic tele-version of an old, old chestnut which seems to have more in common with its director/star's previous outing, *Jack the Ripper*, than it does with Robert Louis Stevenson.
p: Nick Elliott, Patricia Carr for LWT
w/d/exec p: David Wickes
novel: Robert Louis Stevenson
ph: Norman Langley
m: John Cameron
ed: John Shirley
pd: William Alexander
cos: Raymond Hughes
sound: David Crozier, John haywood
2nd unit d/ph: Geoff Glover
stunt co-ordinator: Peter Brayham
Michael Caine, Cheryl Ladd, Joss Ackland, Lionel Jeffries, Ronald Pickup, Diane Keen, Kim Thomson, Kevin McNally, David Schofield, Lee Montague, Miriam Karlin, Lance Percival

Johnson, Laurie (1927-)
British composer and conductor, trained at the Royal College of Music. Best known for his TV themes and scores for *The Avengers*, *The Professionals* and *The New Avengers*. Stage musicals include *The Four Musketeers* and *Lock Up Your Daughters*. A long time friend of composer Bernard Herrmann, he adapted his *It's Alive* score for the sequel after his death. He also conducted a recording of Herrmann's *North by Northwest* in 1979, whilst his own score for *The First Men in the Moon* has more than a touch of Herrmann about it, as does his Hammer score, *Captain Kronos: Vampire Hunter*.
Genre credits:
The First Men in the Moon (1963), *And Soon the Darkness* (1970), *Captain Kronos: Vampire Hunter* (1974 - aka *Kronos*), *It's Alive 2* (1978 - aka *It Lives Again*)

Johnson, Noble (1897-1978)
Tall, imposing African American character actor who, as well as playing countless tribal chiefs, the most famous of which was in *King Kong*, is remembered for playing Man Friday in the silent version of *Robinson Crusoe* (1922) and for playing the zombie in *The Ghostbreakers*. In films from 1914, his other credits include *The Ten Commandments*, *The Navigator*, *The Four Feathers*, *East of Borneo*, *The Jungle Book* and *She Wore a Yellow Ribbon*.
Genre credits:
Murders in the Rue Morgue (1932), *The Mummy* (1932), *King Kong* (1933), *Son of Kong* (1933), *She* (1935), *The Ghost Breakers* (1940)

Johnson, Richard (1927-)
British actor of leading man stature.

Much stage experience, his films include *Operation Crossbow*, *Khartoum* and *Aces High*, as well as two films as Bulldog Drummond: *Deadlier Than the Male* and *Some Girls Do*.
Genre credits:
The Haunting (1963), *The Devil Within Her* (1974 - aka *Beyond the Door/Chi Sei?*), *The Comeback* (1977), *Zombie Flesh Eaters* (1979 - aka *Zombi 2/Zombie/Island of the Living Dead*)

Johnson, Tor (1903-1971)

Hulking Swedish actor working in America, a former wrestler, best known for his appearances in the films of director Edward G. Wood Jr.
Genre credits:
Ghost Catchers (1944), *Bride of the Monster* (1955), *The Black Sleep* (1956), *Plan 9 from Outer Space* (1956), *The Unearthly* (1957), *Night of the Ghouls* (1959), *The Beast of Yucca Flats* (1961)

Jones, Carolyn (1929-1989)

American actress, best known for playing Morticia Addams in the sixties sitcom *The Addams Family*. A former disc jockey, she entered films after stage experience. Her credits include *Bachelor Party*, *Marjorie Morningstar* and *How the West Was Won*.
Genre credits:
House of Wax (1952), *Invasion of the Body Snatchers* (1955), *Death Trap* (1976 - aka *Eaten Alive/Horror Hotel*)

Jones, Darby (1910-1986)

Tall African American actor, remembered for playing the zombie in Val Lewton's *I Walk with a Zombie* (1943), a role he returned to with the inferior *Zombies on Broadway* (1945). His other credits include *Tarzan Escapes* and *Zamba*.

Jones, Duane (1940-1989)

African American actor who played the hero in George Romero's groundbreaking *Night of the Living Dead* in 1968, one of the few positive black leads in horror film history. His only other genre credit is for the rarely seen vampire yarn *Ganja and Hess* (1973 - aka *Blood Couple*).

Jones, Kenneth V. (1924-)

British composer with many credits to his name.
Genre credits:
The Tomb of Ligeia (1964), *Who Slew Auntie Roo?* (1971)

Jones, Robert

British art director with credits for both Hammer and Roger Corman.
Genre credits:
The Masque of the Red Death (1964 - ad), *She* (1965 - co-ad), *Dr Jekyll and Sister Hyde* (1971 - ad), *Captain Kronos - Vampire Hunter* (1972 - aka *Kronos* - ad)

Jordan, Neil (1950-)

Irish writer and director who, between hard-nosed dramas such as *Angel*, *Mona Lisa* and *The Crying Game* (which won him a Best Screenplay Oscar), has dabbled in the horror genre with varying degrees of success.
Genre credits:
The Company of Wolves (1984 - co-w/d), *High Spirits* (1988 - w/d), *Interview with the Vampire* (1994 - co-w/d)

Joseph, Jackie

American actress, a former TV weather girl, remembered for playing Audrey in Roger Corman's original *Little Shop of Horrors*. She is also familiar to TV audiences from *The Doris Day Show*.
Genre credits:
Little Shop of Horrors (1960), *Gremlins* (1984), *Gremlins 2: The New Batch* (1990)

Josephs, Wilfred

British composer with credits in both film and television.
Fanatic (1965 - aka *Die! Die! My Darling*), *The Deadly Bess* (1967), *The Uncanny* (1977)

Julia, Raul (1940-1994)

Puerto Rican actor who became a Hollywood star via such films as *Kiss of the Spider Woman*, *The Morning After* and *Moon Over Parador*, which led his his being cast as Gomez Addams in two big budget films.
Genre credits:
The Eyes of Laura Mars (1978), *Frankenstein Unbound* (1990), *The Addams Family* (1991), *Addams Family Values* (1993)

Julian, Rupert (1889-1943)

New Zealand born director with acting experience, working in America from 1913 where he directed several silent pictures including the Lon Chaney version of *The Phantom of the Opera*.
Genre credits:
The Phantom of the Opera (1925), *The Cat Creeps* (1930)

Juran, Nathan (1907-)

American art director turned director with a penchant for fantasy themes. His credits include *The Seventh Voyage of Sinbad*, *Jack the Giant Killer* and the *First Men in the Moon*.

Genre credits:
The Deadly Mantis (1957), *Twenty Million Miles to Earth* (1957), *The Boy Who Cried Werewolf* (1973)

Jurassic Park **

USA 1993 122m Eastmancolor Dolby
A billionaire invites a group of experts to view his new theme park, a tropical island on which real dinosaurs have been cloned.

Expensive but poorly adapted screen version of a thrilling book redeemed by its brilliant effects work and memorable set pieces, on which count it broke all box office records. Despite the Oscar win for sound, much of the dialogue is unintelligible
p: Kathleen Kennedy, Gerald R. Molen for Universal, Amblin
w: Michael Crichton, David Koepp
novel: MICHAEL CRICHTON
d: Steven Spielberg
ph: Dean Cundey
m: JOHN WILLIAMS
ed: Michael Kahn
pd: Rick Carter
cos: Sue Moore, Eric Sandberg
sp: STAN WINSTON, DENNIS MURREN, PHIL TIPPETT, MICHAEL LANTIERI (AA)
sound: Ron Judkins (aa)
sound effects editing: (aa)
animation: Bob Kurtz
stunt co-ordinator: Gary Hymes
Sam Neill, Laura Dern, Richard Attenborough, Jeff Goldblum, Bob Peck, Martin Ferrero, B. D. Wong, Samuel L. Jackson, Joseph Mazzello, Ariana Richards, Wayne Knight, Jerry Molen, Dean Cundey, Richard Kiley (voice only)

Just Before Dawn

USA 1980 92m Movielab
Teenagers camping on a lonely mountain are stalked and killed by two of the locals.

Despite the pretty scenery this is just another cleaver wielder flick in the *Friday the 13th* manner.
p: David Sheldon, Doro Vlado Hreljanovic for Oakland
w: Harry Aywitz, Gregg Irving
d: Jeff Lieberman
ph: Joel King, Dean King
m: Brad Fiedel
ed: Robert Q. Lovett
ad: Craig Stearns
make-up effects: Matthew Mungle
Chris Lemmon, George Kennedy, Mike Kellin, Gregg Henry, Deborah Benson, Ralph Seymour, Kath Powell, John Hunsaker

K

Das Kabinett von Dr Caligari

see The Cabinet of Dr Caligari

Kadaicha

Australia 1988 87m colour
A group of teenagers find themselves possessed by a malevolent Aboriginal spirit.

Dismal Antipodean shocker utilizing a well-worn theme. Of no interest whatsoever.
p: David Hannay, Charles Hannah for Premiere/Medusa
exec p: Tom Broadbridge
w: Ian Coughlan
d: James Bogle
ph: Stephen F. Windon
m: Peter Westheimer
ed: Andrew Arestides
ad: no credit given
cos: Fiona Spence
sp: Neville Maxwell
sound: Pam Dunne
make-up effects: Deryck De Niese
Natalie McCurry, Eric Oldfield, Zoe Carides, Tom Jennings, Fiona Gauntlett, Kerry McKay, Nicholas Flanagan, Steve Dodd

Kaidan see Kwaidan

Karloff, Boris (1887-1969)

British actor (real name William Henry Pratt) who, after many years of playing bit parts and supports, shot to stardom at the age of forty-four as the Monster in James Whale's Frankenstein, after which he became the pre-eminent horror star of his or any other generation - all very ironic given his own mild-mannered nature and his lisping speech patterns. After studying for the Consular Service he moved to Canada in 1909 where, after experience in several labouring jobs, he broke into rep theatre in both Canada and America. He made his film début in 1916 as a walk on in The Dumb Girl of Portici. Several supporting roles followed with Karloff often portraying a heavy. It was his performance in the prison melodrama Graft in 1931 that brought him to the attention of director James Whale, however, who

• Boris Karloff as Ardath Bey in The Mummy. On the posters he was billed as 'Karloff the Uncanny'.

cast him as the Monster. And the rest, as they say, is history, though at the time of filming, Frankenstein was merely one of thirteen films the busy actor made the same year. More minor roles followed, but once Frankenstein became a hit Karloff confirmed his star status in several other key horror films of the period, including The Old Dark House, The Mummy and The Mask of Fu Manchu, by which time, like Greta Garbo, he was often billed by his surname alone. He played the Monster three times in all (four if one counts his guest appearance in a 1963 episode of TV's Route 66) and when, in the forties, he became too old for the make up he turned to mad doctor films. He also made three films for producer Val Lewton. Though he often appeared in films unworthy of his presence, like Peter Cushing after him, he always brought an air of dignity to the proceedings no matter how shoddy the production. His last taste of glory came in the mid-sixties in several Roger Corman pictures though he is still most remembered for his speechless role in

Frankenstein - a role he made truly his own. His non-genre films include Five Star Final, The Lost Patrol, Mr Wong, Detective (and several sequels), The Secret Life of Walter Mitty and The Venetian Affair, whilst on television he found further popularity in Colonel March of Scotland Yard and Thriller.
Genre credits:
The Mad Genius (1931), Frankenstein (1931), The Old Dark House (1932), The Mummy (1932), The Mask of Fu Manchu (1932), The Ghoul (1933), The Black Cat (1934), The Bride of Frankenstein (1935), The Raven (1935), The Black Cat (1935), The Invisible Ray (1936), The Walking Dead (1936), The Man Who Changed His Mind (1936), Charlie Chan at the Opera (1936), You'll Find Out (1937), Juggernaut (1937), Son of Frankenstein (1939), The Man They Could Not Hang (1939), Tower of London (1939), Black Friday (1940), The Man with Nine Lives (1940 - aka Behind the Door), Doomed to Die (1940 - aka The Mystery of Wentworth Castle), Before I Hang (1940), The Ape (1940), The Devil Commands (1941), The Boogie Man Will Get You (1942), The Climax (1944), House of Frankenstein (1944), The Body Snatcher (1945), Isle of the Dead (1945), Bedlam (1946), Dick Tracy Meets Gruesome (1947 - aka Dick Tracy's Amazing Adventure), Abbott and Costello Meet the Killer, Boris Karloff (1949), The Strange Door (1952), Abbott and Costello Meet Dr Jekyll and Mr Hyde (1953), Monster of the Island (1953 - aka Il Monstro dell'Isola), Voodoo Island (1958), Grip of the Strangler (1958 - aka The Haunted Strangler), Corridors of Blood (1958), Frankenstein 1970 (1958), The Raven (1963), The Terror (1963), The Comedy of Terrors (1963), Black Sabbath (1964), Die, Monster, Die (1964 - aka Monster of Terror), The Ghost in the Invisible Bikini (1966), The Sorcerers (1967), The Mad Monster Party? (1967 - puppetoon, voice only), Targets (1968), The Curse of the Crimson Altar (1968 - aka The Crimson Curse/The Crimson Cult), The Snake People (1970 - aka Isle of the Snake People -unreleased), Cauldron of Blood (1970 - aka El Coleccionista de Cadaveras),

The Fear Chamber (1970 - unreleased), *House of Evil* (1970 - unreleased)

Katzman, Sam (1901-1973)

American producer with countless low-budget films to his credit, including the entire *Jungle Jim* series (*Jungle Jim in the Forbidden Land*, *Voodoo Tiger*, *Jungle Maneaters*, *Cannibal Attack*, *Jungle Moon Men*, etc.). He began his career as a prop boy at Fox's New Jersey studios though it wasn't until he was twenty-three that his career slowly began to take off when he moved to California. He gradually worked his way up the production ladder on such films as *Ship of Wanted Men*, *Brand of Hate* and *A Face in the Fog*, eventually becoming an independent producer in 1936 with *Shadow of Chinatown*, a serial which starred Bela Lugosi. More serials followed (*Blake of Scotland Yard*, etc.), after which Katzman formed Banner Productions in 1940. An arm of Poverty Row studio Monogram, Banner produced a ongoing series of supports starring The East Side Kids (one of several offshoots of The Dead End Kids), including *Boys of the City*, *That Gang of Mine*, *Bowery Blitzkrieg* and *Bowery Champs*. However, Katzman soon began to plumb the depths with a slew of inept no-budgeters, many of which have to be seen to be believed. His biggest hit came in 1956 with *Rock Around the Clock*, the success of which he naturally tried to recapture with *Cha-Cha-Cha Boom*, *Calypso Heat Wave*, *Don't Knock the Rock*, *Juke Box Rhythm*, *Twist Around the Clock*, *Don't Knock the Twist* and *Hootenanny Hoot*. His other credits include *Mr Wise Guy*, *Docks of New York*, *Little Miss Broadway*, *Atom Man vs Superman* (serial), *A Yank in Korea*, *Captain Video*, *The Wizard of Bagdad*, *Riot on Sunset Strip*, *The Fastest Guitar Alive* and two Elvis Presley musicals: *Kissin' Cousins* and *Harum Scarum*.
Genre credits:
Spooks Run Wild (1941 - p), *The Invisible Ghost* (1941 - p), *The Corpse Vanishes* (1942 - aka *The Case of the Missing Brides* - co-p), *The Bowery at Midnight* (1942 - co-p), *The Ape Man* (1943 - aka *Lock Your Doors* - co-p), *Ghosts on the Loose* (1943 - p), *The Voodoo Man* (1944 - co-p), *The Return of the Ape Man* (1944 -co-p), *It Came from Beneath the Sea* (1955 - exec p), *The Creature with the Atom Brain* (1956 - p), *The Werewolf* (1956 - p), *The Man Who Turned to Stone* (1956 - p), *The Giant Claw* (1957 - p), *The Zombies of Mora-Tau* (1957 - aka *The Dead That Walk* - p)

Katz, Fred

American composer with a couple of Corman quickies to his credit.
Genre credits:

Little Shop of Horrors (1961), *The Creature from the Haunted Sea* (1961)

Kay, Edward

American composer and music director whose genre work has been entirely for Monogram.
Genre credits:
The Ape (1940 - md), *The Bowery at Midnight* (1942 - md), *The Ape Man* (1943 - aka *Lock Your Doors* - m), *Return of the Ape Man* (1944 - m), *The Voodoo Man* (1944 - md), *Face of Marble* (1946 - md)

The Keep

GB/USA 1983 93m Metrocolor Panavision Dolby
A platoon of Nazi soldiers is murdered one by one by a mysterious force when they take over a Carpathian keep.
Slow moving, gloom laden, would-be meaningful horror fantasy with echoes of the similarly plotted but almost equally incomprehensible *Castle Keep*. Of chiefly visual interest, it was barely released, despite the huge amounts spent on it.
p: Gene Kirkwood, Howard W. Koch Jr for Paramount/Associates Capital
exec p: Colin M. Brewer
w/d: Michael Mann
novel: F. Paul Wilson
ph: ALEX THOMSON
m: Tangerine Dream
ed: Dov Koenig
pd: JOHN BOX
cos: Anthony Mendleson
sp: Wally Veevers, Robin Browne
sound: Robin Gregory, Doug Turner
stunt co-ordinator: Alf Joint
2nd unit ph: Arthur Lavis
Scott Glenn, Alberta Watson, Jurgen Prochnow, Ian McKellen, Gabriel Byrne, Robert Prosky

Keir, Andrew (1926-)

British (Scottish) character actor, a memorable Professor Quatermass in Hammer's *Quatermass and the Pit*. His other credits include *The Maggie*, *Daleks Invasion Earth: 2150 AD*, *The Viking Queen*, *The Thirty-Nine Steps* and *Rob Roy*.
Genre credits:
Dracula - Prince of Darkness (1966), *Quatermass and the Pit* (1967 - aka *Five Million Years to Earth*), *Blood from the Mummy's Tomb* (1971), *Absolution* (1978), *Dragonworld* (1994)

Keith, Sheila

Stern-looking British character actress, a familiar face on British television in the seventies and eighties. Her genre work has mostly been for low-budget director Pete Walker.

Genre credits:
Venom (1971 - aka *The Legend of Spider Forest*), *House of Whipcord* (1974), *Frightmare* (1975), *House of Mortal Sin* (1975 - aka *The Confessional*), *The Comeback* (1978 - aka *The Day the Screaming Stopped*), *House of the Long Shadows* (1983)

Kellaway, Cecil (1891-1973)

South African born character actor with stage experience in Australia before heading for Hollywood, where he made his film début in 1933 in *The Hayseeds*. His other credits include *Gunga Din*, *Wuthering Heights*, *Mrs Patrington*, *Harvey*, *Female on the Beach*, *Fitzwilly* (aka *Fitzwilly Strikes Back*), *Guess Who's Coming to Dinner* and *Getting Straight*, though he is perhaps best remembered for playing Daniel the mischievous warlock in director Rene Clair's *I Married a Witch*.
Genre credits:
The Invisible Man Returns (1940), *The Mummy's Hand* (1940), *I Married a Witch* (1942), *The Beast from 20,000 Fathoms* (1953)

Kendall, Suzy (1944-)

Decorative British actress (real name Frieda Harrison) who came to attention in such sixties films as *To Sir With Love*, *The Penthouse* and *Up the Junction* after which she made a handful of horror films in Europe, most notably Dario Argento's *The Bird with the Crystal Plumage*. Her other credits include *30 Is a Dangerous Age*, *Cynthia*, *Fraulein Doktor*, *Assault*, *Fear is the Key*, *Darker Than Amber* and *Adventures of a Private Eye*.
Genre credits:
Psycho Circus (1967 - aka *Circus of Fear*), *The Bird with the Crystal Plumage* (1969), *Tales That Witness Madness* (1973), *Craze* (1974), *The Demon Master* (1973), *Torso* (1974), *Spasmo* (1975)

Kenton, Erle C. (1896-1980)

American director who, after experience as an actor and assistant director to Mack Sennett, began directing his own two-reelers in 1919, moving up to features in 1920 with *Down on the Farm*. A routine talent at best, his other credits include *North to the Klondike*, *Who Done It?* and *Should Parents Tell?*
Genre credits:
The Island of Lost Souls (1932), *The Ghost of Frankenstein* (1942), *House of Frankenstein* (1944), *House of Dracula* (1945), *The Cat Creeps* (1946)

Keys, Anthony Nelson (1913-1985)

British producer, associated chiefly with Hammer. Son of actor-comedian Nelson

'Bunch' Keys, brother of editor Roderick Keys, associate producer Basil Keyes and director John Paddy Carstairs. Began his career as a recordist for HMV in 1928. After war service as a paratrooper he went to work for Gainsborough as a production manager later moving to Romulus. His first film for Hammer/Exclusive was *Never Look Back* in 1952, on which he acted as production manager. Joined Hammer full time in 1956 as an associate producer, graduating to fully fledged producer in 1962 with *The Pirates of Blood River*. Was also general manager of Bray Studios in the sixties and co-wrote the screenplay for *Frankenstein Must Be Destroyed* in 1969. Formed Charlemagne Productions with Christopher Lee in 1972, but their only film, *Nothing But the Night*, was poorly received.
Genre credits:
The Curse of Frankenstein (1956 - associate p), *Dracula* (1958 - aka *Horror of Dracula* - associate p), *The Revenge of Frankenstein* (1958 - associate p), *The Man Who Could Cheat Death* (1959 - associate p), *The Terror of the Tongs* (1961 - associate p), *The Gorgon* (1964 - p), *Dracula - Prince of Darkness* (1966 - p), *Rasputin - The Mad Monk* (1966 - p), *Plague of the Zombies* (1966 - p), *The Reptile* (1966 - p), *Frankenstein Created Woman* (1966 - p), *The Mummy's Shroud* (1966 - p), *The Witches* (1966 -aka *The Devil's Own* - p), *Quatermass and the Pit* (1967 - p), *The Devil Rides Out* (1968 - p), *Frankenstein Must Be Destroyed* (1969 - p/co-w), *Nothing But the Night* (1972 - p).

Kidder, Margot (1948-)
Canadian actress, best known for playing Lois Lane in the four Christopher Reeve *Superman* movies. Much television work in the late sixties was followed by her film début in 1969 in the comedy *Gaily, Gaily* (aka *Chicago, Chicago*). Her other credits include *Quackser Fortune Has a Cousin in the Bronx*, *The Great Waldo Pepper*, *Willie and Phil* and *To Catch a Killer* (TVM).
Genre credits:
Sisters (1972), *Black Christmas* (1974 - aka *Silent Night, Evil Night*), *The Reincarnation of Peter Proud* (1974), *The Amityville Horror* (1979), *Vanishing Act* (1986 - TVM)

Kiel, Richard (1939-)
Giant (7' 2") American actor, best known for playing Jaws in two James Bond films, *The Spy Who Loved Me* and *Moonraker*, prior to which he appeared mostly in villainous or monstrous roles. His other credits include *The Nutty Professor*, *Roustabout*, *Silver Streak*, *Force*

Ten from Navarone and *Pale Rider*.
Genre credits:
The Magic Sword (1961 - aka *St George and the Seven Curses*), *The Phantom Planet* (1961), *Eegah!* (1962), *House of the Damned* (1963), *The Human Duplicators* (1965), *The Humanoid* (1979), *Hysterical* (1982), *War of the Wizards* (1983)

Kier, Udo (1944-)
German actor remembered for playing the title roles in both *Andy Warhol's Frankenstein* and *Andy Warhol's Dracula*. A popular figure on the European scene in the seventies, his other credits include *The Salzburg Connection*, *The Story of O*, *Bolweiser*, *The Third Generation* and *Lili Marlene*.
Genre credits:
Mark of the Devil (1969 - aka *Hexen*), *Andy Warhol's Frankenstein* (1974 - aka *Flesh for Frankenstein*), *Andy Warhol's Dracula* (1974 - aka *Blood for Dracula*), *Spermula* (1975), *Suspiria* (1976)

Killbots see Chopping Mall

Killdozer
USA 1974 74m Technicolor TVM
On a remote island off the coast of Africa workmen are attacked by a bulldozer which has been brought to life through contact with a strange meteorite.
Alas, not nearly as much fun as the plotline would suggest. Similarly themed movies include *Duel*, *The Car* and *Christine*.
p: Herbert F. Solow for Universal
w: Theodore Sturgeon, Ed MacKillop
d: Jerry London
ph: Terry K. Meade
m: Gil Melle
ed: Richard Belding
ad: James Martin Rachman
stunt co-ordinator: Carey Loftin
Clint Walker, James Wainwright, Carl Betz, Neville Brand, Robert Urich

Killer Fish
Fr/Brazil 1978 101m Eastmancolor
Thieves hide their loot in a reservoir which turns out to be infested with piranhas.
The title really tells all in this worthless international *Jaws* rip-off with second rate talent.
p: Alex Ponti for Filmardo de Brazil/ITC/Victoria/Fawcett-Majors
w: Michael Rodgers
d: Anthony M. Dawson (Antonio Margheriti)
ph: Alberto Spagholi
m: Guido and Maurizio de Angelis
ed: Roberto Sterbini
ad: Francesco Bronzi

cos: Adrianne Berselli, Salvadore Russo
Lee Majors, Karen Black, Margaux Hemmingway, Marisa Berenson, James Franciscus, Roy Brocksmith, Dan Pastorini, Frank Presce, Charlie Guardino

Killer Klowns from Outer Space *
USA 1987 88m Technicolor Dolby
A small American township is visited by aliens out to replenish their food supplies.
Offbeat horror comedy which is never quite as funny as or as horrific as one expects it to be, but for a low-budget production it gets a mark for trying. It should please late night video addicts.
p: Edward Chiodo, Stephen Chiodo, Charles Chiodo for Trans World/Sarlui/Diamant/Chiodo Brothers
w: Charles Chiodo, Stephen Chiodo
d: Stephen Chiodo
ph: Alfred Taylor
m: John Masari
ed: Chris Roth
pd/klown design: Charles Chiodo
cos: Darcee Olson
sp: Fantasy II, Gene Warre Jr
sound: Patrick Moriarty
Grant Cramer, Suzanne Snyder, John Allen Nelson, Royal Dano, John Vernon, Michael Siegel, Peter Licassi

Killer Nun
It 1978 90m Technicolor Techniscope
The finger of blame seems to point at a mentally ill nun when murder and mayhem breaks out at an asylum
Over the top horror melodrama, supposedly based on actual events.
p: Enzo Gallo for Cinesud
w: Giulio Berruti, Alberto Tarralo
story: Enzo Gallo
d: Giulio Berruti
ph: Tonino Maccoppi
m: Alessandro Alessandroni
ed: Mario Giacco
pd: Franco Vanorio
cos: Alberto Tarallo
sound: Robert Forrest
Anita Ekberg, Alida Valli, Lou Castel, Joe Dallesandro, Massimo Serato, Laura Nucci, Paola Morra, Lee de Barriault

Killer Workout see Aerobicide

King Kong
This 1933 classic is still regarded by many as the greatest monster movie ever made and remains a tribute to the skills of stop motion animator Willis H. O'Brien. A box office smash, a sequel, *Son of Kong*, was rushed into release later the same year. O'Brien was also behind the similarly plotted *Mighty Joe Young*, who appeared to be a cousin of

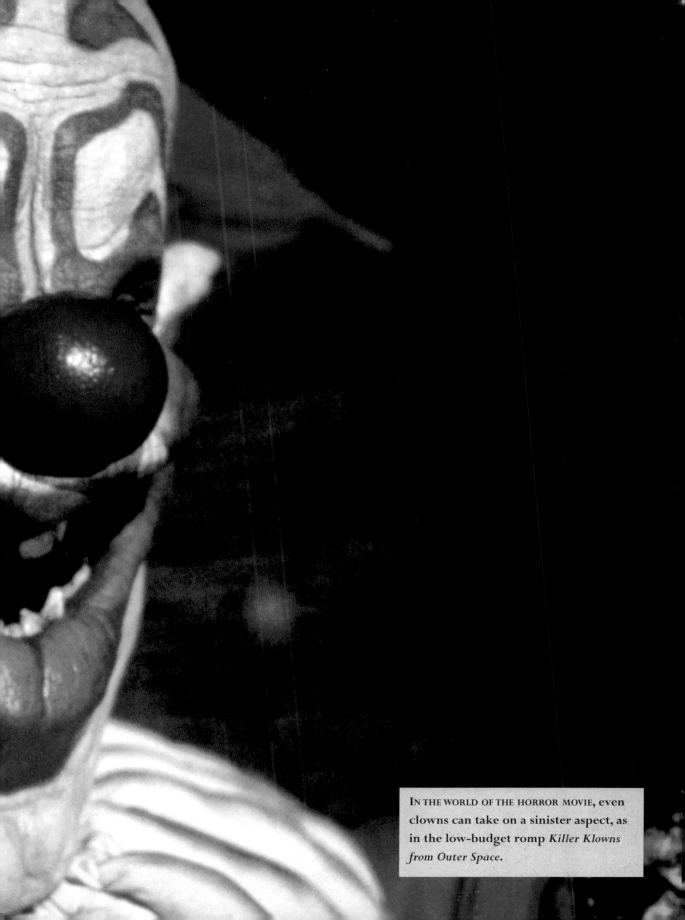

IN THE WORLD OF THE HORROR MOVIE, even clowns can take on a sinister aspect, as in the low-budget romp *Killer Klowns from Outer Space*.

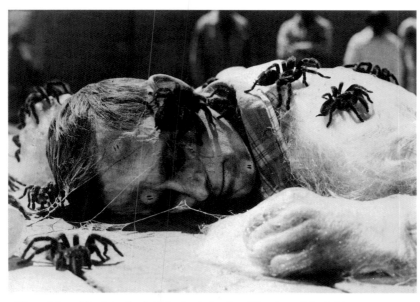

• **The spiders attack in the low budget shocker** *Kingdom of the Spiders*.

Kong's. In the sixties a handful of Japanese films featured Kong, though here he was portrayed by a man in an monkey suit - as was the case with the much-ballyhooed 1976 remake which astonishingly won an Oscar for Best Visual Effects. It even produced a sequel of its own, *King Kong Lives*, about which the less said the better. Ditto the inevitable porn version, *King Dong*.
Key filmography:
King Kong (1933), *Son of Kong* (1933), *Mighty Joe Young* (1949), *Konga* (1960), *King Kong vs Godzilla* (1963 - aka *Kingu Kongu Tai Gojira*), *King Kong Escapes* (1967 - aka *Kingu Kongu No Gyakushu*), *King of Kong Island* (1968 - aka *Eve of the Wild Woman/Eva La Venere Selvaggio*), *Necropolis* (1970), *King Kong* (1976), *Queen Kong* (1976), *A*P*E* (1976 - aka *Attack of the Giant Horny Gorilla*), *King Dong* (1984 - aka *Lost on Adventure Island*), *King Kong Lives* (1986)

King Kong ****
USA 1933 100m bw
An adventurous film producer follows a map to a mysterious island where prehistoric monsters still roam and a giant ape rules the jungle.

Without doubt the most famous monster movie of all time, with some of the most brilliant and painstaking trick effects ever put on film. A fast moving, exciting, thrill-a-minute mixture of action, suspense, romance and thrills, climaxing with the now legendary sequence atop the Empire State Building. An absolute must. *Son of Kong* followed later the same year.

p: Merian C. Cooper for RKO
exec p: David O. Selznick
w: JAMES CREELMAN, RUTH ROSE
story: Edgar Wallace, Merian C. Cooper
d: MERIAN C. COOPER, ERNEST B. SCHOEDSACK
ph: Edward Linden, Vernon L. Walker, J. O. Taylor
m: MAX STEINER
ed: TED CHEESMAN
ad: Carroll Clark, Al Herman, Van Nest Polglase
cos: Walter Plunkett
sp: WILLIS O'BRIEN
sound: Earl A. Wolcott

sound effects: MURRAY SPIVACK
FAY WRAY (as Ann Darrow), ROBERT ARMSTRONG (as Carl Denham), BRUCE CABOT, FRANK REICHER, Sam Hardy, Noble Johnson, James Flavin, Victor Wong, Paul Porcasi, Russ Powell, Merian C. Cooper (cameo as one of the pilots who gun down Kong), Ernest B. Schoedsack (ditto)

King Kong
USA 1976 137m Metrocolor Panavision
Members of an expedition searching for oil on a remote Pacific island discover it to be inhabited by a giant ape which they subsequently capture and take back to New York.

Enjoyably and hilariously awful big-budget remake of the 1933 classic whose Oscar winning (!) effects mostly consist of Rick Baker romping about in a monkey suit. An enormous publicity campaign guaranteed it an audience, most of whom wished they had stayed at home. Some of the dialogue has to be heard to be believed. *King Kong Lives* followed in 1986.

p: Dino de Laurentiis for Paramount
exec p: Federico de Laurentiis, Christian Ferry
w: Lorenzo Semple, Jr
d: John Guillermin
ph: Richard H. Kline
m: John Barry
ed: Ralph E. Winters
pd: Dale Hennesy, Mario Chiari
cos: Moss Mabry
sp: Carlo Rambaldi, Glen Robinson, Frank Van Der Veer (aa)
sound: Jack Solomon
2nd unit d: William Kronick

• **Production artwork for the 1933 classic** *King Kong*.

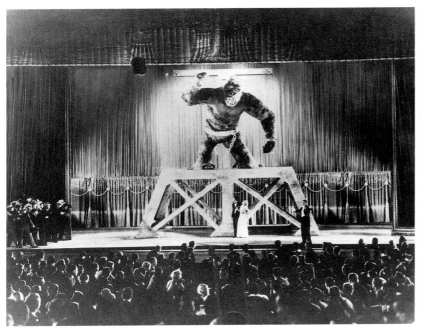

• *King Kong* prepares to go on the rampage in New York.

stunt co-ordinator: Bill Couch
Jeff Bridges, Charles Grodin, Jessica Lange, Rene Auberjonois, Julius Harris, John Randolph, Ed Lauter, Jack O'Halloran, Rick Baker (as Kong)

King, Stephen (1946-)

Best-selling genre novelist turned screenwriter, director and actor. A former English teacher, his first novel, *Carrie*, appeared in 1974, since when a good many of his novels and short stories have been adapted for both the cinema and television, though with the occasional exception (*The Shining*, *Creepshow*, *Misery*) the results have been inconsistent. Nevertheless, he remains one of the genre's modern day linchpins. Occasional non-horror

• Not one of King Kong's finest moments. By the time he appeared in the Japanese-made *King Kong Escapes* he was played by a man in an ape suit.

adaptations include *Stand By Me* and *The Shawshank Redemption*.
Genre credits:
Carrie (1976 - novel), *Salem's Lot* (1979 - TVM - novel), *The Shining* (1980 - novel), *Creepshow* (1982 - w/actor), *The Dead Zone* (1983 - novel), *Christine* (1983 - novel), *Cujo* (1983 - novel), *Firestarter* (1984 - novel), *Children of the Corn* (1984 - novel), *Cat's Eye* (1985 - w), *Silver Bullet* (1985 - w/novella), *Maximum Overdrive* (1986 - w/d), *Creepshow 2* (1987 - story), *Return to Salem's Lot* (1987 - TVM - derived from characters in first film), *Pet Semetary* (1989 - w/novel/actor), *Tales from the Darkside: The Movie* (1989 - co-story), *Misery* (1990 - novel), *It* (1990 - TVM - novel), *Graveyard Shift* (1990 - novel), *Sometimes They Come Back* (1991 - TVM - novel), *Sleepwalkers* (1992 - w/actor), *Pet Semetary 2* (1992 - derived from original characters), *Lawnmower Man* (1992 - novel), *Children of the Corn II: The Final Sacrifice* (1993 - derived from original characters), *The Dark Half* (1993 - novel), *Needful Things* (1993 - novel), *The Tommyknockers* (1993 - TVM - novel), *The Stand* (1994 - TVM - novel), *The Mangler* (1995 - novel), *The Langoliers* (1995 - TVM - novel), *Lawnmower Man 2 - Beyond Cyperspace* (1996 - derived from original characters)

Kingdom of the Spiders

USA 1977 95m Technicolor
An Arizona township finds itself besieged by killer tarantulas.
Old fashioned B shocker which passes the time.
p: Henry Fownes for Dimension/Arachnid
w: Richard Robinson, Alan Caillou
d: John Cardos
ph: John Wheeler, John Morrill
m: Igo Kantor
William Shatner, Woody Stode, Tiffany Bolling, Altovise Davis, Natasha Ryan, Marcy Lafferty, Lieux Dressler, David McLean

Kinnell, Murray (1889-1954)

British actor on stage from 1907. He moved to American in 1923 where much theatre work followed. In films from 1930, he is perhaps best known for playing the carnival barker in Tod Browning's *Freaks*. His other film credits include *Public Enemy*, *Grand Hotel*, *The Great Impersonation* and *Captains Courageous*. He retired from films in 1937 to concentrate on his duties as the assistant treasurer to the Screen Actors' Guild (SAG).
Genre credits:
Freaks (1932), *Mad Love* (1935)

Kinski, Klaus (1926-1991)

Intense-looking, often explosive German actor (real name Claus Gunther Nakszynski) in international films, such as *Doctor Zhivago* and *For a Few Dollars More*, often as a support. In films from 1948 after experience as a cabaret artist, he often appeared in roles unworthy of his talents, though he made several memorable pictures with director Werner Herzog, including *Aguirre Wrath of God*, *Nosferatu* (memorable in the title role), *Fitzcarraldo* and *Cobra Verde*. The father of actress Nastassja Kinski, he also wrote and directed one film, the disastrous biopic *Paganini*.
Genre credits:
The Avenger (1960), *Dead Eyes of London* (1961 - aka *Die Toten Augen von London*), *The Black Abbot* (1961), *Die Tur Mit den Sieben Schlossern* (1962 - *The Door with Seven Locks*), *Dr Mabuse vs Scotland Yard* (1963 - aka *Scotland Yard Jagt Dr Mabuse*), *The Indian Scarf* (1963), *Circus of Fear* (1967), *The Creature with the Blue Hand* (1967), *Marquis de Sade: Justine* (1968 - aka *Justine and Juliet*), *The Devil's Garden* (1968 - aka *Coplan sauve sa Peau*), *Venus in Furs* (1970 - aka *Paroxismus/Black Angel*), *Bram Stoker's Count Dracula* (1970 - aka *El Conde Dracula/Count Dracula*), *La Bestia a Sangue Freddo* (1971 - aka *The Cold-Blooded Beast/Slaughter Hotel*), *Dracula Im Schloss des Schreckens* (1971 - aka *Web of the Spider*), *Nella Stretta Morsa del Ragno* (1971), *Death Smiles on a*

Murderer (1973), *Lifespan* (1973), *Jack the Ripper* (1976), *Nosferatu* (1979 - aka *Nosferatu the Vampyre / Nosferatu: Phantom der Nacht*), *Venom* (1980), *Schizoid* (1980), *Titan Find* (1986 - aka *Creature*), *Deadly Sanctuary* (1986), *Crawlspace* (1986), *Nosferatu in Venice* (1987 - aka *Vampires in Venice / Nosferatu a Venezia*)

Kiss of Evil see Kiss of the Vampire

Kiss of the Vampire *
GB 1964 88m Eastmancolor
In turn-of-the-century Bavaria, a honey-mooning couple inadvertently become involved with a sect of vampires.

Generally lively Hammer horror which makes good use of its restricted budget and settings.
p: Anthony Hinds for Hammer / Universal
w: John Elder (Anthony Hinds)
d: DON SHARP
ph: James Bernard
md: John Hollingsworth
ed: James Needs
pd: Bernard Robinson
ad: Don Mingaye
cos: Molly Arbuthnot
sp: Les Bowie
sound: Ken Rawkins
make-up: Roy Ashton
cam op: Moray Grant
NOEL WILLMAN, Edward de Souza, Clifford Evans, Jennifer Daniel, Isobel Black, Peter Madden, Barry Warren, Brian Oulton, Noel Howlett, Jacquie Wallis

Kneale, Nigel (1922-)
Manx born writer who became a staff writer for the BBC just after the war. Created such television classics as *The Quatermass Experiment* (originally written to fill an unexpected gap in the schedules), *Quatermass 2*, *Quatermass and the Pit*, *The Creature* and, later, *The Sex Olympics*, *Beasts*, *Kinvig* and a fourth Quatermass series (for Thames / Euston). The first three Quatermass series were filmed at various stages by Hammer, the first of which launched the studio on the international scene. Kneale's other screen credits include *Look Back in Anger* and *The Entertainer*. Had his name removed from the credits of *Halloween III: Season of the Witch*.
Genre credits:
The Quatermass Experiment (1955 - aka *The Creeping Unknown* - original series only), *Quatermass 2* (1957 - aka *Enemy from Space* - co-w), *The Abominable Snowman* (1957 - aka *The Abominable Snowman of the Himalayas* - w), *The First Men in the Moon* (1964 - w), *The Witches* (1966 - aka *The Devil's Own* - w), *Quatermass and the Pit* (1967 - aka *Five Million Years to Earth* - w), *Halloween III: Season of the Witch* (1983 - co-w), *The Woman in Black* (1989 - TVM)

Konga
GB 1960 90m Eastmancolor
Spectamation
A biologist injects a serum into a chimpanzee which consequently grows to a monstrous size.

Resolutely silly horror hokum. Some signs of vigour but the acting and the effects (a man in a gorilla suit) don't help.
p: Herman Cohen for Merton Park
w: Aben Kandel (Kenneth Langtry), Herman Cohen
d: John Lemont
ph: Desmond Dickinson
m: Gerard Schurmann
ed: Jack Slade
ad: Wilfred Arnold
Michael Gough, Margo Johns, Jess Conrad, Claire Gordon, Austin Trevor, Jack Watson, Leonard Sachs

Kraus, Werner (1884-1959)
German character actor who appeared in several key silent horror films. An Actor of the State under the Nazi regime, his other credits include *The Brothers Karamazov*, *A Midsummer Night's Dream* and *Jew Suss*.
Genre credits:
The Cabinet of Dr Caligari (1919 - aka *Das Kabinet des Dr Caligari* - as Dr Caligari), *Waxworks* (1924 - aka *Das Wachsfigurenkabinett / The Three Wax Works* - as Jack the Ripper), *The Student of Prague* (1925 - aka *Der Student von Prag / The Man Who Cheated Life*)

Krige, Alice (1955-)
Beautiful South African leading lady in international films (*Chariots of Fire*, *King David*, *Barfly*), memorable as the decaying spectre in *Ghost Story*.
Genre credits:
Ghost Story (1981), *Sleepwalkers* (1992)

Kronos see Captain Kronos: Vampire Hunter

Kubrick, Stanley (1928-)
Celebrated American director, producer and screenwriter whose films include such classics as *Paths of Glory*, *Spartacus*, *Dr Strangelove*, *2001: A Space Odyssey* and *Barry Lyndon*. His only horror movie, *The Shining* (1980), was critically reviled upon its first release, though it has since been re-evaluated and gained something of a cult status.

Kwaidan *
Japan 1964 164m Eastmancolor
Tohoscope
Four ghost stories: *Black Hair*, *Snow Woman*, *Hoichi the Earless* and *In a Cup of Tea*.

A visually arresting collection which nevertheless proves to be something of an endurance test at this length. Perhaps best enjoyed on video, story by story.
p: Shigeru Wakatsuki for Ninjin Club, Bungei
w: Yoko Miszuki
stories: Lafcadio Hearn
d: MASAKI KOBAYASHI
ph: YOSHIO MIYAJIMA
m: Toru Takemitsu
ed: Hisashi Sagara
ad: SHIGEMASA TODA
sound: Hideo Nishizaki
Keiko Kishi, Tatsuya Nakadai, Kazuo Makamura, Tetsuro Tamba, Rentaro Mikuni, Ganjiro Nakamura

L

Le Lac des Mortes-Vivants see
Zombies' Lake

Lacey, Catherine (1904-1979)
British character actress in supporting roles, perhaps most memorably in her début as the nun in high heels in Hitchcock's *The Lady Vanishes*. Other credits include *Cottage to Let*, *I Know Where I'm Going*, *Whisky Galore* (aka *Tight Little Island*) and *The Fighting Prince of Donegal*. She also proved a worthy co-star to Boris Karloff in *The Sorcerers*.
Genre credits:
Shadow of the Cat (1961), *The Mummy's Shroud* (1966), *The Sorcerers* (1967)

Lady in White *
USA 1988 113m DeLuxe
A young boy solves the murder of a little girl after seeing her ghost.

Long and rather complicated ghost story that nevertheless looks good.
p: Frank LaLoggia, Andrew G. La Marca for New Sky/Virgin Vision/Samuel Goldwyn
w/d/m: Frank LaLoggia
ph: Russell Carpenter
ed: Steve Mann
pd: Richard K. Hummel
cos: Jacqueline Saint Anne
sp: Ernest D. Farino, Gene Warren Jr
sound: Robert Anderson Jr
Lukas Haas, Len Cariou, Alex Rocco, Katherine Helmond, Jason Presson, Joelle Jacobi

Laemmle, Carl (1867-1939)
German born producer and mogul who entered films in 1906, going on to found Universal Pictures (originally The Universal Film Manufacturing Company) in 1912 from which small acorn a mighty oak grew. He was the father of producer Carl Laemmle Jr and twelve other children. Sold Universal for $5m in 1935 after it ran into financial difficulties.

Laemmle Jr, Carl (1908-1979)
American producer and production executive, the son of Universal founder Carl Laemmle. As a producer he person-ally oversaw *Dracula* and *Frankenstein*, the success of which launched Universal's horror cycle of the thirties and forties. He also produced *Broadway*, *King of Jazz*, *Imitation of Life* and *Showboat* and won a Best Picture Oscar for producing *All Quiet on the Western Front* in 1930. He resigned from Universal in 1936, becoming an independent producer, but failed to repeat his previous success.
Genre credits:
Dracula (1930), *Frankenstein* (1931), *The Old Dark House* (1932), *The Invisible Man* (1933), *The Bride of Frankenstein* (1935)

The Lair of the White Worm
GB 1988 93m Technicolor Dolby
A lady vampire lures a legendary serpent from its lair with human sacrifices.

Silly horror comic, updated from a Bram Stoker original. Occasional visual pleasures; the acting is pretty dreadful.
p: Ken Russell for Vestron
w/d: Ken Russell
novel: Bram Stoker
ph: Dick Bush
m: Stanislas Syrewicz
ed: Peter Davies
pd: Anne Tilby
sp: Geoff Portass, Alan Whibley
sound: Ray Beckett, Bill Rowe
add ph: Robin Browne
Amanda Donohoe, Hugh Grant, Catherine Oxenberg, Sammi Davis, Stratford Johns, Christopher Gable, Peter Capaldi, Imogen Claire, Paul Brooke

LaLoggia, Frank (1955-)
American writer, director and composer whose work has been primarily in the fantasy-horror genre.
Genre credits:
Fear No Evil (1981 - w/d/m), *The Lady in White* (1988 w/d/m)

Lamont, Charles (1898-1993)
American director long with Universal, where he directed several of Abbott and Costello's comedies. Directing silent shorts from 1923, he made his feature début in 1934 with *The Curtain Falls*. His other credits include *Salome Where She Danced*, *Slave Girl* and several of the *Ma and Pa Kettle* comedies.
Genre credits:
Abbott and Costello Meet the Invisible Man (1951), *Abbott and Costello Meet Dr Jekyll and Mr Hyde* (1953), *Abbott and Costello Meet the Mummy* (1955), *Francis in the Haunted House* (1956)

The Lamp
USA 1987 87m colour Dolby
A malevolent genie kills visitors to the museum where his lamp is on exhibition.

Poor video fodder, not worth renting.
p: Warren Chaney for HIT/Lamp
exec p: Fred T. Kuehnert, M. N. Sanousi
w: Warren Chaney
d: Tom Daley
ph: Herbert Raditschnig
m: Joel Rosenbaum, Bruce Miller
ed: Claudio Cutry
pd: Robert Burns
cos: Rona Lamont
sp: Martin Becker
sound: Tim Himes, Bob Waller, Steve Mann
2nd unit d: Warren Chaney
2nd unit ph: Scott Smith
Deborah Winters, James Huston, Mark Mitchell, Scott Blankston, Andra St Ivanyi, Danny H. Daniels, Jackson Bostwick (voice only, as the genie)

Lanchester, Elsa (1902-1986)
British character actress (real name Elizabeth Sullivan), long married to actor Charles Laughton with whom she co-starred in several films (*The Private Life of Henry VIII*, *Rembrandt*, *The Big Clock*, *Witness for the Prosecution*, etc.). On stage from the age of sixteen, she made her first film, *One of the Best*, in 1927, though she is best remembered by genre fans for her roles as both Mary Shelley and the Monster's mate in *The Bride of Frankenstein*. Her other credits include *David Copperfield*, *Come to the Stable*, *Bell, Book and Candle*, *Mary Poppins*, *Blackbeard's Ghost* and *Murder by Death*.
Genre credits:
The Ghost Goes West (1935), *The Bride of*

• Elsa Lanchester as the bride in director James Whale's *The Bride of Frankenstein*, one of the horror genre's true classics.

Frankenstein (1935), *The Spiral Staircase* (1945), *Willard* (1971), *Arnold* (1973), *Terror in the Wax Museum* (1973)

Landau, Martin (1928-)

American supporting actor, in such films as *North by Northwest*, *Cleopatra*, *Tucker: The Man and His Dreams* and *Crimes and Misdemeanours*. Won a Best Supporting Actor Oscar for his portrayal of Bela Lugosi in Tim Burton's *Ed Wood*. Also known for the TV series *Mission: Impossible* and *Space 1999*.
Genre credits:
The Fall of the House of Usher (1979), *Without Warning* (1980 - aka *It Came Without Warning/The Warning*), *Alone in the Dark* (1982), *The Being* (1983 [previously released as *Easter Sunday* in 1980]), *Ed Wood* (1994)

Landers, Lew (1901-1962)

Prolific American director (real name Lewis Friedlander) with a few interesting B horrors to his name. Other credits include *The Man Who Found Himself*, *The Enchanted Forest* and *Man in the Dark*.
Genre credits:
The Raven (1935), *The Boogie Man Will Get You* (1942), *Return of the Vampire* (1943), *The Ghost That Walks Alone* (1944), *Inner Sanctum* (1948)

Landis, John (1950-)

American writer and director with a penchant for all kinds of comedy, including *Kentucky Fried Movie*, *National Lampoon's Animal House*, *The Blues Brothers*

and three Eddie Murphy vehicles: *Trading Places*, *Coming to America* and *Beverly Hills Cop III*. Began his career in the mailroom at Fox, which he followed with experience as a production assistant and stuntman before going on to star as a prehistoric ape in his first film, *Schlock*, in 1972. Achieved a certain notoriety when three people (actor Vic Morrow and two Vietnamese child actors) were killed in a helicopter crash on the set of his *Twilight Zone* segment. He is now also appearing as a supporting actor in other director's films.
Genre credits:
Schlock (1976 - aka *The Banana Monster* - w/d/actor), *An American Werewolf in London* (1981 - w/d/actor), *The Twilight Zone* (1983 - co-w/co-d/co-p), *Thriller* (1983 - music video - d), *Spontaneous Combustion* (1989 - actor only), *Darkman* (1990 - actor only), *Psycho IV: The Beginning* (1990 -TVM - actor only), *Sleepwalkers* (1992 - actor only), *Innocent Blood* (1992 - aka *A French Vampire in America* - d), *The Stand* (1994 -TVM - actor only)

Landon, Michael (1936-1991)

American actor, best known for the TV series *Bonanza*, *Little House on the Prairie* and *Highway to Heaven*. His occasional films include *These Wilder Years*, *God's Little Acre*, *The Errand Boy* and, of course, *I Was a Teenage Werewolf* (1957) in which he played the title character.

Lang, Charles (1902-)

American cinematographer, a former lab assistant and assistant cameraman from the early twenties. Co-photographed his first film, *The Night Patrol*, in 1926, after which he went on to distinguish himself on such films as *The Lives of a Bengal Lancer*, *Ace in the Hole* (aka *The Big Carnival*), *Some Like It Hot* and *Charade*, winning an Oscar for *A Farewell to Arms* (1932).
Genre credits:
The Cat and the Canary (1939), *The Ghost Breakers* (1940), *The Uninvited* (1944), *The Ghost and Mrs Muir* (1947)

Langella, Frank (1940-)

Handsome American leading man (*The Twelve Chairs*, *Diary of a Mad Housewife*) with much stage experience. Made a mark in the 1979 version of *Dracula* (following playing the role on stage) after which he emerged as a character actor, often in villainous roles (*Masters of the Universe*, *Dave*, etc.).
Genre credits:
Dracula (1979), *Sphinx* (1981), *Brainscan* (1994)

Langenkamp, Heather (1964-)

American actress who came to attention in the first *Nightmare on Elm Street* movie and reappeared in several later episodes. Her other credits include *The Outsiders*, *Rumble Fish* and *Nickel Mountain*.
Genre credits:
A Nightmare on Elm Street (1984), *A Nightmare on Elm Street Part 3: The Dream Warriors* (1987), *Shocker* (1989), *Wes Craven's New Nightmare* (1994)

Larraz, Jose Ramon (1929-)

Spanish director (also known as Joseph Larraz) with a penchant for exploitation subjects often involving sex and horror. Perhaps best known for the British films *Symptoms* and *Vampyres*, he began directing in Britain in 1969 with *Whirlpool* (aka *She Died with Her Boots On*) following fifteen years in Paris where he worked as a comic strip artist and fashion photographer. Since his directorial début he has worked out of both Britain and Spain and his other credits include *Deviation*, *La Fin de la Inocencia*, *Violation of the Bitch* (aka *La Visita del Vicio*), *The Golden Lady* and *Sevilla Connection*. He also occasionally uses the pseudonym Joseph Braunstein.
Genre credits:
Scream and Die (1973 - aka *Psycho Sex Fiend/The House That Vanished*), *Emma, Puertas Oscuras* (1973), *Symptoms* (1974 - aka *The Blood Virgin*), *Vampyres* (1974 - aka *Daughters of Dracula/Vampyres - Daughters of Darkness/The Vampyre Orgy*), *Uncertain Death* (1977 - aka *La Muerte Incierta*), *Povlos Magicos* (1979), *The National Mummy* (1981 - aka *La Momia Nacional*), *The Sex Rites of the Devil* (1982 - *Black Candles/Los Ritos Sexuales del Diabolo*), *Estigma* (1981), *Rest in Pieces* (1987 aka *Descanse en Piezas* [as Joseph Braunstein]), *Edge of the Axe* (1989 - aka *Filo del Hacha* [as Joseph Braunstein]), *Deadly Manor* (1990 - aka *Savage Lust*)

The Last Horror Film

USA 1981 114m colour
A murderous fan follows a beautiful actress to the Cannes Film Festival.
Standard horror flick with a few flashes of local colour. Anoraks will be able to spot the author of this very book in a brief scene by a swimming pool. I'm the one in the striped trunks with my arms folded holding a camera, though you'll have to be quick with the still pause button to catch me. If only I was that slim now!
p: David Winters, Judd Hamilton for Sphere
w: Judd Hamilton, David Winters, Tom Klassen
d: David Winters

ph: Tom de Nove
m: Jesse Frederick, Jeff Koz
ed: Chris Barnes, Edward Salier
Caroline Munro, Joe Spinell, Judd
Hamilton, David Goldenberg, David
Winters, Stanley Susanne Benton, Mary
Spinell

Last House on the Left Part 2
see Bay of Blood

Last Video and Testament
GB 1984 74m Technicolor TVM
An electronic expert fakes his own
death after discovering his wife's
infidelities and extracts an elaborate
revenge.

Mild entry in an apparently endless
series of *Hammer House of Mystery and
Suspense* tele-thrillers.
p: Roy Skeggs for Hammer/TCF
w: Roy Russell
d: Peter Sasdy
ph: Frank Watts
md: Philip Martell
ed: Bob Dearberg
ad: Carolyn Scott
cos: Laura Nightingale
sound: John Bramall, Ernie Marsh
Deborah Raffin, David Langton, Oliver
Tobias, Christopher Scoular, Clifford
Rose, Shane Rimmer

The Late Nancy Irving
GB 1984 74m Technicolor TVM
A lady golfer is kidnapped by an
exclusive clinic because of her rare
blood type.

Another over padded *Hammer House
of Mystery and Suspense* drama.
p: Roy Skeggs for Hammer/TCF
w: David Fisher
d: Peter Sasdy
ph: Brian West
m: Paul Glass
md: Philip Martell
ed: Bob Dearberg
ad: Carolyn Scott
Christina Raines, Marius Goring, Mick
Ford, Simon Williams, Tony Anhalt,
Zienia Merton

Laughton, Charles (1899-1962)
Celebrated British character actor. A
former hotel clerk, he came to acting
via amateur dramatics, which led to his
enrolling at RADA. Made his West End
début in 1925 soon after which he met
and married actress Elsa Lanchester,
who co-starred with him in several
films. He appeared in a couple of British
shorts before making his feature début
in 1929 in *Piccadilly*, after which it was
but a short step to Hollywood. It was,
however, for the British film, *The Private
Life of Henry VIII* (1933), that he won the

Best Actor Oscar. A series of strongly
etched roles followed, including Javert
in *Les Miserables*, Captain Bligh in *Mutiny
on the Bounty* and Quasimodo in *The
Hunchback of Notre Dame*. The latter two,
of course, proved staples for impression-
ists for years. His other credits include
The Barretts of Wimpole Street, *Ruggles of
Red Gap*, *Rembrandt*, *Hobson's Choice*,
Witness for the Prosecution and *Spartacus*,
by which time he'd become a relishable
ham. He also directed one film, the
superbly cinematic *Night of the Hunter*.
Genre credits:
The Old Dark House (1932), *Island of Lost
Souls* (1932), *The Hunchback of Notre
Dame* (1939), *The Canterville Ghost*
(1944), *The Strange Door* (1951), *Night of
the Hunter* (1955 - d)

Laurie, Piper (1932 -)
American actress (real name Rosetta
Jacobs) with a variety of strong credits
to her name, including performances in
The Hustler, *Tim* and *Children of a Lesser
God*, though she is perhaps best
remembered by genre fans for playing
the reli-giously obsessed mother in
Brian de Palma's *Carrie*, which earned
her an Oscar nomination as Best
Supporting Actress.
Genre credits:
Carrie (1976), *Ruby* (1978), *Trauma*
(1993)

Lawrence, Brian (1920-)
British executive and executive producer who joined Exclusive in 1945 after
experience in the Anglo American Film
Corps during the war. Became
Exclusive's sales manager in 1950, then
general manager and assistant to studio
head James Carreras in the late fifties.
Became a Hammer board director in the
1960s. Formed Cinema Arts with partner Roy Skeggs in 1979 with whom he
took control of Hammer when it col-
lapsed in 1979. Executive produced
Hammer House of Horror (1980) and
Hammer House of Mystery and Suspense
(1984) for television. Retired in 1986.

Le Borg, Reginald (1902-1989)
Prolific Austrian director who, after
experience as a stage director in
Europe, moved to America in 1937,
where he found work as a choreograph-
er of musical sequences at Columbia
before moving on to direct shorts at
MGM. He made his first feature, *She's
for Me*, in 1943, after which he became
tied to the lower berths of Universal's
forties horror cycle. Directed seven of
Monogram's *Joe Palooka* series (*Joe
Palooka, Champ, Joe Palooka in the
Knockout, Joe Palooka in the Counterpunch*).

Genre credits:
Calling Dr Death (1943), *Weird Woman*
(1944), *The Mummy's Ghost* (1944), *Dead
Man's Eyes* (1944), *Jungle Woman* (1944),
The Black Sleep (1956), *Voodoo Island*
(1957), *Diary of a Madman* (1963), *The
Eyes of Annie Jones* (1964), *So Evil, My
Sister* (1972 - aka *Psycho Sisters*)

LeFanu, J. (Joseph) Sheridan (1814-1873)
Irish writer whose novella *Carmilla*, first
published in 1872, has been filmed
several times in various guises, most
notably as *Blood and Roses* (1960), *The
Vampire Lovers* (1970) and *Lust for a
Vampire* (1971). Other filmed works
include *Uncle Silas* (1949). Also see
Carmilla.

Leakey, Phil (1908-1992)
British make-up artist who, having
trained at Shepperton Studios in the
mid-forties, joined Hammer/Exclusive
in 1947, where he worked on many of
their second feature
thrillers/programmers, including *Meet
Simon Cherry*, *Room to Let* and *Someone at
the Door*. Worked on several of their key
fifties horror films before leaving, having
become disillusioned with their output.
Other credits include *Only Two Can Play*,
Sammy Going South, *The Ipcress File* and
The Belstone Fox.
Genre credits:
The Quatermass Experiment (1955 - aka
The Creeping Unknown), *The Curse of
Frankenstein* (1956), *X - The Unknown*
(1956), *Quatermass 2* (1957 - aka *Enemy
from Space*), *The Abominable Snowman*
(1957 - aka *The Abominable Snowman of
the Himalayas*), *Dracula* (1958 - aka
Horror of Dracula), *The Revenge of
Frankenstein* (1958), *Vampira* (1974 - aka
Old Dracula)

Lee, Christopher (1922-)
British actor whose prolific output has
mostly been in the horror genre, often
in partnership with Peter Cushing.
Regarded by many as the definitive
screen *Dracula*, he began his career after
military service during the war, winning
a seven year contract with Rank in
1947. However, his height proved a
restriction and he subsequently found
himself playing bit parts in all manner of
films, including *Corridor of Mirrors*,
Hamlet, *Prelude to Fame*, *A Tale of Two
Cities* and *Valley of Eagles*. Ironically, his
height did win him the role of the
Creature in Hammer's *The Curse of
Frankenstein* in 1956, after which it was
but a short step to the title roles in
Dracula and *The Mummy*. International
fame in the horror genre followed,

STRANGE,
FORBIDDING,
THRILLING—

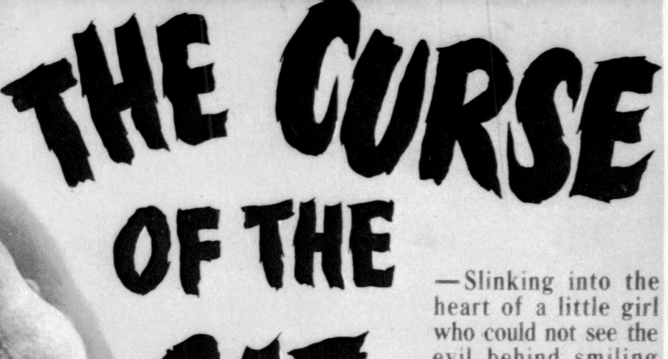

THE CURSE OF THE CAT PEOPLE

— Slinking into the heart of a little girl who could not see the evil behind smiling lips that could snarl, and feline fingers that could rip young flesh to shreds!

VAL LEWTON'S *THE CURSE OF THE CAT PEOPLE* was a follow up to his 1942 classic *Cat People* and marked the directorial debut of former editor Robert Wise, who would go on to helm such diverse classics as *The Body Snatcher*, *The Set-Up*, *The Day the Earth Stood Still*, *West Side Story* and *The Sound of Music*.

Simone
SIMON

Kent
SMITH

ANN CARTER • ELIZABETH RUSSELL • EVE MARCH
JULIA DEAN • ERFORD GAGE • SIR LANCELOT

• Christopher Lee as Lord Summerisle in the classic British shocker *The Wicker Man*. Lee himself regards this as among the highlights of his career.

though his gradual dissatisfaction with Hammer's treatment of the *Dracula* series saw him distance himself from the genre in the seventies with well received performances in *The Three Musketeers*, *The Man with the Golden Gun*, *The Four Musketeers* and *1941*. Formed Charlemagne Productions in 1972 with Hammer producer Anthony Nelson Keyes, but their only film, *Nothing But the Night* (1972), in which he also appeared, was not a success. Also a singer and linguist, he has made films in several languages.
Genre credits:
The Curse of Frankenstein (1956), *Dracula* (1958 - aka *Horror of Dracula*), *Corridors of Blood* (1958 - aka *The Doctor from Seven Dials*), *The Mummy* (1959), *The Hound of the Baskervilles* (1959), *The Man Who Could Cheat Death* (1959), *City of the Dead* (1960 -aka *Horror Hotel*), *The Two Faces of Dr Jekyll* (1960 - aka *House of Fright/Jekyll's Inferno*), *The Hands of Orlac* (1961 - aka *Hands of a Strangler*), *Hard Times for Vampires* (1961 - aka *Uncle Was a Vampire/Tempi Duri Per I Vampiri*), *The Terror of the Tongs* (1961), *Taste of Fear* (1961 - aka *Scream of Fear*), *Hercules in the Centre of the Earth* (1961 - aka *Hercules in the Haunted World/Vampires vs Hercules*), *The Devil's Daffodil* (1961 - aka *The Daffodil Killer/Secret of the Devil's Daffodil*), *The Devil's Agent* (1962 - aka *Im Namen Teufels*), *Castle of Terror* (1963 - aka *Horror Castle/La Vergine di Norimberga*), *Crypt of Horror* (1963 - aka *Terror on the Crypt/The Vampire's Crypt/La Cripta E L'Incubo/La Maldición*

des Los Karlstein), *Castle of Terror* (1963 - aka *Le Vergina di Norimberga*), *Night of ther Phantom* (1963 -aka *The Whip and the Body/What!/La Frustra E Il Corpo*), *Sherlock Holmes and the Deadly Necklace* (1963 - aka *Sherlock Holmes und das Halsband des Todes*), *The Gorgon* (1964), *Dr Terror's House of Horrors* (1964), *Castle of the Living Dead* (1964 - aka *Il Castello dei Morti Vivi*), *The Masque of the Red Death* (1964 - voice only), *The Face of Fu Manchu* (1965), *She* (1965), *Theatre of Death* (1965 - aka *Blood Fiend*), *Circus of Fear* (1965 - aka *Psycho Circus*), *The Skull* (1965), *Dracula - Prince of Darkness* (1966), *Rasputin - The Mad Monk* (1966), *The Brides of Fu Manchu* (1966), *The Vengeance of Fu Manchu* (1967), *Night of the Big Heat* (1967 - aka *Island of the Burning Damned*), *Victims of Terror* (1967 - aka *Victims of Vesuvius* - short), *The Blood Demon* (1967 - aka *Die Schlangengrube und das Pendel*), *The Devil Rides Out* (1967 - aka *The Devil's Bride*), *The Vengeance of Fu Manchu* (1967), *Dracula Has Risen from the Grave* (1968), *The Blood of Fu Manchu* (1968), *The Curse of the Crimson Altar* (1968 - aka *The Crimson Cult*), *The Castle of Fu Manchu* (1968 - aka *Assignment Istanbul/Die Folterkammer des Du Manchu*), *Blood of Fu Manchu* (1968 - aka *Kiss and Kill/Against All Odds/Fu Manchu and the Kiss of Death*), *One More Time* (1969 - gag cameo as Dracula/himself), *The Oblong Box* (1969), *Scream and Scream Again* (1969), *Taste the Blood of Dracula* (1970), *The House That Dripped Blood* (1970), *Bram Stoker's Count Dracula* (1970 - aka *El Conde Dracula/Count Dracula/Dracula '71*), *Scars of Dracula* (1970), *The Bloody Judge* (1970 - aka *Night of the Blood Monster/Throne of Blood/Il Trono di Fuoco*), *In Search of Dracula* (1971 - TV documentary), *I, Monster* (1971), *Dracula AD 1972* (1972), *Horror Express* (1972 -aka *Panico En El Transiberio*), *The Creeping Flesh* (1972), *Death Line* (1972 - aka *Raw Meat*), *Nothing But the Night* (1972), *Poor Devil* (1972 - TVM), *Dark Places* (1973), *The Satanic Rites of Dracula* (1973), *Dark Places* (1973), *The Wicker Man* (1973), *The Keeper* (1975), *Whispering Death* (1975), *To the Devil... A Daughter* (1976), *Revenge of the Dead* (1976 - voice only), *Dracula, Father and Son* (1976 - aka *Dracula, Pere et Fils*), *The End of the World* (1977), *The Meat Cleaver Massacre* (1977), *The House of the Longshadows* (1982), *The Howling II: Your Sister is a Werewolf* (1985), *Gremlins 2: The New Batch* (1990), *Curse III: Blood Sacrifice* (1990), *Funnyman* (1994)

Lee, Rowland V. (1891-1975)
American writer, producer and director with several interesting credits to his name (*The Count of Monte Cristo*, *Cardinal Richelieu*, *The Three Musketeers*), including the third episode in Universal's *Frankenstein* cycle, *Son of Frankenstein*. A former stage actor with experience as a stockbroker on Wall Street, he entered films as an actor in 1915, turning to direction in 1920 with *The Cup of Life*.
Genre credits:
Son of Frankenstein (1939 - p/d), *Tower of London* (1939 - p/d)

The Legend of the Seven Golden Vampires
GB/Hong Kong 1974 88m
Eastmancolor
In 1904 Professor Van Helsing tracks down the six surviving members of a vampire cult in Chung King.
　　Dismal amalgam of poorly staged thrills and karate, the nadir of the Hammer horror cycle.
p: Vee King Shaw, Don Houghton for Hammer
exec p: Michael Carreras
w: Don Houghton
d: Roy Ward Baker
ph: John Wilcox, Roy Ford
m: James Bernard
md: Philip Martell
ed: Chris Barnes, Larry Richmond
ad: Johnson Tsau
cos: Lui Chi-Yu
sp: Les Bowie
sound: Les Hammond
fight ch: Tang Chia, Liu Chia-Liang
Peter Cushing, David Chiang, Julie Ege, John Forbes Robertson (as Dracula), Robin Stewart

The Legacy
GB 1978 102m Technicolor Dolby
An American designer and her boyfriend are invited to stay at a mysterious English country mansion after a car accident and find they cannot leave it.
　　Tired and unimaginative diabolical mumbo jumbo that becomes tedious well before the end.
p: David Foster for Columbia/Pethurst/Turman-Foster
w: Jimmy Sangster, Patrick Tilley, Paul Wheeler
d: Richard Marquand
ph: Dick Bush, Alan Hume
m,: Michael J. Lewis
ed: Anne V. Coates
pd: Disley Jones
cos: John Motherhill
sp: Ian Wingrove
sound: Brian Simmons, Bill Rowe
Katherine Ross, Sam Elliott, John Standing, Ian Hogg, Charles Gray, Margaret Tyzack, Lee Montague, Hildegard Neil, Roger Daltry

The Legend of Hell House **

GB 1973 94m DeLuxe
Four parapsychologists accept £100,000 to investigate a haunted house where several unaccounted murders have taken place.

Genuinely frightening haunted house chiller with just the right style and atmosphere. Not for the nervous.
p: Albert Fennell, Norman T. Herman for TCF/Academy
exec p: James H. Nicholson
w: Richard Matheson from his novel
d: JOHN HOUGH
ph: Alan Hume
m: Brian Hidgson, Delia Derbyshire
ed: GEOFFREY FOOT
ad: Robert Jones
cos: Eileen Sullivan
sp: Tom Howard, Roy Whybrow
sound: BILL ROWE, LES HAMMOND
Pamela Franklin, Roddy McDowall, Clive Revill, Gayle Hunnicutt, Roland Culver, Peter Bowles, Michael Gough

Legend of the Werewolf

GB 1974 90m Eastmancolor
A young man, brought up by wolves, gets a job at a zoo in Paris, but it's not long before he goes on the rampage.

Tolerable low-budget werewolf saga, rather restrictedly set. Okay for fans but the acting's on the wooden side.
p: Kevin Francis for Tyburn
w: John Elder (Anthony Hinds)
d: Freddie Francis
ph: John Wilcox
m: Harry Robinson
ed: Henry Richardson
ad: Jack Shepman, Brian Ackland-Snow
make-up: Graham Freeborn
Peter Cushing, Ron Moody, David Rintoul (as the werewolf), Hugh Griffith, Roy Castle, Stefan Gryff, Lynn Dalby, Renee Houston

Leigh, Janet (1927-)

Glamorous American actress, notable in such films as *Houdini*, *My Sister Eileen*, *Touch of Evil* and *The Vikings*, though most memorable as Marion Crane, the runaway thief in Hitchcock's *Psycho* (1960). However, after her famous encounter with 'mother' in the shower at the Bates Motel, she eschewed horror films until she popped up in John Carpenter's *Fog* in 1978, which starred her daughter, Jamie Lee Curtis.

Leon, Valerie

Glamorous British actress and model familiar to TV audiences in the seventies for a series of commercials for Hai Karate aftershave. Brief appearances on TV (*The Saint*, *The Avengers*, *Randall and Hopkirk*, *The Persuaders*, *The Baron*) and in films (*Carry On Camping*, *Carry On Up the Khyber*, *Carry On Again Doctor*, *The Italian Job*, *Carry on Up the Jungle*, etc.) led to her only leading role in Hammer's *Blood from the Mummy's Tomb* in 1971. Subsequent film appearances include *Carry On Matron*, *The Spy Who Loved Me*, *The Revenge of the Pink Panther* and *Never Say Never Again*.

The Leopard Man **

USA 1943 60m bw
A small Mexican township sees a series of murders which may or may not be attributable to an escaped leopard.

Atmospheric addition to the Lewton gallery of horrors, containing many effective, though not always logical, sequences.
p: VAL LEWTON for RKO
w: Ardel Wray, Edward Dein
novel: Cornell Woolrich
d: JACQUES TOURNEUR
ph: ROBERT DE GRASSE
m: Roy Webb
md: Constantin Bakaleinikoff
ed: Mark Robson
ad: Albert S. D'Agistino, Walter E. Keller
sound: J. C. Grubb
Dennis O'Keefe, Jean Brooks, Margo, James Bell, Isabel Jewell

Leroux, Gaston

French novelist whose 1910 novel *The Phantom of the Opera* has been filmed a number of times, most notably in 1923, 1943, 1962, 1983 (TVM), 1989 and 1990 (TVM). Other variations include *The Phantom of the Paradise*, *The Phantom of Hollywood* (TVM) and *Phantom of the Mall: Eric's Revenge*. Also see *The Phantom of the Opera*.

Let Sleeping Corpses Lie see The

Living Dead at the Manchester Morgue

Leviathan

USA/It 1989 98m Technicolor Dolby
Miners working from a station based on the ocean floor find themselves prey to a genetically created monster.

Tolerable underwater variation on *Alien* and *The Thing*. It passes the time.
p: Luigi de Laurentiis, Aurelio de Laurentiis for Fox/Gordon/Filmauro
exec p: Lawrence Gordon, Charles Gordon
w: David Peoples, Jeb Stuart
story: David Peoples
d: George Pan Cosmatos
ph: Alex Thomson
m: Jerry Goldsmith
ed: Robert Silvi, John F. Burnett
pd: Ron Cobb
cos: April Ferry
sp: Stan Winston, Barry Nolan
sound: Robin Gregory
Peter Weller, Richard Crenna, Amanda Pays, Michael Carmine, Daniel Stern, Ernie Hudson, Hector Elizondo, Lisa Eilbacher, Meg Foster

Lewis, Fiona (1946-)

Glamorous British actress who has appeared in a wide variety of films in both Britain and America, usually in slightly offbeat roles. Her credits include *Otley*, *Where's Jack?* *Lisztomania*, *Stunts*, *Wanda Nevada* and *Innerspace*.
Genre credits:
Dance of the Vampires (1967 - aka *The Fearless Vampire Killers/Pardon Me, But Your Teeth Are in My Neck*), *Dr Phibes Rises Again* (1972), *Dracula* (1973 - TVM), *The Fury* (1978), *Strange Behaviour* (1981 - aka *Dead Kids*), *Strange Invaders* (1983)

Lewis, Herschell Gordon (1926-)

American writer, producer and director of gory and luridly titled exploitation flicks, several of which have gained cult status. A former English professor he produced his first film, *The Prime Time*, in 1960. Dabblings with soft core porn followed (*Lucky Pierre*, *Nature's Playmates*, *B-O-I-N-N-N-G!*, *Goldilocks and the Three Bares*, etc.), after which he turned to the horror genre, sometimes photographing and scoring his films himself, which broke new boundaries with their extreme gore and violence. The first of these, which set the pattern for what was to follow, was *Blood Feast*, filmed in Miami for $70,000 in nine days. He retired from filmmaking in the early seventies to concentrate on business interests, though many still consider him the grandfather of the modern day splatter/gore film. His other credits include *Alley Tramp*, *Santa Visits the Magic Land of Mother Goose*, *The Ecstasies of Women*, *Linda and Abilene* and *Miss Nymphet's Zap-In*.
Genre credits:
Blood Feast (1963 - d/ph/m/sp), *Two-Thousand Maniacs* (1964 -w/d/ph), *Color Me Blood Red* (1964 - w/d/ph), *Monster a Go-Go* (1965 - co-p/co-d), *The Gruesome Twosome* (1965 - p/d/ph), *How to Make a Doll* (1967 - co-w/p/d), *A Taste of Blood* (1967 - p/d), *Something Weird* (1968 - d), *She-Devils on Wheels* (1968 - p/d), *The Wizard of Gore* (1970 - p/d), *The Gore-Gore Girls* (1971 - p/d/m - aka *Blood Orgy*)

Lewis, Michael J. (1939-)

Underrated British composer who has contributed memorable scores to *Julius Caesar* and *The Medusa Touch* and others.
Genre credits:
The Man Who Haunted Himself (1970),

Theatre of Blood (1973), The Medusa Touch (1978), The Legacy (1979), Sphinx (1981), The Unseen (1981)

Lewton, Val (1904-1951)

Russian born producer (real name Vladimir Ivan Leventon), responsible for a series of restrained yet effective low-budget horror thrillers for RKO in the forties. In America from the age of five, he trained as a journalist before turning to writing in the twenties. Began work as a publicist for MGM in 1928, becoming a story editor for David O. Selznick in 1933, for whom he also acted as a production supervisor for the mammoth storming of the Bastille sequence in the 1935 version of A Tale of Two Cities. Turned producer in 1942, his first film being the genre classic Cat People. He also wrote screenplays under the name of Carlos Keith. His non-genre credits include Mademoiselle Fifi, Youth Runs Wild, My Own True Love, Please Believe Me and Apache Drums.
Genre credits:
Cat People (1942 - p), I Walked with a Zombie (1943 - p), The Leopard Man (1943 - p), The Ghost Ship (1943 - p), The Seventh Victim (1943 - p), Curse of the Cat People (1944 - p), The Body Snatcher (1945 - p/w [w as Carlos Keith]), Isle of the Dead (1945), Bedlam (1946 - p/w [w as Carlos Keith])

The Lift

Netherlands 1983 99m Eastmancolor
A newly installed lift unaccountably starts to murder its passengers.
    Fairly slick horror story that does quite well by its silly premise.
p: Matthis Van Heijningen for Sigma
w/m: Dick Maas
d: DICK MAAS
ph: Andre Sjouerman
ed: Hans Van Dongen
ad: Harry Ammerlaan
sp: Leo Chan
Huub Stapel, Willeke Van Ammelrooy, Josine Van Dalsum, Hans Dagelet, Ab Alsopoel

Lindfors, Viveca (1920-1995)

Swedish actress (real name Elsa Viveca Torstedotter Lindfors), in Hollywood from 1946, prior to which she had made a few films in her home country, the first of these being The Spinning Family in 1940. She has done much theatre work in Europe and has appeared in a variety of international productions, including The Adventures of Don Juan, Singoalla, King of Kings, A Wedding and Stargate, though she is perhaps best remembered by genre fans for her performance in Creepshow.

Genre credits:
Cauldron of Blood (1968 - aka Blind Man's Bluff), The Hand (1981), Creepshow (1982), Silent Madness (1984), Frankenstein's Aunt (1986), The Exorcist III (1990)

Link *

GB 1986 103m Technicolor Dolby
An educated chimapnzee goes on the rampage at an isolated research institute.
    Over long gimmick thriller with interesting touches to compensate for the far-fetched plot, which seems to have been borrowed from Poe's Murders in the Rue Morgue.
p: Richard Franklin, Richard McCallum for Cannon/EMI
exec p: Verity Lambert
w: Everet de Roche
story: Lee Zlotoff, Tom Ackerman
d: Richard Franklin
ph: Mike Malloy
m: JERRY GOLDSMITH
ed: Andrew London
pd: Norman Garwood
cos: Catherine Cook
sp: John Gant
sound: David Stephenson
animal trainer: Ray Berwick
wnd unit ph: Mike Proudfoot
Elisabeth Shue, Terence Stamp, Steven Pinner, Richard Garnett, David O'Hara, Joe Belcher, Kevin Lloyd

Lippert, Robert L. (1909-1976)

American producer, director and exhibitor through whom Hammer/Exclusive gained Stateside releases for many of their early films, in return for which Exclusive obtained the rights to release such Lippert produced films as Rocketship XM and The Lost Continent in Britain.

Lisa and the Devil

It 1972 87m Eastmancolor
A lady tourist finds herself stranded in an old Spanish mansion where strange occurrences are the order of the day.
    Foolishly plotted horror film with the odd moment for connoisseurs of its director. It was also re-released in 1975 as House of Exorcism to cash in on the Exorcist boom.
p: Alfred Leone for Leone International
w: Alberto Tintini, Alfred Leone
d: Mario Bava (credited as Mickey Lion)
ph: Cecilio Panigua
m: Carlo Savina
ed: Carlo Reali
ad: Nedo Azzini
sp: Franco Toco
sound: Lamberto Bava
Elke Sommer, Telly Savalas (as a lollipop-sucking butler), Alida Valli, Alessio Orano

Little, Dwight H.

American director who seems to alternate horror films with action films (Lethal, Marked for Death, Rapid Fire).
Genre credits:
Bloodstone (1988), Halloween 4: The Return of Michael Myers (1988), The Phantom of the Opera (1989)

The Little Girl Who Lives Down the Lane

Canada 1976 94m Technicolor
A teenage girl resorts to murder to hide the fact that she's keeping her dead mother's body in the cellar.
    Over stretched would-be thriller which takes a long time getting nowhere in particular. It might have worked better as a TV half hour.
p: Zev Braun, Denis Heroux, Leland Nolan, Eugene Lepicier for ICL
exec p: Harold Greenberg, Alfred Pariser
w: Laird Koenig from his novel
d: Nicholas Gessner
ph: Rene Verzier
m: Christian Gaubert, Chopin
md: Mort Shuman
ed: Yves Langlois
ad: Robert Prevost
cos: Denis Sperdouklis
sp: Charles Harbor
sound: Patrick Rousseau
Jodie Foster, Martin Sheen, Alexis Smith, Scott Jacoby, Mort Shuman

Little Shop of Horrors *

USA/GB 1986 88m Technicolor
In New York's Skid Row, a young florist cultivates a carnivorous plant from outer space.
    Expensive fantasy musical via a cult off-Broadway show and a 1960 Corman quickie. Generally amusing for those in the mood, though not quite in the same league as The Rocky Horror Picture Show.
p: David Geffen for Warner/Geffen
w: Howard Ashman from his musical book
d: Frank Oz
ph: Robert Paynter
m: Alan Menken
ly: Howard Ashman
md: Miles Goodman
ed: John Jympson
pd: Roy Walker
cos: Marit Allen
sp: Bran Ferren, Lyle Conway
sound: Peter Sutton
ch: Pat Garrett
titles: Bran Ferren
Rick Moranis, Ellen Greene, Vincent Gardenia, Steve Martin, James Belushi, Bill Murray, Christopher Guest, John Candy, Tichina Arnold, Tisha Campbell, Michelle Weeks, Stanley Jones, Bertice

Reading, Ed Wiley, Alan Tilvern, John Scott Martin, Vincent Wong, Miriam Margolyes, Bob Sherman, Levi Stubbs (as the voice of Audrey II)

The Live Ghost *
USA 1934 20m bw
Stan and Ollie help the captain of an apparently haunted ship to Shanghai men for his next voyage.

Fairish Laurel and Hardy romp with a few good gags along the way.
p: H. M. Walker (uncredited)
d: Charles Rogers
ph: Art Lloyd
m: no credit given
ed: Lois McManus
sound: James Greene
Stan Laurel, Oliver Hardy, Arthur Housman, Walter Long, Mae Busch, Charlie Hall, Leo Willis

The Living Dead at the Manchester Morgue
Sp 1974 93m Eastmancolor
An experimental sonic device used to kill insects on a farm revives the dead.

Filmed by a Spanish crew in England, this rip-off of George Romero's *Night of the Living Dead*, which exists in varying degrees of goriness, has its moments, but is too long drawn-out to be entirely effective. The English language version is poorly dubbed and the writers' lack of local geography is also glaringly obvious.
p: Edmundo Amati for Flaminia/ Miracle/Star
w: Sandro Continenza, Marcello Coscia

d: Jorge Grau
ph: Francisco Sempere
m: Giuliano Sorgini
ed: Vincenzo Tomassi
pd: Carlo Leva
ad: Rafael Ferri
cos: Carmen de la Casa
sp: Giannetto de Rossi, Luciano Bird
sound: Antonio Cardenas
Ray Lovelock, Arthur Kennedy, Christine Galbo, Roberto Posse, Giorgio Trestini, Aldo Massasso

Living Doll
GB 1989
A medical student kidnaps the dead body of the girl he's loved from afar.

Cheapjack low-budgeter that distinctly fails to amuse.
d: Peter Litten, George Dugdale
Mark Jax, Katie Ogrill, Eartha Kitt, Gary Martin, Freddie Earle

Lloyd, Christopher (1938-)
American character actor with stage experience. Came to note in the TV sit-com *Taxi* as Reverend Jim, after which he tackled a wide variety of eccentric comedy parts on the big screen, most notably as Doc in the *Back to the Future* trilogy. He has also played Uncle Fester in the two big screen *Addams Family* movies. Other credits include *One Flew Over the Cuckoo's Nest*, *Star Trek III: The Search for Spock*, *Who Framed Roger Rabbit?* and *Angels in the Outfield*.
Genre credits:
Schizoid (1980), *The Addams Family* (1991), *Addams Family Values* (1993)

The Lodger ****
GB 1926 85m bw/tinted silent
The new lodger at a London boarding house is suspected of being a Jack the Ripper called The Avenger.

Hitchcock's third film but his first true suspense story features many of the devices he would return to again and again throughout his career. Given its age, the film has barely dated, save a wooden leading performance, and the techniques involved, many of them new at the time, still ensure that the picture retains its grip.
p: Michael Balcon, Carlyle Blackwell for Gaumont
w: Eliot Stannard
novel: Belloc Lowdnes
d: ALFRED HITCHCOCK
ph: Baron Ventimiglia
ed: Ivor Montague
ad: C. Wilfred Arnold, Bertram Evans
titles: E. McKnight Kauffer
ass d: Alma Reville
Ivor Novello, June, Malcolm Keen, Arthur Chesney, Marie Ault

The Lodger *
USA 1944 84m bw
A lodger in a London boarding house is suspected of being Jack the Ripper. And he is…

An atmospheric little thriller with some very effective passages. Neatly done.
p: Robert Bassler for TCF
w: Barre Lyndon
d: JOHN BRAHM
ph: LUCIEN BALLARD
m: Hugo Friedhofer
md: Emil Newman
ed: J. Watson Webb, Jr.
ad: JAMES BASEVI, JOHN EWING
cos: Rene Hubert
LAIRD CREGAR, Merle Oberon, George Sanders, Cedric Hardwicke, Sara Allgood, Aubrey Mather, Queen Leonard, Helena Pickard, Lumsden Hare, Frederick Warlock

LoDuca, Joe
American composer who began his career scoring the films of director Sam Raimi. His other credits include the TV series *Hercules - The Legendary Journeys*.
Genre credits:
The Evil Dead (1983), *Evil Dead 2: Dead by Dawn* (1987), *Army of Darkness* (1992 - aka *Evil Dead III: Army of Darkness/The Medieval Dead*), *Necronomicon* (1993)

Lom, Herbert (1917-)
Czech born character actor (real name Herbert Charles Angelo Kuchacevich ze Schluderpacheru), equally adept at comic or sinister roles, though probably

• The hungry dead prepare to attack in *The Living Dead at the Manchester Morgue*, a Spanish financed, American influenced flick filmed in England.

best known as the twitching Inspector Dreyfus in the *Pink Panther* films. Other films include *The Seventh Veil*, *The Ladykillers*, *Mysterious Island* (as Captain Nemo) and *King Solomon's Mines*.
Genre credits:
The Dark Tower (1943), *The Phantom of the Opera* (1962), *Doppelganger* (1968 aka *Journey to the Far Side of the Sun*), *Mark of the Devil* (1969 - aka *Austria 1700/Hexen Geschandet und zu Tode Gequalt*), *Count Dracula* (1969 - aka *Bram Stoker's Count Dracula/Les Nuits de Dracula/El Conde Dracula*), *Dorian Gray* (1970 - aka *The Secret of Dorian Gray*), *Murders in the Rue Morgue* (1971), *Asylum* (1972), *And Now the Screaming Starts* (1973), *The Dead Zone* (1983), *The Masque of the Red Death* (1990), *The Sect* (1991 - aka *La Setta*)

Lommel, Ulli (1944-)
German director working in America, often photographing his own films. A former actor, he appeared in several of Rainer Werner Fassbinder's films before picking up the megaphone.
Genre credits:
The Tenderness of the Wolves (1973 - aka *Zartlichkeit der Wolfe* - d), *Satan's Brew* (1976 - aka *Satansbraten* - actor only), *The Boogey Man* (1980 - d/actor), *Brainwaves* (1983 - d/ph), *The Devonsville Terror* (1983 - co-w/d/ph), *Overkill* (1986 - d)

The Long Hair of Death
It 1964 98m bw
In the sixteenth century, a woman burned at the stake for witchcraft places a curse on those responsible.

Good looking but rather silly spaghetti horror, somewhat typical of its period.
p: Felice Testa Gay for Cinegay
w: Robert Bohr
story: Julian Berry
d: Anthony M. Dawson (Antonio Margheriti)
ph: Richard Thierry
m: Evirust
ed: Mark Sirandrews
ad: George Greenwood
sound: Robert Tennberg
Barbara Steele, Giorgio, Halina Zalewska, Robert Rains, Jean Rafferty, Laureen Nuyen, John Carey, Jeffrey Darcey

The Long Weekend *
Australia 1977 100m Technicolor Panavision
A young couple camping on a remote beach find themselves at the mercy of the local wildlife.

Ecological thriller which plays like a cross between *The Birds* and *Frogs*.

Unsettling moments.
p: Colin Eggleston for Dugong
exec p: Richard Brennan
w: Everett De Roche
d: COLIN EGGLESTON
ph: Vincent Monton
m: Michael Carlos
ed: Brian Kavanagh
pd: Larry Eastwood
cos: Kevin Reagan
sp: Ivan Durrant
sound: John Phillips
John Hargreaves, Briony Behets, Mike McEwen, Roy Day, Michael Aitkens, Sue Kiss Von Soley

Loomis, Nancy
American actress who played Annie, one of the teenage victims in John Carpenter's *Halloween* (1978), but has made too few films since, her only other genre appearance being in Carpenter's *The Fog* (1979).

Lords, Traci (1968-)
American actress (real name Nora Louise Kuzma) who gained a certain notoriety as an under-age teenage porn star before turning legitimate in 1988 with the remake *Not of This Earth*. Since then she has appeared in a variety of comedy sexpot roles, including two for director John Waters in *Cry-Baby* and *Serial Mom*.
Genre credits:
Not of This Earth (1988), *Shock 'Em Dead* (1990), *The Tommyknockers* (1993 - TVM)

Lorre, Peter (1904-1964)
Much impersonated Hungarian actor (real name Laszlo Lowenstein), in America from 1935 after starring in several German films, including the Fritz Lang classic *M*, as well as Hitchcock's *The Man Who Knew Too Much* in Britain. A memorable supporting actor throughout the thirties and forties in such films as *The Maltese Falcon*, *Casablanca* and *The Mask of Demetrios*, he also appeared as the Japanese sleuth *Mr Moto* in several second features (*Thankyou, Mr Moto*, *Think Fast, Mr Moto*, *Mr Moto's Last Warning*, etc.). His many other credits include *The Secret Agent*, *Casbah*, *20,000 Leagues Under the Sea*, *Around the World in 80 Days* and *Voyage to the Bottom of the Sea*.
Genre credits:
M (1931), *Mad Love* (1935 - aka *The Hands of Orlac*), *You'll Find Out* (1937), *The Face Behind the Mask* (1941), *The Invisible Agent* (1942), *The Boogie Man Will Get You* (1942), *The Beast with Five Fingers* (1946), *Tales of Terror* (1962), *The Raven* (1963), *The Comedy of Terrors* (1963)

The Lost Boys *
USA 1987 91m Technicolor Panavision Dolby
Two teenage brothers move with their mother to the west coast township of Santa Clara and find themselves threatened by a gang of vampires. Trendy modern day vampire saga for the MTV crowd, with effective sequences along the way.
exec p: Richard Donner, Mark Damon, John Hyde
p: Harvey Bernhard for Warner
w: Janice Fischer, James Jeremias, Jeffrey Boam
story: Janice Fischer, James Jeremias
d: Joel Schumacher
ph: Michael Chapman
m: Thomas Newman
ed: Rob Brown
pd: Bo Welch
2nd unit d: James Arnett
2nd unit ph: Paul Goldsmith
cos: Susan Becker
sp: Eric Brevig
make-up: Greg Cannom
sound: David Ronne
titles: Anthony Goldschmidt
aerial ph: Frank Holgate
Jason Patric, Corey Haim, Dianne Wiest, Barnard Hughes, Edward Herrmann, Kiefer Sutherland, Jami Gertz, Corey Feldman, Billy Wirth, Brooke McCarter, Alexander Winter

The Lost Continent
GB 1968 98m Technicolor
Passengers on a tramp steamer come across a strange island governed by the Spanish Inquisition.

Preposterous adventure yarn with a few absurd looking monsters thrown in for good measure. One or two lively moments but the results are mostly tedious. Director Michael Carreras replaced Leslie Norman after just a couple of days.
p: Michael Carreras for Hammer
w: Michael Nash (Michael Carreras)
novel: Dennis Wheatley
d: Michael Carreras
ph: Paul Beeson
m: Gerard Schurmann
md: Philip Martell
ed: James Needs, Chris Barnes
ad: ARTHUR LAWSON
cos: Carl Toms
sp: Robert A. Mattey, Cliff Richardson
Eric Porter, Hildegarde Neff, Suzanna Leigh, Tony Beckley, Nigel Stock, Jimmy Hanley, Michael Ripper

Lost Women see Mesa of Lost Women

Lourie, Eugene (1905-1991)
Russian born art director, a stage painter

and set designer in France from 1921, which led to film work, including several for director Jean Renoir in the thirties (*Madame Bovary*, *La Grande Illusion*, *La Regle du Jeu*, *La Bete Humaine*, etc.). Went to Hollywood in 1942 where he worked on several of Renoir's American films (*The Southerner*, *Diary of a Chambermaid*), acting as associate producer on the director's *This Land Is Mine*. He later turned to direction himself in 1953 with less distinguished results.
Genre credits:
House of Fear (1945 - ad), *The Beast from 20,000 Fathoms* (1953 - d/ad), *The Colossus of New York* (1958 - d), *The Giant Behemoth* (1959 - aka *Behemoth - The Sea Monster* - w/co-d), *Gorgo* (1960 - d/co-story), *The Strangler* (1963 - co-ad), *What's the Matter with Helen?* (1971 - ad), *Haunts of the Very Rich* (1972 - TVM - ad), *Burnt Offerings* (1976 - ad)

Love at First Bite *
USA 1979 96m Technicolor
When the Communists take over his castle, Count Dracula moves to New York where he falls in love with a glamorous model.
    Generally agreeable spoof with a smattering of bright gags, though the production could have been a lot sharper. A popular success, nevertheless.
p: Joel Freeman for Melvin Simon
exec p: Robert Kaufman, George Hamilton
w: Robert Kaufman
story: Mark Gindes, Robert Kaufman
d: Stan Dragoti
ph: Edward Rosson
m: Charles Bernstein
ed: Mort Fallick, Allan Jacobs
pd: Serge Krizman
cos: Oscar de la Renta
sp: Allen Hall
sound: Don Bassman, Ron Cogswell
2nd unit d: Gray Johnson
2nd unit ph: John Elsenbach
GEORGE HAMILTON, Susan Saint James, RICHARD BENJAMIN, ARTE JOHNSON, Dick Shawn, Sherman Helmsley, Isabel Sanford

Lovecraft, H. P. (1890-1937)
American writer whose novels and short stories have popped up in a variety of cinematic guises, not always to their advantage. The following is a list of films inspired by his work.
Genre credits:
The Haunted Palace (1963), *Die, Monster, Die!* (1965 - aka *Monster of Terror*), *The Dunwich Horror* (1969), *Re-Animator* (1985), *From Beyond* (1986 - aka *H. P. Lovecraft's From Beyond*), *The Farm* (1987), *The Gate* (1987), *The Unnameable* (1988 -

• **Bela Lugosi's** *Dracula* **shrinks from the cross held by Edward Van Sloan's Van Helsing in Universal's** *Dracula*, **the success of which launched the golden age of Hollywood horror.**

aka *H. P. Lovecraft's The Unnamable*), *Re-Animator 2* (1989 - aka *Bride of the Re-Animator*), *The Resurrected* (1991), *Gate 2* (1992), *The Unnameable Returns* (1992 - aka *H. P. Lovecraft's The Unnameable Returns*), *Necronomicon* (1993)

Lugosi, Bela (1882-1956)
Celebrated Hungarian horror star (real name Bela Blasco, occasionally known as Arisztid Olt), best remembered as the stage and screen's first Count Dracula, a role which nevertheless typecast him for the rest of his career. Officially, though, it is a role he played only twice in the movies, in *Dracula* and *Abbott and Costello Meet Frankenstein*. Made his film début in Hungary in 1917 with *A Leopard* following stage experience (from 1901) and military service during World War One. Moved to Vienna and then Berlin in 1919 following the collapse of the Bela Kun Communist regime, making his German film début in *Der Fluch der Menschheit* in 1920. Moved to America in 1921, first touring in Hungarian plays for emigres. Made his English-speaking stage début in 1922 in *The Red Poppy*, learning his lines phonetically. His first American film was *The Silent Command* in 1923. It wasn't until 1927, though, when he won the role of *Dracula* in the original Broadway production, that his career took off by which time he was already 45. He reprised the role in 1930 for the film version to general acclaim, but

turned down the opportunity to play the Monster in *Frankenstein* the following year (though he later played the Monster in *Frankenstein Meets the Wolf Man*). Played the part of Igor with distinction in *Son of Frankenstein*, though by the forties he'd been reduced to appearing in Poverty Row horrors and thrillers, spoofing his own Dracula image in *Abbott and Costello Meet Frankenstein*. Descended into drugs in the fifties, seeing out his career in a number of Ed Wood no-budgeters, his final appearance in Wood's *Plan 9 from Outer Space* being completed by a so-called double. He was buried in his Dracula cape and ring. In 1995, Martin Landau won a best supporting actor Oscar for portraying Lugosi in Tim Burton's biopic, *Ed Wood*.
Genre credits:
The Head of Janus (1920 - aka *Dr Jekyll and Mr Hyde*), *The Thirteenth Chair* (1929), *Dracula* (1930), *The Murders in the Rue Morgue* (1932), *White Zombie* (1932), *Chandu the Magician* (1932), *Island of Lost Souls* (1932), *Whispering Shadows* (1933 - serial), *The Black Cat* (1934 - aka *House of Doom*), *The Return of Chandu* (1934 - serial), *Chandu on the Magic Isle* (1934 - serial), *The Mysterious Mr Wong* (1935), *Murder by Television* (1935), *Mark of the Vampire* (1935), *The Raven* (1935), *The Mystery of the Marie Celeste* (1936 - aka *Phantom Ship*), *The Invisible Ray* (1936), *The Dark Eyes of London* (1939), *The Phantom Creeps*

(1939 - serial), *Son of Frankenstein* (1939), *The Gorilla* (1939), *Black Friday* (1940), *The Devil Bat* (1940), *The Wolf Man* (1940), *The Invisible Ghost* (1941), *The Black Cat* (1941), *Spooks Run Wild* (1941), *The Ghost of Frankenstein* (1942), *The Corpse Vanishes* (1942 - aka *The Case of the Missing Brides*), *The Bowery at Midnight* (1942), *Frankenstein Meets the Wolf Man* (1943), *The Ape Man* (1943), *Ghosts on the Loose* (1943), *The Return of the Vampire* (1943), *Voodoo Man* (1944), *Return of the Ape Man* (1944 - aka *Lock Your Doors*), *One Body Too Many* (1944), *The Body Snatcher* (1945), *Zombies on Broadway* (1944 - aka *Loonies on Broadway*), *The Devil Bat's Daughter* (1946), *Scared to Death* (1946), *Abbott and Costello Meet Frankenstein* (1948 - aka *Abbott and Costello Meet the Ghosts*), *Mother Riley Meets the Vampire* (1952 - aka *My Son the Vampire*/*King Robot*), *Bela Lugosi Meets a Brooklyn Gorilla* (1952 - aka *The Monster Meets a Gorilla*), *Glen or Glenda?* (1953 - aka *I Changed My Sex*/*I Led Two Lives*/*He or She?*/*The Transvestite*), *Bride of the Monster* (1954), *The Black Sleep* (1956), *Plan 9 from Outer Space* (1956)

Lust for a Vampire

GB 1970 95m Technicolor
In 1830, an English writer falls foul of the Karnstein family whilst teaching at a girls' school.
    Somewhat typical of Hammer's later output, this rather routine vampire yarn adds elements of lesbianism and nudity in the brew in a bid to spice things up.
p: Harry Fine, Michael Style for Hammer
w: Tudor Gates
d: Jimmy Sangster
ph: David Muir
m: Harry Robinson
md: Muir Mathieson
ed: Spencer Reeve
cos: Laura Nightingale
sound: Ron Barron, Tony Lumkin
Ralph Bates, Michael Johnson, Barbara Jefford, Yutte Stensgaard, Suzanna Leigh, Helen Christie, Mike Raven, Eric Chitty, Christopher Neame, Pippa Steele

Lustig, William (1955-)

American director, perhaps best known for the *Maniac Cop* trilogy. He began his professional career as a production assistant on adult movies, making his directorial début (using the pseudonym Billy Bagg) in 1977 with *The Violation of Claudia*. He turned to horror in 1981 with the notorious *Maniac*, since when he has alternated between horror and action with such films as *Vigilante*, *Hit List* and *Brute Force*.

Genre credits:
Maniac (1981), *Maniac Cop* (1988), *Relentless* (1989), *Maniac Cop 2* (1990), *Maniac Cop 3: Badge of Silence* (1992)

Lutyens, Elizabeth (1906-1983)

British composer, trained at The Royal College of Music. Daughter of architect Sir Edwin Lutyens, she did much work for film, television and radio, as well as for the concert platform.
Genre credits:
Never Take Sweets from a Stranger (1960), *Paranoiac* (1963), *The Earth Dies Screaming* (1964), *The Skull* (1965), *Dr Terror's House of Horrors* (1966), *The Psychopath* (1966), *The Terrornauts* (1967)

Lycanthropy

Werewolves have been baying at the moon in horror movies from as early as 1913, though it wasn't really until Universal made *The Wolf Man* starring Lon Chaney Jr in 1940 that they became an integral part of the genre, despite an earlier effort by the same studio (1935's *Werewolf of London*). Chaney went on to play the character another four times for Universal, thus becoming identified with the role for the rest of his career. He also played a werewolf in the Mexican film *Face of the Screaming Werewolf*. Since Chaney's death the Spanish star Paul Naschy has appeared in several films as 'El Hombre Lobo', whilst in 1981 Rick Baker won the first official make-up effects Oscar for his work on *An American Werewolf in London*, the success of which ushered in a new spate of werewolf flicks. As with *Dracula* and *Frankenstein* there have been spoofs, adult versions and countless variations down the decades. More surprising actors to have donned the crepe hair are Oliver Reed, Michael J. Fox and Jack Nicholson.
Filmography:
The Werewolf (1913), *The White Wolf* (1914), *Le Loup-Garou* (1923), *Werewolf of London* (1935), *The Wolf Man* (1940), *Le Loup de Malveneurs* (1942), *The Mad Monster* (1942), *The Undying Monster* (1943 - aka *The Hammond Mystery*), *The Return of the Vampire* (1943), *Frankenstein Meets the Wolf Man* (1943), *Cry of the Werewolf* (1944), *House of Frankenstein* (1944), *House of Dracula* (1945), *Abbott and Costello Meet Frankenstein* (1948), *The Werewolf* (1956), *El Castillo de los Monstruos* (1956), *I Was a Teenage Werewolf* (1957), *How to Make a Monster* (1958), *Face of the Screaming Werewolf* (1958 - aka *La Casa del Terror*), *Curse of the Werewolf* (1961), *Werewolf in a Girls' Dormitory* (1961 - aka *I Married a Werewolf*/*Lycanthropus*/*Bei Vollmond*

Mord), *House of Bare Mountain* (1962), *El Demonio Azul* (1963), *Bikini Beach* (1964), *Dr Terror's House of Horrors* (1964), *Hercules, Prisoner of Evil* (1964), *House of the Black Death* (1965), *La Loba* (1965), *Orgy of the Dead* (1967), *Dr Terror's Gallery of Horrors* (1967), *Mad Monster Party?* (1967 - puppetoon), *La Marca del Hombre Lobo* (1968 - aka *Frankenstein's Bloody Terror*/*Wolf Man of Dracula*), *El Bosque del Lobo* (1968 - aka *Wolf Man of Galicia*/*Wolf's Forest*), *Las Noches del Hombre Lobo* (1968), *Tore Ng Diyablo* (1969), *The Werewolf vs the Vampire Woman* (1970 - aka *Shadow of the Werewolf*/*La Noche de Walpurgis*), *Dracula vs Frankenstein* (1970 - aka *El Hombre que Vino Ummo*/*Dracula Contra Frankenstein*), *Santo Y Blue Demon Contra los Monstruos* (1970), *Jekyll and the Werewolf* (1971 - aka *Dottor Jekill Y el Hombre Lobo*), *O Homen Lobo* (1971 - aka *The Werewolf*), *Werewolves on Wheels* (1971), *Moon of the Wolf* (1972 - TVM), *The Rats Are Coming! The Werewolves Are Here!* (1972), *Santo Y Blue Demon Contra Dracula Y el Hombre Lobo* (1972), *The Werewolf of Washington* (1973), *The Boy Who Cried Werewolf* (1973), *Curse of the Devil* (1973 - aka *El Ritorno del Hombre Lobo*), *The Beast Must Die* (1974 - aka *Black Werewolf*), *Scream of the Wolf* (1974 - TVM), *Legend of the Werewolf* (1975), *La Maldición de la Bestia* (1975 - aka *The Werewolf and the Yeti*), *La Lupa Mannera* (1976 - aka *Werewolf Woman*/*The Wolf Man*), *Wolfman* (1979), *Cry Wolf!* (1980 - short), *The Monster Club* (1980), *The Howling* (1980), *Wolfen* (1980), *An American Werewolf in London* (1981), *Teen Wolf* (1985), *Silver Bullet* (1985), *Teen Wolf Too* (1987), *The Monster Squad* (1987), *Berserker: The Nordic Curse* (1987 - aka *Berserker*), *The Werewolf of W* (1988 - aka *Der Werwolf von W*), *Full Eclipse* (1994 - TVM), *Wolf* (1994)

Lynley, Carol (1942-)

American actress (real name Carol Jones) whose career was at its busiest in the sixties and early seventies with such films as *Return to Peyton Place*, *The Stripper*, *The Cardinal*, *Harlow* and *The Poseidon Adventure*, though horror fans perhaps know her best from the Otto Preminger thriller *Bunny Lake is Missing*.
Genre credits:
Shock Treatment (1964), *Bunny Lake is Missing* (1965), *The Shuttered Room* (1967), *The Night Stalker* (1971 - TVM), *Son of the Blob* (1972), *If it's a Man, Hang Up!* (1975), *The Cat and the Canary* (1978), *In Possession* (1984 - TVM), *Dark Tower* (1987), *Blackout* (1989), *Howling VI: The Freaks* (1991), *Spirits* (1991)

M **
Ger 1931 117m bw
Berlin criminals track down a child
murderer because police investigations
are hampering their own activities.

Despite its inevitably dated air, this
expressionist melodrama remains its
director's most powerful film, and is
never anything less than a highly
absorbing (and influential) piece of
cinema. It was remade in 1951 by
Joseph Losey, and in 1973 as *Tenderness
of the Wolves* (aka *Zartlichkeit der Wolfe*).
p: Seymour Nebenzal for Nero
w: THEA VON HARBOU, FRITZ LANG
d: FRITZ LANG
ph: Fritz Arno Wagner
m: Grieg
ed: Paul Falkenberg
ad: Karl Vollbrecht, Emil Hasler
sound: Adolf Jansen
PETER LORRE, Otto Wernicke, Gustav
Grundgens, Ellen Widman, Inge
Landgut, Franz Stein, Theodor Loos,
Fritz Gnass, Theo Lingen

MGM see Metro-Goldwyn-Mayer

Maas, Dick (1956-)
Dutch writer, director, producer and
composer who has turned out a number
of interesting European thrillers and
horror films, often in association with
his partner, producer Laurens Geels. A
former cartoonist, he now works in
Hollywood.
Genre credits:
Rigor Mortis (1981 - d), *The Lift* (1983 -
w/d/m), *Amsterdamned* (1987 - w/d/m)

McCambridge, Mercedes (1918-)
American actress who won a Best
Supporting Actress Oscar for her first
film, *All the King's Men* (1949). Her long
experience as a radio actress no doubt
came in handy when, in 1973, she
provided the voice of the Devil for *The
Exorcist*, for which she is perhaps best
known to genre fans. Her other films
include *Johnny Guitar*, *Giant* and *Airport
'79 - The Concorde* (aka *Concorde - Airport
'80*). Her only other genre film is *Echoes*
(1981).

McCarthy, Kevin (1914-)
American actor with countless film
appearances to his credit, now usually in
character cameos in the films of Joe
Dante. He is best known for playing
Miles Bennel in Don Siegel's *Invasion of
the Body Snatchers*, a role he repeated in a
gag cameo in the 1978 remake. His
other credits include *Death of a Salesman*,
The Misfits, *The Prize*, *Captain Avenger*,
Inner Space and *Matinee*.
Genre credits:
Invasion of the Body Snatchers (1956),
Invasion of the Body Snatchers (1978),
Piranha (1979), *The Howling* (1981),
Twilight Zone: The Movie (1983), *Welcome
to Hell* (1984 - TVM), *Ghoulies III:
Ghoulies Go to College* (1991 - aka
Ghoulies Go to College)

McClure, Doug (1935-1995)
American general-purpose actor,
perhaps best known for his role in TV's
The Virginian. In films from 1957, he
appeared mainly in routine productions.
In the mid-seventies he came to Britain,
where he appeared in a number of low-
budget fantasy adventures, including *The
Land That Time Forgot* and *The Warlords of
Atlantis*. His other films include *The
Unforgiven*, *Shenandoah*, *Beau Geste*,
Cannonball Run II and *Maverick*.
Genre credits:
The Land That Time Forgot (1975), *The
People That Time Forgot* (1977),
Humanoids from the Deep (1980), *The
House Where Evil Dwells* (1983)

McCormick, Bret
American exploitation director who
made his début in 1985 with the spoof
Tabloid. He works mostly on action
films, but makes the occasional foray
into horror, sometimes using the
pseudonym Max Raven. His other
credits include *Highway to Hell*, *Macon
County War*, *Armed for Action*, *Blood on the
Badge* and *Timechasers*.
Genre credits
The Abomination (1986 - as Max Raven),
Ozone: Attack of the Redneck Mutants
(1987 - as Max Raven), *Invasion of the
Space Varmints* (1991), *Mardi Gras for the*

Devil (1992), *Children of Dracula* (1994),
Interviews with Real Vampires (1994),
Cyberstalker (1995)

McDowall, Roddy (1928-)
British actor (real name Roderick
Andrew Anthony Jude McDowall) who,
after youthful appearances in a few
British films in the thirties (*Scruffy*,
Murder in the Family, *Poison Pen*, etc.), was
evacuated to America in 1940 to escape
the London Blitz. There, he became a
noted child star in such Hollywood films
as *How Green Was My Valley*, *My Friend
Flicka* and *Lassie, Come Home*. After
experience on Broadway he returned to
the screen as an adult in a wide variety
of roles in such films as *Cleopatra*, *Planet
of the Apes*, *Bedknobs and Broomsticks*, *The
Poseidon Adventure* and *Evil Under the Sun*,
though genre fans perhaps know him
best as the Van Helsing-like horror host
and vampire hunter Peter Vincent in the
two *Fright Night* movies. A celebrated
stills photographer, he has also directed
one (unsuccessful) film, *Tam Lin* (aka *The
Devil's Widow*).
Genre credits:
The Legend of Hell House (1973), *Arnold*
(1973), *Embryo* (1977), *Laserblast* (1978),
Fright Night (1985), *Fright Night 2*
(1989), *Carmilla* (1989 - TVM)

McGillivray, David
British screenwriter and occasional actor,
mostly for directors Pete Walker and
Norman J. Warren. An authority on the
British sex film industry (he wrote a
book, *Doing Rude Things*, on the subject),
he is also a film critic and columnist, and
has long been associated with such
magazines as *Monthly Film Bulletin*, *Films
and Filming* and *Film Review*. His other
writing credits include *White Cargo*, *The
Hot Girls*, *I'm Not Feeling Myself Tonight*
and *Turnaround*.
Genre credits:
House of Whipcord (1974 - w), *Frightmare*
(1975 - w), *House of Mortal Sin* (1975 -
aka *The Confessional* - w), *Schizo* (1976 -
aka *Amok/Blood of the Undead* - w),
Satan's Slave (1976 - w/actor), *Terror*
(1978 - w/actor)

MacGinnis, Niall (1913-)

Irish character actor, memorable as the
sinister Dr Karswell in *Curse of the
Demon*. In films from 1935 with *Turn of
the Tide*, his other credits include *The
Tawny Pipit*, *Henry V*, *Hell Below Zero*,
Helen of Troy, *Billy Budd*, *Jason and the
Argonauts* (as Zeus), *The Shoes of the
Fishermen* and *Darling Lili*.
Genre credits:
Night of the Demon (1957 - aka *Curse of
the Demon*), *Island of Terror* (1966),
Torture Garden (1967)

MacGregor, Scott (1914-1973)

Scottish art director/production
designer who succeeded Bernard
Robinson at Hammer in 1969 to
become their most prolific designer. A
former stage designer, he entered films
in 1941 as an assistant to art director
Edward Carrick, for whom his work
includes *Western Approaches* and *Target for
Tonight*. He also worked, often as an
assistant, on such films as *The Day They
Robbed the Bank of England* and *Cleopatra*.
Genre credits:
Doctor Blood's Coffin (1960), *The Day of
the Triffids* (1962), *The Vengeance of Fu
Manchu* (1968), *The Vengeance of She*
(1968), *Taste the Blood of Dracula* (1969),
Crescendo (1969), *Horror of Frankenstein*
(1970), *The Vampire Lovers* (1970), *Blood
from the Mummy's Tomb* (1971), *Straight
on Till Morning* (1972), *Frankenstein and
the Monster from Hell* (1973)

MacNee, Patrick (1922-)

Dapper British leading man, best known
for his performance as John Steed in the
TV series *The Avengers* and *The New
Avengers*. A stage actor in the thirties, he
served with the Royal Navy during
World War Two, after which he resumed
his career on both stage and screen. His
other credits include *Three Cases of
Murder*, *The Sea Wolves*, *A View to a Kill*
and *Shadey*.
Genre credits:
The Howling (1980), *Waxwork* (1988),
Transformations (1988), *Lobster Man from
Mars* (1989), *The Masque of the Red Death*
(1989), *Waxwork II: Lost in Time* (1991)

The Mad Genius *

USA 1931 81m bw
A club-footed puppeteer turns a
runaway boy into a great dancer.
    Enjoyably dated melodrama in the
Svengali/Trilby manner, of interest
chiefly for its look.
p: Warner
w: J. Grubb Alexander, Harvey Thew
play: Martin Brown
d: MICHAEL CURTIZ
ph: Barney McGill

md: David Mendoza
ed: Ralph Dawson
ad: ANTON GROT
cos: Earl Luick
sound: no credit given
ch: Adolph Bolm
John Barrymore, Marian Marsh, Donald
Cook, Luis Alberni, Carmel Myers,
Charles Butterworth, Frankie Darro,
Boris Karloff

Mad Love **

USA 1935 83m bw
A mad surgeon grafts the hands of a
murderer on to a pianist whose own
hands have been crushed in a train crash.
    Stark horror melodrama with
interesting visuals and a persuasive star
performance.
p: John Considine Jr for MGM
w: Guy Endore, P. J. Wolfson, John L.
Balderston, Florence Crewe Jones
novel: Maurice Renard
d: KARL FREUND
ph: Chester Lyons, Gregg Toland
m: Dimitri Tiomkin
md: Oscar Radin
ed: Hugh Wynn
ad: Cedric Gibbons, William A. Horning
PETER LORRE, Colin Clive, Frances
Drake, Ted Healy, Edward Brophy, Isabel
Jewell, Billy Gilbert, Keye Luke, Sara
Haden

The Mad Magician *

USA 1954 72m bw 3D
An inventor of stage illusions resorts to
murder when he discovers that his own
ambitions as a magician have been
quashed by the contract he has signed.
    Energetic low-budget horror hokum.
p: Bryan Foy for Columbia
w: Crane Wilbur
d: John Brahm
ph: Bert Glennon
m: Emil Newman, Arthur Lange
ed: Grant Whytock
ad: Frank Sylos
cos: Robert Martin
sp: David Koehler
sound: John Kean
Vincent Price, Mary Murphy, Eva
Gabor, Patrick O'Neal, John Emery

The Mad Monster Party?

GB 1966 94m Eastmancolor Animagic
Baron Frankenstein invites the world's
most famous monsters to his castle in
order to announce his retirement.
    Fitfully amusing puppetoon, passable
enough for younger audiences.
p: Arthur Rankin Jr, Jules Bass for
Embassy/Videocraft International
exec p: Joseph E. Levine
w: Len Korobkin, Harvey Kurtzman
story: Arthur Rankin Jr

d: Jules Bass
songs: Maury Laws, Jules Bass
m: Maury Laws
character design: Jack Davis
sound: Eric Tomlinson, Peter Page,
Stephen Frohock
ch: Killer Joe Piro
voices: Boris Karloff, Phyllis Diller, Gale
Garnett, Alan Swift, Ethel Ennis

Maddin, Guy

Canadian director who had a cult hit
with his first feature, *Tales from the Gimli
Hospital*.
Genre credits:
The Dead Father (1987 - short), *Tales from
the Gimli Hospital* (1989), *Archangel*
(1990)

Madhouse *

GB 1974 92m Eastmancolor
When he makes a comeback, an old
horror star finds himself amid a series of
murders that resemble those in his early
films.
    Rather along the lines of the star's *Dr
Phibes* films and *Theatre of Blood*, this
low-budget entry offers a fairly
successful mixture of chills and humour.
p: Milton Subotsky, Max J. Rosenberg
for AIP/Amicus
exec p: Samuel Z. Arkoff
w: Greg Morrison
novel: Angus Hall
d: JIM CLARK
ph: Ray Parslow
m: Douglas Gamley
ed: Clive Smith
ad: Tony Curtis
cos: Dulcie Midwinter
sp: Kress and Spencer
sound: Danny Daniel, Gerry Humphries
associate p: John Dark
VINCENT PRICE, Peter Cushing,
Robert Quarry, Adrienne Corri, Natasha
Pyne, Michael Parkinson, Linda Hayden,
Jenny Lee Wright, Peter Halliday

Magee, Patrick (1924-1982)

British character actor, from the stage,
where he was known for performing in
the works of Samuel Beckett, and for his
performance as the Marquis de Sade in
Marat/Sade, which won him a Tony
when he took the play to Broadway. His
film work, which includes appearances
in *Zulu*, *The Birthday Party*, *King Lear* and
A Clockwork Orange, has mostly been in
supporting roles.
Genre credits:
Dementia 13 (1963 - aka *The Haunted and
the Hunted*), *The Masque of the Red Death*
(1964), *The Skull* (1965), *Die, Monster,
Die!* (1965 - aka *Monster of Terror*), *The
Fiend* (1972), *Demons of the Mind* (1972),
Asylum (1972), *And Now the Screaming*

Starts (1973), *The Monster Club* (1980), *The Black Cat* (1981 - aka *Il Gatto Nero/The Black Cat of Park Lane*)

Magic *
USA 1978 107m DeLuxe
A ventriloquist finds himself increasingly dominated by his dummy, which compels him to murder.

Certainly not a new idea (*Dead of Night*, *Devil Doll*) and rather an odd choice for this director, but not entirely unwatchable.
p: Joseph E. Levine, Richard L. Levine for TCF
w: William Goldman
novel: WILLIAM GOLDMAN
d: Richard Attenborough
ph: Victor J. Kemper
m: JERRY GOLDSMITH
ed: John Bloom
pd: Terence Marsh
cos: Ruth Myers
sound: John Bolz
ANTHONY HOPKINS, Ann-Margret, BURGESS MEREDITH, Ed Lauter, E. J. Andre, David Ogden Stiers

The Magnetic Monster *
USA 1953 75m bw
A radio-active element draws energy to itself, causing a series of implosions of increasing size.

Brisk though now rather dated low-budget sci-fi, one of the better examples of its kind.
p: Ivan Tors for UA
w: CURT SIODMAK, IVAN TORS
d: Curt Siodmak
ph: Charles Van Enger
m: Blaine Sanford
ed: Herbert L. Strock
pd: George Van Marter
Richard Carlson, King Donovan, Byron Foulger, Jean Byron

Malleson, Miles (1888-1969)
Portly, cherubic-looking British character actor, on stage from 1911. In countless films from the early thirties, often as comedy support, he was also a notable screenwriter, penning such important British films as *Nell Gwyn*, *Victoria the Great*, *Rhodes of Africa* and *The Thief of Bagdad*. His credits as an actor include *The Thief of Bagdad*, *Kind Hearts and Coronets*, *The Importance of Being Earnest*, *Private's Progress* and *I'm All Right, Jack!*
Genre credits:
Dead of Night (1945), *Dracula* (1958 - aka *Horror of Dracula* -as the jovial undertaker), *The Hound of the Baskervilles* (1959), *The Brides of Dracula* (1960), *Peeping Tom* (1960), *The Hellfire Club* (1961), *The Phantom of the Opera* (1962)

Man Bites Dog *
Belgium 1992 97m bw
A documentary film crew follow the exploits of a serial killer.

Ultra-black thriller which doesn't quite live up to its notorious reputation. Nevertheless, it's not for the easily offended.
p: Remy Belvaux, André Bonzel, Benoit Poelvoorde for Les Artistes Anasymes
w: Remy Belvaux, André Bouzel, Benoit Poelvoorde, Vincent Tavier
story: Remy Belvaux
d: Remy Belvaux, André Bouzel, Benoit Poelvoorde
ph: André Bonzel
m: Jean-Marc Chenut
ed: Eric Dardill, Remy Belvaux
ad: no credit given
sound: Alain Opezzi, Vincent Tavier Benoit Poelvoorde, Remy Belvaux, André Bonzel, Jenny Drye, Jacqueline Poelvoorde Pappaert, Willy Vandenbroek

The Man in Half Moon Street *
USA 1944 91m bw
A man of ninety keeps his youth through a series of gland transplants.

Dorian Gray-style melodrama, adequately mounted. Remade in 1959 by Hammer as *The Man Who Could Cheat Death*.
p: Walter MacEwan for Paramount
w: Charles Kenyon
play: Barre Lyndon
d: Ralph Murphy
ph: Henry Sharp
m: Miklos Rozsa
ed: Tom Neff
ad: Walter Tyler, Hans Dreier
Nils Asther, Helen Walker, Brandon Hurst, Reinhold Schunzel, Paul Cavanaugh, Edmond Breon

Man Made Monster *
USA 1940 56m bw
Induced with large amounts of electricity, a carnival performer turns into a robotic monster.

Lively horror programmer with adequate credits.
p: Jack Bernhard for Universal
w: Joseph West
d: George Waggner
ph: Elwood Bredell
m: Hans J. Salter
md: Charles Previn
ed: Arthur Hilton
ad: Jack Otterson
sp: JOHN P. FULTON
LON CHANEY JR, LIONEL ATWILL, Anne Gwynne, Frank Albertson, Samuel S. Hinds

The Man They Could Not Hang *
USA 1939 65m bw

A doctor executed for his experiments is brought back to life and murders those responsible for his conviction. Dated horror hokum with a typical part for its star.
p: Columbia
w: Karl Brown
d: Nick Grinde
ph: Benjamin Kline
m: W. M. Stoloff
ed: William Lyon
Boris Karloff, Lorna Gray, Robert Wilcox, Roger Pryor, Don Beddoe, Byron Foulger

The Man Who Changed His Mind
GB 1936 66m bw
A young nurse goes to work for a scientist whose experiments involve brain transplants.

Formularistic mad doctor shenanigans with the credits more interesting than the story.
p: Gainsborough
w: John L. Balderston, Sidney Gilliat, L. DuGarde Peach
d: Robert Stevenson
ph: Jack Cox
md: Louis Levy
ed: Alfred Roome, R. E. Dearing
ad: Alex Vetchinsky
cos: Molyneux
sound: W. Salter
Boris Karloff, Anna Lee, Frank Cellier, Donald Calthrop, Cecil Parker, John Loder, Lyn Harding

The Man Who Could Cheat Death
GB 1959 83m Technicolor
A Parisian sculptor keeps his youth with a series of gland operations, his real age being 104.

Talkative, lethargically handled Hammer horror with very little in the way of interest. A remake of *The Man in Half Moon Street*.
p: Anthony Hinds for Hammer
w: Jimmy Sangster
play: Barre Lyndon
d: Terence Fisher
ph: Jack Asher
m: Richard Rodney Bennett
md: John Hollingsworth
ed: James Needs, John Dunstead
ad: Bernard Robinson
make-up: Roy Ashton
associate p: Anthony Nelson Keys
Anton Diffring, Hazel Court, Christopher Lee, Arnold Marle, Delphi Lawrence, Francis de Wolff

The Man Who Haunted Himself
GB 1970 94m Technicolor
After an emergency operation, a

HAMMER DELIVER ANOT
FOR PARAMOUNT RELEA

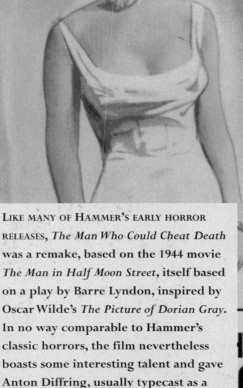

LIKE MANY OF HAMMER'S EARLY HORROR
RELEASES, *The Man Who Could Cheat Death*
was a remake, based on the 1944 movie
The Man in Half Moon Street, itself based
on a play by Barre Lyndon, inspired by
Oscar Wilde's *The Picture of Dorian Gray*.
In no way comparable to Hammer's
classic horrors, the film nevertheless
boasts some interesting talent and gave
Anton Diffring, usually typecast as a
Nazi, a rare leading role.

HAZEL
OURT · CHRISTOPHER
LEE

with ARNOLD MARLE · DELPHI LAWRENCE · FRANCIS DeWOLFF · Screenplay by JIMMY

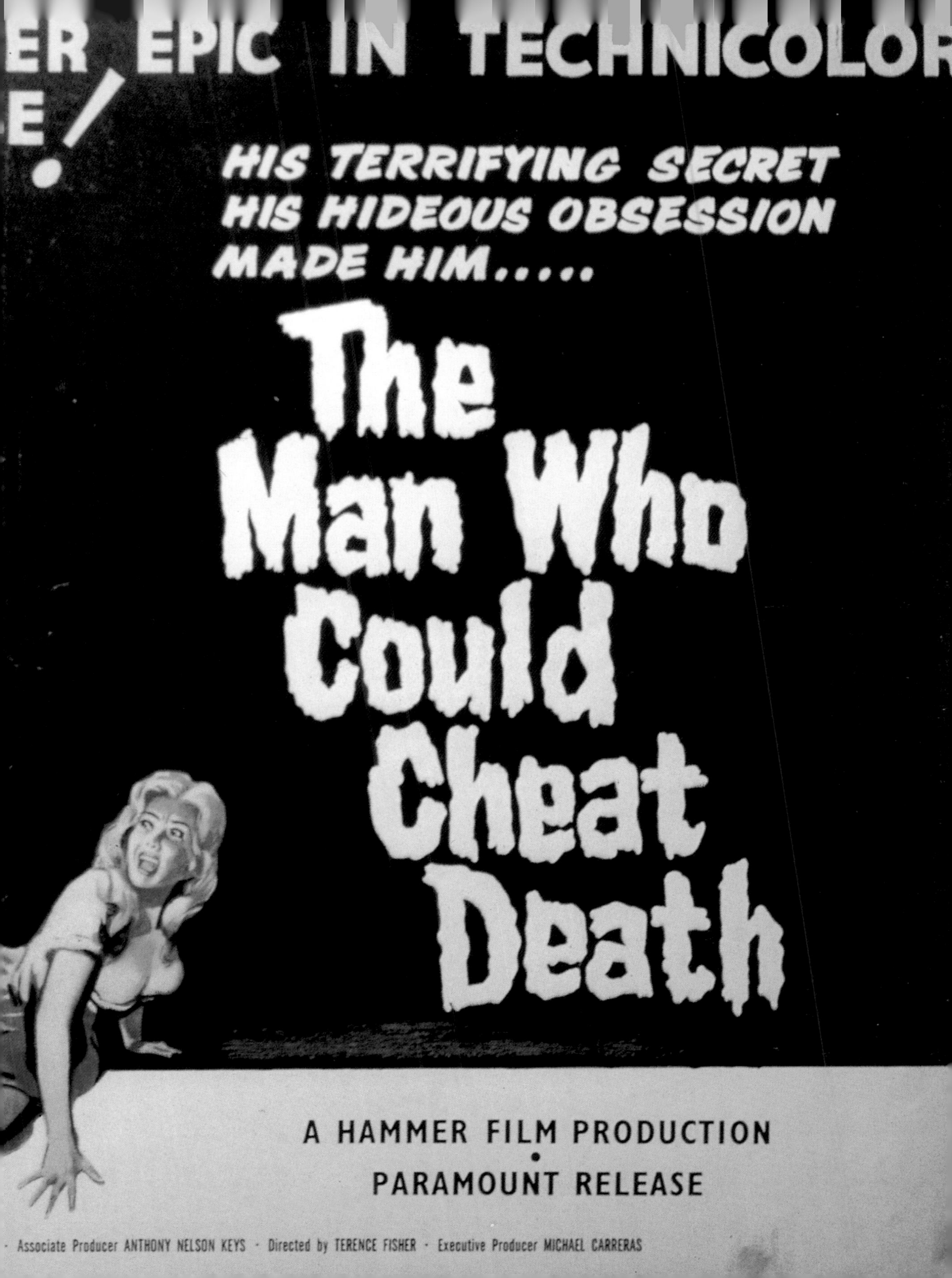

ER EPIC IN TECHNICOLOR

E !

HIS TERRIFYING SECRET
HIS HIDEOUS OBSESSION
MADE HIM.....

The Man Who Could Cheat Death

A HAMMER FILM PRODUCTION
•
PARAMOUNT RELEASE

Associate Producer ANTHONY NELSON KEYS · Directed by TERENCE FISHER · Executive Producer MICHAEL CARRERAS

businessman is haunted by his doppel-ganger, who gradually takes over his life.

Sadly, excessive length finally defeats this mildly interesting anecdote with a surprisingly good performance from a usually bland star.
p: Michael Relph for ABP/Excalibur
w: Basil Dearden, Michael Relph
story: Anthony Armstrong
d: Basil Dearden
ph: Tony Spratling
m: Michael J. Lewis
ed: Teddy Darvas
ad: Albert Whitherick
ROGER MOORE, Hildegarde Neil, Olga Georges-Picot, Anton Rogers, Thorley Walters, Freddie Jones, John Carson, John Welsh

The Man Who Lived Again see
The Man Who Changed His Mind

The Man Who Lived Twice
USA 1936 73m bw
A killer becomes a different person after undergoing brain surgery.

Dated nonsense in the familiar mad scientist manner.
p: Ben Pivar for Columbia
w: Fred Niblo Jr., Tom Van Dycke, Arthur Strawn
story: Tom Van Dycke, Henry Altimus
d: Harry Lachman
ph: James Van Trees
m: no credit given
ed: Byron Robinson
ad: no credit given
sp: Kenneth Wheeler
sound: no credit given
Ralph Bellamy, Marian Marsh, Thurston Hall, Isabel Jewell, Ward Bond

The Man with X-Ray Eyes see X - The Man with X-Ray Eyes

Manfredini, Harry
American composer, perhaps best known for scoring practically all of the *Friday the 13th* shockers as well as all four *House* films. His few non-horror credits include *Here Come the Tigers* and *Aces: Iron Eagle III*.
Genre credits:
Friday the 13th (1980), *Friday the 13th Part 2* (1981), *Friday the 13th Part 3 in 3D* (1982), *Swamp Thing* (1982), *The Returning* (1983), *The Hills Have Eyes Part 2* (1984), *Friday the 13th - The Final Chapter* (1984), *Friday the 13th Part V - A New Beginning* (1985), *House* (1986), *Friday the 13th Part 6 - Jason Lives* (1986), *House II: The Second Story* (1983), *Friday the 13th Part 7 - The New Blood* (1988 - co-m), *The Horror Show* (1989 - aka *House III*), *Deepstar Six* (1989), *House IV* (1992), *Jason Goes to*

Hell (1993 - aka *Friday the 13 Part 9: Jason Goes to Hell*)

Mangiati Vivi see Eaten Alive (1980)

Manhattan Baby see Possessed

Manhunter *
USA 1986 119m Technicolor Dolby
An FBI agent tracks down a serial killer.

Slick but quite ineffective version of a gripping novel, better known these days as the prequel to the Oscar-winning *Silence of the Lambs*.
p: Richard Roth for Dino de Laurentiis
exec p: Bernard Williams
w/d: Michael Mann
novel: THOMAS HARRIS
ph: Dante Spinotti
m: Michael Rubini, The Reds
ed: Dov Hoenig
pd: Mel Bourne
cos: Colleen Atwood
sound: John Mitchell, Bud Knudson
William L. Petersen, Joan Allen, Brian Cox (as Hannibal Lector, here spelled Leckter), Kim Griest

Maniac
USA 1980 85m colour Dolby
A murderer scalps his victims and dresses mannequins with them.

Sleazy killer thriller, one of the most execrable of its kind, though it now seems to be gaining a cult following. Spinell and Munro reteamed the following year for the slightly better *Last Horror Film* (aka *Fanatic*).
p: Andrew Garroni, William Lustig for Magnum
exec p: Joe Spinell, Judd Hamilton
w: C. A. Rosenberg, Joe Spinell
story: Joe Spinell
d: William Lustig
ph: Robert Lindsay
m: Jay Chattaway
ed: Lorenzo Martinelli
ad: Marla Schweppe
cos: Candace Clements
sound: Gary Rich, Rick Dior
make-up effects: Tom Savini
Joe Spinell, Caroline Munro, Gail Lawrence, Kelly Piper, Tom Savini

Maniac Cop
USA 1988 85m Technicolor
New York is threatened by a killer cop.

Dismal low-grade thriller that inspired two sequels: *Maniac Cop 2* (1990) and *Maniac Cop 3: Badge of Silence* (1992).
p: Larry Cohen for Medusa/Shapiro Glickenhaus Entertainment
w: Larry Cohen
d: William Lustig
ph: Vincent J. Rabe

m: Jay Chattaway
ed: David Kern
ad: Jonathan Hodges, Ann Cudworth
Tom Atkins, Bruce Campbell, Richard Roundtree, Sheree North, Robert Z'Dar, William Smith, Laurence Landon

The Manitou
USA 1978 104m CFIcolor Panavision Dolby
The spirit of a 400-year-old Indian manifests itself in the body of an unsuspecting woman.

Ludicrous exploitation horror nonsense, a long, long way behind *The Exorcist* and *The Omen*.
p: William Girdler for Manitou Productions
w: William Girdler, Jon Cedar, Tom Pope
novel: Graham Masterton
d: William Girdler
ph: Michael Hugo
m: Lalo Schifrin
ed: Bud Asman, Gene Ruggiero
pd: Walter Scott Herndon
cos: Michael Freth, Agnes Lyon
sp: Dale Tate, Frank Van Der Veer, Gene Grigg, Tim Smythe
sound: Glenn Anderson
make-up effects: Tom Burman
Tony Curtis, Susan Strasberg, Michael Ansara, Burgess Meredith, Ann Sother, Stella Stevens, Jon Cedar, Paul Mantee

Manners, David (1901-)
Canadian actor (real name Rauff de Ryther Duan Ackolm) who made his film début in James Whale's *Journey's End* in 1930. Stayed in Hollywood until 1936, after which he retired from films and became a novelist. Perhaps best remembered for playing Jonathan Harker in Tod Browning's *Dracula*, he also had an effective smaller part in *The Mummy*, in which he utters the famous line, 'He went for a little walk!'. His other credits include *The Last Flight*, *A Bill of Divorcement* and *The Mystery of Edwin Drood* (as Edwin Drood).
Genre credits:
Dracula (1930), *The Mummy* (1932), *The Black Cat* (1934)

March, Fredric (1897-1975)
American star actor (real name Frederick McIntyre) who won a Best Actor Oscar for his performance(s) in *Dr Jekyll and Mr Hyde* (1932), the only actor to win for a horror role until Anthony Hopkins in *The Silence of the Lambs* (1991). March won a second Best Actor Oscar for *The Best Years of Our Lives* (1946). His other credits include *Les Miserables*, *A Star Is Born*, *The Adventures of Mark Twain*, *Death of a*

Salesman and *Inherit the Wind.*
Genre credits:
The Dummy (1929), *Dr Jekyll and Mr Hyde* (1932), *Death Takes a Holiday* (1934), *I Married a Witch* (1942)

Margheriti, Antonio (1930-)

Prolific Italian director who often works under the pseudonym Anthony M. Dawson, in which guise he has been responsible for a string of undistinguished action and horror films (*The Golden Arrow, Ark of the Sun God* and *Codename: Wild Geese*). He entered films in 1950 as an assistant editor, becoming a director of documentaries and travelogues with *Vecchia Roma* in 1953. He began directing special effects in 1954 and writing screenplays in 1955, then made the jump to direction proper with *Assignment: Outer Space* (aka *Spacemen*), which he also co-wrote, in 1960. His other credits include *Hercules - Prisoner of Evil, The Wild, Wild Planet, War of the Planets, Snow Devils, Mr Superinvisible, The Commander, Indio* and *Indio 2: The Revolt*.
Genre credits:
Castle of Blood (1964 - aka *La Danza Macabra*), *The Virgin of Nuremberg* (1964 - aka *Horror Castle / Back to the Killer / La Vergine di Norimberga*), *The Long Hair of Death* (1964 - aka *I Lunghi Capelli della Morte*), *Schoolgirl Killer* (1967 - aka *The Young, the Evil and the Savage / Nude... Si Muore*), *The Unnaturals* (1969 - aka *The Exterminators / Contronatura*), *Web of the Spider* (1971 - aka *Nella Stretta Morsa del Ragno*), *Seven Deaths in the Cat's Eye* (1973 - aka *La Morte Negli Occhi del Gatto*), *Killer Fish* (1978), *Invasion of the Flesh Hunters* (1980 - aka *Cannibals in the Streets / Cannibal Apocalypse / Apocalisse Domani*)

Mark of the Devil

GB 1984 74m Technicolor TVM
From beyond the grave a tattooist wreaks revenge on the man who killed him.
    More padded nonsense from the disappointing Hammer *House of Mystery and Suspense* series of telefilms.
p: Roy Skeggs for Hammer/TCF
w: Brian Clemens
d: Val Guest
ph: Frank Watts
m: David Bedford
md: Philip Martell
ed: Bob Dearberg
ad: Carolyn Scott
cos: Laura Nightingale
sound: John Bramall, Ernie Marsh
Dirk Benedict, Jenny Seagrove, George Sewell, John Paul, Tom Adams, Burt Kwouk, Reginald Marsh, James Ellis

• Bela Lugosi and Carol Borland in *Mark of the Vampire*, director Tod Browning's remake of his own silent shocker *London After Midnight*.

Mark of the Vampire *

USA 1935 62m bw
A police inspector investigating a murder deploys vaudevillians to pose as vampires to help him with his plans.
    Hammy, leadenly paced remake of the same director's *London After Midnight* (1927) with just a few visual compensations for connoisseurs.
p: E. J. Mannix for MGM
w: Guy Endore, Bernard Schubert

• William Marshall in the classic 'blaxploitation' flick *Blacula*, the success of which provoked a lesser known sequel *Scream, Blacula, Scream.*

d: Tod Browning
ph: James Wong Howe
m: no credit given
ed: Ben Lewis
ad: CEDRIC GIBBONS
sound: Douglas Shearer
Lionel Barrymore, Bela Lugosi, Lionel Atwill, Jean Hersholt, Elizabeth Allan, Henry Wordsworth, Carol Borland, Donald Meek, Jessie Ralph, Holmes Herbert, Ivan Simpson

Marshall, William (1924-)

Distinguished African-American actor with much stage experience (particularly in Shakespeare), though he is remembered by genre fans for playing Count Blacula in two seventies 'blaxploitation' pictures, to which he brought a welcome touch of dignity. His other film credits include *Lydia Bailey, Sabu and the Magic Genie, The Boston Strangler, Twilight's Last Gleaming* and *Maverick*.
Genre credits:
Blacula (1972), *Scream, Blacula, Scream* (1973), *Abby* (1974), *Sorceress* (1994)

Martell, Philip (1915-1993)

British conductor who, in 1964, succeeded John Hollingsworth as Hammer's resident musical supervisor, a role he retained until his death. Worked on all of Hammer's film and television projects, from *The Evil of Frankenstein* onwards, including their records of *Dracula* and *The Seven Golden Vampires*. Also contributed to Silva Screen's *Music from the Hammer Films* (aka *Dracula - Classic Scores from Hammer Horror*). Trained at the Guildhall School of Music in London, entering films in the early thirties as an arranger. Later formed his own orchestra and often performed on BBC radio. Was also the musical director for Tyburn Films.

Martelli, Carlo

British composer (despite the Italianate name) with several routine horror scores to his credit.
Genre credits:
Witchcraft (1964), *The Curse of the Mummy's Tomb* (1964), *Catacombs* (1964), *It* (1966), *Slave Girls* (1968 - aka *Prehistoric Women*)

Martin *

USA 1978 95m colour
A disturbed young boy with an appetite for blood is believed by his elderly cousin to be a vampire.
    Intriguing, curiously memorable and surprisingly well-judged low-budget horror film which works on several levels.
p: Richard Rubinstein for Laurel/Braddock

w/d/ed: George A. Romero
ph: Michael Gornick
m: Donald Rubinstein
ad: no credit given
sp: Tom Savini
sound: Tony Buba
John Amplas, Lincoln Maazel, Christine Forrest, Tom Savini, Elyane Nadeau, Sarah Venable, Fran Middleton, Al Lavistsky

Martin the Vampire see Martin

Martino, Sergio (1938-)
Italian director with a penchant for gory horror films, few of which have been released outside Italy. Other credits include *Mondo Sex*, *The Strange Vice of Mrs Ward* and *Casablanca Express*.
Genre credits:
Demons of the Dead (1972 - aka *They're Coming to get You*/*Tutti I Colori del Buio*), *Torso* (1973), *Slave of the Cannibal God* (1976 - aka *Prisoner of the Cannibal God*/*La Montagna del Dio Cannibale*), *Screamers* (1979 - aka *Island of Mutations*/*L'Isola degli Uomini Pesce*), *Caiman* (1980 - aka *The Great Alligator*)

Mary Shelley's Frankenstein *
GB/USA 1994 123m Technicolor
After the death of his mother, medical student Victor Frankenstein experiments with life itself, but the result of his work, though intelligent, goes on the rampage.

In its attempt to be taken seriously, this adaptation of the oft-filmed novel becomes overly earnest and is certainly no more entertaining for being faithful to the original. There are minor compensations along the way, though the miscasting of Branagh does not help.
p: Francis Ford Coppola, James V. Hart, John Veitch, Kenneth Branagh, David Parfitt for Columbia/American Zoetrope/JSB
exec p: Fred Fuchs
w: Steph Lady, Frank Darabont
novel: MARY SHELLEY
d: Kenneth Branagh
ph: Roger Pratt
m: Patrick Doyle
ed: Andrew Marcus
pd: Tim Harvey
cos: James Acheson
sp: Richard Conway
make-up effects: Daniel Parker
sound: Ivan Sharrock
2nd unit d: Andrew Marcus
Robert de Niro (as the Creature), Kenneth Branagh, Helena Bonham Carter, Tom Hulce, Aidan Quinn, Ian Holm, Richard Briers, John Cleese, Robert Hardy, Celia Imrie, Cherie Lunghi, Trevyn McDowell, Mark

Hadfield, Gerard Horan, Jimmy Yuill, Joanna Roth

The Mask of Fu Manchu *
USA 1932 70m bw
Nayland Smith and his friends find themslves in mortal peril when kidnapped by the nefarious Fu Manchu.

Serial-like thriller, very competently made in the thirties manner, with plenty to take the eye.
p: MGM/Cosmopolitan
w: John Willard, Edgar Woolf, Irene Kuhn
stories: Sax Rohmer
d: Charles Brabin, Charles Vidor
ph: TONY GAUDIO
m: no credit given
ed: Ben Lewis
ad: CEDRIC GIBBONS
cos: Adrian
sound: Douglas Shearer
BORIS KARLOFF, MYRNA LOY, LEWIS STONE, Karen Morley, Charles Sarrett, Jean Hersholt, Lawrence Grant

Mask of the Demon see Black Sunday

Mask of Satan see Black Sunday

The Masque of the Red Death *
GB 1964 89m Pathecolor Pathescope
Turning his back on the plague raging outside his castle, Prince Prospero holds a masked ball, but Death is an uninvited guest.

Over-talkative but visually arresting horror film, one of its director's key works. It was remade much less effectively in 1990.
p: George Willoughby for AIP/Alta Vista/Anglo Amalgamated
exec p: Nat Cohen, Stuart Levy
w: Charles Beaumont, R. Wright Campbell
story: Edgar Allan Poe
d: ROGER CORMAN
ph: NICOLAS ROEG
m: David Lee
ed: Ann Chegwidden
ad; ROBERT JONES
cos: LAURA NIGHTINGALE
sp: George Blackwell
sound: Richard Bird, Len Abbott
ch: Jack Carter
titles: Jim Baker
VINCENT PRICE (as Prospero), Jane Asher, Hazel Court, Patrick Magee, Nigel Green, David Weston, Paul Whitsun-Jones, Robert Brown

Massie, Paul (1932-)
Canadian actor, long in Britain, where he has appeared in such films as *Orders to Kill*, *The Rebel* and *Raising the Wind*,

though genre fans will know him chiefly as the lead(s) in Hammer's *The Two Faces of Dr Jekyll* (1960 - aka *House of Fright*/*Jekyll's Inferno*)

Matheson, Richard (1926-)
American novelist and short-story writer with many genre credits to his name, including several of Roger Corman's celebrated Poe adaptations. Made his screenplay début in 1957 with *The Incredible Shrinking Man*. Other credits include *Somewhere in Time* and *Loose Cannons*.
The House of Usher (1960 - aka *The Fall of the House of Usher*), *Master of the World* (1961), *The Pit and the Pendulum* (1961), *Tales of Terror* (1962), *Burn, Witch, Burn* (1963 - aka *Night of the Eagle*), *The Raven* (1963), *The Comedy of Terrors* (1963), *The Last Man on Earth* (1964), *Fanatic* (1965 - aka *Die! Die! My Darling!*), *The Devil Rides Out* (1968 - aka *The Devil's Bride*), *De Sade* (1969), *The Omega Man* (1971), *The Night Stalker* (1971 - TVM), *Duel* (1971 -TVM), *The Night Strangler* (1972 - TVM), *The Legend of Hell House* (1973), *Dracula* (1973 - TVM), *Scream of the Wolf* (1974 - TVM), *The Stranger Within* (1974 - TVM), *Trilogy of Terror* (1975 - TVM), *The Strange Possession of Mrs Oliver* (1977 - TVM), *Jaws 3D* (1983), *Twilight Zone - The Movie* (1983)

Mathews, Kirwin (1926-)
American leading man, former teacher, perhaps best remembered as Sinbad in *The Seventh Voyage of Sinbad* (1958). Other credits include *The Three Worlds of Gulliver*, *Jack the Giant Killer* and *The Pirates of Blood River*.
Genre credits:
Maniac (1963), *Ghostbreaker* (1967 - TVM), *Battle Beneath the Earth* (1968), *Octaman* (1971), *The Boy Who Cried Werewolf* (1973), *Nightmare in Blood* (1978)

Matthews, Francis (1927-)
Debonair British leading man specializing in superior upper-crust types. Much stage and television work.
Genre credits:
Corridors of Blood (1958 - aka *The Doctor from Seven Dials*), *The Revenge of Frankenstein* (1958), *Dracula - Prince of Darkness* (1966), *Rasputin - The Mad Monk* (1966)

Mausoleum
USA 1982 98m colour
After the death of her mother, a young girl inherits a family curse and is possessed by a demon.

Horror fare of the most ridiculous and boring kind. If it wasn't so bad it

might be funny. But it's not even that.
p: Robert Barich for Western International
exec p: Jerry Zimmerman, Michael Franzese
w: Robert Barich, Robert Madero
d: Robert Madero
ph: Robert Barich
m: Jamie Mendoza-Nava
ed: Richard Christopher Bock
ad: Robert Burns
sp: John Buechler
cos: Nancy Montgomery
sound: John Speak
Marjoe Gortner, Bobbie Bressee, Norman Burton, La Wanda Page, Maurice Sherbanee

Maximum Overdrive
USA 1986 97m Technicolor
A passing comet causes all things mechanical to go haywire in a North Carolina township.
    Sometimes lively though mainly silly hokum.
p: Martha Schumacher for Dino de Laurentiis
w/d: Stephen King
ph: Armando Nannuzzi
m: AC-DC
ed: Evan Lottman
pd: Giorgio Postiglione
cos: Clifford Capone
Emilio Estevez, Pat Hingle, Yeardley Smith, Laura Harrington, John Short, Ellen McElduff

May, Brian
Australian composer, now also working in America following the success of such films as *Mad Max*, *Gallipoli* and *Mad Max 2* (aka *The Road Warrior*). Studied at Adelaide's Elder Conservatorium, after which he worked for the Australian Broadcasting Corporation, breaking into films with *The True Story of Eskimo Nell* in 1975. He should not be confused with the Queen guitarist of the same name.
Genre credits:
Patrick (1979), *Thirst* (1979), *The Day After Halloween* (1979 - aka *Snapshot*), *Harlequin* (1980), *Road Games* (1981), *Bloodmoon* (1989), *Freddy's Dead: The Final Nightmare* (1991), *Dr Giggles* (1992)

Mayne, Ferdy (1916-)
German actor (real name Ferdinand Mayer-Borckel) working in Britain, where he has played distinguished-looking villains in countless films from 1948, including *Where Eagles Dare* and *When Eight Bells Toll*. Perhaps best known to genre fans as the vampire in Roman Polanski's *The Fearless Vampire Killers*.

• A studio portrait of Ferdy Mayne, best remembered for playing the role of Count Von Krolock in director Roman Polanski's horror spoof *The Fearless Vampire Killers*.

Genre credits:
The Fearless Vampire Killers (1968 - aka *Dance of the Vampires/Pardon Me Your Teeth Are in My Neck*), *The Vampire Lovers* (1970), *The Vampire Happening* (1971 - voice only), *The Horror Star* (1982), *Howling II: Your Sister is a Werewolf* (1985 - aka *Howling II: Stirba, Werewolf Bitch*), *Night Train to Terror* (1985), *Frankenstein's Aunt* (1986), *My Lovely Monster* (1989)

The Maze
USA 1953 81m bw 3D
An heir returns to a remote castle to inherit his title only to discover that his predecessor has turned into a giant frog.
    Childishly inept horror comic that has to be seen to be believed.
p: Richard Heermance for Allied Artists
w: Dan Ullman
story: Maurice Sandoz
d/pd: William Cameron Menzies
ph: Harry Neumann
m: Marlin Skiles
ed: John Fuller
ad: David Milton
sp: Augie Lohmann
sound: Charles Cooper
Richard Carlson, Veronica Hurst, Katherine Emery, Michael Pate, Hilary Brooke, Lillian Bond, Owen McGiveney

The Medieval Dead see Army of Darkness - The Medieval Dead

The Medusa Touch **
GB/Fr 1978 109m Technicolor

A novelist discovers that he has the power to cause catastrophe.
    Compelling supernatural thriller, nicely judged all round, especially in its scenes of disaster and mayhem. Worth a look for the cast alone.
p: Anne V. Coates, Jack Gold for ITC/Citeca/Coates-Gold
exec p: Arnon Miclahn, Elliott Kastner
w: John Briley
novel: Peter Van Greenaway
d: JACK GOLD
ph: Arthur Ibbetson
m: MICHAEL J. LEWIS
ed: Anne V. Coates, Ian Crafford
pd: Peter Mullins
cos: Elsa Fennell, Jane Robinson
sp: Brian Johnson, Doug Ferris
sound; Ivan Sharrock, Gordon K. McCallum
stunt co-ordinator: Eddie Stacey
Richard Burton, Lee Remick, Lino Ventura, Harry Andrews, Alan Badel, Marie-Christine Berrault, Jeremy Brett, Michael Hordern, Gordon Jackson, Michael Byrne, Derek Jacobi, Avril Elgar, Robert Flemyng, Jennifer Jayne, Shaw Taylor, Gordon Honeycombe

Meet the Applegates *
USA 1990 82m DuArt
Faced with the destruction of their home in the Brazialian rain forests, a family of giant insects disguise themselves as humans and move to America, their plan being to blow up a nuclear power station. However, they are swayed from their mission by modern-day consumerism.
    Fitfully amusing one-joke movie which wears out its welcome about halfway through.
p: Denise Di Novi for Castle Premier/New World
exec p: Christopher Webster, Steve Wright
w: Redbrad Simmons, Michael Lehmann
d: Michael Lehmann
ph: Mitchell Dubin
m: David Newman
ed: Norman Hollyn
pd: Jon Hutman
cos: Joseph Porro
sound: Douglas Axtell
make-up effects: Kevin Yagher
Ed Begley Jr, Stockard Channing, Dabney Coleman (as Aunt Bea), Cami Cooper, Bobby Jacoby, Glenn Shadix, Adam Bieski, Susan Barnes

Meet the Feebles
New Zealand 1989 96m colour
A temperamental hippo resorts to massacre when she is ousted from a variety show.

Determinedly outrageous puppet show which plays like the Muppets on acid. A few good moments, but the adults-only humour quickly palls.
p: Jim Booth, Peter Jackson for Wingnut
w: Daniel Mulheron, Frances Walsh, Stephen Sinclair, Peter Jackson
d: Peter Jackson
ph: Murray Milne
m: Peter Dasent
ed: Jamie Selkirk
pd: Michael Kane
cos: Glennis Foster
sound: Grant Taylor
puppet design: Cameron Chittock
titles: Sue Rogers
voices: Donna Akersten, Stuart Devenie, Mark Hadlow, Ross Jolly, Peter Vere Jones, Mark Wright, Brian Sergent

Mekagojira No Gyakushu see
Terror of Mechagodzilla

Melford, George (1889-1961)
American actor and director with stage experience. He began his film career as an actor in 1909 before turning to direction in 1911 with *Arizona Bill*. Much work followed (*To Have and To Hold*, *The Call of the East*, *The Sea Wolf*, etc.), though his best-known silent film is *The Sheik*, which starred Rudolph Valentino. In 1930 he directed the Spanish-language version of *Dracula* for Universal; those who have seen it regard it as superior to the Browning/Lugosi version. His other sound credits as director include *The Viking*, *East of Borneo* and *East of Java*. He later returned to acting in such films as *The Robe*, *The Egyptian* and *The Ten Commandments*.

Méliès, Georges (1861-1938)
Pioneering French director, a stage magician who began making simple 'trick' films, such as *A Vanishing Lady* and an incredible seventy-eight short films in the same year as early as 1896. Had built his own studio at Montreuil by 1897 where, under the Star Films banner, he made twenty to thirty films a year. His most famous early film is the elaborate *Voyage to the Moon* (1902), which provided the cinema with its first iconographic image. Business began to decline in 1908, the cinema having moved on, yet Méliès persisted in churning out the same kind of production. He retired from the movies in 1912 to pursue other interests, but never with the same degree of success. After years of obscurity, he was rediscovered in 1929, when he was named the father of fantasy film.

Selected genre credits:
The Haunted Cavern (1998), *The Man with Four Heads* (1998), *Cinderella* (1900), *Indiarubber Head* (1901), *Voyage to the Moon* (1902 - aka *A Trip to the Moon*), *Jupiter's Thunderbolts* (1902), *The Damnation of Dr Faust* (1903), *The Kingdom of the Fairies* (1903), *The Impossible Voyage* (1904), *The Merry Frolics of Satan* (1905), *Tunneling the English Channel* (1906), *20,000 Leagues Under the Sea* (1907), *Baron Munchausen* (1911), *The Conquest of the Pole* (1912)

Melle, Gil (1935-)
American composer, mostly for television. His film scores have generally been undistinguished and include *The Andromeda Strain*, *Starship Invasion* and *Restless*.
Genre credits:
Frankenstein: The True Story (1973 - TVM), *The Sentinel* (1977), *Blood Beach* (1981)

Melly, Andree (1932-)
British actress (the sister of jazz singer George Melly) with a lot of theatre work to her name, but remembered by genre fans for playing Gina the vampire girl in Hammer's *The Brides of Dracula*. Her other film credits include *So Little Time*, *The Belles of St Trinian's* and *The Big Day*.
Genre credits:
The Brides of Dracula (1960), *The Horror of It All* (1963)

Meredith, Burgess (1908-)
American character actor (real name George Burgess), a former merchant seaman and businessman who made his stage début in 1929, moving to Hollywood in 1935 to film his stage success *Winterset*. He has played key roles in several important films, including *Of Mice and Men*, *Tom, Dick and Harry* and *Mine Own Executioner*. Known to TV audiences as The Penguin in *Batman*, his other supporting roles include performances in *Day of the Locust*, *Rocky*, *True Confessions*, *Clash of the Titans* and *Grumpy Old Men*. He has also directed one film, *The Man on the Eiffel Tower* (1949).
Genre credits:
Torture Garden (1967), *Burnt Offerings* (1976), *The Sentinel* (1977), *Magic* (1978), *The Manitou* (1978)

Mesa of Lost Women
USA 1952 70m bw
A mad scientist's experiments include an attempt to cross women with spiders.

Grade Z rubbish, not even enjoyably bad. And as for the music...
p: G. William Perkins, Melvin Gordon for Howco

exec p: Wade Williams
w: Herbert Trevos
d: Herbert Trevos, Ron Ormond
ph: Kark Struss, Gil Warrenton
m: Hoyt S. Curtin
ed: Hugh Winn, Ray H. Lockert, W. Donn Hayes
ad: no credit given
sp: Ray Mercer
sound: Oscar Rodriquez
narrator: Lyle Talbot
Jackie Coogan, Richard Travis, Allan Nixon, Mary Hill, Robert Knapp, Tandra Quinn

Mescall, John (1899-)
American cinematographer, noted for his distinguished work on James Whale's *The Bride of Frankenstein* and *Showboat*. A former lab assistant, he turned to cinematography in 1920 with *It's a Great Life*, going on to photograph such silent films as *Satan in Sables*, *The Student Prince* and *The Wreck of the Hesperus*. His sound films include *Magnificent Obsession* and *Dark Waters*.
Genre credits:
The Black Cat (1934), *The Bride of Frankenstein* (1935), *Not of This Earth* (1957)

Metamorphosis
USA 1988 95m colour
A scientist tries an experimental drug on himself and metamorphoses into a monster.

Amateur-looking rubbish that ends with a series of behind-the-scenes shots chronicling the making of the film, though these by no means make it worth seeking out.
p: Anthony Brewster for BB
exec p: Frank Bresee
w/d: G. L. Eastwood (Luigi Montefiori)
ph: Christopher Condon
m: John Vulich
ed: William Shaffer, Skip Melanowski
ad: Roger McCoin
sp: Dan Bardona, Christopher Ray
sound: David Wilder
make-up effects: Ralph Miller III, Tom Floutz, Cleve Hall
Gene LeBrock, Harry Carson, Catherine Baranov, Jason Arnold, David Wicker, Anna Colona

Metro Goldwyn Mayer (MGM/UA)
From the mid-twenties to the late fifties, MGM was the dominant Hollywood studio, producing top-quality musicals and dramas, though their record with horror has been fairly patchy. MGM began life in 1920 as Loewe's Inc, an exhibition company which merged first with Metro Pictures

and then with Goldwyn Productions to produce the world-famous logo. Genre highlights for the studio include *Freaks*, *Mad Love* and *The Picture of Dorian Gray*. Genre filmography:
London After Midnight (1927 - aka *The Hypnotist*), *Freaks* (1932), *Mad Love* (1935 - aka *The Hands of Orlac*), *Mark of the Vampire* (1935), *The Devil Doll* (1936), *Dr Jekyll and Mr Hyde* (1941), *The Picture of Dorian Gray* (1945), *House of Dark Shadows* (1971), *Night of Dark Shadows* (1971), *Night of the Lepus* (1971), *Species* (1995)

Midnight
USA 1981 88m colour
An abused runaway teenager and the friends she makes while hitch-hiking find themselves prey to a family of blood-drinking backwoods psychopaths.
    Predictable low-budget backwoods thriller, moving at too leisurely a pace to be very effective.
p: Donald M. Redinger for Independent International/Congregation
exec p: Samuel M. Sherman, Daniel Q. Kennis
w/d/novel: John Russo
ph/ed: Paul McCollough
m: The Sound Castle and others
ad: no credit given
cos: Don Di Fonso
sound: Eric Baca, Aaron Nathanson
make-up effects: Tom Savini
Melanie Verlin, John Amplas, Robin Walsh, Charles Jackson, John Hall

The Midnight Movie Massacre
USA 1986 84m colour
In 1956, an audience watching a science-fiction thriller in a run-down theatre finds itself under threat from a man-eating monster from outer space.
    Mild horror spoof with an unnecessary amount of gore. Not a patch on *The Rocky Horror Picture Show*.
p: Wade Williamson for Tower
exec p: Aaron Wilson
w: Roger Branit, John Chadwell, David Houston
d: Mark Stock, Larry Jacobs
ph: David Dart, Nicholas Von Sternberg
m: Bill C. Crain and others
ed: Roger Branit
cos: Christopher Leitch
sound: Ken Ross, Herbert Strock
ch: Ken Stout
Robert Clarke, Ann Robinson, David Staffer, Margie Robbins, Tom Hustler, Brad Bittiker, Susan Murphy, Duke Howze, Mary Stevens

Midnight Offerings
USA 1981 96m Technicolor TVM
A girl student dabbles in witchcraft, and woe betide anyone who gets in her way.

Adequate malarkey, somewhere down the road from *Carrie*.
p: Alex Beaton for Paramount/ABC
exec p: Stephen J. Cannell
w: Juanita Bartlett
d: Rod Holcomb
ph: Hector Figueroa
m: Walter Scharf
ed: Christopher Nelson
ad: John D. Jeffries, Sr
sp: John Coles
sound: Jack May
Melissa Sue Anderson, Cathryn Damon, Mary McDonough, Gordon Jump, Patrick Cassidy, Kym Karath

Mighty Joe Young *
USA 1949 94m bw
A girl befriends a giant gorilla and takes it to New York, where it at first causes panic. However, it later saves the day by rescuing orphans from their burning home.
    Predictable semi-sequel to *King Kong*, with tired dialogue and situations, though it does build to a pretty exciting climax - followed, for once, by a happy ending.
p: Merian C. Cooper for RKO
exec p: John Ford, Merian C. Cooper
w: Ruth Rose
story: Merian C. Cooper
d: Ernest B. Schoedsack
ph: J. Roy Hunt
m: Roy Webb
md: Constantin Bakaleinikoff
ed: Ted Cheesman
ad: James Basevi, Howard Richmond
cos: Adele Balkan
sp: Willis O'Brien (aa), Ray Harryhausen, Peter Peterson
photographic effects: Harold Stine, Bert Willis, Linwood Dunn
sound: Walter Elliott
Terry Moore, Robert Armstrong, Ben Johnson, Frank McHugh, Lora Lee Michel, Douglas Fawley, Regis Toomey

Mikels, Ted V.
American exploitation director (real name Theodore Vincent Mikacevich), a former magician, accordionist(!), editor and stuntman who made his directorial début with *Strike Me Deadly* in 1963. His other credits include *Black Klansman*, *The Doll Squad*, *Ten Violent Women* and *Angel of Vengeance*.
Genre credits:
Day of the Nightmare (1965), *The Astro-Zombies* (1969), *The Corpse Grinders* (1972), *Blood Orgy of the She-Devils* (1973), *The Worm Eaters* (1975)

Milland, Ray (1905-1986)
Welsh actor (real name Reginald Truscott-Jones), a pleasant enough light

leading man until the success of the rather more dramatic *Lost Weekend* (1945), in which he played a dipsomaniac, won him a Best Actor Oscar and altered the course of his career. A former guardsman, he made his film début in Britain in 1929 in *The Plaything* and headed for Hollywood the following year. There he appeared in such films as *Way for a Sailor*, *The Glass Key*, *The Jungle Princess* and *Charlie Chan in London* before being given more substantial roles in the likes of *Beau Geste*, *Arise, My Love*, *Reap the Wild Wind* and *Ministry of Fear*. He later tried his hand at direction, with such pictures as *A Man Alone*, *Lisbon*, *The Safecracker*, *Panic in Year Zero* and *Hostile Witness*. His other films as an actor include Hitchcock's *Dial M for Murder*, *Love Story*, *Gold* and *Escape to Witch Mountain*.
Genre credits:
The Uninvited (1944), *Alias Nick Beal* (1949 - aka *The Contact Man*), *X - The Man With X-Ray Eyes* (1963 - aka *The Man With X-Ray Eyes*), *Daughter of the Mind* (1969 - TVM), *Black Noon* (1971 - TVM), *The Thing With Two Heads* (1972), *Frogs* (1972), *The House in Nightmare Park* (1973), *Terror in the Wax Museum* (1973), *The Dead Don't Die* (1974 - TVM), *Look What Happened to Rosemary's Baby* (1977 - TVM), *The Uncanny* (1977), *The Darker Side of Terror* (1978 - TVM), *Cruise Into Terror* (1978), *The Attic* (1979), *The Sea Serpent* (1986)

Miller, Dick (1928-)
American actor, a long-time fixture of the Roger Corman school. Consequently something of a cult, he has appeared in supporting roles and cameos in the films of a variety of modern filmmakers, particularly those of Joe Dante. A former disc-jockey, semi-pro footballer, psychologist, TV talk-show host and stage actor, he made his film début in 1955 in Corman's *Apache Woman*. Other credits include *The St Valentine's Day Massacre*, *Cannonball* (aka *Carquake*), *1941*, *Explorers*, *After Hours*, *Matinee* and *Pulp Fiction*.
Genre credits:
It Conquered the World (1956), *The Undead* (1956), *Attack of the Crab Monsters* (1956), *Not of This Earth* (1957), *War of the Satellites* (1958), *A Bucket of Blood* (1959 - as Walter Paisley), *Last Woman on Earth* (1959), *The Little Shop of Horrors* (1960), *The Premature Burial* (1962), *The Terror* (1962), *X - The Man With X-Ray Eyes* (1963 - aka *The Man With X-Ray Eyes*), *Piranha* (1978), *The Howling* (1980), *Dr Heckyll and Mr Hype* (1980), *The Twilight Zone* (1983), *The Terminator* (1984), *Lies* (1984), *Gremlins* (1984), *Night of the*

Creeps (1986), *Killbots* (1986 - aka *Chopping Mall* - as Walter Paisley), *Dead Heat* (1988), *Gremlins 2: The New Batch* (1991), *Evil Toons* (1991), *Amityville 1992: It's About Time* (1992 - TVM), *Demon Knight* (1994)

Miller, Jason (1939-)
Intense-looking American actor and playwright, notable as the priest in *The Exorcist* (1973), a role he reprised for the second sequel, *Exorcist III* (1990). His other credits include *The Ninth Configuration* and *That Championship Season*, which he wrote and directed from his stage play.

Milligan, Andy (1929-1991)
American director who made a handful of extremely gory but barely watchable zero-budget films in the sixties and seventies. He began his directorial career in 1963 with the sexploiter *Liz* (aka *The Promiscuous Sex*), which he followed with *The Naked Witch*. In the eighties he directed a few direct-to-video shockers which showed no improvement on his earlier output. His other credits include *Gutter Trash*, *Seeds*, *Fleshpot on 42nd St.*, *The Depraved* and *The Degenerates*.
Genre credits:
The Naked Witch (1964 - aka *The Naked Temptress*), *The Ghastly Ones* (1969), *Bloodthirsty Butchers* (1970), *Torture Dungeon* (1970), *The Body Beneath* (1971), *Guru the Mad Monk* (1971), *The Man with Two Heads* (1972 - aka *Dr Jekyll and Mr Blood*), *The Rats Are Coming! The Werewolves Are Here!* (1972 - aka *Curse of the Full Moon*), *Blood* (1974), *Legacy of Blood* (1978), *Carnage* (1983), *The Weirdo* (1988), *Monstrosity* (1989), *Surgikill* (1990)

Milton, David
American art director whose genre work has been entirely for Monogram.
Genre credits:
The Bowery at Midnight (1942), *The Ape Man* (1943 - aka *Lock Your Doors*), *Return of the Ape Man* (1944), *The Voodoo Man* (1944), *Face of Marble* (1946)

Mindkiller
USA 1987 86m colour Hi-Fi stereo
A librarian's attempts to expand his mind with a machine of his own invention turn him into a monster, with his brain eventually bursting from his head and taking on a murderous life of its own.
Foolish nonsense with echoes of *X - The Man with X-Ray Eyes*. Look for it on the highest and dustiest shelf in the video store.
p: Sarah A. Liles for Flash Features/First Films

exec p: A. B. Goldberg
w: Dave Sipos, Curtis Hannum, Michael Krueger, Doug Olsen
story: Ted A. Bohus, Michael Krueger, Doug Olson
d: Michael Krueger
ph: Jim Kelley
m: Jeffrey Wood
ed: Jonathan Moser
ad: Susan MacDonald Petersen
cos: Margaret Sjobers
sound: Bob Abbott
make-up effects: Vincent J. Gaustini Joe McDonald, Shirley Ross, Christopher Wade, Tom Henry, Kevin Hart

Miner, Steve (1951-)
American producer and director who began his career as a production assistant in 1970. Produced, directed and edited educational films from the mid seventies, turning to features in 1978. Began as a producer of low-budget horrors before progressing to bigger things. His non-genre credits include *Soul Man*, *Forever Young* and *My Father the Hero* (US remake).
Genre credits:
Friday the 13th Part 2 (1981 - co-p/d), *Friday the 13th Part 3 in 3D* (1982 - d), *House* (1986 - d), *Warlock* (1988 - p/d)

Mingaye, Don
British art director, trained at the St Martin's School of Art in London. Began in films in 1945 as a junior scenic artist at Gainsborough's Islington studios. Went to work for Hammer in the late fifties as an assistant art director, gradually working his way up to fully fledged art director, often in association with Hammer's designer-in-chief, Bernard Robinson.
Genre credits:
The Shadow of the Cat (1961 - co-ad), *The Phantom of the Opera* (1962 - co-ad), *Captain Clegg* (1962 - aka *Night Creatures* - co-ad), *The Damned* (1963 - aka *These Are the Damned* - ad), *Paranoiac* (1963 - co-ad), *Kiss of the Vampire* (1964 - aka *Kiss of Evil* - ad), *The Evil of Frankenstein* (1964 - ad), *Nightmare* (1964 - co-ad), *The Gorgon* (1964 - co-ad), *She* (1965 - co-ad), *Dracula - Prince of Darkness* (1966 - ad), *Rasputin - The Mad Monk* (1966 - ad), *Plague of the Zombies* (1966 - ad), *The Reptile* (1966 - ad), *The Witches* (1966 - aka *The Devil's Own* - ad), *The Mummy's Shroud* (1967 - ad), *Lust for a Vampire* (1971 - ad)

Misery **
USA 1990 107m CFIcolor Dolby
A popular romantic novelist is saved from a crippling car accident by his number-one fan, who cares for him in

her isolated home - but she turns out to be homicidal.
Quirky, claustrophobic but well-acted thriller which picks up speed as it moves along and provides a couple of memorable moments.
p: Andrew Schienman, Rob Reiner for Castle Rock/Nelson Entertainment
w: William Goldman
novel: Stephen King
d: Rob Reiner
ph: Barry Sonnenfeld
m: Marc Shaiman
ed: Robert Leighton
pd: Norman Garwood
sp: Phil Cory
sound: Mark Long
2nd unit d: Barry Sonnefeld
2ndd unit ph: Gary Kibbe
stunt co-ordinator: David Ellis
James Caan, Kathy Bates (aa), Frances Sternhagen, Richard Farnsworth, Lauren Bacall, Graham Jarvis, Jerry Potter

Mitchell, Cameron (1918-1994)
American actor (real name Cameron Misell), best known for his long run in the TV western series *High Chaparral*. A former radio commentator and stage actor, he appeared in countless films of variable quality throughout his lengthy career. His better credits include *They Were Expendable*, *Death of a Salesman* and *My Favorite Year*.
Genre credits:
Gorilla at Large (1954), *Face of Fire* (1959), *Blood and Black Lace* (1965), *Man-Eater of Hydra* (1965), *Nightmare in Wax* (1967), *Autopsy of a Ghost* (1967), *Haunts* (1976), *The Toolbox Murders* (1978), *The Swarm* (1978), *Silent Scream* (1980), *Without Warning* (1980), *The Demon* (1981), *Frankenstein Island* (1980), *Blood Link* (1983), *Night Train to Terror* (1985), *The Tomb* (1986), *The Offspring* (1987)

Monkey Shines
USA 1989 113m DeLuxe
A quadroplegic is given a specially trained monkey to help him around the house, but an experimental drug turns it into a razor-wielding killer.
A tasteless premise that provides a few routine shocks towards the end.
p: Charles Evans for Orion
exec p: Peter Grunwald, Gerald S. Paonessa
w/d: George Romero
novel: Michael Stewart
ph: James A. Contner
m: David Shire
ed: Pasquale Buba
pd: Cletus Anderson
cos: Barbara Anderson
sound: John Sutton

make-up effects: Tom Savini
monkey trainer: Alison Pascoe
Jason Beghe, John Pankow, Kate
McNeil, Joyce Van Patten, Christine
Forrest, Stephen Root, Stanley Tucci,
Juanine Turner, William Newman

Monogram

American Poverty Row studio, a subsidiary of Allied Artists, known for low-
budget second features which centred
round the exploits of The Bowery Boys,
The East Side Kids and Charlie Chan,
etc. The studio was also the purveyor of
a number of undistinguished bottom-of-
the-barrel horror films, many of them
starring the downward-sliding Bela
Lugosi. They were often produced and
directed by the double threat of Sam
Katzman and William Beaudine.
Genre filmography:
The Ape (1940), *Bowery at Midnight*
(1942), *The Corpse Vanishes* (1942 - aka
The Case of the Missing Brides), *The Ape
Man* (1943 - aka *Lock Your Doors*), *Return
of the Ape Man* (1944), *Face of Marble*
(1946)

The Monster and the Girl

USA 1940 64m bw
The brain of an executed man is
transplanted into a gorilla which then
goes after the gangsters responsible for
his death.

A curious if incredibly plotted
concoction of gangsterism and horror.
Surprisingly, it's not too badly made,
though its central situation quickly
became a horror cliché.
p: Jack Moss for Paramount
w: Stuart Anthony
d: Stuart Heisler
ph: Victor Milner
m: Sigmund Krumgold
ed: Everett Douglas
ad: Hans Dreier, Haldane Douglas
Paul Lukas, Ellen Drew, George Zucco,
Joseph Calleia, Robert Paige, Rod
Cameron, Onslow Stevens

The Monster Club

GB 1980 97m Technicolor
After being turned into a vampire, a
horror author is invited to a club for
monsters where he is told weird stories.

Poorly assembled all-star
compendium whose mixture of mild
thrills and weak jokes fails to amuse.
p: Milton Subotsky for ITC/Chips/
Sword and Sorcery
exec p: Jack Gill, Bernard J. Kingham
w: Edward Abraham, Valerie Abraham
stories: R. Chetwynd-Hayes
d: Roy Ward Baker
ph: Peter Jessop
m: Douglas Gamley, Alan Hawkshaw,

John Georgiadis
songs: B. A. Robertson and others
ed: Peter Tanner
pd: Tony Curtis
cos: Eileen Sullivan
sound: Norman Polland, Bob Jones
Vincent Price, John Carradine, Donald
Pleasence, Simon Ward, Anthony Steel,
Geoffrey Bayldon, James Laurenson,
Stuart Whitman, Patrick Magee,
Anthony Valentine, Richard Johnson,
Britt Ekland, Barbara Kellerman, Lesley
Dunlop, Warren Saire, B. A. Robertson

The Monster from Green Hell

USA 1957 71m bw/colour
A rocket launched into space to chart
the effects on various insects crash-lands
in Africa where the cargo grows to giant
proportions.

Ludicrous grade-Z science-fiction
horror that seems to consist largely of
stock footage from *Stanley and
Livingstone*, made back in 1939.
p: Al Zimbalist for Gross-Krasne
exec p: Jack J. Gross, Philip N. Krasne
w: Louis Vittes, André Bohen
d: Kenneth Crane
ph: Ray Flin
m: Albert Glasser
ed: Kenneth G. Krane
ad: Ernst Fetge
cos: Joe Dimmutt
sp: Jess Davidson, Jack Brabin, Louis de
Witt
sound: Stanley Codey, Robert W.
Roderick
Jim Davis, Barbara Turner, Eduardo
Cianelli, Robert E. Griffin, Joel Fluellen

The Monster Squad *

USA 1988 82m Metrocolor Panavision
Dolby
Monster-mad youngsters discover that
Dracula, the Wolf Man, the Gill Man
and Frankenstein's Monster have moved
to their neighbourhood to search for
Professor Van Helsing's old diary.

Mild but enjoyable horror comic for
younger audiences - and discerning
older ones.
p: Jonathan A. Zimbert for
Taft/Braveworld
exec p: Peter Hyams, Rob Cohen, Keith
Barish
w: Fred Dekker, Shane Black
d: Fred Dekker
ph: Bradford May
m: Bruce Broughton
ed: James Mitchell
pd: Albert Brenner
cos: Michael Hoffman, Aggie Lyon
sp: Richard Edlund
sound: Richard Church
make-up effects: Stan Winston
André Gower, Robby Kiger, Stephen

Macht, Stan Shaw, Duncan Regehr (as
Dracula), Tom Noonan (as Frankenstein's
Monster), Leonardo Cimino

The Monster That Challenged the World

USA 1957 83m bw
A giant caterpillar threatens an isolated
Californian military base.

Dim monster hokum, one of the
worst giant-insect movies of its period.
p: Arthur Gardner, Jules V. Levy for
UA/Levy-Gardner-Laven
w: Pat Fielder
story: David Duncan
d: Arnold Laven
ph: Lester White
m: Heinz Roemheld
ed: John Faure
ad: James Vance
sp: August Lohman
sound: Charles Althaus, Joel Moss
underwater d: Paul Stader
underwater ph: Scotty Welborn
Tim Holt, Audrey Dalton, Hans
Conreid, Harlan Wade, Casey Adams,
Gordon Jones, Mimi Gibson

Monster Zero see Invasion of the
Astro Monsters

Moorehead, Agnes (1906-1974)

Respected American character actress,
best known to TV audiences as Endora
the witch in *Bewitched*. On stage from the
age of eleven as a dancer, she began
appearing on Broadway from 1928,
though it was on radio that she had her
first real success. She joined Orson
Welles' Mercury Theatre Company in
1940, after which it was but a short step
to roles in *Citizen Kane* and *The
Magnificent Ambersons*. Her other films
include *Journey Into Fear*, *Jane Eyre*, *Since
You Went Away*, *The Lost Moment*, *The
Woman in White* and *Magnificent Obsession*.
Genre credits:
The Woman in White (1948), *The Bat*
(1959), *Hush... Hush, Sweet Charlotte*
(1964), *What's the Matter With Helen?*
(1971), *Night of Terror* (1972 - TVM),
Frankenstein - The True Story (1973 -
TVM)

Mora, Philippe (1949-)

Australian writer, producer and director,
responsible for a number of
undistinguished productions, including
Captain Invincible and two of the dismal
Howling sequels.
Genre credits:
The Beast Within (1981 - d), *Howling II:
Your Sister is a Werewolf* (1985 - aka
Howling II: Stirba, Werewolf Bitch - d),
Howling III: The Marsupials (1987 -
w/co-p/d), *Communion* (1990 - co-p/d)

Morell, André (1909-1978)

Reliable British character actor with a penchant for well-bred authority figures. Was the ideal Watson to Peter Cushing's Holmes in Hammer's *The Hound of the Baskervilles*. Other credits include *Seven Days to Noon*, *Ben-Hur*, *The Slipper and the Rose* and *The First Great Train Robbery*.
Genre credits:
Stolen Face (1952), *The Hound of the Baskervilles* (1959), *Behemoth the Sea Monster* (1959 - aka *The Giant Behemoth*), *The Shadow of the Cat* (1961), *She* (1965), *Plague of the Zombies* (1966), *The Mummy's Shroud* (1967), *The Vengeance of She* (1968)

Morris, John (1926-)

American composer, long associated with the films of Mel Brooks (*The Producers*, *The Twelve Chairs*, *Blazing Saddles*, *Silent Movie*, *High Anxiety*, etc.) and Gene Wilder (*The Adventure of Sherlock Holmes' Smarter Brother*, *The World's Greatest Lover*, *The Woman in Red*, etc.). Came to films via stage and TV and his association with Brooks.
Genre credits:
Young Frankenstein (1974), *The Elephant Man* (1980), *The Doctor and the Devils* (1985), *Haunted Honeymoon* (1986)

Morrissey, Paul (1939-)

American director, long associated with the so-called underground films of Andy Warhol (*Flesh*, *Trash*, *Heat*, etc.), for whom he also wrote and directed two horror films in Italy: *Andy Warhol's Frankenstein* (1973 - aka *Flesh for Frankenstein/Frankenstein 3D/The Frankenstein Experiment*) and *Andy Warhol's Dracula* (1973 - aka *Blood for Dracula/Young Dracula*). He also co-wrote and directed a comic version of *The Hound of the Baskervilles* in 1977; it starred Peter Cook and Dudley Moore and also contained a spoof of *The Exorcist*.

Mortuary

USA 1981 91m DeLuxe
A cloak-clad killer goes about dispatching his victims with a variety of mortician's instruments.
    Dismal slasher pic which adds nothing at all to this overworked sub-genre.
p: Howie Avedis, Marlene Schmidt for Hickmar/Movie Makers
w: Howie Avedis, Marlene Schmidt
d: Howie Avedis
ph: Gary Graver
m: John Cacavas
ed: Standford C. Allen
ad: Randy Ser
cos: Marydith Chase
sp: Jim Gillespie, Diane Seletos

sound: Don Sanders, Jonathan Stein
Mary McDonough, Bill Paxton, Lynda Day George, Christopher George, Alvy Moore, David Wallace

The Most Dangerous Game *

US 1932 63m bw
A mad count hunts down guests, shipwrecked on his island, for his secret trophy room.
    Slow-starting and rather dated chase melodrama with a ripe star performance. The chase itself is often excitingly staged and the whole thing plays like a dress rehearsal for the same team's *King Kong*, which followed a year later.
p: Merian C. Cooper for RKO
exec p: David O. Selznick
w: James Creelman
story: Richard Connell
d: Ernest B. Schoedsack, Irving Pichel
ph: HARRY GERRARD
m: MAX STEINER
ed: Archie Marshek
ad: Carroll Clark
cos: Walter Plunkett
sp: Harry Redmond Jr
sound: Clem Portman
sound effects: Murray Spivack
Leslie Banks, Fay Wray, Joel McCrea, Robert Armstrong, Noble Johnson, Steve Clemento, William Davidson, Hale Hamilton, Dutch Hendrian

Mother Riley Meets the Vampire

GB 1952 74m bw
Mother Riley helps capture a crook known as the Vampire.
    Rather lame final outing for Lucan's famous Irish washerwoman, with Lugosi's presence adding little to the overall effect. Cheap production values only make matters worse.
p: John Gilling for Reknown
w: Val Valentine
d: John Gilling
ph: Stan Pavey
m: Linda Southworth
ed: Len Truman
ad: Bernard Robinson
Arthur Lucan, Bela Lugosi, Dora Bryan, Richard Wattis, Dandy Nichols, Judith Furse, Philip Leaver, Hattie Jacques, Graham Moffatt, Maria Mercedes

Moxey, John Llewellyn (1920-)

British director who has made couple of interesting low-budget films, most notably *City of the Dead* (aka *Horror Hotel*) before moving to America where he became a prolific director of TV movies.
Genre credits:
City of the Dead (1960 - aka *Horror Hotel*), *Circus of Fear* (1967 -aka *Psycho*

Circus), *The House That Would Not Die* (1970 - TVM), *A Taste of Evil* (1971-TVM), *The Night Stalker* (1971 - TVM), *The Strange and Deadly Occurrence* (1974 - TVM), *Sanctuary of Fear* (1979)

The Mummy

Though a handful of films featuring mummies were made during the silent period, it wasn't until Universal made *The Mummy* in 1932, some ten years after the sensational discovery of Tutankhamun's tomb by Lord Carnarvon and Howard Carter, that mummies became popular cinematic fodder. Starring Boris Karloff (billed as 'Karloff the Uncanny') in the title role, the film produced a handful of sequels in the forties before the character inevitably met Abbott and Costello in 1955. Hammer successfully revived the story in 1959 with Christopher Lee playing the central part. Again, several undistinguished sequels followed. Meanwhile, in the late fifties, Mexico instigated a series involving Aztec mummies and, later, wrestling hero Santos. The Karloff and Lee films aside, the character has not been too well served by the movies down the years.
Key filmography:
The Mummy of King Rameses (1909 - aka *La Momie du Roi*), *The Mummy* (1911), *The Eyes of the Mummy* (1918 - aka *Die Augen der Mumie*), *The Mummy* (1932), *Mummy's Boys* (1936), *The Mummy's Hand* (1940), *The Mummy's Tomb* (1942), *The Mummy's Ghost* (1943), *The Mummy's Curse* (1944), *Abbott and Costello Meet the Mummy*

• **Boris Karloff in a classic pose from the 1932 classic *The Mummy*. The painstakingly-applied make-up was the work of Jack P. Pierce.**

• **Before, during and after. Christopher Lee's Kharis pays the ultimate price for entering the tomb of Princess Ananka in** *The Mummy.*

(1955), *The Pharaoh's Curse* (1956), *The Aztec Mummy* (1957 - aka *The Mummy / The Mummy Strikes / La Momia Azteca*), *The Robot vs the Aztec Mummy* (1959 - aka *La Momia Contra el Robot Humano*), *The Curse of the Aztec Mummy* (1959 - aka *La Maldición de la Momia*), *The Mummy* (1959), *Attack of the Malayan Mummy* (1963), *The Curse of the Mummy's Tomb* (1964), *Wrestling Women vs. the Aztec Mummy* (1964 - aka *Las Luchadoras Contra la Momia*), *The Mummy's Shroud* (1966), *Orgy of the Dead* (1966), *Santo y Blue Demon Contra los Monstruos* (1971), *Santo en la Vengenza de la Momia* (1971), *Blood from the Mummy's Tomb* (1971), *Lips of Blood* (1972 - aka *Le Sang des Autres / Le Cheminsole la Violence / Perversions Sexuelles*), *La Venganza de la Momia* (1973 - aka *The Mummy's Revenge / The Mummy's Vengeance*), *The Curse of King Tut's Tomb* (1979 - TVM), *The Awakening* (1980), *Dawn of the Mummy* (1980), *La Momia Bacional* (1981), *Timewalker* (1982), *The Tomb* (1985), *The Lamp* (1987 - aka *The Outing*), *Tales from the Darkside: The Movie* (1991 - segment)

The Mummy **
USA 1932 72m bw
An ancient Egyptian mummy is unwittingly brought back to life by archaeologists.

Slow-moving but well-crafted horror melodrama which provides a splendid part for its star. Full of interest for connoisseurs, though the Mummy itself is glimpsed only briefly at the beginning.
p: Stanley Bergerman for Universal
w: JOHN L. BALDERSTON
d: KARL FREUND
ph: CHARLES STUMAR
m: Tchaikowsky
ed: Milton Carruth
ad: WILLY POGANY
make-up: JACK P. PIERCE
BORIS KARLOFF, ZITA JOHANN, Edward Van Sloane, David Manners, Arthur Byron, Bramwell Fletcher, Noble Johnson

The Mummy **
GB 1959 88m Technicolor
A 4000-year-old mummy returns to life to kill the archaeologists responsible for desecrating the tomb of an Egyptian queen.

Generally competent Hammer horror with a couple of scenes in their best style. Enjoyable nonsense for aficionados.
p: Michael Carreras, Anthony Nelson Keys for Hammer / Universal
w: JIMMY SANGSTER
d: Terence Fisher
ph: Jack Asher
m: FRANK REIZENSTEIN
md: John Hollingsworth
ed: James Needs, Alfred Cox
ad: Bernard Robinson
cos: Molly Arbuthnot
sp: Bill Warrington
sound: Jock May
make-up: Roy Ashton
Peter Cushing, CHRISTOPHER LEE (as the Mummy), Yvonne Furneaux, Felix Aylmer, Raymond Huntley, Michael Ripper, John Stuart, Eddie Byrne, George Woodbridge

The Mummy's Curse
USA 1944 62m bw
Revived yet again, the Mummy goes on the rampage in a Louisiana swamp.

Feeble finale to a relentless series, though eleven years later the Mummy met Abbott and Costello in *Abbott and Costello Meet the Mummy*.
p: Ben Pivar, Oliver Drake for Universal
w: Bernard Schubert
d: Leslie Goodwin
ph: Virgil Miller
m: Oliver Drake, Frank Orth
md: Paul Sawtell
ed: Fred Feitshans
ad: John B. Goodman
sp: John P. Fulton
make-up: Jack P. Pierce
Lon Chaney Jr, Peter Coe, Martin Kosleck, Virginia Christine, Kay Harding, Dennis Moore

The Mummy's Ghost
USA 1943 61m bw
Brought back to life, the Mummy pursues a reincarnated Egyptian princess.

The usual mixture of tanna leaves, fainting heroines and torch-wielding villagers. Strictly routine.
p: Ben Pivar for Universal
w: Griffin Jay, Henry Sucher, Brena Weisberg
d: Reginald LeBorg
ph: William Sickner
md: Hans J. Salter
ed: Saul Goodkind
ad: John B. Goodman, Abraham Grossman
make-up: Jack P. Pierce
Lon Chaney Jr, John Carradine, Robert Lowery, Ramsey Ames, Barton MacLane, George Parker, Eddie Parker, Harry Shannon

The Mummy's Hand
USA 1940 67m bw
A reconstituted mummy is used to kill off various members of an archaeological team.

Routine second-feature sequel to the 1932 classic. The so-called comedy relief, typical of its period, tends to be counter-productive.
p: Ben Pivar for Universal
w: Griffin Jay, Maxwell Shane
d: Christy Cabanne
ph: Elwood Bredell
md: Hans J. Salter
ed: Phil Cahn
ad: Jack Otterson, Ralph M. De Lacy
make-up: Jack P. Pierce
Dick Foran, Wallace Ford, George Zucco, Cecil Kellaway, Tom Tyler (as the Mummy), Peggy Moran, Eduardo Cianelli

The Mummy's Shroud
GB 1966 84m Technicolor
A mummy is brought back to life to wreak vengeance on those who have disturbed the resting place of its young master.

Tedious horror hokum, scuppered by a low budget and an even lower sense of imagination. The climax, in which the Mummy crushes itself to dust, is a long time coming.
p: Anthony Nelson-Keys for Hammer
w/d: John Gilling
ph: Arthur Grant
m: Don Banks
md: Philip Martell
ed: James Needs, Chris Barnes
ad: Don Mingaye
cos: Molly Arbuthnot, Larry Stewart
sp: Les Bowie
sound: Ken Hawkins
cam op: Moray Grant
John Phillips, André Morell, Elizabeth Sellars, David Buck, Catherine Lacey, Michael Ripper, Roger Delgado, Maggie Kimberley, Dickie Owen (as the Mummy)

The Mummy's Tomb
USA 1942 65m bw
A high priest revives the Mummy in order to kill the remaining members of the expedition that defiled the tomb of the princess Ananka.

Fairly lively addition to Universal's Mummy series, using large chunks of The Mummy's Hand in its flashback sequences.
p: Ben Pivar for Universal
w: Griffin Jay, Henry Sucher
d: Harold Young
ph: George Robinson
md: Hans J. Salter
ed: Milton Carruth
ad: Jack Otterson, Ralph M. De Lacy
make-up: Jack P. Pierce
Lon Chaney Jr, Dick Foran, Turhan Bey, George Zucco, John Hubbard, Wallace Ford, Mary Gordon, Virginia Brissac, Frank Reicher

Munro, Caroline (1951-)
British horror starlet and game-show hostess (on British TV's 3,2,1) who has appeared as glamorous support in a variety of films, including The Golden Voyage of Sinbad, At the Earth's Core, Starcrash (as Stella Starr) and The Spy Who Loved Me.
Genre credits:
The Abominable Dr Phibes (1971), Dracula AD 1972 (1972), Captain Kronos - Vampire Hunter (1973 - aka Kronos), The Devil Within Her (1973), Maniac (1981), The Last Horror Film (1982 - aka Fanatic), Don't Open Till Christmas (1983), Slaughter High (1986), Howl of the Devil (1987), Faceless (1988), The Black Cat (1991), Night Owl (1993)

Murder by Decree *
GB/Canada 1978 112m Metroclor Panavision

When Jack the Ripper strikes in London, Sherlock Holmes investigates, only to find royal and masonic links in the case.

Tolerable though rather lengthy variation on an oft-told story (see A Study in Terror, which also linked Holmes with the Ripper legend). Cutting would have helped, but the performances of the two leads compensate.
p: René Dupont, Bob Clark for Avco/Decree Productions/Saucy Jack
w: John Hopkins
d: Bob Clark
ph: Reginald Morris
m: Carl Zittrer, Paul Zaza
ed: Stan Cole
pd: Harry Pottle
cos: Judy Moorcroft
sp: Michael Albrechten
sound: John Mitchell
CHRISTOPHER PLUMMER, JAMES MASON, Anthony Quayle, David Hemmings, John Gielgud, Susan Clark, Geneviève Bujold, Frank Finlay, Donald Sutherland, Robin Marshall

Murders in the Rue Morgue
USA 1932 62m bw
A mad scientist trains an ape to abduct girls whom he then uses in experiments.

Poorly constructed and woodenly acted variation on Poe, occasionally good to look at, but of very little real interest.
p: Carl Laemmle Jr, for Universal
w: Tom Reed, Dale Van Avery, John Huston, Robert Florey
story: Edgar Allan Poe
d: ROBERT FLOREY
ph: KARK FREUND
m: none
ed: Maurice Pivar, Milton Carruth
ad: CHARLES D. HALL
sp: John P. Fulton
BELA LUGOSI, Sidney Fox, Leon Ames, Bert Roach, Brandon Hurst, Noble Johnson

The Murders in the Rue Morgue *
USA 1986 96m Technicolor TVM
In 1899 Paris, a retired inspector solves a series of bizarre murders.

Good-looking tele-version of the oft-told tale. Good suspense sequences are let down by acres of chat.
p: Robert Halmi, Edward J. Pope for Robert Halmi Inc/International
w: David Epstein
story: Edgar Allan Poe
d: Jeannot Szwarc
ph: Bruno de Keyser
m: Charles Gross
ed: Eric Albertson
ad: André Guerin
cos: Christiane Coates
sound: Daniel Brisseau

titles: Greg Webb
make-up effects: Lyle Conway
George C. Scott, Rebecca de Mornay, Val Kilmer, Ian McShane, Neil Dickson, Maud Rayer

Murders in the Zoo *
USA 1933 64m bw
A jealous zoologist uses the animals in his zoo as a means of murdering his wife's suitors.

Occasionally sprightly horror thriller.
p: Paramount
w: Philip Wylie, Seton I. Miller
d: EDWARD SUTHERLAND
ph: Ernest Haller
Lionel Atwill, Kathleen Burke, Charles Ruggles, Randolph Scott, John Lodge, Gail Patrick, Harry Beresford, Edward McWade

Musuraca, Nicholas (1890/1895/1900-1975)
American cinematographer, long with RKO, where he worked on several of the Val Lewton horror films. Began his career in 1918 as a trainee at Vitograph, working his way up the photography ladder, from camera assistant to full-blown cinematographer by the early twenties with contributions to such films as Bride of the Storm and The Tyrant of Red Gulch. His first sound film was The Terror in 1928, which he followed with work on Cracked Nuts, Murder on a Bridle Path, The Swiss Family Robinson, The Bachelor and the Bobbysoxer and The Story of Mankind.
Genre credits:
The Terror (1928), The Stranger on the Third Floor (1940), Cat People (1942), The Seventh Victim (1943), The Curse of the Cat People (1944), Spiral Staircase (1945), Bedlam (1946)

My Best Friend Is a Vampire
USA 1988 89m Technicolor
A teenager becomes a vampire after a sexual encounter with a female vampire in a old mansion.

Mild teen comedy that wastes eighty-nine minutes amiably enough.
p: Dennis Murphy for King's Road Entertainment
w: Tab Murphy
d: Jimmy Huston
ph: James Bartle
m: Steve Dorst
ed: Janice Hampton, Gail Yasunaga
pd: Michael Molly
cos: Rona Lamont
sound: Art Names, Tim Himes, David Parker
Robert Sean Leonard, Evan Mirand, David Warner, Fannie Flagg, Rene Auberjonois, Cheryl Pollack

My Bloody Valentine
Canada 1981 91m colour
Murder and mayhem follow when a mad killer stalks guests at a St Valentine's party.

Predictable slasher fare with the final reel taking place in a disused mine. In Britain it was released on a double bill with *The Funhouse* and accompanied by the tag line, 'Pay to get in, pray to get out!'
p: John Dunning, André Link, Stephen Miller for Paramount
w: John Beard
d: George Mihalka
Paul Kelman, Cynthia Dale, Lori Hallier, Neil Affleck, Keith Knight, Alf Humphreys

The Mystery of Mr X *
USA 1934 84m bw
A jewel thief witnesses one of several police murders, and when he himself is suspected he sets out to find the real murderer.

Tolerable mystery thriller.
p: Lawrence Weingarten for MGM
w: Howard Emmett Rogers, Philip McDonald, Monckton Hoffe
novel: Philip McDonald
d: Edgar Selwyn
ph: Oliver T. Marsh
m: no credit given
ed: Hugh Wynne
ad: Merrill Pye
sound: Douglas Shearer
Robert Montgomery, Elizabeth Allen, Lewis Stone, Ralph Forbes, Henry Stephenson, Forester Harvey

The Mystery of the Wax Museum ***
USA 1933 77m Two-strip Technicolor
A sculptor survives a wax-museum fire to open a new one years later in New York. But this time he uses the bodies of real people as the bases for his exhibits.

Pacy, slickly made horror comic, very typical of the Warner style of film-making in the thirties, with sets and shadows used to maximum effect. Thought lost for many years, it remains historically important for its early use of colour, its various sub-plots and its Germanic influences. A must for buffs, it was remade in 1953 as *House of Wax*.
p: Henry Blanke for Warner
w: Don Mullally, Carl Erickson
story: Charles S. Belden
d: MICHAEL CURTIZ
ph: RAY RENNEHAN
md: Leo F. Forbstein
ed: George Amy
ad: ANTON GROT
cos: Orry-Kelly
sound: no credit given
LIONEL ATWILL, Fay Wray, GLENDA FARRELL, FRANK MCHUGH, Gavin Gordon, Allen Vincent, Edwin Maxwell, Holmes Herbert, Monica Bannister

N

Naha, Ed

American screenplay writer, a former
fanzine journalist and author (*The Making
of Dune*, *The Films of Roger Corman -
Brilliance on a Budget*, etc.). His other
credits include *Honey, I Shrunk the Kids*.
Genre credits:
Troll (1986 - w), *CHUD II: Bud the CHUD*
(1989 - w), *Matinee* (1992 - co-w)

Naked Exorcism

It 1975 88m colour
When a teenage boy shows signs of
being possessed by the Devil, a young
nun helps to exorcize him.

Dismal Italian shocker, a poor
attempt to cash in on the worldwide
box-office success of *The Exorcist* - so
much so that one of its many alternative
titles is *Exorcist III: Cries and Shadows*.
p: Luigi Fedeli for Colosseum/Manila
Cinematografica
w: Aldo Crudo, Franco Brocani, Elo
Pannaccio
story: Guido Albonico
d: Elo Pannaccio
ph: Franco Villa, Maurizio Centini
m: Giuliano Sorgini
ed: Fernanda Papa
Richard Conte, Francoise Prevost, Elena
Svevo, Patrizia Gori, Jean-Claude Verne,
Mimma Monticelli

Naismith, Laurence (1908-1992)

British character actor, perhaps best
remembered for playing the title role in
The Amazing Mr Blunden and with several
other forays into the horror genre to his
name. His non-genre credits include
Trouble in the Air, *Richard III*, *A Night to
Remember*, *Jason and the Argonauts* (as
Argus), *Camelot* and TV's *The Persuaders*.
Genre credits:
The Valley of Gwangi (1968), *Eye of the
Cat* (1969), *Scrooge* (1970), *The Amazing
Mr Blunden* (1972)

The Nanny **

GB 1965 93m bw
A malicious boy continually accuses his
nanny of being a psychopath... and she is.

Mainly enjoyable nut-house melodrama in the Hitchcock manner, smartly

handled and containing one of its star's
better crazy-old-lady performances.
p: Jimmy Sangster for
Hammer/Associated British
w: Jimmy Sangster
novel: Evelyn Piper
d: SETH HOLT
ph: HARRY WAXMAN
m: Richard Rodney Bennett
md: Philip Martell
ed: James Needs, Tom Simpson
pd: Edward Carrick
cos: Mary Gibson
sound: Norman Coggs, Charles Crafford
BETTE DAVIS, WILLIAM DIX, JAMES
VILLIERS, WENDY CRAIG, JILL
BENNETT, Pamela Franklin, Maurice
Denham, Harry Fowler, Jack Watling

Naschy, Paul (1936-)

Prolific (eight films in 1972 alone!)
Spanish horror star (real name Jacinto
Molina Alvarez) with a penchant for
playing werewolves. Sometimes billed as
Paul Nash, he also writes his own
screenplays, often under the pseudonyms
Jack Moll and James Mollin, and
occasionally produces and directs. A
former circus performer and weight-
lifter, he has been a staple of the Spanish
horror industry from the mid-sixties and
has played practically all of the genre's
monsters, though it must be said that
many of his films do not travel well.
Genre credits:
Frankenstein's Bloody Terror (1968 - aka
Hell's Creatures/La Marca del Hombre Lobo -
w/actor), *Night of the Wolf Man* (1968 -
aka *Las Noches del Hombre Lobo* -
co-w/actor), *Dracula vs. Frankenstein*
(1969 - aka *El Hombre Que Vino de
Uommo/Los Monstruos del Terror*
-w/actor), *The Fury of the Wolfman* (1970
- aka *La Furia de Hombre Lobo* - w/actor),
La Messa Nera Della Contessa Dracula (1970
-w/actor), *The Werewolf vs. the Vampire
Woman* (1970 - aka *Shadow of the
Werewolf/La Noche Walpurgis/Nacht der
Vampire* -co-w/co-story/actor), *Jack the
Ripper* (1971 - aka *Jack el Distripador de
Londres* - co-w/actor), *Dr Jekyll and the
Werewolf* (1972 - aka *El Dottor Jekill y el
Hombre Lobo* - w/actor), *Dracula's Great

Love* (1972 - aka *Count Dracula's Great
Love/Dracula's Virgin Lovers/El Gran Amor
del Conde Dracula* - co-w/actor), *Bird of
Blood* (1972 - aka *L'Oiseau de Sang* -
actor), *La Orgio de los Muertos* (1972 -
actor), *The Hunchback of the Morgue* (1972
- aka *The Rue Morgue Massacres/El Jorobado
de la Morgue* - w/actor), *Vengeance of the
Zombies* (1972 - aka *La Rebelión de las
Muertas* - co-w/actor), *Dracula's Daughter*
(1972 - aka *La Hija de Conde Dracula* -
w/actor), *The Night of All Horrors* (1972 -
aka *La Noche de Todos los Horrores* -
w/actor), *The Blue Eyes of the Broken Doll*
(1973 - aka *The House of Psychotic
Women/Los Ojos Azules de la Muneca Rota* -
co-w/actor), *Horror Rises from the Tomb*
(1973 - aka *El Espanto Surge de la Tomba* -
co-w/actor), *The Mummy's Revenge* (1973
- aka *La Venganza de la Momia* - co-w/
actor), *El Asesino Está Entre los Trece* (1973
-actor), *Las Ratas No Duermen de Noche*
(1973 - actor), *Una Libuela Para Cada
Muerto* (1973 - w/actor), *El Mariscal del
Infierno* (1974 - w/actor), *Curse of the
Devil* (1974 - aka *El Retorno de Walpurgis* -
w/actor), *Exorcism* (1974 - aka *Exorcismo* -
co-w/actor), *Todos los Gritos del Silencio*
(1974 - co-w/actor), *The Werewolf and the
Yeti* (1975 - aka *Night of the Howling
Beast/La Maldición de la Bestia* -w/actor),
Muerto de un Quinqui (1975 - co-w/
actor), *Planet Without Eyes* (1975 - aka
Planeta Ciego - actor), *La Balada del
Atracador* (1975 - actor), *La Cruz del
Diablo* (1975 - co-w), *Inquisition* (1976 -
aka *La Inquisición* - w/d/actor), *Pecado
Mortal* (1977 - actor), *El Huerto del Francés*
(1978 - w/d/actor), *The Craving* (1980 -
aka *El Retorno del Hombre Lobo* - w/d/
actor), *The Mystery of Monster Island* (1980
- actor), *Human Beasts* (1980 - aka *El
Carnaval de las Bestias* - w/p/d/actor),
Panic Beats (1983 - actor), *The Beast and
the Magic Sword* (1983 - w/p/d/actor),
Howl of the Devil (1987 - d/actor)

Nascimbene, Mario (1916-)

Italian composer, trained at the
Giuseppe Verdi Conservatory in Milan.
Perhaps best known for his 'sword and
sandal' scores, which include *Alexander
the Great*, *Solomon and Sheba*, *Barabbas*

and, of course, *The Vikings*. Also scored several of Hammer's prehistoric epics. Genre credits:
One Million Years BC (1966), *The Vengeance of She* (1968), *When Dinosaurs Ruled the Earth* (1970), *Creatures the World Forgot* (1971)

Nash, Michael see Carreras, Michael

The Navy vs the Night Monsters
USA 1966 90m Technicolor
A navy experiment which has turned part of the South Pole into a tropical zone produces carnivorous trees into the bargain.

As inept as it sounds, but the appeal of the unintentional hilarity wanes very quickly.
p: George Edwards for Realart/Standard Club of California
w/d: Michael Hoey
ph: Stanley Cortez
m: Gordon Zahler
ed: George White
ad: Paul Sylos
cos: Patrick Cummings
sp: Edwin Tillman
sound: Clarence Peterson
Mamie Van Doren, Anthony Eisley, Pamela Mason, Bobby Van, Bill Gray, Edward Faulkner

Near Dark
USA 1987 95m Technicolor Ultra Stereo
Modern-day vampires roam America's mid-west in search of sustenance.

Slow, tedious horror flick with nothing new to offer, though it has its admirers.
p: Steven Charles-Jaffe for FM Entertainment/Feldman-Meeker
w: Eric Reid, Kathryn Bigelow
d: Kathryn Bigelow
ph: Adam Greenberg
m: Tangerine Dream
ed: Howard Smith
ad: Dan Perryman
sp: Derek Howard, Steve Gallich, Dale Martin
sound: Donald Summer, David Lewis Yewdall
make-up effects: Gordon Smith
Adrian Pasdar, Lance Henriksen, Jenny Wright, Bill Paxton, Jenette Goldstein, Tim Thomerson

Necropolis
USA 1988 76m Cinemacolor
An ancient witch living in the modern world disguises herself as a punk and goes about killing low-lifes.

Dismal low-budgeter, of no possible interest, even to videoholics.
p: Cynthia De Paula, Tim Kincaid for Empire/Tycin
w/d: Bruce Hickey
ph: Arthur D. Marks

m: no credit given
ed: Barry Zetlin, Tom Meshelski
ad: Ruth Lounsburg, Marina Zurkow
cos: Jeffrey Wallach
sp: James Chai, Matt Vogel
sound: Russell C. Fager
2nd unit d: Matt Vogel
make-up effects: Ed French
Leeanne Baker, Jacquie Fitz, William K. Reed, Michael Conte

Needs, James
Busy British editor and editorial supervisor, a Hammer mainstay until the mid-seventies. He seems to have had a hand in nearly every film the studio made, having cut practically every one of their horror classic and a substantial proportion of their non-horrors too.
Genre credits:
The Quatermass Experiment (1955 - aka *The Creeping Unknown* - ed), *The Curse of Frankenstein* (1956 - ed), *X - The Unknown* (1956 - ed), *Quatermass 2* (1957 - aka *Enemy from Space* - ed), *Dracula* (1958 - aka *Horror of Dracula* - co-ed), *The Revenge of Frankenstein* (1958 - co-ed), *The Mummy* (1959 - co-ed), *The Man Who Could Cheat Death* (1959 - co-ed), *The Hound of the Baskervilles* (1959 - co-ed), *The Ugly Duckling* (1959 - co-ed), *The Stranglers of Bombay* (1960 - co-ed), *The Two Faces of Dr Jekyll* (1960 - aka *House of Fright / Jekyll's Inferno* - co-ed), *The Brides of Dracula* (1960 -co-ed), *The Shadow of the Cat* (1961 - ed), *The Curse of the Werewolf* (1961 - co-ed), *Taste of Fear* (1961 - aka *Scream of Fear* - co-ed), *The Terror of the Tongs* (1961 - co-ed), *The Old Dark House* (1962 - ed), *Kiss of the Vampire* (1962 - aka *Kiss of Evil* -ed), *Captain Clegg* (1962 - aka *Night Creatures* - co-ed), *Paranoiac* (1963 - ed), *The Damned* (1963 - aka *These Are the Damned* - co-ed), *Maniac* (1963 - ed), *The Gorgon* (1964 - co-ed), *The Evil of Frankenstein* (1964 - ed), *The Curse of the Mummy's Tomb* (1964 - co-ed), *Hysteria* (1965 - ed), *She* (1965 - co-ed), *Fanatic* (1965 - aka *Die! Die! My Darling!* - co-ed), *Dracula - Prince of Darkness* (1966 - co-ed), *Rasputin - The Mad Monk* (1966 - co-ed), *The Plague of the Zombies* (1966 - co-ed), *The Reptile* (1966 - ed), *The Witches* (1966 - aka *The Devil's Own* - co-ed), *One Million Years BC* (1966 - co-ed), *Frankenstein Created Woman* (1966 - co-ed), *The Mummy's Shroud* (1966 - co-ed), *Quatermass and the Pit* (1967 - aka *Five Million Years to Earth* - co-ed), *Dracula Has Risen from the Grave* (1968 - co-ed), *The Devil Rides Out* (1968 - aka *The Devil's Bride* - co-ed), *Slave Girls* (1968 - aka *Prehistoric Women* - co-ed), *The Lost Continent* (1968 - co-ed), *The Vampire Lovers* (1970 - ed), *Scars of*

Dracula (1970 - ed), *Dr Jekyll and Sister Hyde* (1971 - co-ed), *Captain Kronos - Vampire Hunter* (1972 - aka *Kronos* - ed), *Dracula AD 1972* (1972 - ed), *Frankenstein and the Monster from Hell* (1973 - ed)

Neil, Ve
Award-winning make-up artist who has won Oscars for *Beetlejuice* (with Steve La Porte and Robert Short), *Ed Wood* (with Rick Baker and Yolanda Toussieng) and *Mrs Doubtfire* (with Greg Cannom and Yolanda Toussieng). Other credits include *Batman Returns* and *Hoffa*.
Genre credits:
Beetlejuice (1988 - co-sp), *Edward Scissorhands* (1990 - co-sp), *Ed Wood* (1994 - co-sp)

Neill, Roy William (1886-1946)
Irish director (real name Roland de Gostrie), in Hollywood from 1915 after experience as an actor and a war correspondent. He first worked for producer Thomas Ince, for whom he began directing in 1916. He also directed in England in the thirties, but is best remembered for the string of Sherlock Holmes second features he directed at Universal in the forties, all of which starred Basil Rathbone (*Sherlock Holmes and the Secret Weapon*, *Sherlock Holmes in Washington*, *Sherlock Holmes Faces Death*, *Spider Woman*, *The Scarlet Claw*, *The Pearl of Death*, *House of Fear*, *The Woman in Green*, *Pursuit to Algiers*, *Terror by Night*, *Dressed to Kill*). His other credits include *Whirlpool*, *The Lone Wolf Returns*, *Hoots Mon* and *Black Angel*. He was also lined up to direct *The Lady Vanishes* before Hitchcock took over the project.
Genre credits:
The Black Room (1935), *Dr Syn* (1937), *Frankenstein Meets the Wolf Man* (1943)

The Nest
USA 1988 88m Foto-kem
A seaside township is overrun by killer cockroaches, the result of a scientific experiment gone wrong.

Slick but overpadded shocker with a few gross moments for creepy-crawly haters, who'll want to invest in a roach motel before sitting down to watch it.
p: Julie Corman for Concorde
w: Robert King
novel: Eli Cantor
d: Terence H. Winkless
ph: Ricardo Jacques Gale
m: Rick Conrad
ed: James A. Stewart, Stephen Mark
ad: Carol Bosselman
cos: Vicki Graef
sp: Cary Howe
sound: Chat Gunter
2nd unit d: Jeffrey Delman
2nd unit ph: Jonathan Heap

WOULD YOU TRUST THE NANNY... OR THE BOY?

ASSOCIATED BRITISH PRODUCTIONS LIMITED present A HAMMER FILM PRODUCTION

BETTE DAVIS

THE

By 1965, BETTE DAVIS, once the queen of the American box office, was reduced to playing crazy old ladies in such movies as *The Nanny*. Here, however, the elements gelled perfectly, the result being one of Hammer's classiest shockers. The work of director Seth Holt, the best of his career, has been compared by many to that of Hitchcock.

NANNY
X

Robert Lansing, Franc Luz, Jack Collins, Lisa Langlois, Terri Treas, Stephen Davies

Neumann, Kurt (1908-1958)
German director working in America, mostly on undistinguished low-budget programmers, including several episodes of the Tarzan series (*Tarzan and the Amazons, Tarzan and the Leopard Woman, Tarzan and the Huntress*, etc.). An occasional writer and producer, his other credits include *Ellery Queen - Master Detective, Rocketship X-M, Mohawk* and *Circus of Love*.
Genre credits:
The Secret of the Blue Room (1933 - d), *The Return of the Vampire* (1943 - story only), *She-Devil* (1957 - co-w/p/d), *The Fly* (1958 - p/d)

New Year's Evil
USA 1980 85m colour
A pop-show hostess is threatened by a maniac.
    Awful cheap-jack killer thriller with no redeeming features.
d: Emmett Alston
m: Shadow
Kip Niven, Roz Kelly, Chris Wallace, Grant Cramer, Teri Copley, Taffee O'Connell, Jed Mills, Louisa Moritz

Newbrook, Peter (1916-)
British cinematographer (often in association with producer-director Robert Hartford-Davies) who turned to directing and producing with varying results. His credits include everything from sex dramas (*The Yellow Teddy Bears*) to comedies (*Gonks Go Beat, The Sandwich Man, Press for Time*) to horror.
Genre credits:
The Black Torment (1964 - ph), *Corruption* (1967 - p/ph), *Bloodsuckers* (1970 - aka *Incense for the Damned/Doctors Wear Scarlet* - exec p), *The Asphyx* (1972 - d)

Nicholson, Jack (1937-)
American star actor who won the Best Actor Oscar for *One Flew Over the Cuckoo's Nest* (1975) and Best Supporting Actor for *Terms of Endearment* (1983). Began his career on stage and in television soaps in the mid-fifties before turning to film with the Roger Corman-produced *Cry Baby Killer* in 1958, which he followed with several other Corman quickies, most memorably *Little Shop of Horrors*. It wasn't until 1969 that he achieved stardom, with the cult biker pic *Easy Rider*, by which time he had also written several pictures (*Flight to Fury, Head*, etc.). In the seventies he became a performer of note in such films as *Five Easy Pieces, Carnal Knowledge, The Last Detail* and *Chinatown*. He has directed three films to date (*Drive,*

He Said, Goin' South and *The Two Jakes*) and has periodically returned to the horror genre with several big-budget productions. His other credits include *Reds, Heartburn, Prizzi's Honour, Broadcast News, Batman* (as the Joker), *Hoffa* and *A Few Good Men*.
Genre credits:
Little Shop of Horrors (1962), *The Raven* (1963), *The Terror* (1963), *The Shining* (1980), *The Witches of Eastwick* (1987), *Wolf* (1994)

Nicholson, James H. (1916-1972)
American producer and executive producer, long in association with his partner, Samuel Z. Arkoff, with whom he founded American International Pictures (AIP) in 1955. AIP produced a number of Roger Corman's films, along with dozens of sci-fi and exploitation items.
Genre credits:
I Was a Teenage Frankenstein (1957 - aka *Teenage Frankenstein* -co-exec p), *The Amazing Colossal Man* (1957 - co-exec p), *Blood of Dracula* (1957 - aka *Blood Is My Heritage/Blood of the Demon* -co-exec p), *Attack of the Puppet People* (1958 - co-exec p), *Night of the Blood Beast* (1958 - co-exec p), *The Spider* (1958 - aka *Earth vs. the Spider* - co-exec p), *Terror from the Year 5000* (1958 - co-exec p), *Teenage Caveman* (1958 - aka *Prehistoric World* - co-exec p), *How to Make a Monster* (1958 - co-exec p), *War of the Colossal Beast* (1958 - aka *The Terror Strikes* - co-exec p), *The Headless Ghost* (1959 - co-exec p), *Attack of the Giant Leeches* (1959 - aka *Demons of the Swamp* - co-exec p), *The Ghost of Dragstrip Hollow* (1959 - co-exec p), *A Bucket of Blood* (1959 - co-exec p), *The Fall of the House of Usher* (1960 - aka *House of Usher* - exec p), *The Pit and the Pendulum* (1962 - co-exec p), *Tales of Terror* (1962 -co-exec p), *X - The Man With X-Ray Eyes* (1963 - aka *The Man With X-Ray Eyes* - co-exec p), *The Raven* (1963 - co-exec p), *The Comedy of Terrors* (1963 - co-p), *Die, Monster, Die!* (1965 - aka *Monster of Terror* - co-exec p), *The Dunwich Horror* (1969 - co-p), *The Abominable Dr Phibes* (1971 - co-exec p), *Murders in the Rue Morgue* (1971 - co-exec p), *Dr Phibes Rises Again* (1972 - co-exec p), *The Legend of Hell House* (1973 - exec p)

The Night Caller
GB 1965 84m bw
Scientists find themselves in danger from a curious orb from outer space.
    Straightforward low-budget science fiction with moments of style.
p: Ronald Liles for Armitage/New Art
exec p: John Phillips
w: Jim O'Connolly
novel: Frank Crisp

d: John Gilling
ph: Stephen Dade
m: Johnny Gregory
ed: Philip Barnikel
ad: Harry White
cos: Duncan McPhee.
sound: John Cox, Kevin Sutton
John Saxon, Maurice Denham, Patricia Haines, John Carson, Jack Watson, Alfred Burke, Warren Mitchell, Aubrey Morris, Ballard Berkeley, Marianne Stone

Night Creatures see Captain Clegg

Night Eyes see Deadly Eyes

Night of the Big Heat
GB 1967 94m Eastmancolor
So that they can survive, aliens make a remote Scottish island unbearably hot.
    Unremarkable lower-berth horror, not that dissimilar to the same makers' *Island of Terror*.
p: Ronald Liles for Planet
exec p: Tom Blakeley
w: Ronald Liles, Pip Barker, Jane Barker
novel: John Lymington
d: Terence Fisher
ph: Reg Wyer
m: Malcolm Lockyer
ed: Rod Keys
ad: Alex Vetchinsky
cos: Kathleen Moore
sound: Dudley Messenger, E. Karnon
Christopher Lee, Patrick Allen, Peter Cushing, Sarah Lawson, Jane Merrow, William Lucas, Kenneth Cope

Night of the Comet
USA 1984 96m Technicolor
Two sisters have to fend for themselves when a comet turns the earth's population into carnivorous zombies.
    Amusing low-budget science-fiction horror piece in the B-picture manner.
p: Wayne Crawford, Andrew Wayne for Atlantic
w/d: Thom Eberhardt
ph: Arthur Albert
m: David Richard Campbell
md: Don Perry
ed: Fred Stafford
pd: John Muto
cos: Linda Linn
sp: Court Wizard, John Muto
sound: Steve Nelson
titles: Mark Sawicki
Catherine Mary Stewart, Kelli Maroney, Robert Beltran, Mary Woronov, John Achorn, Sharon Farrell, Michael Bowen

Night of the Creeps *
USA 1986 88m CFIcolor Dolby
College students find themselves prey to a horde of zombies whose heads are full of alien slugs.

Quirky horror comic with some energetically staged sequences and enough exploding heads to keep gorehounds happy. Ideal video viewing.
p: Charles Gordon for Tri-Star/Finnegan
exec p: William Finnegan
w/d: Fred Dekker
ph: Robert C. New
m: Barry De Vorzon
ed: Michael N. Knue
pd: George Costello
cos: Eileen Kennedy
sp: David Stipes
sound: James Thornton
make-up effects: David B. Miller
titles: Ernest D. Farino
Jason Lively, Tom Atkins, Steve Marshall, Jill Whitlow, Allan J. Kayser, Bruce Solomon, Wally Taylor, Dick Miller

The Night of the Dark Full Moon see Silent Night, Bloody Night

Night of the Demon ***
GB 1957 87m bw
An occultist uses various forms of black magic to dispatch his enemies, but reckons without the interference of a sceptical American professor.

Classic supernatural thriller, put together with intelligence and style and containing several genuinely frightening sequences. Required viewing.
p: Frank Bevis for Columbia/Sabre
w: CHARLES BENNETT, HAL E. CHESTER
story: M. R. JAMES
d: JACQUES TOURNEUR
ph: Ted Scaife
m: CLIFTON PARKER
md: Muir Mathieson
ed: Michael Gordon
pd: Ken Adam
sp: George Blackwell, Wally Veevers
sound: Arthur Bradburn
DANA ANDREWS, Peggy Cummins, NIALL MACGINNIS, ATHENE SEYLER, Brian Wilde, Maurice Denham, Ewan Roberts, Liam Redmond, Reginald Beckwith

Night of the Demons
USA 1987 89m colour Ultra Stereo
A group of high-school kids have a Hallowe'en party in a disused mortuary and find themselves possessed by demons.

Quite lively horror comic which picks up speed after a slow start. Nice animated opening credits, too.
p: Joe Augustyn for Hallowe'en Partnership Ltd
exec p: Walter Josten
w: Joe Augustyn
d: Kevin S. Tenney
ph: David Lewis
m: Dennis Michael Tenney

ed: Daniel Duncan
ad: Ken Aichele
cos: Donna Reynolds
sound: Lee Haxall, Bo Harwood
titles: Kathy Zielinski
make-up effects: Steve Johnson
Linnea Quigley, Cathy Podwell, Mimi Kincade, William Gallo, Hal Havins, Lance Fenton

Night of the Eagle *
GB 1961 87m bw
At a select medical school, a professor discovers that he owes much of his success to his wife, a practising witch.

Tolerable late-night horror with some effective sequences.
p: Albert Fennell for Independent Artists
exec p: Julian Wintle, Leslie Parky
w: Charles Beaumont, Richard Matheson, George Baxt
novel: Fritz Leiber
d: Sidney Hayers
ph: Reg Wyer
m: William Alwyn
md: Muir Mathieson
ed: Ralph Sheldon
ad: Jack Shampan
cos: Maude Churchill
sound: Len Shilton, Eric Bayman
cam op: Gerry Turpin
Margaret Johnston, Peter Wyngarde, Janet Blair, Kathleen Byron, Reginald Beckwith, Anthony Nicholls

Night of the Ghouls
USA 1959 78m bw
A fake swami who claims to be able to revive the dead has his bluff called by a crook who really can raise the dead.

Another hilarious example of ineptitude from this celebrated grade-Z director.
p: Edward D. Wood Jr, for Wade Williams
w/d: Edward D. Wood Jr
ph: William C. Thompson
md: Gordon Zahler
Kenne Duncan, Valda Hansen, Duke Moore, Tor Johnson, Jeannie Stevens, Paul Marco, Criswell

Night of the Hunter ****
USA 93m bw
Two children are relentlessly pursued by a psychopathic preacher because they know the whereabouts of $10,000.

Eerie, brilliantly cinematic, frequently sinister nightmare drama, imaginatively conceived and executed. An unexpected delight, well worth seeking out. An unsuccessful TV remake starring Richard Chamberlain appeared in 1991.
p: Paul Gregory for UA
w: JAMES AGEE

novel: David Grubb
d: CHARLES LAUGHTON
ph: STANLEY CORTEZ
m: WALTER SCHUMANN
ed: ROBERT GOLDEN
ad: HILYARD BROWN
cos: Jerry Bos, Evelyn Carruth
sp: Jack Rabin, Louis de Witt
sound: Stanford Naughton
ROBERT MITCHUM, Shelley Winters, LILLIAN GISH, Don Beddoe, Evelyn Varden, Peter Graves, James Gleason, Sally Jane Bruce, Billy Chapin, Gloria Castilo

Night of the Living Dead **
USA 1968 98m bw
Carnivorous zombies lay siege to an isolated farmhouse where several people are stranded.

Low-budget exploitation horror piece let down only by a sag in the middle. Gruesome fun for genre addicts and all the better for being shot in black and white (though a colourized version is available), this seminal film is now very much a cult item. A disappointing remake appeared in 1990.
p: Russell Streiner, Karl Hardman for Target International/Image Ten
w: John Russo
d: GEORGE A. ROMERO
ph/ed: George A. Romero
m: library material
ad: no credit given
sp: Regis Survinski, Tony Pantanello
sound: Garry S. Streiner, Marshall S. Booth
Judith O'Dea, Duane Jones, Karl Hardman, Keith Wayne, Julia Rodley, Marilyn Estman

Night of the Living Dead
USA 1990 89m TVcolor Ultra Stereo
Zombies threaten a group of people stranded in a remote farmhouse.

Over-talkative, lethargically handled remake, rather pointless given that the original has now been colourized.
p: John A. Russo, Russ Steiner for 21st Century/Columbia
exec p: George A. Romero, Menahem Golan
w: George A. Romero
d: Tom Savini
ph: Frank Prinzi
m: Paul McCollough
ed: Tom Dubensky
ad: James Feng
cos: Barbara Anderson
sound: Felipe Borreo
make-up effects: John Vulich, Everett Burrell
Tony Todd, Patricia Tallmann, Tom Towles, McKee Anderson, Bill Mosley, Heather Mazur

The Night Stalker *
USA 1971 74m Technicolor TVM
A Las Vegas newspaper reporter tracks
down a vampire.

Fairly routine horror piece which at
least keeps moving. It was followed by *The
Night Strangler* (1972) and *The Norliss
Tapes* (1973).
p: Dan Curtis for Aaron Spelling
w: Richard Matheson
story: Jeff Rice
d: John Llewellyn Moxey
ph: Michael Hugo
m: Robert Cobert
ed: Desmond Marquette, Mike Crumplar
ad: Trevor Williams
cos: John S. Perry, Betsy Cox
Darren McGavin, Carol Lynley, Simon
Oakland, Claude Akins, Charles McGraw,
Barry Atwater, Elisha Cook Jr, Kent Smith

The Night Strangler *
USA 1972 74m Technicolor TVM
A reporter specializing in the supernatural tracks down a serial killer in Seattle
who turns out to be 144 years old.

Reasonably engaging follow-up to
The Night Stalker, which itself led to *The
Norliss Tapes* and the short-lived TV
series *Kolchak: The Night Stalker*.
p: Dan Curtis for Aaron Spelling
w: Richard Matheson
d: Dan Curtis
ph: Robert Hauser
m: Robert Cobert
ed: Folmar Blangsted
pd: Trevor Williams
cos: John Perry
sound: Harold Lewis
stunt co-ordinator: Dick Ziker
Darren McGavin, Jo Ann Pflug, Simon
Oakland, John Carradine, Margaret
Hamilton, Scott Brady, Al Lewis,
Richard Anderson

Night Train to Terror
USA 1985 93m colour
God and the Devil argue over the fate of
several people while travelling on a train
to heaven/hell.

Dismal portmanteau of three stories
(*The Case of Harry Billings*, *The Case of
Greta Connors*, *The Case of Claire Hansen*)
culled from various uncompleted
features and shorts (hence the many
directors and cinematographers
credited). A real mess.
p: Jay Schossberg-Cohen for Visto
International
w: Philip Yordan
d: John Carr, Jay Schlossberg-Cohen,
Philip Marshak, Gregg Tallas, Tom
McGowan
ph: Susan Maljan, Frank Byers, Byron
Wardlow, Art Fitzsimmons, Bruce
Markoe

md: Ralph Ives
ed: Evan E. Stoliar, Steve Nielsen, Philip
Marshak, Bruce Markoe
ad: Ronald K. Crosby, Robert
Chatterton
cos: Susan Maljan and others
sp: William R. Stromberg
sound: Jon Ferro, David Brownlow,
Bobby D'Amora
John Phillip Law, Cameron Mitchell,
Richard Moll, Marc Lawrence, Ferdy
Mayne, Sharon Ratcliff, Rick Barnes,
Robert Bristol, Meredith Haze

The Night Walker *
USA 1964 86m bw
A recently widowed woman has
nightmares about her disfigured husband
and a tall dark stranger who later turns
up in reality.

Zippy low-budget horror comic with
effective moments of fright.
p: William Castle for Universal
w: ROBERT BLOCH
d: WILLIAM CASTLE
ph: Harold Stine
m: VIC MIZZY
ed: Ewin H. Bryant
ad: Alexander Golitzen, Frank Arrigo
BARBARA STANWYCK, Robert Taylor,
Lloyd Bochner, Rochelle Hudson, Judi
Meredith, Hayden Rorke

Nightmare *
GB 1964 82m bw Hammerscope
A teenage girl fears for her sanity after
witnessing her mother kill her father.

A variation on Hammer's own *Taste
of Fear* - and a good one, making the
most of all the expected twists and
turns.
p: Jimmy Sangster for
Hammer/Universal
w: JIMMY SANGSTER
d: FREDDIE FRANCIS
ph: John Wilcox
m: Don Banks
md: John Hollingsworth
ed: James Needs
ad: Bernard Robinson
cos: Rosemary Burrows
sound: Ken Rawkins
Moira Redmond, JENNIE LINDEN,
David Knight, Brenda Bruce, John Welch

A Nightmare on Elm Street *
USA 1984 91m DeLuxe
A young girl dreams that her life is being
threatened by a disfigured maniac, only to
find her dreams mingling with reality.

Quite reasonable horror comic with a
few new twists. A genre hit, it produced a
new horror hero in the guise of Freddy
Krueger and practically spawned an
industry. It was followed by *A Nightmare
on Elm Street Part 2: Freddy's Revenge*

(1985), *A Nightmare on Elm Street Part 3:
The Dream Warriors* (1987), *A Nightmare on
Elm Street Part 4: The Dream Master* (1988),
*A Nightmare on Elm Street 5: The Dream
Child* (1989), *Freddy's Dead: The Final
Nightmare* (1991) and *Wes Craven's New
Nightmare* (1994). There was also a TV
series, *Freddy's Nightmares*.
p: Robert Shaye, Sara Risher for New
Line/Elm Street Ventures/Media/Smart
Egg
w/d: Wes Craven
ph: Jacques Haitkin
m: Charles Bernstein
ed: Rick Shaine
pd: Greg Fonsecca
cos: Dana Lyman
sp: Jim Doyle
sound: James La Rue, Jack Cooley
make-up effects: David Miller
stunt co-ordinator: Tony Cecere
John Saxon, Ronee Blakeley, Heather
Langenkamp, Robert Englund (as Freddy
Krueger), Amanda Wyss, Nick Corri,
Johnny Depp, Charles Fleischer

A Nightmare on Elm Street
Part 2: Freddy's Revenge *
USA 1985 87m DeLuxe
A new family moves on to Elm Street and
the eldest son finds himself being
taken over by the spirit of Freddy
Krueger.

Zippy sequel, perhaps even a couple
of marks up on its predecessor.
p: Robert Shayer for New Line/Heron
Communications/Smart Egg
w: David Chaskin
d: Jack Sholder
ph: Jacques Haitkin
m: Christopher Young
ed: Arline Garson, Bob Brady
pd: Mick Strawn
Mark Patton, Kim Myers, Robert
Englund, Robert Rusler, Hope Lange,
Clu Gulagher

A Nightmare on Elm Street
Part 3: The Dream Warriors *
USA 1987 96m DeLuxe
Freddy Krueger insinuates himself into
the dreams of a group of teenage hospital
patients.

Lively third episode in the on-going
series, with plenty of imaginative special
effects.
p: Robert Shaye for New Line/Heron
Communications/Smart Egg
exec p: Wes Craven, Stephen Diener
w: Wes Craven, Bruce Wagner
story: Wes Craven
d: Chuck Russell
ph: Roy Wagner
m: Angelo Badalamenti
ed: Terry Stokes
pd: Mick Strawn, C. J. Strawn

cos: Camile Schroeder
sp: Dream Quest, Doug Beswick
sound: William Fiege, David Lewis Yewdall
make-up effects: Kevin Yagher, Greg Cannom
stunt co-ordinator: Rick Barker
2nd unit d/titles: Dan Perri
2nd unit ph: Glen Kershaw
Heather Langenkamp, Robert Englund, Craig Wasson, Patricia Arquette, Larry Fishburne, John Saxon, Priscilla Pointer, Dick Cavett, Zsa Zsa Gabor

A Nightmare on Elm Street 4: The Dream Master

USA 1989 93m Metrocolor Dolby
Freddy Krueger returns from the grave (reconstituted by a fire-pissing dog!) to wreak havoc on yet more teenagers.

Flashy but otherwise uninspired regurgitation of the previous films, lacking any thrills or surprises of its own.
p: Robert Shaye, Rachel Talalay for New Line/Heron Communications/Smart Egg
exec p: Sara Risher, Stephen Diener
w: Brian Helgeland, Scott Pierce
story: William Kotzwinkle, Brian Helgeland
d: Renny Harlin
ph: Steven Fierberg
m: Craig Safan
ed: Michael K. Knue, Chuck Weiss
pd: Mick Strawn, C. J. Strawn
cos: Audrey Bansmer
sp: Dream Quest Images, Image Engineering
sound: Nicholas Allen
make-up effects: Kevin Yagher, Screaming Mad George, Steve Johnson, Christopher Biggs
2nd unit d: Peter Chesney, T. G. Vijovich
stunt co-ordinator: Rick Barker
Robert Englund, Rodney Eastman, Danny Hassel, Andras Jones, Tuesday Knight, Lisa Wilcox, Brooke Bundy, Nicholas Mele

A Nightmare on Elm Street 5: The Dream Child

USA 1989 90m Metrocolor Dolby
Freddy Krueger attacks a girl through the dreams of her unborn child.

Risible entry which all too frequently abandons plot in favour of an overabundance of special effects... and not enough Freddy.
p: Robert Shaye, Rupert Harvey for New Line
exec p: Sarah Risher, John Turtle
w: Leslie Boehm
story: John Skip, Craig Spector, Leslie Boehm
d: Stephen Hopkins
ph: Peter Levy
m: Jay Ferguson
ed: Chuck Weiss, Brent Schoenfeld

pd: C. J. Strawn
sp: Alan Munro, Ted Rae, Doug Beswick, Peter Kurran, Philip Downey, Andre Ellington, Eddie Paul
make-up effects: David Miller
2nd unit ph: Chris Nibley
Robert Englund, Lisa Wilcox, Danny Hassel, Whitby Hertford, Kelly Jo Minter, Erika Anderson, Nick Mele, Beatrice Boepple, Joe Seely

Nightmares

US 1983 96m Technicolor TVM
Four tales of horror and the supernatural.

Familiar portmanteau, well enough put together. It was also released theatrically with additional footage.
p: Christopher Crowe for Universal
exec p: Andrew Mirisch, Alex Beaton
w: Christopher Crowe, Jeffrey Bloom
d: Joseph Sargent
ph: Gerald Perry Finnerman, Mario DiLeo
m: Craig Safan
ed: Rod Stephens, Michael Brown
pd: Dean Edward Mitzner
cos: Nancy McArolle, Nick Mezzanotti
sp: Michael L. Griffin
sound: Jim Alexander
Cristina Raines, Joe Lambie, Anthony James, Emilio Estevez, Lee James Jude, Mariclare Costello, Louis Giambalvo, Moon Zappa, Billy Jacoby, Richard Masur, Veronica Cartwright, Albert Hague, Robin Gammell, Tony Plana, Timothy Scott, Lance Henriksen

Nightwing

USA 1979 105m Metroclor
A plague of vampire bats hits a small Arizona community.

Thoroughly boring and predictable shocker, a long, long way behind *Jaws* and *The Birds*.
p: Martin Ransohoff for Columbia/Polyc
w: Steve Shagan, Bud Shrake
novel: Martin Cruz Smith
d: Arthur Hiller
ph: Charles Rosher
m: Henry Mancini
ed: John C. Howard
pd: James Vance
sp: Carlo Rambaldi, Milt Rice
David Warner, Kathryn Harrold, Steven Macht, Strother Martin, Ben Piazza, Nick Mancuso

976 Evil

USA 1988 97m Technicolor
A put-upon teenager changes into a vicious monster after telephoning a dial-a-horoscope number.

Over-padded horror hokum in which too little happens too late, despite being directed by Freddy Krueger himself,

Robert Englund. *976 Evil: The Astral Factor* followed in 1992.
p: Lisa Hansen for Cinetel
exec p: Paul Hertzberg
w: Rhet Topham, Brian Helgeland
d: Robert Englund
ph: Paul Elliott
m: Tom Chase, Steve Rucker
ed: Stephen Myers
pd: David Bryan Miller
cos: Elizabeth Gower-Gruzinski
sp: Kevin Yagher
sound: Beau Franklin
Stephen Geoffreys, Sandy Dennis, Patrick O'Bryan, Jim Metzler, Maria Rubel, Leslie Deane, J. J. Cohen, Jim Thiebaud

The Ninth Configuration *

USA 1980 104m Metroclor
The new psychiatrist at a remote military hospital discovers that his patients are not all they claim to be.

Shoddy-looking but quite curious psycho-thriller with compensations in the script.
p: William Peter Blatty for Lorimar
w/d: William Peter Blatty from his novel
ph: Gerry Fisher
m: Barry DeVorzon
ed: Battle Davis, Peter Lee-Thompson, Roberto Silvi
pd: Bill Malley
Stacy Keach, Scott Wilson, Jason Miller, Ed Flanders, Moses Gunn, Neville Brand, George DiCenzo, Joe Spinell

Non Si Seve Profanare ol Sonne die Morte see The Living

Dead at the Manchester Morgue

The Norliss Tapes *

USA 1973 74m Technicolor TVM
A writer investigates the case of a woman who claims that her sculptor husband has risen from the dead.

Slick supernatural thriller with production well above average by television standards. The projected series unfortunately failed to materialize.
p: Dan Curtis for Metromedia
w: WILLIAM F. NOLAN
d: DAN CURIS
ph: Ben Colman
m: Robert Cobert
ed: John F. Link II
ad: Trevor Williams
Roy Thinnes, Angie Dickinson, Hurd Hatfield, Claude Akins, Vonetta McGee, Michele Carey

Norton, Edgar (1868-1953)

British character actor who, after stage experience in Britain, travelled to America in late 1889, where an equally prolific stage career ensued. He made his film début in 1916 in *The Ocean Waif*, which was followed by such silents as *The Amazons*, *A Pair of Cupids* and *The Light in the Dark*. In the thirties he came into his own as a supporting actor in films, often playing fussy servants. His other films include *Bachelor Father*, *Squaw Man*, *East of Java*, *Top Hat*, *A Chump at Oxford*, *Kitty* and countless others.

Genre credits:
Dr Jekyll and Mr Hyde (1932), *Dracula's Daughter* (1936), *Son of Frankenstein* (1939)

The Nose Picker

USA 1988 76m colour
A low-life learns 'morphosynthesis', a means by which he hypnotizes people into thinking he's someone else, and adopts various female guises under the security of which he goes about murdering young girls.

Quirky low-budgeter with a high quota of gory stabbings. It's certainly different (even if the overall quality is poor) and the twist ending is for once worth waiting for.
p: Steven Hodge, Patrick J. Matthews, Mark Nowicki for Front Porch
w: Steven Hodge
d: Mark Norwicki
ph: Patrick J. Matthews
m: Clinton Clark
ed: Michael Mayne, Gary Shifflet
ad: no credit given
sp: Gary Jones
sound: D. B. Greer
Carl Zschering, Edward Tanner, Lura Cummings

Nosferatu **

Ger 1922 72m bw silent
Vampire count Graf Orlok moves from his crumbling castle in Transylvania to seek fresh victims in the city of Bremen.

Eerie, still effective silent variation on Bram Stoker's *Dracula*, which brought lengthy legal action from Stoker's widow for breach of copyright. Its inevitably dated air only adds to its other-worldly atmosphere and the central performance is riveting.
p: Prana
w: Henrik Galeen
d: F. W. MURNAU
ph: FRITZ ARNO WAGNER
ed: Symon Gould
ad: ALBIN GRAU
MAX SCHRECK, Alexander Granach, Gustav Von Waggenheim, Greta Schroder-Matray, G. H. Schnell, Ruth Landshoff

Nosferatu a Venezia see Vampires in Venice

• **Klaus Kinski makes an excellent vampire in director Werner Herzog's remake of** Nosferatu.

Nosferatu, Phantom der Nacht

see Nosferatu the Vampyre

Nosferatu the Vampyre

Ger/Fr 1979 107m Eastmancolor
A vampire count travels to the city of Bremen, taking a plague of rats along with him.

A lot of care has been taken to achieve the right look and atmosphere in this expensive remake of the 1922 classic (which was itself an unofficial variation on Bram Stoker's *Dracula*). However, despite occasional visual pleasures, the pace is too slow and the film finally bores rather than chills. A major disappointment from this director, though the star's performance stays in the mind.
p: Werner Herzog for Gaumont/Werner Herzog Filmproduktion
exec p: Michael Gruskoff
w/d: Werner Herzog
ph: Jorg Schmidt-Reitwein
m: Popol Vuh, Florian Fricke
ed: Beate Mainka-Jellinghaus
pd: Henning Von Girke
cos: Gisela Storch
sp: Cornelius Siegel
sound: Harold Maury
make-up: Reiko Kruk, Dominique Colladant
KLAUS KINSKI, Isabelle Adjani, Bruno Ganz, Roland Topper, Walter Ladengast, Dan Van Husen, Jacques Dufilio, Werner Hersoz

Nothing But the Night

GB 1972 98m Eastmancolor
A group of orphans kill off their trustees for diabolical purposes.

Straightforward horror movie in the British tradition. More wit and style would not have gone amiss. Its box-office failure saw an end to Christopher Lee and Anthony Nelson Keys' Charlemagne Productions, whose first and only film this proved to be.
p: Anthony Nelson Keys for Rank/Charlemagne
w: Brian Hayles
novel: John Blackburn
d: Peter Sasdy
ph: Ken Talbot
m: Malcolm Williamson
md: Philip Martell
ed: Keith Palmer
ad: Colin Grimes
cos: Rosemary Burrows
sp: Les Bowie
sound: Danny Daniel, Ken Barker
Christopher Lee, Peter Cushing, Diana Dors, Georgia Brown, Keith Barron, Gwyneth Strong, Fulton Mackay, John Robinson, Michael Gambon

Notre Dame de Paris see The Hunchback of Notre Dame (1956)

Nurmi, Maila see Vampira

O

O'Bannon, Dan (1946-)
American writer (*Dark Star*, *Blue Thunder*, *Invaders from Mars*, *Total Recall*) who has also directed a couple of genre films.
Genre credits:
Alien (1979 - w), *Dead and Buried* (1981 - co-w), *Lifeforce* (1985 -co-w), *The Return of the Living Dead* (1985 - w/d), *The Resurrected* (1992 - d)

O'Brien, Richard (1942-)
New Zealand-born actor, writer and composer, best known for the musical *The Rocky Horror Show*, filmed in 1975 as *The Rocky Horror Picture Show*, in which he plays the hunchbacked assistant Riff Raff. Also known to television audiences for the game show *The Crystal Maze*, his other credits as an actor include *Carry On Cowboy*, *The Odd Job* and *Flash Gordon*.
Genre credits:
The Rocky Horror Picture Show (1975 - co-w/actor/songs), *Shock Treatment* (1982 - co-w/actor/co-songs)

O'Brien, Willis H. (1886-1962)
Pioneering American special-effects wiz, a stop-motion expert whose work on *King Kong* was and still is an industry milestone. He turned to film comparatively late in life after experience as a rancher, poultry farmer, draughtsman and cartoonist. An experiment with stop motion in 1914 led to a film contract, the result being the short film *The Dinosaur and the Missing Link*, made in 1915 and released in 1917. Further shorts followed, all of which led to his first feature film, *The Lost World*, in 1925. He was working on a film called *Creation*, which was never completed, when he received the call from RKO to work on *King Kong*. A sequel quickly followed. After sixteen years trying to get various other projects of the ground, in 1949 O'Brien received an Oscar for his effects work on the *Kong*-like *Mighty Joe Young*, on which he was assisted by the young Ray Harry-hausen, who eventually inherited his crown as Hollywood's special-effects king. Sadly, O'Brien's subsequent work never quite matched his achievements on *Kong*.
Genre credits:
The Dinosaur and the Missing Link (1915 - short), *RFD 10,000 BC* (1917 - short), *Prehistoric Poultry* (1917 - short), *Curious Pets of Our Ancestors* (1917 - short), *The Ghost of Slumber Mountain* (1919 - short), *The Lost World* (1925), *Creation* (1931 - uncompleted), *King Kong* (1933), *Son of Kong* (1933), *Mighty Joe Young* (1949), *The Animal World* (1956), *The Beast of Hollow Mountain* (1956 - story only), *The Black Scorpion* (1957), *The Giant Behemoth* (1958 - aka *Behemoth the Sea Monster*), *The Lost World* (1960 - adviser only)

O'Connolly, Jim (1926-)
British director with a variety of credits (*The Traitors*, *Smokescreen*, *The Little Ones*, *Crooks and Coronets*) to his name, including the odd foray into horror.
Genre credits:
Berserk! (1967 - aka *Circus of Blood*), *The Valley of Gwangi* (1968), *Horror on Snape Island* (1972 - aka *Beyond the Fog/Tower of Evil*)

O'Connor, Una (1880-1959)
Irish character actress, in British films from 1929 with *Dark Red Roses*. Other early credits include *Timbuctoo*, *Murder* and *Cavalcade*. In 1932 she went to Hollywood, where she popped up in all manner of films, usually as a gossip or busybody, most notably in *The Bride of Frankenstein*. An actress with the Abbey Theatre in Dublin, she also appeared on the stage both in the West End and on Broadway before films beckoned. Her many other credits include *The Barretts of Wimpole Street*, *The Informer*, *The Adventures of Robin Hood*, *The Sea Hawk*, *The Bells of St Mary's* and *Witness for the Prosecution*.
Genre credits:
The Invisible Man (1933), *The Bride of Frankenstein* (1935), *The Cavnterville Ghost* (1944), *The Corpse Came COD* (1947)

O'Dea, Judith
American actress whose only leading role was as Barbara in George Romero's ground-breaking *Night of the Living Dead*, after which nothing was heard from her.

O'Herlihy, Dan (1919-)
Irish actor with much stage (the Abbey Theatre, Dublin) and radio experience. His film roles have mostly been as a supporting actor, though this hasn't prevented him from leaving his mark, most notably in *Halloween III: Season of the Witch* and *Robocop*. His other credits include *Odd Man Out*, *The Adventures of Robinson Crusoe*, *The Virgin Queen*, *Fail Safe*, *QB VII* (TVM), *The Last Starfighter*, *The Dead* and *Robocop 2*.
Genre credits:
The Cabinet of Caligari (1962 - as Caligari), *Halloween III: Season of the Witch* (1983)

The Oblong Box *
GB 1969 95m Eastmancolor
One of two nineteenth-century brothers is driven to madness and buried alive as a result of African tribal ritualism.
Good-looking period horror melodrama with effective touches of style. Hessler took over the project following the death of its original director, Michael Reeves.
p: Gordon Hessler for AIP
w: Lawrence Huntington, Christopher Wicking
d: GORDON HESSLER
ph: JOHN COQUILLON
m: Harry Robinson
md: Philip Martell
ed: Max Benedict
pd: George Provis
cos: Kay Gilbert
sound: Bob Peck, Bob Jones
titles: Peter Howitt
Vincent Price, Christopher Lee, Alastair Williamson, Rupert Davies, Hilary Dwyer, Peter Arne, Maxwell Shaw, Michael Balfour

Obzina, Martin
American art director, long with Universal, where he worked on several of the studio's Sherlock Holmes adventures (*Sherlock Holmes and the Secret Weapon*, *Sherlock Holmes in Washington*, *Spider Woman*, *Pursuit to Algiers*, etc.) as well as a handful of their forties horror films.
Genre credits:
The Invisible Man Returns (1940 - co-ad), *The Mad Ghoul* (1943 - co-ad), *House of Frankenstein* (1944 - co-ad), *House of Dracula* (1945 - co-ad)

L'Occi del Male see Possessed

Ogilvy, Ian (1943-)
British actor, best known for playing the Saint in TV's *The Return of the Saint*, prior to which he played the young hero in a couple of horror films, including three

RUSSIAN CHARACTER ACTRESS MARIA
OUSPENESKAYA cropped up in many a
Hollywood movie, from *Dodsworth* to
King's Row, though she was never more
memorable than as Maleva the Gypsy in
the *Wolf Man*, uttering the famous
warning:
'Even a man who is pure in heart,
And says his prayers at night,
May become a wolf when the wolfbane
blooms,
And the autumn moon is bright.'

for director Michael Reeves. His other credits include *Wuthering Heights* and *No Sex Please, We're British*.
Genre credits:
The Revenge of the Blood Beast (1965 - aka *The She-Beast* / *La Sorella di Satana*), *The Sorcerers* (1967), *Witchfinder General* (1968 - aka *The Conqueror Worm*), *And Now the Screaming Starts* (1972), *From Beyond the Grave* (1973), *Menace Unseen* (1988 - TVM), *Death Becomes Her* (1992), *Puppetmaster 5: The Final Chapter* (1995)

Ogle, Charles (1865-1940)

American actor of the silent period (*The Honour of His Family*, *Treasure Island*, *The Covered Wagon*) who deserves a footnote in history for being the first actor to play Frankenstein's Monster on screen - in Thomas Edeson's *Frankenstein* (1909).

The Ogre see Demons 3: The Ogre

Old Dracula see Vampira

Oldman, Gary (1958-)

Dynamic British actor (*Sid and Nancy*, *Prick Up Your Ears*, *True Romance*) who played the title role in director Francis Ford Coppola's overblown *Bram Stoker's Dracula* (1992).

O'Mara, Kate (1939-)

Glamorous British actress with much stage and television experience, including stints on both *Triangle* and *Dynasty* (as Joan Collins' sister). Her other film credits include *Great Catherine* and *The Desperados*.
Genre credits:
Corruption (1967), *Horror of Frankenstein* (1970), *The Vampire Lovers* (1970)

The Omega Man *

USA 1971 98m Technicolor Panavision
After germ warfare has devastated the world, the only survivor battles for his life against plague-carrying zombies.
Lack-lustre science fiction, lethargically handled and with a surplus of talk.
p: Walter Seltzer for Warner
w: John William Corrington, Joyce M. Corrington
novel: Richard Matheson
d: Boris Sagal
ph: Russell Metty
m: Ron Grainer
ed: William Ziegler
ad: Arthur Loel, Walter M. Simonds
cos: Margo Baxley
sound: Bob Martin
Charlton Heston, Rosalind Cash, Anthony Zerbe, Paul Koslo, Lincoln Kilpatrick, Gill Giraldi

The Omen **

USA/GB 1976 111m DeLuxe Panavision

• You little devil. Gregory Peck attempts to kill the anti-Christ (Harvey Stephens) in the blockbuster *The Omen*.

After the mysterious death of his son at birth, the American Ambassador to Great Britain has the boy secretly replaced with another child, who turns out to be the Anti-Christ himself.
Well-mounted variation on *Rosemary's Baby* and *The Exorcist*, all the more persuasive for its use of biblical prophecy. Goldsmith's atmospheric, Oscar-winning score is an asset, as are some spectacularly staged deaths. A box-office hit, it provoked three sequels: *Damien: Omen II*, *The Final Conflict* and *Omen IV: The Awakening*.
p: Harvey Bernhard for TCF
exec p: Mace Neufeld
w: DAVID SELTZER
d: RICHARD DONNER
ph: Gilbert Taylor
m: JERRY GOLDSMITH (AA)
md: Lionel Newman
ed: Stuart Baird
ad: Carmen Dillon
cos: G. W. Nicholls
sp: John Richardson
sound: Gordon Everett, Doug Turner
stunt co-ordinator: Alf Joint
make-up: Stuart Freeborn
Gregory Peck, Lee Remick, Billie Whitelaw (as Mrs Baylock), David Warner, Harvey Stevens (as Damien), Patrick Troughton, Martin Benson, Anthony Nichols, Don Stride

Omen IV: The Awakening

US 1991 96m Technicolor TVM
An adopted girl turns out to be the Anti-Christ.
Distaff version of *The Omen*, a poor attempt to continue a series that had already run its course. Released in cinemas outside America.
p: Harvey Bernhard for TCF/FNM Films
exec p: Mace Neufeld
w: Brian Taggert
d: Dominique Othenin-Gerard, Jorge

Montesi
ph: Martin Fuhrer
m: Jonathan Sheffer
ed: Frank Irvine
pd: Richard Wilcox
Michael Woods, Faye Grant, Madison Mason, Asia Vieira, Michael Lerner

One Dark Night

USA 1981 90m DeLuxe
The dead body of a psychic wreaks havoc in a morgue and terrorizes three girls hiding there on a dare.
Low-grade horror of the cheapest, most tedious kind.
p: Michael Schroeder for UPM
w: Thomas McLoughlin, Michael Hawes
d: Thomas McLoughlin
ph: Hal Trussel
m: Bob Summers
ed: Charles Tetoni, Michael Spence
pd: Craig Stearns
make-up effects: Tom Burman, Ellis Burman, Bob Williams
Meg Tilley, Melissa Newman, Robin Evans, Leslie Speights, Adam West

One Million BC *

USA 1940 81m bw
In prehistoric times a warrior is befriended by a peaceful tribe and shows them how to defend themselves from dinosaurs.
Dated, anachronistic monster hokum, of interest chiefly for the talent involved.
p: Hal Roach
w: Mickell Novak, George Baker, Joseph Frickert, Grover Jones
d: Hal Roach, Hal Roach Jr (and, some say, D. W. Griffith)
ph: Norbert Brodine
m: Werner B. Heyman
ed: Ray Snyder
ad: Charles D. Hall, Nicolai Remisoff
cos: Harry Black
sp: Roy Seawright
sound: William Randall
narrator: Conrad Nagel
Victor Mature, Carole Landis, Lon Chaney Jr, Nigel de Brulier, Conrad Nagel, John Hubbard

One Million Years B.C. **

GB 1966 100m Technicolor
In prehistoric times, a cave girl abandons her tribe to look for a mate.
Lively remake of Hal Roach's *One Million B.C.*, here benefitting from lively action sequences and excellent effects work. Keep an eye out for the doe skin bikinis, the 60s hair dos and the mascara.
p: Michael Carreras for Hammer
w: Michael Carreras
d: DON CHAFFEY
ph: Wilkie Cooper
m: MARIO NASCIMBENE
md: Philip Martell

ed: James Needs, Tom Simpson
ad: Robert Jones
cos: Carl Toms
sp: RAY HARRYHAUSEN, Les Bowie
sound: Bill Rowe , Len Shilton
2nd unit ph: Jack Mills
Raquel Welch, John Richardson, Robert Brown, Martine Beswick, Percy Herbert, Lisa Thomas, Malya Nappil

Onibaba **

Japan 1964 1014m bw Tohoscope
A woman and her daughter-in-law survive in the marshlands by killing passing soldiers and selling their armour.

Visually striking folk tale with moments of violence and horror. A Japanese classic, it makes the very most of its eerie marshland setting.
p: Kazuo Kuwahara for Kindai Eiga Kyokai/Tokyo Eiga
w/d: KANETO SHINDO
ph: KIYOMI JURODA
m: Hikaru Hayashi
ed: Kazao Enoki
sound: Tetsuya Ohashi
Nobuko Otowa, Jitsuko Yoshimura, Kei Sat

Open House

USA 1987 97m Foto-Kem
A madman with a penchant for eating dog food goes about killing female real-estate agents and their clients.

Bottom-of-the-barrel stalk and slash, indifferently presented.
p: Sandy Cobe for Intercontinental
exec p: Victor Bhalla, Sultan Allaudin
w: David Mickey Evans
d/story: Jag Mundhra
ph: Robert Hayes
m: Jim Studer
pd: Naomi Shohan
cos: Leslie Peters Ballard
sound: David Waelder
Joseph Bottoms, Adrienne Barbeau, Rudy Ramos, Darwyn Swalve, Scott Thompson Baker, Mary Stavin

Opera

It 1987 90m Technicolor
A young opera singer finds herself forced to witness a series of vicious murders by a madman.

Flashy, over-plotted killer thriller with touches typical of its director, but no overall narrative grip. Also known as *Terror at the Opera*.
p: Mario Cecci Gori, Vittorio Cecci Gori for Cecci Gori/Gruppo Tiger Cinematografica
w: Dario Argento, Franco Ferrini
d/story: Dario Argento
ph: Ronnie Taylor
m: Claudio Simonetti
ed: Franco Fraticelli

pd: Sergio Stivaletti
Cristina Marsillach, Urbano Barberini, Ian Charleson, Daria Nicolodi, Antonella Vitale, William McNamara

Orca - Killer Whale

USA 1977 92m Technicolor Panavision
When a calf-bearing killer whale is shot, its mate avenges her death.

Occasionally repellent shocker, obviously inspired by the success of *Jaws*, to which it is in no way comparable.
p: Dino de Laurentiis for Famous Films
w: Luciano Vincenzoni, Sergio Donati
d: Michael Anderson
ph: Ted Moore, Ron Taylor, J. Barry Herron, Vittorio Dragonetti
m: Ennio Morricone
ed: Ralph E. Winetrs, John Bloom, Marion Rothman
pd: Mario Garbuglia
Richard Harris, Charlotte Rampling, Will Sampson, Bo Derek, Keenan Wynn, Scott Walker, Robert Carradine, Peter Hooten

The Other Hell

It 1980 88m Augustuscolor
A convent of nuns becomes demonically possessed after one of them gives birth to a girl with diabolical powers.

Risible low-grade amalgam of various well-worn themes. Even videoholics will find themselves reaching for the fast-forward button with this one.
p: Arcangelo Picchi for Cinemec
w: Claudio Fragasso
story: Claudio Fragasso, Bruno Mattei
d: Stefan Oblowsky
ph: Giuseppe Bernardini
m: Goblin
ed: Lilliana Serra
Franca Stoppi, Carlo de Mejo, Andrew Ray, Francesca Carmeno, Frank Garfield

Otterson, Jack

American art director, long with Universal, where he worked on many key forties horror films as well as several episodes in the Sherlock Holmes series (*Sherlock Holmes and the Secret Weapon*, *Sherlock Holmes in Washington*, etc).
Genre credits:
Son of Frankenstein (1939 - co-ad), *Tower of London* (1939 - ad), *The Mummy's Hand* (1940 - co-ad), *The Invisible Man Returns* (1940 -co-ad), *The Wolf Man* (1941 - ad), *Hold That Ghost* (1941 - co-ad), *Man Made Monster* (1941 - aka *The Electric Man* - ad), *The Mad Doctor of Market Street* (1942 - ad), *The Mummy's Tomb* (1942 - ad), *The Ghost of Frankenstein* (1942 - ad)

Ouspeneskaya, Maria (1876-1949)

Diminutive, heavily accented Russian actress who appeared in all manner of

Hollywood films in the thirties, either as a dowager or, most memorably, as Maleva the gypsy in *The Wolf Man*, a role she reprised two years later. She came to America in 1923 on a tour with the Moscow Art Theatre, remaining to work on Broadway. She turned to films in 1936 with *Dodsworth*, which earned her a Best Supporting Actress Oscar nomination. Early Russian films (all silents) include *The Cricket on the Hearth*, *Worthless* and *Dr Torpokov*. Her Hollywood credits include *Love Affair*, *The Rains Came*, *King's Row* and *Tarzan and the Amazons*.
Genre credits:
The Wolf Man (1941), *Frankenstein Meets the Wolf Man* (1943)

Outback Vampires

Australia 1987 86m colour
Travellers in the Australian outback find themselves prey to a family of vampires.

Quirky but undernourished variation on a well-worn theme.
p: Jan Tyrell, James Michael Vernon for Cine-Funds/Somerset
exec p: Peter Ramster, Robert Sanders, Grahame Jennings
w: David R. Young, Colin Eggleston
d: Colin Eggleston
ph: Garry Wapshott
m: Colin Bayley, Kevin Bayley, Murray Burns
ed: Josephine Cooke
pd: Michael Ralph
cos: Helen Hooper
sp: Steve Courtney
sound: Tim Lloyd, Michael Thomas
make-up effects: Debbie Lanser
Richard Morgan, Angela Kennedy, Brett Climo, John Doyle, Maggie Blingo

Outbreak *

USA 1995 120m colour Dolby
Scientists race against time to contain a highly contagious and very deadly virus.

Slick thriller slightly let down by its conventional human interest (the characters played by Hoffman and Russo are recently divorced) and a predictable nick-of-time ending.
p: Arnold Kopelson, Wolfgang Petersen, Gail Katz for Warner/Punch
exec p: Duncan Henderson, Anne Kopelson
w: Laurence Dworet, Robert Roy Pool
d: Wolfgang Petersen
ph: Michael Ballhaus
m: James Newton Howard
ed: Neil Travis, Lynzee Klingman, William Hoy
pd: William Sandell
Dustin Hoffman, Rene Russo, Morgan Freeman, Donald Sutherland, Cuba Gooding Jr, Patrick Dempsey, Kevin Spacey

The Outing see The Lamp

P

PRC
American Poverty Row production company which, like Monogram, produced low-budget bottom-of-the-barrel second features.
Genre filmography:
The Devil Bat (1940), *The Mad Monster* (1942), *The Monster Maker* (1944), *The Brute Man* (1946), *The Devil Bat's Daughter* (1946)

Palance, Jack (1920-)
American actor (real name Walter Palanuik, first billed as Walter Palance), in films from 1950 with *Panic in the Streets*, though most memorable as the villain in the western classic *Shane*. Has tackled all manner of roles in all manner of films (*Barabbas*, *Che*, *They Came to Rob Las Vegas*, *Batman*), including that of a rather well fed-looking Dracula in a 1973 TV movie, though he seems to be known mostly for westerns (*The Professionals*, *The Desperados*, *The McMasters*, *Monte Walsh*, etc.). He finally won a Best Supporting Actor Oscar for the 1991 western spoof *City Slickers*.
Genre credits:
Torture Garden (1967), *Dr Jekyll and Mr Hyde* (1968 - TVM), *Justine: Marquis De Sade* (1969 - aka *Deadly Sanctuary*), *Craze* (1973), *Dracula* (1973 - TVM), *Hawk the Slayer* (1980), *Alone in the Dark* (1982), *Evil Stalks the House* (1983 - TVM)

Palmentola, Paul
American art director whose work has been primarily at the low-budget end of the market, including a couple of films for producer Sam Katzman.
Genre credits:
The Devil Bat (1940), *The Monster Maker* (1944), *It Came from Beneath the Sea* (1955), *The Creature with the Atom Brain* (1955), *The Werewolf* (1956), *The Man Who Turned to Stone* (1956), *The Giant Claw* (1957), *The Zombies of Mora-Tau* (1957 - aka *The Dead That Walk*)

Palmer, Betsy (1929-)
American actress (real name Patricia Brumek), remembered by genre fans for playing Mrs Voorhees in the first *Friday the 13th* movie (1980). She was also seen in the sequel, *Friday the 13th Part 2* (1981), though only in the flashback. Her other credits include *Queen Bee*, *The Tin Star* and TV's *Knots Landing*.

Pandemonium *
USA 1982 82m Technicolor Panavision
A maniac threatens a group of kids at cheerleading camp.
Airplane!-style horror spoof, often genuinely funny, despite the low budget. Worth renting from the video shop for the sequence involving Godzilla as an air hostess alone.
p: Doug Chapin for UA/Krost-Chapin
w: Richard Whitley, Jaime Klein
d: Alfred Sole
ph: Michael Hugo
m: Dana Kaproff
ed: Eric Jenkins
pd: Jack de Shields
Carol Kane, Miles Chapin, Marc McClure, Candy Azzard, Eve Arden, Tab Hunter, Donald O'Connor, Gary Hunter, Kaye Ballard, Eileen Brennan, Terry Landrum, Dabralee Scott, Tom Smothers

Pánico en el Transiberiano see Horror Express

Paramount
American studio formed in 1912 by Adolf Zukor. Paramount first went by the name of Famous Players, then Famous Players Lasky before becoming Paramount Pictures in 1914 following a series of mergers and takeovers. In the thirties they made slick, sophisticated comedies highlighting such stars as Maurice Chevalier and the Marx Brothers. Paramount was also the home of director Cecil B. de Mille, who made a series of racy biblical epics for the studio. More recent hits include the *Indiana Jones* series and the *Star Trek* franchise. Genre highlights include *Dr Jekyll and Mr Hyde*, *The Uninvited* and *Rosemary's Baby*. Paramount also distributed and later invested in the successful *Friday the 13th* series.
Genre filmography:
Dr Jekyll and Mr Hyde (1920), *Dr Jekyll and Mr Hyde* (1932), *The Island of Lost Souls* (1932), *Supernatural* (1933), *Murders in the Zoo* (1933), *The Ghost Breakers* (1940), *The Monster and the Girl* (1941), *The Man in Half Moon Street* (1943), *The Uninvited* (1944), *Rosemary's Baby* (1968), *Bug* (1975), *The Addams Family* (1991), *Addams Family Values* (1993)

Paranoiac *
GB 1963 80m bw Cinemascope
The apparently dead brother of an heiress turns up to claim his inheritance, but is he really who he claims he is?
Commendably brief shocker with sufficient twists and revelations to keep one watching.
p: Anthony Hinds for Hammer/Universal
w: JIMMY SANGSTER
d: FREDDIE FRANCIS
ph: Arthur Grant
m: Elizabeth Lutyens
md: John Hollingsworth
ed: James Needs
ad: Bernard Robinson
OLIVER REED, JANETTE SCOTT, Alexander Davion, Sheila Burrell, Liliane Brousse, Maurice Denham, John Bonney

Pardon Me, But Your Teeth Are in My Neck see The Fearless Vampire Killers

Parker, Eddie (1900-1960)
American actor and stuntman who stunted for many of Universal's monsters in the forties and fifties, often uncredited.
Genre credits:
The Mummy's Tomb (1942), *The Mummy's Ghost* (1943), *Frankenstein Meets the Wolf Man* (1943), *The Mummy's Curse* (1944), *Abbott and Costello Meet Dr Jekyll and Mr Hyde* (1953), *Abbott and Costello Meet the Mummy* (1955)

Partleton, George
British make-up artist who worked on three of Hammer's last films at Bray Studios.

Genre credits:
The Masque of the Red Death (1964), *The Witches* (1966 - aka *The Devil's Own*), *Frankenstein Created Woman* (1966), *The Mummy's Shroud* (1966), *Berserk!* (1967), *The Comeback* (1977)

Patrick *

Australia 1978 96m Colorfilm
A young nurse discovers that a comatose patient has deadly psycho-kinetic powers.
    Predictable but quite lively low-budget shocker.
p: Anthony I. Ginnane, Richard Franklin for AIFC
exec p: William Fayman
w: Everett de Roche
d: RICHARD FRANKLIN
ph: Don McAlpine
m: Brian May (Goblin for the Italian release)
ed: Edward McQueen-Mason
ad: Leslie Binns
cos: Kevin Regan
sp: Conrad C. Rothman
sound: Paul Clark, Peter Fenton
Susan Penhaligon, Robert Helpmann, Julia Blake, Bruce Barry, Rod Mullinar, Robert Thompson (as Patrick)

Paynter, Robert (1928-)

British cinematographer, familiar for his work with the directors Michael Winner (*Hannibal Brooks*, *The Games*, *Chato's Land*, *The Mechanic*, *The Big Sleep*, *Firepower*, etc.) and John Landis (*An American Werewolf in London*, *Trading Places*, *Spies Like Us*, *Into the Night*). His other credits include *Scorpio*, *Saturn 3*, *Superman 2*, *Superman 3*, *The Muppets Take Manhattan* and *National Lampoon's European Vacation*.
Genre credits:
The Nightcomers (1971), *The Final Conflict* (1981 - co-ph), *An American Werewolf in London* (1981), *Curtains* (1983), *Scream for Help* (1984), *Little Shop of Horrors* (1986)

Pearce, Jacqueline

British actress who made a mark as the title character in Hammer's *The Reptile*. Other credits include *Sky West and Crooked*, *White Mischief* and TV's *Blake's Seven*.
Genre credits:
Plague of the Zombies (1966), *The Reptile* (1966)

The Pearl of Death *

USA 1944 67m bw
Sherlock Holmes retrieves a valuable pearl and captures a back-breaking killer called the Creeper.
    Lively Holmes adventure with good detail and plenty of incident.

p: Roy William Neill for Universal
w: Bertram Millhauser
novel: Arthur Conan Doyle
d: ROY WILLIAM NEILL
ph: Virgil Miller
md: Paul Sawtell
ed: Ray Snyder
ad: John B. Goodman, Martin Obzina
cos: Vera West
sound: Bernard B. Brown, Joe Lapis
BASIL RATHBONE, Nigel Bruce, Dennis Hoey, Miles Mander, Rondo Hatton (as the Hoxton Creeper), Evelyn Ankers, Mary Gordon

Peel, David (1920-1982)

British actor whose only leading role was that of Baron Meinster in Hammer's *The Brides of Dracula*. On stage in both London and New York, his film appearances were few and far between, the first being in *We Dive at Dawn* in 1942. His other film credits include *Escape to Danger*, *Squadron Leader X*, *Gaiety George* and *They Who Dare*. After *The Brides of Dracula* he retired and became an antiques dealer.
Genre credits:
The Hands of Orlac (1960), *The Brides of Dracula* (1960)

The People That Time Forgot *

GB 1977 90m Technicolor
Backed by a London newspaper, Major McBride searches for the lost continent of Caprona, where two of his friends disappeared in 1916.
    Silly but quite lively sequel to *The Land That Time Forgot*. Okay for younger audiences, but the effects are hardly convincing.
p: John Dark for AIP/Amicus
exec p: Samuel Z. Arkoff, Max J. Rosenberg
w: Patrick Tilley
novel: Edgar Rice Borroughs
d: Kevin Connor
ph: Alan Hume
m: John Scott
ed: John Ireland, Barry Peters
pd: Maurice Carter
sp: John Richardson, Ian Wingrove
Patrick Wayne, Sarah Douglas, Doug McClure, Tony Britton, Thorley Walters, Dana Gillespie, Shane Rimmer

The People Under the Stairs

USA 1991 102m DeLuxe Dolby
Slum tenants decide to rob their landlord's house only to discover it to be full of lunatics.
    Idiotic horror rubbish put together with its director's usual lack of subtlety, though championed in some quarters.
p: Marianne Maddalena, Stuart M. Besser for Alive

exec p: Wes Craven, Shep Gordon
w/d: Wes Craven
ph: Sandi Sissel
m: Don Peake
ed: James Coblentz
pd: Bryan Jones
cos: Ileane Meltzer
sp: Image Engineering Inc.
sound: Donald Summer
2nd unit ph: Tony Cutrono
titles: Kathie Broyles, Jeff Okun
Brandon Adams, Everett McGill, Wendy Robie, A. J. Langer, Bill Cobbs, Ving Rhames, Kelly Jo Minter, Sean Whalen, Jeremy Roberts

Perkins, Anthony (1932-1992)

American actor who, despite strong performances in such films as *Desire Under the Elms*, *This Angry Age*, *On the Beach*, *Murder on the Orient Express* and *Crimes of Passion* (aka *China Blue*), will always be remembered as the mother-fixated Norman Bates in Hitchcock's *Psycho* and its sequels, one of which he directed. He also co-wrote the script (with Stephen Sondheim) for the brilliant comedy whodunnit *The Last of Sheila*.
Genre credits:
Psycho (1960), *The Fool Killer* (1965), *How Awful About Allan* (1970 - TVM), *Psycho 2* (1983), *The Sins of Dorian Gray* (1983 - TVM), *Psycho III* (1986 - and d), *Lucky Stiff* (1988 - d only), *Edge of Sanity* (1989), *Psycho IV - The Beginning* (1990 - TVM), *Daughter of Darkness* (1990), *I'm Dangerous Tonight* (1990), *A Demon in My View* (1992), *In the Deep Woods* (1992)

Persecution

GB 1974 96m Eastmancolor

• Anthony Perkins as Norman Bates in Alfred Hitchcock's classic *Psycho*.

The son of a wealthy, cat-loving American woman living in England uncovers a grisly family secret.

Over-ripe horror melodrama, too familiar to be effective.
p: Kevin Francis for Tyburn/Fanfare
w: Robert B. Hutton, Rosemary Wootten
d: Don Chaffey
ph: Kenneth Talbot
m: Paul Ferris
ed: Mike Campbell
ad: Jack Shampan
cos: Anthony Mendleson
sound: John Brommage, Ken Barker
Lana Turner, Ralph Bates, Olga Georges-Picot, Trevor Howard, Patrick Allen, Suzan Farmer, Ronald Howard

Pet Sematary
USA 1989 102m Technicolor Dolby
A grief-stricken father reburies his young son in an ancient Indian burial ground with recuperative properties, but the results are tragic.

Passably well made but over-extended horror story which might have made a good television half-hour. It was followed by *Pet Sematary 2* in 1992.
p: Richard P. Rubinstein, Mitchell Galin for Paramount
exec p: Tim Zinnemann
w: Stephen King from his novel
d: Mary Lambert
ph: Peter Stein
m: Elliot Goldenthal
ed: Michael Hill, Daniel Hanley
pd: Michael Z. Hanan
cos: M. Stewart
sp: Fantasy II
sound: Mark Ulanop
make-up effects: Lance Anderson, David Anderson
titles: Neal Thompson
Dale Midkiff, Fred Gwynne, Denise Crosby, Brad Greenquist, Michael Lombardo, Miko Hughes, Blaze Berdahl, Stephen King

Phantasm
USA 1979 89m Technicolor
Teenagers encounter grave robbing and murder at the Morningside Mortuary, where death lurks in the guise of a mysterious tall man and a brain-drilling sphere.

Silly but occasionally energetic low budget shocker, though not quite in the same league as *The Evil Dead*. Very much a cult item, its success, particularly on video, led to two increasingly unsatisfactory sequels: *Phantasm II* (1988) and *Phantasm III* (1995 - aka *Phantasm, Lord of the Dead*), both of them directed by Coscarelli.
p: Don Coscarelli for New Breed/Avco

w/d/pf/ed: Don Coscarelli
m: Fred Myrow, Malcolm Seagrave
pd: S. Tyer, DAvid Gavin Brown
sp: Paul Pepperman
sound: Lorane Mitchell, Gene Corso
Michael baldwin, Angus Scrimm (as the Tall Man), Bill Thornbury, Rggie Bannister, Susan Harper, Terrie Kalbus, Kathy Lester, Lynn Eastman

The Phantom Empire
USA 1988 85m Unitedcolor Prehistoric Stereo
Explorers discover a hidden valley where monsters still roam.

Dim adventure hokum that ends with the caption: 'Coming soon, Phantom of the Empire II - The Land Where Time Said Fuck It.' The same goes for this.
p: Fred Olen Ray for American Independent
w: Fred Olen Ray, T. L. Lankford
d: Fred Olen Ray
ph: Gary Graver
m: Robert Garrett
ed: Robert A. Ferretti, William Shaffer
pd: Cory Kaplan
cos: Jill Conner
sp: Kevin McCarthy, Bret Mixon
sound: Dennis Fuller
stunt co-ordinator: Bob Ivy
make-up effects: Paul M. Rinehard
Ross Hagen, Jeffrey Combs, Robert Quarry, Sybil Danning, Michelle Bauer, Russ Tamblyn, Dawn Wildsmith, Susan Stokey

The Phantom Light
GB 1934 75m bw
A gang of wreckers use a 'phantom light' to scare off a new lighthouse keeper.

Archetypal British comedy thriller in the *Ghost Train* manner. A little dated now, it remains of interest for its credits.
p: Jerome Jackson for Gainsborough
w: Ralph Smart, Jefferson Farjon, Austin Melford
play: Evadne Price, Joan Roy Byford
d: MICHAEL POWELL
ph: Roy Kellino
m: no credit given
ed: D. N. Twist
ad: Alex Vetchinsky
sound: A. Birch
GORDON HARKER, Binnie Hale, Ian Hunter, Herbert Lomas, Donald Calthrop, Milton Rosmer, Fawlass Llewellyn, Alice O'Day, Reginald Tate, Mickey Brantford

The Phantom of Hollywood *
USA 1974 74m Technicolor TVM
A masked figure haunts an old film studio threatened with destruction.

Sometimes sprightly variation on *The Phantom of the Opera*, making good use of

• Lon Chaney as Erik the Phantom in *The Phantom of the Opera*. The superb make-up was created by Chaney himself.

MGM's decaying backlot.
p: Gene Levitt for MGM
exec p: Burt Nodella
w: George Schenck
story: Robert Thom, George Schenck
d: Gene Levitt
ph: Gene Polito
m: Leonard Rosenman
ed: Henry Batista
ad: Edward C. Carfagno
cos: James Linn, Floydine Alexander
sound: Jerry Jost, Hal Watkins
make-up: William Tuttle
Jack Cassidy, Peter Lawford, Skye Aubrey, Broderick Crawford, John Ireland, Peter Haskell, Billy Halop

The Phantom of the Opera
Gaston Leroux's 1910 novel has been filmed several times down the decades. The key versions are 1925 (with Lon Chaney as the Phantom), 1943 (with Claude Rains) and 1989 (with Robert Englund). There have also been two television adaptations (1983 with Michael York, 1990 with Charles Dance), a popular stage musical (with music by Andrew Lloyd Webber) as well as a handful of variations, including *The Climax* (1944), *The Vampire of the Opera* (1964 - aka *Il Mostro dell'Opera*), *Phantom of the Paradise* (1974), *The Phantom of Hollywood* (1974 - TVM), *Opera* (1987 - aka *Terror at the Opera*) and *Phantom of the Mall: Eric's Revenge* (1989)

Phantom of the Opera **
USA 1926 94m bw/tinted
A deformed musician haunts the Paris

Opera House, where he abducts a prima donna to teach her the secrets of music.

Probably the star's best vehicle, tailor-made to display his unique talents to the full. A major production of its day, aficionados will still find much to admire, though padding is occasionally evident. A sound version, with music and fragments of dialogue, appeared in 1930.
p: Carl Laemmle for Universal
w: Elliott Clawson, Raymond Schrock
novel: Gaston Leroux
d: RUPERT JULIAN (and Edward Sedgewick, Lon Chaney)
ph: CHARLES VAN ENGER, VIRGIL MILLER
m: David Broekman, Max Hayman (added in 1930)
ed: Gilmore Walker, Maurice Pivar
ad: DAN HALL
LON CHANEY, Mary Philbin, Norman Kelly, Gibson Gowland, Arthur Edmund Carew, John Sainpolis

The Phantom of the Opera *
USA 1943 92m Technicolor
A composer disfigured by acid kills those who stand in the way of a prima donna with whom he is in love.

Slow, over-padded retread of the 1926 movie, further hampered by an over-abundance of music. Decor and colour are well enough used, however.
p: George Waggner for Universal
w: Erich Taylor, Samuel Hoffenstein, John Jacoby
novel: Gaston Leroux
d: Arthur Lubin
ph: W. HOWARD GREENE, HAL MOHR (aa)
m: Edmund Ward
ed: Russell Schoengarth
ad/set decoration: JOHN B. GOODMAN, ALEXANDER GOLITZEN, Russell A. Gowsman, Ira S. Webb (aa)
cos: Vera West
make-up: Jack P. Pierce
Claude Rains, Nelson Eddy, Susanne Foster, Edgar Barrier, Leo Carrillo, J. Edward Bromberg, Jane Ferrer, Hume Cronyn, Miles Mander

Phantom of the Opera *
GB 1962 90m Technicolor
A disfigured composer abducts a prima donna and coaches her in his lair below the opera house.

Reasonable Hammer remake of the old story, well enough mounted for its purpose. Herbert Lom replaced Cary Grant, who pulled out of the project at the eleventh hour.
p: Anthony Hinds for Hammer/Universal
w: John Elder (Anthony Hinds)

novel: Gaston Leroux
d: TERENCE FISHER
ph: Arthur Grant
m: Edwin Astley
md: John Hollingsworth
ed: Alfred Cox
ad: Bernard Robinson
Herbert Lom, Edward de Souza, Heather Sears, Thorley Walters, Michael Gough, Ian Wilson, Martin Miller, John Harvey, Miriam Karlin, Michael Ripper

Phantom of the Opera
USA 1983 96m Technicolor TVM
A disfigured conductor moulds the career of a singer who resembles his dead wife.

Adequate but uninspired TV version of a story already told once too often.
p: Robert Halmi for CBS
w: Herman Yellen
novel: Gaston Leroux
d: Robert Markowitz
ph: Larry Pizer
m: Ralph Burns
ed: Caroline Ferriol
ad: Tivadar Bertalan
cos: Alice Hetlay
make-up: Stan Winston
Maximilian Schell, Michael York, Jane Seymour, Jeremy Kemp, Diana Quick, Philip Stone

Phantom of the Opera *
USA/Hungary 1989 93m Rankcolor Ultra Stereo
A young singer finds herself transported back through time to Victorian England, where her career is championed by the Phantom of the Opera.

Surprisingly tolerable variation on the oft-filmed story. The sewer chase finale compensates for any longueurs, though the time-travel element is regrettable.
p: Harry Alan Towers for Castle Premier/21st Century/Breton
exec p: Menahem Golan
w: Duke Sandefur, Gerry O'Hara
novel: Gaston Leroux
d: Dwight H. Little
ph: Elemer Ragalyi
m: Misha Segal
ed: Charles Bornstein
ad: Tivadar Bertalan
cos: John Bloomfield
make-up effects: Kevin Yagher
sound: Cyril Collick
titles: Wenden Baldwin
stunt co-ordinator: Tamas Pinter
2nd unit ph: Peter Collister
ch: Gyorgy Gaal
Robert Englund, Jill Schoelen, Alex Hyde-White, Bill Nighy, Terence Harvey, Peter Clapham, Nathan Lewis, Stephanie Lawrence

The Phantom of the Opera
GB/Fr/It 1990 2x96m Technicolor TVM
A disfigured composer lurking beneath the Paris Opera House creates a new singing star.

Tedious and unnecessary tele-version of an over-filmed story. Handling unremarkable.
p: Ross Milloy, William W. Wilson, Arthur Kopit for Saban/Scherick/Hexatel/Starcom
w: Arthur Kopit from his play
d: Tony Richardson
ph: Steve Yaconelli
m: John Addison
ed: Robert K. Lambert
pd: Timian Alsaker, Jacques Bugnoir
cos: Jacqueline Moreau
sound: Jeramy Hoenack
stunt co-ordinator: Daniel Verite
Charles Dance, Burt Lancaster, Teri Polo, Ian Richardson, Adam Storke, Andrea Ferreol

Phantom of the Paradise
USA 1974 91m Movielab
A rock palace is haunted by a madman who had his face disfigured in a record press.

Dated, half-successful, satirical update of The Phantom of the Opera in rock-opera terms. There are moments of interest for those who can stick with it.
p: Edward R. Pressman for TCF/Pressman-Williams
w/d: Brian de Palma
ph: Larry Pizer
songs: Paul Williams
m: Paul Williams, George Aliceson Tipton
md: Julie Chalkin, Michael Arciaga
ed: Paul Hirsch
pd: Jack Fisk
cos: Rosanna Norton
sp: Greg Auer
sound: James Tanenbaum, Al Gramaglia
ch: Harold Oblong
Paul Williams, William Finley, Jessica Harper, George Memmoli, Gerrit Graham, William Shepherd

Phantom of the Rue Morgue *
USA 1954 84m Warnercolor 3D
In 1890s Paris, murders attributed to a madman turn out to be the work of an ape under the control of a zoologist.

Garish horror melodrama, plainly presented. It passes the time tolerably enough for addicts.
p: Henry Blanke for Warner
w: Harold Medford, James R. Webb
story: Edgar Allan Poe
d: Roy del Ruth
ph: Peverell Marley
m: David Buttolph
ed: James Moore

Phantoms Inc.

ad: Bertram Tutu
cos: Moss Mabry
sound: Stanley Jones
make-up: Gordon Bau
Karl Malden, Claude Dauphin, Steve
Forrest, Patricia Medina, Dolores Dorn,
Allyn McLerie

Phantoms Inc.

USA 1945 20m bw
The police reveal a fake spiritualist.
   Lively addition to MGM's long-
running *Crime Does Not Pay* series of
supports which were popular from the
mid-thirties to the mid-forties.
p: MGM
w: Edward Brock
story: Brian Duffield
d: Harold Young
ph: Jackson Rose
m: Max Terr
ed: Harry Komer
ad: Richard Duce
sound: no credit given
Frank Reicher, Ann Shoemaker, Arthur
Shields, Dorothy Adams

Phase IV *

GB 1973 85m Technicolor
Scientists investigating the behaviour patterns of ants in the Arizona Desert find
themselves isolated and under attack.
   Silly but visually arresting science-
fiction hokum, to be avoided by haters
of creepy-crawlies.
p: Paul Radin for Paramount/Alced
w: Mayo Simon
d: SAUL BASS
ph: Dick Bush
m: Brian Gascoyne
ed: Willy Kemplen
pd: John Barry
sp: John Richardson
2nd unit ph: Jack Mills
ant ph: KEN MIDDLEHAM
Nigel Davenport, Michael Murphy,
Lynne Frederick, Alan Gifford, Robert
Henderson, Helen Horton

Phenomena

It 1984 114m Technicolor Panavision
Dolby
A girl who possesses a strange power
over insects tracks down a mad killer.
   Ludicrous fantasy thriller whose
occasional vestiges of style fail to
compensate for its ridiculous plot.
p: Angelo Jacono for Dacfilm
w: Dario Argento, Franco Ferrini
d: Dario Argento
ph: Romano Albani
m: Claudio Simonetti, Fabio Pgnatelli
and others
ed: Franco Fraticelli
pd: Maurizio Garrone, Nello Giorgetti,
Luciano Spadoni, Umberto Turco

cos: Giorgio Armani
Jennifer Connelly, Donald Pleasence,
Daria Nicolodi, Patrick Bauchau, Dalila
di Lazzaro, Michele Soavi

Philbin, Mary (1903-1993)

American actress of the silent screen,
most notably as Christine Dade, the
abducted prima donna in the Lon
Chaney version of *The Phantom of the
Opera* (1925). A discovery of director
Erich von Stroheim, her only other
genre credit was *The Man Who Laughs*
(1928). Her other films include *The
Blazing Trail*, *Merry Go Round*, *Drums of
Love* and *Love Me and the World is Mine*.

Phobia

Canada 1980 89m Technicolor
A psychiatrist's patients, each with their
own specific phobia, are killed one by
one by an unknown assailant.
   Poorly executed thriller which belies
the talent involved.
p: Zale Magder for Borough Park
exec p: Larry Stuegel, Mel Bergman
w: Lew Lehman, Jimmy Sangster, Peter
Ballwood
story: Gary Sherman, Ronald Shusett
d: John Huston
ph: Reginald Morris
m: André Gagnon
ed: Stan Lee
pd: Ben Edwards
cos: Aleida MacDonald
sp: Martin Maliveire
sound: Paul Coombs, Mike
Hodgenboom
Paul Michael Glaser, John Colicos, Susan
Hogan, David Bolt, Alexandra Stewart

The Picture of Dorian Gray **

USA 1945 110m bw/Technicolor
A Victorian gentleman keeps locked up
in his attic a portrait of himself which
reveals his true age and depravity whilst
he remains eternally young.
   Slow, elegant, handsomely
photographed adaptation of an overly
epigrammatical novel. All very civilized,
though sometimes a bit of a bore.
p: Pandro S. Berman for MGM
w/d: ALBERT LEWIN
novel: Oscar Wilde
ph: HARRY STRADLING (AA)
m: HERBERT STOTHART
ed: Ferris Webster
ad: CEDRIC GIBBONS, HANS PETERS
cos: Irene, Valles, Marion Heywood
Keyes
sound: Douglas Shearer
make-up: Jack Dawn
HURD HATFIELD, GEORGE
SANDERS, Donna Reed, ANGELA
LANSBURY, Peter Lawford, Lowell
Gilmore, Richard Fraser, Miles Mander

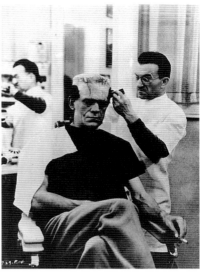

• **Make-up man Jack P. Pierce applies
the putty to Boris Karloff in this
behind the scenes still from *The Bride
of Frankenstein*. Pierce was also
responsible for the classic make-ups
of *Dracula*, *The Mummy* and *The Wolf
Man*.**

Pierce, Jack P. (1889-1968)

Celebrated American make-up artist,
responsible for the accepted look of
Dracula, Frankenstein's Monster, the
Wolf Man and the Mummy, all of which
he created while at Universal. He went
on to head the studio's make-up department from 1936 to 1946. After this he
went freelance, though he never
matched his earlier achievements, which
in any case were copyrighted to
Universal. A former actor on both stage
and screen, he also worked as a cameraman and stuntman before turning to
make-up in the mid-twenties. His monster designs feature on merchandising
and Hallowe'en masks to this day.
Genre credits:
Dracula (1930), *Frankenstein* (1931), *The
Mummy* (1932), *Murders in the Rue Morgue*
(1932), *White Zombie* (1932), *The Old
Dark House* (1932), *The Bride of
Frankenstein* (1935), *Werewolf of London*
(1935), *Dracula's Daughter* (1936), *Son of
Frankenstein* (1939), *Tower of London*
(1939), *The Mummy's Hand* (1940),
Man-Made Monster (1941), *The Wolf Man*
(1941), *The Ghost of Frankenstein* (1942),
The Mummy's Tomb (1942), *The Phantom
of the Opera* (1943), *Captive Wild Woman*
(1943), *Son of Dracula* (1943),
Frankenstein Meets the Wolf Man (1943),
The Mummy's Ghost (1943), *The Mad
Ghoul* (1943), *House of Frankenstein*
(1944), *The Mummy's Curse* (1944), *House*

of Dracula (1945), *Jungle Captive* (1945), *The Spider Woman Strikes Back* (1945), *House of Horrors* (1946 - aka *Joan Medford is Missing*), *The Time of Their Lives* (1946), *The Master Minds* (1949), *Teenage Monster* (1957), *The Devil's Hand* (1958), *Giant from the Unknown* (1959), *Beyond the Time Barrier* (1960), *The Creation of the Humanoids* (1962), *Beauty and the Beast* (1963)

Piper, Brett (1955-)

American writer, producer, director and special-effects technician working at the low-budget end of the horror market. He directed his first film, *Mysterious Planet*, in 1982. His other credits include *Battle for the Lost Planet* and *The Return of Captain Sinbad*.
Genre credits:
Raiders of the Living Dead (1983, released 1989 - aka *Dying Day* -w/p/d), *Mutant War* (1988 - w/p/d/sp), *A Nymphoid Barbarian in Dinosaur Hell* (1990 - aka *Dark Fortress* - w/p/d/sp), *They Bite* (1993 - w/p/d)

Piranha *

US 1978 92m Metrocolor
Searching for two missing persons, a young woman accidentally drains a pool of man-eating piranha into a river at the end of which is a holiday resort.
Spoofy variation on *Jaws* and all the other hungry fish films of the period. Lively low-budget nonsense.
p: Jan Davison, Chako Van Leeuwen for New World
exec p: Roger Corman, Jeff Schechtman
w: John Sayles
story: Richard Robinson, John Sayles
d: Joe Dante
ph: Jamie Anderson
m: Pino Donaggio
md: Natale Massara
ed: Mark Goldblatt, Joe Dante
ad: Bill Mellin, Kerry Mellin
cos: Linda Pearl
sp: Phil Tippett, Jon Berg
sound: Joel Goldsmith
make-up effects: Rob Botton, Vincent Prentice, Phil Tippett
2nd unit d: Dick Lowry
2nd unit ph: M. Todd Henry
stunt co-ordinator: Conrad Palmisano
Bradford Dillman, Heather Menzies, Kevin McCarthy, Bruce Gordon, Barbara Steele, Keenan Wynn, Dick Miller, Belinda Balask, Melody Thomas, Paul Bartel, Barry Brown, Richard Deacon

Piranha II: The Flying Killers

US/It 1982 94m Technicolor
A holiday resort is attacked by piranha fish with the ability to fly.

Not quite as awful as some have made it out to be, this unnecessary sequel nevertheless is something of a disappointment. Astonishingly, director Cameron survived the critical onslaught and went on to helm such blockbusters as *The Terminator*, *Aliens*, *Terminator 2* and *True Lies*.
p: Chako Van Leevwew, Jeff Schechtman for Chako
exec p: Ovidio G. Assonitis
w: H. A. Milton
d: James Cameron
ph: Roberto D'Ettore Piazzoli
m: Steve Powder
ed: Robert Silvi
pd/sp: Gianetto de Rossi
cos: Nicoletta Ercole
sound: Piero Fondi, Danilo Sterbini
Tricia O'Neil, Lance Henriksen, Steve Marachuk, Ted Richert, Leslie Graves, Ricky G. Paull

Piranha II: The Spawning see

Piranha II: The Flying Killers

The Pit and the Pendulum *

USA 1961 85m Pathecolor Panavision
Investigating the mysterious death of his sister, a Spanish nobleman finds himself locked up in her husband's torture chamber.
Good-looking but slow-moving horror film that, even at this length, seems padded. The torture-chamber finale is worth waiting for.
p: Roger Corman for AIP/Alta Vista
exec p: James H. Nicholson, Samuel Z. Arkoff
w: Richard Matheson
story: Edgar Allan Poe
d: Roger Corman
ph: FLOYD CROSBY
m: Les Baxter
ed: Anthony Carras
pd/ad: Daniel Haller
cos: Marjorie Corso
sp: Pat Dinga, Ray Mercer, Butler-Glouner
sound: Roy Meadows
Vincent Price, Barbara Steele, John Kerr, Luana Anders, Anthony Carbone, Charles Victor

The Pit and the Pendulum

USA/It 1990 90m Technicolor Ultra Stereo
In 1492, an innocent young couple are tortured by the Grand Inquisitor, Torquemada.
Boring low-budget horror, poorly presented.
p: Albert Band for Full Moon Entertainment
exec p: Charles Band
w: Dennis Paoli

• **Countess Dracula herself, Ingrid Pitt, one of the genre's most beautiful yet most underused talents.**

story: Edgar Allan Poe
d: Stuart Gordon
ph: Adolfo Bartoli
m: Richard Band
ed: Andy Horvitch
ad: Giovanni Natalucci
cos: Michela Gisotti
sp: Giovanni Corridori
sound: Giuseppe Muratori
make-up effects: Greg Cannom
Lance Henriksen, Rona de Ricci, Jonathan Fuller, Oliver Reed, Jeffrey Combs, Frances Bay, Stephen Lee

Pitt, Ingrid (1937-)

Glamorous Polish actress in international films, with experience in East Germany and Spain, where she was a member of the Spanish National Theatre. Broke into films in Spain in 1964 with *The Prehistoric Sound* (*El Sonido Prehistórico*), which led to work on *The Omegans* and *Where Eagles Dare*. Became one of Hammer's vampire queens in the early seventies. Other credits include *Who Dares Wins*, *Wild Geese II* and *Parker*. Also writes novels and screenplays.
Genre credits:
The Prehistoric Sound (1964 - aka *El Sonido Prehistórico*), *The Omegans* (1968), *The Vampire Lovers* (1970), *Countess Dracula* (1970), *The House That Dripped Blood* (1971), *Nobody Ordered Love* (1971), *The Wicker Man* (1973)

Pivar, Maurice

American editor, long with Universal, where he supervised the editing of many of their thirties horror classics.
Genre credits:

The Phantom of the Opera (1925 - co-ed), *Frankenstein* (1931 -supervising editor), *The Old Dark House* (1932 - sup ed), *The Invisible Man* (1933 - co-ed), *The Bride of Frankenstein* (1935 - sup ed), *The Raven* (1935 - sup ed), *Dracula's Daughter* (1936 - sup ed)

Pizer, Larry

British cinematographer (*Four in the Morning*, *Morgan - A Suitable Case for Treatment*, *Our Mother's House*, *Isadora*) who went to work in America in the mid-seventies.
Genre credits:
The Phantom of the Paradise (1974), *The Killing Hour* (1981 - aka *The Clairvoyant* - TVM), *Too Scared to Scream* (1982 - aka *The Doorman*), *The Phantom of the Opera* (1983 - TVM)

The Plague of the Zombies *

GB 1966 91m Technicolor
In a small Cornish village, the local squire resurrects the dead to work in his tin mine.

Spirited Hammer horror with a strong central performance and plenty of atmosphere. It was filmed back-to-back with *The Reptile* with much the same cast and crew.
p: Anthony Nelson Keys for Hammer
w: John Bryan
d: JOHN GILLING
ph: ARTHUR GRANT
m: James Bernard
md: Philip Martell
ed: James Needs, Chris Barnes
pd: Bernard Robinson
ad: Don Mingaye
cos: Rosemary Burrows
sp: Les Bowie
sound: Ken Rawkins
make-up: Roy Ashton
ANDRÉ MORELL, John Carson, Diane Clare, Jacqueline Pearce, Alex Davison, Brook Williams, Michael Ripper, Marcus Hammond

Pleasence, Angela

British character actress, the daughter of Donald Pleasence, with whom she appeared in *From Beyond the Grave* (1973). Her other notable genre appearance was in Joseph Larraz's *Symptoms* (1974 - aka *The Blood Virgin*).

Pleasence, Donald (1919-1995)

British actor, the father of Angela Pleasence, long associated with the horror genre, most notably with the *Halloween* series. Prior to service in the RAF in World War Two (during which he was a POW), he began his career in rep in Jersey, making his West End début in 1939. He returned to the stage after

the war, though it wasn't until 1954 that he appeared in his first film, *The Beachcomber*. He then became familiar to TV audiences as Prince John in *Robin Hood*. More films followed, in which he often seemed to play the bad guy, especially after taking the title role in *Dr Crippen* and portraying super-villain Blofeld in the James Bond outing *You Only Live Twice*. He had important non-sinister roles in *The Great Escape* and *Cul-de-Sac*, and was also notable in such films as *Hell Is a City*, *The Caretaker* (recreating his acclaimed stage role), *Fantastic Voyage*, *The Eagle Has Landed* (as Himmler), *Escape from New York* (as the US president) and *Ground Zero*. He also appeared as Count Plasma in the Australian comedy *Barry Mackenzie Holds His Own*.
Genre credits:
The Flesh and the Fiends (1959 - aka *Mania/The Fiendish Ghouls*), *Circus of Horrors* (1960), *The Hands of Orlac* (1960), *What a Carve Up* (1961), *Eye of the Devil* (1966), *Death Line* (1972 - aka *Raw Meat*), *Tales That Witness Madness* (1973), *Dr Jekyll and Mr Hyde* (1973 - TVM), *From Beyond the Grave* (1973), *The Mutations* (1974), *I Don't Want to be Born* (1975 - aka *The Devil Within Her*), *Land of the Minotaur* (1976 - aka *The Devil's Men*), *The Uncanny* (1977), *Night Creature* (1978 - aka *Devil Cat*), *The Dark Secret of Harvest Home* (1978 - TVM - voice only), *Halloween* (1978), *Dracula* (1979 -as Dr Seward), *The Monster Club* (1980), *Witch Hunt* (1980), *Halloween II* (1981), *Alone in the Dark* (1982), *The Devonsville Terror* (1983), *Frankenstein's Great Aunt Tillie* (1983), *Terror in the Aisles* (1983), *Reel Horror* (1985), *Phenomena* (1985 - aka *Creepers*), *Nothing Underneath* (1986), *Phantom of Death* (1987), *Nosferatu in Venice* (1987 - aka *Vampires in Venice*), *Ghosts* (1987), *Prince of Darkness* (1987), *Specters* (1987), *Halloween 4: The Return of Michael Myers* (1988), *Halloween 5: The Revenge of Michael Myers* (1989), *The House of Usher* (1989), *The Raven* (1990), *Buried Alive* (1990), *Halloween 6: The Curse of Michael Myers* (1995)

Poe, Edgar Allan (1809-1849)

Celebrated American novelist, short story-writer and poet whose macabre tales of terror and the supernatural have been filmed by various film-makers down the decades, most notably by Roger Corman in the sixties, though he tended to be fairly liberal with the original storylines, often discarding them completely. Among Poe's filmed stories are *The Black Cat*, *The Raven*, *The Fall of the House of Usher*, *The Pit and the Pendulum*, *The Murders in the Rue Morgue*,

The Premature Burial, *Tales of Terror* (compendium featuring *The Black Cat*, *Morella* and *The Facts in the Case of M. Valdemar*), *The Tomb of Ligeia* and *The Masque of the Red Death*. Poe's own story has been told several times, most notably by D. W. Griffith in *The Life of Edgar Allan Poe* and by Harry Lachman in *The Loves of Edgar Allan Poe*. He was also the inspiration for one of the segments in the horror portmanteau *Torture Garden*, which went by the title *The Man Who Collected Poe*.

Polanski, Roman (1933-)

Polish-born actor, writer and director who, after several acclaimed shorts and one Polish feature, *Knife in the Water* (1961), came to Britain in the mid-sixties, where he worked on several key films (*Repulsion*, *Cul-de-Sac*, *Dance of the Vampires*), before moving to America. There he met with even greater success with *Rosemary's Baby* and *Chinatown*. Also famous for the fact that his first wife, actress Sharon Tate, was murdered by the Manson gang in 1969, and for leaving America in 1979 prior to being sentenced for having had unlawful sexual intercourse with a minor. He has since worked in Europe, though success has been intermittent (*Tess*, *Frantic*, *Death and the Maiden*). His other credits include *Macbeth*, *What?*, *The Tenant*, *Pirates* and *Bitter Moon*.
Genre credits:
Repulsion (1965 - co-w/d), *Dance of the Vampires* (1967 - aka *The Fearless Vampire Killers or Pardon Me, But Your Teeth Are in My Neck* - actor/co-w/d), *Rosemary's Baby* (1968 - w/d)

Pollexfen, Jack

American writer and producer, responsible for a handful of undistinguished low-budgeters.
Genre credits:
Son of Dr Jekyll (1951 - co-w), *The Neanderthal Man* (1953 - co-w/co-p), *Daughter of Dr Jekyll* (1957 - w/p), *Monstrosity* (1963 - co-p)

Poltergeist **

USA 1982 112m Technicolor Panavision Dolby
A suburban family is plagued by spirits from the cemetery on which their house is built; playful at first, the spirits soon turn nasty and abduct one of the children.

Slick modern-day ghost story with superior technical effects and enough going on to keep one glued. It was followed by *Poltergeist II: The Other Side* (1986) and *Poltergeist III* (1988).
p: Steven Spielberg, Frank Marshall, Kathleen Kennedy for MGM/UA
w: Steven Spielberg, Michael Grain,

Mark Victor
story: Steven Spielberg
d: Tobe Hooper
ph: Matthew F. Leonetti
m: JERRY GOLDSMITH
ed: Michael Kahn
pd: James H. Spencer
cos: Ann Gray Lambert
sp: RICHARD EDLUND
sound: Art Rochester, Bill Varney, Steve
Maslow, Kevin Connell
sound effects: ALAN HOWARTH
sound effects ed: Bonnie Koehler,
Warren Hamilton Jr.
make-up effects: Craig Reardon
stunt co-ordinator: Glenn H. Randall Jr.
Craig T. Nelson, JoBeth Williams,
BEATRICE STRAIGHT, Dominique
Dunne, Oliver Robbins, HEATHER
O'ROURKE (as Carol Anne), Martin
Casello, Richard Lawson, ZELDA
RUBINSTEIN

Poltergeist II: The Other Side *
USA 1986 87m Metrocolor Panavision
Dolby
The Freeling family find themselves
threatened by more spirits, this time
from an Indian burial tomb.
    Technically adroit rehash of
Poltergeist. Good to look at and with the
expected plethora of effects, though the
climax is perhaps a bit of a let-down.
p: Freddie Fields for
MGM/UA/Victor-Grais
w: Mark Victor, Michael Grais
d: Brian Gibson
ph: Andrew Laszlo
m: Jerry Goldsmith
ed: Thom Noble
pd: Ted Haworth
cos: April Ferry
sp: RICHARD EDLUND
sound: Adrian Rachin
make-up effects: Michael J. Kohut,
Carlos del Arios
effects design: H. R. Giger
JoBeth Williams, Craig T. Nelson, Will
Sampson, Zelda Rubinstein, Heather
O'Rourke, Oliver Robbins, Julian Beck,
Geraldine Fitzgerald

Poltergeist III
USA 1988 98m Technicolor Dolby
Demons follow little Carol Anne to the
Chicago apartment building of her aunt
and uncle.
    Tired rehash of the old formula with
dull effects work and too much chat.
p: Barry Bernardi for MGM/UA
exec p: Gary Shearman
w: Gary Shearman, Brian Taggert
d: Gary Shearman
ph: Alex Nepomniaschy
m: Joe Renzetti
ed: Paul Albert

pd: Paul Eads
make-up effects: Dick Smith
Nancy Allen, Tom Skerritt, Heather
O'Rourke, Richard Fire, Zelda
Rubinstein, Lara Flynn Boyle, Kip Wentz

Popcorn
USA 1990 91m Eastmancolor Dolby
A maniac goes on the rampage during a
horror-film festival.
    Initially intriguing but sadly
disappointing horror film with spoofy
elements.
p: Torben Johnke, Gary Croch, Ashok
Amritraj for Filmhouse
International/Movie Partners/Century
Films
w: Tod Hackett (Alan Ormsby)
story: Mitchell Smith
d: Mark Herrier
ph: Ronnie Taylor
m: Paul J. Zaza
ed: Stan Cole
pd: Peter Murton
cos: Heidi Kaezenski
sp: George Ferrari
sound: Oscar Lawson
make-up effects: Bob Clark
2nd unit ph: John Harris
Jill Schoelen, Tom Villard, Dee Wallace
Stone, Tony Roberts, Ray Ralston,
Malcolm Danare, Derek Rydall

Portrait of Jennie ***
USA 1948 86m bw/Technicolor
An artist down on his luck meets a
strange but beautiful young girl who he
later discovers was killed many years
earlier in a storm at sea.
    Charming ghost story put together
with great pictorial style, so that even
the silly story carries conviction.
p: David O. Selznick
w: Peter Berneis, Paul Osborn, Leonard
Bernovici
novel: Robert Nathan
d: WILLIAM DIETERLE
ph: JOSEPH AUGUST
m: DIMITRI TIOMKIN, after Debussy
ed: no credit given
ad: J. McMillan Johnson, Joseph B. Platt
cos: Lucinda Ballard, Anna Hill
Johnstone
sp: CLARENCE SLIFER
sound: no credit given
JENNIFER JONES, JOSEPH COTTEN,
ETHEL BARRYMORE, Lillian Gish,
Florence Bates, Henry Hull, CECIL
KELLAWAY, Albert Sharpe, Felix
Bressart

The Possessed
USA 1977 74m Technicolor TVM
A dying priest who has lost his faith is
brought back to life in order to combat
evil.

Moderate horror nonsense, clearly
derived from The Exorcist.
p: Philip Mandelker for Warner/NBC
exec p: Jerry Thorpe
w: John Sacret Young
d: Jerry Thorpe
ph: Charles G. Arnold
m: Leonard Rosenman
ed: Michael A. Hoey
ad: Frank Hope
cos: Henry Salley, Marie Brown
James Farentino, Joan Hackett,
Claudette Nevins, Harrison Ford, P. J.
Soles, Diana Scarwid, Eugene Roche,
Ann Dusenberry, M. Emmett Walsh

Possessed
It 1983 87m colour
The daughter of an archaeologist becomes
possessed by a malevolent spirit.
    Ludicrous horror mish-mash with an
over-abundance of incident. Not one of
its director's greatest moments.
p: Fabrizio de Angelis for Lightning
w: Elisa Livia Briganti, Dardano
Sacchetti
d: Lucio Fulci
ph: Guglielmo Mancori
ed: Vincenzo Tomassi
pd/cos: Massimo Lentini
Christopher Connelly, Martha Taylor,
Brigitta Boccoli, Giovanni Frezza,
Cinziade Ponti

Possession
Fr/Ger 1981 80m Kodak 300
A young woman leaves her husband for
what appears to be another man but
turns out to be a slithering monster.
    Hysterical matrimonial melodrama
which switches halfway through into
fantasy horror. Despite much blood-
letting and some pretensions to style, it
bores well before the end and the story
makes no sense at all.
p: Marie-Laurie Reyre for
Oliane/Mariane/Soma
w: Andrzej Zulawski, Frederic Tuten
d: Andrzej Zulawski
ph: Bruno Buytten
m: Andrzej Korznyski
ed: Marie-Sophie Dubus, Suzanne
Lang-Willar, Jutta Omura, Sabine
Marang
ad: Holger Gross, Barbara Kloth
sp: Carlo Rambaldi
Isabelle Adjani, Sam Neill, Margrit
Carstense, Heinz Bennett, Johanna
Hofer, Carl Duering, Shawn Lawton

The Possession of Joel Delany *
USA 1971 108m Eastmancolor
A New York woman discovers that her
brother may have been taken over by a
Puerto Rican spirit which is driving him
to violence and murder.

An incomprehensible and unsatisfactory horror movie with socio-political undertones. Occasional flashes of interest (the head in the fridge is memorable), but it's hardly entertaining.
p: George Justin for ITC/Haworth
w: Matt Robinson, Grimes Grice
novel: Ramona Stewart
d: Waris Hussein
ph: Arthur J. Ornitz
m: Joe Raposo
ed: John Victor Smith
pd: Peter Murton
Shirley MacLaine, Perry King, David Elliott, Lisa Kohane, Miriam Colon

Powell, Eddie (1927-)
British stunt man, long associated with Hammer, where he often doubled for Christopher Lee. A despatch rider for the Grenadier Guards during World War Two, he turned to stunt work in 1948, his largest role being that of Prem the Mummy in Hammer's *The Mummy's Shroud*. His other credits include *Daleks Invasion Earth: 2150 AD*, *Where Eagles Dare*, *Flash Gordon*, *Krull* and *Legend*.
Genre credits:
The Mummy (1959), *She* (1965), *Dracula - Prince of Darkness* (1966), *The Mummy's Shroud* (1967), *Dracula Has Risen from the Grave* (1968), *The Devil Rides Out* (1968 - aka *The Devil's Bride* - as the Goat of Mendes), *The Lost Continent* (1968), *Dracula* (1973 - TVM), *The Omen* (1976), *To the Devil... A Daughter* (1976), *Alien* (1979 - uncredited work as the alien), *Dracula* (1979), *Howling II: Your Sister is a Werewolf* (1982), *The Keep* (1983), many more

The Power
USA 1983 84m colour
An amulet wreaks havoc on those who come into contact with it.
Undernourished low-budgeter.
p: Jeff Obrow for Jeff Obrow Productions
w/d/ed: Jeff Obrow, Stephen Carpenter
ph: Stephen Carpenter
m: Chris Young
pd: Chris Hopkins
make-up effects: Matthew Mungle
Susan Stokey, Warren Lincoln, Lisa Erickson, Chad Christian

Pranks
USA 1981 85m colour
Students staying on a deserted college campus are murdered one by one by a maniac who turns out to be one of them.
Independent cheapjack horror, the usual let's-kill-the-kids fare, unimaginatively presented.

p: Jeff Obrow for Death Dorm
w: Jeff Obrow, Stephen Carpenter, Stacey Glachino
d/ed: Jeff Obrow, Stephen Carpenter
ph: Stephen Carpenter
m: Chris Young
Laurie Lapinski, Stephen Sachs, David Snow, Pamela Holland, Dennis Ely, Woody Roll, Daphne Zuniga

Predator
USA 1987 115m DeLuxe
Mercenaries on a secret mission in the jungle are picked off one by one by a chameleon-like creature from outer space.
Relentlessly elongated science-fiction actioner which very quickly outstays its welcome. The dialogue is ridiculous. However, it made a pot of money and produced a sequel, *Predator 2*, in 1990.
p: Laurence Pereira, Jim Thomas for TCF
exec p: Lawrence Gordon, Joel Silver, John Davis
w: Jim Thomas, John Thomas
d: John McTiernan
ph: Donald McAlpine
m: Alan Silvestri
ed: John F. Link, Mark Helrich
pd: John Vallone
cos: Marilyn Vance Straker
sp: R. Greenberg, Joel Hynek
sound: Kevin Carpenter, Don Bassman, Kevin Cleary, Richard Overton
make-up effects: Stan Winston
2nd unit d/stunt co-ordinator: Craig R. Baxley
2nd unit ph: Frank E. Johnson
Arnold Schwarzenegger, Carl Weathers, Kevin Peter Hall (as the Predator), Shane Black, Sonny Landham, Jesse Ventura, Bill Duke, Elpidia Carrillo

Predator 2
USA 1990 107m DeLuxe Dolby
In 1997, a second predator treats Los Angeles as its own private game park.
Sickeningly expensive follow-up in which plot and character take second place to relentless action, special effects, noise and foul language. It caters to the lowest possible denominator - and then some.
p: Lawrence Gordon, Joel Silver, John Davis for TCF
w: Jim Thomas, John Thomas
d: Stephen Hopkins
ph: Peter Levy
m: Alan Silvestri
ed: Mark Goldblatt
pd: Lawrence G. Paul
cos: Marilyn Vance-Straker
sp: R. Greenberg
sound: Richard Raguse
make-up effects: Stan Winston

stunt co-ordinator: Gary Davis
Danny Glover, Gary Busey, Maria Conchita, Alonso Ruben Blades, Bill Paxton, Robert Davi, Adam Baldwin, Kevin Peter Hall (as the Predator), Ken McCord, Morton Downey Jr, Calvin Lockhart, Steve Kahan

The Premature Burial ✲
USA 1961 80m Eastmancolor Panavision
A cataleptic afraid of being buried alive becomes obsessed with the subject.
Good-looking horror melodrama in the established Corman-Poe manner, with the studio dry-ice machine working overtime.
p: Roger Corman for AIP
exec p: Gene Corman
w: Charles Beaumont, Ray Russell
story: Edgar Allan Poe
d: Roger Corman
ph: FLOYD CROSBY
m: Ronald Stein
ed: Ronald Sinclair
ad: Daniel Haller
cos: Margo Corso
sound: John Bury
Ray Milland, Hazel Court, Heather Angel, Alan Napier, John Dierkes, Richard Ney, Dick Miller

Prettykill
USA 1987 96m colour
Someone is murdering prostitutes, so a cop uses his hooker girlfriend as bait to catch the killer.
Dismal shocker with nothing whatsoever to recommend it. The surprisingly good cast is completely wasted.
p: John R. Bowen, Martin Walters for Dax Avant
w: Sandra K. Bailey
d: George Kaczender
ph: Joao Fernandes
m: Robert O. Ragland
ed: Tom Merchant
ad: Andris Hausmanis
cos: Trish Bakker
sound: Daniel Latour
David Birney, Season Hubley, Susannah York, Suzanne Snyder, Yaphet Kotto, Germaine Houde

Price, Dennis (1915-1973)
British actor (real name Dennistoun Franklyn John Rose-Price), on stage from 1937, though remembered chiefly for playing the urbane killer in *Kind Hearts and Coronets*. A light leading man in the forties and fifties (*A Canterbury Tale*, *A Place of One's Own*, *Holiday Camp*, *Snowbound*, *The Bad Lord Byron*, *Private's Progress*, *I'm All Right, Jack*, etc.), he turned to character roles later in life, often appearing in horror films which

did little for his dignity. His other credits include *The Naked Truth*, *Tunes of Glory*, *Victim*, *Tamahine*, *The Magic Christian* and *Alice's Adventures in Wonderland*.
Genre credits:
What a Carve Up (1961), *The Horror of It All* (1964), *The Earth Dies Screaming* (1964), *The Haunted House of Horror* (1969 - aka *The Horror House/The Dark*), *The Horror of Frankenstein* (1970), *Twins of Evil* (1971), *Dracula - Prisoner of Frankenstein* (1972 - aka *Dracula Contra Frankenstein/The Screaming Dead*), *Venus in Furs* (1972 - aka *Paroxismus*), *Horror Hospital* (1973), *Theatre of Blood* (1973)

Price, Vincent (1911-1993)

Inimitably voiced American horror star, one of the genre's giants. An art connoisseur with a degree in Art History and English and an MA in Fine Arts, he turned to acting in 1935, making his stage début in London at the Gate Theatre Club. More theatre followed in Britain and America (most notably with *Victoria Regina*, in which he played Prince Albert to Helen Hayes' Victoria), along with a stint with Orson Welles' Mercury Theatre Workshop. He made his first Hollywood appearance in 1938 in director Rowland V. Lee's comedy *Service DeLuxe*. The following year he appeared in *The Private Lives of Elizabeth and Essex* before returning to work with Lee on his first genre film, *Tower of London*. Supporting roles in all manner of films followed (*The House of Seven Gables*, *Green Hell*, *The Song of Bernadette*, *Laura*, *The Keys of the Kingdom*), along with the occasional horror film (*The Invisible Man Returns*), though it wasn't until he starred in *House of Wax* in 1953 that he became irrevocably identified with the genre. An association with producer/director William Castle brought further appearances in horror films, as did his collaboration in the sixties with director Roger Corman on his popular Poe series and a remake of *Tower of London*, with Price now playing Crookback instead of Clarence. Price's penchant for tongue-in-cheek roles seemed to develop during this period, though he proved he was an actor of range with the much-mentioned *Witchfinder General* (aka *The Conqueror Worm*). In the seventies he also displayed an inclination for black comedy with the *Dr Phibes* films and their variations, including the superb *Theatre of Blood*. A legend long before his death, Price did many commercial voice-overs towards the end of his career and provided

vocals for Tim Burton's tribute short *Vincent*, the Michael Jackson music video *Thriller* and the Disney cartoon *Basil - The Great Mouse Detective* (aka *The Adventures of the Great Mouse Detective*), in which he played the villain Professor Ratigan with relish. His final film was Tim Burton's Frankenstein spoof *Edward Scissorhands*, in which he made a brief but telling appearance as the Creator. His other non-horror credits include *The Three Musketeers*, *Casanova's Big Night*, *Dr Goldfoot and the Bikini Machine*, *Dr Goldfoot and the Girl Bombs* and *The Whales of August*.
Genre credits:
Tower of London (1939), *The Invisible Man Returns* (1940), *Abbott and Costello Meet Frankenstein* (1948 - voice only, as the Invisible Man), *House of Wax* (1953), *The Mad Magician* (1954), *The Fly* (1958), *The House on Haunted Hill* (1958), *The Bat* (1959), *The Tingler* (1959), *The Return of the Fly* (1959), *The Fall of the House of Usher* (1960 - aka *House of Usher*), *Master of the World* (1961), *The Pit and the Pendulum* (1961), *The Last Man on Earth* (1961), *Tales of Terror* (1962), *Tower of London* (1962), *The Raven* (1963), *The Comedy of Terrors* (1963), *Twice Told Tales* (1963), *Diary of a Madman* (1963), *The Haunted Palace* (1963), *The Masque of the Red Death* (1964), *The Tomb of Ligeia* (1965), *City Under the Sea* (1965), *Witchfinder General* (1968 - aka *The Conqueror Worm*), *The Oblong Box* (1969), *Annabel Lee* (1969 - short - voice only), *Scream and Scream Again* (1970), *Cry Banshee* (1970), *The Abominable Dr Phibes* (1971), *Dr Phibes Rises Again* (1972), *Theatre of Blood* (1973), *Madhouse* (1974), *The Monster Club* (1980), *House of the Long Shadows* (1983), *Vincent* (1982 - short - voice only), *Bloodbath at the House of Death* (1983), *Thriller* (1983 - music video - voice only), *From a Whisper to a Scream* (1986 - aka *The Offspring*), *Dead Heat* (1988), *Edward Scissorhands* (1990)

Priestley, J. B. (1894-1984)

Celebrated British novelist and playwright (*The Good Companions*, *Dangerous Corner*, *When We Are Married*, *An Inspector Calls*), whose novel *Benighted* has been filmed twice as *The Old Dark House* (1932 and 1962).

Primal Rage

USA 1988 87m Technicolor Dolby
A student goes on the rampage after being attacked by a laboratory monkey on which mind-altering experiments have taken place.

Poor on every conceivable level, this dismal shocker is a complete waste of space.
p: William J. Immerman for Elpico/Laguna
exec p: Josi W. Konsiki
w: Harry Kirkpatrick
d: Vittorio Rambaldi
ph: Antonio Climati
m: Claudio Simonetti
ed: John Rawson
ad: Federico Padovan
cos: France Carretti
sp: Carlo Rambaldi, Alex Rambaldi
sound: Lenny Hirschtriff
Patrick Lowe, Cheryl Arutt, Sarah Buxton, Mitch Watson, Doug Sloan, Bo Svenson

Prince of Darkness

USA 1987 101m DeLuxe Panavision Ultra Stereo
Scientists carrying out experiments on an ancient cannister discover it to contain the spirit of the Devil himself.

Slow-moving, rather po-faced horror that compares unfavourably with its director's earlier successes in the genre.
p: Larry Franco for Universal/Alive/Northern Distributors Inc.
exec p: Shep Gordon, Andre Blay
w: Martin Quatermass (John Carpenter)
d: John Carpenter
ph: Gary K. Kibbe
m: John Carpenter, Alan Howarth
ed: Steve Mirkovich
pd: Daniel Lomino
cos: Deahdra Scarno
sp: Dane Davis, John Paul Fasal, Kevin Quibell, Jim Danforth
sound: David Gertz
make-up: Frank Carrisosa
Donald Pleasence, Jameson Parker, Victor Wong, Lisa Blount, Susan Blanchard, Anne Howard, Alice Cooper, Ann Yen, Ken Wright, Dirk Blocker, Jessie Lawrence Ferguson

Prison *

USA 1988 103m Foto-Kem Ultra Stereo
The vengeful spirit of an executed criminal returns to cause havoc at a state penitentiary.

Lively, often well-staged low-budget hokum, the success of which led its director on to increasingly bigger things (*Die Hard 2*, *Cliffhanger*, *Cutthroat Island*, etc.).
p: Irwin Yablans for Empire
w: C. Courtnay Joyner
story: Irwin Yablans
d: Renny Harlin
ph: Michael Ballhaus
m: Richard Band, Christopher Stone
md: Richard Band
ed: Ray Lovejoy

pd: Phillip Duffin
cos: Stephen Chudej
sp: Eddie Surkin
sound: Jon Brodin
make-up effects: John Buechler
2nd unit ph: David Boyd
Viggo Mortensen, Lane Smith, Chelsea
Field, Ivan Kane, Tom Everett, Lincoln
Kilpatrick

Probyn, Brian
British cinematographer who worked on
several of Hammer's seventies
productions, including *Man at the Top*
and the unreleased *Shatter* (aka *Call Him
Mr Shatter*).
Genre credits:
Straight on Till Morning (1972), *The Satanic
Rites of Dracula* (1973), *Frankenstein and the
Monster from Hell* (1973)

Profondo Rosso see Deep Red

The Projected Man *
GB 1966 90m Technicolor Techniscope
A scientist working on the transmission
of matter subjects himself to the
experiment only to turn into a monster
with the ability to kill on contact.

Fitfully diverting low-budget science-
fiction romp marred by some
predictable clichés.
p: John Croydon, Maurice Foster for
MLC
w: John C. Cooper, Peter Bryan
story: Frank Quattrocchi
d: Ian Curteis
ph: Stan Pavey
m: Kenneth V. Jones
ed: Derek Holding
ad: Peter Mullins
cos: Kathleen Meore
sp: Flo Nordhoff, Robert Hedges, Mike
Hope
sound: S. G. Rider, Red Law
Bryant Halliday, Mary Peach, Norman
Wooland, Derek Farr, Ronald Allen,
Derrick de Marney, Sam Kydd

Prophecy
USA 1979 102m Movielab Panavision
A mercury leak causes the local wildlife
in Maine to mutate and a giant monster
threatens tourists.

Silly horror story with an ecological
angle and a rather ridiculous-looking
monster.
p: Robert L. Rosen for Paramount
w: David Seltzer
d: John Frankenheimer
ph: Harry Stradling
m: Leonard Rosenman
ed: Tom Rolf
pd: William Craig Smith
Talia Shire, Robert Foxworth, Armand
Assante, Richard Dysart

**Dave 'Darth Vader' Prowse as the
Monster in *Horror of Frankenstein*, one
of the lesser entries in the Hammer
series.**

Prowse, Dave
Tall (6'7") British actor and stunt man,
best remembered for playing Darth
Vader in the *Star Wars* trilogy. He has also
played Frankenstein's Monster three
times (including a gag cameo in the
Bond spoof *Casino Royale*). His other
film credits include *Up the Chastity Belt*.
Genre credits:
Horror of Frankenstein (1970), *Vampire
Circus* (1971), *Frankenstein and the Monster
from Hell* (1973), *Jabberwocky* (1977)

Psychic Killer
USA 1975 90m colour
A mental patient uses psychic means in
order to avenge himself on those who
put him away.

Tolerable supernatural thriller building up to a reasonably shocking climax
in which the killer is cremated alive.
p: Mardi Rustam
exec p: Mohammed Rustam
w: Greydon Clark, Mikel Angel,
Raymond Danton
d: Raymond Danton
ph: Herb Pearl
m: William Kraft
ed: Michael Brown
ad: Joel Leonard
cos: Monika Henreid
sound: Robert Dietz, Ted Gomillion
Jim Hutton, Julie Adams, Paul Burke,
Whit Bissell, Aldo Ray, Neville Brand,
Nehemiah Persoff, Della Reese, Rod
Cameron, Mary Wilcox

Psycho ****
USA 1960 109m bw

A trusted secretary absconds with
$40,000 but is later murdered at a
remote motel, apparently by the
owner's mother.

One of Hitchcock's most celebrated
thrillers and deservedly so. The visuals
(including the now legendary shower
sequence) are stunning and are effectively backed by Bernard Herrmann's
atmospheric 'black and white' music.
Disdained by the critics of the day, the
film has since taken on classic status -
and all without the graphic detail so
heavily relied upon today. It was followed, at a distance, by *Psycho II* (1983),
Psycho III (1986), *Bates Motel* (1987 -
TVM) and *Psycho IV* (1990 - TVM).
p: Alfred Hitchcock for Shamley
w: Joseph Stefano
novel: Robert Bloch
d: ALFRED HITCHCOCK
ph: JOHN L. RUSSELL
m: BERNARD HERRMANN
ed: GEORGE TOMASINI
ad: Joseph Hurley, Robert Clatworthy
cos: Helen Colvig
sp: Clarence Champagne
sound: Waldon O. Watson, William
Russell
titles/pictorial consultant: SAUL BASS
ANTHONY PERKINS, VERA MILES,
JANET LEIGH, John Gavin, John
McIntire, MARTIN BALSAM, Simon
Oakland, Pat Hitchcock

Psycho II *
USA 1983 118m Technicolor Dolby
Norman Bates is let out of the asylum
after twenty-two years, only to find

**• Vera Miles and John Gavin wonder
where Mother can be in this posed
publicity still from Alfred Hitchcock's
masterpiece *Psycho*.**

himself caught up a bizarre plot to have him recommitted.

Slick but some would argue unnecessary sequel which, while in no way comparable to the original, adds a good many twists of its own to the proceedings.
p: Hilton A. Green for Universal/Oak Industries
exec p: Bernard Schwartz
w: Tom Holland
d: Richard Franklyn
ph: Dean Cundey
m: Jerry Goldsmith
ed: Andrew London
pd: John W. Corso
cos: Robert Ellsworth, Brian O'Dowd, Denise Schlom
sp: Albert Whitlock
sound: Jim Alexander, Roger Heman, Philip Fland, Rex Slinkard, Mark B. Server, Andrew London
make-up effects: Michael McCracken, Chuck Crafts
Anthony Perkins, Vera Miles, Meg Tilly, Robert Loggia, Dennis Franz, Hugh Gillin, Claudia Briar, Robert Alan Browne, Ben Hartigan, Tim Maier, Tom Holland, Osgood Perkins (as the young Norman Bates)

Psycho III *
USA 1986 93m Technicolor Dolby
A suicidal novice takes refuge at the Bates Motel, where murder is the order of the day.

Lively third instalment, a few marks up on No. 2.
p: Hilton A. Green for Universal
w: Charles Edward Pogue
d: ANTHONY PERKINS
ph: Bruce Surtees
m: Carter Burwell
ed: David Blewitt
pd: Henry Bumstead
cos: Peter V. Saldutti, Maria Denise Schlom
sp: Syd Dutton, Bill Taylor, Karl G. Miller, Louis R. Cooper, Dan Lester
sound: John Stacy, Jim Thompson
make-up effects: Michael Westmore
Anthony Perkins, Diana Scarwid, Jeff Fahey, Roberta Maxwell

Psycho IV *
USA 1990 96m Technicolor TVM
Norman Bates recalls his teenage years to a radio talk-show hostess.

Mildly diverting addition to a series that had already run its course.
p: George Zaloom, Les Mayfield for Universal/Smart Money
exec p: Hilton A. Green
w: Joseph Stefano
d: Mick Garris
ph: Rodney Charters

m: Graeme Revell
ed: Charles Bornstein
pd: Michael Hanan
cos: Mary Ellen Winston
sp: Rick Jones, Bruce Block
sound: Henri Lopez, Rick Alexander
Anthony Perkins, Henry Thomas (as the young Norman Bates), Olivia Hussey (as Mother), Warren Frost, C. C. H. Pounder, Donna Mitchell, Thomas Schuster, John Landis

Psychomania
GB 1972 91m Technicolor
A Hell's Angel and his gang are brought back to life after his mother makes a pact with the devil.

Idiotic horror comic, something of an embarrassment for all concerned, though not without its choice moments for connoisseurs of the truly dreadful.
p: Andrew Donally for Benmar
w: Armand D'Usseau, Julian Halevy
d: Don Sharp
ph: Ted Moore
m: David Whitaker
ed: Richard Best
ad: Maurice Carter
cos: Jean Farlie
sp: Patrick Moore
sound: Buster Ambler, Bob Jones
stunt co-ordinator: Gerry Crampton
Nicky Henson, Beryl Reid, George Sanders, Mary Larkin, Roy Holder, Robert Hardy, Patrick Holt, Bill Pertwee, June Brown

The Psychopath
GB 1966 82m Technicolor Techniscope

A Scotland Yard detective tracks down a mad killer who leaves miniature dolls of his victims by their bodies.

Lunatic would-be thriller, slackly handled and hammily performed.
p: Max J. Rosenberg, Milton Subotsky for Paramount/Amicus
w: Robert Bloch
d: Freddie Francis
ph: John Wilcox
m: Elizabeth Lutyens
md: Philip Martell
ed: Oswald Hafenrichter
ad: Bill Constable
cos: Mary Gibson
sp: Ted Samuels
sound: Baron Mason, John Cox
titles: Sam Suliman
Patrick Wymark, John Standing, Margaret Johnston, Alexander Knox, Thorley Walters, Colin Gordon, Judy Huxtable, Don Borisenko

Pulse *
USA 1988 95m DeLuxe Dolby
Electrical surges turn everyday domestic items into murderous objects.

Derivative but reasonably slick horror hokum.
p: Patricia A. Stallone for Columbia/Aspen
exec p: William E. McEuen
w/d: Paul Golding
ph: Peter Lyons
m: Jay Ferguson
ed: Gib Jaffe
pd: Holger Gross
cos: Jacqueline Saint Anne
sp: Richard O. Helmer

• Gina Gianelli succumbs to *The Psychopath*, which had a screenplay by *Psycho* author Robert Bloch.

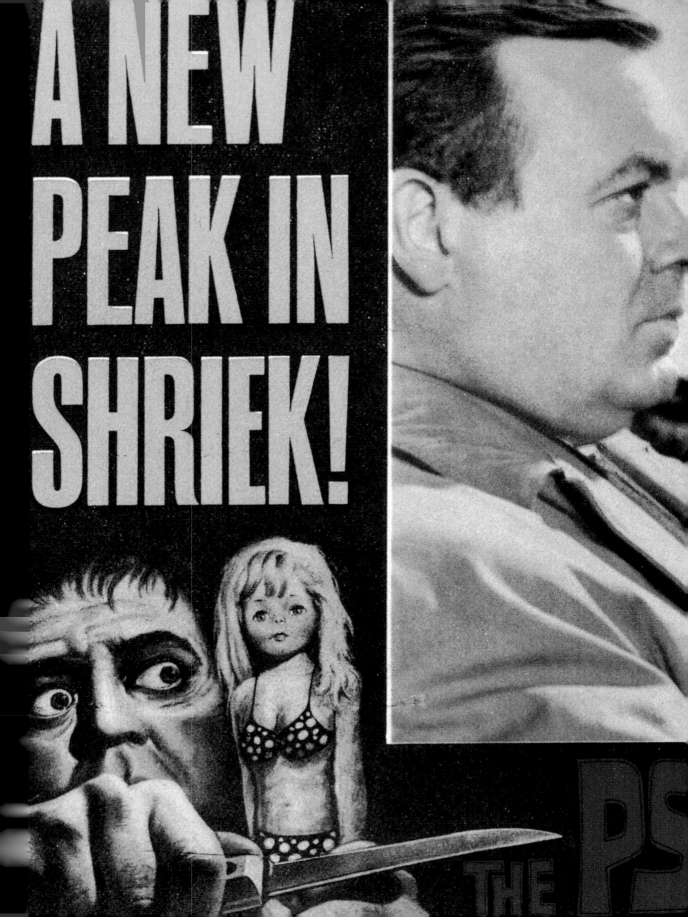

THOUGH NOT QUITE 'A NEW PEAK IN SHRIEK' *The Psychopath* was one of several workmanlike shockers directed by Oscar winning cinematographer Freddie Francis in the 1960s. His career saw him direct for Hammer, Amicus and Tyburn before he finally returned to photography in the eighties with such largescale productions as *The Elephant Man, Dune, Glory* and *Cape Fear*.

YCHOPATH

sound: Susumu Tokunow
titles: Wayne Fitzgerald, David Oliver Pfeil
2nd unit ph: Gary Wagner
stunt co-ordinator: Mike Cassidy
Joey Lawrence, Cliff de Young, Roxanne Hart, Myron Healey, Charles Tyner

The Puppet Masters

USA 1994 109m DeLuxe Dolby
An alien spaceship crash-lands near a small American township and the creatures within begin to take over the local populace at an alarming rate. The army is brought in to contain the situation before it becomes one of national importance.

The Tommyknockers meets Invasion of the Body Snatchers meets Aliens meets Invaders from Mars meets Outbreak. Slickly enough done for those who don't mind (or perhaps enjoy spotting) clichés.
p: Ralph Winter for Hollywood
exec p: Michael Engelberg
w: Ted Elliott, Terry Rossio, David S. Gayer
novel: Robert A. Heinlein
d: Stuart Orme

ph: Clive Tickner
m: Colin Towns
ed: William Goldenberg
pd: Daniel Lomino
cos: Tom Brosnan
sp: Buena Vista Visual Effects, Roy Arbogast
sound: Robert Anderson Jr, John Pospisil
make-up effects: Greg Cannom
stunt co-ordinator: Jeffrey Danshaw
Donald Sutherland, Eric Thal, Julie Warner, Keith David, Will Patton, Yaphet Kotto, Richard Belzer

Puppetmaster

USA/It 1989 90m DeLuxe
A group of psychics converge on an old hotel where a series of murders, apparently committed by puppets, have taken place.

Relentlessly padded horror comic with an overabundance of chat between the effects. Unbelievably, it was followed by Puppetmaster II (1990), Puppetmaster III (1990), Puppetmaster IV (1994) and Puppetmaster V: The Final Chapter (1995).
p: Hope Perello for Full Moon

exec p: Charles Band
w: Joseph G. Collodi
story: Charles Band, Kenneth J. Hall
d: David Schmoeller
ph: Sergio Salvati
m: Richard Band
ed: Tom Meshelski
pd: John Myhre
cos: Robin Lewis
sp: David Allen
sound: William Fiege
2nd unit d: Hope Perello
Paul Le Mat, William Hickey, Irene Miracle, Jimmy F. Skaggs, Robin Frates, Matt Roe, Kathryn O'Reilly, Marrya Small, Barbara Crampton

Pyun, Albert

American director with a penchant for low-budget fantasy films, though few of them have lived up to the promise of one of his earliest, The Sword and the Sorcerer. His other credits include Cyborg, Spiderman, Kickboxer II and Deceit.
Genre credits:
The Sword and the Sorcerer (1982), Dollman (1990), Nemesis (1992), Brain Smasher (1993), Arcade (1994), Nemesis (1994)

Q

Q - The Winged Serpent *
USA 1982 100m Technicolor
A flesh-eating prehistoric serpent
threatens New York City.
   Offbeat horror hokum with old-
fashioned stop-frame animation. For
the most part it at least keeps moving
and is not without its amusing touches.
p: Larry Cohen for UFD
exec p: Dan Sandburg, Richard de
Bona
w/d: Larry Cohen
ph: Fred Murphy
m: Robert O. Ragland
ed: Armand Lebowitz
ad: no credit given
cos: Tim D'Arcy
sp: David Allen, Randy Cook, Peter
Kuram
sound: Jeff Hayes
Michael Moriarty, David Carradine,
Candy Clark, James Dixon, Richard
Roundtree

Quarry, Robert (1923-)
Velvety-voiced American actor, best
known for his role as Count Yorga,
which he played in two films. After
training at the Hollywood Actors' Lab,
he made his film début in 1943 in
Hitchcock's *Shadow of a Doubt*, in a
small part which was subsequently cut
from the finished film. Much stage
work followed, peppered with the
occasional film (*A Kiss Before Dying*),
though it wasn't until the seventies
that he came into his own with horror
roles. His other film credits include
Rollercoaster, *Phantom Empire* and
Warlords.
Genre credits:
Count Yorga, Vampire (1970), *The Return
of Count Yorga (1971)*, *Dr Phibes Rises
Again (1972)*, *The Deathmaster (1972)*,
Madhouse (1973), *Sugar Hill (1974 -
aka Voodoo Girl)*, *Beverly Hills Vamp
(1988)*, *Sexbomb (1989)*, *Evil Spirits
(1991 - aka Spirits)*, *Haunting Fear
(1991)*, *Teenage Exorcist (1991)*

Quatermass and the Pit **
GB 1967 87m Technicolor
During extension work on London's

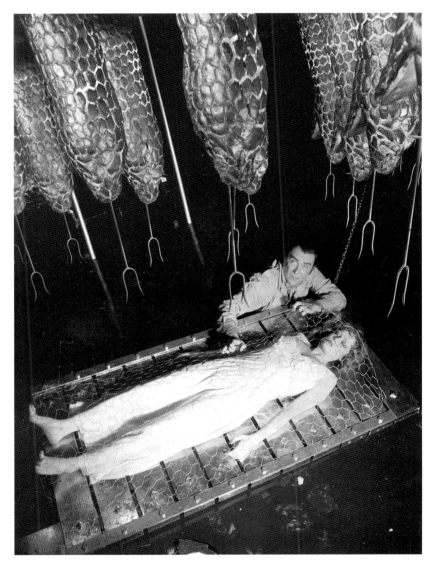

• **Robert Quarry and Fiona Lewis in a tense moment from the stylish horror
comedy *Dr Phibes Rises Again*.**

underground, an impenetrable space-
craft is unearthed and a mysterious
force makes itself felt.
   Intellectually exciting and compul-
sively watchable science-fiction thriller
with many gripping moments, only
occasionally let down by unconvincing
effects and dated terminology.
Certainly the best of the Hammer
Quatermass films.

p: Anthony Nelson Keys for Hammer/Associated British
w: NIGEL KNEALE, from his TV series
d: ROY WARD BAKER
ph: Arthur Grant
m: Tristam Carey
md: Philip Martell
ed: James Needs, Spencer Reeve
ad: Bernard Robinson
cos: Rosemary Burrows
sp: Les Bowie
sound: Sash Fisher
ANDREW KEIR, JAMES DONALD, BARBARA SHELLEY, Julian Glover, Duncan Lamont, Edwin Richfield, Peter Copley, Sheila Steafel, Brian Marshall

The Quatermass Experiment ***
GB 1955 82m bw
The only surviving member of a space expedition begins to mutate once back on earth, goes on the rampage and is eventually cornered in Westminster Abbey.

Though the script and concept have dated somewhat, this remains an eerily effective and sometimes quite frightening science-fiction horror whose success in both Britain and America helped to put Hammer films on the map. Required viewing for genre addicts.
p: Anthony Nelson Keys for Hammer/Exclusive
w: Richard Landau, Val Guest
TV series: NIGEL KNEALE
d: VAL GUEST

ph: Jimmy Harvey
m: JAMES BERNARD.
md: John Hollingsworth
ed: James Needs
ad: J. Elder Wills
cos: Molly Arbuthnot
sp: Les Bowie
sound: H. C. Pearson
Brian Donlevy, Jack Warner, Margia Dean, RICHARD WORDSWORTH, David King Wood, THORA HIRD, Gordon Jackson, Lionel Jeffries, Harold Lang, Maurice Kauffmann, Sam Kydd

Quatermass 2 **
GB 1957 85m bw
Professor Quatermass discovers that an industrial plant supposedly making synthetic food is in fact harbouring aliens from outer space.

Imaginatively plotted follow-up to The Quatermass Experiment, betrayed only by its low budget, general scientific naiveté and a monster that looks like a walking mud pie. Plenty of interest for genre addicts.
p: Anthony Hinds for Hammer
w: Nigel Kneale, Val Guest
TV series: NIGEL KNEALE
d: Val Guest
ph: Gerald Gibbs
m: James Bernard
md: John Hollingsworth
ed: James Needs
ad: Bernard Robinson
cos: Rene Cooke
sp: Bill Warrington, Henry Harris, Frank George

sound: Cliff Sandell
Brian Donlevy, John Longden, Sid James, Bryan Forbes, William Franklyn, Michael Ripper, Charles Lloyd Pack, Percy Herbert, Tom Chatto

Quigley, Linnea (1959-)
American actress, a horror babe who came to note in Return of the Living Dead (1985), in which she danced semi-naked in a cemetery at midnight. Much genre work has followed since, including a workout video, Linnea Quigley's Horror Workout (1989). Her non-genre credits include Cheech and Chong's Nice Dreams, The Young Warriors, Cheech and Chong: Still Smokin', Vice Academy, Assault of the Party Nerds, Virgin High and Rock 'n' Roll Detective.
Genre credits:
Psycho from Texas (1974), Fairy Tales (1976), Don't Go Near the Park (1980), Graduation Day (1981), The Black Room (1983), Fatal Games (1984), Silent Night, Deadly Night (1984), Return of the Living Dead (1985), Creepzoids (1987), Sorority Babes in the Slime Bowl-O-Rama (1987), Nightmare Sisters (1987), A Nightmare on Elm Street 4: The Dream Master (1988), Night of the Demons (1988), Dead Heat (1988), Hollywood Chainsaw Hookers (1988), Drive-In Madness (1988), Murder Weapon (1989), Witch Trap (1989), Sexbomb (1989), Blood Church (1990), Innocent Blood (1992), Beach Babes from Beyond Infinity (1993), Pumpkinhead II (1993)

R

RKO Radio Pictures
American studio renowned for glossy musicals starring Ginger Rogers and Fred Astaire and comedies featuring such talents as Katharine Hepburn and Cary Grant. RKO was formed in 1921 as an adjunct to the Keith Orpheum circuit and produced top-quality, family-orientated entertainment for almost three decades before running into financial difficulties. It was bought by Lucille Ball and Desi Arnaz's Desilu TV production outfit in 1953. During its heyday RKO did produce several horror milestones, most notably *King Kong* and the Val Lewton-produced shockers of the early forties.
Genre filmography:
King Kong (1933), *Son of Kong* (1933), *Cat People* (1942), *I Walked with a Zombie* (1943), *The Leopard Man* (1943), *The Seventh Victim* (1943), *The Ghost Ship* (1943), *Curse of the Cat People* (1944), *The Body Snatcher* (1945), *Isle of the Dead* (1945), *Bedlam* (1946), *Cat People* (1982 - remake)

Rabid
Canada 1976 91m Technicolor
Untried surgery techniques are used on a young woman who has been in a motorcycle accident. As a result she is turned into a blood-craving monster with the ability to infect others.
  Cult horror with only the gore to sustain it for anyone other than Cronenberg anoraks.
p: John Dunning for Cinema Entertainment Enterprises
exec p: Ivan Reitman, Andre Link
w/d: David Cronenberg
ph: Rene Verzier
m: Ivan Reitman
ed: Jean Lafleur
ad: Claude Marchand
sound: Richard Lightstone
make-up effects: Joe Blasco
Marilyn Chambers, Frank Moore, Joe Silver, Howard Ryshpan, Patricia Gage, Susan Roman, Terry Schonblum

Rabin, Jack
American special-effects technician who worked on several low-budget schlockers in the fifties, always in collaboration. Genre credits:
The Neanderthal Man (1953), *The Pharaoh's Curse* (1956), *The Black Sleep* (1956), *Macabre* (1957), *The Monster from Green Hell* (1957), *The Giant Behemoth* (1958 - aka *Behemoth the Sea Monster*)

Race with the Devil *
USA 1975 88m DeLuxe
Diabolists give chase to four holiday-makers who have witnessed a black mass in which a young girl was sacrificed.
  Lively chase melodrama in which the horror elements take a back seat to the car stunts. An adequate late-night offering.
p: Wes Bishop for TCF/Saber
exec p: Paul Maslansky
w: Lee Frost, Wes Bishop
d: JACK STARRETT
ph: Robert Jessup
m: Leonard Rosenman
ed: Allan Jacobs, John Link
ad: no credit given
cos: Nancy McArdle
sp: Richard Helmer
sound: William Randall, Don Bassman
stunt co-ordinator: Paul Knuckles
titles: Jack Cole
Peter Fonda, Loretta Swit, Warren Oates, Lara Parker, R. G. Armstrong, Wes Bishop, Jack Starrett

Rage see Rabid

Raimi, Sam (1960-)
American actor, writer, producer and director whose first feature film, *The Evil Dead*, was much praised for its low-budget energy and ingenuity, yet was banned on video in Britain for several years after an initial outcry. Often working with producer Robert Tappert and actor Bruce Campbell (with whom he formed Renaissance Motion Pictures), his subsequent work hasn't quite matched his début, but remains of interest for its surface technique. His other credits as a director include *The Quick and the Dead*.
Genre credits:

• Claude Rains as Jack Griffin, the 'Invisible One', in director James Whale's *The Invisible Man*. Though his face was seen for only a few moments, the film made Claude Rains a star.

The Evil Dead (1980 - w/d/co-exec p), *Crimewave* (1985 - co-w/d), *Evil Dead II: Dead by Dawn* (1987 - co-w/d), *Darkman* (1990 - story/co-w/d), *Army of Darkness* (1992 - aka *The Medieval Dead/Evil Dead III: The Medieval Dead* - co-w/d), *The Stand* (1994 - TVM -actor)

Rains, Claude (1889-1967)
Urbane British actor, long in Hollywood, where he shot to stardom as *The Invisible Man*, in which his face is seen but for a few fleeting moments at the end. He made his professional stage début at the age of eleven, went to America for the first time in 1914 and made one film, *Build Thy House*, in Britain in 1920. It would be thirteen years before he made his second. Long at Warner Bros, he was the supporting actor supreme in such films as *The Adventures of Robin Hood*, *Here Comes Mr Jordan*, *King's Row*, *Casablanca*, *Mr Skeffington*, *Notorious*, *The Passionate Friends* and *Lawrence of Arabia*.

Genre credits:
The Invisible Man (1933 - title role), *The Clairvoyant* (1934 - title role), *The Wolf Man* (1941), *The Phantom of the Opera* (1943 - title role)

Rambaldi, Carlo

Italian special-effects technician now working mostly in Hollywood. So far he has won three Oscars for his effects work (all in conjunction with others) for, incredibly, *King Kong* (1976), *Alien* (1979) and *E. T.* (1982).
Genre credits:
Deep Red (1976 - aka *Profundo Rosso/The Hatchet Murders* - sp), *King Kong* (1976 - co-sp), *Alien* (1979 - co-sp), *Nightwing* (1979 - co-sp), *Possession* (1981 - sp), *The Hand* (1981 - sp), *King Kong Lives* (1986 - sp), *Primal Rage* (1988 - co-sp)

Rasputin - The Mad Monk

GB 1966 92m Technicolor Cinemascope
Rasputin insinuates himself into the court of Tsar Nicholas II.

A coloured view of history played chiefly for shocks in the Hammer manner. A little tired, despite a wide-eyed star performance.
p: Anthony Nelson Keys for Hammer/Associated British
w: John Elder (Anthony Hinds)
d: Don Sharp
ph: Michael Reed
m: Don Banks
md: Philip Martell
ed: James Needs, Roy Hyde
ad: Bernard Robinson
cos: Rosemary Burrows
sound: Ken Rawkins
make-up: Roy Ashton
Christopher Lee, Barbara Shelley, Richard Pasco, Francis Matthews, Dinsdale Landen, Renée Asherson, Derek Francis, Joss Ackland, Robert Duncan, John Welsh

Rathbone, Basil (1892-1967)

South African-born character actor (real name Philip St John Basil Rathbone), as adept at villainous roles as heroic ones. He began his acting career in Britain in 1911, but it was interrupted by military service during World War One. He made his film début in Britain in 1921 with *Innocent*, which was followed by *The Fruitful Vine*, *The School for Scandal* and *The Masked Bride*. He then headed for Hollywood, where his first film was *Trouping with Ellen* (1924). A notable villain in *David Copperfield* (as Murdstone), *Captain Blood* (as Levasseur) and, most memorably, *The Adventures of Robin Hood* (as Sir Guy of Gisbourne), he was also the screen's definitive Sherlock Holmes, appearing in the role fourteen times (*The*

Hound of the Baskervilles, *The Adventures of Sherlock Holmes*, *Sherlock Holmes and the Voice of Terror*, *Sherlock Holmes and the Secret Weapon*, *Sherlock Holmes in Washington*, *Sherlock Holmes Faces Death*, *Spider Woman*, *The Scarlet Claw*, *The Pearl of Death*, *The House of Fear*, *The Woman in Green*, *Pursuit to Algiers*, *Terror by Night*, *Dressed to Kill*). The first two of these were produced by Fox, after which Universal took over the series, often imbuing the stories with horror elements. A respected actor throughout his career, Rathbone's other credits include *The Dawn Patrol*, *The Mark of Zorro*, *The Court Jester* and *Pontius Pilate*, as well as two films for Roger Corman.
Genre credits:
Love from a Stranger (1937), *Son of Frankenstein* (1939 - title role), *Tower of London* (1939), *The Hound of the Baskervilles* (1939), *The Mad Doctor* (1941), *The Black Cat* (1941), *The Scarlet Claw* (1944), *Spider Woman* (1944), *The Pearl of Death* (1944), *The House of Fear* (1945), *The Black Sleep* (1956), *The Magic Sword* (1962), *Tales of Terror* (1962), *The Comedy of Terrors* (1963), *Queen of Blood* (1966), *The Ghost in the Invisible Bikini* (1966), *Voyage to a Prehistoric Planet* (1967), *Autopsy of a Ghost* (1967 - aka *Autopsia de un Fantasma*), *Hillbillies in a Haunted House* (1967)

The Rats (1982) see Deadly Eyes

The Rats (1983) see Rats Night of Terror

Rats Night of Terror

It/Fr 1983 80m Telecolor Technovision
In 225 AB (after the bomb!), a new breed of 'primitives' has to defend themselves against a plague of man-eating rats.

Poorly dubbed post-apocalyptic nonsense with just a couple of well-staged attack sequences in its favour.
p: (no producer credit) for Beatrice/Imp
w: Claudio Fragasso, Herve Piccini
story: Bruno Mattei
d: Vincent Dawn, Clyde Anderson
ph: Franco Delli Colli
m: Luigi Ceccarelli
ed: Gilbert Kikoine
ad: Maurizio Mammi, Charles Fimelli
cos: Elda Chinellato
sound: no credit given
Richard Raymond, Janna Ryann, Richard Crost, Alex McBride, Ann Gisel Glass, Tony Lombardo

The Raven *

USA 1935 61m bw
A mad surgeon mutates a convict on the run and tortures his guests in a

Poe-inspired torture chamber.

Hammy but occasionally effective horror melodrama, typical of its period and building to a fairly exciting climax.
p: David Diamond for Universal
w: David Boem
story: Edgar Allan Poe
d: LEW LANDERS (credited as Louis Friedlander)
ph: Charles Stumar
md: Gilbert Kurland
ed: Albert Akst, Maurice Pivar
ad: Albert D'Agostino
cos/sp/sound: no credits given
BELA LUGOSI, Boris Karloff, Samuel S. Hinds, Irene Ware, Lester Matthews, Spencer Charters, Inez Courtnay, Ian Wolfe, Maidel Turner

The Raven *

USA 1963 86m Pathecolor Panavision
A fifteenth-century magician is visited by a talking raven who persuades him into a duel with a fellow sorcerer.

Hammily performed and sluggishly staged oddball horror comic which doesn't quite live up to its reputation, though the duel itself helps to compensate and the cast is interesting. The link with Poe is tenuous to say the least.
p: Roger Corman for AIP/Alta Vista
exec p: James H. Nicholson, Samuel Z. Arkoff
w: Richard Matheson
story: Edgar Allan Poe
d: Roger Corman
ph: Floyd Crosby
m: Les Baxter
ed: Ronald Sinclair
pd/ad: Daniel Haller
cos: Marjorie Corso
sp: Pat Dinga, Butler-Glouner
sound: John Bury
raven trainer: Moe Disesso
Vincent Price, BORIS KARLOFF, Peter Lorre, Hazel Court, Jack Nicholson, Olive Sturgess, Connie Wallace, William Raskin, Aaron Saxon

Raven, Mike (1924-)

British actor, a former disc jockey (Radio Atlanta, Radio Luxembourg, Radio One) and author. In the early seventies he looked set for a career in horror films but never quite made it, so retired to become a sheep farmer. He also played minor parts in such forties films as *On Approval*.
Genre credits:
I, Monster (1970), *Crucible of Terror* (1971), *Lust for a Vampire* (1971 - as Count Karnstein, but dubbed by Valentine Dyall), *Disciple of Death* (1972 - also w/co-p)

Raw Meat see Death Line

• One time DJ and horror star wannabe Mike Raven in *The Crucible of Terror*.

Ray, Fred Olen (1954-)

Prolific American producer and director, a former TV station engineer and make-up man who works at the low-budget end of the exploitation and horror market, much of his output going straight to video. His other credits include *Commando Squad*, *Deep Space*, *Terminal Force*, *Bulletproof* and *Mob Boss*.
Genre credits:
Alien Dead (1979 - aka *It Fell from the Sky* - d), *The Brain Leeches* (1978 - d), *Scalps* (1983 - d), *Biohazard* (1985 - d), *Death Farm* (1985 - d), *The Tomb* (1986 - d), *Phantom Empire* (1987 - d), *Warlords* (1988 - d), *Hollywood Chainsaw Hookers* (1988 - d), *Evil Spawn* (1989 - p), *Alienator* (1989 - d), *Beverly Hills Vamp* (1989 -d), *Bad Girls from Mars* (1991 - d), *Empire of the Dark* (1991 - d), *Evil Toons* (1991 - d), *Inner Sanctum* (1991 - d), *Haunting Fear* (1992 - d), *Wizards of the Demon Sword* (1992 - d), *Witch Academy* (1992 - d), *Demon Cop* (1992 - d), *The Coven* (1993 - d), *Possessed by the Night* (1993 - d), *Dark Universe* (1993 - d), *Biohazard II* (1993 - d), *Step Monster* (1993 - d), *Inner Sanctum II* (1994 - d), *Dark Is the Night* (1994 - d), *Mind Twister* (1994 - d), *Dinosaur Island* (1994 - d), *Sorceress* (1995 - p)

Razorback

Australia 1984 95m Technicolor
Panavision
A razorback boar terrorizes a small Australian township.
    Slick-looking but derivative horror, watchable enough of its kind.
p: Hal McElroy for UAA/Western
w: Everett de Roche
novel: Peter Brennan
d: Russell Mulcahy
ph: Dean Semler
m: Iva Davies
ed: William Anderson

pd: Bryce Wimsley
cos: Helen Hooper
sp: Mary Conny
sound: Tim Lloyd
2nd unit d: Arch Nicholson
2nd unit ph: Billy Grimrod
make-up effects: Bob McCarron
Gregory Harrison, Arkie Whiteley, Chris Heywood, Bill Kerr, David Argue, Judy Morris

Re-Animator *

USA 1985 DeLuxe
A medical student discovers a serum that can re-animate the dead.
    Quirky low-budget update of an old situation with plenty of carnage for gorehounds. *Re-Animator 2* (aka *Bride of the Re-Animator*) followed in 1989.
p: Brian Yuzna for Empire/Re-Animator
w: Dennis Paoli, William J. Norris, Stuart Gordon
story: H. P. Lovecraft
d: Stuart Gordon
ph: Mac Ahlberg
m: Richard Band (doing a variation on Bernard Herrmann's *Psycho* theme)
ed: Lee Percy
ad: Robert A. Burns
cos: Robin Burton
sp: Anthony Doublin, John Nalilin
sound: Don Summer
titles: Robert Dawson
add ph: Robert Frederic Ebinger
Jeffrey Combs (as Herbert West), Bruce Abbott, Barbara Crampton, David Gale, Robert Sampson, Gerry Black, Peter Kent

Re-Animator 2 *

USA 1989 96m DeLuxe
Herbert West continues his experiments, his intention this time being to create a woman from spare body parts.
    Cheeky update of *The Bride of Frankenstein*, a few marks up on its predecessor.
p: Brian Yuzna for Medusa/Wildstreet
w: Woody Keith
story: Woody Keith, Rick Fry, Brian Yuzna
d: Brian Yuzna
ph: Rick Fichter
m: Richard Band
ed: Peter Teschner
pd: Philip J. C. Duffin
cos: Norma Jean Austin, C. T. Nelli
sp: Thomas C. Rainone, David Allen, Anthonou Doublin
sound: Mary Jo Devenney
titles: David McCutchen
make-up effects: Screaming Mad George
Jeffrey Combs, Bruce Abbott, Claude Earl Jones, Fabiana Volenio, Davis Gale, Kathleen Kinmont, Mel Stewart, Irene Forrest, Michael Strassner

Reed, Michael (1929-)

British cinematographer with several large-scale productions to his credit, including *On Her Majesty's Secret Service*, *The Mackenzie Break*, *Shout at the Devil* and *Wild Geese II*.
Genre credits:
The Gorgon (1964), *Dracula - Prince of Darkness* (1966), *Rasputin -The Mad Monk* (1966), *Slave Girls* (1968 - aka *Prehistoric Women*)

Reed, Oliver (1938-)

British actor, nephew of director Sir Carol Reed (for whom he played Bill Sikes in the film version of *Oliver!*). Began his film career as an extra, graduating to bit parts in such films as *The League of Gentlemen*, *The Bulldog Breed* and *The Rebel*. A brief role as a nightclub rowdy in Hammer's *The Two Faces of Dr Jekyll* led to his being cast as the wolfman in the same studio's *Curse of the Werewolf*. Several more Hammer projects followed, including a handful of swashbucklers (*The Pirates of Blood River*, *The Scarlet Blade*, etc.), after which he found international fame in such productions as *The Jokers*, *Hannibal Brooks*, *Women in Love* and *The Three Musketeers*, though he has appeared in other genre films since. Narrated the Hammer compilation series *The World of Hammer* in 1990.
Genre credits:
The Two Faces of Dr Jekyll (1960 - aka *House of Fright/Jekyll's Inferno*), *The Curse of the Werewolf* (1961), *Captain Clegg* (1962 - aka *Night Creatures*), *The Damned* (1962 - aka *These Are the Damned*), *Paranoiac* (1963), *The Shuttered Room* (1967), *The Devils* (1970), *Burnt Offerings* (1976), *The Brood* (1979), *Dr Heckyl and Mr Hype* (1980), *Venom* (1981), *Spasms* (1983), *The Pit and the Pendulum* (1990), *The House of Usher* (1990), *The Mummy Lives* (1992)

Reeve, Spencer

British editor whose genre work has been solely for Hammer, often under supervising editor James Needs.
Genre credits:
Frankenstein Created Woman (1966), *The Devil Rides Out* (1967 - aka *The Devil's Bride*), *Dracula Has Risen from the Grave* (1968), *Lust for a Vampire* (1970), *Twins of Evil* (1971)

Reeves, Michael (1944-1969)

British writer and director whose burgeoning career was sadly cut short after his greatest success, *Witchfinder General*. He was an assistant in various capacities before co-writing and co-directing his first film, *Castle of the Living Dead* (aka *Il Castello dei Morti Vivi*) in Italy at the age

• A moment from *Revenge of the Blood Beast*, director Michael Reeves' first film. Sadly, his career was abruptly terminated.

of twenty - he handled the second unit for the film's credited director (listed as either Herbert Wise or Luciano Ricci, depending on which cut you see, both being pseudonyms for co-writer/director Warren Kiefer). Reeves' work impressed the film's executive producer, Paul Maslansky, so much that he was given his own film to direct. Originally to have been titled *Vardella*, this became *Revenge of the Blood Beast*, and was made for just £13,000, a low budget even by 1965 standards! Reeves had just begun work on his fifth film, *The Oblong Box* (which was completed by Gordon Hessler), when he died from a drugs overdose.
Genre credits:
Castle of the Living Dead (1964 - aka *Il Castello dei Morti Vivi* -co-w/2nd unit d [credited as 1st assistant director]), *Revenge of the Blood Beast* (1965 - aka *Sister of Satan/The She-Beast/La Sorella di Satana* - w/d [w as Michael Byron]), *The Sorcerers* (1967 - co-w/d), *Witchfinder General* (1968 - aka *The Conqueror Worm* - co-w/d), *The Oblong Box* (1969 - part d, uncredited)

Reid, Beryl (1920-)
British character actress and comedienne with much stage experience. Remembered for both the stage and the film versions of *The Killing of Sister George*, her other credits include *The Belles of St Trinian's*, *Star*, *Entertaining Mr Sloane* and *No Sex Please, We're British*.
Genre credits:
The Beast in the Cellar (1971), *Dr Phibes Rises Again* (1972), *Psychomania* (1972), *The Doctor and the Devils* (1985)

The Reincarnation of Peter Proud *
USA 1974 105m Technicolor
A young man has dreams about a previous life in which he was murdered by his wife. He then learns that she is still alive.
   Intriguing supernatural drama, very competently done.
p: Frank P. Rosenberg for Avco Embassy/Bing Crosby Productions
w: Max Ehrlich from his novel
d: J. Lee-Thompson
ph: Victor J. Kemper
m: Jerry Goldsmith
ed: Michael Anderson
ad: Jack Martin Smith
Michael Sarrazin, Jennifer O'Neill, Margot Kidder, Cornelia Sharpe, Paul Hecht

Reitman, Ivan (1946-)
Canadian director, composer and producer with a penchant for all kinds of comedy, from the supernatural antics of the *Ghostbusters* films to such Arnold Schwarzenegger vehicles as *Twins*, *Kindergarten Cop* and *Junior*. He began his career directing shorts, his first feature being *Columbus of Sex* (aka *My Secret Life*) in 1970, which he produced and scored. He then produced for fellow countrymen David Cronenberg and William Fruet before hitting the big time as the co-producer of *National Lampoon's Animal House* in 1978. His other credits include *Meatballs*, *Stripes*, *Legal Eagles* and *Dave*.
Genre credits:
Cannibal Girls (1972 - d), *Shivers* (1974 - aka *The Parasite Murders/They Came from Within* - p), *Death Weekend* (1976 - aka *The House by the Lake* - p), *Rabid* (1976 - aka *Rage* - co-exec p/m), *Ghostbusters* (1984 - p/d), *Ghostbusters II* (1989 - p/d)

Reizenstein, Franz (1911-1968)
German composer/concert pianist whose score for Hammer's *The Mummy* is among the studio's most memorable (parts of it were even re-used for *Curse of the Mummy's Tomb*).
Genre credits:
The Mummy (1959), *Circus of Horrors* (1960)

Repossessed
USA 1990 85m CFIcolor
A young housewife finds herself possessed by the devil.
   Over-the-top spoof of *The Exorcist* in the *Airplane!* manner. Some of the gags work, but it very quickly becomes embarrassing and is seventeen years too late anyway.
p: Steve Wizan, Jean Higgins for Carolco
w/d: Bob Logan
ph: Michael D. Margulies
m: Charles Fox
ed: Jeff Freeman
pd: Shay Austin
cos: Timothy D'Arcy
sp: Reel EFX
sound: Clancy T. Troutman
make-up effects: Steve Laporte
Linda Blair, Leslie Nielsen, Ned Beatty, Anthony Starke, Thom J. Sharp, Lana Schwab, Benj Thall, Dove Dellos, Willie Garson

The Reptile *
GB 1966 90m Technicolor
The daughter of a Cornish doctor turns into a murderous reptile.
   The usual veiled warnings and something nasty up at the manor house, quite neatly done in this case.
p: Anthony Nelson Keys for Hammer
w: John Elder (Anthony Hinds)
d: JOHN GILLING
ph: Arthur Grant
m: Don Banks
md: Philip Martell

ed: James Needs, Roy Hyde
ad: Bernard Robinson
cos: Rosemary Burrows
sp: Les Bowie
make-up: Roy Ashton
sound: William Bulkles
Noel Willman, Ray Barrett, Jennifer
Daniel, Jacqueline Pearce, Michael
Ripper, John Laurie, Marne Maitland,
George Woodbridge

Republic

American studio, formed in 1935 by
Herbert J. Yates and known for producing countless serials and second-feature
westerns in the thirties, forties and
fifties. The studio's dabblings with mainstream horror were minimal, however,
and included such undistinguished
efforts as *The Vampire's Ghost* (1945) and
The Catman of Paris (1946).

Repulsion **

GB 1965 105m bw
Left to her own devices whilst her sister
is away on holiday, a Belgian beautician
with a pathological fear of men locks
herself into her flat and retreats into a
nightmare world of her own making.
  Extremely well-handled
psycho-melodrama with moments of
genuine shock. An unsettling
experience, it established its director
firmly on the international scene.
p: Gene Gutowski for Compton-Tekli
w: Gerard Brach, Roman Polanski,
David Stone
d: ROMAN POLANSKI
ph: GILBERT TAYLOR
m: Chico Hamilton
ed: Alastair McIntyre
ad: Seamus Flannery
sound: Leslie Hammond, Stephen Dalby,
Gerry Humphreys
titles: Maurice Binder
CATHERINE DENEUVE, Ian Hendry,
Yvonne Furneaux, John Fraser, Patrick
Wymark, James Villiers, Helen Fraser,
Renée Houston

Retribution

USA 1988 107m Fujicolor Dolby
After a failed suicide attempt, an artist
finds himself possessed by the evil spirit
of a dead killer.
  Straightforward variation on a by
now hackneyed theme. A few minor
pretensions to style, though not enough
to make it memorable.
p: Guy Maga for Unicorn/Renegade
exec p: Scott Lavin, Brian Christian
w: Guy Magar, Lee Wasserman
d/ed: Guy Magar
ph: Gary Thieltges
m: Alan Howarth
pd: Robb Wilson King

cos: Hilary Wright
sound: Peter Bentley, Mark Sheret
make-up effects: Kevin Yagher
stunt co-ordinator: Bob Yerkes
Dennis Lipscomb, Leslie Wing, Pamela
Dunlap, Suzanne Snyder, George
Murdock, Susan Peretz

The Return of Count Yorga *

USA 1971 97m Movielab
Count Yorga vampirizes the staff of an
orphanage.
  Ghoulish follow-up to *Count Yorga -
Vampire*, with a few good frissons to
counterbalance the longueurs.
p: Michael Macready for
AIP/Peppertree
w: Robert Kelljan, Yvonne Wilder
d: Robert Kelljan
ph: Bill Butler
m: Bill Marx
ed: Fabien Tordjimann, Laurette Odney
ad: Vince Cresceman
cos: Jeannie Anderson
sp: Roger George
sound: Rod Sutton
ROBERT QUARRY, Mariette Hartley,
Roger Perry, Yvonne Wilder, Tom Toner,
Rudy del Uca

The Return of Dr X *

USA 1939 62m bw
A reporter tracks down a vampire-like
killer in New York.
  Mild comedy thriller, economically
but not especially imaginatively made.
Nothing to do with *Dr X*, though of
passing interest for containing Bogart's
only horror role.
p: Bryan Foy for Warner
w: Lee Katz
novel: William J. Makin
d: Vincent Sherman
ph: Sid Hickox
m: Bernard Kaun
ed: Thomas Pratt
ad: Esdras Hartley
Humphrey Bogart, Rosemary Lane,
Wayne Morris, Dennis Morgan, John
Litel, Lya Lys, Huntz Hall, Creighton
Hale

The Return of Dracula

USA 1958 77m bw
A European vampire murders a painter
and goes to America in his stead.
  Mild low-budgeter. A few interesting
touches along the way, though the
emphasis on small-town life soon
becomes tedious.
p: Jules V. Levy, Arthur Gardner for
UA/Gramercy
w: Pat Fielder
d: Paul Landres
ph: Jack Mckenzie
m: Gerald Fried

ed: Sherman Rose
ad: James Vance
sound: Jack Goodrich, Frank Morgan
Francis Lederer, Norman Eberhardt,
Ray Stricklyn, Jimmie Baird, John
Wengraf

Return of the Living Dead

USA 1985 90m DeLuxe
A dangerous gas with the ability to
reanimate the dead is accidentally
allowed to escape.
  Trashy shlocker which caters to the
most jaded end of the teenage market,
though it's regarded as a cult item in
some quarters.
p: Tom Fox, Graham Henderson for
Orion/Tartan/Fox Films
w/d: Dan O'Bannon
ph: Jules Brenner
m: Matt Clifford
ed: Robert Gordon
pd: William Stout
make-up effects: Bill Munns, Tony
Gardner
Clu Gulager, James Karen, Don Calfa,
Thom Matthews, Beverly Randolph,
Jewell Shepard, Brian Peck, John
Philbin, Jonathan Terry, Cathleen
Cordell

Return of the Living Dead Part II

USA 1987 89m Photolab
Teenagers inadvertently release a
zombie from its holding canister.
  More from the same bowl, though
even less effective the second time
round. For staunch genre addicts only.
p: Tom Fox for Lorimar/Greenfox
w/d: Ken Widerhorn
ph: Robert Elswit
m: J. Peter Robinson, Vladimir
Horunzhy
ed: Charles Bornstein
pd: Dale Allan Pelton
sp: Kenny Myers
James Karen, Thom Matthews, Dana
Ashbrook, Michael Kenworthy, Marsha
Dietlein, Suzanne Snyder, Philip Bruns

Return of the Living Dead Part III

USA 1993 92m Foto-Kem Dolby
A teenager discovers that his father is
trying to turn zombies into weapons for
the military and exposes his girlfriend,
killed in a motorcycle accident, to the
gas used in the process.
  Gory addition to the series. An
improvement on its predecessors, but
with rather too many longueurs
between the effects.
p: Brian Yuzna, Gary Schmoeller for
Trimark/Ozla/Bandai Visual
w: John Penney

d: Brian Yuzna
ph: Gerry Lively
m: Barry Goldberg
ed: Christopher Roth
pd: Anthony Tremblay
cos: Jananicole Mincer
make-up effects: Steve Johnson, Tim Ralston, Kevin Brennan, Christopher Nelson, Wayne Toth
sound: Geoffrey Lucas Patterson
J. Trevor Edmond, Sarah Douglas, Kent McCord, Mindy Clarke, James T. Callahan, Mike Moroff, Sal Lopez, Basil Wallace

The Return of the Vampire ∗

USA 1943 69m bw
A vampire count, staked in a London graveyard, is brought back to life after a bomb attack during the Blitz.

Minor horror comic, not without its moments of style.
p: Sam White for Columbia
w: Griffin Jay
story: Kurt Neumann
d: Lew Landers
ph: John Stumar, L. J. O'Connell
m: Mario Tedesco
md: Morris Stoloff
ed: Paul Borofsky
ad: Lionel Banks
sp: Aaron Nadley
Bela Lugosi, Nina Foch, Frieda Inescort, Miles Mander, Matt Willis (as a were-wolf), Roland Verno, Ottola Nesmith

Return to Glennescaul ∗∗

Eire 1951 23m bw
On his way home, Orson Welles gives a man a lift and is told a ghost story.

Neat short story with effective touches along the way. Made during a break in the filming of Welles' Othello.
p: Micheal MacLiammoir for Dublin Gate Theatre
w/d: HILTON EDWARDS
ph: Georg Fleischmann
m: Hans Gunther Stumpf
ed: Joseph Sterling
ad: Tony Inglis
cos: Paul Smith
sound: Digby Jones
Orson Welles, Michael Lawrence, Helen Hughes, Sheila Richards, John Dunne, Isobel Causer, Ann Clery

The Revenge of Billy the Kid

GB 1991 87m Eastmancolor
A randy farmer impregnates his goat and the resultant offspring goes on the rampage.

Dismal comedy horror which relies almost totally for its laughs on flatulence, defecation and the sexual act. The sort of crap that could finish off the cinema for good.

p: Tim Dennison, Richard Lake for Powerhouse/Montage
exec p: Tim Dennison, Jim Groom
w: Tim Dennison, Jim Groom, Richard Matthews
d: Jim Groom
ph: David Read
m: Tony Flynn
ed: James Groom
ad: Jon Wright
sound: Peter Kyle, Trevor Barber
make-up effects: Neill Gorton, Steven M. Painter
stunt co-ordinator: Derek Ware
Michael Balfour, Samantha Perkins, Jackie D. Broad, Bryan Heeley, Trevor Peake, Michael Ripper, Norman Mitchell, Dean Williamson

The Revenge of Frankenstein ∗

GB 1958 89m Technicolor
The good baron continues his experiments within the confines of a hospital - with the expected results.

Rather tame follow-up to The Curse of Frankenstein, with a few unwise attempts at humour and a dull monster.
p: Anthony Hinds for Hammer/Columbia
exec p: Michael Carreras
w: Jimmy Sangster, Hurford Janes
d: Terence Fisher
ph: Jack Asher
m: Leonard Salzedo
ed: James Needs, Alfred Cox
pd: BERNARD ROBINSON
cos: Rosemary Burrows
sound: Jock May
make-up: Phil Leakey
associate p: Anthony Nelson Keys
PETER CUSHING, Michael Gwynne, Francis Matthews, Eunice Gayson, Oscar Quitak, John Welsh, Lionel Jeffries, Richard Wordsworth, Charles Lloyd Pack, Arnold Diamond, Michael Ripper, John Stuart

Revenge of the Creature

USA 1955 85m bw 3D
The Gill-Man is captured and put on show in a Florida aquarium, but he escapes and causes the expected havoc.

Run-down sequel to The Creature from the Black Lagoon. Strictly for drive-ins.
p: William Alland for Universal
w: Martin Berkeley
d: Jack Arnold
ph: Charles S. Welbourne
md: Joseph Gershenson
ed: Paul Weatherwax
ad: Alexander Golitzen, Alfred Sweeney
cos: Jay A. Morley Jr
sound: Leslie I. Carey, Jack Bolger
make-up: Bud Westmore
John Agar, Lori Nelson, John Bromfield, Robert B. Williams, Nestor Pavia, Ricou

Browning (as the Creature), Clint Eastwood

Revenge of the Dead see Night of the Ghouls

The Rhode Island Murders see The Demon Murder Case

Richardson, John (1934-)

Handsome British leading man on the international scene, with much work in Europe. Perhaps best remembered as Raquel Welch's love interest in One Million Years BC. Made his movie début in 1952 in Ivanhoe. His other credits include Bachelor of Hearts, The Chastity Belt, On a Clear Day You Can See Forever, Duck in Orange Sauce and Cosmos: War of the Planets.
Genre credits:
Black Sunday (1961 - aka Mask of the Demon/Revenge of the Vampire/Maschera del Demonio), She (1965), One Million Years BC (1966), The Vengeance of She (1968), Frankenstein '80 (1973 - aka Frankenstein Mosaic), Torso (1974), Eyeball (1974 - aka The Devil's Eye/Red Cat in a Glass Maze/Gatto Rossi in un Labirinto)

Ripper, Michael (1913-)

British character actor who began his career in rep in 1924. Broke into films in 1935 with Twice Banned, which he followed with countless minor roles in the likes of Prison Breaker, The Heirloom Mystery and If I Were Boss, often as a crook, cabby or comic relief. Best known for his brief appearances in seemingly all of the Hammer horrors,

• Michael Ripper, one of Hammer's busiest character actors, here seen in a pose from Curse of the Werewolf.

either as a coachman or as bait for their various monsters. Other films include *The Belles of St Trinian's*, *Blue Murder at St Trinian's*, *Geordie*, *Richard III*, *Sink the Bismarck* and *No Sex Please, We're British*.
Genre credits:
X - The Unknown (1956), *Quatermass 2* (1957 - aka *Enemy from Space*), *The Revenge of Frankenstein* (1958), *The Man Who Could Cheat Death* (1959), *The Ugly Duckling* (1959), *The Mummy* (1959), *The Brides of Dracula* (1960), *The Curse of the Werewolf* (1960), *Captain Clegg* (1962 - aka *Night Creatures*), *The Phantom of the Opera* (1962), *The Curse of the Mummy's Tomb* (1964), *Plague of the Zombies* (1966), *The Reptile* (1966), *The Deadly Bees* (1966), *Torture Garden* (1967), *The Mummy's Shroud* (1967), *The Lost Continent* (1968), *Dracula Has Risen from the Grave* (1968), *Mumsy, Nanny, Sonny and Girly* (1969 - aka *Girly*), *Taste the Blood of Dracula* (1970), *Scars of Dracula* (1970), *The Creeping Flesh* (1972), *Legend of the Werewolf* (1974), *The Revenge of Billy the Kid* (1992)

Roadgames *
Australia 1981 98m Technicolor Panavision
A truck driver making his way across Australia tracks down a vicious sex killer.
    Quirky little Hitchcock pastiche with plenty of inventive detail. *Rear Window* on wheels.
p: Richard Franklin, Barbi Taylor for Essaness/Australian Film Corporation/Victorian Film Commission/Western Australian Film Council/GUO Film Distributors
exec p: Bernard Schwartz
w: Everett de Roche
story: Everett de Roche, Richard Franklin
d: RICHARD FRANKLIN
ph: Vincent Monton
m: Brian May
ed: Edward McQueen-Mason
ad: Jon Dowding
cos: Aphrodite Kondos
sound: Paul Clark
stunt co-ordinator: Grant Page
STACY KEACH, Jamie Lee Curtis (as Hitch), Marion Edward, Bill Stacey, Grant Page, Thaddeus Smith, Robert Thompson

Robertson, Harry see Robinson, Harry

Robinson, Andrew
American actor with a penchant for off-the-wall villains, most notably in *Dirty Harry*, in which he played the sniper Scorpio, the punk blown away by Clint

Eastwood's Dirty Harry Callahan. His other credits include *Charley Varrick*, *Cobra* and *Prime Target*.
Genre credits:
Hellraiser (1987), *Child's Play 3* (1991), *Pumpkinhead II* (1993), *The Puppetmasters* (1994)

Robinson, Bernard (1912-1970)
Distinguished British art director and production designer, noted for his contributions to countless Hammer horrors, to which he brought both visual flair and a sense of Victorian clutter. Educated at the Liverpool School of Art, he began his film career as a draughtsman at Warner's Teddington studios, but quickly graduated to art director for British Lion, which he joined in 1939. During the war he became a camouflage and decoy expert, after which he returned to films with the likes of *The Shop at Sly Corner*, *Carve Her Name with Pride* and *Reach for the Sky*. He joined Hammer in 1956, staying with them until 1969.
Genre credits:
Old Mother Riley Meets the Vampire (1952 - aka *My Son the Vampire*), *The Curse of Frankenstein* (1956), *X - The Unknown* (1956), *Quatermass 2* (1957 - aka *Enemy from Space*), *The Abominable Snowman* (1957 - aka *The Abominable Snowman of the Himalayas*), *Dracula* (1958 - aka *Horror of Dracula*), *The Revenge of Frankenstein* (1958), *The Mummy* (1959), *The Ugly Duckling* (1959), *The Man Who Could Cheat Death* (1959), *The Stranglers of Bombay* (1960), *The Two Faces of Dr Jekyll* (1960 - aka *House of Fright*/*Jekyll's Inferno*), *Never Take Sweets from a Stranger* (1960), *The Brides of Dracula* (1960), *The Shadow of the Cat* (1961), *Taste of Fear* (1961 - aka *Scream of Fear*), *Terror of the Tongs* (1961), *The Curse of the Werewolf* (1961), *The Phantom of the Opera* (1962), *The Old Dark House* (1962), *Captain Clegg* (1962 - aka *Night Creatures*), *The Damned* (1963 - aka *These Are the Damned*), *Paranoiac* (1963), *Kiss of the Vampire* (1964 - aka *Kiss of Evil*), *Nightmare* (1964), *The Curse of the Mummy's Tomb* (1964), *Dracula - Prince of Darkness* (1966), *Rasputin - The Mad Monk* (1966), *Plague of the Zombies* (1966), *The Reptile* (1966), *The Witches* (1966 - aka *The Devil's Own*), *Frankenstein Created Woman* (1967), *The Mummy's Shroud* (1967), *Quatermass and the Pit* (1967 - aka *Five Million Years to Earth*), *The Devil Rides Out* (1968 - aka *The Devil's Bride*), *Dracula Has Risen from the Grave* (1968), *Frankenstein Must Be Destroyed* (1969)

Robinson, George (1895-1958)
American cinematographer who began

his career as a camera assistant in the early twenties, rising quickly up the ladder to become a cinematographer soon after. Long with Universal, he photographed many of their key horror films, which were all the more atmospheric for his efforts. His other credits include *The Mystery of Edwin Drood*, *Son of Monte Cristo* and *The Naughty Nineties*.
Genre credits:
Dracula (1930 - Spanish language version only), *The Invisible Ray* (1936), *Dracula's Daughter* (1936), *Son of Frankenstein* (1939), *Tower of London* (1939), *Son of Dracula* (1943), *Frankenstein Meets the Wolf Man* (1943), *Captive Wild Woman* (1943), *The Scarlet Claw* (1944), *House of Frankenstein* (1944), *House of Dracula* (1945), *The Cat Creeps* (1946), *The Creeper* (1948), *Abbott and Costello Meet the Invisible Man* (1950), *Abbott and Costello Meet Dr Jekyll and Mr Hyde* (1953), *Abbott and Costello Meet the Mummy* (1955), *Francis in the Haunted House* (1956)

Robinson, Harry
Scottish musician, former pop arranger/composer/producer, also known as Harry Robertson, under which name he produced the sword and sorcery adventure *Hawk the Slayer* in 1980. Television work includes Hammer's *Journey to the Unknown*.
Genre credits:
The Oblong Box (1969), *The Vampire Lovers* (1970), *Lust for a Vampire* (1971), *Countess Dracula* (1971), *Twins of Evil* (1971), *Fright* (1971), *Demons of the Mind* (1972), *Legend of the Werewolf* (1974), *The Ghoul* (1975), *Hawk the Slayer* (1980 - p/m)

Robson, Mark (1913-1978)
Canadian director and, later, producer, a former editor who, after experience as a prop boy at Fox, began working at RKO in 1935. There he gradually turned to editing, working (uncredited) with Robert Wise on the cutting of *Citizen Kane* and (credited) *The Magnificent Ambersons* before receiving his first solo credit for *Journey Into Fear* in 1942. The same year he began working with producer Val Lewton, editing several of his horror films before going on to direct four himself, as well as Lewton's social drama *Youth Runs Wild*. A director of variable quality, his work ranged from solid (*Champion*, *Peyton Place*, *The Prize*, *Von Ryan's Express*) to stolid (*Valley of the Dolls*, *Earthquake*, *Avalanche Express*).
Genre credits:
The Cat People (1942 - ed), *I Walked with a Zombie* (1943 - ed), *The Leopard Man* (1943 - ed), *The Seventh Victim* (1943 -

SOMETHING WICKED THIS WAY COMES. The monster is let out of its box in director George Romero's horror comedy *Creepshow*.

d), *The Ghost Ship* (1943 - d), *Isle of the Dead* (1945 - d), *Bedlam* (1946 - d), *Daddy's Gone A-Hunting* (1969 - p/d)

The Rocky Horror Picture Show *
GB 1975 101m Eastmancolor
A young couple take refuge in a creepy castle during a thunderstorm, only to discover that their host is a mad transvestite scientist on the verge of creating life.

High-camp rock musical horror spoof whose legion of followers has turned it into *the* cult phenomenon of the late-night circuit. Mildly amusing for those in the mood, though most will probably wonder what all the fuss is about. It's certainly energetically performed.
p: Michael White for TCF
exec p: Lou Adler
w: Richard O'Brien, Jim Sharman
d: Jim Sharman
ph: Peter Suschitsky
songs: Richard O'Brien
m/md: Richard Hartley
ed: Graeme Clifford
ad: Brian Thomson, Terry Ackland-Snow
cos: Sue Blane
sp: Wally Veevers, Colin Chilvers
sound: Keith Grant, Ron Barron, Bill Rowe
ch: David Toguri
make-up: Peter Robb-King
TIM CURRY (as Frank N. Furter), Susan Sarandon (as Janet), Barry Bostwick (as Brad), Richard O'Brien (as Riff Raff), Jonathan Adams, Nell Campbell, Meatloaf, Peter Hinwood, Patricia Quinn, CHARLES GRAY (teaching The Timewarp), Christopher Biggins, Koo Stark, John Marquand, Mark Johnson

Roemheld, Heinz (1901-1985)
German-born composer and music director, long in Hollywood, especially at Universal and Warner Bros. He won an Oscar (with Ray Heindorf) for his work on the George M. Cohan musical *Yankee Doodle Dandy* in 1942.
Genre credits:
The Black Cat (1934 - aka *House of Doom* - md), *Dracula's Daughter* (1936 - m), *The Monster That Challenged the World* (1957 - m)

Rollin, Jean (1938-)
French director with a tendency towards sex-filled vampire films, some of which make little sense but contain passing moments of arresting imagery. After experience as a film extra, he began directing in 1958 with the short *Les Amours Jaunes* (aka *The Yellow Loves*). Work as a television editor and an assis-

tant director followed, after which he made a handful of shorts and documentaries (*Ciel de Cuivre*, *Vivre en Espagne*, *Les Pays Loins*, etc.) before turning to features in 1968 with *Le Viol du Vampire*. Using the pseudonym Michael Gentil, he also directed *Jeunes Filles Impudiques*, *Tout le Monde Il y en a Deux*, *Vibrations Sexuelles* and *Petites Pensionnaires Impudiques*.
Genre credits:
Le Viol du Vampire (1968), *The Naked Vampire* (1969 - aka *The Nude Vampire/La Vampire Nue*), *Terror of the Vampires* (1970 - aka *Sex and the Vampire/Les Frissons des Vampires*), *Requiem for a Vampire* (1971 - aka *Virgins and Vampires/Crazed Virgins/Requiem Pour Une Vampire*), *The Crystal Rose* (1973 - aka *La Rose de Fer/La Nuit du Cimetière*), *Demoniacs* (1974 - aka *Les Demoniaques*), *Once Upon a Virgin* (1975 - aka *Phantasmes/Phantasmes Pornigraphiques*), *Lips of Blood* (1976 - aka *Lèvres de Sang*), *Pesticide* (1978 - aka *Les Raisins de la Mort*), *Fascination* (1979), *La Nuit Traquée* (1980 -aka *Filles Traquées*), *Zombie Lake* (1980 - aka *Lake of the Living Dead/El Lago de Los Muertos Vivientes* [as J. A. Laser]), *Les Echappées* (1981 - aka *Les Paumées du Petit Matin/Fugue Minuere/Les Meutrières/A Couteaux Tirés*), *The Living Dead Girl* (1980 - aka *La Morte Vivante*), *Killing Car* (1993 - aka *La Femme Dangereuse*), *Les Deux Orphelines Vampires* (1995)

Romain, Yvonne (1938-)
Sultry-looking British actress (real name Yvonne Warren) who added sex appeal to a number of early-sixties horrors. Her other credits include *The Bay and the Battleship*, *The Brigand of Kandahar*, *The Last of Sheila* (as Sheila). She is married to composer/lyricist Leslie Bricusse.
Genre credits:
Corridors of Blood (1958), *Chamber of Horrors* (1960), *Curse of the Werewolf* (1961), *The Devil Doll* (1963)

Romero, George (1940-)
American writer, producer and director with a penchant for gory horror films, particularly those involving zombies. Studied design and drama, then began his career making television commercials and industrial films, which he wrote, directed, photographed and edited. His first film, *Night of the Living Dead* (1968), was and is a genre milestone and was followed by two sequels: *Dawn of the Dead* and *Day of the Dead*. His occasional non-genre films, such as *Knightriders* and *The Affair* (aka *There's Always Vanilla*), have generally been met

• Director George Romero at the time of *Dawn of the Dead*, the sequel to his 1968 classic *Night of the Living Dead*, after which zombie flicks were never quite the same.

with indifference. In 1990 he co-directed *Two Evil Eyes* (taking the episode titled *The Truth About the Valdemar Case*) with Dario Argento, who had worked on the European cut of *Dawn of the Dead*.
Genre credits:
Night of the Living Dead (1968 - d/ph/ed), *Season of the Witch* (1971 - aka *Hungry Wives/Jack's Wife* - w/d/ph/ed), *The Crazies* (1973 - aka *Code Name: Trixie* - w/d/ed), *Martin* (1977 - w/d/ed), *Dawn of the Dead* (1978 - aka *Zombies* - w/d/ed), *Creepshow* (1982 - d/co-ed), *Day of the Dead* (1985 - w/d), *Creepshow 2* (1987 - w), *Monkey Shines* (1988 - w/d), *Two Evil Eyes* (1990 - aka *Due Occhi Diabolici* - co-d), *Tales from the Darkside: The Movie* (1990 -co-w), *Night of the Living Dead* (1990 - remake - w/co-exec p), *The Dark Half* (1991 - w/d/co-exec p), *Unholy Fire* (1994 - d)

Ronay, Edina
Sultry-looking French actress, the daughter of food critic Egon Ronay. She popped up in a handful of sixties movies, including *Carry On, Cowboy*, and is now a respected clothes designer.
Genre credits:
The Black Torment (1965), *A Study in Terror* (1965), *Prehistoric Women* (1967 - aka *Slave Girls*)

Rosenberg, Max J.
American producer who, with his partner, writer and producer Milton Subotsky, founded Amicus Films in

• Director George Romero and friends on the set of *Day of the Dead*, the third entry in his zombie trilogy.

Britain, giving Hammer a run for their money from the mid-sixties to the early seventies. They began a trend for compendium horrors with the *Dead of Night*-style *Dr Terror's House of Horrors* in 1965 and followed it with several other compendiums and shockers, many of them directed by either Freddie Francis or Roy Ward Baker. Rosenberg's other credits include *Dr Who and the Daleks*, *Daleks Invasion Earth: 2150 AD*, *The Terrornauts*, *They Came from Beyond Space* and *The Mind of Mr Soames*, all co-produced with Subotsky.
Genre credits:
Dr Terror's House of Horrors (1965 - co-p), *The Deadly Bees* (1965 - co-p), *The Psychopath* (1965 - co-p), *The Skull* (1965 - co-p), *Torture Garden* (1967 - co-p), *They Came from Beyond Space* (1967 - co-p), *Scream and Scream Again* (1970 - co-p), *The House That Dripped Blood* (1970 - co-p), *I, Monster* (1970 - co-p), *Asylum* (1972 - co-p), *And Now the Screaming Starts* (1973 - co-p), *Vault of Horror* (1973 - co-p), *Madhouse* (1974 - co-p), *The Beast Must Die* (1974 - aka *Black Werewolf* - co-p), *The Land That Time Forgot* (1974 -co-p)

Rosemary's Baby **
USA 1968 137m Technicolor
The young wife of an ambitious actor is impregnated by the Devil after moving into an apartment building with a history of diabolism.
Persuasively understated horror melodrama with excellent production and performances. A modern genre classic.
p: William Castle for Paramount
w/d: ROMAN POLANSKI
novel: IRA LEVIN
ph: WILLIAM A. FRAKER
m: Christopher Komeda
ed: Sam O'Steen, Bob Wyman
pd: Richard Sylbert
cos: Anthea Sylbert
sp: Farciot Edouart
sound: Harold Lewis
MIA FARROW, JOHN CASSAVETES, RUTH GORDON (AA), SIDNEY BLACKMER, Maurice Evans, Ralph Bellamy, Elisha Cook Jr, Emmaline Henry, Charles Grodin, Patsy Kelly, William Castle

Rubinstein, Zelda
Diminutive, squeaky-voiced American character actress, memorable as the psychic Tangina in *Poltergeist* and its two inferior sequels.
Genre credits:
Poltergeist (1982), *Poltergeist II: The Other Side* (1986), *Anguish* (1987), *Poltergeist III* (1988)

Russell, Chuck (Charles)
American writer and director of slick-looking fantasy and horror pictures, the most successful of which have been the Jim Carrey comedy *The Mask* and the Arnold Schwarzenegger action-thriller *Eraser*.
Genre credits:
Dreamscape (1984 - co-w), *A Nightmare on Elm Street Part 3: The Dream Warriors* (1987 - co-w/d), *The Blob* (1988 - co-w/d)

Russell, Elizabeth (1916 -)
American actress who appeared in a handful of producer Val Lewton's horror films in the forties, most memorably in *Cat People* and its sequel. Her other credits include *Hitler's Madmen*, *Girl of the Ozarks* and *Youth Runs Wild*.
Genre credits:
Cat People (1942), *The Corpse Vanishes* (1942), *The Seventh Victim* (1943), *Curse of the Cat People* (1944), *Weird Woman* (1944), *Bedlam* (1946)

S

Salem's Lot *

USA 1979 2x96m Technicolor TVM
A plague of vampires infects a small
New England town and a writer and his
young friend set out to destroy them.

Fairly slick, often quite frightening
adaptation of the Stephen King novel.
Riveting stuff, despite the length,
though the condensed theatrical version,
Salem's Lot: The Movie, running at 112m,
is much too rushed and does the plot no
favours at all. *Return to Salem's Lot*
followed in 1989.
p: Richard Kobritz for
Warner/Serendipity
exec p: Stirling Silliphant
w: Paul Monash
novel: Stephen King
d: TOBE HOPPER
ph: Jules Brenner
m: Harry Suckman
ed: Carol Sax, Tom Pryor
pd: Mort Rabinowitz
cos: Phyllis Carr, Barry Kellog
sp: Frank Torro
sound: Richard Raguse
make-up up: Jack Young
titles: Gene Krall
David Soul, JAMES MASON, Lance
Kerwin, Bonnie Bedelia, Lew Ayres,
Kenneth McMillan, Julie Cobb, Elisha
Cook Jr, George Dzunda, Ed Flanders,
Clarissa Kaye, Geoffrey Lewis

Salter, Hans J. (1896-1994)

Prolific German-born composer and
music director, in Hollywood from
1938, where he worked on the
Universal comedy *The Rage of Paris*. He
trained at Vienna's Academy of Music,
after which he became the musical
director at two European opera houses:
the Volksoper in Vienna and the State
Opera in Berlin. While in Berlin he also
scored a number of early sound films for
UFA. Long at Universal, he worked on
many of their key horror films of the
forties and fifties, often in collaboration
(mostly with Charles Previn, Frank
Skinner, Paul Desau and Joseph
Gershenson) and often uncredited, scoring certain sections of a movie, snatches
of which subsequently popped up in all

manner of films. The following genre list
includes Salter's uncredited and pirated
contributions. His other scores/contri-
butions include *It Started with Eve*, *Scarlet
Street*, *The Web*, *The Incredible Shrinking
Man*, *Come September* and *Beau Geste*.
Genre credits:
Tower of London (1939), *The Invisible Man
Returns* (1940), *Black Friday* (1940), *The
Mummy's Hand* (1940), *The Wolf Man*
(1941), *Man Made Monster* (1941 - aka
The Electric Man), *The Black Cat* (1941),
Hold That Ghost (1941), *The Ghost of
Frankenstein* (1942), *The Invisible Agent*
(1942), *The Mad Doctor of Market Street*
(1942), *The Night Monster* (1942), *The
Strange Case of Dr. RX* (1942), *The
Mummy's Tomb* (1942), *The Mummy's
Ghost* (1943), *Frankenstein Meets the Wolf
Man* (1943), *Son of Dracula* (1943), *The
Mad Ghoul* (1943), *Captive Wild Woman*
(1943), *Calling Dr Death* (1943), *House
of Frankenstein* (1944), *The Spider Woman*
(1944), *The Invisible Man's Revenge*
(1944), *The Scarlet Claw* (1944), *House of
Fear* (1944), *The Pearl of Death* (1944),
Weird Woman (1944), *Jungle Captive*
(1944), *Jungle Woman* (1944), *House of
Dracula* (1945), *The Frozen Ghost* (1945),
House of Horrors (1946), *The Brute Man*
(1946), *The Strange Door* (1951), *Abbott
and Costello Meet the Invisible Man* (1951),
The Black Castle (1952), *Abbott and
Costello Meet Dr Jekyll and Mr Hyde*
(1953), *The Creature from the Black Lagoon*
(1954), *This Island Earth* (1955), *Abbott
and Costello Meet the Mummy* (1955), *The
Mole People* (1956), *The Creature Walks
Among Us* (1956), *The Land Unknown*
(1957)

Salzedo, Leonard (1921-)

British composer, studied at the Royal
College of Music. Scored several of
Hammer/Exclusive's early pre-horror
programmers in the fifties. His only
horror score for them was for *The
Revenge of Frankenstein* (1958).

Samuels, Ted

British special-effects technician, the
majority of whose credits have been for
Amicus.

Genre credits:
The Tomb of Ligeia (1964), *Dr Terror's
House of Horrors* (1964), *The Psychopath*
(1965), *The Skull* (1965), *The Asphyx*
(1972)

Sanders, George (1906-1972)

Distinguished British (but Russian-born)
actor, the archetypal cad in countless
Hollywood films. After experience in
the textile and tobacco industries, he
turned to the stage and radio.
Appearances in several British films of
the early thirties followed (*Find the Lady*,
Strange Cargo, *The Man Who Could Work
Miracles*), though it was with his
Hollywood début in *Lloyd's of London* in
1936 that his star began to rise. Known
for playing both the Saint and the Falcon
in two popular crime series, he became
an increasingly sought-after character
actor after performing in such films as
Rebecca, *The Moon and Sixpence* and *The
Picture of Dorian Gray*, going on to win a
Best Supporting Actor Oscar for his role
as Addison de Witt in *All About Eve*
(1950). His career began to decline in
the sixties, however, and he found
himself appearing in films unworthy of
his talents, all of which inexorably led to
his suicide ('Dear World, I am leaving
you because I am bored,' read his suicide
note). His other credits include
Hitchcock's *Foreign Correspondent*, *Forever
Amber*, *Solomon and Sheba*, *A Shot in the
Dark* and *The Kremlin Letter*.
Genre credits:
The Lodger (1944), *The Picture of Dorian
Gray* (1944), *Hangover Square* (1944),
The Ghost and Mrs Muir (1947), *Village of
the Damned* (1960), *The Body Stealers*
(1969), *Doomwatch* (1972), *Psychomania*
(1972)

Sands, Julian (1957-)

British actor working in Britain,
Hollywood and Europe, where he is
equally at home in art-house films and
more commercial ventures. His credits
include *The Killing Fields*, *A Room with a
View*, *Impromptu*, *Night Sun* (aka *Il Sole
Anche di Notte*), *Boxing Helena* and *The
Browning Version*.

Genre credits:
The Doctor and the Devils (1985), *Gothic* (1986), *Warlock* (1989), *Arachnophobia* (1990), *The Naked Lunch* (1991), *Warlock 2: The Armageddon* (1993), *Witch Hunt* (1994)

Sangster, Jimmy (1927-)
British writer, producer and director who scripted many of Hammer's classic genre films. He joined Hammer/Exclusive as a third assistant director after World War Two (during which he served in the RAF) and gradually worked his way up to first assistant at the age of just nineteen. In 1954, he began work as a production manager, then became assistant to Hammer's executive producer, Michael Carreras. His first script was for the short *A Man on the Beach* (1956), with his first full-length screenplay, *X - The Unknown*, following in the same year. Still in 1956, *The Curse of Frankenstein* put both Sangster and Hammer on the international map. Further genre scripts followed for Hammer and other studios, who billed him Jimmy 'Frankenstein' Sangster on their posters. In the sixties he turned with equal success to psychological thrillers, the first of which, *Taste of Fear* (aka *Scream of Fear*), he also produced. He turned director with less success with *Horror of Frankenstein* (1970), then in the mid-seventies left Hammer for America, where much television work followed. Sometimes uses the pseudonym John Sansom.
Genre credits:
X - The Unknown (1956 - w), *The Curse of Frankenstein* (1956 - w), *Dracula* (1958 - aka *Horror of Dracula* - w), *The Revenge of Frankenstein* (1958 - w), *The Trollenberg Terror* (1958 - aka *The Crawling Eye* - w), *Blood of the Vampire* (1958 - w), *The Mummy* (1959 - w), *The Man Who Could Cheat Death* (1959 - w), *Jack the Ripper* (1959 - w), *The Brides of Dracula* (1960 - co-w), *Taste of Fear* (1961 - aka *Scream of Fear* - w/p), *Maniac* (1963 - w/p), *Hysteria* (1965 - w/p), *The Nanny* (1965 - w/p), *Dracula - Prince of Darkness* (1966 - w [as John Sansom]), *Crescendo* (1969 - w/p), *Horror of Frankenstein* (1970 - w/p/d), *Lust for a Vampire* (1971 - w/d), *A Taste of Evil* (1971 - TVM - w), *Fear in the Night* (1972 -co-w/p/d), *Scream, Pretty Peggy* (1973 - TVM - co-w), *Good Against Evil* (1977 - TVM - w), *The Legacy* (1978 - co-w), *The Devil and Max Devlin* (1980 - co-story)

Sarandon, Susan (1946-)
American actress who first came to attention playing Janet in *The Rocky Horror Picture Show*, though it was some years before she achieved true star status - in such films as *Atlantic City*, *The Witches of Eastwick*, *Bull Durham*, *White Palace*, *Thelma and Louise*, *Lorenzo's Oil*, *The Client* and *Dead Man Walking*, which won her a Best Actress Oscar.
Genre credits:
The Rocky Horror Picture Show (1975), *The Hunger* (1983), *The Witches of Eastwick* (1987)

Sarrazin, Michael (1940-)
Canadian actor, in Hollywood from the mid-sixties after experience on stage in New York and on American television. Perhaps best remembered by genre fans for playing Frankenstein's Monster in *Frankenstein: The True Story*. His other credits include *The Flim Flam Man*, *They Shoot Horses, Don't They?*, *Sometimes a Great Notion* (aka *Never Give an Inch*), *For Pete's Sake* and *The Gumball Rally*.
Genre credits:
Eye of the Cat (1968), *Frankenstein: The True Story* (1973 - TVM), *The Reincarnation of Peter Proud* (1975)

Sasdy, Peter (1934-)
Hungarian director in Britain, with many TV credits to his name. Also experience as a theatre producer and critic. Came to Britain after the 1956 uprising and studied drama at Bristol University before joining the BBC. His first feature film was Hammer's *Taste the Blood of Dracula* in 1970, after which he found himself labelled a horror director.
Genre credits:
Taste the Blood of Dracula (1970), *Countess Dracula* (1970 - & co-story), *Hands of the Ripper* (1971), *Nothing But the Night* (1972), *Doomwatch* (1972), *I Don't Want to Be Born* (1975 - aka *The Devil Within Her*), *Welcome to Blood City* (1977), *Last Video and Testament* (1984 - TVM), *The Late Nancy Irving* (1984 - TVM), *The Sweet Smell of Death* (1984 - TVM)

The Satanic Rites of Dracula *
GB 1973 88m Technicolor
Professor Van Helsing discovers that Dracula is at the head of business empire intent on destroying the world via a deadly bacteria.
Avengers-style finish to the Hammer series. A few marks up on the same director's *Dracula A. D. 1972*, though vampires and motorcycles don't really go together. Worth a look for Lee's impersonation of American tycoon D. D. Denham.
p: Roy Skeggs for Hammer/Warner
w: Don Houghton
d: ALAN GIBSON
ph: Brian Probyn
m: John Cacavas
md: Philip Martell
ed: Chris Barnes
ad: Lionel Couch
cos: Rebecca Reed
sp: Les Bowie
sound: Claude Hitchcock, Dennis Whitlock
Christopher Lee, Peter Cushing, Michael Coles, Joanna Lumley, William Franklyn, Freddie Jones, Patrick Barr, Richard Vernon, Lockwood West, Barbara Yu Ling, Valerie Van Ost

Satan's Skin see The Blood on Satan's Claw

The Savage Bees
USA 1976 96m colour TVM
A swarm of killer bees threatens New Orleans.
Lame thriller, tediously executed. Worse, even, than *The Swarm*, which is saying something.
p: Bruce Geller for NBC
exec p: Alan Landsburg, Don Kirschner
w: Guerdon Trueblood
d: Bruce Geller
ph: Richartd C. Glouner
m: Walter Murphy
md: Don Kirschner
ed: George Hively, Bud Friedgen
ad: no credit given
cos: Bucky Rous
sp: Norman Gary, Kenneth Lorenzen
Ben Johnson, Michael Parks, Paul Hecht, Horst Buchholz, Gretchen Corbett

Savini, Tom
Italian-American make-up effects artist (a splatter expert) who has also tried his hand at acting and directing. Known chiefly for his work with director George Romero, he did much influential work within his field in the eighties.
Genre credits:
Deathdream (1972 - assistant sp), *Deranged* (1974 - sp), *Martin* (1977 - sp/actor), *Dawn of the Dead* (1979 - sp/actor), *Effects* (1980 - actor), *Maniac* (1980 - sp/actor), *Friday the 13th* (1980 -sp), *Midnight* (1981 - sp), *The Burning* (1981 - sp), *Eyes of a Stranger* (1981 - sp), *The Prowler* (1981 - sp), *Knightriders* (1981 - actor), *Alone in the Dark* (1982 - sp), *Creepshow* (1982 -sp/actor), *Friday the 13th Part Four: The Final Chapter* (1984 -sp), *Day of the Dead* (1985 - sp), *The Texas Chainsaw Massacre Part 2* (1986 - sp), *The Ripper* (1986 - sp), *Creepshow 2* (1987 -sp/actor), *Monkey Shines* (1988 - sp), *Night of the Living Dead* (1990 - d), *The Bloodsucking Pharaohs of Pittsburgh* (1990 - sp), *Two Evil Eyes* (1991 - aka *Due Occhi Diabolici* - sp/actor), *Trauma* (1993 - sp), *Necronomicon* (1994 - sp), *From Dusk Till Dawn* (1996 - actor)

Sawtell, Paul (1906-1971)

Prolific Polish composer and music director, long in America, where he tackled all manner of middle- to low-budget productions, including several Tarzans. His other credits include *The Gay Falcon*, *Tarzan Triumphs*, *Dick Tracy Meets Gruesome*, *Stopover Tokyo* and *Five Weeks in a Balloon*.

Genre credits:

The Mummy's Curse (1944 - md), *Jungle Woman* (1944 - m), *Jungle Captive* (1944 - m), *Son of Dr Jekyll* (1959 - m), *The Black Scorpion* (1957 - co-m), *The Fly* (1958 - m), *The Return of the Fly* (1959 -co-m), *The Last Man on Earth* (1964 - aka *L'Ultimo Uomo Della Terra* - co-m)

Saxon, John (1935-)

American actor (real name Carmen Orrico), a reliable support since the mid-fifties. A former model, he made his film début in 1955 with *Running Wild*. Also familiar on television in such series as *Park Avenue* and *Falcon Crest*, his films credits include *The Cardinal*, *Joe Kidd*, *Enter the Dragon* and *Beverly Hills Cop III*. He has also directed one film, *Death House*.

Genre credits:

The Evil Eye (1962), *The Night Caller* (1965 - aka *Blood Beast from Outer Space*), *Queen of Blood* (1966), *Black Christmas* (1975 - aka *Silent Night, Evil Night*), *The Bees* (1978), *Beyond Evil* (1980), *Blood Beach* (1981), *Tenebrae* (1982 - aka *Unsane/Ténèbres*), *A Nightmare on Elm Street* (1984), *A Nightmare on Elm Street Part 3: The Dream Warriors* (1987), *Death House* (1988 - actor/d), *My Mom's a Werewolf* (1989), *Blood Salvage* (1989), *The Arrival* (1991), *Hellmaster* (1992), *Wes Craven's New Nightmare* (1994)

Scanners

Canada 1980 103m Eastmancolor
A renegade scientist trains a group of people with exceptional telepathic powers to take over the world.

Long and tediously talkative science-fiction mumbo-jumbo, quite highly regarded in certain circles, though mostly remembered for a scene involving an exploding head, on which count it did well enough at the box office. It was followed by *Scanners 2: The New Order* (1991), *Scanners 3: The Takeover* (1992), *Scanner Cop* (1993) and *Scanner Cop 2: Volkin's Revenge* (1995).

p: Claude Heroux for Filmplan International/Canadian Film Development Corporation
exec p: Victor Solnicki, Pierre David
w/d: David Cronenberg
ph: Mark Irwin
m: Howard Shore
ed: Ronald Sanders
ad: Carol Spier
cos: Delphine White
sp: Gary Zeller, Henry Pierrig
sound: Don Cohen
make-up effects: Dick Smith, Tom Schwartz, Chris Walas, Stephen Dupuis
Patrick McGoohan, Jennifer O'Neill, Stephen Lack, Lawrence Dane, Michael Ironside, Adam Ludwig, Robert Silverman, Mavor Moore

Scared Stiff

USA 1953 108m bw
A nightclub singer and a busboy accompany an heiress to her haunted Cuban castle.

Flat and unamusing remake of *The Ghost Breakers*, with none of the sparkle of the original.

p: Hal B. Wallis for Paramount
w: Herbert Baker, Walter de Leon, Ed Simmons, Norman Lear
play: Paul Dickey, Charles W. Goddard
d: George Marshall
ph: Ernest Laszlo
m: Leith Stevens
songs: Mack David, Jerry Livingston
md: Joseph J. Lilley
ed: Warren Low
ad: Hal Pereira, Franz Bachelin
cos: Edith Head
sp: Gordon Jennings, Paul Lerpae, Farciot Edouart
sound: Hugo Grenzbach, Walter Oberst
ch: Billy Daniel
Dean Martin, Jerry Lewis, Lizabeth Scott, Carmen Miranda, Dorothy Malone, William Ching, Jack Lambert, George Dolenz

The Scarlet Claw **

USA 1944 74m bw
Sherlock Holmes investigates a series of murders apparently committed by a glowing phantom.

One of the liveliest of the Rathbone Holmes adventures, the plot being little more than a thinly disguised variation on *The Hound of the Baskervilles*, though the script is not without its incongruities.

p: Roy William Neill for Universal
w: Edmund L. Hartmann, Roy William Neill
story: Paul Gangelin, Brenda Weisberg
d: ROY WILLIAM NEILL
ph: GEORGE ROBINSON
md: Paul Sawtell
ed: Paul Landres
ad: Ralph M. De Lacy, John B. Goodman
cos: Vera West
sp: John P. Fulton
sound: Bernard B. Brown, Robert Pritchard
BASIL RATHBONE, Nigel Bruce, Miles Mander, Gerald Hamer, Paul Cavanaugh, Kay Harding, Arthur Hohl

Scars of Dracula

GB 1970 96m Technicolor
A young man and his fiancée trace his missing brother to Castle Dracula.

Unimaginative variation on the original story, with too little invention in the script to sustain its length, and the low budget does show.

p: Aida Young for Hammer
w: John Elder (Anthony Hinds)
d: Roy Ward Baker
ph: Moray Grant
m: James Bernard
md: Philip Martell
ed: James Needs
ad: Scott MacGregor
cos: Laura Nightingale
sp: Roger Dicken
sound: Ron Barron, Tony Lumkin
Christopher Lee, Dennis Waterman, Jenny Hanley, Christopher Matthews, Patrick Troughton, Michael Gwynne, Bob Todd, Michael Ripper

Schizo

GB 1976 108m Technicolor
An ice-skating star finds her life in peril following her recent marriage.

Tolerable but overpadded and wholly predictable shocker in its director's tried and tested style (i.e. not too much style at all).

p: Pete Walker for Peter Walker Ltd/Heritage
w: David McGillivray
d: Pete Walker
ph: Peter Jessop
m: Stanley Myers
ed: Alan Brett
ad: Chris Burke
sound: Peter O'Connor, Tony Anscombe
Lynne Frederick, Stephanie Beacham, John Leyton, John Fraser, Queenie Watts, Jack Watson, Terry Duggan, Colin Jeavons, John McEnery

Schizoid

USA 1980 88m colour
A man in fear of his daughter's sanity turns out to be schizophrenic himself. Artless cheapie hingeing on an ancient wheeze.

d: David Paulsen
Klaus Kinski, Craig Wasson, Marianna Hill, Donna Wilkes, Christopher Lloyd, Flo Gerrish, Richard Herd, Joe Regalbuto

Schmoeller, David

American director who, while working at the low-budget end of the horror market, manages to turn out slick-looking productions, his best work being for

Charles Band's Empire outfit.
Genre credits:
Crawlspace (1986 - w/d), *Puppetmaster* (1989), *Catacombs* (1990 - aka *Curse IV: The Ultimate Sacrifice*), *Netherworld* (1990)

Schoedsack, Ernest B. (1893-1979)

American writer, producer, director and cinematographer who, with his partner Merian C. Cooper (whom he met in Poland in 1920), made a number of documentaries in the twenties (*Grass, Chang*) before going on to make a series of spectacular big-budget features, including *The Four Feathers* and, of course, the legendary *King Kong* (in fact, Schoedsack and Cooper can be spotted briefly during the Empire State climax as two of the pilots who gun Kong down). He began his film career as a cameraman for comedy producer Mack Sennett, which led to his becoming a combat cameraman during World War One. His other credits include *Rango, Long Lost Father, The Last Days of Pompeii* and *Outlaws of the Orient*.
Genre credits:
The Most Dangerous Game (1932 - aka *The Hounds of Zaroff* - co-p/co-d), *King Kong* (1933 - co-p/co-d), *Son of Kong* (1933 - d), *Dr Cyclops* (1939 - d), *Mighty Joe Young* (1949 - d)

Schoelen, Jill (1970-)

American actress who has appeared in a handful of shockers.
Genre credits:
Chiller (1985 - TVM), *The Stepfather* (1987), *Curse II: The Bite* (1989), *The Phantom of the Opera* (1989), *Cutting Class* (1989), *Popcorn* (1991), *When a Stranger Calls Back* (1993)

Schreck, Max (1879-1936)

German character actor, remembered soley for his portrayal of the vampire count Graf Orlok in *Nosferatu* (1922), though he appeared in many other films, including *The Street, The Strange Case of Captain Ramper, Rasputin - The Holy Devil, Ludwig II* and *The Tunnel*.

Schurmann, Gerard (1928-)

Dutch-born orchestrator (*The Vikings, Exodus, Lawrence of Arabia, Cross of Iron*, etc.) and composer working in Britain. Formerly an assistant to composer Alan Rawsthorne, he has also composed operas and for the concert platform. His other film scores include *The Long Arm, The Bedford Incident* and *Dr Syn - Alias the Scarecrow*, though he is best known for the throat-grabbing *Horrors of the Black Museum*.

Genre credits:
The Headless Ghost (1958), *Horrors of the Black Museum* (1959), *Konga* (1961), *The Lost Continent* (1968)

Scoones, Ian

British special-effects technician with much television experience (*Thunderbirds, Dr Who, Terrorhawks, Hammer House of Horror*, etc.). Began his career as an assistant to Les Bowie, with whom he worked on a number of Hammer films. He became an effects supervisor in his own right in the early eighties.
Genre credits:
Shadow of the Cat (1960 - assistant), *Taste of Fear* (1961 - aka *Scream of Fear* - ass), *The Old Dark House* (1962 - ass), *Paranoiac* (1963 - ass), *The Damned* (1963 - aka *These Are the Damned* - ass), *Kiss of the Vampire* (1964 - aka *Kiss of Evil* - ass), *Nightmare* (1964 - ass), *The Evil of Frankenstein* (1964 - ass), *Frankenstein Created Woman* (1966 - ass), *The Mummy's Shroud* (1966 - ass), *Quatermass and the Pit* (1967 - aka *Five Million Years to Earth* -ass), *Haunted Honeymoon* (1986 - sp sup), *Hardware* (1990 - sp sup)

Scott, John (1930-)

British composer, conductor and arranger, comfortable in most genres. His scores include *Doctor in Clover, The Long Duel, Girl Stroke Boy, Antony and Cleopatra, The Shooting Party, The Final Countdown, The Legend of Tarzan, Lord of the Apes* and *The Deceivers*.
Genre credits:
A Study in Terror (1965), *Trog* (1970), *Doomwatch* (1972), *Symptoms* (1974 - aka *The Blood Virgin*), *Satan's Slave* (1976), *The People That Time Forgot* (1977), *Inseminoid* (1980 - aka *Horror Planet*), *King Kong Lives* (1986)

Scream and Scream Again *

GB 1969 94m Eastmancolor
Police investigating a series of murders discover them to be the work of superhuman beings, created by a mad scientist.
  Silly but fast-moving *Avengers*-style horror hokum, though the starry cast has little to do.
p: Max J. Rosenberg, Milton Subotsky for AIP/Amicus
exec p: Louis M. Heyward
w: Christopher Wicking
novel: Peter Saxon
d: GORDON HESSLER
ph: John Coquillon
m: David Whitaker (though the video version has an electronic score by Kendall Schmidt for some reason)
ed: Peter Elliott
pd: Bill Constable

ad: Don Mingaye
cos: Evelyn Gibbs
sound: Hugh Strain, Bert Ross
Vincent Price, Christopher Lee, Peter Cushing, ALFRED MARKS, Anthony Newlands, Christopher Matthews, Yutte Stensgaard, Julian Holloway, Peter Sallis, Michael Gothard

Scream of Fear see Taste of Fear

Scream of the Wolf *

USA 1974 74m Technicolor
A specialist is called in to help solve a series of murders that have apparently been committed by a werewolf.
  An above-average tele-thriller from a well-practised hand.
p: Dan Curtis for MPC
exec p: Charles Fries
w: Richard Matheson
story: David Case
d: Dan Curtis
ph: Paul Lohmann
m: Robert Cobert
ed: Richard A. Harris
ad: Walter Simon
cos: Nat Tolmak
sp: Roger George
sound: Gene Garvin
Peter Graves, Clint Walker, Jo Ann Pflug, Phil Carey

Scream, Pretty Peggy *

USA 1973 74m Technicolor TVM
A girl student takes a part-time job at a secluded house and discovers that murder and deception are the order of the day.
  Familiar screamer with an obvious twist ending in the *Psycho/Taste of Fear* manner.
p: Lou Morheim for Universal
w: Jimmy Sangster, Arthur Hoffe
d: Gordon Hessler
ph: Leonard J. South
m: Bob Prince
md: Hal Mooney
ed: Larry Strong, Richard Belding
ad: Joseph Alves Jr
cos: Burton Miller
sound: L. Ralph Zerbe
Bette Davis, Ted Bessell, Sian Barbara Allen, Charles Drake, Allen Arbus, Tovah Fledshuh, Jessica Rains

Screaming Mimi

USA 1958 79m bw
A murder witness believes that she has committed the crime herself and takes herself to the brink of insanity.
  Ho-hum plot twister, indifferently scripted and presented. The novel was later used as the basis for Dario Argento's directorial début, *The Bird with the Crystal Plumage*, to rather better effect.

JOEL SCHUMACHER'S HOMOEROTIC MODERN DAY VAMPIRE SAGA *THE LOST BOYS* – Bela Lugosi's Dracula was never like this. 'Sleep all day, party all night – it's fun to be a vampire!'

p: Harry Joe Brown, Robert Fellows for Columbia/Sage
w: Robert Blees
novel: Fredric Brown
d: Gerd Oswald
ph: Burnett Guffey
md: Mischa Bakaleinikoff
ed: Gene Havlick, Jerome Thoms
ad: Cary Odell
sound: John Livardy, Josh Westmoreland
ch: Lee Scott
Anita Ekberg, Gypsy Rose Lee, Harry Townes, Alan Gifford, Romney Brent

Scrooged *
USA 1988 101m Technicolor Dolby
A mean-spirited television executive is visited on Christmas Eve by three ghosts who persuade him to be kinder to his fellow man.

Mildly amusing if somewhat indulgent comic update of the Dickens story for fans of the star.
p: Richard Donner, Art Linson for Paramount/Mirage
exec p: Steve Roth
w: Mitch Glazer, Michael O'Donoghue
d: Richard Donner
ph: Michael Chapman
m: Danny Elfman
ed: Fredric and William Steinkamp
pd: J. Michael Riva
cos: Wayne Finkelman
sp: Dream Quest
sound: Willie Burton
make-up effects: Tom Burman
titles: Anthony Goldschmidt
stunt co-ordinator: Mic Rodgers
Bill Murray, Karen Allen, Robert Mitchum, John Forsythe, Bobcat Goldthwaite, John Houseman, Buddy Hackett, Michael J. Pollard, Carol Kane, Lee Majors, Mary Lou Retton

The Secret of the Blue Room
USA 1933 66m bw
An apparently haunted room, locked for twenty years, causes the guests of an heiress to have a sleepless night.

Dated spooky-house thriller that needed more wit and style.
p: Carl Laemmle Jr for Universal
w: William Hurlbut
story: Erich Philippi
d: Kurt Neumann
ph: Charles Stumar
m: Heinz Letton
ed: Philip Cahn
ad: Stanley Fleischer
sound: no credit given
Lionel Atwill, Edward Arnold, Paul Lukas, Gloria Stuart, Onslow Stevens, Robert Barrat, William Janney, Muriel Kirkland, Elizabeth Patterson, Russell Hopton

Secrets of the Phantom Caverns
GB 1984 89m colour
Archaeologists discover a long-lost albino race living in a South American cavern.

Low-budget hokum which fails to live up to its title or its idea. Its director's weakest film.
p: Sandy Howard, Robert D. Bailey for Adams Apple
exec p: Mel Pearl, Don Levin
w: Christy Marx, Robert Vincent O'Neil
story: Ken Barnett
d: Don Sharp
ph: Virgil Harper
m: Michel Rubini, Denny Jaeger
ed: John R. Bowey
ad: Stephen Marsh
Robert Powell, Lisa Blount, Timothy Bottoms, Richard Johnson, Anne Heywood, A. C. Weary

The Sect
It 1993 102m Technicolor
A schoolteacher finds herself pursued by a sect who wish to mate her with their god, a giant pterodactyl-like bird.

Slick-looking but foolishly plotted horror hokum in which the director again tries to immitate the style of his producer/mentor Dario Argento.
p: Dario Argento, Mario Cecchi Gori, Vittorio Cecchi Gori for Silvio Berlusconi Communications/Penta/ADC
exec p: Andrea Tinnirello
w: Dario Argento, Michele Soavi, Giovanni Romoli
d: Michele Soavi
ph: Raffaele Mertes
m: Pino Donaggio
ed: Franco Fraticelli
pd: M. Antonello Geleng
cos: Vera Cozzolini
sp: Massimo Crostofanelli, Sergio Stivaletti
sound: Giancarlo Laurenzi
Kelly Curtis, Herbert Lom, Maria Angela Giordano, Michel Adatte, Carla Cassola, Tomas Arana

See No Evil see Blind Terror

Seltzer, David (1940-)
American writer (*One Is a Lonely Number*, *The Other Side of the Mountain*, *Table for Five*), now also directing (*Punchline*, *Shining Through*). Best known for writing *The Omen* (1976). His only other genre script has been for *Prophecy* (1979).

The Sentinel *
USA 1976 92m Technicolor

A young woman discovers that her apartment house is a gateway to hell and that she is to be its next sentinel.

Smart horror drama whose lapses into bad taste (which include a masturbation scene involving Sylvia Miles and the use of real freaks in the climactic scenes) may not be to everyone's liking.
p: Jeffrey Konvitz for Universal
w: Michael Winner, Jeffrey Konvitz
novel: Jeffrey Konvitz
d: MICHAEL WINNER
ph: Dick Kratina
m: Gil Melle
ed: Bernard Gribble, Terence Rawlings
pd: Philip Rosenberg
sp: Albert Whitlock
make-up effects: Dick Smith, Bob Laden
Cristina Raines, Chris Sarandon, Jerry Orbach, Ava Gardner, Martin Balsam, John Carradine, Jose Ferre, Arthur Kennedy, Burgess Meredith, Sylvia Miles, Deborah Raffin, Eli Wallach, Christopher Walken, Tom Berenger

The Serpent and the Rainbow *
USA 1987 98m DuArt Dolby
An American pharmaceutical company sends one of its employees to Haiti to get hold of the drug used by witch doctors to zombify people.

Reasonably watchable horror hokum, more so than most of its director's output.
p: David Ledd, Doug Claybourne for Universal
w: Richard Maxwell, A. R. Simoun
novel: Wade Davis
d: Wes Craven
ph: John Lindley
m: Brad Fiedel
ed: Glenn Farr
pd: David Nichols
cos: Peter Mitchell
sp: Guy Guitierz
sound: Jay Boekelheide
make-up effects: Lance Anderson, David Anderson
stunt co-ordinator: Tony Cecere
Bill Pullman, Cathy Tyson, Zakes Mokae, Paul Winfield, Michael Gough, Brent Jennings, Conrad Roberts, Badja Djola, Theresa Merritt

La Setta see The Sect

Seven *
USA 1995 125m Technicolor Dolby
Two cops, one of them young and ambitious, the other tired and on the verge of retirement, track down a serial killer who is using the seven deadly sins as the theme for his killings.

Darkly lit and poorly recorded thriller that nevertheless continued the public's fascination with serial killers

and also found great favour with the critics. Disturbing moments, though not quite as shocking as some would have one believe.
p: Arnold Kopelson for New Line
w: Andrew Kevin Walker
d: David Fincher
m: Howard Shore
cos: Michael Kaplan
Brad Pitt, Morgan Freeman, Kevin Spacey

The Seven Brothers Meet Dracula see The Legend of the Seven Golden Vampires

The Seventh Seal ***
Sweden 1957 95m bw
In medieval Sweden, a wandering knight is challenged by Death to a game of chess.

Visually striking mixture of fantasy and religiosity which quickly took on classic status and is best remembered for its stark tableaux-like imagery. A must for students of the director's work.
p: Allan Ekelun for Svenks Filmindustri
w/d: INGMAR BERGMAN
ph: GUNNAR FISCHER
m: Erik Nordgren
md: Sixten Ehrling
ed: Lannart Wallen
ad: P. A. Lundgren
cos: Manne Lindholm
sound: Abby Wedin, Lennart Wallin
ch: Else Fischer
MAX VOV SYDOW, BENGT EKEROT, Gunnar Bjornstrand, Bibi Andersson, Nils Poppe, Gunnel Lindblom

The Seventh Victim *
USA 1943 71m bw
A young woman goes to New York to trace her sister who has mysteriously disappeared.

Interesting minor thriller, part of the celebrated Lewton series for RKO, though not quite the best of them.
p: Val Lewton for RKO
w: Charles O'Neal, DeWitt Bodeen
d: MARK ROBSON
ph: Nicholas Musuraca
m: Roy Webb
md: Constantin Bakaleinikoff
ed: John Lockert
ad: Albert S. D'Agistino, Walter E. Keller
cos: Irene
sound: John C. Grubb
Kim Hunter, Tom Conway, Jean Brooks, Hugh Beaumont, Erford Gage, Isabel Jewell, Evelyn Brent

Sewage Baby
USA 1989 85m colour
An aborted baby, flushed down a toilet, goes on the rampage in a brothel, having grown to an enormous size after ingesting toxic waste.

Poorly acted semi-professional exploitation piece with a few energetic moments.
p: Michael Helman, Francis Teri for Suckling
exec p: Peter Lewnes, Miljan Peter Ilich
w: no credit given
d: Francis Teri
ph: Harry Eisenstein
m: Joseph Teri
ed: no credit given
pd: Mike Rich
cos: Norma Trivelli
make-up effects: Ralph Cordero Frank Reeves, Marie Michaels, Lisa Patruno, Janet Sovey, Gerald Preger, Michael Logan

Sewell, Vernon (1903-)
British director with experience as an assistant cameraman, art director and editor. Has many undemanding low-budget pictures to his name, and much TV work. His other credits include Silver Fleet, Latin Quarter Frenzy, Jack of Diamonds and Strongroom.
Genre credits:
The Ghosts of Berkeley Square (1947), The Ghost Ship (1952), House of Mystery (1961), The Bloodbeast Terror (1967), The Curse of the Crimson Altar (1968 - aka The Crimson Cult), Burke and Hare (1971)

The Shadow of the Cat *
GB 1961 79m bw
When its mistress is murdered by greedy relatives, a pet cat takes revenge.

Well-mounted if somewhat foolish horror hokum with an insufficiently frightening monster.
p: Jon Penington for BHP
w: George Baxt
d: JOHN GILLING
ph: Arthur Grant
m: Mikis Theodorakis
ed: James Needs, John Pomeroy
ad: Bernard Robinson, Don Mingaye
cos: Molly Arbuthnot
sp: Les Bowie
sound: Ken Cameron
Barbara Shelley, André Morell, William Lucas, Freda Jackson, Catherine Lacey, Vanda Godsell, Richard Warner, Alan Wheatley, Conrad Phillips

Shallow Grave **
GB 1994 92m Technicolor
Three flatmates conspire to do away with the dead body of a fourth when they discover that he has a suitcase full of money under his bed.

Gripping low-budget thriller that makes the very most of its situations, on which count it did well both critically and commercially.
p: ANDREW MACDONALD for Film Four/Glasgow Film Fund/Figment
w: JOHN HODGE
d: DANNY BOYLE
ph: Brian Tufano
m: Simon Boswell
ed: Masahiro Hirakubo
pd: Kave Quinn
Kerry Fox, Christopher Eccleston, Ewan McGregor, Colin McCredie, Keith Allen

Shampan, Jack
British art director with a handful of genre titles to his name.
Genre credits:
Circus of Horrors (1960), Night of the Eagle (1961 - aka Burn, Witch, Burn!), The Ghoul (1974), Legend of the Werewolf (1975)

Sharp, Don (1922-)
Tasmanian-born director who began his career as an actor. He came to Britain after World War Two and went to work with Group Three. In the fifties he began writing then directing low-budget thrillers and musicals, such as The Golden Disc, It's All Happening and Hal 5. He graduated to genre films with Hammer's Kiss of the Vampire (aka Kiss of Evil) and was also responsible for the stunning second-unit work on both Those Magnificent Men in Their Flying Machines and Puppet on a Chain. His other credits include The Devil-Ship Pirates, Rocket to the Moon, Callan, The Thirty-Nine Steps, Bear Island and TV's A Woman of Substance.
Genre credits:
Kiss of the Vampire (1964 - aka Kiss of Evil), Witchcraft (1964), The Face of Fu Manchu (1965), The Curse of the Fly (1965), Rasputin - The Mad Monk (1966), The Brides of Fu Manchu (1966), Psychomania (1973), The Secret of the Phantom Caverns (1984)

She *
USA 1935 89m bw
Old documents lead an explorer and his friends to a mysterious Arctic country ruled by a queen who cannot age.

Occasionally striking fantasy adventure, reshaped from the original in the manner of the same producer's King Kong. Of interest chiefly for its art direction.
p: Merian C. Cooper for RKO
w: Ruth Rose, Dudley Nichols
novel: H. Rider Haggard
d: Irving Pichel, Lansing G. Holden
ph: J. Roy Hunt
m: MAX STEINER
ed: Ted Cheesman
ad: VAN NEST POLGLASE, AL HERMAN

cos: Aline Bernstein, Harold Miles
sp: Vernon L. Walker
sound: John L. Cass
sound effects: Walter Elliott
ch: Benjamin Zemach
Randolph Scott, Nigel Bruce, Helen Gahagan (as She - her only film), Helen Mack

She *

GB 1965 105m Technicolor
Hammerscope
Explorers discover a remote colony in Africa governed by a queen who cannot die unless she falls in love...

Claustrophobic, ill-adapted Hammer remake lacking the sense of mystery of its predecessor. A few moments of interest along the way, but the sluggish pace is self-defeating.
p: Michael Carreras for Hammer/Associated British
w: David T. Chantler
novel: H. Rider Haggard
d: Robert Day
ph: Harry Waxman
m: JAMES BERNARD
md: Philip Martell
ed: James Needs, Eric Boyd-Perkins
ad: Robert Jones, Don Mingaye
cos: Carl Toms
sp: George Blackwell, Les Bowie
sound: Claude Hitchcock, A. W. Lumkin
make-up: Roy Ashton
associate p: Aida Young
ch: Cristyne Lawson
cam op: Ernest Day
make-up: John O. Gorman, Roy Ashton
Ursula Andress, Peter Cushing, Bernard Cribbins, Christopher Lee, John Richardson, André Morell, Rosenda Monteros, The Oo-Bla-Da Dancers (!)

The She-Creature

USA 1956 77m bw
A hypnotist conjures up a monster from the id of a lady volunteer.

Dull horror nonsense with a risible monster.
p: Alex Gordon for Golden State
exec p: Samuel Z. Arkoff
w: Lou Rusoff
story: Jerry Zigmond
d: Edward L. Cahn
ph: Frederick E. West
m: Ronald Stein
ed: Ronald Sinclair
ad: Don Ament
cos: Marjorie Corso
sp: Paul Blaisdell
sound: Ben Winkler
Chester Morris, Tom Conway, Marla English, Cathy Downs, Lance Fuller, Ron Randell, Frieda Inescort, Paul Blaisdell, El Brendel

• Barbara Shelley, one of the horror genre's most beautiful actresses, here seen in a studio portrait taken during the making of *The Masque of the Red Death*.

Shefter, Bert (1904-)

Russian-born composer, long in America, where he worked on all manner of films, including *Danger Zone*, *M*, *Cattle Empire*, *Jack the Giant Killer* and *The Christine Jorgensen Story*. Most of his genre scores were written in association with Paul Sawtell.
Genre credits:
The Black Scorpion (1956 - co-m), *The Return of the Fly* (1959 -co-m), *The Curse of the Fly* (1965 - m), *The Last Man on Earth* (1964 - aka *L'Ultimo Uomo Della Terra* - co-m)

Shelley, Barbara (1933-)

Beautiful, sadly underused British actress who began her career as a model before films beckoned. She first made brief apearances in a number of Italian films, returning to Britain in 1957, where she made her genre debut in *Cat Girl*. Other credits include *The Camp on Blood Island*, *Postman's Knock* and *The Secret of Blood Island*.
Genre credits:
Cat Girl (1957), *Blood of the Vampire* (1958), *Village of the Damned* (1960), *The Shadow of the Cat* (1961), *Dracula - Prince of Darkness* (1966), *Rasputin - The Mad Monk* (1966), *Quatermass and the Pit* (1967 - aka *Five Million Years to Earth*), *Ghost Story* (1974 - aka *Madhouse Mansion*)

Shelley, Mary Wollstonecraft (1797-1851)

British novelist, the wife of the poet

Shelley, whose novel *Frankenstein* (aka *The Modern Prometheus*), which was published in 1818, has been filmed countless times, most notably in 1931 (with Boris Karloff as the Creature and Colin Clive as the Baron), 1956 (as *The Curse of Frankenstein*, with Christopher Lee as the Creature and Peter Cushing as the Baron) and 1994 (with Robert de Niro as the Creature and Kenneth Branagh as the Baron). Sequels, variations and rip-offs have been legion. Also see *Frankenstein*.

The Shining **

USA 1980 119m or 146m Technicolor
Panavision
The winter caretaker of an enormous hotel cut off by snow goes mad and tries to kill his wife and son.

Overblown and overhyped horror drama which seemed to disappoint at the time chiefly because it didn't live up to the ballyhoo. Seen today, however, one can better appreciate the great technical flair with which it is made, the splendid sets and slick photography being of particular note. Even Nicholson's performance, once deemed well over the top, now seems better suited to the story (which was much altered from the original, to the consternation of King fans).
p: Stanley Kubrick for Warner/ Peregrine/ The Producer Circle Company
exec p: Jan Harlan
w: Stanley Kubrick, Diane Johnson
novel: Stephen King
d: STANLEY KUBRICK

• 'Here's Johnny!' Jack Nicholson goes over the top in director Stanley Kubrick's underrated shocker *The Shining*.

ph: JOHN ALCOTT
m: Bela Bartok, Wendy Carlos, Krzysztof Penderecki, Rachel Elkind, Gyorgy Ligeti
ed; Ray Lovejoy
pd: ROY WALKER
cos: Milena Canonero
sound: Ivan Sharrock, Richard Daniel, Bill Rowe, Ray Merrin
make-up: Tom Smith
2nd unit ph: Douglas Milsome
Jack Nicholson, Shelley Duvall, Danny Lloyd, Barry Nelson, Scatman Crothers, Philip Stone, Anne Jakcson, Joe Turkel, Tony Burton

Shock!
It 1977 92m colour
A house with a mysterious past has a strange effect on the son of its new owners.

Childish shocker, quite unwatchable. An unfortunate tailpiece to its director's career.
p: Eagle/Lazer
w: Dardano Sacchetti, Frank Barber, Lamberto Bava
d: Mario Bava (and Lamberto Bava)
Daria Nicolodi, John Steiner, David Colin Jr, Ivan Rassimov

Shock 'Em Dead
USA 1991 95m RGBcolor
In order to become a rock star, a pizza delivery boy sells his soul.

Dim blend of heavy metal and would-be horror, clearly aimed at the brain dead.
p: Eric Louzil for Noma
exec p: Al Lapin Jr, Clair Higgins
w: Mark Freed, David Tedder, Andrew W. Cross
d: Mark Freed
ph: Ron Chapman
m: Robert Decker
ed: Terry Blythe
pd: Randy Lapin
cos: Jacqueline Aronson
sound: Bruce Hively
Traci Lords, Stephen Quadros, Aldo Ray, Troy Donohue

Shock Waves
GB 1976 87m TVCcolor
Shipwreck survivors find themselves prey to Nazi zombies with the ability to breathe underwater (yes, you read that right).

Perversely ridiculous nonsense with a few well-staged underwater sequences.
p: Reuben Trane for Zopix/Joseph Brenner Associates
w: John Harrison, Ken Wiederhorn
d: Ken Wiederhorn
ph: Reuben Trane
m: Richard Einhorn
ed: Norman Gray
pd: Jessica Sack
cos: Jacquie Kegeles
sound: Stephen Manners
underwater ph: Irving Pare
make-up: Alan Ormsby
Peter Cushing, John Carradine, Brooke Adams, Luke Halpin, Fred Buch, D. J. Sidney

Shocker
USA 1989 110m Technicolor
A serial killer escapes the electric chair and goes after one of his surviving victims.

Lively but rather stupid horror comic, practically a remake of the same director's *A Nightmare on Elm Street*.
p: Marianne Maddalena, Barin Kumar for Alive/Carolco
exec p: Wes Craven
w/d: Wes Craven
ph: Jacques Haitkin
m: William Goldstein
ed: Andy Blumenthal
pd: Cynthia Kay Charette
cos: Isis Mussenden
Mitch Pileggi, Michael Murphy, Peter Berg, Cami Cooper, Heather Langenkamp, Jessica Craven, John Tesh, Richard Brooks, Bingham Ray

Shonteff, Lindsay (1940-)
Canadian director working in Britain. He began his directorial career in his homeland with a 1958 short titled *The Bum*. Work as a production assistant followed, after which he directed his first feature, *The Hired Gun*, in 1960. Perhaps best known for his first British film, *Devil Doll*, his other credits include *Licensed to Kill* (aka *The Second Best Secret Agent in the Whole Wide World*), *The Million Eyes of Su-Muru*, *Permissive*, *Big Zapper* and such unwatchable drivel as *Spy Story*, *Number One of the Secret Service*, *Licensed to Love and Kill*, *Number One Gun* and *The Gunfighter*.
Genre credits:
Devil Doll (1963), *Curse of Simba* (1964 - aka *Curse of the Voodoo/Lion Man*), *Night After Night After Night* (1969 - aka *Evil Is...*)

Shore, Howard
Canadian composer known for his collaborations with director David Cronenberg. Formerly with the Canadian rock band Lighthouse, he came to films via radio and television (first for the Canadian Broadcasting System), having been the music director on NBC's *Saturday Night Live* for many years, from its inception in 1975. His other movie credits include *Places in the Heart*, *After Hours*, *A Kiss Before Dying*, *Single White Female*, *Sliver*, *Mrs Doubtfire*, *M Butterfly*, *Philadelphia* and *The Client*.
Genre credits:
The Brood (1979), *Scanners* (1980), *Videodrome* (1983), *The Fly* (1986), *Dead Ringers* (1988), *The Silence of the Lambs* (1991), *The Naked Lunch* (1991), *Ed Wood* (1994)

The Shuttered Room
GB 1967 110m Technicolor
A young woman returns with her new husband to her island home, where they are menaced by a gang of youths and something nasty in the attic.

Slickly made variation of an oft-used plot which still manages a frisson or two.
p: Philip Hazelton for Warner
exec p: Tony Schenck
w: D. B. Ledrov, Nathaniel Tanchunck
story: H. P. Lovecraft, August Derleth
d: DAVID GREENE
ph: KEN HODGES
m: Basil Kirchin
md: Jack Nathan
ed: Brian Smedley-Aston
ad: Brian Eatwell
cos: Caroline Mott
sound: Kenneth Osborn, C. Humphreys
titles: Derek Nice
make-up: Harry Frampton
Gig Young, Carol Lynley, Flora Robson, Oliver Reed, William Devlin, Ann Bell, Rick Jones, Judith Arthy, Charles Lloyd Pack, Bernard Kay

The Silence of the Lambs ****
USA 1991 119m Technicolor Dolby
(AA, BEST PICTURE)
A trainee FBI agent is sent to interview a convicted serial killer in order to expose another one, and subsequently finds herself in mortal danger.

Instantly absorbing, genuinely harrowing character thriller, put together with great flair. Impossible to forget, with the performance of a lifetime from Hopkins as the urbane killer Hannibal Lecter. Unmissable for those who can take it.
p: Edward Saxon, Kenneth Utt, Ron Bozman for Orion/Strong Heart-Demme
exec p: Gary Goetzman
w: TED TALLY (AA)
novel: THOMAS HARRIS
d: JONATHAN DEMME (AA)
ph: TAK FUJIMOTO
m: HOWARD SHORE
ed: CRAIG MCKAY
pd: KRISTI ZEA
cos: Colleen Attwood
sound: SKIP LIEVSAY
make-up effects: Carl Fullerton, Neal Martz

JODIE FOSTER (AA), ANTHONY HOPKINS (AA), SCOTT GLENN, TED LEVINE, ANTHONY HEALD, Roger Corman, Brooke Smith, Diane Baker, Pat McNamara

Silent Night, Bloody Night

USA 1972 87m DeLuxe
A mad killer lurks in an old New England house where a series of murders took place.

Horror exploitation of the cheapest and most tedious kind.
p: Jeffrey Konvitz, Ami Artzi for Amor
w: Theodore Gershuny, Jeffrey Konvitz, Ira Teller
d: Theodore Gershuny
ph: Adam Gifford
m: Gershon Kingsley
ed: Tom Kennedy
Patrick O'Neal, James Patterson, Mary Woronov, Astrid Heeren, John Carradine, Walter Abel

Silent Night, Evil Night see Black Christmas

Simon, Simone (1911-)

French actress working in both Europe and America. A former fashion designer and model, she made her film début in 1931 in Le Chanteur Inconnu, though she is best remembered by genre fans for playing the mysterious Irena Dubrovna in Cat People and its sequel. Her other films include Dark Eyes (aka Les Yeux Noirs), Mademoiselle Fifi and The Extra Day.
Genre credits:
All That Money Can Buy (1941 - aka The Devil and Daniel Webster / Daniel and the Devil / Here is a Man), Cat People (1942), The Curse of the Cat People (1944)

Simonetti, Claudio

Brazilian-born composer, record producer and keyboard player who moved to Italy. After studying at the Conservatory of Santa Cecilia in Rome, he began scoring horror movies with his band Goblin, most notably for director Dario Argento. Since the split-up of Goblin, Simonetti has pursued a solo career as both composer and recording artist. His other scores include Roller and Il Fantastico Viaggio del Bagarozzo Mark.
Genre credits:
Deep Red (1975 - aka Profundo Rosso / The Hatchet Murders - co-m), Suspiria (1976 - co-m), Dawn of the Dead (1970 - aka Zombies - co-m), Tenebrae (1982 - aka Ténèbres / Unsane - co-m), Phenomena (1984 - aka Creepers - co-m), Demons (1985 - co-m), Opera (1988 -aka Terror at the Opera - co-m), Primal Rage (1988 - m)

Siodmak, Curt (1902-)

German writer and director who, after experience as a journalist, wrote a number of screenplays in Europe, the first of which was the much-mentioned People on Sunday (aka Menschen am Sonntag) in 1929, which he co-wrote with Billy Wilder and which was co-directed by his brother Robert Siodmak and Edgar G. Ulmer. He went to America in 1938, first working on the story for the Dorothy Lamour saronger Her Jungle Love. Much genre work followed, as did several novels, one of which, Donovan's Brain, has been filmed a number of times in various guises (The Lady and the Monster, Vengeance, Hauser's Memory, etc.). He turned to direction in 1951 with Bride of the Gorilla. His other credits include The Tunnel (aka Transatlantic Tunnel), Aloma of the South Seas, Berlin Express, Tarzan's Magic Fountain and Love Slaves of the Amazon.
Genre credits:
The Invisible Man Returns (1940 - co-story / co-w), The Ape (1940 - co-w), Black Friday (1940 - co-w), The Invisible Woman (1940 - co-story), The Wolf Man (1941 - w), The Invisible Agent (1942 - w), I Walked With a Zombie (1943 - co-w), Son of Dracula (1943 - story), Frankenstein Meets the Wolf Man (1943 - w), The Climax (1944 - co-w), House of Frankenstein (1944 - story), The Lady and the Monster (1944 - aka The Lady and the Doctor - novel), The Beast with Five Fingers (1946 - w), Bride of the Gorilla (1951 - w/d), Donovan's Brain (1953 - novel), The Magnetic Monster (1953 - co-w/d), Riders to the Stars (1953 - w), The Creature with the Atom Brain (1955 - w), Curucu, Beast of the Amazon (1956 - w/d), Earth vs. the Flying Saucers (1956 - story), The Devil's Messenger (1962 - co-d), Vengeance (1962 - aka The Brain / Ein Toter Sucht Seinen Morder - novel), Hauser's Memory (1970 - TVM - novel)

Siodmak, Robert (1900-1973)

American-born director, brother of Curt Siodmak. Brought up in Germany, he entered the film industry in the mid-twenties after experience as an actor in rep. Working his way up through the ranks, he began his film career as a title writer, moving on to editing and, in 1929, directing, his first film being People on Sunday (aka Menschen am Sonntag), which he co-directed with Edgar G. Ulmer (the film was also scripted by his brother Curt Siodmak and Billy Wilder). Several more German films followed, as did a number of films in France following his exile there after the Nazis came to power in Germany in 1933. In 1940 he moved to America, where his first film

was West Point Window the same year. He went on to direct several classic noirist thrillers, including The Phantom Lady, The Killers, The Suspect, Dark Mirror and Criss Cross, with the occasional foray into horror.
Genre credits:
Son of Dracula (1943), Cobra Woman (1944), The Spiral Staircase (1946)

Det Sjunde Inseglet see The Seventh Seal

Sisters *

USA 1972 90m colour
One of a pair of Siamese twins is a schizophrenic murderess. But which one?

One of de Palma's best early works, a well-crafted and constructed thriller with sequences that would not disgrace a Hitchcock picture.
p: Edward R. Pressman for American International / Pressman-Williams
w: Brian de Palma, Louisa Rose
d: BRIAN DE PALMA
ph: Gregory Sandor
m: BERNARD HERRMANN
ed: PAUL HIRSCH
pd: Gary Weist
Margot Kidder, Jennifer Salt, Charles Durning, Bill Finley, Lisle Wilson, Barnard Hughes, Mary Davenport

Skeggs, Roy (1934-)

British producer and executive who began his career as an accountant, first working for Douglas Fairbanks Productions in 1956. In 1963 he became Hammer's production accountant, then company accountant and secretary. Became a production supervisor in 1970 on such films as Blood from the Mummy's Tomb and Hands of the Ripper, after which it was but a short step to producing, his first film in this capacity being Hammer's Straight on Till Morning in 1972. Formed Cinema Arts in 1979 with his partner Brian Lawrence and produced George and Mildred and Rising Damp. Took control of Hammer (with Brian Lawrence, whom he bought out after his retirement) after its collapse in 1979 and produced Hammer House of Horror and Hammer House of Mystery and Suspense for television. Is now working in conjunction with a number of American backers on proposed remakes of classic Hammer films. Other producer credits include Love Thy Neighbour, Man at the Top and Man About the House.
Genre credits:
Straight on Till Morning (1972), The Satanic Rites of Dracula (1973), Frankenstein and the Monster from Hell (1973), To the Devil... A Daughter (1976), And the Wall Came Tumbling Down (1984 - TVM), Black

Carrion (1984 - TVM), *Child's Play* (1984 - TVM), *The Corvini Inheritance* (1984 - TVM), *Czech Mate* (1984 - TVM), *A Distant Scream* (1984 - TVM), *In Possession* (1984 - TVM), *Last Video and Testament* (1984 - TVM), *The Late Nancy Irving* (1984 - TVM), *Mark of the Devil* (1984 - TVM), *Paint Me a Murder* (1984 - TVM), *The Sweet Smell of Death* (1984 - TVM), *Tennis Court* (1984 - TVM)

Skinner, Frank (1898-1968)

Prolific American composer, conductor and arranger, long with Universal, where he contributed to a handful of their horror films, often in association with music director Charles Previn. His other credits include *Destry Rides Again*, *Hellzappoppin*, *Saboteur*, *Francis* and *Shenandoah*.
Genre credits:
Son of Frankenstein (1939), *Tower of London* (1939), *Abbott and Costello Meet Frankenstein* (1948)

The Skull

GB 1965 Technicolor Techniscope
Two antiquarians find themselves diabolically inspired by the skull of the Marquis de Sade.
　　Silly but sometimes endearing horror hokum with familiar faces.
p: Milton Subotsky, Max J. Rosenberg for Paramount/Amicus
w: Milton Subotsky
story: Robert Bloch
d: Freddie Francis
ph: John Wilcox
m: Elizabeth Lutyens
md: Philip Martell
ed: Oswald Hafenrichter
ad: Bill Constable
cos: Jackie Cummins
sp: Ted Samuels
sound: Buster Ambler, John Cox
Peter Cushing, Christopher Lee, Patrick Wymark, Nigel Green, Jill Bennett, Michael Gough, Patrick Magee, Peter Woodthorpe, April Orlich, Anna Palk

Slaney, Ivor (1921-)

British composer who worked on many of Hammer/Exclusive's early programmers (*The Gambler and the Lady*, *Spaceways*, *The Saint's Return*, *The House Across the Lake*, etc.), but none of their horror films.
Genre credits:
Prey (1977 - aka *Alien Prey*), *Terror* (1979), *Death Ship* (1980)

Slaughter, Tod (1885-1956)

Swaggering British character actor (real name N. Carter Slaughter) of the hammy 'fie thee' variety, on stage in countless Victorian barnstormers, several of which he filmed, among them *Maria Marten*, *The Ticket of Leave Man*, *The Curse of the Wraydons* and *The Greed of William Hart*.
Genre credits:
Maria Marten (1935 - aka *Murder in the Red Barn*), *Sweeney Todd - The Demon Barber of Fleet Street* (1936), *Sexton Blake and the Hooded Terror* (1938), *The Face at the Window* (1939), *Crimes at the Dark House* (1940), *The Curse of the Wraydons* (1946), *The Greed of William Hart* (1948)

Slave Girls from Beyond Infinity

USA 1987 76m Foto-Kem
On a distant planet, a group of bikini-clad girls are hunted down like animals by an evil lord.
　　Stupid sci-fi variation on *The Most Dangerous Game* (aka - *The Hounds of Zaroff*) with plenty of attractive babes for the six-pack crowd.
p: Ken Dixon for Titan
w/d: Ken Dixon
ph: Ken Wiataak, Tom Calloway
m: Carl Dante
md: Jonathan Scott Bogner
ed: Bruce Stubblefield, James A. Stewart
ad: E. Scott Morton
sp: Mark Wolf, John Eng
sound: Rick Fin, Paul Bacca
make-up effects: John Buechler, Joe Reader
Elizabeth Clayton, Don Scribner, Cindy Beale, Brinke Stevens, Carl Horner

Sleepwalkers

USA 1992 91m Technicolor Dolby
Mother and son shape-shifters move to a small American township where they proceed to prey on the locals.
　　Silly but quite lively horror nonsense, helped along by some nifty effects (including death by corn cob!) and a number of gag cameos.
p: Mark Victor, Michael Grais, Nabeel Zahid for Columbia/Ion
exec p: Dimitri Logothetis, Joseph Medawar
w: Stephen King
d: Mick Garris
ph: Rodney Charters
m: Nicholas Pyke
ed: O. Nicholas Brown
pd: John De Cuir Jr
cos: Michael Hoffman
sp: Jeffrey Okun, Tom Hester and others
sound: Don H. Matthews
2nd unit d: Richard Senta, Rexford Metz
add ph: Bert Dunk
Brian Kraus, Alice Krige, Madchen Amick, Jim Haynie, Ron Perlman, Cindy Pickett, Dan Martin, Stephen King, Clive Barker, Tobe Hooper, John Landis, Joe Dante

Slocombe, Douglas (1913-)

Distinguished British cinematographer, a former journalist, stills photographer and newsreel cameraman. Long with Ealing, he photographed many of their key films (*Hue and Cry*, *It Always Rains on Sunday*, *Kind Hearts and Coronets*, *The Lavender Hill Mob*, *Mandy*, *The Titfield Thunderbolt*, etc.), before going on to work on a string of large-scale international productions including *Freud*, *The Blue Max*, *The Music Lovers*, *The Great Gatsby*, *Rollerball*, *Never Say Never Again* and the Indiana Jones trilogy.
Genre credits:
Dead of Night (1945 - co-ph), *Circus of Horrors* (1960), *Dance of the Vampires* (1967 - aka *The Fearless Vampire Killers/Pardon Me, But Your Teeth Are in My Neck*)

Slumber Party Massacre

USA 1983 76m colour
Teenagers holding a pyjama party are killed off one by one by a maniac.
　　Sleazy exploitation flick that fails completely to create any suspense out of its overused premise. Nevertheless, it was followed by *Slumber Party Massacre II* (1987) and *Slumber Party Massacre III* (1990).
w: Rita Mae Brown
d: Amy Jones
Michele Michaels, Michael Vilela, Robin Stille, Jennifer Meyers, Debra Deliso, Brinke Stevens, Andree Honore

Smith, Dick (1922-)

American make-up effects specialist, regarded as the grandfather of modern make-up effects. Smith began experimenting in his teenage years, which led in 1945 to his first professional appointment, with NBC, where he remained for fourteen years. His first feature film was *Misty* in 1959, which he followed with *Requiem for a Heavyweight* and further television work. It wasn't until 1971, however, that he attracted widespread attention with his highly convincing old age make-up (his speciality) for *Little Big Man*, in which he transformed Dustin Hoffman into a 121-year-old. *The Godfather* followed, though it was *The Exorcist* that catapulted Smith to superstar status, his ground-breaking work on Linda Blair's possessed child Regan and his old-age make-up for Max Von Sydow's Father Merrin setting a new high for effects make-up. His work has since influenced several make-up artists, many of whom first worked as his assistants. He finally won a Best Make-Up Oscar for his work on *Amadeus* (1984), since when he has worked mostly in a supervisory capacity. His non-genre work includes *The*

247

Cardinal, *The World of Henry Orient*, *Midnight Cowboy*, *Who Is Harry Kellerman and Why Is He Saying Those Terrible Things About Me?*, *The Sunshine Boys*, *Taxi Driver*, *Marathon Man*, *The Godfather Part 2*, *Dad* and *Forever Young*.
Genre credits:
House of Dark Shadows (1970), *The Exorcist* (1973), *The Stepford Wives* (1974), *Burnt Offerings* (1976), *The Sentinel* (1976), *Exorcist II: The Heretic* (1977), *The Fury* (1978), *Altered States* (1980), *Scanners* (1980), *Ghost Story* (1981), *The Hunger* (1983), *Poltergeist III* (1988), *Tales from the Darkside: The Movie* (1990), *Death Becomes Her* (1992)

Smith, Madeleine (1949-)

Innocent-looking British actress, in films from 1967. Her credits include *Up Pompeii*, *Up the Front*, *Live and Let Die* and *The Bawdy Adventures of Tom Jones*, though she is perhaps best known for the handful of Hammer films she made in the early seventies. Much TV work.
Genre credits:
Taste the Blood of Dracula (1969), *The Vampire Lovers* (1970), *The Amazing Mr Blunden* (1972), *Theatre of Blood* (1973), *Frankenstein and the Monster from Hell* (1973), *Bloodbath at the House of Death* (1983)

Soavi, Michele (1958-)

Italian actor and director whose work has been much influenced by that of Dario Argento, whose former assistant he was on such films as *Tenebrae* and *Phenomena* (he also directed the documentary *Dario Argento's World of Horror* in 1985). In films from 1979 with *Bambule*, his other credits include the second unit work for Terry Gilliam's *The Adventures of Baron Munchausen*.
Genre credits:
Alien Terror (1980 - aka *Alien 2: Sulla Terra* - actor), *City of the Living Dead* (1980 - aka *Paura Nella Citta dei Morti Viventi* -actor), *Creepers* (1985 - aka *Phenomena* - ass d/actor), *Demons* (1986 - aka *Demoni* - ass d/actor), *Opera* (1987 - aka *Terror at the Opera* - 2nd unit d/actor), *Stage Fright* (1987 - aka *Deliria* - actor/d), *The Church* (1989 - aka *La Chiesa* - actor/d), *La Mascha del Demonio* (1990 - actor), *The Black Cat* (1990 - actor), *The Sect* (1991 - aka *La Setta* - actor/co-w/d), *Dellamorte Dellamore* (1994 -co-p/d)

Society

USA 1989 99m Technicolor
A teenage boy gradually comes to realize that his parents are aliens who prey on the lower classes.
    Boring horror junk that builds to an obscene climax, on which count it has gained a certain following.
p: Keith Walley for Medusa/Wild Street
exec p: Paul White, Keizo Kabata, Terry Ogisu
w: Woody Keith, Ricky Fry
d: Brian Yuzna
ph: Rick Fichter
m: Mark Ryder, Phil Davis
ed: Peter Teschner
pd: Mathew P. Jacobs
make-up effects: Screaming Mad George Billy Warlock, Connie Danese, Ben Slack, Evan Richards, Patrice Jennings, Tim Bartell, Charles Lucia, Heidi Kozak, Brian Bremer, Ben Meyerson, Devin de Vazquez, Pamela Matheson

Soles, P. J. (1956-)

American actress (real name Pamela Jayne Soles) who specialized in obnoxious teenage roles in the seventies, most notably as Norma Watson in Brian de Palma's *Carrie* (1976), in which she helps to engineer Carrie's soaking in pig blood at the high-school prom, and as the gum-chewing Lynda, one of the victims in John Carpenter's *Halloween*. Her other credits include *Rock 'n' Roll High School*, *Private Benjamin*, *Stripes* and *Saigon Commandos*.
Genre credits:
Carrie (1976), *The Possessed* (1977 - TVM), *Halloween* (1978)

Something Evil *

USA 1971 74m Technicolor TVM
A married couple and their children move to a remote farmhouse and discover it contains 'something evil'.
    Fairly smart supernatural thriller which does quite well by its oft-used theme and helped to display its director's emerging talent.
p: Alan Jay Factor for CBS/Bedford
w: Robert Clouse
d: STEVEN SPIELBERG
ph: Bill Butler
m: Wladimir Selnisky
ed: Allan Jacobs
ad: E. Albert Heschong
cos: Stephen Lodge, Agnes Ryan
sound: George Ronconi
Sandy Dennis, Darren McGavin, Ralph Bellamy, Jeff Corey, Johnnie Whittaker, John Rubinstein

Something Wicked This Way Comes **

USA 1982 94m Technicolor Panavision Dolby
At the turn of the century, a sinister carnival visits a small American town and two boys help to destroy the evil carnival owner, who is out to get them because they have stumbled across his secrets.
    Skilfully made macabre fantasy whose elements come together most satisfactorily. Unfortunately, it failed find an appreciative audience.
p: Peter Vincent Douglas for Walt Disney/Bryna
w: RAY BRADBURY from his novel
d: JACK CLAYTON
ph: STEPHEN H. BURUM
m: JAMES HORNER (after a score by Georges Delerue was rejected)
ed: Argyle Nelson, Barry Mark Gordon
pd: Richard MacDonald
cos: Ruth Myers
sp: LEE DYER and others
sound: Bob Hathaway
sound effects: Richard R. Portman, David M. Horton
make-up effects: Robert J. Schiffer
JASON ROBARDS JR, Jonathan Pryce, Shawn Carson, Vidal Peterson, Pam Grier, Diane Ladd, Royal Dano, Angelo Rossitto, Jill Carroll, Tony Christopher, Mary Grace Canfield, Richard Davalos

Son of Dracula *

USA 1943 80m bw
Under the name of Alucard (yes, that old chestnut), Count Dracula is the guest of an unsuspecting family in America's deep south.
    Enjoyable, eerily effective addition to Universal's gallery of horrors, with sequences in the genre's best style.
p: Forde Beebe for Universal
w: Eric Taylor
story: Curtis Siodmak
d: ROBERT SIODMAK
ph: GEORGE ROBINSON
m: Hans J. Salter
ed: Saul Goodkind
ad: John B. Goodman, Martin Obzina
cos: Vera West
sp: John P. Fulton
sound: Bernard B. Brown, Charles Carroll
Lon Chaney Jr, Louis Allbritton, Robert Paige, Samuel S. Hinds, Evelyn Ankers, Fran Craven Jr, J. Edward Bromberg

Son of Frankenstein **

USA 1939 99m bw
After the death of his father, Baron Frankenstein's son returns to the family fold only to pick up the experiments where his father left off.
    Stylish but halting third instalment in Universal's celebrated Frankenstein series, much of which now seems unintentionally funny thanks to Mel Brooks' later parody, *Young Frankenstein*. Connoisseurs of the genre will no doubt be able to appreciate its finer points.
p: Rowland V. Lee for Universal
w: Willis Cooper
d: ROWLAND V. LEE
ph: GEORGE ROBINSON

m: FRANK SKINNER
md: Charles Previn
ed: Ted Kent
ad: JACK OTTERSON, RICHARD RIEDEL
cos: Vera West
sound: Bernard B. Brown, William Hedgecock
make-up: Jack P. Pierce
BASIL RATHBONE, BORIS KARLOFF, Lionel Atwill, BELA LUGOSI (as Ygor), Josephine Hutchinson, Donnie Dunagan, Emma Dunn, Edgar Norton, Lawrence Grant

Son of Godzilla
Japan 1967 86m Technicolor
Godzilla protects his motherless son from a giant praying mantis and spider.

Enjoyably ludicrous monster hokum which has to be seen to be believed.
p: Tomoyuki Tanaka for Toho
w: Shinichi Sekizawa, Kazue Shiba
d: Jun Fukuda
ph: Kazuo Yamada
m: Masaru Soto
ed: Ryohei Fujuii
ad: Takeo Kita
sp: Sadamas Arikawa, Eiji Tsuburaya
sound: Shin Hatari, Toshiya Ban
Tadaeo Takashima, Bibara Maeda, Akira Kubo, Akihiko Hirata, Kenji Sahara

Son of Kong *
USA 1933 69m bw
After the death of King Kong, Carl Denham returns to Skull Island, only to discover another giant ape which later saves him from drowning in a storm.

Rushed sequel made to cash in on the success of King Kong. The effects have their interest, but the whole is relentlessly padded and generally disappointing. Even at this length, it is tedious to sit through.
p: Merian C. Cooper for RKO
w: Ruth Rose
d: Ernest B. Schoedsack
ph: Eddie Linden, Vernon L. Walker, J. O. Taylor
m: Max Steiner
ed: Ted Cheesman
ad: Van Nest Polglase, Al Herman
cos: Walter Plunkett
sp: WILLIS O'BRIEN
sound: Earl A. Wolcott
sound effects: Murray Spivack
ROBERT ARMSTRONG, Helen Mack, Frank Reicher, John Marston, Victor Wong, Ed Brady, Katherine Ward, Noble Johnson, Clarence Wilson, Lee Kohlmar

Sondergaard, Gale (1899-1985)
American actress, the archetypal sinister housekeeper, who won the first ever Best Supporting Actress Oscar for

Anthony Adverse (1936). She came to films via the stage (stock and Broadway), though investigation by the House Un-American Activities Committee halted her career for several years. Her other credits include The Bluebird, The Letter, Anna and the King of Siam, The Road to Rio and The Return of a Man Called Horse.
Genre credits:
The Cat and the Canary (1939), The Black Cat (1941), Spider Woman (1944), The Invisible Man's Revenge (1944), The Climax (1944), Spider Woman Strikes Back (1946), The Cat Creature (1974 - TVM), Echoes (1981)

The Sorcerers
GB 1967 85m Eastmancolor
An elderly couple discover a way of experiencing other people's pleasures via hypnosis and thought transferral. But something goes wrong...

Silly horror hokum, of passing interest to buffs for its credits.
p: Patrick Curtis, Tony Tenser for Tigon/Curtwel/Global
exec p: Arnold L. Miller
w: Michael Reeves, Tom Baker
story: John Burke
d: Michael Reeves
ph: Stanley Long
m: Paul Ferris
ed: David Woodward, Susan Michie
ad: Tony Curtis
sound: Ken Osbourne
Boris Karloff, Catherine Lacey, Ian Ogilvy, Elizabeth Ercy, Victor Henry, Susan George, Alf Joint, Meier Tzelniker

Spasmo *
It 1974 86m colour
A businessman accused of murder is helped by a beautiful girl, but it's a set-up to get him committed to an asylum.

Absurdly over-plotted shocker with a few pretensions to style for connoisseurs.
p: Ugo Tucci for UTI Produzione Associate
w: Masimo Franciosa, Luisa Montagnano, Pino Boller, Umberto Lenzi
d: Umberto Lenzi
ph: Guguelmo Mancori
m: Ennio Morricone
ed: Eugenio Ababiso
pd: Giacomo Galo Garalucci
Robert Hoffman, Suzy Kendall, Ivan Rassimov, Adolfo Lastretti, Franco Silva, Mario Erpichini, Monica Monet

Species
USA 1995 108m DeLuxe DTS Stereo
A shape-shifting alien escapes from a research institute and goes on the run in the guise of a beautiful young woman.

Tired, overtalkative, not to mention wholly predictable variation on Alien and The Thing. Nevertheless, it did surprisingly well at the box office.
p: Frank Mancuso Jr, Dennis Feldman for MGM/UA
exec p: David Streit, Lee Orloff
w: Dennis Feldman
d: Roger Donaldson
ph: Adrzej Bartkowiak
m: Charistopher Young
ed: Conrad Buff
pd: John Muto
cos: Joe I. Tompkins
sp: Richard Edlund
sound: Jay Boekelheide
make-up effects: Steve Johnson
alien design: H. R. Giger
titles: Dan Perri
stunt co-ordinator: Glenn Randall Jr, Max Kleven
Ben Kingsley, Michael Madsen, Forest Whitaker, Alfred Molina, Marg Helgenberger, Natasha Henstridge

Specters
It 1988 96m Kodak Dolby
Archaeologists unearth an evil spirit when they discover an ancient Roman catacomb.

Half-baked horror nonsense, typical of the Italian genre.
p: Maurizio Tedesco for Avtar/Reteitalia/Trio Cinema
w: Marcello Avallone, Andrea Purgatori, Dardano Sacchetti, Maurizio Tedesco
idea: Andrea Purgatori, Dardano Sacchetti, Maurizio Tedesco
d: Marcello Avallone
ph: Silvano Ippoliti
m: Lele Marchitelli, Danilo Rea
ed: Adriano Tagliavia
ad: Carmelo Agate
cos: Paola Collaccini Bonucci, Maurizio Marchitelli
sp: Sergio Stivaletti
sound: Danilo Moroni
Donald Pleasence, John Pepper, Katrine Michelson, Massimo de Rossi, Lavinia Grizi

Spellbinder
USA 1988 99m colour
A young lawyer rescues a young woman from muggers and falls in love with her only to discover that she is a witch.

Wholly unremarkable hocus-pocus.
p: Joe Wizan, Brian Russell for MGM/UA
w: Tracy Torme
d: Janet Greek
ph: Adam Greenberg
m: Basil Poldedouris
ed: Steve Mirkovich
pd: Roger Maus
Timothy Daly, Kelly Preston, Rick

Rossovich, Diana Bellamy, Audra
Lindley, Roderick Cook

Sphinx

USA 1980 118m Technicolor Panavision
Murder and intrigue follow the path of
several archaeologists as they search for
a hidden tomb.

Fairish horror drama which only
occasionally comes to life, despite the
talent involved.
p: Stanley O'Toole for
Warner/Orion/Schaffner-O'Toole
w: John Byrum
novel: Robin Cook
d: Franklin J. Schaffner
ph: Ernest Day
m: Michael J. Lewis
ed: Robert E. Swink, Michael E.
Anderson
pd: Terence Marsh
cos: Judy Moorcroft
Lesley-Anne Down, Frank Langella,
Maurice Ronet, John Gielgud, Vic
Tablian, John Rhys Davies, Martin
Benson, Saeed Jaffrey

Spielberg, Steven (1947-)

Commercially successful American
writer, producer, director and executive,
responsible for a string of blockbusting
action and adventure films which caused
him to be dismissed by serious critics.
More recently he has displayed a maturer
side with such films as *The Color Purple*,
Empire of the Sun and *Schindler's List*, which
finally won him Best Director and Best
Picture Oscars. His genuine
understanding of all things cinematic has
occasionally been squandered a little too
freely (*1941*, *Hook*), but when in top form
(*Jaws*, *Close Encounters of the Third Kind*,
Raiders of the Lost Ark, *E. T.*) his films can
transport millions. Into making home
movies from an early age, Spielberg went
professional in 1969 (after studying film
at California's State College) with the
short *Amblin*, a name he later used for his
production company, founded in 1984
with producers Kathleen Kennedy and
Frank Marshall. Several episode segments
(*Night Gallery*, *Columbo*) and TV movies
followed at Universal, climaxing with the
acclaimed thriller *Duel*, which led to his
big-screen directorial début, *The Sugarland
Express*. *Jaws* followed, and the rest, as they
say, is cinema history. His latest venture is
Dreamworks SKG, a new studio which he
created with producers Jeffrey
Katzenberg and David Geffen. His films
as a producer include such hits as the *Back
to the Future* trilogy, *An American Tail*, *Who
Framed Roger Rabbit?* and *Joe vs. the Volcano*.
Genre credits:
Something Evil (1971 - TVM -d), *Jaws*
(1975 - d), *Poltergeist* (1982 -

story/co-w/co-p), *Twilight Zone: The
Movie* (1983 - co-p/co-d), *Gremlins* (1985
- co-p), *Arachnophobia* (1990 - co-p),
Gremlins 2: The New Batch (1990 - co- p),
Jurassic Park (1993 - co-p/d), *Casper* (1995
- exec p), *The Lost World* (1997 - co-exec
p/d)

Spinell, Joe (1936-1989)

American actor (real name Joseph
Spagnuolo) with stage experience. A
minor support in such big films as *The
Godfather*, *The Godfather Part II*, *Farewell,
My Lovely*, *Taxi Driver*, *Rocky*, *Rocky II*,
Nighthawks and *Married to the Mob*,
though he is better remembered for
playing the lead in the low-budget slash-
er pic *Maniac*, which he also co-wrote.
Genre credits:
The Ninth Configuration (1980), *Maniac*
(1980 - also co-w/story/co-exec p), *The
Last Horror Film* (1984 - aka *Fanatic*),
Deadly Illusion (1987)

Splatter

Splatter movies - horror films with a high
gore content and much gratuitous violence, often in loving close up - came into
their own in the late seventies following
the success of *Halloween*, *Friday the 13th*
and their countless derivatives. By no
means the first examples of their kind
(Hammer's *Curse of Frankenstein* and the
many films of director Herschell Gordon
Lewis in the sixties were the splatter films
of their day), the term came into public
usage in the eighties, along with 'stalk
and slash' and 'video nasty', though splatter itself can be traced back to the plays
and illusions staged at the Theatre du
Grand Guigol in Paris in the late 1800s.
Key filmography:
The Curse of Frankenstein (1956), *Color Me
Blood Red* (1964), *2000 Maniacs* (1964), *A
Taste of Blood* (1967), *Night of the Living
Dead* (1968), *Mark of the Devil* (1969 - aka
Hexen), *The Corpse Grinders* (1971), *The
Gore Gore Girls* (1971), *Death Line* (1972 -
aka *Raw Meat*), *Sisters* (1973), *Andy
Warhol's Frankenstein* (1974), *Andy Warhol's
Dracula* (1974), *The Texas Chainsaw
Massacre* (1974), *Carrie* (1976), *Suspiria*
(1976), *Martin* (1978), *Halloween* (1978),
Dawn of the Dead (1979 - aka *Zombies*),
Zombie Flesheaters (1979 - aka *Zombi 2*),
Friday the 13th (1979), *The Burning*
(1981), *Halloween II* (1981), *The Funhouse*
(1981), *Maniac* (1981), *Scanners* (1981),
The Evil Dead (1983), *A Nightmare on Elm
Street* (1984), *Re-Animator* (1985),
Hellraiser (1987), *Braindead* (1992), etc.

Spook Louder

USA 1942 20m bw
Three door-to-door salesmen inadvertently catch some spies posing as ghosts.

Tame Three Stooges romp which fails
to make the most of an old chestnut.
p: Del Lord, Hugh McCollum for
Columbia
w: Clyde Bruckman
d: Del Lord
ph: John Stumar
ed: Paul Borofsky
ad: Carl Anderson
Curly Howard, Larry Fine, Moe
Howard, Stanley Blystone, Lew Kelly

Spookies

USA 1985 86m colour
Partying teenagers fall foul of a sorcerer
and zombies when they break into a
crumbling mansion.

Nothing we haven't seen a hundred
times before (and usually better done).
p: Eugenie Joseph, Thomas Doran,
Brendan Faulkner, Frank M. Farel for
Twisted Souls Inc.
w: Eugenie Joseph, Thomas Doran,
Brendan Faulkner, Joseph Burgund
d: Eugenie Joseph, Thomas Doran,
Brendan Faulkner
ph: Robert Chappel, Ken Kelsch
m: Kenneth Higgins, James Calabrese
ed: Eugenie Joseph
ad: Anne Burgund, Cecilia Consetini
cos: Tom Molinelli, Anne Burgund
sp: John Dods
sound: Judy Carp, Scott Breindell,
Alexandra Balyarzuk
make-up effects: Arnold Gargiulo and
others
Felix Ward, Lisa Friede, Maria Pechukes,
Alec Remser, Nick Gionta

Spooks Run Wild

USA 1941 65m bw
The East Side Kids are sent off to
summer camp and find themselves
involved with spooks and murderers.

Poverty Row time-filler, hard to sit
through for anyone but fans of the gang.
Lugosi isn't even the monster.
p: Sam Katzman for
Monogram/Banner/Astor
w: Carl Foreman, Charles Marion
d: Phil Rosen
ph: Marcel Le Piccard
ed: Robert Golden
Bela Lugosi, Leo Gorcey, Huntz Hall,
Bobby Jordan, David Gorcey, Sammy
Morrison, Donald Haines, David
O'Brien, Dorothy Short, Rosemary
Portia, George Pembroke, Guy
Wilkerson, Ava Gardner

Spoorloos see The Vanishing (1989)

Stage Fright

It 1987 90m colour
Actors rehearsing a musical are
murdered by an escaped lunatic.

• Horror icon Barbara Steele in her most famous film, director Mario Bava's *Black Sunday*.

Unremarkable shocker that doesn't quite make the most of its situations or setting.
p: Filmirage
w: Lew Cooper (Joe D'Mato)
d: Michele Soavi
ph: Renato Tafuri
m: Simon Boswell
sp: Don Maklansky, Robert Gould and others
sound: Hubrecht Nijhuis, David Lee David Brandon, Barbara Cupisti, Don Fiore, Robert Gligrow, Mickey Knox, Clain Parker, Lori Parrel, Martin Phillips, James Sampson

Stannard, Roy
British art director, solid contributor to two of Hammer's later films.
Genre credits:
Hands of the Ripper (1971), *Twins of Evil* (1971)

Steckler, Ray Dennis (1939-)
American director and actor (using the name Cash Flagg) with a penchant for wildly titled low-budgeters, several of which have gained cult status. A former army photographer in Korea, he began his movie career by photographing a handful of low-budget films, including *Frenzy*, *Secret File: Hollywood* and *Drivers in Hell* (aka *Wild Ones on Wheels*). His first stab at directing was *Wild Guitar* in 1961, followed by *The Incredibly Strange Creatures...* His other credits include *Rat Pfink a-Boo-Boo* and *Body Fever*.
Genre credits:
The Incredibly Strange Creatures Who Stopped Living and Became Mixed-Up Zombies (1962), *Scream of the Butterfly*

(1965), *The Lemon Grove Kids Meet the Monsters* (1966), *The Hollywood Strangler Meets the Skid Row Slasher* (1979)

Steele, Barbara (1938-)
Striking-looking British actress who, after rep experience, made a few minor films for Rank (*Bachelor of Hearts*, *Sapphire*, etc.) before going to Italy, where she became a star in director Mario Bava's *Black Sunday*. Many other horror outings followed in the sixties, a number of them in Europe. Then came several exploitation items in the seventies (*Caged Heat*, etc.) before she retired from the screen and turned to producing with the epic TV series *The Winds of War* and its sequel, *War and Remembrance*. Her other acting credits include *I Never Promised You a Rose Garden*, *Pretty Baby* and *La Clé Sur La Porte*.
Genre credits:
Black Sunday (1960 - aka *Mask of the Demon*/*La Maschera del Demonio*), *The Pit and the Pendulum* (1961), *The Horrible Dr Hitchcock* (1962 - aka *The Terror of Dr Hitchcock*/*L'Orrible Segreto del Dottore Hitchcock*), *The Spectre* (1963 - aka *The Ghost*/*Lo Spettro de Dr Hitchcock*), *Castle of Blood* (1964 - aka *La Danza Macabra*), *The Maniacs* (1964 - aka *I Maniaci*), *The Long Hair of Death* (1964 - aka *I Lunghi Capelli della Morte*), *Terror Creatures from the Grave* (1965 - aka *Cinque Tombe per un Medium*), *Revenge of the Blood Beast* (1965 - aka *She-Beast*/*La Sorella di Satana*), *The Faceless Monster* (1965 - aka *Nightmare Castle*/*Gli Amanti D'Oltre Tomba*), *An Angel for Satan* (1966 - aka *Un Angelo per Satana*), *The Curse of the Crimson Altar* (1968 - aka *The Crimson Cult*), *Shivers* (1974 - aka *The Parasite Murders*/*They Came from Within*), *The Space Watch Murders* (1978 - TVM), *Piranha* (1978), *The Silent Scream* (1980)

Steele, Pippa (1948-1992)
Pretty British actress remembered chiefly for her two Hammer appearances. Her other film credits include *Mr Forbush and the Penguins* and *Young Winston*, as well as appearances in TV's *Saturday Night Theatre*, *Public Eye* and *Z Cars*.
Genre credits:
The Vampire Lovers (1970), *Lust for a Vampire* (1971)

Stein, Ronald
Prolific American composer with many B movies to his credit, the first of which was Roger Corman's *Apache Woman* in 1955. Several more films for Corman followed, along with all manner of low-budget drive-in schlockers. His other credits include *The Day the World Ended*,

It Conquered the World, *Not of This Earth*, *Gunslinger*, *Tank Commandos*, *Hot Rod Gang*, *Getting Straight*, *The Rain People* and *Razzle Dazzle*.
Genre credits:
The She-Creature (1957), *Attack of the Crab Monsters* (1957), *Attack of the Fifty-Foot Woman* (1958), *The Ghost of Dragstrip Hollow* (1959), *The Devil's Partner* (1959), *The Undead* (1959), *The Premature Burial* (1961), *Dementia 13* (1963 - aka *The Haunted and the Hunted*), *The Haunted Palace* (1963), *The Terror* (1963), *Spider Baby* (1964 - aka *Cannibal Orgy*)

Steiner, Max (1888-1971)
Prolific Austrian composer and music director with over 200 films to his credit, rightly regarded by many as the grandfather of the symphonic film score, one of his earliest being the ground-breaking *King Kong*. A child prodigy, he trained at Vienna's Imperial Academy of Music and studied with Mahler, after which he became a conductor. Emigrating to America in 1914, he quickly found work as a conductor on Broadway. He went to Hollywood in 1929 where his influence as a composer was far-reaching, his development of the *leitmotif* way of scoring (whereby which each major character has a musical theme of his or her own) still being in use today, particularly in the scores of John Williams, whom many regard as Steiner's successor. A Best Score Oscar winner for *The Informer* (1935), *Now, Voyager* (1942) and *Since You Went Away* (1944), his other credits include *The Charge of the Light Brigade*, *Gone with the Wind*, *Casablanca*, *The Big Sleep* and *The Dark at the Top of the Stairs*.
Genre credits:
The Most Dangerous Game (1932 - aka *The Hounds of Zaroff*), *King Kong* (1933), *Son of Kong* (1933), *She* (1935), *Two on a Guillotine* (1965)

Stensgaard, Yutte (1946-)
Danish actress (real name Jytte Stensgaard) in Britain from 1963. A former au pair and model, she gained some experience on British television (*A Play in the Darkness*, *The Saint*, etc.) before making her film début in *Girl with a Pistol* (aka *La Ragazza con la Pistola*) in Italy in 1967. Fleeting appearances in *Some Girls Do*, *This, That and the Other* (aka *Promise of a Bed*), *Carry On Again Doctor*, *Doctor in Trouble* and *Zeta One* (aka *The Love Factor*) followed. However, she is best known for her largest role, as the vampire Mircalla in Hammer's *Lust for a Vampire* - though this is more because of the iconographic publicity

still featuring her sitting topless in a coffin, covered in blood, than because of the performance itself. Her other television work includes appearances in *Jason King*, *On the Buses*, *The Persuaders* and the quiz show *The Golden Shot*.
Genre credits:
Scream and Scream Again (1970), *Lust for a Vampire* (1970), *Burke and Hare* (1971)

The Stepfather *
USA 1986 88m CFIcolor Ultra Stereo
A teenage girl comes to believe that her stepfather is a mass murderer. He is...
   Low-budget shocker that generally makes the most of its opportunities. Certainly a cut above the average. It was followed by *Stepfather 2* (1989) and *Stepfather 3* (1992 - TVM).
p: Jay Benson for ITC/New World
w: Donald E. Westlake
story: Carolyn Lefcourt, Brian Garfield, Donald E. Westlake
d: Joseph Ruben
ph: John Whindley
m: Patrick Moraz
ed: George Bowers
pd: James William Newport
cos: Mina Mittletown
sp: Bill Orr, Don Harriss
sound: Larry Sutton
stunt co-ordinator: V. John Wardlow
Terry O'Quinn, Jill Schoelen, Shelley Hack, Charles Lanyer, Stephen Shellen, Stephen E. Miller, Robyn Stevan

Stepfather 2
USA 1989 88m Technicolor
Jerry Blake escapes from the mental institution in which he's been incarcerated and attempts to marry into another family.
   Reasonably slick sequel-cum-remake with a bigger budget in evidence after the surprise success of the first film.
p: Darin Scott, William Burr for ITC/Part II Productions
exec p: Carol Lapman
w: John Aurbach
d: Jeff Burr
ph: Jacek Laskins
m: Jim Nazie, Pat Regan
ed: Pasquale A. Buba
pd: Byrnadette Disanto
cos: Julie Carnatham
sound: David Brownlow
Terry O'Quinn, Meg Foster, Caroline Williams,, Jonathan Brandis, Henry Brown

Stepfather 3
USA 1992 96m Eastmancolor TVM
Jerry Blake descends upon yet another family after undergoing plastic surgery.
   Juvenile third instalment, amateurishly written and performed.
p: Guy Magar, Paul Moen for New Line

w: Guy Mager, Marc B. Kay
d: Guy Mager
ph: Alan Caso
m: Patrick C. Regan
ed: Patrick Greaston
pd: Richard B. Lewis
cos: Judy Sarafian
sp: Andre Ellingson
sound: William Fiege
Robert Wightman, Priscilla Barnes, Season Hubley, David Tom, John Ingle

Stephen King's It see It

Stevenson, Robert Louis (1850-1894)
British novelist whose novella *The Strange Case of Dr Jekyll*, published in 1886, has been filmed many, many times, most notably in 1931 (Fredric March won an Oscar for his dual role) and in 1941 (with Spencer Tracy). Variations include *Abbott and Costello Meet Dr Jekyll and Mr Hyde*, *I, Monster*, *Dr Jekyll and Sister Hyde* and *Dr Jekyll and Ms Hyde*. Other filmed works include *The Body Snatcher*, *Kidnapped*, *The Wrong Box*, *Ebb Tide* and countless versions of *Treasure Island*. See also *Dr Jekyll and Mr Hyde*.

Stine, Clifford
American special-effects technician and effects photographer, long with Universal, where he worked on several of their lesser genre entries.
Genre credits:
Tarantula (1955), *Abbott and Costello Meet the Mummy* (1955), *The Deadly Mantis* (1957), *Monster on the Campus* (1958), *The Thing That Couldn't Die* (1958)

Stoker, Bram (1847-1912)
Irish novelist, author of *Dracula*, published in 1897, one of the screen's most oft-filmed novels. A former civil servant and theatre reviewer for the *Dublin Mail*, Stoker became the manager of actor Henry Irving's Lyceum Theatre in London in 1878, remaining there for almost thirty years. Countless variations on *Dracula* have proliferated down the decades, most notably in 1922 (as *Nosferatu*, with Max Schreck), 1930 (with Bela Lugosi), 1958 (with Christopher Lee), 1979 (with Frank Langella), 1979 (as *Nosferatu the Vampyre*, with Klaus Kinski) and 1992 (with Gary Oldman). His novella *Jewel of the Seven Stars* has been filmed twice, as *Blood from the Mummy's Tomb* (1971) and *The Awakening* (1980). *The Lair of the White Worm* was filmed in 1988. See also *Dracula*.

Stolen Face
GB 1952 72m bw

• A rare studio portrait of Glenn Strange without his Frankenstein Monster make-up.

A plastic surgeon attempts to change the scarred face of a criminal into that of the girl he really loves.
   Very tolerable if ultimately rather silly melodrama with echoes of *Vertigo* to come.
p: Anthony Hinds for Hammer/Exclusive
w: Martin Berkeley, Richard Landau
story: Alexander Paal, Steven Vas
d: Terence Fisher
ph: Walter Harvey
m: Malcolm Arnold
ed: Maurice Rootes
ad: Wilfred Arnold
cos: Edith Head
sound: Bill Salter
make-up: Phil Leakey
ass d: Jimmy Sangster
Paul Henreid, Lizabeth Scott, André Morell, John Wood, Susan Stephen, Arnold Ridley, Mary Mackenzie

Stoler, Shirley (1929-)
Ample American character actress, remembered for playing murderous nurse Martha Beck in *The Honeymoon Killers* (1969). Her only other genre appearance to date is in *Frankenhooker* (1990), though she has popped up as a supporting actress in a wide variety of films, including *Seven Beauties*, *The Displaced Person* and *Miami Blues*.

Stone, Dee Wallace see Wallace, Dee

Strange, Glenn (1899-1973)
Tall American actor, a former rancher and stuntman, familiar to TV audiences

for his role as Sam in the long-running western series *Gunsmoke*. He appeared in countless minor westerns (*Hurricane Express, Border Law, Hard Hombre, Cattle Thief, The Lonely Trail*, etc.) and serials (*The Law of the Wild, Flash Gordon, Flying G-Men, The Lone Ranger Rides Again*), though he is perhaps best remembered by genre fans for his portrayal of the Monster in three of Universal's Frankenstein films.
Genre credits:
The Mad Monster (1941), *House of Frankenstein* (1944), *House of Dracula* (1945), *Abbott and Costello Meet Frankenstein* (1948)), *Master Minds* (1949)

The Strange World of Planet X
GB 1957 75m bw
A scientist's experiments with magnetic fields causes insects to mutate into giant man-eaters.

Talkative low-budget science-fiction hokum with (when they finally appear) some pretty dismal monsters.
p: George Maynard for Eros//Artistes Alliance
w: Paul Ryder
novel: Rene Ray
d: Gilbert Gunn
ph: Joe Ambor
m: Robert Sharples
ed: Francis Bieber
ad: Bernard Sarron
cos: Irma Birch
sp: Anglo-Scottish Pictures
sound: Cecil Mason
Forrest Tucker, Gaby Andre, Martin Benson, Hugh Latimer, Alec Mango, Wyndham Goldie, Dandy Nicholls, Richard Warner

The Stranger Within *
USA 1974 74m Technicolor TVM
Despite all precautions, a woman becomes pregnant and finds herself curiously controlled by her unborn child.

Watchable thriller with a dash of *Rosemary's Baby* and a pinch of *The Exorcist*.
p: Neil T. Maffeo for ABC
exec p: Phil Capice, Neil Rich
w: Richard Matheson from his story
d: Lee Philips
ph: Michael Margulies
m: Charles Fox
ed: Gene Fowler Jr, Samuel E. Beetley
ad: Hilyard Brown
cos: Patricia Norris
sound: Dwight Mobley
Barbara Eden, George Grizzard, Joyce Van Patten, Nehemiah Persoff, David Doyle

The Strangler
USA 1963 80m bw

A mother-dominated lab technician goes about strangling women.

Tolerable low-budget thriller.
p: Samuel Bischoff, David Diamond for Allied Artists
w: Bill S. Ballinger
d: Burt Topper
ph: Jacques Marquette
m: Martin Skiles
ed: Robert S. Eisen
ad: Hal Pereira, Eugene Lourie
sound: Hugo Grenzbach, Charles Grenzbach
Victor Buono, Ellen Corby, Diane Sayer, David McLean

Strickfaden, Kenneth (1896-1984)
American special-effects technician (often working uncredited) remembered for creating the lab equipment and electrical effects seen in Universal's 1931 version of *Frankenstein* (so much so that he was asked to recreate them in 1974 for the Mel Brooks parody *Young Frankenstein*). A US Marine during World War One, he began his film career in the twenties working as an electrician for several Hollywood studios. His early credits as an effects technician include *Wings* and *The Return of Sherlock Holmes*, though it was his breakthrough work on *Frankenstein* that established his reputation. His other credits include the serials *The Phantom Empire, The Clutching Hand, Flash Gordon, Buck Rogers* and *The Mysterious Dr Satan,* as well as contributions to such films as *Showboat* and *The Wizard of Oz.*
Genre credits:
Frankenstein (1931 - lab equipment), *Chandu the Magician* (1932 -electrical effects), *The Mask of Fu Manchu* (1932 - electrical effects), *The Bride of Frankenstein* (1935 - lab equipment), *Son of Frankenstein* (1939 - lab eqipment), *Monstrosity* (1963 - sp), *Dracula vs. Frankenstein* (1971 - aka *Blood of Frankenstein* - sp), *Young Frankenstein* (1974 - lab equipment), etc.

Strock, Herbert L. (1918-)
American director with a penchant for low-budget horrors. Turned to direction after experience as a movie publicist and editor. His other credits include *Gog, Battle Taxi* and *Rider on a Dead Horse*.
Genre credits:
The Magnetic Monster (1953 - ed), *I Was a Teenage Frankenstein* (1957 - aka *Teenage Frankenstein* - d), *Blood of Dracula* (1957 - aka *Blood Is My Heritage/Blood of the Demon* - d), *How to Make a Monster* (1958 - d), *The Devil's Messenger* (1959 - co-d), *The Crawling Hand* (1963 - d), *Monster* (1978 - aka *Monsteroid/The Legend That*

Became a Terror/It Came from the Lake - co-d), *Witches' Brew* (1979 - TVM - aka *Witch is Which?/It's a Charmed Life* - co-d)

Struss, Karl (1891-1981)
American cinematographer, a former portrait photographer who entered films in 1919 as a cameraman for director Cecil B. de Mille. Went on to win (with Charles Rosher) the first Oscar for Best Photography for work on *Sunrise* (1927). Other credits include *Ben-Hur, Coquette, The Sign of the Cross, Journey Into Fear, Limelight* and *Rocketship XM.*
Genre credits:
Dr Jekyll and Mr Hyde (1932), *Island of Lost Souls* (1932), *The Fly* (1958), *The Alligator People* (1959)

Studios
Those studios most identified with the horror genre are A. I. P., Amicus, Hammer and Universal, all of which have their own entries.

A Study in Terror *
GB 1965 95m Eastmancolor
Sherlock Holmes investigates the case of Jack the Ripper.

An odd mixture of Hammer-style horror and parody which doesn't always seem to know whether or not to take itself seriously. On the whole Basil Rathbone is still preferable, but the production is adequate enough.
p: Henry E. Lester for Compton-Tekli/Sir Nigel
exec p: Herman Cohen
w: Donald Ford, Derek Ford
novel: Ellery Queen
d: James Hill
ph: DESMOND DICKINSON
m: John Scott
ed: Henry Richardson
ad: Alex Vetchinsky
cos: Motley
sp: Wally Veevers
sound: H.L. Bird, John Cox
John Neville, Donald Houston, John Fraser, Cecil Parker, Anthony Quayle, Robert Morley (as Mycroft Holmes), Barbara Windsor, Adrienne Corri, Judi Dench, Frank Finlay, Kay Walsh, Georgia Brown, Jeremy Lloyd

Styles, Michael (1933-)
British producer who, after a time in Canada, returned to Britain in 1958. He joined ATV as a sports producer, graduating to drama with productions of *A Month in the Country* and *Luther*. His first film as a producer was *Monique* for Tyburn, after which came Hammer's *Carmilla* trilogy, which he co-produced with his partner Harry Fine, with whom he also formed Fantale Films.

Genre credits:
The Vampire Lovers (1970 - co-p), *Lust for a Vampire* (1971 - co-p), *Twins of Evil* (1971 - co-p), *Fright* (1971 - co-p)

Subotsky, Milton (1921-1991)

American writer and producer who began his career making documentaries and industrial films, which he wrote, directed and edited. This led to a stint as an editor with the US Army's Signal Corps Photographic Centre during World War Two. Experience as an 'ideas man' for impresario Billy Rose and work as a sales manager for a distribution company followed, though it was in television (in which he'd already had experience in 1941) that he finally began to make inroads as a writer in 1949. In 1953 he met distributor Max J. Rosenberg while working on the children's TV series *Junior Science* (which he wrote and produced and Rosenberg financed) and the two decided to go into partnership. The outcome was *Rock, Rock, Rock* (1957), a musical exploitation item (which they produced together and which Subotsky wrote) modelled on the success of the previous year's *Rock Around the Clock*. The two men formed Amicus Pictures in Britain in 1965, giving Hammer a run for its money with a series of chillers and *Dead of Night*-style horror compendiums, a good many of them written by Subotsky and directed by Freddie Francis and Roy Ward Baker. Subotsky left Amicus in 1975 and went on to produce either solo or with others. He remained pretty much in the horror genre, though the results of his efforts were more variable. His other credits include *Dr Who and the Daleks, Daleks Invasion Earth: 2150 AD, The Terrornauts, At the Earth's Core* and *The Martian Chronicles* (TVM).
Genre credits:
City of the Dead (1960 - aka *Horror Hotel* - story/co-exec p), *Dr Terror's House of Horrors* (1964 - w/co-p), *The Skull* (1965 - w/co-p), *The Deadly Bees* (1965 - co-p), *The Psychopath* (1965 - co-p), *They Came from Beyond Space* (1967 - w/co-p), *Torture Garden* (1967 - co-p), *Scream and Scream Again* (1970 - co-p), *The House That Dripped Blood* (1970 - co-p), *I, Monster* (1970 - w/co-p), *Tales from the Crypt* (1971 - w/co-p), *Asylum* (1972 - co-p), *And Now the Screaming Starts* (1972 - co-p), *Vault of Horror* (1973 - w/co-p), *Madhouse* (1974 - co-p), *From Beyond the Grave* (1974 - co-p), *The Beast Must Die* (1974 - aka *Black Werewolf* - co-p), *The Land That Time Forgot* (1974 - co-p), *The Uncanny* (1977 - co-exec p), *Dominique* (1977 - p), *The Monster Club*

(1980 - p), *Cat's Eye* (1985 - co-p), *Maximum Overdrive* (1986 - co-p), *Sometimes They Come Back* (1991 - TVM - co-p), *Lawnmower Man* (1992 - co-p)

Suopr Omicidi see Killer Nun

Suspiria **

It 1976 97m Eastmancolor Technovision
A young ballerina discovers that her academy is really a front for a witches' coven.

Required viewing for fans of its director, this visually flamboyant horror film has plenty to take the eye, though the dialogue often leaves much to be desired. The set pieces (which are basically what the film is about) are superbly staged, though they may not be for the squeamish.
p: Claudio Argento for Sedda Spettacoli
exec p: Salvatore Argento
w: Dario Argento, Dario Nicolodi
d: DARIO ARGENTO
ph: Luciano Tovoli
m: Goblin, Dario Argento
ed: Franco Fraticelli
pd: GIUSEPPE BASSAN
cos: Pierangelo Ciccoletti
sp: Germano Natali
sound: Mario Dallimonti, Federico Savina
Jessica Harper, Joan Bennett, Alida Valli, Stefania Casini, Udo Kier, Miguel Bose, Susanna Javicoli, Margherita Horowitz

Sutherland, Donald (1935-)

Canadian actor who appeared in a handful of horror films before finding international stardom in the seventies in such films as *M*A*S*H, Kelly's Heroes, Klute* and *Don't Look Now*. His other films include *1900, Casanova, National Lampoon's Animal House, Ordinary People, A Dry White Season* and *Six Degrees of Separation*.
Genre credits:
Castle of the Living Dead (1964), *Dr Terror's House of Horrors* (1964), *Fanatic* (1965 - aka *Die! Die, My Darling!*), *Don't Look Now* (1973), *Invasion of the Body Snatchers* (1978), *Murder by Decree* (1979), *Buffy the Vampire Slayer* (1992), *The Puppet Masters* (1994), *Outbreak* (1995)

Svengali *

USA 1931 81m bw
A musician with the power to hypnotize turns a Parisian model into a great opera star.

Dated and often stilted melodrama whose interest lies mainly in the imaginative art direction, though the star and director have their moments, too.
p: Warner
w: J. Grubb Alexander
novel: George du Maurier
d: ARCHIE MAYO
ph: Barney McGill
md: Leo F. Forbstein

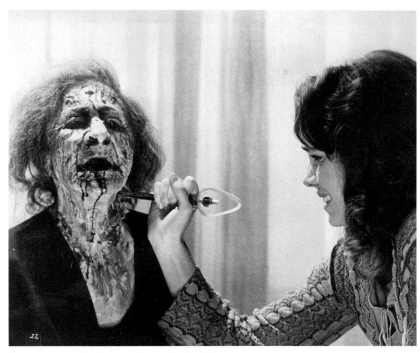

Dario Argento's *Suspiria*: Susy (Jessica Harper) reaches a gory moment in her struggle with the powers of evil.

ed: William Goldman
ad: ANTON GROT
sp: Fred Jackman
JOHN BARRYMORE, Marian Marsh,
Luis Alberni, Lumsden Hare, Paul
Porcasi, Donald Crisp

Svengali

GB 1954 82m Eastmancolor
At the turn of the century, a mysterious
musician turns a model into a great
singer.

Low-budget remake which fails to
make the most of a golden opportunity.
p: George Minter for Renown/
Alderdale
w/d: Noel Langley
novel: George du Maurier
ph: Wilkie Cooper
m: William Alwyn
md: Muir Mathieson
ed: John Pomeroy
ad: FRED PUSEY
cos: Beatrice Dawson
sound: Sash Fisher
ass d: Denis O'Del
cam op: Alan Hume
Donald Wolfit, Hildegarde Neff, Terence
Morgan, David Kossoff, Paul Rogers,
Derek Bond, Hubert Gregg, Alfie Bass,
Harry Secombe, Richard Pearson

Swamp Thing

USA 1982 92m Technicolor
A scientist working in the Everglades on
a top-secret formula is turned into a
half-human half-plant monster when his
experiment goes wrong.

Foolish sci-fi hokum from the DC
comic strip, ludicrous even by the standards of its own genre. *Return of the
Swamp Thing* followed in 1989.
p: Benjamin Melniker, Michael E. Uslan
for UA
w/d: Wes Craven
ph: Robin Goodwin
m: Harry Manfredini

ed: Richard Bracken
ad: David Nichols, Robb Wilson King
cos: Patricia Bolomet, Bennett Choate
sound: David Dockendorf, John Mack,
Bob Deschaine
make-up: William Munns
stunt co-ordinator: Ted Duncan
Louis Jourdan, Adrienne Barbeau, Ray
Wise, David Hess, Nicholas Worth, Dick
Durock (as Swamp Thing)

Sweeney Todd - The Demon Barber of Fleet Street *

GB 1936 68m bw
A London barber robs and murders his
clients and uses their bodies to make
meat pies.

Stilted star melodrama with acting
and direction alike wooden. Of passing
interest for Slaughter's rantings.
p: George King
w: H. F. Maltby
novel: Frederick Hayward
d: George King
ph: Jack Parker
m: no credit given
ed: John Seabourne
ad: Percy Bell
sound: J. Byers
Tod Slaughter, Bruce Seton, Eve Lister,
Stella Rho, Ben Soutten, D. J. Williams,
Jerry Verno, John Singer.

Sykes, Peter (1939-)

Australian-born director, a former
actor and dancer. Came to Britain in
1963, where he contributed to such TV
series as *The Avengers* before turning to
films in 1968 with *The Committee*. He
directed Hammer's last genre film, *To
the Devil... A Daughter*. Other credits
include *Steptoe and Son Ride Again*, *Jesus*
and TV's *The Irish RM*.
Genre credits:
Venom (1971 - aka *The Legend of Spider
Forest*), *Demons of the Mind* (1972), *The*

House in Nightmare Park (1973), *To the
Devil... A Daughter* (1976), *Crazy House*
(1977)

Sylos, Paul

American art director with a handful of
low-budgeters to his credit.
Genre credits:
Billy the Kid vs. Dracula (1965), *Jesse
James Meets Frankenstein's Daughter*
(1966), *The Dunwich Horror* (1969)

Sylvester, William (1922-1995)

American actor whose film career took
off in Britain in 1949 (after three years
at RADA), though it is perhaps for his
role as Dr Heywood Floyd in *Kubrick's
2001: A Space Odyssey* that he is best
remembered. His other credits include
They Were Not Divided, *Whirlpool*, *The Last
Safari*, *The Hindenberg* and *Heaven Can
Wait*.
Genre credits:
Gorgo (1960), *The Devil Doll* (1964),
Devils of Darkness (1965), *The Hand of
Night* (1967 - aka *The Beast of Morocco*)

Symptoms

GB 1974 92m Eastmancolor
A madwoman goes on a killing spree in
a lonely house.

Uneventful low-budget thriller which
might have made an acceptable half-hour
for TV. It is nevertheless held in high
esteem in some quarters.
p: Jean Dupuis for Finiton
w: Joseph Larraz, Stanley Miller
d: Joseph Larraz
ph: Trevor Wrenn
m: John Scott
ed: Eric Boyd-Perkins
ad: Kenneth Bridegwater
Angela Pleasence, Lorna Heilbron, Peter
Vaughan, Ronald O'Neil, Raymond
Huntley, Michael Grady, Nancy
Nevinson, Marie-Paul Mailleux

T

Tales from the Crypt *

GB 1972 92m Eastmancolor
Five people are separated from their
party during a trip to the catacombs,
and whilst trying to find their way out
they meet a mysterious old man who
tells them their futures.

Superior Amicus horror comic with
one or two good jolts, the best story
involving a murderous Father Christmas.
p: Milton Subotsky for
Amicus/Metromedia
w: Milton Subotsky
d: FREDDIE FRANCIS
ph: Norman Warwick
m: Douglas Gamley
ed: Teddy Darvas
ad: Tony Curtis
Ralph Richardson, Joan Collins,
Geoffrey Bayldon, Peter Cushing, Ian
Hendry, Robin Phillips, Richard Greene,
Barbara Murray, Roy Dotrice, Nigel
Patrick, Patrick Magee

Tales from the Darkside - The Movie *

USA 1990 93m Technicolor
A young boy about to be cooked alive by
a witch tells her three stories to occupy
her long enough for him to plan his
escape.

Mildly amusing horror compendium
via a long-running TV series. Nothing
really new, but adequately presented.
p: Richard P. Rubinstein, Mitchell Galin
for Paramount
w: Michael McDowell, George A.
Romero
stories: Stephen King, Sir Arthur Conan
Doyle
d: John Harrison
ph: Robert Draper
m: Donald P. Rubinstein, Jim Manzie,
Pat Regan, Chaz Jankell, John Harrison
ed: Harry B. Miller
ad: Ruth Amon
cos: Ida Gearon
make-up effects: Dick Smith
Deborah Harry, Christian Slater, David
Johansen, William Hickey, James Remar,
Rae Dawn Chong, Matthew Lawrence

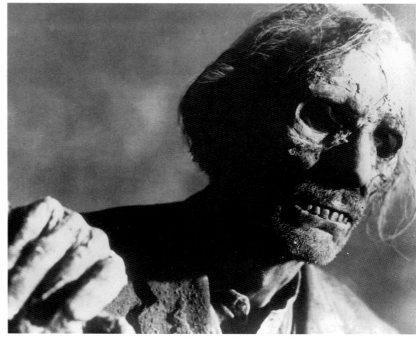

• Peter Cushing as Arthur Grimsdyke in *Tales from the Crypt*, one of the better
Amicus horror anthologies.

Tales of Terror *

USA 1962 89m Pathecolor Panavision
Three tales of terror inspired by the
writings of Edgar Allan Poe: *Morella*, *The
Black Cat* and *The Facts in the Case of M.
Valdemar.*

A variable collection, of which the
first is undoubtedly the most effective.
p: Roger Corman for AIP
exec p: James H. Nicholson, Samuel Z.
Arkoff
w: Richard Matheson
stories: Edgar Allan Poe
d: Roger Corman
ph: Floyd Crosby
m: Les Baxter
ed: Anthony Carras
pd/ad: Daniel Haller
cos: Marjorie Corso
sp: Pat Dinga
sound: John Bury
titles: Murray Laden

VINCENT PRICE, Peter Lorre, Basil
Rathbone, Debra Paget, Maggie Pierce,
Leona Gage, Joyce Jameson, Wally
Campo, David Frankham, Dick Miller

Tales That Witness Madness *

GB 1973 91m Eastmancolor
An asylum keeper tells a friend four
tales of madness involving an imaginary
tiger, a time-travelling penny-farthing, a
'living' tree and a human sacrifice.

Watchable if somewhat tenuously
linked collection of stories from a by
now familiar stable.
p: Norman Priggen for Amicus/World
Film Services
w: Jay Fairbank
d: Freddie Francis
ph: Norman Warwick
m: Bernard Ebbinghouse
ed: Bernard Gribble
ad: Roy Walker

cos: Bridget Sellers
sound: Ken Ritchie, Nolan Roberts
cam op: Ronnie Taylor
Kim Novak, Joan Collins, Donald
Pleasence, Jack Hawkins, Georgia
Brown, Michael Petrovitch, Michael
Jayston, Mary Tamm, Peter McEnery,
Suzy Kendall, Donald Houston, Russell
Lewis, David Wood, Leon Lissek

Tamblyn, Russ (1934-)

American actor, dancer and singer who,
after small roles in such films as *Samson
and Delilah*, *Father of the Bride* and *As
Young as You Feel* (in which he was billed
as Rusty Tamblin), came into his own as
a sprightly juvenile lead in *Seven Brides
for Seven Brothers*, *Peyton Place*, *Tom
Thumb* and *West Side Story* before his star
began to diminish in the mid-sixties. He
then appeared in a number of low-
budget exploitation films before making
a comeback of sorts in the TV series
Twin Peaks.
Genre credits:
The Haunting (1963), *War of the
Gargantuas* (1966 - aka *Sanda vs. Gailah/
Sanda Tai Gailah*), *Blood of Frankenstein*
(1970 - aka *Dracula vs. Frankenstein*),
Satan's Sadists (1971), *Blood Scream*
(1986 - aka *Les Monjes Sangrientos*), *The
Phantom Empire* (1987), *Demon Sword*
(1989), *Wizards of the Demon Sword*
(1991)

Tanner, Peter (1914-)

British editor whose genre work has
mostly been for Amicus. His non-genre
credits include *Scott of the Antarctic*, *Kind
Hearts and Coronets*, *The Blue Lamp*, *Sodom
and Gomorrah*, *Stevie*, *Without a Clue* and
Danny, Champion of the World.
Genre credits:
The House That Dripped Blood (1970), *I,
Monster* (1970), *Asylum* (1972), *And Now
the Screaming Starts* (1973), *The Monster
Club*

Tarantula

USA 1955 80m bw
Scientists experimenting on a new
serum infect a tarantula which
subsequently escapes into the desert
where it grows to an enormous size.

Standard low-budget sci-fi-horror
hokum for the fifties drive-in market,
let down by risible effects work. For
connoisseurs of the genre.
p: William Alland for Universal
w: Robert M. Fresco, Martin Berkeley
d: Jack Arnold
ph: George Robinson
md: Joseph Gershenson
ed: William A. Morgan
ad: Alexander Golitzen, Alfred Sweeney
sp: Clifford Stine

make-up: Bud Westmore
Leo G. Carroll, John Agar, Mara Corday,
Nestor Piava, Ross Eliott, Clint
Eastwood (glimpsed briefly as a bomber
pilot)

Targets **

USA 1967 91m Pathecolor
A sniper is finally cornered at a drive-in
by an ageing horror-film star.

Curious, compelling, offbeat, low-
budget horror melodrama which
launched its director's career and gave
its star his last really good role, a gentle
spoof of his own screen image.
p: Peter Bogdanovich for Paramount
w/d: PETER BOGDANOVICH
ph: Laszlo Kovacs
m: no credit given
ed: Mae Woods
pd: Polly Platt
sound: Sam Kofetzky
sound ed: Verna Fields
ass d: Frank Marshall
BORIS KARLOFF (as Byron Orlok),
Tim O'Kelly, Nancy Hsueh, James
Brown, Peter Bogdanovich, Sandy
Baron, Frank Marshall

Taste of Fear **

GB 1961 82m bw
An heiress confined to a wheelchair goes
to the South of France to visit the father
she has not seen for ten years. When she
gets there she discovers that he has
mysteriously disappeared.

Coiled-spring shocker, rather typical
of Sangster's they're-trying-to-drive-me-
insane output for Hammer (other
variations being *Maniac*, *Paranoiac*,
Crescendo and *Fear in the Night*). Quite
stylishly done for all that, and with
enough twists to keep one watching.
p: Jimmy Sangster for
Hammer/Columbia
w: JIMMY SANGSTER
d: SETH HOLT
ph: DOUGLAS SLOCOMBE
m: Clifton Parker
md: John Hollingsworth
ed: James Needs, Eric Boys-Perkins
ad: Bernard Robinson
cos: Dora Lloyd
sound: Leslie Hammond, E. Mason, Len
Shilton
Susan Strasberg, Ann Todd, Ronald
Lewis, Christopher Lee, Leonard Sachs

Taste the Blood of Dracula *

GB 1969 95m Technicolor
Three Victorian gentlemen in search of
excitement become involved in black
magic and the resurrection of Count
Dracula.

One of the better sequels in
Hammer's Dracula series, with

everything grist to its familiar mill.
p: Aida Young for Hammer
w: John Elder (Anthony Hinds)
d: Peter Sasdy
ph: Arthur Grant
m: James Bernard
md: Philip Martell
ed: Chris Barnes
ad: Scott MacGregor
cos: Brian Owen Smith
sp: Brian Johncock
sound: Rod Barrod, Tony Lumkin
Christopher Lee, Geoffrey Keen, Gwen
Watford, Linda Hayden, Peter Sallis, Isla
Blair, Ralph Bates, Roy Kinnear, John
Carson, Martin Jarvis, Madeleine Smith,
Michael Ripper

Taylor, Gilbert (1914-)

Distinguished British cinematographer
whose list of credits includes such
important films as *The Guinea Pig*, *Ice
Cold in Alex*, *Dr Strangelove*, *A Hard Day's
Night*, *The Bedford Incident*, *Frenzy*, *Star
Wars* and *Flash Gordon*. Began as a camera
assistant in 1929.
Genre credits:
Repulsion (1965), *The Omen* (1976),
Dracula (1979), *Venom* (1982)

Teague, Lewis (1941-)

American director who began his career
as an editor for Roger Corman before
going on to co-direct (with Howard
Freen) his first film, *Dirty O'Neill*, in
1974. Second unit work on such films as
Death Race 2000, *Thunder and Lightning*
and *Avalanche* followed before his solo
début in 1979 with *The Lady in Red*
(which he also edited). He had a small-
scale hit with the *Jaws* spoof *Alligator* in
1980, which led to a couple of Stephen
King adaptations. He then successfully
moved on to big-budget action films like
The Jewel of the Nile and *Navy SEALS*.
Genre credits:
Alligator (1980), *Cujo* (1983), *Cat's Eye*
(1984)

Teen Wolf

USA 1985 90m Labcolor
A high-school basketball player
habitually turns into a werewolf and
helps lead his team to victory.

Puerile teenage dross, of interest
only to pubescent werewolves. The
presence of Michael J. Fox, fresh from
his success in *Back to the Future* and TV's
Family Ties, was enough to turn it into a
box-office hit, however. An even worse
sequel, *Teen Wolf Too*, starring Jason
Bateman, followed in 1987.
p: George Perkins, Mark Levinson,
Scott Rosenfelt for Atlantic
exec p: Thomas Coleman, Michael
Rosenblatt

w: Joseph Loeb III, Matthew Weisman
d: Rod Daniel
ph: Tim Suhrstedt
m: Miles Goodman
ed: Lois Freeman-Fox
ad: Chester Kaczenski
make-up effects: Tom Burman
Michael J. Fox, Scott Paulin, Susan
Ursitti, James Hampton, Jerry Levine,
Matt Adler

Teenage Frankenstein see I Was a Teenage Frankenstein

Teenage Monster

USA 1957 69m bw
In 1880, a teenage boy turns into a hairy
monster after being struck by a ball of
fire from outer space.

Amateurish grade Z rubbish.
p: Jacques Marquette for Howco
International/Marquette
w: Ray Buffum
d: Jacques Marquette
ph: Taylor Bijars
m: Walter Greene
ed: Irving Schoenberg
ad: no credit given
cos: Jerry Bos
sound: Philip Miotchell
Anne Gwynne, Charles Courtney,
Gloria Castillo, Stuart Wade, Norman
Leavitt, Gilbert Perkins (as the
monster), Stephen Parker

The Tell-Tale Heart *

GB 1960 81m bw
When his best friend falls in love with
his fiancée, a Victorian gentleman
resorts to murder, hiding the body
under the floorboards, only to be
tormented by the apparent beating of
the dead man's heart.

Mildly diverting low-budget horror
piece with restricted sets. However,
even at this length, padding is evident.
p: Edward Danziger, Harry Lee
Danziger for Danziger
w: Brian Clemens, Eldon Howard
story: Edgar Allan Poe
d: Ernest Morris
ph: James Wilson
m: Tony Combie, Bill Le Sage
ed: Derek Parsons
ad: Peter Russell
cos: Rene Jerrold Coke
sound: W. A. Howell, George Adams
Laurence Payne, Adrienne Corri,
Dermot Walsh, Selma Vas Diaz, John
Scott, John Martin, Annette Carell

10 Rillington Place *

GB 1970 111m Eastmancolor
Just after World War Two, a tenant in a
shabby apartment building gases and
strangles several women, but the wrong

man is executed for the crimes.

Claustrophobic and dingily realistic
account of a real-life case, complement-
ed by a chilling performance from its
star. Commendable but depressing.
p: Leslie Linder, Martin Ransohoff for
Columbia/Filmways
w: Clive Exton
book/technical adviser: Ludovic
Kennedy
d: RICHARD FLEISCHER
ph: Denys Coop
m: John Dankworth
ed: Ernest Walter
ad: MAURICE CARTER
cos: Tiny Nicholls
sound: Bob Allen, Ken Scrivener
RICHARD ATTENBOROUGH, JOHN
HURT, Pat Heywood, Judy Geeson,
Isobel Black, Geoffrey Charter, André
Morell, Robert Hardy, Sam Kydd

The Tenant *

Fr 1976 126m Eastmancolor
A man moves into an apartment building, fears that he is being persecuted by
the other tenants, and gradually takes
on the persona of his flat's previous
occupant.

Initially intriguing but finally
exhausting psycho-drama with echoes of
the same director's Repulsion. Too long
to be wholly effective, but with
interesting touches.
p: Andrew Braunsberg for Paramount/
Marianne
w: Gerard Brach, Roman Polanski
novel: Roland Topor
d: Roman Polanski
ph: Sven Nykvist
m: Philippe Sarde
ed: Françoise Bonnot
pd: Pierre Guffroy
cos: Jacques Schmidt
sp: Jean Fochet
sound: Jean-Pierre Ruh
Roman Polanski, Shelley Winters,
Melvyn Douglas, Isabelle Adjani, Jo Van
Fleet, Lila Kedrova, Claude Dauphin

Tenebrae *

It 1983 104m Technicolor Techniscope
Whilst in Rome to promote his latest
novel, a thriller writer finds himself
amid a series of grizzly murders similar
to those described in his books.

Involved mystery thriller in its
director's best high-tech style. Of note
for its set pieces, one of which involves
an intricate single-take Louma crane
shot in, over and around a house, finally
coming to rest on the murderer as he
attempts to break in. Certainly not for
the squeamish.
p: Claudio Argento for Sigma
exec p: Salvatore Argento

w: Dario Argento, George Kemp
story: Dario Argento
d: DARIO ARGENTO
ph: Luciano Tovoli
m: Simonetti, Pignatelli, Morante
ed: Franco Fraticelli
pd: Giuseppe Bassan
cos: Pierangelo Cicoletti
sp: Giovanni Corridori
sound: Mario Dallimonti, Romano
Pampaloni
ass d: Lamberto Bava, Michele Soavi
Anthony Franciosa, John Saxon,
Guillano Gemma, Daria Nicolodi, Ania
Peroni, Mirella Dangelo, Isabella
Amadeo, Mirella Banti

Ténèbres see Tenebrae

Tenser, Tony

British producer and production execu-
tive who, in 1967, founded Tigon
British, a production company specializ-
ing in low-budget horror films, the most
successful of which was Witchfinder
General.
Genre credits:
The Sorcerers (1967 - exec p), The Bloodbeast
Terror (1967 - aka The Vampire-Beast Craves
Blood - exec p), Witchfinder General (1968 -
aka The Conqueror Worm - exec p), The
Curse of the Crimson Altar (1968 - aka The
Crimson Cult/The Crimson Altar - exec p),
The Haunted House of Horror (1969 - aka
Horror House -p), The Beast in the Cellar
(1970 - exec p), The Creeping Flesh (1972 -
co-exec p)

The Terminal Man

USA 1974 107m Technicolor Panavision
After a series of black-outs during which
he becomes excessively violent, a
computer genius is given an implant to
suppress his urges. Unfortunately, it
exaggerates them.

Technically competent but otherwise
slow and rather boring fantasy thriller.
p: Mike Hodges for Warner
w/d: Mike Hodges for Warner
novel: Michael Crichton
ph: Richard H. Kline
m: Bach
ed: Robert L. Woolfe
ad: Fred Harpman
George Segal, Joan Hackett, Richard
Dysart, Jill Clayburgh, Donald Moffat,
Michael C. Gwynne, James B. Sikking

The Terror

GB 1938 73m bw
The hooded terror lurking in the cellars
of an old country house turns out to be
the criminal who masterminded a gold
bullion robbery.

Stilted thriller with writing and
performances that must have seemed

dated even at the time.
p: Walter C. Mycroft for ABP
w: William Freshman
novel/play: Edgar Wallace
d: Richard Bird
ph: Walter Harvey
m: no credit given
ed: Lionel Tomlinson
ad: Cedric Dawe
cos/sound: no credit given
Wilfred Lawson, Arthur Wontner,
Linden Travers, Alastair Sim, Henry
Oscar, Bernard Lee, Irene Handl,
Kathleen Harrison, Richard Murdoch.

Terror at the London Bridge
USA 1985 96m colour TVM
Jack the Ripper re-appears at London
Bridge in present-day Arizona.

A rather desperate idea for a
tele-thriller. Needless to say, it doesn't
work on any level.
w: William F. Nolan
d: E. W. Swackhamer
ph: Gil Hubbs
m: Lalo Schifrin
ed: Tom Fries, Leslie Dennis
ad: Tom McAllister
David Hasselhoff, Stephanie Kramer,
Randolph Mantooth, Adrienne Barbeau,
Clu Gulagher, Lane Smith, David
Fox-Brenton, Paul Rossilli

Terror at the Opera see Opera

Terror from the Year 5,000
USA 1958 74m bw
Scientists working on a time machine
inadvertently transport a monster back
from the future.

Grade Z sci-fi rubbish with horror
elements.
p: Robert J. Guerney Jr for AIP
exec p: James H. Nicholson, Samuel Z.
Arkoff
w/d: Robert J. Guerney Jr
ph: Arthur Florman
m: no credit given
ed: Dede Allen
ad: Bill Hoffman
sound: Bob Hathaway
Ward Costello, Joyce Holden, John
Stratton, Frederic Downs, Fred Herrick

Terror in the Wax Museum
USA 1973 94m DeLuxe
Murders that take place in a Victorian
wax museum are initially attributed to
the waxworks themselves…

Cheapjack horror farrago, inept on
every level. How the starry cast was
roped in is anyone's guess.
p: Andrew J. Fenady for Bing Crosby
Productions
exec p: Charles A. Pratt
w: Jameson Brewer

story: Andrew J. Fenady
d: George Fenady
ph: William Jurgensen
m: George Duning
ed: Melvin Shapiro
pd: Stan Jolley
Ray Milland, Broderick Crawford, Elsa
Lanchester, Louis Hayward, Maurice
Evans, Shani Wallis, Nicole Shelby, Mark
Edwards, Patric Knowles, John
Carradine, Lisa Lu, Steven Marlo, Don
Herbert

Terror of Mechagodzilla
Japan 1975 88m colour
Godzilla finds himself pitted against a
giant mechanical version of himself.

Lunatic monster epic in the Japanese
manner.
p: Tomoyuki Tanaka for Toho/Miracle
w: Yukiko Takayama
d: Inoshiro Honda
ph: Mototaka Tomanu
m: Akira Ifukube
ed: Yoshitami Kuroiwa
sp: Teruyoshi Nakano
sound: Fumio Yanoguchui
Katsuhiko Sasaki, Tomoko Ai, Akihito
Hirata, Katsumasa Uchida, Goro Mutsu,
Kenji Sahara

The Terror of Sheba see
Persecution

The Terror of the Vampires see
Le Frisson des Vampires

Terror Train
Canada 1979 98m DeLuxe
During a train-bound party, a college
student avenges himself by murdering all
those who played a cruel prank on him
several years earlier.

Formula killer thriller which doesn't
quite make the most of its setting, though
a few routine shocks are provided on the
way. Includes a rare movie appearance by
David Copperfield, who later became
one of the world's top illusionists.
p: Sandy Howard, Harold Greenberg,
Daniel Grodnik for Astral Bellevue
Pathe/Triple T/Lamar Card
w: T. Y. Drake
d: Roger Spotiswoode
ph: John Alcott
m: John Mills-Cockell
ed: Anne Henderson
pd: Glenn Bydwell
cos: Penny Hadfield
sp: Josef Élsner
sound: Bo Harwood
Ben Johnson, Jamie Lee Curtis, Hart
Bochner, David Copperfield, Derek
McKinnon, Sandee Currie, Timothy
Webber, Anthony Sherwood

• Edwin Neal taunts Marilyn Burns in
director Tobe Hooper's notorious
Texas Chainsaw Massacre.

Terry-Thomas (1911-1990)
British comedy actor (real name Thomas
Terry Hoar-Stevens) whose supercilious
manner and gap-toothed smile livened
up many a film (*Private's Progress, Those
Magnificent Men in Their Flying Machines,
It's a Mad, Mad, Mad, Mad World, The
Last Remake of Beau Geste*, etc.). His
genre work was mostly as comic
support, though in *Vault of Horror* he was
dismembered by his wife and placed in a
row of pickle jars, one of which
contained his gap teeth!
Genre credits:
Munster, Go Home! (1966 - TVM), *The
Abominable Dr Phibes* (1971), *Dr Phibes
Rises Again* (1972), *Vault of Horror*
(1973), *The Hound of the Baskervilles*
(1978)

The Texas Chainsaw Massacre
USA 1974 80m CFIcolour
A group of teenagers are brutally slain
by a family of cannibals whilst driving
through Texas.

Notorious, much banned, but highly
influential exploitation piece whose
occasional pretensions to style and
humour make it seem even more revolting and sadistic. A must for splatter fans.
It was followed by *The Texas Chainsaw
Massacre Part 2* (1986) and *Leatherface:
Texas Chainsaw Massacre III* (1990).
p: Tobe Hooper for
Vortex/Henkel/Hooper
w: Kim Henkel, Tobe Hooper
d: Tobe Hooper
ph: Daniel Pearl, Tobe Hooper
m: Wayne Bell, Tone Hooper
ed: Sallye Richardson, Larry Carroll
ad: Robert A. Burns
make-up: Dorothy Pearl, W. E. Barnes

MAKE-UP MAESTRO ROB BOTTIN poses
with one of his creations for the John
Carpenter remake of *The Thing*.
Slated by the critics on its release, the
film has since been recognized as a
classic by fans.

Marilyn Burns, Allan Danzinger, Paul A. Partain, William Vail, Teri Mominn, Edwin Neal, Jim Siedow, Gunner Hansen (as Leatherface), John Dugan

The Texas Chainsaw Massacre Part 2

USA 1986 90m TVColor Ultra Stereo
A lady disc-jockey falls foul of a family of cannibals living in a condemned fairground.

Determinedly gruesome sequel whose vestiges of ultra-black humour make it seem all the more deplorable. Strictly for gorehounds.
p: Tobe Hooper, Menahem Golan, Yoram Globus for Cannon
exec p: Henry Holmes, James Jorgensen
w: L. M. Kit Carson
d: Tobe Hooper
ph: Richard Kooris
m: Tobe Hooper, Jerry Lambert
ed: Alain Jaknbowicz
pd: Cary White
cos: Carin Hooper
sound: Wayne Bell
make-up effects: Tom Savini
Dennis Hopper, Caroline Williams, Bill Johnson, Bill Moseley, Jim Siedow

Theatre of Blood **

GB 1973 103m DeLuxe
A Shakespearian actor, thought to have been drowned, comes back to murder those critics who gave him bad notices.

Rather black blend of camp humour and grizzly horror in the Dr Phibes tradition, with cherishable moments for those who can take it.
p: John Kohn, Stanley Mann for UA/Cineman/Harbor
exec p: Gustav Berne, Sam Jaffe
w: Anthony Grevill-Bell
idea: Stanley Mann, John Kohn
d: DOUGLAS HICKOX
ph: Wolfgang Suschitzky
m: Michael J. Lewis
ed: Malcolm Cooke
pd: Michael Seymour
cos: Michael Baldwin
sp: John Stears
sound: Simon Kaye, Douglas Turner
cam op: Ronnie Taylor
ch: Tutte Lemkow
stunt co-ordinator: Terry York
make-up: George Blackler
VINCENT PRICE, Diana Rigg, Ian Hendry, Harry Andrews, Coral Browne, Robert Coote, Jack Hawkins, Michael Hordern, Arthur Lowe, Diana Dors, Robert Morley, Dennis Price, Joan Hickson, Renee Asherson, Milo O'Shea, Eric Sykes, Madeleine Smith, Tutte Lemkow

Ernest Thesiger, one of the horror genre's most cherished character actors.

Thesiger, Ernest (1879-1961)

Gaunt-looking British character actor and noted embroiderer, remembered for his portrayal of Dr Praetorius in *The Bride of Frankenstein*. A former artist, he became an actor in 1909 and began making films as early as 1916, though it was his appearance as Horace Femm in James Whale's *The Old Dark House* in 1932 that brought him to the public's attention. His other films include *The Man Who Could Work Miracles*, *My Learned Friend*, *Caesar and Cleopatra*, *Quartet*, *Last Holiday*, *The Man in the White Suit*, *Father Brown* and *Sons and Lovers*.
Genre credits:
The Old Dark House (1932), *The Ghoul* (1933), *The Bride of Frankenstein* (1935), *A Place of One's Own* (1944), *The Ghosts of Berkeley Square* (1947), *Scrooge* (1951 - aka *A Christmas Carol*)

They Live

USA 1988 94m DeLuxe Panavision Dolby
In the near future, a wanderer discovers that the world has been infested by aliens who have disguised themselves as humans, and can only be seen for what they really are through special sunglasses.

Promising science-fiction thriller which works in fits and starts. Good sequences along the way, though on the whole it doesn't quite come off and certainly isn't among its director's best efforts.
p: Larry Franco for Alive
exec p: Shep Gordon, Andre Blay
w: Frank Armitage
story: Ray Nelson
d: John Carpenter
ph: Gary B. Kibbe
m: John Carpenter, Alan Howarth
ed: Gib Jaffe, Frank E. Jimenez
ad: William J. Durrell Jr, Daniel Lomino
cos: Robin Bush
sp: Roy Arbogast
sound: John Judkins
Roddy Piper, Keith David, Meg Foster, George 'Buck' Flower, Peter Jason, Raymond St Jacques, Jason Robards III, John Lawrence, Larry Franco

They Saved Hitler's Brain

USA 1963 74m bw
Having saved Hitler's brain in a pickle jar, a group of Nazi scientists plan his comeback.

Stupefyingly inept horror hokum without even the saving grace of humour. A turkey if ever there was one.
p: Carl Edwards
w/d: David Bradley
ph: Stanley Cortez
m: Leon Seletze, Alan Marks
ad: Frank Sylos
Walter Stocker, Audrey Caine, Carlos Rivas, John Holland, Dani Lynn, Marshall Reed, Nestor Paiva

The Thing **

USA 1951 87m bw
Members of a scientific expedition in the Arctic find themselves menaced by a monster from another world.

Semi-classic science-fiction thriller, a little slow to start with, but building up to sequences of genuine tension and alarm.
p: Howard Hawks for RKO/Winchester
w: Charles Lederer
story: J. W. Campbell Jr
d: Christian Nyby
ph: Russell Harlan
m: Dimitri Tiomkin
ed: Roland Gross
ad: Albert S. D'Agostino, John J. Hughes
cos: Michael Woulfe
sp: Donald Steward, Linwood Dunn
sound: Phil Brigand, Clem Portman
Kenneth Tobey, Robert Cornthwaite, Margaret Sheridan, Bill Self, Dewey Martin, James Arness (as The Thing)

The Thing **

USA 1982 109m Technicolor Panavision Dolby
A monstrous creature from another world, able to take the form of its victims, is unwittingly let into an isolated Arctic research station, where it subsequently runs amok.

Technically adroit, genuinely frightening remake of the 1951 movie, with superior make-up effects. Not for the squeamish, it is now rightly ranked among its director's best work, though

at the time of release it was a critically derided box-office flop.
p: David Foster, Lawrence Turman, Stuart Cohen for Universal
exec p: Wilbur Stark
w: Bill Lancaster
story: J. W. Campbell Jr
d: JOHN CARPENTER
ph: DEAN CUNDEY
m: Ennio Morricone
ed: Tony Ramsey
pd: John L. Lloyd
cos: Ronald I. Caplan, Gilbert Loe
sp: Albert Whitlock, Roy Arbogast
sound: Thomas Causey
make-up effects: ROB BOTTIN
stunt co-ordinator: Dick Warlock
Kurt Russell, J. Wilford Brimley, T. K. Carter, David Clenon, Richard Dysart, Richard Masur

The Thing from Another World
see The Thing (1951)

Thirst
Australia 1979 98m Eastmancolor Panavision
A young woman is initiated into a modern-day vampire cult, the members of which believe her to be descended from Elizabeth Bathory.
    Initially promising variation on a well-worn theme, but too leisurely in its telling to be entirely effective, and further hampered by a let-down ending.
p: Anthony I. Ginnane for New South Wales Film Corporation/Victorian Film Corporation/VG
exec p: William Fayman
w: John Pinkney
d: Rod Hardy
ph: Vincent Manton
m: Brian May
ed: Philip Reid
ad: Don Dowding
cos: Aphrodite
sp: Conrad C. Rothman, Chris Murray
sound: Paul Clark, Peter Fenton
David Hemmings, Chantal Rod Mullinar, Max Phipps, Shirley Cameron, Henry Silva

Thomerson, Tim
American actor, best known for playing Jack Deth in the Trancers series. His other film credits include Car Wash, A Wedding, Carny, Uncommon Valor, Rhinestone and Air America, as well as much television work (Cos, The Associates, The Two of Us, Sirens, etc.).
Genre credits:
Fade to Black (1980), Jekyll and Hyde: Together Again (1982), Metalstorm: The Destruction of Jared Syn (1983), Trancers (1984 - aka Future Cop), Zone Troopers (1984), Ratboy (1986), Near Dark

(1987), Pulsepounders (1988), After Midnight (1989), Trancers II: The Return of Jack Deth (1990), Dollman (1990), Trancers III: Deth Lives (1993), Dollman vs. Demonic Toys (1993), Trancers IV: Jack of Swords (1994), Nemesis (1994 - TVM), Trancers V: Sudden Death (1995)

Thriller *
USA 1983 13m Technicolor
A teenager turns into a werewolf whilst on a date with his girlfriend.
    Phenomenally successful video version of the phenomenally successful Michael Jackson single. Gruesome fun, put together with a certain amount of flair.
p: Michael Jackson, George Folsey Jr, John Landis for Optimum
w: Michael Jackson, John Landis
d: John Landis
ph: Robert Paynter
song: ROD TEMPERTON
m: Elmer Bernstein
ed: George Folsey Jr, Malcolm Campbell
ad: Charles Hughes
cos: Deborah Nadoolman, Kelly Kimball
sound: Bruce Sweiden
make-up effects: Rick Baker
ch: Michael Jackson, Michael Peter
narrator: Vincent Price
Michael Jackson, Ola Ray

Tigon (Tigon British)
British production company founded in 1967 by Tony Tenser, who either produced or executive produced all the films. Tigon's output was mostly low budget and often low grade, the company's one moment of true glory being director Michael Reeves's Witchfinder General.
Genre filmography:
The Sorcerers (1967), The Bloodbeast Terror (1967 - aka The Vampire-Beast Craves Blood), Witchfinder General (1968 - aka The Conqueror Worm), The Curse of the Crimson Altar (1968 - aka The Crimson Cult / The Crimson Altar), The Haunted House of Horror (1969 - aka Horror House), The Beast in the Cellar (1970), The Creeping Flesh (1972)

Time After Time **
USA 1979 112m Metrocolor Panavision
Jack the Ripper escapes to the future in H. G. Wells' time machine. When the machine returns, Wells gives chase...
    Charming fantasy adventure, quite inventively handled.
p: Herb Jaffe for Warner/Orion
story: Karl Alexander, Steve Hayes
w/d: NICHOLAS MEYER
ph: Paul Lohmann
m: MIKLOS ROZSA

ed: Don Cambern
pd: Edward Carfagno
cos: Sal Antonio, Yvonne Rubis
sp: Richard F. Taylor
sound: Jerry Jost
stunt co-ordinator: Everett Creach
MALCOLM MCDOWELL, David Warner, Mary Steenburgen, Charles Cioffi, Kent Williams, Andonia Katsaros, Corey Feldman

Time Walker *
USA 1982 75m DeLuxe
A re-animated mummy proves to be an alien who visited earth 3,000 years ago.
    Occasionally atmospheric low-budgeter which does quite well by its story.
p: Jason Williams for Byzantine/Wescom
exec p: Dimitri Villard
w: Tom Friedman, Karen Levitt
d: Tom Kennedy
ph: Robbie Greenberg
m: Richard H. Band
md: David Franco
ed: Maria Digiovani, Lucile Jones
ad: Robert A. Burns, Joe Garrity
Ben Murphy, Nina Axelrod, Shari Belafonti-Harper, Kevin Brophy, Royce Alexander, Michelle Avonne, Annie Barbieri, Sam Chew Jr

The Tingler
USA 1959 82m bw
A scientist experimenting with fear discovers it to be a parasite which lodges itself at the base of the spine.
    Crudely made shocker with gimmicks in the Castle manner (on its release, some cinema seats were wired to produce mild electric shocks during the fright sequences).
p: William Castle for Columbia
w: Robb White
d: William Castle
ph: Wilfred Cline
m: Von Dexter
ed: Chester W. Schaeffer
ad: Phil Bennett
sound: Harry Mills, John Livardy
Vincent Price, Judith Evelyn, Darryl Hickman, Patricia Cutts, Philip Coolidge

To the Devil... A Daughter *
GB/Ger 1976 93m Technicolor
An occult writer protects a young girl from Satanists.
    Late Hammer horror which moves fast enough to disguise its silly plot. Sadly, it fared badly at the box office and effectively finished off the studio as a going concern.
p: Roy Skeggs for Hammer/EMI/Terra Filmkunst

• Christopher Lee's Father Rayner oversees a black ritual in Hammer's last horror film to date, *To the Devil... A Daughter.*

w: Christopher Wicking
novel: Dennis Wheatley
d: PETER SYKES
ph: David Watkin
m: Paul Glass
md: Philip Martell
ed: John Trumper
pd: Don Picton
sp: Les Bowie
Richard Widmark, CHRISTOPHER LEE, Denholm Elliott, Nastassja Kinski, Honor Blackman, Anthony Valentine, Derek Francis, Michael Goodliffe

Tobey, Kenneth (1919-)

American general-purpose actor, popular as either lead or support in fifties science fiction and monster films. Familiar to TV audiences from *The Whirlybirds*, he now pops up mostly in cameo roles. His other credits include *Dangerous Venture, Davy Crockett - King of the Wild Frontier, The Great Locomotive Chase, Walking Tall* and *Airplane!*
Genre credits:
The Thing (1952), *The Beast from 20,000 Fathoms* (1953), *It Came from Beneath the Sea* (1956), *The Vampire* (1957), *Ben* (1972), *Homebodies* (1974), *The Howling* (1980), *The Creature Wasn't Nice* (1981 - aka *Spaceship*), *Strange Invaders* (1983), *Gremlins* (1984), *Gremlins 2: The New Batch* (1990)

Todd, Holbrook N.

American editor, mostly of forties low-budgeters for PRC.
Genre credits:
The Devil Bat (1940), *The Mad Monster* (1942), *The Monster Maker* (1944), *Daughter of Dr Jekyll* (1957)

Todd, Tony

African-American actor, known to genre fans for his portrayal of the Candyman in the two Clive Barker movies.
Genre credits:
Night of the Living Dead (1990), *Candyman* (1992), *Candyman 2: Farewell to the Flesh* (1995)

The Tomb

USA 1985 84m colour
When her tomb is disturbed by two spoilers, an Egyptian queen returns to life with vengeance on her mind.
    Tame low-budget romp with a few unwise attempts at humour. Nevertheless, it did fairly well on video.
p: Fred Olen Ray, Ronnie Hadar for Transworld Entertainment
exec p: Richard Kaye, Paul Hertzberg
w: Kenneth J. Hall, T. L. Lankford
d: Fred Olen Ray
ph: Paul Elliott
m: Drew Neumann
ed: Miriam L. Preissel
ad: Maxine Shepard
cos: Elizabeth A. Reid, Renee Dorian
sp/titles: Bret Mixon
sound: Stephen Von Hase
2nd unit ph: Scott Ressler

Cameron Mitchell, Sybil Danning, John Carradine, Richard Alan Hench, David Pearson, Kitten Navidad

Torso *

It 1974 90m Technicolor
Four art students are threatened by a maniac with a penchant for dismembering his victims with a hacksaw.
    Fairly stylish but rather necrophiliac shocker, watchable enough of its gruesome kind.
p: Antonio Servi for Joseph Brenner Associates
exec p: Carlo Ponti
w: Ernesto Castaldi, Sergio Martino
d: Sergio Martino
ph: Giancarlo Ferrando
Suzy Kendall, Tina Aumont, Luc Merendo, John Richardson, Roberto Bisacco, Angela Covello

Torture Garden *

GB 1967 93m Technicolor
Visitors to a fairground sideshow are shown their futures.
    Flatly handled and overlit horror compendium which just about passes the time, though some of the stories are on the silly side. One involves a possessed piano which pushes a woman out of a window!
p: Max J. Rosenberg, Milton Subotsky for Amicus/Columbia
w: Robert Bloch
d: Freddie Francis
ph: Norman Warwick
m: Don Banks, James Bernard
md: Philip Martell
ed: Peter Elliott
pd: Bill Constable
ad: Don Mingaye, Don Slimon
cos: Evelyn Gibbs
sound: Ken Rawkins
Burgess Meredith, Jack Palance, Peter Cushing, Michael Ripper, John Standing, Beverly Adams, Michael Bryant, Bernard Kay, Ursula Howells, Barbara Ewing, Niall MacGinnis

Tourneur, Jacques (1904-1977)

French director working mostly in America, where he came to prominence with a handful of the Val Lewton-produced horrors at RKO. The son of director Maurice Tourneur, with whom he emigrated to America in 1914, he began his film career ten years later working as an office boy at MGM. He began to work his way up the ladder, first as an actor, then as a script clerk. In 1928 he returned to France for a short period where he gained experience as an editor and directed his first film, *Tout Vaut pas L'Amour*, in 1931. After directing several more films in France, he returned to

America in 1934, where he directed many shorts at MGM, including several Pete Smith Specialties (*Harnessed Rhythm, Jonker Diamond, Killer Dog, Grand Bounce, The Romance of Radium*), two of John Nesbitt's 'Passing Parade' shorts (*Yankee Doodle Goes to Town, The Magic Alphabet*) and one of the studio's highly regarded "Crime Does Not Pay" shorts (*Think It Over*). He made his American feature début with *Nick Carter, Master Detective* in 1939, following this with *Phantom Raiders* and *Doctors Don't Tell* before teaming up with Lewton. His other credits include *Experiment Perilous, The Flame and the Arrow* and *City Under the Sea* (aka *War Gods of the Deep*), though his best film is undoubtedly *Night of the Demon*, one of the genre's highlights.
Genre credits:
The Cat People (1942), *I Walked with a Zombie* (1943), *The Leopard Man* (1943), *Night of the Demon* (1957 - aka *Curse of the Demon*), *The Comedy of Terrors* (1963)

Tovar, Lupita

Mexican actress, seen in the Spanish-language versions of Universal's *The Cat Creeps* (1930 - aka *La Voluntad del Muerto*) and *Dracula* (1930). Her other credits include the Spanish-language version of *The King of Jazz* (1930).

Towers, Harry Alan (1920-)

Prolific British producer and writer (always using the name Peter Welbeck), a former child actor, radio scriptwriter and television producer (*Dial 999, The Scarlet Pimpernel*, etc.). He began producing films in 1962 with *Invitation to Murder*, though he is best known for the series of Fu Manchu films he produced in the mid-sixties starring Christopher Lee. Since then he has been involved in all manner of low-budget thrillers and horrors in both Britain and Europe, including three versions of Agatha Christie's *Ten Little Indians* (1966, 1975, 1989). Since the mid-seventies, though, his films have rarely risen above the routine. His other credits include *Mozambique, Our Man in Marrakesh* (aka *Bang, Bang, You're Dead!*), *Rocket to the Moon, Treasure Island, Call of the Wild* and *The Hitman*.
Genre credits:
The Face of Fu Manchu (1965 - w/p), *The Brides of Fu Manchu* (1966 - w/p), *The Vengeance of Fu Manchu* (1967 - w/p), *The Castle of Fu Manchu* (1968), *Psycho Circus* (1967 - aka *Circus of Fear* -w/p), *The Blood of Fu Manchu* (1968 - aka *Kiss and Kill*), *Justine* (1968 - w/p), *Throne of the Blood Monster* (1970 - aka *Night of the Blood Monster/Throne of Fire/The Bloody Judge* - story/co-p), *Bram Stoker's Count Dracula* (1970 - aka *Count Dracula/El Conde*

Dracula - co-w/p), *Venus in Furs* (1970 - aka *Paroxismus* - p), *Dorian Gray* (1970 - aka *The Secret of Dorian Gray* - p), *The Night Hair Child* (1971 - p), *House of the Damned* (1975 - p), *Gor* (1985 - p), *Buried Alive* (1988 - p), *The Howling IV* (1989 - exec p), *Edge of Sanity* (1989 - co-p), *The Phantom of the Opera* (1989 - co-exec p), *The House of Usher* (1990 - p), *The Raven* (1990 - p), *The Masque of the Red Death* (1990 - p), *The Lost World* (1992 - unreleased - p), *Return to the Lost World* (1992 - p), *Night Terrors* (1993 - aka *Tobe Hooper's Night Terrors/Tobe Hooper's Nightmare* - p), *The Mangler* (1995 - co-w/co-exec p)

Towns, Colin

British composer with much television work to his credit (*Blind Justice, The Fear, Capital City, Chillers, Pat and Margaret*), including many commercials and idents. His film scores include *Bellman and True, Fellow Traveller* and *Getting It Right*.
Genre credits:
Full Circle (1976 - aka *The Haunting of Julia*), *The Wolves of Willoughby Chase* (1988), *Vampire's Kiss* (1988), *The Puppet Masters* (1994)

The Toxic Avenger

USA 1985 76m colour
A nerdy, much-mocked gymnasium janitor is transformed into a monstrous-looking superhero after falling into a barrel of toxic waste.

Determinedly and unashamedly crude and self-mocking low-budgeter which succeeded in its bid to become a cult item. It was followed by *The Toxic Avenger Part II* (1989), *The Toxic Avenger Part III: The Last Temptation of Toxie* (1989) and a children's cartoon series (accompanied by the expected merchandizing, of course).
p: Lloyd Kaufman, Michael Herz for Troma
w: Joe Ritter, Gay Terry, Lloyd Kaufman, Stuart Strutin
story: Lloyd Kaufman
d: Michael Herz, Samuel Weil
ph: James London, Michael Kaufman
m: various
ed: Richard W. Haines
ad: Barry Shapiro, Alexandra Masur
make-up: Jennifer Aspinal
Mitchell Cohen, Pat Ryan Jr, Andree Maranda, Cindy Manion, Jennifer Babtist, Robert Prichard, Mark Torgi, Gary Schneider

The Transvestite see Glen or Glenda

Trauma *

USA 1993 105m Technicolor Dolby

A disturbed young girl is helped by a young reporter to track down a serial killer with a penchant for beheadings.

Convoluted thriller, watchable enough in itself, though rather more sober in style than some of its director's previous outings.
p: Dario Argento for ADC/Overseas Filmgroup
exec p: T. David Pash, Andrea Tinnirello
w: Dario Argento, T. E. D. Klein
story: Franco Ferrini, Gianni Romoli, Dario Argento
d: Dario Argento
ph: Raffaele Mertes
m: Pino Donaggio
ed: Bennett Goldberg
pd: Billy Jett
cos: Leesa Evans
sound: Paul Coogan
make-up effects: Tom Savini
Asia Argento, Christopher Rydell, Piper Laurie, Brad Dourif, Frederic Forrest, Laura Johnson, James Russo, Dominique Serraud

The Treasure of Abbot Thomas **

GB 1974 40m colour TVM
A nineteenth-century cleric and his pupil pursue the whereabouts of treasure hidden by an abbot in the fourteenth century - but there is something nasty guarding it.

Engaging period mystery which certainly keeps one watching. One of the BBC's better *Ghost Story for Christmas* adaptations.
p: Rosemary Hill for BBC
w: John Bowen
story: M. R. James
d: Laurence Gordon Clark
ph: John McGlashan
m: Geoffrey Burgon
ed: Roger Waugh
ad: Stuart Walker
cos: Janet Tharby
sound: Dick Manston, Stanley Morcom
Michael Bryant, Sheila Dunn, Anne Blake, Frank Mills, Virginia Balfour, Paul Lavers, John Herrington, Peggy Aitchison

Tremors *

USA 1989 96m DeLuxe Dolby
A small desert community is attacked by giant worms.

It sounds silly, but this is actually an energetic horror piece with good effects work. *Tremors II* followed in 1995.
p: Brent Maddock, S. S. Wilson for Universal
w: Brent Maddock, S. S. Wilson
story: Brent Maddock, S. S. Wilson, Ron Underwood
d: Ron Underwood
ph: Alexander Gruszynski
m: Ernest Troost
ed: O. Nicholas Brown

pd: Ivo Cristante
cos: Abigail Murray
sp: Tom Woodruff, Alec Gillis
sound: Walt Martin
2nd unit d: S. S. Wilson
titles: Neal Thompson
Kevin Bacon, Fred Ward, Finn Carter,
Reba McEntirte, Michael Gross, Bobby
Jacoby, Tony Genaro, Charlotte Stewart

Trog

GB 1970 91m Technicolor
A Neanderthal man is discovered down
a pot-hole and trained by a lady scientist
who wants to discover the missing links
in history.
  Stupefyingly inept nonsense, with the
star battling to save her face. So bad it's
almost good.
p: Herman Cohen for Warner
w: Aben Kandel
d: Freddie Francis
ph: Desmond Dickinson
m: John Scott
ed: Oswald Haffenrichter
Joan Crawford (her last film), Michael
Gough, Bernard Kay, David Griffin, Joe
Cornelius

Tsuburaya, Eiji (1901-1970)

Japanese special-effects technician, a for-
mer cameraman, in films from as early as
1919, though it is for his work on the
Godzilla films of the fifties and sixties that
he is best remembered.
Genre credits:
Carnival of Blood (1929 - aka Chimatsuri),
Tales of Monsters (1929 - aka Yoma Kidan),
Kwaidan Yanagi Zoshi (1932), Godzilla
(1954 - aka Godzilla, King of the
Monsters/Gojira), Rodan (1956 - aka
Radan), The Mysterians (1957 - aka Chikyu
Boeigun), The H-Man (1958 - aka Bijyo To
Ekitai), Varan the Unbelievable (1958 - aka
Daikaiju Baran), The Secret of the Telegian
(1960 - aka Denso Ningen), The Human
Vapour (1960 - aka Gasu Mingen Dai
Ichi-Go), Mothra (1961 - aka Mosura), The
Last War (1961 - aka Sekai Dai Senso),
Gorath (1962 - aka Yosei Gorasu), King Kong
vs. Godzilla (1962 - aka King Kong Tai
Gojira), Attack of the Mushroom People (1963 -
aka Matango, Fungus of Terror/Matango), The
Lost World of Sinbad (1963 - aka Samurai
Pirate/Daitozoku), Atragon (1963 - aka
Atragon the Flying Sub/Kaitei Gunkan),
Mothra vs. Godzilla (1964 - aka Godzilla vs.
the Thing/Mosura Tai Gojira), Dagora the
Space Monster (1964 - aka Uchu Daikaiju
Dogora), Ghidrah the Three-Headed Monster
(1964 - aka Sandai Kaiju Chikyu Saidai No
Kessen), Frankenstein Conquers the World
(1965 - aka Furankenstein Tai Baragon),
Daiboken (1965), Invasion of the Astro Monsters
(1965 - aka Monster Zero/Battle of the
Astros/Kaiju Daisenso), War of the

Gargantuas (1966 - aka Sanda Tai
Gailah/Furankenshutan No Kaiju/Sanda Tai
Gailah), Godzilla vs. the Sea Monster (1966 -
aka Ebirah, Horror of the Deep/Namkai No
Dai Ketto), King Kong Escapes (1967 - aka
Kingu Kongi No Gyakushu), Son of Godzilla
(1967 - aka Gojira No Musuko), Destroy All
Monsters (1968 - aka Kaiju Soshingeki),
Latitude Zero (1969 - aka Ido Zero Daisakusen)

Turn of the Screw

USA 1973 74m Technicolor TVM
A governess believes her wards to be
diabolically inspired.
  Miscast, poorly produced and directed
adaptation of the Henry James novel,
definitively filmed in 1961 as The
Innocents, to which this version is in no
way comparable.
p: Dan Curtis for Dan Curtis Productions
w: William F. Nolan
novel: Henry James
d: Dan Curtis
ph: Colin Callow
m: Robert Cobert
ed: Bill Breashers, Gary Anderson
ad: Trevor Williams
Lynn Redgrave, Megs Jenkins, John
Baron, Eva Griffith, Jasper Jacob,
Benedict Taylor

Twentieth Century Fox

American studio formed in 1935
following a merger between Twentieth
Century Pictures and the Fox Film
Corporation. TCF is renowned for a wide
variety of productions, ranging from
musicals (The King and I, The Sound of
Music, Hello, Dolly!) and science-fiction
blockbusters (three Star Wars episodes to
date, the Planet of the Apes series) to
comedies (Home Alone) and all manner of
Golden Age classics. The studio's major
contributions to the horror genre have
been more recent, however, and have
included the Omen, Fly and Alien series.
Like Warner Bros, they also released and
invested in a number of Hammer films in
the sixties.
Genre filmography:
The Gorilla (1939), I Wake Up Screaming
(1941), Dr Renault's Secret (1942),
A-Haunting We Will Go (1942), The
Undying Monster (1943 - aka The Hammond
Mystery), The Ghost and Mrs Muir (1947),
Gorilla at Large (1954), The Fly (1958), The
Return of the Fly (1959), The Alligator People
(1959), The Lost World (1960), Curse of the
Living Corpse (1963), The Curse of the Fly
(1965), The Mephisto Waltz (1971), Young
Frankenstein (1974), Phantom of the Paradise
(1974), The Omen (1976), The Fury (1978),
Damien: Omen II (1978), Alien (1979), The
Final Conflict (1981 - aka Omen III: The
Final Conflict), Aliens (1986), The Fly
(1986), The Fly II (1989), Omen IV: The

Awakening (1991 - TVM), Alien 3 (1992)

Twilight of the Dead see City of
the Living Dead

Twilight Zone - The Movie *

USA 1983 101m Technicolor Dolby
Four tales of the imagination based on the
cult science-fiction series of the sixties.
  At best a rather bland concoction,
lacking the wit, style and intelligence of
the original series. The last episode is
better than its predecessors, but the
whole enterprise is a considerable
disappointment given the talent involved.
p: Steven Spielberg, John Landis, Frank
Marshall, Kathleen Kennedy, Michael J.
Finnell, George Folsey Jr, Jon Davidson
for Warner
w: John Landis, George Clayton, Josh
Rogan, Richard Matheson
d: John Landis, Steven Spielberg, Joe
Dante, George Miller
ph: Stevan Larner, Allen Daviau, John
Hora
m: Jerry Goldsmith
ed: Malcolm Campbell, Tina Hirsch,
Michael Kahn, Howard Smith
pd: James D. Bissell
make-up effects: Rob Bottin, Craig
Reardon, Michael McCracken
narrator: Burgess Meredith
Dan Aykroyd, Albert Brooks, Scatman
Crothers, Vic Morrow (who was killed
during filming, along with two small
children, in a notorious accident involving
a helicopter), Bill Quinn, Kevin
McCarthy, JOHN LITHGOW, Dick
Miller, Jeremy Light, Abbe Lane, Donna
Dixon, Martin Garner

Twins of Evil *

GB 1971 87m Eastmancolor
One of a beautiful pair of twins staying
with their puritanical uncle is turned into
a vampire by the evil Count Karnstein.
  Tolerable vampire yarn with moments
of atmosphere, though more overall style
and pace were needed. The third of
Hammer's Carmilla films, the first two
being The Vampire Lovers and Lust for a
Vampire.
p: Harry Fine, Michael Style for Hammer
w: Tudor Gates
d: John Hough
ph: Harry Robinson
md: Philip Martell
ed: Spencer Reeve
ad: Roy Stannard
cos: Rosemary Burrows
sp/2nd unit d: Jack Mills
sound: Ron Barron, Ken Barker
Peter Cushing, Madeleine Collinson,
Mary Collinson, Dennis Price, Kathleen
Byron, Isobel Black, Damien Thomas

Twitch of the Death Nerve see
Bay of Blood

Two Evil Eyes
USA 1990 120m Technicolor
Two tales inspired by Edgar Allan Poe:
The Facts in the Case of M. Valdemar, in
which a hypnotist keeps a dying
millionaire alive, and *The Black Cat*, in
which a police photographer murders his
girlfriend and bricks her up behind the
wall in his apartment.

Disappointing horror package. The
first episode passes the time adequately
enough, but Argento's segment sadly
lacks the flair of his earlier films. Also
known as *Due Occhi Diabolici*.
p: Achille Manzotti, Dario Argento for
ADC
exec p: Claudio Argento
w/d: George Romero, Dario Argento
stories: Edgar Allan Poe
ph: Peter Reniers
m: Keith Emerson
ed: Pat Buba
pd: Cletus Anderson
cos: Barbara Anderson
make-up effects: Tom Savini
Adrienne Barbeau, E. G. Marshall, Ramy
Zada, Tom Atkins, Christine Forrest,
Bingo O'Malley, Harvey Keitel,
Madeleine Potter, Martin Balsam, Kim
Hunter, John Amos, Chuck Aber, Barbara
Byrne, Anthony DiLeo

Twisted
USA 1986 82m Technicolor
A psychotic teenager torments the
babysitter looking after his young sister.

Fright meets *Halloween* in this dim
thriller that lay on the shelf until 1992,
when it re-emerged following Slater's rise
to stardom.
p: Bruce Graham for Greenroom Features
w: Glenn Kershaw, Bruce Graham
play: Jack Harrisgan
d: Adam Holdender
ph: Alexander Gruszynski
m: Michael Bacon
ed: Peter Hammer
ad: George Brown
cos: Oscar de la Renta, Maureen Hogan
sound: Gary Rich
Christian Slater, Lois Smith, Tandy Cronyn,
Dina Merrill, Brooke Tracy, Dan Ziskie

Twisted Souls see Spookies

The Two Faces of Dr Jekyll *
GB 1960 88m Technicolor Megascope
Dr Jekyll experiments with a potion
which separates good from evil and
turns him into a handsome sadist.

Promising variation on the old, old
story, with an unusual emphasis on sex,

• **Tom Tyler as the Mummy in Universal's** *The Mummy's Hand*, **the first of several
sequels to** *The Mummy*.

vitiated by dull handling and the wide
screen.
p: Michael Carreras, Anthony Nelson
Keys for Hammer
w: Wolf Mankowitz
novel: Robert Louis Stevenson
d: Terence Fisher
ph: Jack Asher
m/songs: Monty Norman, David
Heneker
md: John Hollingsworth
ed: James Needs, Eric Boyd-Perkins
cos: Mayo
sound: Jock May
make-up: Roy Ashton
ch: Julie Mendez
sound ed: Archie Ludski
Paul Massie, Dawn Addams, Christopher
Lee, David Kossoff, Francis de Wolff,
Oliver Reed

Two on a Guillotine
USA 1965 107m bw Panavision
A famous magician vows to perform the
ultimate trick: to come back from the
dead.

Overstretched thriller which takes
forever getting to a predictable twist
ending.
p: William Conrad for Warner
w: Henry Slesar, John Kneubuhl
story: Henry Slesar
d: William Conrad
ph: Sam Leavitt
m: Max Steiner (his last film score)
ed: William Ziegler
ad: Arthur Loel

sound: Francis E. Stahl
Connie Stevens, Dean Jones, Cesar
Romero, Parley Bear, Virginia Gregg,
Connie Gilchrist, John Hoyt

Tyburn
British production company founded in
1972 by producer Kevin Francis. A small-
scale Hammer-style outfit, they turned
out a handful of gothic shockers in the
seventies, two of which (*Legend of the
Werewolf* and *The Ghoul*) were directed by
Francis's father Freddie, who also
photographed the company's
documentary, *Peter Cushing - Gentleman of
Horror*. Tyburn also produced the TV
movie *The Masks of Death*, which starred
Peter Cushing as Sherlock Holmes.
Genre filmography:
Persecution (1974 - aka *The Terror of Sheba*),
Legend of the Werewolf (1974), *The Ghoul*
(1975)

Tyler, Tom (1903-1954)
American actor (real name Vincent
Markowsky) who appeared in countless
B westerns and serials, among them *The
Phantom of the West* (serial), *Battling with
Buffalo Bill* (serial), *Riding the Lonesome
Trail*, *Pinto Rustlers*, *Roamin' Wild*, *The
Westerner* and *She Wore a Yellow Ribbon*.
He also played the Mummy in *The
Mummy's Hand* (1940).

U

Ulmer, Edgar G. (1900-1972)
Austrian director working in Hollywood. A former actor and scenic artist for Max Reinhardt, he also worked on some of the effects sequences for the 1920 version of *The Golem* in Berlin. After experience as a set designer in America with Reinhardt, he returned to Germany, where he worked with F. W. Murnau on *Faust*, following the director to America in 1927 and working with him again on *Sunrise* and several other films. Made his own directorial début back in Germany in 1929 with *People on Sunday* (which he co-directed with Robert Siodmak), after which he returned to America again, his first film there as a director being *Damaged Lives* in 1933. The majority of his career was subsequently spent directing second features, and though several of these have their interest, they are barely worthy of the reverence heaped upon them by French cinéastes in more recent years. His other credits include *Detour*, *Ruthless*, *Atlantis*, *The Lost Kingdom* and *The Cavern*.
Genre credits:
The Black Cat (1934), *Bluebeard* (1944), *The Man from Planet X* (1954), *Daughter of Dr Jekyll* (1957), *Beyond the Time Barrier* (1960), *The Amazing Transparent Man* (1960)

The Uncanny
GB/Canada 1977 85m colour
An author tells his publisher three stories about malevolent cats.

Unremarkable portmanteau with familiar ingredients.
p: Claude Heroux, René Dupont for Rank/Cinevideo/Tor
exec p: Milton Subotsky, Harold Greenberg, Richard R. St. John, Riobert A. Kanfor
w: Michael Parry
d: Dennis Heroux
ph: Harry Waxman, James Bawden
m: Wilfred Josephs
md: Philip Martell
ed: Peter Weatherley, Keith Palmer, Michael Guay

pd: Wolf Kroeger, Harry Pottle
cos: Nicolette Massone, Joyce Stoneman
sound: no credit given
titles: Robert Ellis
Peter Cushing, Ray Milland, Susan Penhaligon, Simon Williams, Joan Greenwood, Roland Culver, Alexander Stewart, Donald Pleasence, Samantha Eggar, John Vernon, Cloe Franks, Catherine Begin, Sean McCann, Donald Pilon

The Undead
USA 1956 71m bw
A hypnotist sends a young woman back to the Middle Ages, where it transpires that she was a witch.

Fairly lively Corman quickie, shot in ten days in a disused supermarket.
p: Roger Corman for AIP/Balboa
w: Charles B. Griffith, Mark Hanna
d: Roger Corman
ph: William Sickner
m: Ronald Stein
ed: Frank Sullivan
Pamela Duncan, Richard Garland, Allison Hayes, Val Dufour, Dorothy Neuman, Billy Barty, Dick Miller, Richard Devon

The Understudy: Graveyard Shift II
USA 1988 88m colour
A vampire resurrects himself on the set of a horror movie.

Slick but overplotted sequel to *Graveyard Shift*. A tolerable video offering.
p: Michael Kravitz, Stephen R. Flaks, Arnold H. Bruck for Cinema Ventures
w/d/pd: Gerard Ciccoretti
ph: Barry Stone
m: Philip Stern
ed: Neil Grieve
cos: Lorrine La Borde
sound: Gordon Thompson
Silvio Olivero, Wendy Gazelle, Ilse Von Glatz, Mark Soper, Leslie Kelly, Tim Kelleher

The Undying Monster *
USA 1943 63m bw

A Scotland Yard detective tries to discover which member of the Hammond family is turning into a werewolf and murdering the locals.

Old-fashioned but handsomely mounted horror mystery obviously patterned after the success of Universal's *The Wolf Man* (there's even a similar curse: 'When the stars are bright on a frosty night, Beware thy bane on the rocky lane').
p: Bryan Foy for TCF
w: Lillie Hayward, Michael Jacoby
novel: Jessie D. Kerruish
d: JOHN BRAHM
ph: LUCIEN BALLARD
m: David Raksin, Emil Newman
ed: Harry Renolds
ad: RICHARD DAY, LEWIS CREBER
cos: Billy Livingston
sound: George Leverett, Harry M. Leonard
James Ellison, John Howard, Heather Angel, Bramwell Fletcher, Halliwell Hobbes, Aubrey Mather, Heather Thatcher, Eily Maylon

Unearthly Stranger *
GB 1963 78m bw
A research scientist discovers that his wife is an alien.

Better-than-average low-budget horror with a few neat touches.
p: Albert Fennell for Anglo Amalgamated/Independent Artists
exec p: Julian Wintole, Leslie Parkyn
w: Rex Carlton
story: Jeffrey Stone
d: John Kirsch
ph: Reg Wyer
m: Edward Williams
md: Marcus Dods
ed: Tom Priestley
ad: Harry Pottle
cos: Vi Murray
sound: Simon Kaye, Ken Cameron
Mark Davidson, Gabriella Licudi, Patrick Newell, Jean Marsh, Warren Mitchell

The Unholy
USA 1987 94m CFI Dolby
A priest finds himself in posession of

miraculous powers after surviving a fall, and later uses them to thwart the Devil.

Flashy mumbo-jumbo which never begins to make sense. A long, long way behind *The Exorcist*.
p: Mathew Hayden for Vestron/Limelight/Team Effort/Unholy Film Partners
exec p: William J. Quigley, Dan Ireland, Frank D. Tolin, Duke Siotkas
w: Philip Yordan, Fernando Fonseca
d: Camilo Vila
ph: Henry Vargas
m: Roger Bellon
ed: Mark Melnick
pd: Fernando Fonseca
cos: Beverly Saffer
sp: Bob Keen
sound: Henri Lopez
Ben Cross, Ned Beatty, William Russ, Jill Carroll, Hal Holbrook, Trevor Howard

The Unholy Three *
USA 1930 70m bw
A ventriloquist teams up with a strong man and a dwarf to carry out a series of robberies, but it ends in murder.

Curious but now dated star vehicle, a remake of a story he also filmed as a silent in 1925. Chaney's first and only sound film; he died of throat cancer before its release.
p: MGM
w: Jack Conway, Elliott Nugent, J. C. Nugent
story: Clarence Robbins
d: Jack Conway
ph: Percy Hilburn
m: no credit given
ed: Frank Sullivan
ad: Cedric Gibbons
LON CHANEY, Lila Lee, Elliott Nugent, Harry Earles, Ivan Linow

The Uninvited **
USA 1944 98m bw
A music critic and his sister take over a Cornish house which proves to be haunted.

A careful but rather slow-moving ghost story with one or two nicely judged shivers along the way.
p: Charles Brackett for Paramount
w: Dodie Smith
novel: Dorothy Macardle
d: Lewis Allen
ph: Charles Lang
m: Victor Young
ed: Doane Harrison
ad: Hans Dreier, Ernst Fetge
sp: Farciot Edouart
RAY MILLAND, RUTH HUSSEY, GAIL RUSSELL, Donald Crisp, Cornelia Otis Skinner, Dorothy Stickney, Alan Napier, Barbara Everest

Universal
Though now one of the biggest film companies in the world, Universal began as something of a family affair. Founded in 1912 by German-born Carl Laemmle, the studio churned out all manner of films during the silent period, one of their most popular stars being the romantic idol Rudolph Valentino. Also under contract was Lon Chaney, who starred in several of the studio's early brushes with horror (*The Hunchback of Notre Dame*, *The Phantom of the Opera*), though it wasn't until the early thirties that they became identified with the horror genre following the success of *Dracula* and *Frankenstein*, both of which were produced by Laemmle's son, Carl Jr. A close brush with bankruptcy occurred in the mid-thirties, from which the studio was rescued by a string of musicals starring Deanna Durbin. Series featuring the Mummy, the Wolf Man, the Invisible Man, Dracula and Frankenstein's Monster starring such horror luminaries as Boris Karloff, Bela Lugosi and Lon Chaney Jr also helped to keep the coffers filled during the forties, as did a series of comedies starring Abbott and Costello, who went on to spoof the studio's monsters in the fifties. The Gill Man (*The Creature from the Black Lagoon*) helped to maintain the studio's horror output through the fifties, whilst *Jaws* and its sequels kept the shocks coming in the seventies and eighties. Meanwhile, in 1993, the studio had the industry's biggest hit with Spielberg's monster epic *Jurassic Park*.
Key genre filmography:
The Hunchback of Notre Dame (1923), *The Phantom of the Opera* (1925), *Dracula* (1930), *Frankenstein* (1931), *Murders in the Rue Morgue* (1932), *The Old Dark House* (1932), *The Mummy* (1932), *The Invisible Man* (1933), *The Secret of the Blue Room* (1933), *The Black Cat* (1934 - aka *House of Doom*), *The Raven* (1935), *The Invisible Ray* (1935), *The Bride of Frankenstein* (1935), *Dracula's Daughter* (1936), *Son of Frankenstein* (1939), *Tower of London* (1939), *The Invisible Man Returns* (1940), *The Mummy's Hand* (1940), *The Wolf Man* (1940), *Man Made Monster* (1941 - aka *The Electric Man*), *Hold That Ghost* (1941), *The Invisible Woman* (1941), *Captive Wild Woman* (1942), *The Mummy's Tomb* (1942), *The Invisible Agent* (1942), *The Ghost of Frankenstein* (1942), *The Mad Doctor of Market Street* (1942), *The Mummy's Ghost* (1942), *Frankenstein Meets the Wolf Man* (1943), *The Phantom of the Opera* (1943), *Sherlock Holmes Faces Death* (1943), *Son of Dracula* (1943), *The Invisible Man's Revenge* (1944), *Jungle Woman* (1944), *Sherlock Holmes and the Spider Woman* (1944), *Jungle Captive* (1944), *House of Frankenstein* (1944), *The Mummy's Curse* (1944), *The Scarlet Claw* (1944), *The Pearl of Death* (1944), *House of Fear* (1945), *House of Dracula* (1945), *The Woman in Green* (1945), *House of Horrors* (1946 - aka *Joan Medford Is Missing*), *Abbott and Costello Meet Frankenstein* (1948), *Abbott and Costello Meet the Killer, Boris Karloff* (1949), *Abbott and Costello Meet the Invisible Man* (1950), *Abbott and Costello Meet Dr Jekyll and Mr Hyde* (1953), *The Creature from the Black Lagoon* (1954), *Cult of the Cobra* (1955), *Abbott and Costello Meet the Mummy* (1955), *Tarantula* (1955), *The Revenge of the Creature* (1955), *The Creature Walks Among Us* (1956), *The Deadly Mantis* (1957), *Monster on the Campus* (1958), *The Thing That Couldn't Die* (1958), *Psycho* (1960), *The Night Walker* (1964), *The Boy Who Cried Werewolf* (1973), *Scream, Pretty Peggy* (1973 - TVM), *Frankenstein: The True Story* (1973 -TVM), *Killdozer* (1974 - TVM), *Jaws* (1975), *The Invisible Man* (1975 - TVM), *The Sentinel* (1976), *The Gemini Man* (1976 - TVM), *The Car* (1977), *Jaws 2* (1978), *Dracula* (1979), *The Island* (1980), *Ghost Story* (1981), *The Thing* (1982), *Psycho 2* (1983), *Nightmares* (1983 - TVM), *Jaws 3D* (1983), *Psycho 3* (1986), *Jaws: The Revenge* (1987), *The Serpent and the Rainbow* (1987), *Bates' Motel* (1987 - TVM), *Prince of Darkness* (1987), *Child's Play* (1987), *Tremors* (1989), *Darkman* (1990), *The Guardian* (1990), *Ghost Dad* (1990), *Child's Play 2* (1990), *Psycho IV* (1990 - TVM), *Child's Play 3* (1991), *Jurassic Park* (1993), *The Lost World* (1997)

The Unnamable
Canada 1988 87m Foto-Kem Ultra Stereo
Students staging a fraternity initiation ceremony in a spooky house are killed off one by one by a monster who has been locked in there for 300 years.

Straightforward shocks and gore. Nothing at all special, and certainly nothing warranting a sequel.
p: Jean-Paul Oullette, Dean Ramser for Yankee Classic
w/d: Jean-Paul Oulette
story: H. P. Lovecraft
ph: Tom Fraser
m: David Bergeuad
ed: Wendy J. Plump
pd: Gene Abel
make-up effects: R. Christopher Biggs
Charles King, Mark Kinsey Stephenson,

Alexandra Durrell, Laura Albert, Eden Ham, Mark Parra, Blane Wheatley, Katrine Alexandre, Alyda Winthrop (as the Unnamable)

The Unnamable Returns
Canada 1992 92m Foto-Kem Ultra Stereo
A college student tracks down the 300-year-old monster responsible for a series of grisly murders and frees the spirit of a young girl trapped inside it.

Talkative sequel, as tedious as it is silly.

p: Jean-Paul Oullette for Yankee Classic/AM East/Prism/New Age/Unnamable Production Company
w/d: Jean-Paul Oulette
ph: Greg Gardiner
m: David Bergeaud
ed: William C. Williams
pd: Tim Keating
make-up effects: R. Christopher Biggs
sound: Geoffrey Patterson
John Rhys-Davies, Charles Klausmeyer, David Warner, Mary Kinsey Stephenson, Maria Ford, Julie Strain (as the Unnamable), Peter Breck

Un Urlo dalle Tenebre see Naked Exorcism

The Valley of Gwangi
USA 1968 95m Technicolor Dynamation
Cowboys discover prehistoric monsters
in a valley in Mexico and catch one for
their wild west show. But it escapes and
goes on the rampage.

Flatly made, routinely scripted slice
of monster hokum, with only the trick
effects to hold one's interest. Originally
intended as a Willis O'Brien project
after his success with *King Kong*.
p: Charles H. Schneer for
Warner/Morningside
w: William E. Bast, Julian More
d: James O'Connelly
ph: Erwin Hillier
m: Jerome Morros
ed: Henry Richardson
ad: Gil Parrondo
sp: RAY HARRYHAUSEN
sound: Malcolm Stenai
titles: Antonia Saura
Richard Carlson, Laurence Naismith,
James Franciscus, Gila Golan, Freda
Jackson, Dennis Kilbane

Vamp
USA 1986 95m colour
Three college students find themselves
in mortal danger from vampires when
they go in search of a stripper for their
frat house party.

Mildly amusing horror comic for
addicts.
p: Donald P. Borchers for New
World/Balcor
w/d: Richard Wenk
story: Donald P. Borchers, Richard
Wenk
ph: Elliot Davis
m: Jonathan Elias
ed: Marc Grossman
pd: Alan Roderick Jones
cos: Betty Pecha Madden
sound: Gregg Barbanell
make-up effects: Greg Cannom
Grace Jones, Chris Makepeace, Sandy
Baron, Robert Russler, Dedee Pfeiffer,
Gedde Watanabe, Billy Drago, Brad
Logan

Vampira (1921-)
Exotic-looking Finnish-born character

actress and TV horror hostess (real name
Maila Nurmi) who moved to America as
a child. Remembered chiefly for her
performance as the vampire in Edward
D. Wood Jr's engagingly inept *Plan 9
from Outer Space*. Her other credits
include *Beat Generation*, *The Big Operator*
and *Sex Kittens Go to College*.
Genre credits:
Plan 9 from Outer Space (1958 - aka *Grave
Robbers from Outer Space*), *The Magic
Sword* (1961 - aka *St George and the Seven
Curses*)

Vampira
GB 1974 88m Eastmancolor
To revive his dead wife, a vampire count
lures young women to his castle so as to
use their blood. However, the blood of a
black girl has a rather odd effect…

Abysmal would-be comedy which
degrades its star.
p: Jack H. Warner for Columbia
w: Jeremy Lloyd
d: Clive Donner
ph: Tony Richmond
song: Anthony Newley
m: David Whitaker
ed: Bill Butler
ad: Philip Harrison
make-up: Phil Leakey
David Niven, Teresa Graves, Peter
Bayliss, Jennie Linden, Linda Hayden,
Nicky Henson, Bernard Bresslaw,
Veronica Carlson, Freddie Jones

Vampire
USA 1980 96m colour TVM
A vampire emerges in modern-day San
Francisco and wreaks the expected
havoc.

Sub-standard vampire yarn without
the necessary style to carry it off.
p: Gregory Hoblitt for ABC/MTM
w: Steven Bochco, Michael Kozoll
d: E. W. Swackhamer
ph: Dennis Dalzell
m: Fred Karlin
ed: Ray Daniels, Christopher Nelson
Jason Miller, Richard Lynch, Kathryn
Harrold, E. G. Marshall, Jessica Walter,
Barrie Youngfellow

Vampire at Midnight
USA 1987 89m colour
A cop hunts down a psychic who may or
may not be a vampire.

Dire thriller that fails to make the
most of its central situation. Avoid.
p: Dulaney Ross Clements for Vampire
Limited Partners
w: Dulaney Ross Clements
story: Jason Williams, Tom Friedman
d: Gregory McClatchy
ph: Daniel Yarussi
m: Robert Etoll
ed: Kaye Davis
ad: Beau Peterson
cos: Sarah Bardo
sound: Vic Carpenter
make-up effects: Mecki Heussen
Jason Williams, Gustav Vintas, Esther
Alise, Jeanie Moore, Lesley Milne,
Robert Random

The Vampire Bat *
USA 1932 70m bw
A series of vampire attacks in a small
middle European village turn out to be
the work of a mad doctor.

Dated low-budget horror comic with
a few well-handled moments amongst
the talk.
p: Phil Goldstone for Majestic
w: Edward T. Lowe
d: Frank Strayer
ph: Ira Morgan
m: no credit given
ed: Otis Garrett
ad: Daniel Hall
sound: Dick Tyler
Lionel Atwill, Fay Wray, Melvyn
Douglas, Dwight Frye, Maude Eburne,
George E. Stone, Lionel Belmore

Vampire Circus *
GB 1971 87m Eastmancolor
A cursed village is visited by the plague
and a circus of vampires.

Lively later Hammer horror with a
few neat touches and a lush musical
score. The twelve-minute pre-credit
sequence is a movie in itself.
p: Wilbur Stark for Hammer
w: Judson Kinberg
d: ROBERT YOUNG

The Vampire Lovers

ph: Moray Grant
m: DAVID WHITAKER
md: Philip Martell
ed: Peter Musgrave
ad: Scott MacGregor
cos: Brian Owen-Smith
sp: Les Bowie
sound: Claude Hitchcock
Adrienne Corri, Laurence Payne,
Thorley Walters, John Moulder Brown,
Lynne Frederick, Elizabeth Seal, Robert
Tayman, Robin Hunter, Dave Prowse,
Robin Sachs

The Vampire Lovers

GB 1970 91m Movielab
A beautiful vampire insinuates herself
into a nobleman's household and feeds
off his impressionable daughter.

Despite a promising start, this is a
slow and rather dull variation on
Carmilla, with the studio's old style sadly
lacking. Two sequels followed: *Lust for a
Vampire* (1970) and *Twins of Evil* (1971).
p: Harry Fine, Michael Stles for
Hammer / American International
w: Tudor Gates, Harry Fine, Michael
Styles
novel: J. Sheridan Le Fanu
d: Roy Ward Baker
ph: Moray Grant
m: Harry Robinson
md: Philip Martell
ed: James Needs
ad: Scott MacGregor
cos: Brian Cox
sound: Claude Hitchcock, Tony Lumkin,
Dennis Whitlock
Ingrid Pitt, Peter Cushing, Pippa Steele,
Madeleine Smith, George Cole, Kate
O'Mara, Dawn Addams, Jon Finch,
Ferdy Mayne, Douglas Wilmer, Janet
Key, John Forbes-Robertson

Vampire Thrills see Le Frisson des
Vampires

Vampire Woman see Crypt of the
Living Dead

Vampires

Though a handful of films featuring
vampires appeared during the silent
period, it wasn't until 1922 and the
advent of *Nosferatu*, an uncredited variation of Bram Stoker's *Dracula*, that they
gradually became a movie staple. The
floodgates, of course, opened following
the successful release of Universal's
Dracula in 1930, since when audiences
have thrilled to all manner of bloodsuckers. *Dracula* aside, there have also been
several versions of J. Sheridan LeFanu's
Carmilla and the Elizabeth Bathory
legend (*Countess Dracula, Daughters of
Darkness*), as well as spoofs (*Abbott and

• Jan Francis's Lucy rises from the dead in the 1979 remake of *Dracula*. Luckily
her father, Professor Van Helsing (Laurence Olivier) is at hand with a stake.

*Costello Meet Frankenstein, Love at First
Bite*), porn films (*Dracula Sucks, Dracula
Exotica*), blaxploitation films (*Blacula,
Vampira*) and countless variations
(*Vampire Circus, Martin, Fright Night, The
Hunger, The Lost Boys, Once Bitten,
Interview with the Vampire*, etc.). Also see
Dracula and *Carmilla*.
Filmography:
The Haunted Castle (1896 - aka *La Manoir
du Diable / The Manor of the Devil*), *The
Vampire* (1914), *Nosferatu* (1922 - aka
Nosferatu - Eine Symphonie des Graunes),
London After Midnight (1927 - aka *The
Hypnotist*), *Dracula* (1930), *Vampyre*
(1932 - aka *David Gray / The
Vampire / Castle of Doom*), *The Vampire Bat*
(1933), *Condemned to Live* (1935), *Mark
of the Vampire* (1935), *Dracula's Daughter*
(1936), *The Macabre Trunk* (1936 - aka *El
Baúl Macabro*), *The Return of Dr X* (1939),
The Devil Bat (1940 - aka *Killer
Bats / Devil Bats*), *The Return of the Vampire*
(1943), *Son of Dracula* (1943), *House of
Frankenstein* (1944), *House of Dracula*
(1945), *Isle of the Dead* (1945), *The Spider
Woman Strikes Back* (1945), *The Vampire's
Ghost* (1945), *Valley of the Zombies*
(1945), *The Face of Marble* (1945), *Les
Vampires* (1947 - short), *Abbott and
Costello Meet Frankenstein* (1948), *Mother
Riley Meets the Vampire* (1952 - aka *My
Son the Vampire / Vampire Over London*),
Drakula Istambula (1953), *The Bowery Boys
Meet the Monsters* (1954), *Pontianak*
(1956), *The Devil's Commandment* (1956 -

aka *I Vampiri / Lust of the Vampire*), *The
Return of Dracula* (1957 - aka *The Curse of
Dracula / The Fantastic Disappearing Man*),
Dendam Pontianak (1957), *Not of This
Earth* (1957), *The Vampire's Coffin* (1957
- aka *El Castillo de los Monstruos*), *The
Vampire* (1957 - aka *Mark of the Vampire*),
Blood of Dracula (1957 - aka *Blood Is My
Heritage*), *Sumpah Pontianak* (1958), *Anak
Pontianak* (1958), *Dracula* (1958 - aka
Horror of Dracula), *Blood of the Vampire*
(1958), *The First Men into Space* (1958),
It! The Terror from Beyond Space (1958),
Curse of the Undead (1958), *Onna
Kyuketsuki* (1959), *Uncle Was a Vampire*
(1959 - aka *Tempi Duri Per I
Vampiri / Hard Times for Vampires*)
The Vampire and the Ballerina (1960 - aka
L'Amante del Vampiro), *La Traite du
Vampire* (1960 - short), *Mill of the Stone
Women* (1960 -aka *Icon / Drops of Blood / Il
Mulino delle Donne di Pietra*), *Little Shop of
Horrors* (1960), *The Playgirls and the
Vampire* (1960 - aka *Curse of the
Vampire / L'Ultima Preda del Vampiro*),
Creature of the Walking Dead (1960),
Blood and Roses (1960 - aka *Et Mourir et
Plaisir*), *The Brides of Dracula* (1960),
*Little Red Riding Hood and Tom Thumb vs.
the Monsters* (1960 - aka *Caperucita y
Pulgarcito Contra los Monstruos*), *Atom Age
Vampire* (1960 - aka *Seddok, L'Erede di
Satana / Seddok*), *Black Sunday* (1960 - aka
*The Mask of Satan / Revenge of the
Vampire / La Maschera del Demonio*), *The
Invasion of the Vampires* (1961 - aka *La

Invasión de los Vampiros), The Naked Witch (1961 - aka The Naked Temptress), The Last Man on Earth (1961), Bring Me the Vampire (1961 - aka Echenme al Vampiro), Samson vs. the Vampire Women (1961 - aka Santo Contra las Mujeres Vampiro), Frankenstein el Vampiro y Cia (1961), The Magic Sword (1961 - aka St George and the Seven Curses), Goliath and the Vampires (1961 - aka Maciste Contro il Vampiro), Hercules in the Haunted World (1961 - aka Hercules in the Centre of the Earth / Ercole al Centro della Terra), The Bloody Vampire (1962 - aka El Vampiro Sangriento / El Conde Frankenhausen), Slaughter of the Vampires (1962 - aka Curse of the Blood Ghouls), El Vampiro Aechecha (1963), Black Sabbath (1963 - aka I Tre Volti della Paura), Insomnia (1963 - aka Insomnie - short), The Horror of It All (1963), Sexy Proibitissimo (1963), Pontianaka Kembali (1963), Crypt of Horror (1963 - aka Terror of the Crypt / La Cripta e L'Incubo / La Maldición de los Karnstein), Devils of Darkness (1964), Kiss Me, Quick! (1964 - aka Dr Breedlove or How I Learned to Stop Worrying and Love), Kiss of the Vampire (1964 - aka Kiss of Evil), The Vampire of the Opera (1964 - aka Il Mostro dell'Opera), Mga Manugang Ni Drakula (1964), Pontianka Gua Musang (1964), El Hacha Diabolica (1964), Castle of Blood (1964 - aka Castle of Terror / La Danza Macabra), Cave of the Living Dead (1964 - aka Der Flucyhder Gruenen Augen), Billy the Kid vs. Dracula (1965), El Baron Brakola (1965 - aka Santo Contra el Baron Brakola), Blood Thirst (1965), Charro de las Calaveras (1965), Dr Terror's House of Horrors (1965), A Vampire for Two (1965 - aka Un Vampiro Para Dos), Planet of the Vampires (1965 - aka Demon Planet / Terrore nella Spazio), The Worst Crime of All (1966 - aka Mondo Keyhole), El Imperio de Dracula (1966), The Hand of Night (1966 - aka The Beast of Morocco), Queen of Blood (1966 - aka Planet of Blood), Blood Bath (1966 - aka Track of the Vampire), Chappaqua (1966), Blood Suckers (1966 - aka Island of the Doomed / Man-Eater of Hydra / Island of Death / La Isla de la Muerte), Island of Terror (1966), Dracula - Prince of Darkness (1966), The Lemon Grove Kids Meet the Monsters (1966), Theatre of Death (1966 - aka Blood Fiend), The Blood Drinkers (1966 - aka Vampire People), Mad Monster Party? (1966 - puppetoon), A Taste of Blood (1967 - aka The Secret of Dr Alucard), The Naked World of Harrison Marks (1967), Frankenstein's Bloody Terror (1967 - aka Hell's Creatures / La Marca del Hombre Lobo), Goke, Body Snatcher from Hell (1967), Dr Terror's Gallery of Horrors (1967 - aka The Blood Suckers / Return from the Past / Gallery of Horrors / Alien

Massacre), Blood of Dracula's Castle (1967), The Blood Beast Terror (1967 - aka The Vampire Beast Craves Blood), Batman Fights Dracula (1967), Vampirisme (1967 - short), Vig (1967), The Vampire's Rape (1967 - aka Le Viol du Vampire / La Reine des Vampires), Dance of the Vampires (1967 - aka The Fearless Vampire Killers / Pardon Me, But Your Teeth Are in My Neck), Dracula Has Risen from the Grave (1968), The Torture Zone (1968 - aka The Fear Chamber / The Torture Chamber / La Camara del Terror), Kuroneko (1968 - aka Yabu No Naka Kuroneko), Malenka, the Niece of the Vampire (1968 - aka Fangs of the Living Dead / La Nipote del Vampiro), Sangre de Virgenes (1968), Las Vampiras (1968), Yokai Daisenso (1968), Santo y el Tesoro de Dracula (1968 - aka El Vampiro y el Sexo), Dracula, the Dirty Old Man (1969), La Venganza de las Mujeres Vampiro (1969), Dracula vs. Frankenstein (1969 - aka El Hombre Que Vino del Ummo / Assignment Terror), Men of Action Meet Women of Dracula (1969) Drakulita (1969), Hiroku Kaibyoden (1969), A Vampire's Dream (1969 - aka Um Sonho de Vampiros), Tore Ng Diyablo (1969), The Maltese Bippy (1969), Santo y el Blue Demon Contra los Monstruos (1969), The Nude Vampire (1969 - aka La Vampire Nue), Taste the Blood of Dracula (1969), The Magic Christian (1970), Le Frisson des Vampires (1970 - aka The Vampire's Thrill / Sex and the Vampire), The Murder Mansion (1970 - aka La Mansion de la Niebla / Quando Marta Urlo dalla Tomba), Sadique aux Dents Rouges (1970), Necropolis (1970), Jonathan (1970 - aka Jonathan, Vampire Sterben Nicht), Bloodsuckers (1970 - aka Incense of the Damned), Vampyros Lesbos die Erbin des Dracula (1970 - aka El Signo del Vampiro / Las Vampiras), The Horrible Sexy Vampire (1970), Horror of the Blood Monsters (1970 - aka Vampire Men of the Lost Planet / Horror Creatures of the Prehistoric Planet / Creatures of the Prehistoric Planet / Creatures of the Red Planet), House of Dark Shadows (1970), Guess What Happened to Count Dracula? (1970 - aka The Master of the Dungeon), Dracula's Lusterne Sex Vampire (1970), One More Time (1970), Dracula vs. Frankenstein (1970 - aka Blood of Frankenstein / The Revenge of Dracula / They're Coming to Get You), Santo Contra los Cazadores de Cabezas (1970), Countess Dracula (1970) The Vampire Lovers (1970), Web of the Spider (1970 - aka Nella Stretta Morsa del Ragno), The Werewolf vs. the Vampire Woman (1970 - aka Blood Moon / Shadow of the Werewolf), Scars of Dracula (1970), Count Yorga, Vampire (1970), The Devil's Skin (1970), Night of the Vampire (1970 - aka Chi O Suu Ning Yo), The House That

Dripped Blood (1970), Creatures of Evil (1970 - aka Curse of the Vampires), Bram Stoker's Count Dracula (1970 - aka El Conde Dracula / Il Conte Dracula / Count Dracula), The Mad Love Life of a Hot Vampire (1970), The Body Beneath (1971), Lake of Dracula (1971 - aka Chi O Suu Me), Let's Scare Jessica to Death (1971), In Search of Dracula (1971 - aka In Search of the Real Dracula - documentary), The Curse of the Vampire (1971 - aka La Llamada del Vampiro), Lust for a Vampire (1971), Tombs of the Blind Dead (1971 - aka The Blind Dead / La Noche del Terror Ciego), Twins of Evil (1971 - aka The Gemini Twins), El Retorno de los Vampiros (1971), Requiem for a Vampire (1971 - aka Requiem Pour un Vampire / Caged Virgins / Crazed Vampires / Vierges et Vampires), Pastel de Sangre (1971 - segment), The Case of the Full Moon Murders (1971 - aka The Case of the Smiling Stiffs / Sex on the Groove Tube), The Velvet Vampire (1971 - aka The Waking Hour), Daughters of Darkness (1971 - aka Children of the Night / La Rouge aux Lèvres), Chantoc Contra el Tigre y el Vampiro (1971), Count Erotica, Vampire (1971), The Night Stalker (1971 - TVM), The Return of Count Yorga (1971), The Vampire Happening (1971) Santo y Blue Demon Contra Dracula y el Hombre Lobo (1972), Capulina Contra los Monstruos (1972), Invasion of the Blood Farmers (1972), Blacula (1972), Lips of Blood (1972 - aka Le Sang des Autres / Perversions Sexuelles / Les Chemins de la Violence / El Segretto de la Momia), Alamaba's Ghost (1972), The Night Strangler (1972 - TVM), Invasión de los Muertos (1972), Night of the Devils (1972 - aka La Notte dei Diavoli), Capulina Contra los Vampiros (1972), The Mystery in Dracula's Castle (1972 - TVM), Angeles y Querubines (1972), La Fille de Dracula (1972 - aka La Hija de Dracula), Grave of the Vampire (1972), The Vampire's Bite (1972), The Vampire's Night Orgy (1972 - aka Orgy of the Vampires / La Orgia Nocturna de los Vampiros / La Noche de los Vampiros), Vampire Kung-Fu (1972), The Legend of Blood Castle (1972 - aka Blood Ceremony / The Female Butcher / Ceremonia Sangrienta), Dracula's Great Love (1972 - aka Dracula's Virgin Lovers / Vampire Playgirls / Cemetery Girls), The Dracula Saga (1972 - aka Saga of the Draculas / Dracula - The Bloodline / La Saga de los Dracula), Dracula Prisoner of Frankenstein (1972 - aka Dracula Contra Frankenstein / The Screaming Dead), The Deathmaster (1972), Dracula AD 1972 (1972), The Blood-Spattered Bride (1972 - aka Till Death Do Us Part / La Novia Ensangrentada), Crypt of the Living Dead (1972 - aka Vampire Woman / Hannah:

Queen of the Vampires / Young Hannah, Queen of the Vampires), Pepito y Chanelo vs. los Monstruos (1973), The Norliss Tapes (1973 - TVM), Vault of Horror (1973), The Devil's Wedding Night (1973), Ganja and Hess (1973 - aka Black Evil / Blackout: The Moment of Terror / Black Vampire / Possession), The Legendary Curse of Lemora (1973 - aka Lady Dracula / Lemora: A Child's Tale of the Supernatural), El Retorno de Walpurgis (1973 - aka Curse of the Devil), Return of the Evil Dead (1973 - aka Attack of the Blind Dead / El Ataque de los Muertos Sin Ojos), House of Dracula's Daughter (1973), Sons of Satan (1973), Los Vampiros de Coyoacan (1973), The Satanic Rites of Dracula (1973), Scream, Blacula, Scream (1973), The Reincarnation of Isabel (1973 - aka The Ghastly Orgies of Count Dracula), Andy Warhol's Dracula (1973 - aka Blood for Dracula), Dracula (1973 - TVM), Son of Dracula (1973 - aka Count Downe), Vaarwhel (1973), The Devil's Plaything (1973 - aka Veil of Blood), Night of the Sorcerers (1973), The Bare-Breasted Countess (1973 - aka Erotikill / The Loves of Irina / La Comtesse Noire), Captain Kronos: Vampire Hunter (1973 - aka Kronos), Chosen Survivors (1973), Vampyres (1973 - aka Satan's Daughter / Blood Hunger / Vampyres: Daughters of Dracula), Vampira (1974 - aka Old Dracula), The Thirsty Dead (1974 - aka Blood Cult of Shangri-la), Those Cruel and Bloody Vampires (1974 - aka Las Alegres Vampiras de Vogel), Tender Dracula (1974 - aka La Grand Trouille / Tendre Dracula), Quem tem Medo de Lobisomen (1974), The Bat People (1974), The Legend of the Seven Golden Vampires (1974 - aka The Seven Brothers Meet Dracula), Immoral Tales (1974 - aka Three Immoral Women), Blood (1974), Il Cavaliere Costante Nicosia Demoniaco Ovvero Dracula In Brianza (1975), The Evil of Dracula (1975 - aka Chi Suu Bara), El Jovencito Dracula (1975), Mrs Amworth (1975 - TV short), Lèvres de Sang (1975 - aka Lips of Blood), Kathavai Thatteeya Mohni Paye (1975), Sisters of Satan (1975 - aka Innocents from Hell), Mary, Mary, Bloody Mary (1975), Sex Express (1975 - segment), Spermula (1975), Deafula (1975), Night of the Seagulls (1975), Leonor (1975), Suck Me, Vampire (1975), Bloodlust (1976), Dead of Night (1976 - TVM), Martin (1976), Dracula and Son (1976 - aka Dracula, Père et Fils), Rabid (1976), El Pobrecito Draculín (1976), The Bride's Initiation (1976), Tiempos Duros Para Dracula (1976), Rabid (1976 - aka Rage), Blood Relations (1977), Lady Dracula (1977), Dracula's Dog (1977 - aka Zoltan, Hound of Dracula), Doctor Dracula (1977), Sturmtruppen (1977), Count Dracula (1977 - TVM), A Deusa de Marmore -

Escrava do Diabo (1978), Vlad Tepes (1978), La Dinastia Dracula (1978), Nightwing (1979), Nocturna (1979 - aka Nocturna, Granddaughter of Dracula (1979), Nightmare in Blood (1979), Dracula (1979), Dracula Blows His Cool (1979), The Vampire Hookers (1979 - aka Sensuous Vampires), Love at First Bite (1979), Thirst (1979), Star Virgin (1979), Dracula Sucks (1979 - aka Lust at First Bite / Dracula's Bride), Mamma Dracula (1979), Fascination (1979), Vampire (1979 -TVM), People (1979 - segment), Nosferatu the Vampyre (1979 - aka Nosferatu, Phantom der Nacht), Salem's Lot (1979 - TVM), Wolnyoui Han (1980) Les Charlots Contra Dracula (1980), The Games of the Countess Dolingen of Gratz (1980), Deadline (1980 - aka Anatomy of a Horror), The Monster Club (1980), Dracula's Last Rites (1980 - aka Last Rites), Blood Lust (1980), The Craving (1980 - aka El Retorno del Hombre Lobo), Krvava Pani (1981 - cartoon), Dracula Exotica (1981 - aka Love at First Gulp), The Black Room (1981), La Momia Nacional (1981), Saturday the 14th (1981), Buenos Noches, Señor Monstruo (1982), Cafe Flesh (1982), Hysterical (1982), I, Desire (1982 - TVM), La Morte Vivante (1982), One Dark Night (1982), Vincent Price's Dracula (1982 - aka Dracula - The Great Undead - TV documentary), Dracula Rises from the Coffin (1982), Ferat Vampire (1982), La Belle Captive (1983), Geek Maggot Bingo (1983), A Polish Vampire In Burbank (1983 - aka Polish Vampire), Dracula Tan Exarchia (1983), The Trial (1983), Gayracula (1983), The Hunger (1983), Haunted Cop Shop (1984), Bloodsuckers from Outer Space (1984), Loves of the Living Dead (1984), Lust in the Fast Lane (1984), Carne de Tu Carne (1984), I Married a Vampire (1984), Wicked Wife (1984 - aka Curse of the Wicked Wife), Evils of the Night (1984 - aka Space Monsters), Billy the Kid and the Green Baize Vampire (1985), I Like Bats (1985), The Midnight Hour (1985 - TVM), Mixed Up (1985), Mr Vampire (1985), The Tomb (1985), Who Is Afraid of Dracula? (1985) Vampire Hunter D (1985 - cartoon), Dragon Against Vampire (1985 -aka Dragon vs. Vampire), Hello, Dracula (1985), Transylvania 6-500 (1985), Once Bitten (1985), Lifeforce (1985), Fright Night (1985), Graveyard Shift (1986), Mr Vampire II (1986), Red and Black (1986), Haunted Cop Shop 2 (1986), The Close Encounter of the Vampire (1986), Body Double (1986), Kung-Fu Vampire Buster (1986), Anemia (1986), The Seven Vampires (1986 - aka As Sete Vampiros), Vamp (1986), Little Shop of Horrors (1986), Graveyard Shift (1986), Outback

Vampires (1987 - aka The Wicked), Love Me, Vampire (1987), Mr Vampire III (1987), The Lost Boys (1987), Return to Salem's Lot (1987 - TVM), Near Dark (1987), My Best Friend Is a Vampire (1987), Trampire (1987), Elusive Song of the Vampire (1987), The Monster Squad (1987), Outback Vampires (1987 - aka The Wicked), Toothless Vampires (1987), Vampire Knights (1987), Vampire at Midnight (1987), Graveyard Disturbance (1987 - aka Dentro il Cimitrio), Dinner with the Vampire (1988), Sundown (1988 - aka Sundown, the Vampire in Retreat), Teen Vamp (1988), To Die For (1988), The Mysterious Death of Nina Chereau (1988), Vampires (1988 - aka Abadon / Fright House), Saturday the 14th Strikes Back (1988), Howl of the Devil (1988 - aka El Aullido del Diablo), Mr Vampire IV (1988), The Jitters (1988), The Kiss (1988), Lair of the White Worm (1988), Vampires On Bikini Beach (1988), Vampire's Kiss (1988), Not of This Earth (1988), Vampires in Venice (1988 - aka Nosferatu a Venezia), Dracula's Widow (1988), Midnight (1988), The Understudy: Graveyard Shift II (1988), Beverly Hills Vamp (1988), Fright Night Part 2 (1988), The Understudy: Graveyard Shift II (1988), Daughter of Darkness (1989), The Lost Platoon (1989), Shadows in the Dark (1989), Spirit vs. Zombi (1989), Spooky Family (1989), Magic Cope (1989 - aka Mr Vampire V), Mom (1989), Nightlife (1989 - TVM), Pale Blood (1989), Transylvania Twist (1989), The First Vampire in China (1990), I Bought a Vampire Motor Cycle (1990), Banglo 666 (1990), Crazy Safari (1990), Dawn (1990), La Maschera del Demonio (1990), DEF By Temptation (1990), Bandh Darwaza (1990), Baby Blood (1990), Encounters of the Spooky Kind II (1990), Red Blooded American Girl (1990), Children of the Night (1990), Nightbreed (1990), Out for Blood (1990), The Arrival (1990), Vampyre (1990), Streets (1990), Vampire Buster (1990), Vampire Cop (1990), Subspecies (1990), The Reflecting Skin (1990), Rockula (1990), Demon Cop (1991), Doctor Vampire (1991), The Malibu Beach Vampires (1991), The Vampire's Embrace (1991), Spooky Family 2 (1991), Trilogy of Fear (1991 - segment), The Ultimate Vampire (1991), Undying Love (1991), Valerie (1991), Son of Darkness: To Die For 2 (1991), Bloodsuckers (1991 - aka Those Feedy on Blood), Moon Legend (1991), My Granpa Is a Vampire (1991), Vampire Trailer Park (1991), Bite (1991), Bram Stoker's Dracula (1992), Fangs (1992), Buffy the Vampire Slayer (1992), Project Vampire (1992), Sorority House Vampires (1992), To Sleep with a Vampire (1992),

The Reluctant Vampire (1992), *The Vampire's Rope* (1992), *Dracula Rising* (1992), *Dracula's Hair* (1992), *Innocent Blood* (1992), *In the Midnight Hour* (1992), *Sleepwalkers* (1992), *Back to the USSR* (1992), *Tale of a Vampire* (1992), *Bloodlust* (1992), *Darkness* (1992), *Bloodthirsty* (1992), *The Unearthing* (1993), *Night Owl* (1993), *Children of Dracula* (1994), *Interviews with Real Vampires* (1994), *Cronos* (1994), *Interview With the Vampire* (1994), *Vampire Vixens from Venus* (1995), *The Nosferatu Diaries* (1995 - aka *Vampire's Embrace*), *Dracula -Dead and Loving It* (1996), *From Dusk Till Dawn* (1996), *Nadja* (1996), *A Vampire in Brooklyn* (1996)

Vampires in Venice see Nosferatu in Venice

Vampyr **
Fr/Ger 1931 83m bw
A traveller staying at a country inn suspects the locals of being vampires.

A strange and atmospheric horror film which makes excellent use of camera and lighting, its curious dream-like quality being achieved by filming through a layer of gauze. Memorable sequences include the hero's vision of his own death.
p: Carl Dreyer for Tobis Klangfilm/Dreyer Filmproduktion
w: Carl Dreyer, Christian Jul
d: CARL DREYER
ph: RUDOLPH MATÉ, LOUIS NEE
m: Wolfgang Zeller
ad: Hermann Warm, Hans Bittman, Cesare Silvagni
sound: Hans Bittman, Paul Falkenberg
Julian West, Henriette Gerard, Jan Hieronimko, Maurice Schutz, Jane Mora, Rena Mandel, Sibylle Schmitz

Van Enger, Charles (1890-1980)
American cinematographer who worked on several distinguished silents (most notably *The Phantom of the Opera*, which he co-photographed with Virgil Miller). He later found himself assigned to increasingly routine productions to which he occasionally brought a certain flair. His credits include *Fox Movietone Follies*, *Never Give a Sucker an Even Break*, *The Wistful Widow* and *Pa Kettle on the Farm*.
Genre credits:
The Phantom of the Opera (1925 - co-ph), *Night Monster* (1942), *Sherlock Holmes Faces Death* (1943), *Abbott and Costello Meet Frankenstein* (1948), *The Magnetic Monster* (1953)

Van Eyssen, John (1925-)
British actor, best remembered for playing Jonathan Harker in Hammer's 1958 version of *Dracula*. He later retired from acting and became firstly an agent and then a production executive for Columbia Picture's British office. His other credits include *I'm Alright, Jack*, *The Criminal* and *Exodus*.
Genre credits:
Quatermass 2 (1956 - aka *Enemy from Space*), *Dracula* (1958 - aka *Horror of Dracula* - as Jonathan Harker)

Van Sloan, Edward (1882-1964)
American character actor, remembered as the screen's first Van Helsing in the 1930 version of *Dracula*, a role which he created on the Broadway stage and repeated in the 1936 sequel, *Dracula's Daughter*. He consequently found himself playing elderly professor types in all manner of films, including several of Universal's other key horror productions of the thirties. His other credits include *Behind the Mask*, *The Last Days of Pompeii*, *The Doctor Takes a Wife* and *A Foreign Affair*.
Genre credits:
Dracula (1930 - as Van Helsing), *Frankenstein* (1931), *The Mummy* (1932), *The Black Room* (1935), *Dracula's Daughter* (1936 - as Van Helsing), *The Phantom Creeps* (1939), *Before I Hang* (1940), *The Monster and the Girl* (1941), *The Mask of Dijon* (1947)

The Vanishing *
Netherlands 1988 105m colour
A man spends years trying to discover what became of his girlfriend who mysteriously disappeared from a roadside filling station.

Intriguing suspenser which pretty much holds the attention through to the shocking dénouement. It was remade in 1993, less effectively, in America by the same director (see below).
p: Anne Lordo, George Sluizer for Golden Egg/Ingrid/MGS
w: Tim Krabbe from his novel
d: George Sluizer
ph: Tonu Kuhn
m: Henry Vrienten
ed: George Sluizer, Lin Friedman
ad: Isidro Pin, Cor Spijk
Gene Bervoets, Bernard-Pierre Donnadieu, Johanna Ter Steege, Gwen Eckhaus, Tania Latarjet, Bernadette Le Sache

The Vanishing *
USA 1993 109m DeLuxe Dolby
Hollywood remake of the above (from the same director), this time with a 'happy' ending.

Tolerable enough if you haven't seen the original, barely comparable if you have.
p: Larry Brezner, Paul Schiff for TCF
exec p: Peter Jan Brugge, Lauren Weissman
w: Todd Graff
novel: Tim Krabbe
d: George Sluizer
ph: Peter Suschitsky
m: Jerry Goldsmith
ed: Bruce Green
pd: Jannine C. Oppewall
cos: Duirinda Wood
sound: Jeff Wexler
Jeff Bridges, Kiefer Sutherland, Nancy Travis, Sandra Bullock, Park Overall, Maggie Linderman, Lisa Eichhorn, George Hearn, Lynn Hamilton

Vault of Horror *
GB 1973 86m Eastmancolor
Five men find themselves trapped in the basement of a skyscraper. While they wait to be released they tell each other about their nightmares.

Reasonably lively though wholly typical horror compendium.
p: Max J. Rosenberg, Milton Subotsky for Metromedia/Amicus
w: Milton Subotsky
stories: Alf Feldstein, Bill Gaines
d: Roy Ward Baker
ph: Denys Coop
m: Douglas Gamley
ed: Oswald Haffenrichter
ad: Tony Curtis
cos: John Briggs
sound: Danny Daniel, Gerry Humphreys
Terry-Thomas, Daniel Massey, Anna Massey, Curt Jurgens, Denholm Elliott, Tom Baker, Michael Craig, Glynis Johns, Edward Judd, Dawn Addams, Erik Chitty

Veidt, Conrad (1893-1943)
Handsome German leading man with a penchant for sinister parts. After stage experience in Berlin (with Max Reinhardt) he made his film début in 1916 in *Der Spion*, finding stardom three years later as the somnambulist in *The Cabinet of Dr Caligari*. Famous in Germany throughout the twenties, he began making films in Hollywood in 1927, becoming a star in both America and Britain, where he appeared in such classics as *Rome Express*, *The Passing of the Third Floor Back*, *The Spy in Black*, *Contraband*, *The Thief of Bagdad* (as the wicked Caliph) and *Casablanca*. In the thirties he was publicized with the tag line, 'Women fight for Conrad Veidt!'
Genre credits:
The Cabinet of Dr Caligari (1919 - aka *Das Kabinett Von Dr Caligari*), *Satanas* (1919), *Dr Jekyll and Mr Hyde* (1920 - aka *Der Januskopf*), *The Hands of Orlac* (1924 - aka *Orlacs Hande*), *Waxworks*

• **Conrad Veidt as the somnabulist Cesare in** *The Cabinet of Dr Caligari*. **Its expressionist approach had much influence on the Universal horror films of the thirties.**

(1924 - aka *Wachsfigurenkabinett*), *The Student of Prague* (1926 -aka *Der Student Von Prag*), *The Man Who Laughs* (1927), *The Passing of the Third Floor Back* (1935)

Venom
GB 1981 92m Technicolor
An escaped black mamba causes a kidnap plan to go awry.

Hackneyed thriller with a few routine shocks. The script is beyond redemption.
p: Martin Bregman for Aribage/Morison/Venom
w: Robert Carrington
novel: Alan Scholefield
d: Piers Haggard
ph: Gilbert Taylor, Denys Coop
m: Michael Kamen
ed/2nd unit d: Michael Bradsell
ad: Tony Curtis
cos: David Murphy
sp: Alan Whibley, Richard Dean
sound: Bill Rowe, Rene Boriwitz, Simon Kaye
2nd unit ph: Frank Watts
Sterling Hayden, Klaus Kinski, Oliver Reed, Susan George, Sarah Miles, Nicol Williamson, Cornelia Sharpe, Rita Webb

Vernon, Howard
German-born actor, long associated with the films of director Jesus (Jess) Franco, on which he sometimes also acted as stills photographer (often using the pseudonym Mario Lippert).

Genre credits:
The Awful Dr Orloff (1961 - aka *The Demon Doctor/L'Horrible Dr Orloff/Gritos en la Noche*), *La Mano de un Hombre Muerto* (1962), *Sex Charade* (1970), *Virgin Among the Living Dead* (1970 - aka *Christina, Princesse de L'Erotisme*), *Sie Totete in Ekstase* (1970 - aka *Ms Hyde*), *El Diablo que Vino de Akasava* (1970 - aka *The Devil Came from Akasava*), *Dracula Contra Frankenstein* (1971 - aka *Dracula, Prisoner of Frankenstein*), *La Fille de Dracula* (1972), *La Maldición de Frankenstein* (1972 - aka *The Erotic Rites of Frankenstein/Les Experiences Erotiques de Frankenstein*), *Plaisir à Trois* (1973 - aka *How to Seduce a Virgin/Ultra Tumba*), *Comtesse Perverse* (1973), *Lorna, L'Exorciste* (1974 - aka *Lorna/Les Possedées du Diable/Sexy Diabolic Story*), *El Hundimiento de la Casa Usher* (1983 - aka *Revenge in the House of Usher/Nevrose/Neurosis*), *Les Predateurs de la Nuit* (1988 - aka *Faceless*)

Vesota, Bruno (1922-1976)
Rotund American actor who appeared in many a Corman quickie, including *Apache Woman*, *Oklahoma Woman*, *Gunslinger*, *Rock All Night* and *Teenage Doll*. His other film credits include *The Wild One*, *Hot Car Girl*, *Code of Silence* and *Hell's Angels on Wheels*, as well as a handful of genre pictures, again mostly for Roger Corman.
Genre credits:
The Undead (1956), *War of the Satellites*

(1959), *Attack of the Giant Leeches* (1959), *The Wasp Woman* (1959), *Night Tide* (1961), *The Haunted Palace* (1963)

Vetri, Victoria (1944-)
American-born actress of Italian descent who began in television and films using the name Angela Dorian. Remembered for playing Sanna in Hammer's *When Dinosaurs Ruled the Earth*, her other film appearances have been few (*Group Marriage*, *Chuka*, etc.).
Genre credits:
Rosemary's Baby (1968 - as Angela Dorian), *When Dinosaurs Ruled the Earth* (1970), *Invasion of the Bee Girls* (1973 - aka *Graveyard Tramps*)

Victor, Katherine (1928-)
American actress and singer (real name Katena Ktenavea) who appeared in several low-budget horror films in the fifties and sixties, mostly for producer-director Jerry Warren. She at first went by the name Vea, in which guise she had brief roles in *Sabrina* and *The Eddy Duchin Story*, etc.
Genre credits:
Mesa of Lost Women (1952 - aka *Lost Women*), *Teenage Zombies* (1957), *The Cape Canaveral Monsters* (1959), *Curse of the Stone Hand* (1965), *House of the Black Death* (1965), *Creature of the Walking Dead* (1966), *The Wild World of Batwoman* (1966 - aka *She Was a Hippie Vampire*)

Vidgeon, Robin (1939-)
British cinematographer who has worked on several of Clive Barker's films. A camera assistant from the mid-fifties, he turned to photography himself in the early eighties.
Genre credits:
Mr Corbett's Ghost (1986), *Hellraiser* (1987), *Hellbound: Hellraiser II* (1988), *Parents* (1988), *The Fly II* (1989), *Highway to Hell* (1989), *Nightbreed* (1990)

Village of the Damned **
GB 1960 78m bw
Women in a small English village simultaneously give birth to offspring whose origins are from another planet.

Clever low-budget science-fiction thriller which makes the very most of its situations and proves what can be achieved with a low budget if the talent involved is right.
p: Ronald Kinnoch for MGM
w: STIRLING SILLIPHANT, WOLF RILLA, GEOFFREY BARCLAY
novel: JOHN WYNDHAM
d: WOLF RILLA
ph: GEOFFREY FAITHFULL
m: Ron Goodwin
ed: Gordon Hales

• The children take control in *Village of the Damned*, a low budget gem if ever there was one.

ad: Ivan King
cos: Eileen Sullivan
sp: Tom Howard
sound: A. W. Watkins, Cyril Swern
2nd unit ph: Gerald Moss
GEORGE SANDERS, Barbara Shelley, Michael Gwynn, Martin Stephens, Laurence Naismith, Peter Vaughan

Village of the Damned *
USA 1995 98m Eastmancolor DTS Stereo
All the women in the township of Midwich find themselves simultaneously pregnant with children who grow up with mysterious powers.
  Passable video fodder, not quite as bad as some make out, but otherwise a pointless remake lacking the effect of the original.
p: Michael Presser, Sandy King for Universal/Alphaville
w: David Himmelstein
novel: JOHN WYNDHAM
d: John Carpenter
ph: Gary K. Kibbe
m: John Carpenter, Dave Davies
ed: Edward Warschilka
pd: Rodger Maus
sp: Bruce Nicholson, ILM
sound: Thomas Causey
make-up effects: KNB

2nd unit d: Jeff Imada
2nd unit ph: Arthur K. Botham
Christopher Reeve, Kirstie Alley, Mark Hamill, Linda Kozlowski, Michael Pare, Meredith Salenger, Pippa Pearthree, John Carpenter

Villarias, Carlos (1892-?)
Mexican actor with much stage experience, known chiefly for playing Dracula in Universal's Spanish-language version of the Bram Stoker classic, shot simultaneously with the 1930 Lugosi version. His other film credits include *Bordertown*.

The Virgin Witch
GB 1971 84m Rankcolour
Two sisters find themselves in the hands of Satanists while one of them is working as a model at a country house one weekend.
  Surprisingly well staged low-budget tits-and-bum horror in the seventies tradition.
p: Ralph Solomons for Univista
w: Klaus Vogel
d: RAY AUSTIN
ph: Gerald Moss
m: Ted Dicks
md: Bernard Wibley
ed: Philip Barniker

ad: Paul Pernara
cos: Ken Lewington
sound: Derek Ball
Michelle, Ann Michelle, Keith Buckley, Patricia Haines, James Chase, Paula Wright, Christopher Strain, Neil Hallett, Esme Smythe, Garth Watkins

Visiting Hours
Canada 1981 105m DeLuxe Panavision
A mad killer stalks a lady TV reporter in a city hospital.
  Sick slasher pic with revolting detail.
p: Claude Heroux for TCF/Filmplan International
exec p: Victor Samdi, Pierre David
w: Brian Taggart
d/ed: Jean-Claude Lord
ph: Rene Verzier
m: Jonathan Goldsmith
ad: Michael Proulx
cos: Delphine White
sp: Gary Zeller
sound: Don Cohen, Marcel Pothier
stunt co-ordinator: Jim Arnett
Lee Grant, Michael Ironside, William Shatner, Linda Purl, Lenore Zann, Harvey Atkin

Volk, Stephen
British writer who, after scripting *Gothic* for director Ken Russell, found himself labelled a horror writer.
Genre credits:
Gothic (1986 - w), *The Kiss* (1988 - co-w), *The Guardian* (1990 -co-w)

Von Sydow, Max (1929-)
Swedish actor (real name Carl Adolf Von Sydow), noted for his work with director Ingmar Bergman (*The Seventh Seal*, *Wild Strawberries*, *The Face*, *The Virgin Spring*, *Through a Glass Darkly*, *Winter Light*, etc.), though perhaps best known to horror fans as Father Merrin in *The Exorcist*. Since playing Jesus in *The Greatest Story Ever Told* in 1965, he has appeared in all manner of international productions (often bringing a note of much-needed dignity). His credits include *Hawaii*, *Three Days of the Condor*, *Flash Gordon* (as Ming the Merciless), *Hannah and Her Sisters*, *Pelle the Conqueror* and *Judge Dredd*. He has also directed one film, *Katinka*.
Genre credits:
The Seventh Seal (1956), *The Exorcist* (1973), *Exorcist II: The Heretic* (1977), *A Kiss Before Dying* (1991), *Needful Things* (1993)

Wacko

USA 1984 81m Movielab
The 'Lawnmower' killer returns to seek
revenge after a thirteen-year absence.
    Dismal spoof of the slasher genre.
p: Greydon Clark for OSM
exec p: Michael S. Sarita
w: Dana Olsen, Michael Spound, James
Kouf Jr, David Greenwalt
d: Greydon Clark
ph: Nicholas J. Van Sterberg
m: Arthur Kempel
ed: Earl Watson, Curtis Burch
ad: Chester Kaczenski
cos: Kristin Nelson
sp: Joe Quinlivan
sound: William McCoughy, Howard
Wollman, Robert Harman
Joe Don Baker, George Kennedy, Stella
Stevens, Julia Duffy, Scott McGinnis,
Elizabeth Daily, Andrew Clay, Michele
Tobin

Waggner, George (1894-1984)

American producer and director who
worked on a number of Universal's
horror films of the early forties, most
notably *The Wolf Man*. He began his
film career in 1920 as an actor in such
films as *The Sheik*, *Desert Driven* and *The
Iron Horse*, though with the coming of
sound he turned first to songwriting
and then to screenplay writing (*City
Limits*, *The Line Up*, *The Spy Ring*, etc.).
He began directing in 1938 with *Border
Wolves*, and followed this with a
number of other low-budget westerns
(*Western Trails*, *Outlaw Express*, *Prairie
Justice*, *Ghost Town Riders*, *The Phantom
Stage*, etc.) before turning to horror.
His other credits include *The Fighting
Kentuckian*, *Bitter Creek* and *Pale Arrow*.
Genre credits:
Man Made Monster (1940 - aka *The
Electric Man* - d), *The Wolf Man* (1940 -
p/d), *Horror Island* (1941 - d), *The
Ghost of Frankenstein* (1942 - p), *The
Invisible Agent* (1942 - p), *Frankenstein
Meets the Wolf Man* (1943 - p), *The
Phantom of the Opera* (1943 - p), *The
Climax* (1944 - p/d), *Cobra Woman*
(1944 - p)

Walas, Chris

American make-up effects artist who
(with Stephen DuPuis) won an Oscar for
his work on *The Fly*, which led to his
directing the sequel. His only other film
to date as a director is *The Vagrant*. His
work is frequently in collaboration and
also includes *Raiders of the Lost Ark*,
Caveman and *Enemy Mine*.
Genre credits:
Pirahna (1978), *Galaxina* (1980), *Scanners*
(1980 - co-sp), *Caveman* (1981), *Gremlins*
(1984), *The Fly* (1986), *House II: The
Second Story* (1987), *The Kiss* (1988), *The
Fly II* (1989 - d/make-up), *Arachnophobia*
(1990), *Naked Lunch* (1991), *The Vagrant*
(1992 - d)

Walker, Pete (1935-)

British producer-director who, after
directing several sexploitation films (*I
Like Birds*, *For Men Only*, *The Big Switch*,
School for Sex, *Cool It*, *Carol*) turned to
low-budget horror, several of which
have gained cult followings. His one shot
at the big time, *House of the Long
Shadows*, was not the hoped-for success.
His other credits include *Man of Violence*,
The Four Dimensions of Greta, *Tiffany Jones*
and *Home Before Midnight*.
Genre credits:
Die Screaming, Marianne (1971), *The Flesh
and Blood Show* (1971), *House of Whipcord*
(1974), *Frightmare* (1975), *House of
Mortal Sin* (1975 - aka *The Confessional*),
Schizo (1976), *The Comeback* (1977),
House of the Long Shadows (1983)

Walker, Vernon L. (1894-1948)

American cameraman and special-effects
technician, long with RKO. His
countless credits include *Flying Down to
Rio*, *The Last Days of Pompeii*, Hitchcock's
Notorious and *Sinbad the Sailor*.
Genre credits:
The Most Dangerous Game (1932 - aka *The
Hounds of Zaroff* - co-sp), *Son of Kong* (1933
- co-ph), *She* (1935 - sp), *The Hunchback of
Notre Dame* (1939 - sp), *The Spiral
Staircase* (1946 - sp), *Bedlam* (1946 - sp)

The Walking Dead *

USA 1936 66m bw

Brought back to life, a wrongly executed
convict wreaks vengeance against those
who framed him.
    Economically handled chiller in the
Germanic manner, with Karloff's
performance owing much to his
Frankenstein's Monster character.
p: Lou Edelman for Warner
w: Ewart Adamson, Peter Milne, Robert
Adams, Lillie Hayward
story: Joseph Fields, Ewart Adamson
d: MICHAEL CURTIZ
ph: HAL MOHR
m: no credit given
ed: Thomas Pratt
ad: Hugh Reticker
cos: Orry-Kelly
sound: no credit given
BORIS KARLOFF, Edmund Gwenn,
Marguerite Churchill, Ricardo Cortez,
Barton MacLane, Warren Hull, Henry
O'Neill

Wallace, Dee (1949-)

American actress (also known as Dee
Wallace Stone), best known for playing
the mother in Steven Spielberg's *E.T.*
After experience as a teacher and dancer
she began working in television, which
eventually led to film roles.
Genre credits:
The Stepford Wives (1975), *The Hills Have
Eyes* (1977), *The Howling* (1980), *Cujo*
(1983), *Critters* (1986), *Shadow Play*
(1986), *Popcorn* (1991)

Wallace, Tommy Lee

American writer and director who
began his career as both editor and art
director, mostly for John Carpenter. He
worked on several of Carpenter's key
films before turning to direction himself
with the Carpenter-produced *Halloween
III: Season of the Witch* in 1983.
Genre credits:
Halloween (1978 - ad/co-ed), *The Fog*
(1980 - ad/co-ed), *Halloween III: Season
of the Witch* (1983 - d), *Fright Night 2*
(1988 - co-w/d), *It* (1990 - aka *Stephen
King's It* - co-w/d)

Walters, Thorley (1913-1991)

British character actor with a penchant

for buffoons and fussy officials. A welcome supporting actor in several Hammer horrors, his other credits include *Blue Murder at St Trinian's*, *Carlton-Browne of the FO*, *Two-Way Stretch* and *The Sign of Four* (TVM).
Genre credits:
The Phantom of the Opera (1962), *Sherlock Holmes and the Deadly Necklace* (1963 - aka *Sherlock Holmes und das Halsband des Todes*), *The Earth Dies Screaming* (1964), *A Study in Terror* (1965), *The Psychopath* (1966), *Dracula - Prince of Darkness* (1966), *Frankenstein Created Woman* (1967), *Twisted Nerve* (1968), *Frankenstein Must Be Destroyed* (1969), *The Man Who Haunted Himself* (1970), *Trog* (1970), *Vampire Circus* (1972), *The People That Time Forgot* (1977)

Ward, Simon (1941-)

British actor with much stage experience. Began his film career in 1969 in Hammer's *Frankenstein Must Be Destroyed*. Stardom came in 1972 when he was chosen for the title role in Richard Attenborough's Churchill biopic *Young Winston*, which was followed by roles in *The Three Musketeers*, *The Four Musketeers*, *All Creatures Great and Small* and *Supergirl*.
Genre credits:
Frankenstein Must Be Destroyed (1969), *Dracula* (1973 - TVM), *Holocaust 2000* (1977 - aka *The Chosen*), *Dominique* (1978), *The Monster Club* (1980)

Warhol, Andy (1927-1987)

Celebrated American pop artist who also produced and directed several 'underground' films, among them *The Chelsea Girls*, *Trash*, *Flesh* and *Bad*. He also produced two horror films: *Andy Warhol's Dracula* (1974 - aka *Dracula / Blood for Dracula*) and *Andy Warhol's Frankenstein* (1974 - aka *Flesh for Frankenstein / The Frankenstein Experiment*), both of which were directed by Paul Morrissey. When asked about his involvement in these two films, Warhol replied, "I just turned up for the parties!"

Warlock

USA 1988 100m colour
A witch hunter from the seventeenth century follows a warlock through time to modern-day America.
Juvenile horror comic with echoes of *Time After Time*, though totally lacking the right touch. A sequel, *Warlock II: The Armageddon*, followed in 1993.
p: Steve Miner for New World
exec p: Arnold Kopelson
w: David Twohy
d: Steve Miner
ph: David Eggby

• David Warner loses his head (literally) in *The Omen*, the best of his horror film appearances.

m: Jerry Goldsmith
ed: David Finfer
pd: Roy Forge Smith
make-up effects: Carl Fullerton
Julian Sands, Richard E. Grant, Lori Singer, Kevin O'Brien, David Carpenter, Mary Woronov, Richard Kuss, Harry Johnson, Juli Burkhart

Warner Bros

American studio, formed in 1923 by brothers Jack L., Harry M., Albert and Sam. Known mostly for the cinema's first talkie, *The Jazz Singer*, its Golden Age of gangster melodramas featuring the likes of James Cagney, Edward G. Robinson and Humphrey Bogart, as well as for more recent blockbusters such as the *Batman* and *Lethal Weapon* series rather than for its horror output. Down the years it has contributed the occasional key film to the genre, however, most notably *The Mystery of the Wax Museum*, *House of Wax*, *The Devils*, *The Exorcist* and *The Shining*. Warner Bros also released and invested in many of Britain's Hammer films in the fifties, sixties and early seventies.
Genre filmography:
The Terror (1928), *The Haunted House* (1928), *House of Horror* (1929), *The Mad Genius* (1931), *Dr X* (1932), *The Mystery of the Wax Museum* (1933), *The Return of the Terror* (1934), *The Walking Dead* (1936), *Sh! The Octopus* (1937), *The*

Return of Dr X (1939), *The Beast with Five Fingers* (1946), *The Beast from 20,000 Fathoms* (1953), *House of Wax* (1953), *Whatever Happened to Baby Jane?* (1962), *The Shuttered Room* (1967), *The Valley of Gwangi* (1968), *The Devils* (1970), *The Omega Man* (1971), *The Exorcist* (1973), *It's Alive* (1974), *The Pack* (1977), *Exorcist II: The Heretic* (1977), *It's Alive 2* (1978 - aka *It Lives Again*), *The Shining* (1980), *Little Shop of Horrors* (1986), *The Lost Boys* (1987), *It's Alive III: Island of the Alive* (1988), *The Exorcist III* (1990), *Innocent Blood* (1992), *Body Snatchers* (1993)

Warner, David (1941-)

British actor with much stage experience. Made his film début in *Tom Jones* in 1963, though it was his portrayal of Morgan in *Morgan - A Suitable Case for Treatment* that made him a star. He now works primarily as a supporting actor in Hollywood and is perhaps best remembered by genre fans for his decapitation scene in *The Omen*. His other credits include *The Bofors Gun*, *Straw Dogs*, *The Thirty-Nine Steps*, *Time Bandits*, *Star Trek V* and *Star Trek VI*.
Genre credits:
From Beyond the Grave (1973), *The Omen* (1976), *Time After Time* (1979 - as Jack the Ripper), *Nightwing* (1979), *The Island* (1980), *The Company of Wolves* (1984), *My Best Friend Is a Vampire* (1988), *Waxwork* (1988), *Grave Secrets*

(1989), *Cast a Deadly Spell* (1991 -aka *Lovecraft* - TVM), *Dark at Noon* (1992 - aka *Le Terreur de Midi*), *The Unnameable Returns* (1992), *Necronomicon* (1993), *In the Mouth of Madness* (1994)

Warren, Jerry

American producer and director of zero-budget horror films, few of which are watchable.
Genre credits:
Teenage Zombies (1957), *Curse of the Stone Hand* (1965), *House of the Black Death* (1965), *Creature of the Walking Dead* (1966), *The Wild World of Batwoman* (1966 - aka *She Was a Hippie Vampire*)

Warren, Norman J.

British director with a penchant for gorily overstated low-budget horror films. He began his career in 1959 as an assistant to producers Anatole and Dimitri de Grunwald, first in the production office, then as an assistant cutter. He later worked as an assistant director on a handful of films before graduating to editing commercials. He directed his first film, a short entitled *Fragment*, in 1965. Two sexploitation dramas (*Her Private Hell* and *Loving Feeling*) followed, as did many television commercials. His first genre film as director, *Satan's Slave*, came in 1976. His other credits include *Outer Touch* (aka *Spaced Out*), *Gunpowder* and various pop promos and television projects, mostly in a supervisory capacity.
Genre credits:
Satan's Slave (1976), *Prey* (1977 - aka *Alien Prey*), *Terror* (1978), *Inseminoid* (1980 - aka *Horror Planet*), *Bloody New Year* (1986 - aka *Time Warp Terror*).

Wasson, Craig (1954-)

American actor who rose to semi-star status in the eighties, though he is now seen mostly in supporting roles. His credits include *Rollercoaster*, *Go Tell the Spartans* and *Malcolm X*.
Genre credits:
Schizoid (1980), *Ghost Story* (1981), *Body Double* (1984), *A Nightmare on Elm Street 3: The Dream Warriors* (1987), *Midnight Fear* (1990)

The Watcher in the Woods

GB/USA 1980 100m Technicolor Dolby
A young girl is haunted by ghosts from the past when she and her family move into a secluded English house.

Old-fashioned scare story made by the Disney people in an attempt to break away from their old image. After a poor reception it was quickly withdrawn, re-edited and re-released in 1982 with additional footage. The script

still makes very little sense, though the woodland photography is pleasant enough.
p: Ron Miller, Tom Leetch for Walt Disney
w: Brian Clemens, Harry Spaulding, Rosemary Anne Sisson
novel: Florence Engel Randall
d: John Hough (additional d: Vincent McEveety)
ph: Alan Hume (additional ph: Basil Rayburn)
m: Stanley Myers
ed: Geoffrey Foot
pd: Elliott Scott
cos: Emma Porteous
sp: Harrison Ellenshaw, Art Cruickshank and others
sound: Claude Hitchcock, Gerry Humphreys
sound ed: Jim Shields
stunt co-ordinator: Vic Armstrong
Bette Davis, Carroll Baker, David McCallum, Lynn-Holly Johnson, Kyle Richards, Ian Bannen, Richard Pasco, Frances Cuka, Benedict Taylor, Eleanor Summerfield, Georgina Hale

Watchers

USA 1988 91m colour
A dog with psychic powers (it says here) escapes a government laboratory and is pursued by another escapee, a monstrous mutant. But a teenage boy who befriends the dog helps to save the day.

Ludicrous but straight-faced nonsense, as artless as it is stupid. Astonishingly, it was followed by *Watchers II* in 1990.
p: Damian Lee, David Mitchell for Concorde/Centaure/Rose & Ruby
exec p: Roger Corman
w: Bill Freed, Damian Lee
novel: Dean R. Koonitz
d: Jon Hess
ph: Richard Leiterman, Curtis Petersen
m: Joel Goldsmith
ed: Bill Freda, Carolle Alain, Rick Fields
pd: Richard Wilcox
cos: Monique Stranon
sound: Frank Griffiths
2nd unit d: Damian Lee
Corey Haim, Michael Ironside, Barbara Williams, Duncan Fraser, Blu Mankuma

Waxman, Franz (1906-1967)

Celebrated German composer (real name Franz Wachsmann) who contributed a memorable score to *The Bride of Frankenstein*. Studied at the Dresden Music Academy and the Berlin Music Conservatory, after which he joined UFA in 1930 as an orchestrator (*Der Blau Engel* - aka *The Blue Angel*, etc.) and, eventually, a composer (*Liliom*, etc.). When anti-Semitism grew rife in

Germany he left for Paris and then America, arriving in Hollywood in 1934. He won Oscars for *Sunset Boulevard* (1950) and *A Place in the Sun* (1951); his other scores include *The Philadelphia Story*, *Rebecca*, *Mr Skeffington*, *The Paradine Case*, *Rear Window*, *Peyton Place* and *The Nun's Story*.
Genre credits:
The Bride of Frankenstein (1935), *Dr Jekyll and Mr Hyde* (1941), *Alias Nick Beal* (1949 - aka *The Contact Man*)

Waxworks

USA 1989 97m Technicolor Dolby
A group of teenagers find themselves involved in various horrific adventures when they visit a mysterious wax museum.

Slow-starting horror comic with a few lively touches among the longueurs. A sequel, *Waxwork II: Lost in Time*, followed in 1991.
p: Staffan Ahrenberg for Vestron
w/d: Anthony Hickox
ph: Gerry Lively
m: Roger Bellon
ed: Christopher Cibelli
pd: Gianni Quaranta
cos: Leonard Pollock
sound: Robert Janiger
make-up effects/2nd unit d: Bob Keen
2nd unit ph: John Schwartzman
stunt co-ordinator: Bobby Bragg
Zach Galligan, Deborah Foreman, Michelle Johnson, David Warner, Patrick Macnee, Miles O'Keefe, Charles McCaughin, J. Kenneth Campbell, John Rhys-Davies, Anthony Hickox, Staffan Ahrenberg

We Want Our Mummy *

USA 1938 20m bw
The Three Stooges are sent to Egypt to find the lost mummy of Rooten Tooten III.

Anything-for-a-laugh Stooges comedy.
p: Jules White for Columbia
w: Elwood Ullman, Searle Kramer
d: Del Lord
ph: Allen G. Siegler
ed: Charles Nelson
Curly Howard, Larry Fine, Moe Howard, Bud Jamison, James C. Morton, Dick Curtis, Robert Williams

Weaver, Sigourney (1949-)

American star actress (real name Susan Alexandra Weaver) who, after brief appearances in *Annie Hall* and *Madman*, shot to international stardom as Ripley in *Alien* in 1979 and earned a Best Actress Academy Award nomination for the same role in the sequel. Her other credits include *The Year of Living Dangerously*, *Gorillas in the Mist*, *Working*

• Henry Hull attacks Warner Oland (better known for playing Charlie Chan) in *Werewolf of London*, Universal's first stab at the lycanthropy legend.

Girl, *1492*, *Dave* and *Death and the Maiden*.
Genre credits:
Alien (1979), *Ghostbusters* (1984), *Aliens* (1986), *Ghostbusters II* (1989), *Alien 3* (1992)

Webb, Roy (1888-1982)

Prolific but underrated American composer (over 300 scores), long with RKO, where he worked on many of the Val Lewton horrors. He studied music at Columbia University, where he scored and conducted a number of Varsity shows, after which he became a Broadway conductor. Went to work for RKO in 1929, his first film being *Rio Rita*, which he orchestrated. Subsequent scores include *Quality Street*, *Bringing Up Baby*, *Journey Into Fear*, *Notorious*, *Farewell, My Lovely*, *Sinbad the Sailor* and *The Flying Leathernecks*.
Genre credits:
The Cat People (1942), *The Leopard Man* (1943), *The Seventh Victim* (1943), *I Walked With a Zombie* (1943), *The Ghost Ship* (1943), *The Curse of the Cat People* (1944), *The Body Snatcher* (1945), *The Spiral Staircase* (1946), *Bedlam* (1946), *Mighty Joe Young* (1949)

Weeks, Stephen (1948-)

British director who helmed some interesting low-budget entries in the seventies, one of which, *Sir Gawain and the Green Knight* (1972), he later remade as *Sword of the Valiant* (1984), since which

little has been heard from him.
Genre credits:
I, Monster (1970), *Ghost Story* (1974)

Wegener, Paul (1874-1948)

German actor-writer-director from the stage, a former member of Max Reinhardt's Berlin troupe. Turned to film in 1913 with a version of *The Student of Prague*, which he also co-wrote. One of the pioneers of German expressionist cinema, he is perhaps best remembered for his three 'Golem' films, the style of which had a great influence on Hollywood's horror cycle of the thirties, particularly on James Whale's *Frankenstein*. Later, during the Nazi era, he was named Actor of the State.
Genre credits:
The Student of Prague (1913 - actor/co-w), *The Golem* (1914 - actor/co-d), *The Pied Piper of Hamelin* (1916 - actor/co-d), *Der Golem und die Tanzerin* (1916 - actor/co-d), *The Golem* (1919 - actor/w/co-d), *The Magician* (1926 - actor), *Svengali* (1927 - actor), *The Living Dead* (1932 - aka *Funf Unheimliche Gesichten* - actor)

Wells, H. G. (1866-1946)

Celebrated British novelist (*The Man Who Could Work Miracles*, *The Shape of Things To Come*, *Kipps*, *The History of Mr Polly*). Filmed genre works include *The Island of Dr Moreau*, *The Invisible Man*, *The War of the Worlds* and *The Time Machine*.

Wendkos, Paul (1922-)

American director who graduated to feature films in 1957 with *The Burglar* after experience in the theatre and directing documentaries. His more recent work has primarily been for television. His credits include *Gidget Goes to Rome*, *Guns of the Magnificent Seven* and *A Cannon for Cordoba*.
Genre credits:
The Mephisto Waltz (1971), *The Haunts of the Very Rich* (1972 -TVM), *Good Against Evil* (1977 - TVM), *The Bad Seed* (1985 - TVM)

The Werewolf see Lycanthropy

Werewolf of London ⋆

USA 1935 75m bw
Whilst in Tibet searching for a rare flower, a botanist is bitten by a werewolf.
  Dated horror comic with effective sequences along the way. Of interest chiefly for being Universal's first dabble with lycanthropy, later the basis for *The Wolf Man* with Lon Chaney Jr.
p: Stanley Bergerman for Universal
w: Robert Harris
d: STUART WALKER
ph: Charles Stumar
m: Karl Kajos
ed: Milton Carruth, Russell Schoengarth
ad: Albert S. D'Agostino
make-up: Jack P. Pierce
Henry Hull, Warner Oland, Valerie Hobson, Spring Byington, Ethel Griffies, Zeffie Tilbury

The Werewolf of Washington

USA 1973 90m colour
A presidential aide is bitten by a werewolf whilst in Hungary.
  Fairly lively low-budget horror spoof with a little more wit and style than most.
p: Nina Schulman for Millco
w/d/ed: Milton Moses
ph: Bob Baldwin
m: Arnold Freed
ad: Nancy Miller-Corwin
make-up effects: Bob O'Bradovich
Dean Stockwell, Biff Maguire, Clifton James, Beeson Carroll, Jane House, Michael Dunn, Barbara Speigel, Stephen Cheng, Thayer David

Wes Craven's New Nightmare ⋆

USA 1994 112m Foto-Kem
Actress Heather Langenkamp and her young son begin to have nightmares about Freddy Krueger who, it transpires, is trying to break into the real world.
  Reasonably original if somewhat incestuous shocker that mixes supposed reality with the fantasy world of the

A RARE COLOUR STILL OF STARS BETTE DAVIS AND JOAN CRAWFORD on the set of the black and white classic *Whatever Happened to Baby Jane?* Crawford hated Davis so much she actively campaigned against her winning the Best Actress Oscar for the movie, even though a win would have added to the film's box office take and the percentage share of it her contract gave her.

Nightmare on Elm Street movies. Certainly an improvement on some of its predecessors.
p: Marianne Madalenna for New Line
exec p: Robert Shaye, Wes Craven, Sarah Risher
w/d: Wes Craven
ph: Mark Irwin
m: J. Peter Robinson
ed: Patrick Lussier
pd: Cynthia Charette
cos: Mary Jane Fort
sp: Flash Filmworks
sound: Paul B. Clay
2nd unit d: Mickey Gilbert
Heather Langenkamp, Robert Englund, John Saxon, Miko Hughes, David Newsome, Wes Craven, Tracy Middendorf, Robert Shaye, Sarah Risher

West, Roland (1887-1952)

American writer, producer and director (real name Roland van Ziemer) who helmed several visually arresting genre pictures, two of which were based on *The Bat*, the 1920 play by Mary Roberts Rinehart. On stage as an actor from 1899, he later toured in a sketch of his own devising called *The Underworld*, in which he played five parts. He turned to films in 1916, his first directorial credit being *A Woman's Honour* (aka *Lost Souls*). Other credits include *De Luxe Annie*, *The Silver Lining*, *Nobody*, *The Unknown Purple*, *The Dove*, *Alibi* and *Corsair*.
Genre credits:
The Monster (1925 - co-w/d), *The Bat* (1926 co-w/p/d/), *The Bat Whispers* (1930 - w/p/d)

Westmore, Bud (1918-1973)

American make-up artist (real name Hamilton Adolph Westmore), part of the Westmore dynasty of make-up artists, founded by his father George (who created Valentino's famous look) and continued by himself and his brothers Monty, Perc, Ern, Wally and Frank. Long at Universal, where he succeeded Jack P. Pierce, Bud worked on many of the studio's horror films from the mid-forties onwards, including several of the Abbott and Costello spoofs. He also re-created a number of Lon Chaney's famous make-ups for the biopic *Man of a Thousand Faces*.
Genre credits:
The Flying Serpent (1945), *Strangler of the Swamp* (1945), *The Devil Bat's Daughter* (1946), *Abbott and Costello Meet Frankenstein* (1948), *Abbott and Costello Meet the Killer, Boris Karloff* (1949), *Abbott and Costello Meet the Invisible Man* (1951), *It Came from Outer Space* (1953), *Abbott and Costello Meet*

Dr Jekyll and Mr Hyde (1953), *The Creature from the Black Lagoon* (1953 - co-make-up), *Revenge of the Creature* (1954), *This Island Earth* (1954), *Abbott and Costello Meet the Mummy* (1955), *Cult of the Cobra* (1955), *Tarantula* (1955), *The Creature Walks Among Us* (1956), *The Mole People* (1956), *The Monolith Monsters* (1957), *The Land Unknown* (1957), *Man of a Thousand Faces* (1957), *The Deadly Mantis* (1957), *Monster on Campus* (1958), *The Monster That Couldn't Die* (1958), *Curse of the Undead* (1959), *The Leech Woman* (1960), *The Night Walker* (1964), *Dark Intruder* (1965 - TVM), *Munster, Go Home!* (1966 - TVM), *Games* (1967), *Eye of the Cat* (1969), *Hauser's Memory* (1970 - TVM), *Skullduggery* (1970)

Westmore, Perc (1904-1970)

American make-up artist (real name Percival Harry Westmore), brother of Bud, Monty, Ern, Wally and Frank Westmore. His horror films were few, though he made important contributions to *The Hunchback of Notre Dame* and the popular sixties sitcom *The Munsters*, creating the make-ups for Herman, Lily, Eddie and Grandpa Munster.
Genre credits:
The Hunchback of Notre Dame (1939), *The Return of Dr X* (1939)

Westmore, Wally (1906-1973)

American make-up artist (real name Walter James Westmore), brother of Bud, Monty, Ern, Wally, Frank and Perc Westmore. Long at Paramount, his most notable work for the horror genre was for the 1932 version of *Dr Jekyll and Mr Hyde*.
Genre credits:
Dr Jekyll and Mr Hyde (1932), *Island of Lost Souls* (1932), *The Most Dangerous Game* (1932 - aka *The Hounds of Zaroff*), *The Man in Half Moon Street* (1943), *Alias Nick Beal* (1949 - aka *The Contact Man*), *The Colossus of New York* (1958)

Whale, James (1889-1957)

Celebrated British director, responsible for four of the genre's most influential films. A former cartoonist, after World War One (during which he was a POW), he turned to acting, chiefly with the Birmingham Repertory Company. He later became a theatrical producer and director of some note, his greatest success being the World War One trench drama *Journey's End*: he was invited to Hollywood to film the play in 1930. A film version of *Waterloo Bridge* followed the same year, and its success prompted Universal to offer Whale carte blanche for his next project. Whale chose

Frankenstein, and the rest is history. Noted for their style and their quirky humour, his subsequent forays into the genre are cited as models of their kind, though his other films of the same period (*The Impatient Maiden*, *The Kiss Before the Mirror*, *By Candlelight*, *One More River*, etc.) frequently fell below these high standards. After *The Bride of Frankenstein*, Whale renounced the horror genre and went on to direct several other classics, including *Remember Last Night*, *Showboat*, *The Great Garrick* and *The Man in the Iron Mask*, though again these were peppered with more routine work, including *Wives Under Suspicion*, *Green Hell* and *Hello Out There*. He was found drowned in his swimming pool following a stroke after several years in oblivion.
Genre credits:
Frankenstein (1931), *The Old Dark House* (1932), *The Invisible Man* (1933), *The Bride of Frankenstein* (1935)

What a Carve Up

GB 1961 88m bw
A timid proof-reader and his friend go to a spooky house on the Yorkshire moors for the reading of a will.

Mild British farce, not much different from a *Carry On*, though *The Old Dark House* it ain't.
p: Robert S. Baker, Monty Berman for Baker-Berman
w: Ray Cooney, Tony Hilton
novel: Frank King
d: Pat Jackson
ph: Monty Berman
m: Muir Mathieson
ed: Gordon Pilkington
ad: Ivan King
sound: George Adams
Kenneth Connor, Sid James, Shirley Eaton, Dennis Price, Donald Pleasence, Michael Gough, Valerie Taylor, Esma Cannon, George Woodbridge, Michael Gwynne, Philip O'Flynn, Timothy Bateson, Frederick Piper

What Became of Jack and Jill?

GB 1971 90m DeLuxe
A young man plots to kill his grandmother with the help of his girlfriend.

Abysmal would-be thriller which absolutely no one will want to sit through.
p: Max J. Rosenberg, Milton Subotsky for Paolmar/Amicus
w: Roger Marshall
novel: Laurence Moody
d: Bill Bain
ph: Gerry Turpin
m: Carl Davis
ed: Peter Tanner
ad: Tony Curtis

Vanessa Howard, Paul Nicholas, Mona Washbourne, Peter Copley, Peter Jeffrey

Whatever Happened to Baby Jane? **

USA 1962 132m bw Panavision
An alcoholic ex-child star, now in middle age, torments her invalid sister, and when her deeds are discovered murder follows…

Entertaining horror melodrama show-casing two memorable star performances, whose on-set battles were legendary. Delightfully macabre and something of a camp classic.
p: Robert Aldrich for Warner/Associates and Aldrich
exec p: Kenneth Hyman
w: Lukas Heller
novel: Henry Farrell
d: ROBERT ALDRICH
ph: ERNEST HALLER
m: Frank de Vol
ed: Michael Luciano
ad: William Glasgow
cos: Norma Koch (aa)
sound: Jack Solomon
ch: Alex Romero
BETTE DAVIS, JOAN CRAWFORD, VICTOR BUONO, Anna Lee, MARJORIE BENNETT, Barbara Merrill, Julie Alfred, Gina Gillespie, Bert Freed, Ann Barton, Dave Willock, William Aldrich, B. D. Merrill, Russ Conway

Wheatley, Dennis (1897-1977)

British novelist with a penchant for occult subjects. Those turned into films include *The Devil Rides Out* (aka *The Devil's Bride*), *The Lost Continent* (from the book *Uncharted Seas*) and *To the Devil… A Daughter*, all of which were made by Hammer.

When a Stranger Calls

USA 1979 97m Technicolor
A babysitter is threatened by a murderous maniac.

Woefully overstretched killer-on-the-loose stuff of which half an hour would have been more than enough.
p: Doug Chapin, Steve Feke for Melvin Simon Films
exec p: Barry Krost
w: Steve Feke, Fred Walton
d: Fred Walton
ph: Don Peterman
m: Dana Kaproff
ed: Sam Vitale
pd: Elayne Barbara Cedar
cos: Dick Bruno
sound: Martin Bolger, Walter Goss
Charles Durning, Carol Kane, Rachel Roberts, Colleen Dewhurst, Ron O'Neal, Tony Beckley, Steven Anderson, Rutanya Alda

When Dinosaurs Ruled the Earth

GB 1969 100m Technicolor
A prehistoric girl escapes sacrifice and befriends a small dinosaur.

Childish but occasionally lively prehistoric nonsense, let down by its low budget and some poorly integrated studio work.
p: Aida Young for Hammer/Warner
w/d: Val Guest
ph: Dick Bush
m: Mario Nascimbene
md: Philip Martell
ed: Peter Curran
ad: John Blezard
cos: Carl Toms
sp: Jim Danforth, Allan Bryce, Roger Dicken, Brian Johncock
sound: Kevin Sutton
2nd unit ph: Johnny Cabrera
narrator: Patrick Allen
Victoria Vetri, Patrick Allen, Robin Hawdon, Imogen Hassall, Patrick Holt, Sean Caffrey, Magda Konopka, Carol Hawkins, Drewe Henley

Whistle and I'll Come to You **

GB 1968 40m bw TVM
An absent-minded professor has a ghostly encounter.

Persuasively handled adaptation of an M. R. James story, quite frightening in parts, despite the fact that not a lot really happens. Originally made for the BBC-TV documentary series *Omnibus*.
p: Jonathan Miller for BBC
w/d: Jonathan Miller
story: M. R. James
ph: Dick Bush
m: none
ed: Pam Bosworth
ad: Judy Steele
cos: Ken Morey
MICHAEL HORDERN, Ambrose Coghill, George Woodbridge, Nora Gordon, Freda Dowie

Whitaker, David

British composer, conductor, arranger and songwriter who trained at London's Guildhall School of Music. His first film score was for the Jerry Lewis 'comedy' *Don't Raise the Bridge, Lower the River* in 1967.
Genre credits:
Scream and Scream Again (1969), *Dr Jekyll and Sister Hyde* (1971), *Blind Terror* (1971 - aka *See No Evil*), *Vampire Circus* (1972), *Vampira* (1974 - aka *Old Dracula*), *Dominique* (1978), *The Sword and the Sorcerer* (1982)

White, Robb

American writer, often in association with producer/director William Castle.

Genre credits:
Macabre (1957 - w), *The House on Haunted Hill* (1958 - w/associate p), *The Tingler* (1959 - w), *Thirteen Ghosts* (1960 - w), *Homicidal* (1961 - w),

White Zombie *

USA 1932 75m bw
A master sorcerer who uses the living dead to work a Haitian sugar mill abducts a husband and wife newly arrived to the island.

Stilted horror melodrama which hasn't dated too well and which might have played better as a silent. Some eerie moments, however, on which count some consider it a classic.
p: Edward Halperin for UA/ASC
w: Garnett Weston
d: Victor Halperin
ph: Arthur Martinelli
md: Abe Meyer
ed: Howard McLernon
ad: Ralph Berger
sound: no credit given
make-up: Jack P. Pierce
Bela Lugosi, Madge Bellamy, Joseph Cawthorne, Joseph Frazer, John Harron, Clarence Muse, Brandon Hurst

The Wicked see Outback Vampires

Wicked Stepmother

USA 1989 92m DeLuxe Ultra Stereo
A witch moves in with a suburban family and causes chaos.

Fitfully amusing but fatally overstretched supernatural comedy, notable chiefly for the last appearance of its star, who walked off the set in mid-production, causing all manner of problems for the film's creators, who had to rewrite the plot to accommodate her disappearance.
p: Robert Littman for MGM/Larco
exec p: Larry Cohen
w/d: Larry Cohen
ph: Bryan England
m: Robert Folk
ed: David Kern
ad: Gene Abel
cos: Julie Weiss
sp: Joseph Wallikas, Larry Arpin, Mark Williams
sound: Kim Ornitz
Bette Davis, Colleen Camp, Lionel Stander, David Rasche, Barbara Carrera, Tom Bosley, Richard Moll, Seymour Cassell, Evelyn Keyes

The Wicker Man **

GB 1973 86m/102m Eastmancolor
A policeman investigating the disappearance of a young girl on a remote Scottish island finds himself the focus of an ancient pagan ritual.

THE CHILLING CLIMAX TO *THE WICKER MAN*, one of the British horror genre's true moments of glory. Sadly the film was much cut to fit on a double bill with *Don't Look Now*, though fuller prints have thankfully since surfaced, making it a late night must.

Literate and intelligently conceived horror story with strong sexual and religious overtones, building to a shocking and disturbing climax. Well worth seeking out on the late show, though it is often shown in an abbreviated 86m version.

p: Peter Snell for British Lion/Summerisle
w: ANTHONY SHAFFER
d: ROBIN HARDY
ph: Harry Waxman
m: Paul Giovanni
md: Cary Carpenter
ed: ERIC BOYD-PERKINS
ad: Seamus Flannery
cos: Sue Yelland
sound: Robin Gregory, Bob Jones
2nd unit ph: Peter Allwork
ch: Stewart Hopps
EDWARD WOODWARD, CHRISTOPHER LEE, Britt Ekland, Ingrid Pitt, Diane Cilento, Lesley Mackie, Walter Carr, Lindsay Kemp, Ian Campbell

Wickes, David

British director, mostly for television, where he has handled a number of genre projects. His big screen credits include *The Sweeney* and *Silver Dream Racer*.
Genre credits:
Jack the Ripper (1988 - TVM), *Jekyll and Hyde* (1990 - TVM), *Frankenstein - The Real Story* (1993 - TVM)

Wicking, Christopher (1944-)

British screenwriter, a former journalist, who also acted as one of Hammer's story editors. Has worked on several of director Gordon Hessler's films.
Genre credits:
The Oblong Box (1969 - additional dialogue only), *Scream and Scream Again* (1969 - w), *Cry of the Banshee* (1970 - co-w), *Murders in the Rue Morgue* (1971 - co-w), *Blood from the Mummy's Tomb* (1971 - w), *Demons of the Mind* (1972 - w/co-story), *To the Devil... A Daughter* (1976 - co-w)

Wiene, Robert (1881-1938)

German director, best known for the influential *The Cabinet of Dr Caligari*. A screenwriter from 1914, he turned to direction later the same year, co-directing *Arme Eva* with A. Berger. His other films include *Salome*, *Crime and Punishment* and *Ultimatum* (completed by Robert Siodmak after his death).
Genre credits:
The Cabinet of Dr Caligari (1919 - aka *Das Kabinett des Dr Caligari*), *The Hands of Orlac* (1924 - aka *Orlacs Hande*)

Wilcox, John (1905-1984)

British cinematographer who worked on a variety of productions, from low-

budget horror to large-scale actioners. His entire genre output was in association with director Freddie Francis. Other credits include *Where's Jack?*, *The Chairman* (aka *The Most Dangerous Man in the World*) and *The Last Valley*.
Genre credits:
Nightmare (1963), *The Evil of Frankenstein* (1964), *The Psychopath* (1965), *The Skull* (1965), *Craze* (1973), *The Ghoul* (1974), *Legend of the Werewolf* (1975)

Wilder, Gene (1935-)

Popular American comedy actor (*Bonnie and Clyde*, *The Producers*, *Willy Wonka and the Chocolate Factory*, *Blazing Saddles*, *Stir Crazy*, *The Woman in Red*, etc.) who made a memorable Frederick Frankenstein (né Fronkensteen) in Mel Brooks' affectionate horror parody *Young Frankenstein* (1974) which he co-wrote with Brooks. His only other genre credit is *Haunted Honey Moon* (1984), which he also directed and co-wrote.

Wildsmith, Dawn

American actress who mostly appears in the low-budget films of her director husband Fred Olen Ray.
Genre credits:
Surf Nazis Must Die (1987), *The Phantom Empire* (1987), *Beverly Hills Vamp* (1988), *It's Alive III: Island of the Alive* (1988), *Star Slammer* (1988)

Willard

USA 1971 95m DeLuxe
A repressed young man trains a pack of rats to kill his enemies.
Stolid horror flick which fails to do for rats what Hitchcock did for birds. A sequel, *Ben*, followed in 1972.
p: Mort Briskin for Cinerama/Bing Crosby Productions
w: Gilbert Ralston
novel: Stephen Gilbert
d: Daniel Mann
ph: Robert B. Hauser
m: Alex North
ed: Warren Low
ad: Howard Hollander
rat trainer: Moe de Sesso
BRUCE DAVISON, Elsa Lanchester, Ernest Borgnine, Sondra Locke, Michael Dante, J. Pat O'Malley

Williams, JoBeth (1953-)

American actress, with stage and daytime soap experience, remembered by genre fans for playing the mother in *Poltergeist*. Made her film début in 1979 in *Kramer vs. Kramer*. Her other films include *The Big Chill*, *Switch* and *Wyatt Earp*.
Genre credits:
Poltergeist (1982), *Endangered Species* (1982), *Poltergeist II* (1986)

Williams, John (1932-)

Celebrated American composer, conductor and musical director, an Oscar winner for *Fiddler on the Roof* (musical director), *Jaws*, *Star Wars*, *E. T.* and *Schindler's List*. Trained at the Juilliard School of Music, after which he became a jazz pianist. He began scoring for television in the late fifties, and moved on to work as an orchestrator and composer for films from the early sixties onwards (*I Passed for White*, *Bachelor Flat*, *Diamond Head*, etc.). Associated chiefly with the films of director Steven Spielberg and producer George Lucas, he is perhaps the most important and influential musical force working in films today, a good many of his themes having entered the public consciousness. Other key scores include *The Reivers*, *The Cowboys*, *The Poseidon Adventure*, *The Towering Inferno*, *Earthquake*, *Family Plot*, *Close Encounters of the Third Kind*, *Superman*, *1941*, *Raiders of the Lost Ark* (and sequels), *Born on the Fourth of July*, *JFK*, *Hook*, *Home Alone* and *Nixon*.
Genre credits:
Images (1972), *Jaws* (1975), *Jaws 2* (1978), *The Fury* (1978), *Dracula* (1979), *The Witches of Eastwick* (1987), *Jurassic Park* (1993), *The Lost World* (1997)

Williamson, Malcolm (1931-)

Australian-born composer/conductor who came to Britain in 1953. Was made Master of the Queen's Music in 1975. He has many documentary scores to his credit, as well as operas, ballets and work for the concert platform.
Genre credits:
The Brides of Dracula (1960), *Crescendo* (1969), *Horror of Frankenstein* (1970), *Nothing But the Night* (1972)

Willman, Noel (1918-1988)

British character actor with much theatre experience, including work as a director. Best remembered by genre fans for playing Dr Ravna in Hammer's *Kiss of the Vampire*, his other film credits include *The Pickwick Papers*, *Cone of Silence*, *Doctor Zhivago* and *The Odessa File*.
Genre credits:
Kiss of the Vampire (1963 - aka *Kiss of Evil*), *The Reptile* (1966), *The Vengeance of She* (1968)

Windsor, Marie (1922-)

Busty American actress (real name Emily Marie Bertleson), a former beauty queen who appeared mostly in fifties B pictures, though she occasionally made the grade in such A films as *The Three Musketeers*, *Force of Evil*, *The Narrow Margin* and *The Killing*. Her other credits

include *Dakota Lil*, *Japanese War Bride*, *The Story of Mankind*, *Cahill: US Marshal* and *Freaky Friday*.
Genre credits:
Cat Women of the Moon (1954), *Swamp Women* (1955), *Abbott and Costello Meet the Mummy* (1955), *The Day Mars Invaded the Earth* (1962), *Chamber of Horrors* (1966), *Salem's Lot* (1979 - TVM)

The Winged Serpent see Q - The Winged Serpent

Winston, Stan

Celebrated American make-up effects expert who won Oscars for his work on *Aliens* (1986), *Terminator 2: Judgement Day* (1992) and *Jurassic Park* (1993). Began his career as a make-up trainee at the Walt Disney Studios in 1969 and came to attention four years later when, with Rick Baker, he won an Emmy for his work on the TV movie *The Autobiography of Miss Jane Pittman*. He has also directed two films: *A Gnome Named Gnorm* (aka *Upworld*) and *Pumpkinhead*, for which he also co-wrote the story. His other films include *W. C. Fields and Me*, *The Wiz*, *Heartbeeps*, *Alien Nation* and *Batman Returns*.
Genre credits:
Gargoyles (1974 - TVM), *Blacula* (1972), *Mansion of the Doomed* (1977), *Zoltan - Hound of Dracula* (1977 - aka *Dracula's Dog*), *The Entity* (1981), *Dead and Buried* (1981), *Parasite* (1982), *The Entity* (1983), *Phantom of the Opera* (1983 - TVM), *Something Wicked This Way Comes* (1983), *The Terminator* (1984), *Chiller* (1985 - TVM), *Aliens* (1986), *Invaders from Mars* (1986), *Predator* (1987), *The Monster Squad* (1988), *A Gnome Named Gnorm* (1988 - aka *Upworld* - d), *Pumpkinhead* (1988 - d/co-story), *Leviathan* (1989), *Predator 2* (1990), *Edward Scissorhands* (1990), *Terminator 2: Judgement Day* (1992), *Jurassic Park* (1993), *Interview with the Vampire* (1994)

Winters, Shelley (1922-)

Once voluptuous, now matronly American actress who twice won a Best Supporting Actress Oscar for *The Diary of Anne Frank* (1959) and *A Patch of Blue* (1963). On stage from 1941 and in films from 1943 with *What a Woman*, her countless credits include *A Double Life*, *A Place in the Sun*, *The Big Knife*, *Lolita*, *Alfie*, *Bloody Mama*, *The Poseidon Adventure*, *Stepping Out* and TV's *Roseanne*. Now a reliable supporting character actress, she turned to horror (like many other female stars of her generation) in the early seventies when her leading-actress status began to wane.
Genre credits:

Night of the Hunter (1955), *The Mad Room* (1969), *What's the Matter with Helen?* (1969), *Who Slew Auntie Roo?* (1971), *The Devil's Daughter* (1972 - TVM), *The Tenant* (1976), *Tentacles* (1977 - aka *Tentacoli*)

Wise, Robert (1914-)

Though known primarily as the Oscar-winning producer and director of both *West Side Story* and *The Sound of Music*, Wise, an editor with RKO from 1933 (*The Hunchback of Notre Dame* [co-ed], *Citizen Kane*, *The Magnificent Ambersons*, *All That Money Can Buy*, etc.), began his directorial career working for horror producer Val Lewton, co-directing *The Curse of the Cat People* with Gunther Frisch in 1944. He followed this later the same year with solo duties on Lewton's *Madmoiselle Fifi* (he also directed several scenes for *The Magnificent Ambersons* when it was taken out of Orson Welles' hands). Wise went on to direct a wide variety of films, including the boxing drama *The Set-Up*, *Executive Suite*, *Sand Pebbles*, *Star!* and *The Hindenberg*, along with several key science-fiction films, including *The Day the Earth Stood Still*, *The Andromeda Strain* and *Star Trek: The Motion Picture*.
Genre credits:
The Hunchback of Notre Dame (1939 - co-ed), *All That Money Can Buy* (1941 - aka *The Devil and Daniel Webster/Daniel and the Devil/Here Is a Man* - ed), *The Curse of the Cat People* (1944 - co-d), *The Body Snatcher* (1945 - d), *The Haunting* (1963 - p/d), *Audrey Rose* (1977 - p/d)

Witchcraft *

GB 1964 79m bw
When a graveyard is disturbed to make way for a new housing development, a witch wreaks havoc on those responsible.

Cheaply produced British horror film with just a couple of effective moments among the tedium.
p: Robert Lippert, Jack Parsons for TCF/Lippert
w: Harry Spaulding
d: Don Sharp
ph: Arthur Lavis
m: Carlo Martelli
ed: Robert Winter
ed: Robert Winter
ad: George Provis
cos: Jean Fairlie
sound: Buster Ambler
Lon Chaney Jr, Jack Hedley, Marie Ney, Jill Dixon, David Weston, Diane Clare, Viola Keats, Yvette Rees

Witchcraft

USA 1988 90m colour
A young woman discovers that her

husband and mother-in-law are satanists out to use her baby for diabolical purposes.

Dull supernatural nonsense that spends too much time with characters we care little about and not enough time on special effects. Astonishingly, it was followed by *Witchcraft II: The Temptress* (1989), *Witchcraft III: The Kiss of Death* (1990), *Witchcraft IV: The Virgin Heart* (1992), *Witchcraft V: Dance With the Devil* (1993) and *Witchcraft VI* (1994). Oh dear.
p: Academy
d: Robert Spera
Anat Topol-Barzilai, Gary Sloan, Deborah Scott, Mary Shelley (!), Lee Kisman, Alexander Kirkwood

Witchcraft (1989) see Witchery

Witchery

USA/It 1989 95m Telecolor
Death at the hands of a witch follows a group of people stranded in a deserted beachside hotel.

Standard creepy-house shocker with one memorable scene involving a woman who has her lips sewn together. Otherwise nothing special. Also released as *Ghosthouse II*.
p: Filmirage/Production Group
w: Daniel Davis
d: Martin Newlin (Fabrizio Laurenti)
ph: Lorenzo Battaglia
m: Carlo Maria Cordio
ed: Kathleen Stratton
ad: Alex Colby
sp: Maurizio Trani
sound: Keith Young, Michael Barry
Linda Blair, David Hasselhoff, Catherine Hick, Annie Ross, Leslie Cumming, Bob Champagne, Hildegard Knef

The Witches

GB 1966 91m Technicolor
Having been subjected to witchcraft in Africa, a schoolteacher retreats to a quiet English village, where she discovers more of the same.

Genteel horror story with little in the way of surprise, given the talent involved.
p: Anthony Nelson Keys for Hammer/Warner
w: Nigel Kneale
novel: Peter Curtis
d: Cyril Frankel
ph: Arthur Grant
m: Richard Rodney Bennett
md: Philip Martell
ed: James Needs, Chris Barnes
pd: Bernard Robinson
cos: Molly Arbuthnot
sound: Ken Rawkins
ch: Denys Palmer

Joan Fontaine, Kay Walsh, Alec
McCowen, Gwen Frangcon Davies,
Ingrid Brett, John Colin, Martin
Stephens, Carmel McSharry, Leonard
Rossiter, Michele Dotrice

The Witches *

USA/GB 1990 91m Eastmancolor
A young boy and his grandmother manage
to dispatch an evil witch and her cronies
before they succeed with their plan to
turn all the children in England into mice.

Engagingly macabre fantasy for
youngsters who like a scare or two.
p: Mark Shivas for Warner/Lorimar
exec p: Jim Henson
w: Allan Scott
novel: Roald Dahl
d: Nicolas Roeg
ph: Harvey Harrison
m: Stanley Myers
ed: Tony Lawson
pd: Andrew Sanders
cos: Marit Allen
sp: Jim Henson's Creature Shop
sound: Peter Sutton, Gerry Humphreys
2nd unit d/ph: John Palmer
sp ph: Paul Wilson
Anjelica Huston, MAI ZETTERLING,
Jason Fisher, Rowan Atkinson, Brenda
Blethyn, Jane Horrocks, Anne Lambton,
Charlie Potter

The Witches of Eastwick **

USA 1987 118m Technicolor Panavision
Dolby
An enigmatic stranger with mysterious
powers arrives in a quiet New England
township where he seduces three
women who later resort to witchcraft
to destroy him.

Expensive serio-comic fantasy, a
little long, but always good to look at.
p: Jon Peters, Peter Guber, Neil
Canton for Warner/Kennedy
Miller/Guber-Peters
exec p: Rob Cohen, Don Devlin
w: Michael Cristofer
novel: John Updike
d: George Miller
ph: VILMOS ZSIGMOND
m: JOHN WILLIAMS
ed: Richard Francis Bruce, Hubert C.
de la Bouillerie
pd: Polly Platt
cos: Aggie Guerard Rodgers
sp: Michael Owens, ILM
sound: Art Rochester
make-up effects: Rob Bottin
titles: Anthony Goldschmidt
stunt co-ordinator: Alan Gibbs
JACK NICHOLSON, CHER, SUSAN
SARANDON, MICHELLE PFEIFFER,
VERONICA CARTWRIGHT, Richard
Jenkins, Keith Jochim, Carel Struycken,
Helen Lloyd Breed, Caroline Struzik

• Claude Rains, Lon Chaney Jr and Evelyn Ankers in a still from *The Wolf Man*.

Witchfinder General *

GB 1969 87m Eastmancolor
In 1645, lawyer Matthew Hopkins roams
the countryside, torturing and hanging
those he believes to be guilty of
witchcraft.

Well-crafted and photographed
horror film with sufficient gruesomeness
to keep one watching. Its director's last
film.
p: Arnold Miller, Louis M. Heyward for
Tigon
exec p: Tony Tenser
w: Michael Reeves, Tom Baker, Louis M.
Heyward
novel: Ronald Bassett
d: MICHAEL REEVES
ph: JOHN COQUILLON
m: Paul Ferris
ed: Howard Lanning
ad: Jim Morahan
cos: Jill Thomson
sp: Roger Dicken
sound: Hugh Strain, Paul Le Mare
Vincent Price, Ian Ogilvy, Hilary Dwyer,
Rupert Davies, Robert Russell, Patrick
Wymark, Wilfred Brambell, Michael
Beint, Tony Selby, Derek Ware

The Wolf Man see Lycanthropy

The Wolf Man *

USA 1940 70m bw
Bitten by a werewolf, Lawrence Talbot
himself becomes one whenever the
moon is full.

Slow-moving but atmospheric semi-
classic horror movie, with a couple
of effective sequences in the genre's
best style.
p: George Waggner for Universal
w: CURT SIODMAK
d: George Waggner
ph: JOSEPH VALENTINE
m: Hans J. Salter, Frank Skinner
md: Charles Previn
ed: Ted Kent
ad: JACK OTTERSON, ROBERT
BOYLE
sp: John P. Fulton
make-up: JACK P. PIERCE
LON CHANEY Jr, CLAUDE RAINS,
Warren William, Bela Lugosi, Ralph
Bellamy, MARIA OUSPENESKAYA,
Patrick Knowles, Evelyn Ankers, Fay
Helm

Wolfen *

USA 1981 115m Technicolor Panavision
Dolby
A New York cop and a lady journalist
trace a series of grizzly murders to a
subterranean pack of wolfmen.

Slick modern-day variation on the
wolf-man theme with added gore,
though ultimately the sound one hears is
that of old wine being poured into new
bottles.
p: Rupert Hitzig for
Warner/Orion/King-Hitzig
exec p: Alan King
w: David Eyre, Michael Wadleigh
novel: Whitley Strieber
d: Michael Wadleigh
ph: Gerry Fisher
m: James Horner
ed: Chris Lebenzon, Dennis Dolan
pd: Paul Sylbert

cos: John Boxer
sp: Robert Blalock
sound: Michael Minkler
stunt co-ordinator: Vic Magnotta
cam op: Garret Brown
Albert Finney, Diane Venora, Gregory Hines, Edward James Olmos, Tom Noonan, Dick O'Neil, Peter Michael Goelz, James Tolkan

The Wolves of Willoughby Chase *

GB 1988 93m Eastmancolor Dolby
In Victorian times, a wicked governess attempts to wrest a large family estate from the two young girls who are its only surviving inheritors.

Engaging family film of the kind all too rarely attempted these days.
p: Mark Forstater for Zenith/Entertainment/Subatomic
w: William M. Ankers
novel: Joan Aiken
d: Stuart Orme
ph: Paul Beeson
m: COLIN TOWNS
ed: Martin Walsh
pd: Christopher Hobbs
cos: Monica Howe
sound: Peter Glossop
Stephanie Beecham, Mel Smith, Geraldine James, Richard O'Brien, Emily Hudson, Jane Horrocks, Eleanor David, Jonathan Coy, Aleks Darowska

The Woman in Black *

GB 1989 96m colour TVM
Sent to a small seaside town to tie up the estate of a recently deceased client, a young solicitor finds himself haunted by a mysterious woman in black.

Watchable but padded ghost story with a couple of goodish frissons, though one expects more from the talent involved.
p: Chris Burt for Central/Carglobe
exec p: Ted Childs
w: Nigel Kneale
novel: Susan Hill
d: Herbert Wise
ph: Michael Davis
m: Rachel Portman
ed: Laurence Mery Clark
pd: Jon Bunker
cos: Barbara Kronig
sp: Ace Effects
sound: Tony Dawe, Richard King
titles: Trevor Bond
Adrian Rawlins, Bernard Hepton, David Daker, Pauline Moran, David Ryall, Clare Holman, John Cater, John Franklyn-Robbins, Fiona Walker

Wood Jr, Edward D. (1924-1978)

Cult American actor, writer, producer and director, celebrated for the sheer ineptitude of his output. Unfortunately, he died a few years before his cult status emerged. He was the subject of the 1994 Tim Burton biopic Ed Wood, in which he was portrayed by Johnny Depp. His own films include Jail Bait, The Violent Years and Fugitive Girls.
Genre credits:
Glen or Glenda (1953 - He or She?/I Changed My Sex/I Led Two Lives/The Transvestite - actor/w/p/d), Bride of the Monster (1955 - w/d), The Bride and the Beast (1958 - w), Plan 9 from Outer Space (1959 - actor/w/d), Night of the Ghouls (1960 - aka Revenge of the Dead - w/d), Orgy of the Dead (1965 - w), Necromancy (1975 - w/d)

Woodbridge, George (1907-1973)

Portly, gravel-voiced British character actor, perhaps best remembered for playing Stryker of the Yard in a number of fifties featurettes. Popped up in several Hammer horrors, usually as an innkeeper or policeman.
Genre credits:
The Revenge of Frankenstein (1958), Dracula (1958 - aka Horror of Dracula), Jack the Ripper (1959), The Mummy (1959), The Flesh and the Fiends (1959 - aka Mania), The Brides of Dracula (1960), The Curse of the Werewolf (1961), What a Carve Up (1961), Dracula -Prince of Darkness (1966), The Reptile (1966), Doomwatch (1972)

Woolley, Stephen (1956-)

British producer who, with his partner Nik Powell, set up Palace Pictures in the eighties. When this ran into financial difficulties, they went independent. Credits include A Letter to Brezhnev, Absolute Beginners, Mona Lisa, Scandal and The Crying Game.
Genre credits:
The Company of Wolves (1985 - co-p), High Spirits (1988 co-p), Interview with the Vampire (1994 - p)

Wordsworth, Richard (1915-1993)

British actor, the great-great-grandson of the poet. On stage from 1938, he didn't make a film until 1955. However, this was Hammer's The Quatermass Experiment, in which he played the doomed astronaut Victor Caroon. His other credits include The Man Who Knew Too Much, The Camp on Blood Island, Time Without Pity, Lock Up Your Daughters and Song of Norway. His genre appearances were exclusively for Hammer.
Genre credits:
The Quatermass Experiment (1955 - aka The Creeping Unknown), The Revenge of Frankenstein (1958), The Curse of the Werewolf (1961)

Woronov, Mary (1940-)

American actress who made a few films for Andy Warhol in the sixties (The Chelsea Girls, etc.) before turning to genre pictures in the seventies and eighties. Her credits include Death Race 2000, Hollywood Boulevard, Jackson County Jail, Rock 'n' Roll High School and Scenes from the Class Struggle in Beverly Hills.
Genre credits:
Silent Night, Bloody Night (1972), Sugar Cookies (1973), Seizure (1974), Eating Raoul (1982), Night of the Comet (1984), Hellhole (1985), The Movie House Massacre (1985), Nomads (1986), Terrorvision (1986), Killbots (1986 - aka Chopping Mall), Warlock (1989), Mortuary Academy (1989), Watchers II (1990)

Wray, Fay (1907-)

Canadian-born actress, once the genre's greatest screamer. Remembered above all for her role as Ann Darrow in King Kong, she began her career in 1923 as an extra in Hal Roach two-reelers before graduating to leading roles in such films as The Four Feathers, Dirigible and The Texan. Her other credits include The Bowery, Queen Bee, Tammy and the Bachelor and Gideon's Trumpet (TVM).
Genre credits:
The Most Dangerous Game (1932 - aka The Hounds of Zaroff), Dr X (1932), The Vampire Bat (1933), King Kong (1933), The Mystery of the Wax Museum (1933), The Clairvoyant (1934)

Wymark, Patrick (1920-1970)

British actor (real name Patrick Cheesman) who popped up as support in a variety of films, often in sinister roles.
Genre credits:
Repulsion (1965 - as the landlord), The Psychopath (1966), Blood on Satan's Claw (1970 - aka Satan's Skin)

Wyndham, John (1903-1969)

British novelist whose filmed books include The Day of the Triffids and The Midwich Cuckoos (twice, as Village of the Damned).

Wynorski, Jim (1950-)

American writer and director with a penchant for all manner of exploitation items. A former campaign manager for Doubleday, he became a TV production assistant in 1980, which he followed with promotional work for Roger Corman's trailer department. He began writing

• **Fay Wray, the genre's greatest screamer, seen here as Ann Darrow in** *King Kong*.

screenplays for Corman in 1981 with *Forbidden World*, which he followed with *Sorceress* and the teen sex romp *Screwballs*. He turned to direction in 1986 with *Lost Empire*. His other credits include *Big Bad Mamma II*, *Hollywood Scream Queen Hot Tub Party*, *Hard to Die*, *Body Chemistry II*, *Sins of Desire*, *Little Miss Zillions* (aka *Home for Christmas*) and *Body Chemistry III*.
Genre credits:
Forbidden World (1981 - aka *Mutant* - w), *Sorceress* (1982 - w), *The Lost Empire* (1986 - w/d), *Chopping Mall* (1986 - aka *Killbots* -co-w/d), *Deathstalker II: Duel of the Titans* (1987 - d), *Not of This Earth* (1988 - d), *Return of the Swamp Thing* (1989 - d), *Transylvania Twist* (1989 - d), *The Haunting of Morella* (1990 -w/d), *976 Evil: The Return* (1991 - d), *Sorority House Massacre II* (1992 - d), *House IV* (1992 - co-story), *Ghoulies IV* (1992 - d), *Dinosaur Island* (1994 - d)

X

X - The Man with X-Ray Eyes *
USA 1963 80m Pathecolor Spectarama
A scientist experiments on himself with
X-ray vision only to find the process
irreversible.

Silly but engaging Corman horror in
his typically cheap but cheerful manner.
p: Roger Corman for AIP
exec p: James H. Nicholson, Samuel Z.
Arkoff
w: Robert Dillon, Ray Russell
story: Ray Russell
d: ROGER CORMAN
ph: Floyd Crosby
m: Les Baxter
ed: Anthony Carras
ad: Daniel Haller
cos: Marjorie Corso
sp: John Howard, Butler-Glouner
sound: John Bury
RAY MILLAND, Diana van der Vlis,
Harold J. Stone, John Hoyt, Don
Rickles, John Dierkes, Dick Miller

X - The Unknown *
GB 1956 81m bw
Whilst on training exercises in Scotland,
the army unearths a strange force which
feeds off radioactive energy.

Overpadded variation on *The
Quatermass Experiment*, let down by poor
effects work and a restricted budget.
Sci-fi fans may enjoy the clichés.
p: Anthony Hinds for
Hammer/Exclusive
w: Jimmy Sangster
d: Leslie Norman
ph: Gerald Gibbs
m: James Bernard
md: John Hollingsworth
ed: James Needs
ad: Bernard Robinson
cos: Molly Arbuthnot
sp: Jack Curtis, Les Bowie
sound: Jock May
production manager: Jimmy Sangster
Dean Jagger, Edward Chapman, Leo
McKern, William Lucas, John Harvey,
Peter Hammond, Michael Ripper,
Anthony Newley, Michael Brook,
Marianne Brauns

Xtro
GB 1982 83m Technicolor
An alien visits earth in the guise of a
man abducted three years earlier.

Low-budget shocker with moments
of rape and gore which found a certain
success on video. Inevitably, it was
followed by *Xtro II: The Second Encounter*
(1991) and *Xtro III* (1994).
p: Mark Forstarter for Amalgamated
Film Enterprises/Ashley/New Realm
w: Harry Bromley Davenport, Iain
Cassie, Robert Smith, Michel Parry, Jo
Ann Kaplan
d/m: Harry Bromley Davenport
ph: John Metcalfe
ed: Nicolas Gaster
Philip Sayer, Bernice Stegers, Danny
Brainin, Anna Wing, Maryam D'Abo,
David Cardy, Peter Mandell

Y

Yarborough, Jean (1900-1975)

American director of strictly routine talent. A former prop man, he worked for comedy producer Hal Roach from 1922, graduating to assistant director and then director in full with *The Devil Bat* in 1940. His other credits include several Abbott and Costello comedies, among them *In Society*, *The Naughty Nineties*, *Lost in Alaska* and *Jack and the Beanstalk*.
Genre credits:
The Devil Bat (1940), *King of the Zombies* (1941), *Joan Medford is Missing* (1946 - aka *House of Horrors*), *She-Wolf of London* (1946 - aka *The Curse of the Allenbys*), *The Brute Man* (1946), *The Creeper* (1948), *Master Minds* (1949), *Hillbillies in a Haunted House* (1967)

Yates, George Worthing (1901-)

American writer, perhaps best remembered for writing the story for the giant ant shocker *Them!* 1958 seems to have been a busy year for him.
Genre credits:
Them! (1954 - story), *It Came from beneath the Sea* (1955 -story/co-w), *Frankenstein 1970* (1958 - co-w), *War of the Colossal Beast* (1958 - w), *Earth vs. the Spider* (1958 - aka *The Spider* -co-w), *Attack of the Puppet People* (1958 - aka *Six Inches Tall*), *The Flame Barrier* (1958 - story/co-w), *Tormented* (1960 - w)

Young, Aida

British producer who worked her way up from third to second assistant director on Hammer's *The Quatermass Experiment* (aka *The Creeping Unknown*). Joined Capricorn Productions in 1963 and acted as an associate to producer Michael Carreras on *What a Crazy World* and several of his Hammer films. Graduated to fully fledged producer with *Dracula Has Risen from the Grave* in 1968.
Genre credits:
She (1965 - associate p), *One Million Years BC* (1966 - associate p), *Slave Girls* (1968 - aka *Prehistoric Women* - associate p), *The Vengeance of She* (1968 - associate p), *Dracula Has Risen from the Grave* (1968 - p), *Taste the Blood of Dracula* (1970 - p), *Scars of Dracula* (1970 - p), *When Dinosaurs*

• Puttin' on the Ritz. Gene Wilder as Professor Frankenstein (or should that be Fronkensteen?) and Peter Boyle as the Monster in director Mel Brooks' spot-on *Frankenstein* spoof *Young Frankenstein*.

Ruled the Earth (1970 - p), *Hands of the Ripper* (1971 - p)

Young, Christopher

American composer who studied music with David Raksin at UCLA. He then graduated from synth scores for exploitation films (his first being for the low-budget slasher pic *Pranks* in 1981) to fully fledged symphonic soundtracks, most notably for the first two *Hellraiser* films and *The Fly II*. His other credits include *Wheels of Fire* (aka *The Desert Warrior*), *Invaders from Mars*, *Bat-21*, *Jennifer 8*, *Dream Lover* and *Copycat*.
Genre credits:
Pranks (1981 - aka *The Dorm That Dripped Blood/Death Dorm*), *The Power* (1983), *A Nightmare on Elm Street Part 2: Freddy's Revenge* (1985), *Hellraiser* (1987), *Haunted Summer* (1988), *Hellbound: Hellraiser II* (1988), *The Fly II* (1989), *The Dark Half* (1991), *The Vagrant* (1992), *Species* (1995)

Young Frankenstein **

USA 1974 108m bw
After the death of his infamous grandfather, Victor Frankenstein (né Fronkensteen) returns to Transylvania and has a go at creating his own monster.
   On the whole a very enjoyable and affectionate parody of the old Universal Frankenstein movies, with sets and photography more than compensating for the inconsistent supply of jokes. A must for buffs.
p: Michael Gruskoff for TCF/Gruskoff/ Crossbow/Venture/Juer
w: Mel Brooks, Gene Wilder
d: MEL BROOKS
ph: GERALD HIRSCHFELD
m: JOHN MORRIS
ed: John C. Howard
ad: DALE HENNESY
cos: Dorothy Jeakins
sp: Henry Millar Jr, Hal Millar
sound: Gene Cantamessa, Richard Portman

titles: Anthony Goldschmidt
make-up: WILLIAM TUTTLE
GENE WILDER, MARTY FELDMAN,
PETER BOYLE, MADELEINE KAHN,
CLORIS LEACHMAN (as Frau Blücher
- all together now!), Kenneth Mars,
Gene Hackman, Richard Haydn, TERI
GARR, Anne Beesley, Liam Dunn,
Danny Goldman

Young Hannah, Queen of the Vampires see Crypt of the Living Dead

The Young Poisoner's Handbook
GB/Ger 1994 94m colour
A teenager with an unhealthy obsession
with toxicology begins to poison his
family and workmates.

Generally entertaining black comedy
based on actual events, though it might
have benefitted from being even blacker
than it is.
p: Sam Taylor for Mass/Kinowlet and
Haut et Court/British Screen
exec p: Caroline Hewitt, Eric
Stonestran, Cameron McCracken
w: Jeff Rawle, Benjamin R oss
d: Benjamin Ross
ph: Hubert Taczanowski
m: Robert Lane, Frank Strobel
ed: Anne Sopel
pd: Maria Djurkovic
cos: Stewart Meacham
sound: Eckhard Kuckenbecker
Hugh O'Connor, Antony Sher, Roger
Lloyd Pack, Frank Mills, Charlotte
Coleman, Ruth Sheen, Tobias Arnold

Younger, Henry see Carreras, Michael

Yuzna, Brian (1949-)
Philippine-born writer, producer and
director working in America, often in
association with director Stuart Gordon,
with whom he has produced a number
of cult items. He also co-wrote the story
for the fantasy comedy, *Honey, I Shrunk
the Kids.*
Genre credits:
Re-Animator (1985 - p), *From Beyond*
(1986 - aka *H. P. Lovecraft's From Beyond*
- p/co-adaptation), *Dolls* (1986 - p),
Re-Animator 2 (1989 - aka *Bride of
Re-Animator* - d), *Society* (1989 - d),
Return of the Living Dead III (1993 -
co-p/d), *Necronomicon* (1993 p/co-d),
Ticks (1994 - exec p)

Z

Zaza, Paul

Canadian composer, often associated with the films of director Bob Clark (*Murder by Decree*, *Porky's*, *A Christmas Story*, *From the Hip*, *Turk 182*, etc.).
Genre credits:
Murder by Decree (1978 - co-m), *Prom Night* (1980 - co-m), *My Bloody Valentine* (1981 - m), *Curtains* (1983 - m), *The Brain* (1988 - m), *Popcorn* (1991 - m)

Zito, Joseph

American director who has 'graduated' from low-budget horrors to low-budget action pictures. His credits include *Missing in Action*, *Invasion USA* and *Red Scorpion*.
Genre credits:
Rosemary's Killer (1981 - aka *The Prowler* / *The Graduation*), *Friday the 13th: The Final Chapter* (1984)

Zoltan - Hound of Dracula

USA 1977 88m DeLuxe
Dracula's manservant takes his master's dog to America to search for the last in the Dracula line.

Ridiculously plotted screamer betrayed by its low budget and a lack of humour.
p: Albert Band, Frank Ray Perelli for Vic
w: Frank Ray Perelli
d: Albert Band
ph: Bruce Logan
m: Andrew Belling
ed: Harry Keramidas
ad: F. P. O. M
make-up effects: Stan Winston, Zoltan Elek
2nd unit ph: Ron Johnson
Jose Ferrer, Reggie Nalder, Michael Pataki, Jan Shutan, Libbie Chase

Zombi 2 see Zombie Flesh-Eaters

Zombie see Zombie Flesh-Eaters

Zombie Aftermath see The Aftermath

Zombie Flesh-Eaters

It 1979 93m or 85m Eastmancolor Panavision

• The cast decide they don't like being on the menu in *Zombie Flesh Eaters*.

A young woman travels to a remote tropical island in search of her missing father, only to discover the place overrun with flesh-eating zombies.

Ludicrous, gut-churning zombie flick, wholly typical of its director's output, and much cut outside his home country. A must for gore-hounds.
p: Ugo Tucci, Frabrizio De Angelis for Variety
w: Elisa Briganti
d: Lucio Fulci
ph: Sergio Salvati
m: Fabio Frizzi, Giorgio Tucci
ed: Vincenzo Tomassi
pd: Walter Salvati
sound: Ugo Celani
make-up effects: Giannetto de Rossi
underwater ph: Ramon Bravo
Tisa Farrow, Richard Johnson, Ian McCulloch, Al Cliver, Auretta Gay, Stefania D'Amario

Zombie Holocaust

It 1980 85m Technicolor
A lady doctor and a scientist trace a zombie sect to a Pacific island.

Gory grade-Z schlocker, of no possible interest, even for video-nasty lovers.
p: Gianfranco Coujoumdjian, Frabrizio De Angelis for Flora/Fulvia/Gico Cinematografia
w: Romano Scandariato
story: Fabrizio De Angelis
d: Frank Martin (Marino Girolami)
ph: Fausto Zuccoli
m: Nico Fidenco
ed: Alberto Moriani
pd: Walter Patriarca
cos: Silvana Scandariato
sp: Maurizio Trani
sound: Giacomo Delli Orso
Ian McCulloch, Alexandra Delli Colli, Sherry Buchanan, Peter O'Neal, Donald O'Brien

Zombie Nightmare

USA 1987 84m Pathecolor
A baseball player is resurrected from the dead by voodoo magic and sets out to kill the teenagers responsible for running him down in their car.

Silly zombie flick with elementary gore - and acting and plotting.
p: Pierre Grise for Starmaker

exec p: Sheldon S. Goldstein
w: David Wellington
d: Jack Bravman
ph: Roger Racine
m: Jon Mikl Thor
ed: David Franko
ad: no credit given
cos: Terry Joseph
sound: Michel Gvzelek
Adam West, Jon Mikl Thor, Shawn Levy, Tia Carrere, Frank Dietz, Manuska Rigaud

Zombies see Dawn of the Dead

Zombies

Films featuring zombies, or the walking dead, have become increasingly visceral down the decades, particularly since the release of George Romero's landmark *Night of the Living Dead* in 1968. According to Haitian folklore, the zombie is a corpse brought back to somnambulistic life via voodoo so as to provide cheap labour for the sugar-cane fields. In movie terms, prior to Romero's film, zombies were little more than shuffling creatures, as easy to outrun as their cousin, the mummy. Since 1968, however, they have also taken on cannibalistic qualities, the result being such gore-filled sagas as *Zombie Holocaust* and *The Return of the Living Dead*. Of the more sedate variety, *White Zombie*, *I Walked with a Zombie* and Hammer's *Plague of the Zombies* remain key works.
Genre filmography:
White Zombie (1932), *Crime of Voodoo* (1935 - aka *Ouangu*), *Revolt of the Zombies* (1936), *The Walking Dead* (1936), *The Ghost Breakers* (1940), *King of the Zombies* (1941), *I Walked with a Zombie* (1943), *Dead Men Walk* (1943), *Revenge of the Zombies* (1943), *Voodoo Man* (1944), *Zombies on Broadway* (1945), *Valley of the Zombies* (1946), *Zombies of the Stratosphere* (1952 - serial), *Scared Stiff* (1953), *Zombies of Mora-Tau* (1957 - aka *The Dead That Walk*), *Voodoo Island* (1957), *Quatermass 2* (1957 - aka *The Enemy from Space*), *Teenage Zombies* (1958), *The Curse of the Doll People* (1960 - aka *Muñecos Infernales*), *The Dead One* (1960), *Santo Contra los Zombies* (1961), *The Last Man on Earth* (1961), *The War of the Zombies* (1963 - aka *Roma Contra Roma*), *The Incredibly Strange Creatures Who Stopped Living and Became Mixed-Up Zombies* (1963), *Dr Terror's House of Horrors* (1964 - segment), *The Plague of the Zombies* (1966), *El Dr Satan* (1966), *Orgy of the Dead* (1966), *El Dr Satan y la Magia Negra* (1967), *Night of the Living Dead* (1968), *Blood of Ghastly Horror* (1970), *Cabezas* (1970), *The Omega Man* (1971), *I Eat Your Skin* (1971 - aka *Zombie*), *La Invasión de los Muertos* (1972), *La Rebelión de los Muertos* (1972), *Santo Contra la Magia Negra* (1972), *Tombs of the Blind Dead* (1972 - aka *Those Cruel and Bloody Vampires / Night of the Blind Dead / The Blind Dead / La Noche del Terror Ciego*), *Return of the Blind Dead* (1973 - aka *Revenge of the Evil Dead / Attack of the Eyeless Dead / El Ataque de los Muertos Sin Ojos*), *Horror Hospital* (1973), *Messiah of Evil* (1973 - aka *Dead People / Return of the Living Dead / Revenge of the Screaming Dead*), *The Living Dead at the Manchester Morgue* (1974 - aka *Fin de Semano para los Muertos*), *Sugar Hill* (1974 - aka *Voodoo Girl*), *Horror of the Zombies* (1974 - aka *Ghost Ship of the Blind Dead / The Ghost Galleon / El Buque Maldito*), *Bloodfeast of the Blind Dead* (1975 - aka *Terror Beach / Night of the Death Cult / Night of the Seagulls / La Noche de las Gaviotas*), *The Child* (1977 - aka *Zombie Child*), *Dawn of the Dead* (1978 - aka *Zombies,*) *Zombie Flesh-Eaters* (1979 - aka *Zombie / Zombi 2 / Island of the Living Dead*), *The Beyond* (1980 - aka *The Seven Doors of Death / L'Adela*), *Zombies' Lake* (1980), *Zombie Holocaust* (1980 - aka *La regina dei Cannibali*), *Le Notti del Terrore* (1980 - aka *Zombi 3*), *The Evil Dead* (1980), *City of the Living Dead* (1980 - aka *The Gates of Hell / Paura Nella Citta dei Morti Viventi*), *The Aftermath* (1980 - aka *Zombie Aftermath*), *The House by the Cemetery* (1981), *Zombie Creeping Flesh* (1981 - aka *Cannibal Virus / Hell of the Living Dead / Cannibal Apocalypse / Inferno dei Morti Viventi / Apocalipsis Canibal / Virus Canibale*), *An American Werewolf in London* (1981), *I, Desire* (1982 - TVM), *Thriller* (1983 - music video), *Mutant* (1983), *Night of the Comet* (1984), *Zombie Island Massacre* (1984), *Return of the Living Dead* (1985), *Day of the Dead* (1985), *Re-Animator* (1985), *Spookies* (1985 - aka *Twisted Souls*), *Deadly Friend* (1986), *Return of the Living Dead Part II* (1987), *The Serpent and the Rainbow* (1987), *Zombie High* (1987), *Demonwarp* (1987), *Zombie Nightmare* (1987), *Evil Dead 2: Dead by Dawn* (1987), *Re-Animator 2* (1989 - aka *Bride of the Re-Animator*), *Night of the Living Dead* (1990 - remake), *Zombie '90: Extreme Pestilence* (1990), *Army of Darkness* (1992 - aka *Evil Dead 3 / The Medieval Dead*), *Return of the Living Dead Part III* (1993), *Weekend at Bernie's II* (1993), *My Boyfriend's Back* (1993)

Zombies see Dawn of the Dead

Zombies' Lake
Fr 1980 93m colour
Nazis killed during the war return as zombies to terrorize a small town.
    Abysmal addition to the zombie cycle, amateur in all departments.
p: Modern / Eurocine
d: J. A. Laser (Jean Rollin)
Howard Vernon, Pierre Escourrou, Annouchka, Anthony Mayans, Nadine Pscale, Jean Rollin

Zucco, George (1886-1960)
British actor, long in Hollywood, where he appeared mostly in horror films, to which he brought a note of often-needed dignity. A stage actor in both Britain and Canada, he made his film début in Britain in 1931 with a supporting role in *Dreyfus* (aka *The Dreyfus Case*). His Hollywood début came in 1935 with an appearance in *After the Thin Man*. His other films include *The Good Companions*, *Marie Antoinette*, *The Adventures of Sherlock Holmes* (in which he played Moriarty), *Madame Bovary* and *David and Bathsheba*.
Genre credits:
The Cat and the Canary (1939), *The Hunchback of Notre Dame* (1939), *The Mummy's Hand* (1940), *The Monster and the Girl* (1941), *Dr Renault's Secret* (1942), *The Mad Monster* (1942), *The Mummy's Tomb* (1942), *Dead Men Walk* (1943), *Voodoo Man* (1944), *The Mummy's Ghost* (1944), *The Return of the Ape Man* (1944), *House of Frankenstein* (1944), *Fog Island* (1945), *The Flying Serpent* (1946)

ZOMBIES ARE PERHAPS THE GENRE'S cheapest monster. All you need is a convincing mask or make-up job for the actors' heads. The makers of *Astro-Zombies* failed even in this basic requirement, however. Despite his own low budget, George Romero managed to pull the trick off in his ground-breaking Zombie flick *Night of the Living Dead*.

Acknowledgements

The author and publishers would like to thank the following picture sources:

Alan Frank
19, 25, 28, 48b, 50, 52, 53, 79, 80, 83, 92, 97, 103, 106, 119, 138, 139, 141, 147, 152, 157, 162a, 162b, 163a, 163b, 166, 174, 175, 183a, 191a, 191b, 191c, 196, 206, 209, 210, 213, 218a, 219, 223, 225, 228, 230, 244, 251, 256, 259, 267, 274, 278, 281, 283, 288, 292, 294

Joel Finler
14, 20, 21, 29, 34, 35, 43, 48a, 69, 84, 86a, 86b, 91, 102, 113, 115a, 115b, 116, 127, 131, 141, 144, 144, 164a, 149, 151, 168, 173, 180, 183b, 190, 202, 204, 212, 218b, 220, 227, 234 , 235, 264, 279, 284, 296, 298

The Kobal Collection
36, 56, 64, 104, 105, 128, 160, 232, 240, 260, 272

The following pictures are reproduced by kind permission of Hammer Films Inc.
84, 86, 98, 106, 180, 191, 196, 218a, 230, 264 , cover [Christopher Lee]